THE INFORMED READER

THE
INFORMED READER

Contemporary Issues in the Disciplines

Charles Bazerman

Baruch College • City University of New York

Houghton Mifflin Company • Boston
Dallas • Geneva, Illinois • Palo Alto • Princeton, New Jersey

The following permissions acknowledgments are made to publishers and authors:

Richard Bernstein: "In Dispute on Bias, Stanford Is Likely to Alter Western Culture Program." From *The New York Times*. January 19, 1988. Copyright © 1988 by The New York Times Company. Reprinted by permission.

Floyd E. Bloom, Arlyne Lazerson, and Laura Hofstadter: "Brain Systems and Memory." From *Brain, Mind and Behavior* by Floyd E. Bloom et al. Copyright © 1985 by Educational Broadcasting Company. Reprinted with the permission of W. H. Freeman and Company.

Laura Bohannan: "Shakespeare in the Bush." From *Natural History*, August–September 1966. Copyright © Laura Bohannan. Reprinted with permission of the author.

Charles N. Cofer: "Two Experimental Traditions in the Study of Memory." From *The Structure of Human Memory*
(continued on page 599)

Cover painting by Jim Baldwin

Printed in the U.S.A.
Library of Congress Catalog Card Number: 88-81322
ISBN: 0-395-40718-4

ABCDEFGHIJ-AP-9543210-898

Contents

UNIT 2
HISTORY
Upward Mobility in America: How Much and for Whom?
111

UNIT 3
SOCIAL SCIENCES
Memory: The World We Carry with Us
193

UNIT 4
BUSINESS
Productivity: Organizing Work, Motives, and Goals
275

UNIT 5
NATURAL SCIENCES
The Greenhouse Effect: A Change in the Weather
355

UNIT 6
ENGINEERING
Nuclear Power Safety: Containing Terrifying Forces
451

UNIT 7
INTERDISCIPLINARY STUDIES
Artificial Intelligence: Changing the Way We Think
523

To the Teacher

THE INFORMED READER IS an anthology designed to show students how ideas evolve through the written "conversations" of professionals in actual discourse communities. The book's fifty-eight readings are organized into six disciplinary units and one interdisciplinary unit, each of which takes up an issue of contemporary relevance to the teacher and the students:

- Literary Studies: Why are some books considered to be great while other works are ignored?
- History: How likely is it that I will lead a more prosperous life than my parents?
- Social Sciences: What is memory? How does it work?
- Business: How can we increase our productivity as individuals and as a society?
- Natural Sciences: Is worldwide industrialization causing a greenhouse-like heating of the earth's atmosphere? What will the consequences of this global warming be?
- Engineering: Can nuclear power plants be designed and built safely?
- Interdisciplinary Studies: Can computers be taught to think like humans? How does artificial intelligence affect our lives?

The introduction, "Reading in the Disciplines and Writing with Knowledge," provides the student with guidelines for reading authentic disciplinary materials and for responding to them through writing summaries, journal entries, response essays, syntheses, analyses, and documented statements.

Features

Challenging material, if it is to be read with understanding and enjoyment, must be accessible. *The Informed Reader* provides students and teachers with context-setting information and helpful apparatus:

- The **introduction** to each unit acquaints the reader with the discipline and its typical method of inquiry.
- The **headnote** for each reading gives further background on the unit's issue and orientation to the selection's rhetorical purposes.
- **Glosses** explain unfamiliar names and discipline-specific terms.
- **Rhetorical analysis through annotation** exercises show students how to identify rhetorical features of the selection and relate those features to the selection's overall aims.
- **Discussion questions** guide students through each selection's development and highlight significant arguments.
- **Writing suggestions** for each selection and unit encourage students to apply their disciplinary knowledge to a variety of more familiar contexts and situations.
- An extensive **Instructor's Manual** provides a synopsis and discussion of each issue and selection, suggestions for alternative groupings of selections, approaches for classroom discussions, and answers to each selection's analysis and discussion questions.

Consultants for *The Informed Reader*

I am particularly indebted to the consultants who helped me select material for various units, gave me background knowledge in their areas, and corrected substantive errors in the manuscript: Selma Berrol, John Andreassi, and Donald Vredenburgh, Baruch College, City University of New York; Shirley Lim, Westchester Community College, State University of New York; Cynthia Rosenzweig, Goddard Space Center; and George Grochowski, Power Authority of the State of New York.

This book is dedicated to my son, Gershom Kean Bazerman. May the world be his domain.

C.B.

Acknowledgments

I am grateful to the following reviewers for their comments and suggestions:

Larry W. Beason, Texas A&M University
Pam Besser, Jefferson Community College, Kentucky
Patricia Bizzell, College of the Holy Cross, Massachusetts
Lydia Blanchard, Southwest Texas State University
Beth Burch, Purdue University
Janet H. Carr, Northeastern University, Massachusetts
Jean Chimsky, University of Cincinnati
Ken Davis, Indiana University-Purdue University at Indianapolis
R. Edward Davis, Sinclair Community College, Ohio
Christine R. Farris, University of Missouri at Columbia
Cheryl Giuliano, University of California at Los Angeles
Donna Gorrell, St. Cloud State University, Minnesota
Joan Graham, University of Washington
Kristine Hansen, Brigham Young University
Robert Hemenway, The University of Oklahoma
Doug Hunt, University of Missouri at Columbia
Michael L. Keene, University of Tennessee, Knoxville
Malcolm Kiniry, Rutgers University, Newark
James L. Kinneavy, The University of Texas at Austin
Robert G. Lesman, Northern Virginia Community College
Thomas E. Martinez, Villanova University, Pennsylvania
George Miller, University of Delaware
Susan Miller, University of Utah
Constance M. Perry, St. Cloud State University, Minnesota
Louise Wetherbee Phelps, Syracuse University
James A. Preston, Jr., Miami-Dade Community College
Karen Spear, University of South Florida
Teresa Vilardi, Bard College, New York
Ray Wallace, University of Tennessee, Knoxville

THE INFORMED READER

INTRODUCTION
Reading in the Disciplines and Writing with Knowledge

Increasingly, our world is becoming one of specialists. There are experts in cardiac research, urban planning, economic history, solid-state engineering, and thousands of other areas of knowledge. Specialists have information and ideas about issues that affect our lives. If we are going to make intelligent decisions about such issues, we must become informed about what specialists have learned and what they are doing.

It is not always easy, however, for us to gain access to specialized knowledge because specialists communicate among themselves in unusual and seemingly difficult ways. For good reasons, specialized languages develop to deal with the problems that specialists are trying to solve, the objects and concepts they work with, and the dynamics of their discussions. Although it is not deliberate, non-specialists may have a hard time getting the information they need to make decisions themselves. As a result, we must be satisfied with what we can learn from simplified versions written for nonexperts (popularizations) or we must consult professionals who can interpret or act for us (a doctor, lawyer, or engineer, for example).

Reliance on intermediaries or on simplified versions may not always tell us what we need to know. Moreover, we then lose control over significant decisions. We then have no other intelligent course of action than to blindly accept our doctor's opinion or our lawyer's advice.

Of course, we can dismiss the role of specialized knowledge in our private, public, and professional lives. We can pretend that we can understand fully who we are and how we relate to one another without the help of the humanities and social sciences. We can pretend that we can intelligently criticize trade policy without an understanding of international economics and politics. We can even pretend that we can build a bridge without learning about the physics of materials and structures, as well as the political, economic, and social environment in which bridges get built. We can take stands and make common-sense decisions, but without the information we need our bridges will fall down and our trade policies will fail. We would be doing without important knowledge that could help us make better informed statements and make wiser decisions.

On the other hand, we could admit powerlessness and leave all decisions to the experts. We could earn our living doing work chosen by others, passively enjoy entertainments produced by professional media experts, and live according to governmental decisions in which we have no say. Fortunately, there is a middle choice. We can gain access to the specialized knowledges that grant power in our modern specialized society. We cannot become experts in every field, but we can learn how to *communicate* with the experts of any field. Through communication we will be able to make personal use of specialized knowledge and make our public concerns known in languages the professionals will respect. We do not need to be limited to the language we have grown up with or the language of the one career we choose to follow.

College as an Entry into Professional Communities

A college education offers you access to specialized knowledge for your personal growth, public participation, and professional training. Unlike your earlier education, which was largely devoted to providing basic information and the skills you need just to get by in the world, a college education is meant to introduce you to the knowledge, language, and activities of specialized academic communities, which are called disciplines.

College courses are structured socializations into the various disciplines, beginning with the freshman introductory survey courses and ending with senior seminars devoted to specific problem areas within your major discipline. In these courses you become familiar with the style of communication of each discipline you study, often mediated through a textbook or the instructor's lectures and sometimes directly by reading the articles and books of the disciplinary literature. Through class discussions, exams, and assigned papers, you will be asked to produce statements appropriate to the discipline's style of communication. If you go on to graduate school, you will go through an apprenticeship that develops your ability to contribute to the knowledge-building conversation of the discipline.

After college, you will likely find disciplinary knowledge useful in three aspects of your lives: professional, public, and personal. No matter which area of work you choose it is likely to require knowledge of one or more disciplines. For example, in order to practice medicine, first you need to know biology, anatomy, chemistry, and mathematics before you enter specialized training; it also does not hurt to know some psychology, cultural history, and literature, for such knowledge will help you to understand your patients better as people. To be a business manager, you need to be skilled in economics, finance, organizational sociology, industrial psychology, and communications, and have some awareness of the humanities in order to understand the human side of the work. No matter what the career, it will be enhanced by certain kinds of disciplinary knowledge.

In addition to a professional life, we all lead a public life. We vote in elections, get involved in community issues, do volunteer work, or join organizations. Typically, we follow the news and express our opinions because the news relates to real issues and choices facing us. Medical breakthroughs, air travel safety, economic policy, educational programs, gun control legislation, antidrug programs, and all the other issues reported in the news affect our daily lives. Rarely, however, do we get sufficiently detailed and complete information about what is going on from the newspaper and television news to make informed judgments. For example, in order to make a serious decision about a welfare reform proposal for your city, you will need some knowledge of sociology, economics, and political science, as well as the detailed, local information contained in agency reports. To be able to decide whether to support or oppose the construction of an incinerator to convert garbage to energy, you need to understand a variety of technical, biological, and ecological factors. Even your desire to help out some troubled kids in your neighborhood would be aided by knowledge of education, psychology, urban anthropology, and perhaps the legal system.

Ultimately, we all have private lives in which we attempt to gain some understanding of who we are, the lives we lead, and the choices we make. Humanistic liberal arts education traditionally has been aimed at helping us lead an "examined life." Philosophy, the arts, literature, and history help us view ourselves and enrich our personal experiences. So do the social sciences, such as anthropology, which extends our view of what it means to be human, and psychology, which helps us consider how we think, feel, and act. The natural sciences, as well, help us to understand the world we live in and our physical relationships with the environment. All of these disciplines enrich our personal experiences and inform our choices if we can make the connection between these school disciplines and our own lives.

Disciplinary Questions and Significant Issues

Disciplines address significant human issues. This book, *The Informed Reader*, looks at issues of concern to six contemporary disciplines and one interdisciplinary issue. Each unit presents articles that show how people within a discipline attempt to solve a significant problem. Each of the issues has an obvious impact on our lives:

> Why do we consider some books great works and teach them widely, while other works are not given attention?

> What is the likelihood of our leading more prosperous lives than our parents?

> What is memory and how does it work?

> How can we be more productive as individuals and as a society?

> Is the earth heating up because of what humans do to the atmosphere and what will the consequences be of this global warming trend?

> Can nuclear power plants be constructed safely enough?

> Can computers be made to think like humans and what is the effect of computer intelligence on our lives?

Most units begin with a selection that discusses the direct impact of the issues on our lives, and then selections of actual disciplinary writing explore the issues more fully. In *The Informed Reader* you will have the opportunity to read the actual work of professionals in the disciplines who are grappling with these issues every day.

Although disciplines start with basic human issues, they often pursue them in rather specialized conversations using specialized language. Each unit's series of articles demonstrates how members of a discipline discuss an issue among themselves. The articles literally speak to each other in a conversation. One article answers another as the members of a discipline work out answers to important questions. The articles implicitly and explicitly refer to each other as they build on prior statements to develop an answer or consensus that then becomes disciplinary knowledge.

These specialized conversations are not that difficult to follow once you recognize the issues and see how the articles speak to each other. If you walk into the middle of a conversation and you do not know what the individuals are talking about, you will have a difficult time of it, even if they use very familiar language. If, however, you listen in on a conversation from the beginning and you have some sense of the issues being discussed, you can follow complicated arguments back and forth simply by paying normal, careful attention. The selections in each unit are organized so as to lead you into the issue gradually, following the development of the discussion in the discipline. The introduction to each of the units explains the issue discussed in the selections and describes how the discipline talks about the issue. The notes for each selection give you any background you may need to know and help orient you to how each article contributes to the disciplinary conversation. The questions and annotation exercises that follow each selection will lead you to a deeper understanding of the articles and the issues.

If you read with care and use the support of the introductions, notes, and questions, you may be surprised at how well you can understand material that at first appeared as though only a specialist could make sense of. Once you understand the core issue and how each selection attempts to advance the discussion of that issue, the reading of the article will be an intelligible, rewarding activity. Difficulties people have in reading specialized articles usually come from picking up an article out of context, with no idea of what the issue is or how it fits with what other specialists have said. By presenting a tightly organized cluster of articles around an issue—a chunk of disciplinary conversation—*The Informed Reader* helps you understand specialized writing in the context in which it originally appeared. Specialists are not much different from the rest of us; they just know the context of their specialty.

Reading into Writing

With any piece of writing we usually do not read to memorize the text. Rather we transform it for our own understanding and purposes. Even an actress who must memorize the script of her part must then interpret that part through her delivery of the lines, gestures, and actions. Just as the actress must create life on stage out of the dead words on the page, we must do the same with our reading: convert someone else's words into our own meanings, thoughts, and actions. We start with the dead page and end with the statements of our own life.

Reading becomes meaningful to us when we link it up to our personal, public, academic, or professional interests. One of the main ways we make this link is through making new statements—talking and writing about what we read, connecting it with other things we know and think, applying it to questions we wonder about, using it to support our choices and activities. After each of the selections of this anthology, reading questions and writing suggestions help you formulate your own understanding of the readings and use that understanding to make a variety of statements, both spoken and written. These questions and assignments sometimes ask for responses very close to the text (as in summary and synthesis questions) and sometimes they ask you to take a more distant approach to the reading (as in analytical writing and in developing your own statements).

Writing Tasks and Distance from Reading

In school or on the job, our new statements and actions may stay rather close to the text, reproducing much of what the text says. We need to be able to repeat information from a textbook on an examination or we need to be able to explain to others concisely what a long report recommends. In such cases we need to be able to summarize a text, pick out the important parts, and restate it to show its overall flow of ideas and information.

In a **summary** you reproduce the meaning of the original text in a shorter form (usually one-fifth of the original or less, depending on the purpose of the summary). You must stay close to the ideas and information of the original text, but you should delete the less important information and phrasing. You should not add any ideas, information, reactions, or comments of your own. You can, however, select material from the original and vary the emphasis of presentation to fit the summary's purpose.

The following suggestions should help you write a compact, focused summary.

How to Write Summaries

1. Read the original carefully, so that you understand both its overall point and its specific details.
2. Identify the purpose of the summary.
3. Select the most important ideas and information of the original for the purpose of the summary. Either mark up the original or take notes to identify the selected material.
4. Delete repetitions of ideas and information.
5. Gather groups of details, examples, or minor ideas under more general terms that cover an entire group in a single word or phrase.
6. Locate a statement of the main idea of the original. If there is none, write your own.
7. Rewrite the material in concise, coherent sentences and paragraphs. Begin the summary with the main idea statement (see step 6). Combine several ideas, where appropriate, in a single sentence. Use paragraphs to identify large divisions in the summary. Use transitional words and phrases to show the connections between different parts of the summary. Make sure the summary fits together and does not break down into a lot of unconnected information. Do not, however, use unnecessary words or roundabout phrasing.
8. Identify the text summarized (including author) in a heading, the opening sentence, or a source line at the end. (See "Documenting Sources.")
9. Rewrite or retype to make a clean copy and proofread for typographical errors.

At other times, we may gain more distance on the reading by expressing our own thoughts or responses to it. To develop personal thoughts in response to reading, we may keep a **reading journal**. In school, public life, and our professions we may have to argue in support of or against statements made by others.

In school we sometimes are asked to write an essay relating the ideas of the reading to our personal experiences.

In writing responses you develop your own ideas and experiences in relation to the text you have read. Your response may be a judgment about some opinion stated in the text: you might directly agree or disagree, or you might have a more balanced judgment. Or your response may explore associations you make from the reading, perhaps considering how the incidents or opinions expressed in the text compare with experiences you have had, a current situation you are familiar with, or other readings.

Keeping a reading journal will allow you to identify and develop your responses informally without having to worry about how your ideas will all fit together and how well you have expressed yourself. Then later you can use the journal entries to develop formal writing for more public situations. The following guidelines will help you develop your responses in reading journals and more formal essays.

How to Write Reading Journals

1.   Set aside a separate notebook or folder for your journal.
2.   Immediately after you read an assignment or anything that you find interesting, turn to a blank page in the journal and put the date at the top.
3.   Do not worry about spelling, grammar, or coherence of your writing. If in the middle of writing the journal entry you make a new association or shift an opinion, do not worry. Just write down and explore that new thought.
4.   Begin writing by identifying what you were reading and by identifying one specific idea, incident, or detail in the reading that evoked in you some response (either positive or negative) or association.
5.   Then directly state that response or association. Develop your response in as much detail as possible. Avoid just giving the headlines; tell the full story. What are the reasons you agree or disagree? Do you have any experiences or other knowledge that lie behind your opinion? If you associate the reading with a memory, situation, or other text, give full details about the association.
6.   Ask yourself further questions about how your associations and responses relate to the reading, perhaps putting the original statement in a different light or connecting it with other statements in the text. Or find some point in your response that can be
(continued)

(continued)

developed more. Or ask what your response reveals about your own way of thinking. If you keep pushing your ideas further, asking yourself new questions, comparing specific details to general comments, you will then deepen your responses and will have more developed things to say. If, however, you are satisfied with only briefly labeling your idea and moving on, you will be left with only a superficial catalogue of top-of-the-head opinions.

7.   After you have finished writing, read over the journal entry to see where your thinking has led you.

You may have to adapt these guidelines to fit the situation you are writing for, your specific goals in presenting responses, and the exact nature of the responses.

How to Write Response Essays

1.   Before you begin writing, think through your reactions and opinions about the reading, perhaps by using a journal, freewriting, or notes.

2.   Of all your many responses to the reading, select the single most important one to form the main point of your essay. Several closely related responses may be combined into a single overall idea only if you can show how they are all parts of that main thought. You must be careful that your essay does not break down into a laundry list of unconnected and undeveloped points.

3.   Formulate your main response into a single statement which will become the thesis statement of your essay. Then in notes or an outline, plan how you will develop that idea in the essay. The plan should follow an orderly sequence of steps so the reader will be led from point to point, without having to jump between disconnected points or to fill in missing logical connections.

4.   In the opening paragraph of the essay identify the text you are responding to, the specific point in the text that you are discussing (see "Referring to Sources"), and the main response you have to that point. You may also characterize the original text in a way

(continued)

(continued)

appropriate to the point you are going to make, or you may suggest how you will develop your response in the essay.

5. In each paragraph or section of the essay you should develop one step in your reasoning. You should explain your idea at each step fully enough for the reader to understand you; then you should provide enough examples, details, and arguments for the reader to accept your point. If you just state your point and then do not develop it, the reader may neither understand exactly where you are leading, nor wish to follow you down a path he or she has not been prepared for.

6. In the closing paragraph reemphasize your main point and tie the various stages of your reasoning together. This can be done by developing conclusions out of the argument you have developed, by describing an incident that illustrates how all the ideas you have been developing fit together, or by returning to a discussion of the original text in light of all the points you have made.

7. Revise the essay to make sure that your ideas are logically and fully developed and that you present them so that they can be clearly understood. Then edit on the sentence level to eliminate wordy and awkward phrasing, to correct grammatical and spelling errors, and to develop more pointed and elegant wording.

8. Rewrite or retype to make a clean copy and proofread for typographical errors.

Synthesis is a third type of writing task, which requires you to bring a number of different things you have read together into a coherent pattern. In school you may be asked to bring together several assigned readings or sources you found through library research to address an issue or reveal what is known on a subject. In academic or other professional life, you may have to put together a review of the literature on a subject or write a report tying together a number of previous reports. In your personal life, as well, as you think through the various things you have read and experienced, you may see connections that you want to pull together into some form of informal writing.

In a synthesis you put together the ideas and information of a number of sources to see an overall pattern. In a **review of the literature** the focus of the synthesis is on the different ways the various sources treat the subject. In a **synthesis report**, the focus is on how the information fits together to lead to conclusions or an overview of the subject. The following guidelines are useful for both kinds of writing.

How to Write Syntheses

1.   Determine your purpose in writing the synthesis. Is there a specific question you need to answer for your audience, such as, "What is the consensus of current medical experts on what constitutes a healthy diet?" Or is the synthesis to demonstrate to the instructor that you are familiar with important statements and research in a specific area?

2.   Identify the appropriate texts to use. The texts may be assigned by the teacher or in course textbooks, such as this anthology. Or you may need to search out appropriate sources through bibliographic search methods. Library bibliographic tools such as card catalogues, periodical indexes, bibliographies, and computer searches are useful. But also let one source lead you to another: use the notes and references in one appropriate source to find other relevant sources.

3.   Read the sources carefully in relation to your purpose. Take notes or annotate your own copies to be able to retrieve relevant information easily.

4.   Think about the connections among the various sources. Do any sources agree or disagree on any points? Does one source provide background for another? Does one source take up where another leaves off? Does one source provide general ideas that apply to the more specific information of the other sources? Does one source provide an example of some idea discussed in another source? Do any common ideas or viewpoints run through all the sources?

5.   Based on the pattern of connections you have seen among the various sources, develop an overall point or conclusion to serve as the organizing thesis of your synthesis. If you are writing a review of the literature, your thesis statement should focus on how the various texts relate to each other. If you are writing a synthesis report, your thesis statement should focus on your conclusions about the topic itself.

6.   Develop a plan for presenting the various parts of the information in a unified way. In a review of the literature, you will likely organize your discussion around separate discussions of each article (or group of closely related articles); you would then need to develop an intelligent order for the discussions of the various articles. In a synthesis report, you will likely organize your discussion around the various parts of the subject; you would then need to find an appropriate order for these parts.

(continued)

(continued)

7. Write the first draft of the synthesis. Develop the points made in each of the paragraphs through details from your various sources. Use quotation, paraphrase, and summary to present the information from the sources. (See "Referring to Sources.")

8. Document the sources of your information, using an appropriate parenthetical reference or footnote method. (See "Documenting Sources.")

9. Revise the draft, paying particular attention to the transitions that tie the various parts of the synthesis together and to the overall coherence of the presentation. Make sure you maintain a consistency of tone and focus throughout the paper. Do not let the variety of sources you use lead the writing in different directions. Finally, edit for correctness.

10. Rewrite or retype to make a clean copy and proofread for typographical errors.

In **analytical writing** you move beyond reacting to or using the content of the text to look at how the text was put together or how the ideas and information were developed. You take apart the reading piece by piece according to some analytical framework or set of critical ideas that helps you to see different parts or aspects of the text. Analysis, by giving you even greater objective and critical distance on the reading, helps you evaluate what you read and decide on how you will use the information, if at all.

In school you may have to write analyses of literary or philosophical readings, but you may also need to analyze business cases, social science theories, or even computer programs. In professional work you may often be called on to analyze the work of other people or problems described in other documents; you will, of course, use the analytic methods of your particular profession. In public life, the ability to analyze a problem or the statements of your opponents may help persuade others to agree with your own position. Even in your private life, an informal analysis of something you have read may help you to understand something that puzzled you.

In analytical writing you view a text or some other object critically, by examining it through some analytical framework. The framework used most often in this book is rhetorical: that is, considering the features of a text in relation to the intended effect on its audience. Texts may be analyzed in many other ways, including from grammatical, metaphoric, and philosophic perspectives. Not only texts, but anything else may be analyzed from an appropriate perspective, from chemicals and rocks to musical compositions.

The following guidelines should aid in writing all varieties of analyses.

How to Write Analyses

1.   Consider your purpose in carrying out an analysis. Is it to understand how a text works or to criticize it for using some deceptive or faulted technique? Is it to evaluate whether a new coffee maker is worth the price or is it to be able to copy some of the design features in a competing model your company will produce?

2.   Identify what specifically you are analyzing and the method or set of concepts (the analytical framework) you are using for analysis. Consider why the analytical framework is appropriate for your purposes and whether it is likely to reveal much of interest about the text or object it is applied to. A rhetorical analysis is appropriate if you want to understand how texts are designed to achieve their purposes, but it will not tell you whether the texts have actually been successful. For that you need to analyze the responses of the audience through some sort of impact framework.

3.   Each analytical framework asks you to consider particular categories, features, or parts of the object or text you are analyzing. Identify exactly what the analytical framework asks you to look for in the text or object.

4.   Examine the text or object carefully in relation to the categories, features, or parts specified by the analytical framework. Take notes on all relevant details.

5.   Find patterns in how the various details and categories fit together. Do all the various parts seem to support the same overall rhetorical purpose? Or do some details suggest one aim, while others suggest a contradictory one?

6.   Draw overall conclusions about the patterns you have found through analysis. This overall conclusion will become the thesis statement of your analytical paper.

7.   Write the opening paragraph of the analysis. This paragraph should announce what you are analyzing and why, the analytical framework you are using, and the overall conclusions you have come to.

8.   Write the body of the analysis. Each paragraph or section should examine a single category or group of features exposed through the analysis. The topic sentence of each paragraph should relate the details of the paragraph to the overall pattern described in your conclusions. The largest part of each paragraph should be devoted to examining details of the text or object in relation to the analytical categories. Give many specific examples. In analyzing a text you should probably quote specific passages, but make sure

(continued)

(continued)

you do not simply repeat the content or ideas of the text; maintain an analytical focus.

9.   Write the closing section of the analysis to draw together the pattern found in all the detailed analysis of the body sections of the paper.

10.   In revising, pay special attention to make sure that the overall pattern of the analysis comes out strongly, that sufficient details are offered in support of the analysis, and that clear connections are always made between the details and the overall pattern.

11.   Edit for sentence style and correctness.

12.   Rewrite or retype to make a clean copy and proofread for typographical errors.

Finally, the most creative use of reading is to help you make **your own statements**. Out of all you have read, thought about, put together, and analyzed, you may say something new that represents your own ideas and goals, whether in private, public, academic, or other professional realms. As part of making your own statements you may use summary, response, synthesis, and analysis, but the overall result will be to move beyond the readings, which were your starting point, to establish a new position of your own. Some suggestions are offered in the text on how to rely on your reading, yet still establish sufficient distance and originality to create your own statements.

In becoming informed on a subject you become familiar with statements by other people, which you have put together and analyzed in various ways. However, at some point you can move beyond what you have read to ask new questions about the material or make the material serve some new purpose. You must then come up with some new kind of statement to satisfy these different questions or purposes. Using everything you have learned about the subject, you must put the information and ideas together in a new way. In this new statement your own ideas and interpretations will dominate. The source materials will only serve to support your ideas or provide points of discussion to allow you to develop your ideas further. The organization of the statement should be built on the development of your ideas. The following guidelines should help you keep the focus on the development of your own ideas.

Writing New Statements Using Sources

1.   Identify the purpose of your statement. Write a question that, if answered, will serve your purpose.

(continued)

(continued)

2.   Ask yourself what you would need to know to be able to answer this question. Then locate source materials that will inform you about what you need to know. These materials may already be familiar to you, such as through assigned reading, or you may need to carry out a library search. (See item 2 under "How to Write Syntheses.")

3.   Take notes on relevant materials.

4.   Ask yourself how you would now answer your question in light of the information from the sources. Write out the answer in as brief and direct a form as possible. This answer will form the thesis of your statement.

5.   Ask yourself what your audience would need to know in order to understand and agree with your answer. Look carefully at your brief written answer (see step 4) to find all the topics implied in your statement. Use this analysis of the audience's need for information as the basis for your plan for the statement.

6.   Outline your statement to lead the audience in an orderly way through the ideas and information they need to know to comprehend and accept your answer.

7.   Write a first draft, making sure that each section develops only material that directly relates to answering your main question. Do not get lost in any intriguing side-subjects that wander from your primary purpose. Use material from your sources to develop your answer, but avoid repeating unrelated information from your sources. Refer to material from your sources by quotation, paraphrase, and summary. (See "Referring to Sources.")

8.   Document your source materials using a parenthetical reference or footnote system. (See "Documenting Sources.")

9.   When revising pay special attention to keeping the main focus on answering your question. Also consider whether you have clearly indicated how the source materials support your answer. Edit at the sentence level.

10.   Rewrite or retype to make a clean copy and proofread.

No matter how much distance you gain from your reading or how much you transform the readings into your own writing, you must cite any material you are using and document the source of that material. The following guidelines for **referring to sources** and **documenting sources** will enable you to identify your source material more effectively and accurately.

Referring to Sources

You may bring material from your reading into your own writing in several ways.

Direct quotation has the advantage of using the author's exact words, but this means that the flow of your own statement is interrupted to let the source's author speak through the quotation. If you quote too much, you could easily lose control of the writing, as the voices of your sources take over. You should, therefore, only quote directly when it is important to have the exact words of the original, and you should never extend the quotation beyond the length that is absolutely needed. Whenever you use exact words you must identify them with quotation marks or block indentation for longer passages. Introduce quotations with a phrase or sentence indicating the person being quoted; for example, *Smith argues that "the problem arises from . . ."* or *"The cause," contends Jones, "can be found. . . ."*

By **paraphrasing**, restating the original in your own words, you can vary the phrasing to fit in with the flow of your writing and to emphasize the aspect of the source material most relevant to the point you are making. You retain control of the voice of the writing. Paraphrased material, even though not using original words, must be documented; moreover, the paraphrase ought to be introduced by identifying the person paraphrased.

Summarizing also allows you to maintain control over the voice of the writing and the topic focus. It further allows you to mention only the main points relevant to your discussion. Usually most reference to sources in your writing will be through summary. Summarized material must also be documented, and the author of the original in most cases should also be identified in a phrase introducing the summary.

Documenting Sources

Whenever you use information, ideas, or other material from a source you must give credit to that source. There are several methods to document sources.

In-text mention   In the sentence introducing the source material you can mention the source. In-text mentions are particularly appropriate when you are using just one or two sources in a response essay, when you are writing a review of the literature where it is important to emphasize each source you are discussing, and when you are speaking to a nonprofessional audience and want to highlight the authority of your sources. Usually you will need to include full bibliographic information in the mention, perhaps using parentheses as shown here:

> Donald McCloskey in *The Rhetoric of Economics* (Madison: University of Wisconsin Press, 1985) states that "Economists have two attitudes toward discourse, the official and the unofficial, the explicit and the implicit" (5).

If you are writing about assigned material in a class assignment, it is often sufficient just to give author, title, and page number:

> In the selection from our text, "Restoring the Traditional Black Family," Eleanor Holmes Norton asks, "What would society be like if the family found it difficult to perform its most basic functions?" (181)

Tag line or heading   When you write a separate summary, you may identify the source of the material summarized in either a heading

> Summary of Robert Solow, "Technical Change and the Aggregate Production Function," *Review of Economics and Statistics* 36 (1981): 312–320.

or a tag line.

> . . . summarized from Laura Bohannan, "Shakespeare in the Bush" in our textbook, pp. 44–53.

Parenthetical reference systems   In parenthetical reference systems a short reference in parenthesis immediately follows the material to be documented, and complete bibliographical information appears at the end in an alphabetically arranged reference list. The exact format of the short reference and the reference lists varies from discipline to discipline, and a number of varieties appear in this book. Examples of the American Psychological Association style appear on pages 219–231, and examples of the Modern Language Association style appear on pages 66–75. Check other units for styles used in other disciplines.

In the MLA system, the basic parenthetical reference consists only of the author's last name and a page number (Spacks 61), with other information (such as first initial or short title of the work) added only to differentiate similar references. The basic reference list format follows the following two examples, the first for a book, the second for an article.

> Spacks, Patricia Meyer. *The Female Imagination*. New York: Knopf, 1975.

> Doheny-Farina, Stephen. "Writing in an Emerging Organization." *Written Communication* 3 (1988):158–185.

Notes   Footnotes and endnotes are becoming less popular in most disciplines as they are replaced with parenthetical reference systems, but they are still widely used in history and some other fields. Examples of documentation through endnotes appear on pages 104–107.

Rhetorical Forums and Forms

You transform your reading into new statements to take part in a particular conversation or activity in the academic, professional, public, or private realms. These conversations or activities occur in specific forums. You write your essay for an art history class that meets three times a week, led by a professor and attended by twenty-five students. You write legal arguments for a client to be presented in a court of law. You protest the town board's master development plan by writing a petition to be distributed among your neighbors for their signature and then to be submitted to the board. You consider how some ideas you learned in sociology have changed how you understand some of your relationships by confiding to a friend or talking privately with your teacher during office hours.

Each realm of our life has specific forums associated with it. These forums are regularized places, occasions, or situations where you can make a statement or otherwise carry your interests forward. Business meetings, internal communications systems, letters to the editor columns in newspapers, academic journals, regular exchanges of letters with friends—these are all forums to carry on particular kinds of activities. Even an ordinary dinner with family members is a kind of personal forum, where you know certain issues are raised and certain problems are solved while other issues or problems are out of bounds.

Within each of these forums, people have developed particular ways of communicating that have been successful for them in carrying out their work. Newspaper articles are written to answer the four W's—who, what, where, when—within the opening paragraph and then to elaborate in the remainder of the article. Business memos follow standard formats within each organization and often use standard wording. Scientific experimental reports have standard sections for introduction, review of the literature, methods, results, discussion, and conclusions. Economists use economic terms that help them convey their specialized ideas most efficiently. Even private journals and diaries develop certain styles and patterns of development, sometimes particular to each author. If you are familiar with the typical features, or conventions, of each type of document, you can often figure out which type of forum and activity any piece of writing comes from, even if the text itself is not identified.

Features of This Book

In this volume the selection headnotes identify the situation and forum for each reading and discuss the special features of writing that help the text operate within this context. Moreover, the clustering of articles within a disciplinary conversation helps establish the context of each selection, so that the whole cluster reveals the situation of each of the selections. The unit introductions discuss the overall dynamics of the conversation and the general features of writing appropriate to the situation.

As well, each assignment you are asked to write has a situation and forum, so that you know who you are writing for in what kind of context, and you can choose an appropriate form for your writing. The situations and forums for the writing assignments are all chosen to be familiar to you. In the personal realm, writing situations are developed around private journals, letters to friends and parents, and communications of social, church, and college organizations. In the academic realm, writing situations reflect the typical classroom assignments that are likely to occur in undergraduate courses: note-taking and summaries, exam essays, evaluations and analyses, syntheses of several readings, speculative essays asking you to consider implications of the reading, and essays applying concepts from reading to your life and experiences. Public situations are designed around forums of newspapers, magazines, and community meetings. Since you are likely not to be too familiar yet with the forums of professional life, you are not asked to do much in the way of professional writing, but some assignments are offered that use easily imagined situations or translate some of the dynamics of professional situations into more familiar contexts, such as using the classroom as a research community, or the college administration as a corporate hierarchy.

Some of the readings are from the kinds of forums and in the kinds of forms you will be asked to write, such as newspaper articles and personal essays from magazines. But since most of the readings are from professional forums, which you will be transforming for use in other realms, you often will not be writing in the same forms you are reading. Unless the teacher assigns you professional writing, your writing will not usually imitate the forms and conventions of your reading. Several writing assignments, nonetheless, point to special features of the reading that may be applied to other kinds of situations; in those cases you will be specifically asked to imitate particular features of the selection, such as persuasive techniques, use of narratives, or organizational patterns.

Using "Rhetorical Analysis Through Annotation" Exercises

Each writer selects and arranges words to accomplish some purpose within a particular situation. Rhetoric is the art of writing and speaking so as to affect your readers and listeners in the way you desire, so that you will accomplish your goals. Rhetorical analysis points out the rhetorical choices made by a writer or speaker and relates those choices to the overall purpose of the text within the situation. By learning to analyze texts rhetorically you will understand more fully what each text attempts to accomplish and can evaluate how successful it is in achieving those ends. Moreover, you will become more aware of the rhetorical means available for you to use in your own writing.

Each selection in this anthology is followed by an annotation exercise that will help you examine the language and structure of the selection. The exercise begins with an observation about some rhetorical pattern in the selection. For example, the exercise about Gilbert Highet's essay "Compulsory Reading" begins by noting that Highet, to reach an audience of nonspecialists, uses common personal experiences throughout his discussion. Highet's audience can relate to his experiences and are therefore drawn into his article.

The annotations and discussion topics that follow pursue in detail the opening general observation. By asking you to underline, mark up, make marginal comments, or otherwise identify and characterize specific features of the text, the annotation exercises will highlight some choices made by the writer. For the Highet essay, for example, you are asked to note in the margin where the author uses personal anecdotes and common experiences, where he identifies problems arising from these examples, and where he puzzles over these problems. With these instructions you might annotate the opening lines of the essay as follows.

Every now and then, at a party, you meet someone who tells you about a book she has read. She describes its tremendous reception and the growing fame of its author. Finally, in a tone of friendly authority, she says 'You *must* read it. Do remember its title, now, and don't forget. You *must* read it.' } common experience

At once your stomach—assisted by the canapés—turns. You thank her civilly. You fix the name of the book in your memory. You resolve never, never on any account, to read it.

Yet it might have been quite a good book. She explained how important it was. What made you feel it must be revolting? Was the evidence in its favor inadequate? No. The evidence was fairly sound. But you were biased against the book simply because someone told you that you must *must* MUST read it. } turns experience into problem

We have all felt like this. It goes back to the days when we were in school, when we were told that we were obliged to read some book about which we usually knew nothing, nothing whatever, except that it was a Must. } puzzles over the problem

Issues for class discussion then explore how the features you have annotated are related to other features of the author's writing and to the overall purpose of the text. Sometimes one of the discussion questions or writing suggestions then asks you to develop the rhetorical analysis you began in the annotation exercises. In the Highet example, the eighth discussion question follows up on the rhetorical analysis by asking you to compare the rhetorical choices of this essay with those of another selection.

The annotation exercise, nonetheless, focuses only on some small part of the rhetorical choices of the selection. Each piece of writing is the product of many choices that the author has made at many different levels. After you annotate a number of selections, you will begin to see how the features pointed out in one selection also operate in others. By annotating many examples for many different features you will become aware of a wide variety of techniques that writers use in different situations to achieve their purposes. In addition to expanding your repertoire of rhetorical techniques to add depth to your reading and to use in your writing, the analysis will help you understand how every piece of writing is shaped by underlying purposes. This fundamental understanding will give you much greater control over both reading and writing.

UNIT

1

LITERARY STUDIES
The Literary Canon: Why Do We Read This Stuff?

As you have gone through school, you have been assigned stories, novels, poems, and plays to read. At first you probably gave little thought to why teachers chose to assign certain works of literature rather than others. By the time you reached high school, however, you likely realized that certain pieces were considered great classics and essential reading. You study Shakespeare's *Hamlet* or Hawthorne's *The Scarlet Letter*, for example, not only because they are thought-provoking and enjoyable to read, but also because an educated person in our culture is expected to have read them.

Collectively such acknowledged masterpieces form what is known as the literary canon. The term *canon* is borrowed from the Roman Catholic church, where it refers to the authoritative list of saints and the books accepted as Holy Scripture. Within the disciplines of English and literary studies, however, canon refers to works of literature that are widely held in high regard. Until a few years ago, most literary critics and professors would have agreed that there was a fairly well defined list of literary texts that designated the masterpieces of our culture. Some might have argued over the selection of some individual works, but most would have agreed on the works of well-established, great authors like

Homer, Sappho, Dante, Shakespeare, Milton, Austen, Wordsworth, and more recently Dickens, Twain, Ibsen, Woolf, Orwell. These texts would make up the syllabi for courses, fill the anthologies, and define excellence and taste. In short, these texts would be the canon.

In the last decade, however, the canon has become a matter of dispute in literary studies, for it has been recognized that the canonical works are largely written by white males of European-dominated cultures. Demands have followed that the canon of American literature include more works by women and minorities, and that the canon of world literature include works from Asia, Africa, South America, the Islamic world, and other less familiar places. In the past few years, a serious conflict has developed between those arguing for an extensive opening up of the canon and those arguing that the traditional great works of Western literature should remain the core of education. The most dramatic confrontation took place on the Stanford University campus. Richard Bernstein's article from the *New York Times*, the first selection in this unit, describes the uproar that was caused by students' efforts to change the list of required books taught in the core curriculum. As the newspaper piece makes clear, a debate that began as a local problem at Stanford soon attracted national attention and the comments of well-known authors and politicians. On many other campuses the same issues are being worked out, although perhaps not with as much noise and national attention.

The choice of which works are taught is not just a matter of how class hours are filled. As the Spanish novelist Miguel de Cervantes noted almost four hundred years ago, our reading shapes our vision of life. His famous character, Don Quixote, sets out on his adventures because he had spent most of his time

> reading books of chivalry with such pleasure and devotion as to lead him almost wholly to forget the life of a hunter and even the administration of his estate. . . .
>
> In short, our gentleman became so immersed in his reading that he spent whole nights from sundown to sunup and his days from dawn to dusk in poring over his books, until, finally, from so little sleeping and so much reading, his brain dried up and he went completely out of his mind. He had filled his imagination with everything that he had read, with enchantments, knightly encounters, battles, challenges, wounds, with tales of love and its torments, and all sorts of impossible things, and as a result had come to believe that all these fictitious happenings were true; they were more real to him than anything else in the world. (From Miguel de Cervantes Saavedra, *The Ingenious Gentleman Don Quixote de la Mancha*, trans. Samuel Putnam, New York: Viking, 1949, 26–27.)

Believing the world was the noble conflict between good and evil described in romantic tales of the adventures of bold knights, Don Quixote puts on rusty armor, gets on a creaky old horse, and goes off to battle with windmills.

More recently, the literary critic F. R. Leavis, lecturer at Cambridge University, showed concern for how literature influences our imagination and thereby our sense of life. In his book *The Great Tradition*, written in 1948, he argued that the great novelists and poets "not only change the possibilities of art for practitioners and readers, but they are significant in terms of that human awareness they promote; awareness of the possibilities of life" (London: Stewart, 10). Leavis suggested that the great writers not only write better, but have a deeper vision of life, a greater wisdom. Similarly the poet T. S. Eliot in his essay "What Is a Classic?" (excerpted in this unit) argued the classics show a maturity of art, thought, and culture.

If we believe in the wisdom and beauty of certain works, we will want to understand these works accurately and in detail, so as to be able to appreciate them fully. Accordingly, interpretation of literature became a major task in the middle of the century. Through detailed textual analyses, critics and teachers showed students the way to mine meanings from the deep texts; students, through their own interpretations, demonstrated their competence in reading the great works. Most likely, your high school and college courses in literature were based on such principles.

Identifying particular works as great creates difficulties. As Mark Twain commented, "A classic is a book everyone wants to have read, but no one wants to read." The classics may seem like medicine, good for you but with an unpleasant taste. Gilbert Highet supports the canon, although he writes of it in an irreverent way. Like Eliot, Highet distinguishes different levels of greatness within the canon and urges us to cherish that which is best. In "Compulsory Reading," Highet advises that students be assigned only works by "an absolutely first-rate writer" or by "an author who is close to them in time and in interest." (He assumes that there will be widespread agreement on what works fit these categories.) Students should be encouraged to sift the good from the bad in a classic, rather than put the whole thing on a pedestal. And they should learn to see a work's overall structure and plan, or how the parts fit together into a whole.

After Highet's, the next three selections reassess common assumptions about the Western canon's universal relevance and expose prejudice embedded in it. Laura Bohannan tells the story of Hamlet to African tribespeople and learns that the interpretation she thought universal was actually just a culture-bound Western one. Ngugi Wa Thiong'o argues that the canon of Western literature has no place in the developing nations of Africa. Some canonical works are merely irrelevant; many contain materialistic values and racist attitudes that are highly offensive to nations trying to escape their colonial past. Ngugi wants Africans to read African literature and works that are anti-imperialistic and humanistic. His essay makes us question why we in the West would want the objectionable works in our own canon. Richard Yarborough surveys the issue of why so few Afro-American works have been accepted into the canon of American literature. He urges teachers and critics to redouble their efforts to right this wrong. He sees the struggle to enlarge and enrich the canon as part of a larger struggle for social equality.

Despite these problems of cultural limitation, value perpetuation, and exclusions, E. D. Hirsch, Jr. counters that we need some form of canon to create a common culture, for without a common culture we cannot communicate with each other; nor can we learn to read and think, unless we have something to read and think about.

The dilemma and meaning of canon formation is vividly revealed by Shirley Lim's personal essay. While the power of a canonical work opens up the imagination, experience, and understanding of new worlds, it may also create a distance between the reader and his or her native culture.

The many strands of the debate over the canon are pulled together in Barbara Herrnstein Smith's theoretical essay, "Contingencies of Value." She connects canon formation with one of our most basic forms of interaction: making evaluations for our own good and the good of our group. From the subject of individual judgments, she turns to the larger social mechanisms of evaluation, charting the complex processes by which a book can come to be valued as great within a culture. Artists, readers, reviewers, publishers, librarians, bookstore owners, scholars, awarders of prizes, editors of anthologies, imitators—all can have a significant effect on whether the "literary value" of a book will increase or decrease. Once value is firmly established and a work is canonized, there is a tendency for the discipline to, in a sense, protect its investment and preserve the classic's stature. Tradition-minded scholars will tend to push to the background any racism, sexism, or national chauvinism that may be contained in the work, focusing instead on the safer discussion of its form or structure. In a final selection, "Male Critics and Female Readers," Deborah Pope brings to the foreground sexist assumptions in contemporary literary studies.

Since literary culture is shared by many people, and not just experts in literature, literary critics and scholars often write for general educated audiences or mixed audiences of students and scholars. The selections by Gates, Eliot, Highet, Bohannon, Ngugi, and Lim rely on the reader's literary experiences and knowledge, but do not use specialized technical vocabulary; nor do they argue narrow technical points. These writers refer to fundamental experiences and broad questions. The main specialized knowledge they rely on is simply familiarity with the literary texts of the canon.

The essays by Yarborough, Hirsch, Smith, and Pope were written for a more specialized audience. Yet neither the Yarborough nor the Hirsch essay depends on a complex technical and conceptual vocabulary, even though they do rely on a knowledge of the history of literature and literary studies. The essays by Smith and Pope, on the other hand, are more typical of a philosophical technical style common to literary theory of recent years. Although the style may be difficult, it allows a fundamental analysis of the cultural processes of canon formation.

In Dispute on Bias, Stanford Is Likely to Alter Western Culture Program

Richard Bernstein

In the following 1987 article, *New York Times* reporter Richard Bernstein looks into the conflict at Stanford University over a required undergraduate course in Western culture. He sees the local conflict over curriculum as part of a larger debate over what the role of the canon of great works should play in education. The heart of the problem is that almost all of the accepted canonical works in philosophy and literature used in the course were written by white males. Does this mean that such a course will foster racist and sexist biases? Will an attempt to bring in the works of minorities and women weaken the quality of a great works course? Is it ethical to require a course that does not seem to represent the viewpoints of many of the students? If indeed these are the important works of our Western culture, should all students be required to read them, despite the racial and sexual imbalance? Through extended quotations from national and local figures, the reporter presents the arguments of people on all sides of the issue.

———————————

AT STANFORD UNIVERSITY, THEY still talk of the day nearly a *1* year ago when some 500 students, on a march with the Rev. Jesse Jackson, came up with a slogan for the next generation.

The students were celebrating a new course at Stanford, one that *2* would stress the contributions of minorities and women to Western culture, and, they chanted: "Hey hey, ho ho, Western culture's got to go."

Student and faculty members these days assert that the slogan ex- *3* pressed no hostility to the likes of Plato and Saint Augustine, Rousseau and John Stuart Mill, all of whom are on Stanford's current list of required reading for freshmen. But in claiming a kind of equal time for minority contributions to American civilization, the chant did reflect a demand that is expected to be accepted by the faculty in the weeks ahead.

Responding to charges that the core reading list reflects what some *4* have referred to as a "European-Western and male bias" and what others call "sexist and racist stereotypes," the Stanford faculty seems likely to approve a measure that would eliminate the Western culture course that is required of all freshmen. The course, which has been offered since

1980, is based on a list of 15 acknowledged masterpieces of philosophy and literature.

In its place would be a new yearlong requirement called "culture, *5* ideas, and values" that would include the study of at least one non-Western culture and "works by women, minorities and persons of color."

Return to Core Curriculums

The turmoil over the curriculum, with its overtones of 1960's protest, *6* promises to reawaken a longstanding debate in American education. Some argue that by ignoring classics of Western culture, universities risk leaving students ignorant of the works of genius that lie at the heart of their own civilization. Others have said that Western culture is too restrictive a concept to be adequate in an ever more diverse world, and that students should be grounded, not just in the West, but also in a global culture.

In the past decade, as universities have returned to the idea of core *7* curriculums, many of them, from Brooklyn College to Harvard, from Berkeley to Columbia, have tried to thread their way between the two alternatives, offering students a selection of courses in both Western and non-Western cultures.

Stanford seems to be unusual these days in the sharpness of the anti- *8* Western attitudes among some students, who are asserting not only that the study of the West is incomplete, but also that it represents nothing less than the dominance of a particular white male view of history.

"I don't see black students at Harvard getting excited about this sort *9* of thing," said Nathan Huggins, chairman of the Afro-American studies department at Harvard. "It seems to me that the students at Stanford are expressing the sense of ethnic diversity that is more conspicuous in California, which is close to one-third non-white, than elsewhere in the country."

'Policy by Intimidation'

The anti-Western rhetoric at Stanford comes just as conservative *10* voices—such as those of Prof. Allan Bloom in his best-selling "The Closing of the American Mind" and William J. Bennett, the Secretary of Education—have contended that the failure of students to know the great works of the West's past has left them impoverished.

"This kind of debate has gone on before, and since it's going on at *11* Stanford, it may have a ripple effect," Mr. Bennett said in a telephone interview.

"They are moving confidently and swiftly into the late 1960's, and *12* why anybody would want to do that intentionally I don't know," he said. "It looks to me as though policy by intimidation is at work. Unfortunately, a lot of academic leadership is readily intimidated by the noisiest of its students and faculty."

Stanford's proposed new curriculum was forged at the end of a two- *13* year discussion, involving numerous public meetings, written exchanges in various campus publications and a special student-faculty task force. The debate was spurred by the major black student organization, which was joined in its demand for change by feminists and groups represent- ing other minority students.

The new course will begin in 1989 and, while its exact content remains *14* undetermined, will presumably spur a search for relatively unknown or underrated works by women and Africans to be included in the core list of acknowledged classics. But, whatever the course's final form, many students and faculty members believe, or at least hope that the decision to include the works of women and minority group members in no way is a repudiation of the idea that all students should be familiar with great works of Western civilization.

The set of suggestions expected to be adopted by the faculty were *15* formulated by the student-faculty task force. Members of the panel say they represent a middle ground, retaining many of the elements of the old Western culture course while paying more attention to the contri- butions to American civilization made by groups other than white males.

"Plato will not be banned from our republic of letters," said Barry *16* M. Katz, a historian and member of the task force. "Freshmen will not emerge from their first year steeped in the lore of Eskimos and Pygmies but ignorant of English composition."

"Put simply and bluntly," he added, "the existing course requirement *17* asserts that we have a common culture and it asserts that it can be defined by a bit of reading in the great works. This has been an affront to a large number of students and faculty, to women and members of minority groups."

Nonetheless, it is clear that the recommendations have produced *18* plenty of unease, even what William M. Chace, an English professor and vice provost for academic planning, called a mood of "disappoint- ment and polite alienation" on the part of many in the faculty. Dr. Chace and others have indicated that the faculty, which is due to discuss the issue at a meeting this month, will vote for the changes, but more out of a sense of necessary compromise than intellectual enthusiasm.

Opponents of the changes have raised several objections. They say *19* the old requirement, installed as part of Stanford's back-to-basics move- ment in the late 1970's, was among the most popular and successful in the university's 100-year history. They believe student pressure should play no role in devising curriculum. And, they think that to label history's most influential works as examples of a white male culture and little else is to make a travesty of Western culture itself.

'Education Is Not a Democracy'

"It's a version of academic populism° and populism is always dangerous 20 for a university," Dr. Chace said. "Education is not a democracy. Students don't come here thinking that they know as much as their professors. There is a system of deference, and if the system breaks down, we're in real trouble.

"We owe it to our students to tell them, 'Here's the kind of thing you 21 will find of long-term value. These are the things that thousands of people have lived their lives by.' To relegate them to the status of white male writing may be factually true, but it's of low significance."

Some maintain that dropping the old Western culture course marks 22 the triumph of a kind of tyranny of the minority. They say proponents of the change were quick to label opposition as "racist."

"The overriding motivation for the change is political expediency," 23 said Isaac D. Barchas, a classics student. "I think that the consequences will be the impoverishment of the undergraduate experience."

"What is a liberal education?" he asked. "It's an education that liberates 24 people. And if there's a liberating idea in the Western tradition, it is that it doesn't matter if you're black or white or Jewish or Chinese, that there are truths that transcend the accident of birth. That's why the great books are important."

Many faculty members, including supporters and opponents of the 25 new plan, contend the demands of minority students, who constitute about one-third of freshmen classes, stemmed from a desire simply to be represented in a curriculum that excluded their own heritage's great figures.

The resentment and estrangement of some was expressed by Amanda 26 Kemp, former president of the Black Student Union who wrote in the student newspaper, The Stanford Daily, that the implicit message of the current curriculum is "nigger go home."

William King, the current president of the Black Student Union, said: 27 "The Western culture requirement has had a very significant impact because it's a course that every student at the university has to take. It's the one requirement that really says to us, we're different."

He added: "We want a sense that America, where we are now, is not 28 just the progress that came from England and France, that it wasn't only Thomas Jefferson and the Founding Fathers. Other groups contributed significantly."

In the debate other themes arose. Carolyn C. Lougee, a faculty mem- 29 ber and member of the task force, wrote that "the Western civ course is not a timeless, eternal distillate of human wisdom," which happens to be precisely what the core reading list's advocates believe it to be.

Populism—a political appeal to the interest and opinions of the common people.

Instead, she contended that it arose from a need of the United States, flooded by new immigrants after World War I, to forge "a myth of a West that transcended every ethnicity and embraced them all."

Faculty members here, aware of their university's importance and *30* prestige, have bristled at criticism of the change from elsewhere. The novelist Saul Bellow, for example, remarked in a recent issue of The New York Times Magazine that he did not know "the Tolstoy° of the Zulus, the Proust° of the Papuans°." His remark provoked the ire of some professors, who charged him with insensitivity to the feelings of non-whites.

"I don't know much about the Zulus," John R. Perry, a philosophy *31* professor and task force member, said, "but if his never having heard of a great author among them suggests that it's pointless to look for great ideas or things to teach from the whole African continent, then I find it sad."

Rhetorical Analysis Through Annotation

This story is presented as both a political conflict and a conflict of ideas, involving nationally prominent figures and local Stanford University faculty and students. Circle each person or group who is mentioned as taking part in the debate. Note in the margin whether these people are national figures, Stanford University faculty, or Stanford University students. Further, note whether each supports the traditional Western canon or desires a more open selection of readings. Finally, based on what each says, mark whether each believes the conflict is predominantly political or intellectual.

When are people mentioned as groups ("some," "others"), rather than as individuals? Why?

Is equal space devoted to both sides of the conflict? With what figures and with what viewpoint does the article begin and end? Why? Are both sides presented as offering equally good arguments? Do the people quoted offer reasons in support of their positions? Do they see their opposition as driven by politics or bias or do they give credit to their opposition's intellectual position?

How is the local conflict related to national issues? Where and why are other campuses and national political and intellectual figures mentioned in the story? Do the national figures tend to favor one side or the other? Do the Stanford figures tend to favor one side or another? Is there a difference in the types of arguments used by the national and the Stanford figures? Are either presented as being more reasonable? How do the local Stanford situation and mood compare to the broader national mood?

Leo Tolstoy (1828–1910)—Russian novelist, author of *War and Peace*.   **Marcel Proust** (1871–1922)—French novelist, author of *Remembrance of Things Past*.   **Papuans**—a Pacific aboriginal people from the island of Papua New Guinea.

Discussion Questions

Interpreting the Text

1. Why do proponents of the change believe that the traditional canon of great works of Western culture should not be the basis of a required course?

2. In what ways do the proposals create unease, even mild alienation, among the faculty? To what extent do the proposals address an alienation among the students? To what extent should either or both of these considerations enter into an academic decision?

Considering the Issues

3. In what way does the story represent the conflict as between sixties radicalism and eighties conservatism? To what extent does the story move beyond that characterization to a deeper exploration of the issues?

4. Why do some faculty members feel that students should not influence curriculum choices? Whom do you believe should have a say in determining college curriculum: faculty, students, or some combination of both? If students should have some say but only under special conditions, what should those conditions be?

5. To what extent do you believe we share a common culture? To what extent has that culture been shaped by the work of the acknowledged great thinkers and writers of Western culture? What other elements have gone into shaping that culture? On the other hand, do you believe that different populations in the United States live within separate cultures? If so, should such a separation remain as part of our cultural diversity?

6. Is there a required great works or Western culture course at your college? Do you agree with the requirement or lack of it? If your college has such courses, are minorities, women, and non-Western cultures represented in the readings? Do you believe there should be more or less representation? If you have no such required course, how well do you feel writings of women, minorities, and non-Western culture are represented elsewhere in the curriculum? Have you ever read such works in any of your courses? Do you feel there should be more or fewer such works taught at your college?

7. Are you acquainted with the works of any of the authors of great works mentioned in this article? If so, what important ideas have you learned from that author? How has reading that author helped you understand yourself and our culture? Which works by women, minorities, or members of non-Western cultures are you familiar with? How have reading those works increased your understanding of yourself and others?

8. In April 1988 Stanford's faculty senate voted 39–4 to keep only six of the original fifteen names on the required list (the Bible's Abraham, Plato, St. Augustine, Machiavelli, Rousseau, and Marx). Professors will supplement works by these authors with others of their own choosing, making sure to give "substantial attention to issues of race, gender, and class" (*Time*, April 11, 1988,

pp. 66–67). Is this compromise fair? Will it satisfy everyone or no one? Who "won" this debate?

Writing Suggestions

1. You have been appointed to a faculty–student committee to consider revising your college's current base curriculum requirements. If your college does not have a Western culture course, the committee is to consider whether to institute one. If your college does have such a requirement, the committee is to consider whether to modify it. Write a three-hundred word statement to the committee setting forth your position on the course.

2. Your college newspaper has a column called, "News Briefs from Other Campuses." Write a fifty-word summary of the Stanford controversy to appear in that column.

3. As part of this course's concern for how information is presented, write a critique of the Bernstein article in which you discuss whether either side is presented in this article more favorably than the other. To what extent and in what way does the reporter maintain or violate journalistic objectivity? How can the reporter establish a viewpoint for a story without explicitly stating a position? Does the news story offer balanced coverage to satisfy readers holding a wide range of opinions on the subject? In what other way might this story have been reported to be either more objective or more supportive of one view or another?

What Is a Classic?

T. S. Eliot

> By the time T. S. Eliot made the following address to the Virgil Society in London in 1944, he was a famous literary figure. Born in St. Louis in 1888, Eliot attended Harvard and afterwards received a scholarship to study in Germany and England. He took up permanent residence in England, became a naturalized citizen in 1927, and lived there until his death in 1965. In addition to writing such famous poems as "The Love Song of J. Alfred Prufrock" (1915), *The Wasteland* (1922), and *Four Quartets* (1943), Eliot wrote a large amount of influential criticism, carrying the recurring message that we ought to understand why we appreciate literature, and that we ought to appreciate only the best.
>
> The Virgil Society was a group of scholars dedicated to the study of that ancient Latin poet. Eliot begins his essay by commenting on the centrality of Virgil to European values and the comprehensiveness

of his writing. He turns to the question "What is a classic?" because
he thinks Virgil contains all the defining qualities: maturity of mind,
manners, and language. Maturity, however, remains an elusive quality
of the human spirit, recognizable only by those who themselves have
attained it.

IF THERE IS ONE word on which we can fix, which will suggest the   1
maximum of what I mean by the term 'a classic', it is the word *maturity*
I shall distinguish between the universal classics like Virgil, and the
classic which is only such in relation to the other literature in its own
language, or according to the view of life of a particular period. A classic
can only occur when a civilization is mature; when a language and a
literature are mature; and it must be the work of a mature mind. It is
the importance of that civilization and of that language, as well as the
comprehensiveness of the mind of the individual poet which gives the
universality. To define *maturity* without assuming that the hearer already
knows what it means, is almost impossible: let us say then, that if we
are properly mature, as well as educated persons, we can recognize
maturity in a civilization and in a literature, as we do in the other human
beings whom we encounter. To make the meaning of maturity really
apprehensible—indeed, even to make it acceptable—to the immature, is
perhaps impossible. But if we are mature we either recognize maturity
immediately, or come to know it on more intimate acquaintance. No
reader of Shakespeare, for instance, can fail to recognize, increasingly as
he himself grows up, the gradual ripening of Shakespeare's mind: even
a less developed reader can perceive the rapid development of Elizabethan literature and drama as a whole, from early Tudor° crudity to the
plays of Shakespeare, and perceive a decline in the work of Shakespeare's
successors. We can also observe, upon a little conversance, that the plays
of Christopher Marlowe° exhibit a greater maturity of mind and of style
than the plays which Shakespeare wrote at the same age: it is interesting
to speculate whether, if Marlowe had lived as long as Shakespeare, his
development would have continued at the same pace. I doubt it: for we
observe some minds maturing earlier than others, and we observe that
those which mature very early do not always develop very far. I raise
this point as a reminder, first that the value of maturity depends upon
the value of that which matures, and second, that we should know when
we are concerned with the maturity of individual writers, and when
with the relative maturity of literary periods. A writer who individually
has a more mature mind may belong to a less mature period than
another, so that in that respect his work will be less mature. The maturity

---

Tudor—referring to the rough style of the mid-sixteenth century.   **Christopher Marlowe** (1564–1593)—English dramatist and contemporary of William Shakespeare.

of a literature is the reflection of that of the society in which it is produced: an individual author—notably Shakespeare and Virgil—can do much to develop his language: but he cannot bring that language to maturity unless the work of his predecessors has prepared it for his final touch. A mature literature, therefore, has a history behind it: a history, that is not merely a chronicle, an accumulation of manuscripts and writings of this kind and that, but an ordered though unconscious progress of a language to realize its own potentialities within its own limitations.

It is to be observed, that a society, and a literature, like an individual *2* human being, do not necessarily mature equally and concurrently in every respect. The precocious child is often, in some obvious ways, childish for his age in comparison with ordinary children. Is there any one period of English literature to which we can point as being fully mature, comprehensively and in equilibrium? I do not think so: and, as I shall repeat later, I hope it is not so. We cannot say that any individual poet in English has in the course of his life become a more mature man than Shakespeare: we cannot even say that any poet has done so much, to make the English language capable of expressing the most subtle thought or the most refined shades of feeling. Yet we cannot but feel that a play like Congreve's° *Way of the World* is in some way more mature than any play of Shakespeare's: but only in this respect, that it reflects a more mature society—that is, it reflects a greater maturity of *manners*. The society for which Congreve wrote was, from our point of view, coarse and brutal enough: yet it is nearer to ours than the society of the Tudors: perhaps for that reason we judge it the more severely. Nevertheless, it was a society more polished and less provincial: its mind was shallower, its sensibility more restricted; it has lost some promise of maturity but realized another. So to maturity of *mind* we must add maturity of *manners.*

The progress towards maturity of language is, I think, more easily *3* recognized and more readily acknowledged in the development of prose, than in that of poetry. In considering prose we are less distracted by individual differences in greatness, and more inclined to demand approximation towards a common standard, a common vocabulary and a common sentence structure: it is often, in fact, the prose which departs the farthest from these common standards, which is individual to the extreme, that we are apt to denominate 'poetic prose'. At a time when England had already accomplished miracles in poetry, her prose was relatively immature, developed sufficiently for certain purposes but not for others: at that same time, when the French language had given little promise of poetry as great as that in English, French prose was much more mature than English prose. You have only to compare any Tudor

---

William Congreve (1670–1729)—English dramatist.

writer with Montaigne°—and Montaigne himself, as a stylist, is only a precursor, his style not ripe enough to fulfil the French requirements for the classic. Our prose was ready for some tasks before it could cope with others: a Malory° could come long before a Hooker°, a Hooker before a Hobbes°, and a Hobbes before an Addison°. Whatever difficulties we have in applying this standard to poetry, it is possible to see that the development of a classic prose is the development towards a *common style*. By this I do not mean that the best writers are indistinguishable from each other. The essential and characteristic differences remain: it is not that the differences are less, but that they are more subtle and refined. To a sensitive palate the difference between the prose of Addison and that of Swift° will be as marked as the difference between two vintage wines to a connoisseur. What we find, in a period of classic prose, is not a mere common convention of writing, like the common style of newspaper leader writers, but a community of taste. The age which precedes a classic age, may exhibit both eccentricity and monotony: monotony because the resources of the language have not yet been explored, and eccentricity because there is yet no generally accepted standard—if, indeed, that can be called eccentric where there is no centre. Its writing may be at the same time pedantic and licentious. The age following a classic age, may also exhibit eccentricity and monotony: monotony because the resources of the language have, for the time at least, been exhausted, and eccentricity because originality comes to be more valued than correctness. But the age in which we find a common style, will be an age when society has achieved a moment of order and stability, of equilibrium and harmony; as the age which manifests the greatest extremes of individual style will be an age of immaturity or an age of senility.

Maturity of language may naturally be expected to accompany maturity of mind and manners. We may expect the language to approach maturity at the moment when men have a critical sense of the past, a confidence in the present, and no conscious doubt of the future. In literature, this means that the poet is aware of his predecessors, and that we are aware of the predecessors behind his work, as we may be aware of ancestral traits in a person who is at the same time individual and unique. The predecessors should be themselves great and honoured: but their accomplishment must be such as to suggest still undeveloped resources of the language, and not such as to oppress the younger writers with the fear that everything that can be done has been done, in their language. The poet, certainly, in a mature age, may still obtain stimulus from the hope of doing something that his predecessors have not done:

Michel de Montaigne (1533–1592)—French essayist. **Thomas Malory**—Fifteenth-century English translator of tales of King Arthur. **Richard Hooker** (1554–1600)—English theologian. **Thomas Hobbes** (1588–1679)—English philosopher. **Joseph Addison** (1672–1719)—English essayist. **Jonathan Swift** (1667–1745)—Irish satirist.

he may even be in revolt against them, as a promising adolescent may revolt against the beliefs, the habits and the manners of his parents; but, in retrospect, we can see that he is also the continuer of their traditions, that he preserves essential family characteristics, and that his difference of behaviour is a difference in the circumstances of another age. And, on the other hand, just as we sometimes observe men whose lives are overshadowed by the fame of a father or grandfather, men of whom any achievement of which they are capable appears comparatively insignificant, so a late age of poetry may be consciously impotent to compete with its distinguished ancestry. We meet poets of this kind at the end of any age, poets with a sense of the past only, or alternatively, poets whose hope of the future is founded upon the attempt to renounce the past. The persistence of literary creativeness in any people, accordingly, consists in the maintenance of an unconscious balance between tradition in the larger sense—the collective personality, so to speak, realized in the literature of the past—and the originality of the living generation.

Rhetorical Analysis Through Annotation

This essay may be viewed as an extended definition of the word maturity, but the definition proceeds more by associating maturity with other concepts, experiences, and examples than by giving a straightforward formal dictionary definition.

To examine how the definition works, circle all uses of the words *mature* and *maturity*. Box other concepts Eliot sees related to maturity, and underline all examples and experiences that reflect maturity.

Then discuss what you think Eliot means by maturity, how he builds up that definition, and whether you think the definition is clear. Finally discuss whether you agree with his definition.

Discussion Questions

Interpreting the Text

1. How does Eliot's definition of maturity compare with the more ordinary meanings of that word? What assumptions does Eliot's definition rest on? What purpose does he have in developing his definition?

2. In what ways can Eliot's language be called evaluative? What are some specific words and phrases he uses to make evaluations and assert judgments?

Considering the Issues

3. Which books have you read that seem to have the kind of maturity Eliot describes? Which books do not have it at all? Does maturity in literature appeal to you? Is it a proper measure for literature? Does maturity as a measure for literature suggest that literature is primarily to be appreciated by older people,

and that the works that appeal to more youthful tastes do not qualify as serious literature? If so, what do you think of that?

4. How mature is our current cultural period? Consider movies, television, music, art, and other forms of cultural expression as well as books. Are there certain creative artists you consider more mature than others? Why?

Writing Suggestions

1. Based on your own literary experience and taste, write an answer to Eliot, defining what a classic means to you and giving examples.

2. Write an article for the arts page of your college newspaper on one of the following:
"What Makes a Rock and Roll Classic a Classic"
"It's Junk and I Love It"
"Maturity and Immaturity on Television"
"The Classics of Advertising"

3. Look at the second sentence in the first paragraph, in which Eliot distinguishes two kinds of classics. For a course in contemporary art, literature, or music write a short paper in which you identify some artistic product of our time that you think will have lasting greatness and one that is now thought great, but later ages will scorn or forget. Give reasons for your evaluations.

4. Imagine you are part of a discussion group examining your own values. The group could be church-related, part of a philosophy course, attached to college counselling, or just an informal collection of friends. For this group write an informal essay exploring your thoughts on the value of maturity or value of immaturity.

Compulsory Reading

Gilbert Highet

Gilbert Highet (1906–1978), scholar of classical languages at Columbia University, followed in the tradition of T. S. Eliot. He firmly believed that the books comprising the canon were more worthy and beautiful than others. These works, he believed, offered deep insights into the human mind and spirit.

To help share the riches of literature with a broader public, Highet gave weekly radio talks in the 1950s. These talks brought the classics of literature to the public's attention and helped explain what was special about each writer and text. In one of his talks in 1957, however, he recognizes a fundamental problem in what he does: people react against being told what to do. Good literature then becomes something to be dreaded, like medicine that leaves you groggy. Highet offers some suggestions for bringing enjoyment back to the great works.

EVERY NOW AND THEN, at a party, you meet someone who tells *1* you about a book she had just read. She describes its tremendous reception and the growing fame of its author. Finally, in a tone of friendly authority, she says 'You *must* read it. Do remember its title, now, and don't forget. You *must* read it.'

At once your stomach—assisted by the canapés—turns. You thank *2* her civilly. You fix the name of the book in your memory. You resolve never, never on any account, to read it.

Yet it might have been quite a good book. She explained how im- *3* portant it was. What made you feel it must be revolting? Was the evidence in its favor inadequate? No. The evidence was fairly sound. But you were biased against the book simply because someone told you that you must *must* MUST read it.

We have all felt this. It goes back to the days when we were in school, *4* when we were told that we were obliged to read some book about which we usually knew nothing, nothing whatever, except that it was a Must. Now, there are some people who naturally hate reading because of some psycho-physical quirk in their make-up: they live through their hands, they can hit a ball anywhere or fix anything, but they are made dizzy by looking at print on paper. Still, such people are few. Most people can read, most people like to read; yet many of them are discouraged from reading, in school. Surely that is worse than a blunder: it is a crime. Reading, for most people, is a natural pleasure. They would enjoy it without any suspicion or reluctance—in fact, it would be difficult to keep them away from it. But compulsion does so: for some, completely; for all, partially.

Surely, if we wanted to make boys disgusted with baseball, one very *5* good way would be to institute baseball classes in every school, to make baseball efficiency compulsory for graduation, to set up baseball curricula and baseball quizzes and baseball Regents' Examinations,° to distribute lists of baseball facts which had to be learned off by heart and interpretations of baseball trends which had to be discussed, to work out long courses in pitching, catching, fielding, and strategy, to treat the entire game as something deadly systematic and deadly serious, and to build it up as a painful dedicated occupation to a Ph.D. degree. Of course, a few noble souls would take it all in, and stay with it; the others

---

Regents' Examinations—state-wide secondary school examinations.

would be sickened of baseball, and never think of it again for the rest of their lives.

However, it is not only the repellent force of compulsion that makes **6** the young disgusted with the books they are forced to read. Partly it is the quality of the books. They are often bad.

The other day, one of my friends showed me a book of modern **7** Spanish short stories which he was expected to use in teaching Spanish. I read some of them. It would be a compliment to call them mediocre. Any sensitive boy or girl who read them would be forced to conclude that Spain had no modern literature worth a *caramba*, that Spanish was not worth learning for its own sake, and that his or her teachers were tasteless idiots. It is often the same in English literature. A month of my life at the age of fifteen or sixteen was blighted by one of the books of that distinguished bore, George Eliot.° *The Mill on the Floss*, I think it was: a decent enough little work for its time, but now utterly without relevance or distinction. They tell me that some schools are still plagued by another work of that obsolete author (or authoress), called *Silas Marner*. It is the same in other tongues. My wife still speaks with horror of the endless tedium of Balzac's° social-documentary novels, which she was compelled to read when studying French in school. I myself like Latin; but all the time my classmates were reading the works of Caesar in Latin, I (having read them the night before) was working through Victor Hugo° in French, under the desk. A dashed good book, too, *The Toilers of the Sea*. But I was detected. The schoolmaster saw that something must be wrong. Instead of looking as consumedly bored as the other members of the class, I was actually showing signs of interest. No wonder. I was not reading about Caesar building a bridge across the Rhine. I was reading about a diver being attacked in a submarine cave by a gigantic octopus: *la Pieuvre!*°

But how about the plays of Shakespeare? Surely they are different. I **8** enjoyed the plays of Shakespeare, even at school, even under compulsion. So did most of us. We talked about them. We went downtown to see an amateur performance of *The Merchant of Venice*, and talked about that. And then there were a few other books which, even although obligatory, did not appear boring. We did penetrate to their value.

It is the same in other countries. We do not hear that French school- **9** boys object bitterly to reading Molière° and Racine;° that German boys despise Goethe° when they are directed to study *Faust*; that the Italian youngsters think it is a waste of time when they begin Dante.° They

---

George Eliot (1819–1880)—pen name of English novelist Mary Ann Evans. **Honoré de Balzac** (1799–1850)—French novelist. Victor Hugo (1802–1885)—French poet, playwright, and novelist. *la Pieuvre*—the poor thing. Molière (1622–1673)—pen name of Jean Baptiste Poquelin, French playwright. **Jean Racine** (1639–1699)—French playwright. **Johann Wolfgang von Goethe** (1749–1832)—German poet, dramatist, and novelist. Dante Alighieri (1265–1321)—Italian poet.

may kick at other compulsory books; but at those, no. On the whole, the young will read good books even if they are made compulsory, while they will object bitterly to reading inferior or obsolete books under the slightest degree of obligation.

Now, why is this? Is all compulsion hopeless in leading boys and girls *10* to read? Or are there some books which ought to be compulsory, and can be made compulsory without creating permanent disgust? If so, what are they? Are there any methods of urging boys and girls to read which will gradually dispense with compulsion—in fact, change external pressure into self-perpetuating interest? Surely there must be some way of getting the young to read, without using Chinese tortures on them. Bribery, perhaps? No. A friend of mine recently told me that he paid his daughter ten dollars to read Walter Scott's° *Ivanhoe.* Half way through she came and offered to return him five dollars if he would not make her finish the book. You see, bribery is expensive, and it does not work. There must be some other methods.

The first essential, it seems to me, is to choose books which are not *11* only good, but appealing: books which are authoritative, books which are already partly known, partly 'sold' to the young. Boys and girls have very narrow horizons. They know few books; they know few authors. Therefore it is no good giving them something remote and obsolete. They have never heard of George Eliot. Most of them have never even heard of T. S. Eliot (if you can imagine such a thing). The bright ones may care about T. S. None of them will care about George, and there is no real reason whey they should. If they are to be interested in literature, they must be given *either* something by an absolutely firstrate writer, or *else* something by an author who is close to them in time and in interest. They will not reject Shakespeare. They will not reject Ernest Hemingway.° With the one, they will know they are reading something of almost universal appeal. With the other, they will know that they are reading a lively and energetic contemporary. Most of them are not going to be professional students of literature. They will never write Ph.D. theses on 'The development of social consciousness in the nineteenth-century English novel as illustrated by George Eliot.' But Shakespeare will always be playing somewhere—on the stage, in motion pictures, or in other media; and every lively youngster will enjoy meeting the Nobel Prize winners of his own generation and his own country.

Then the second essential in this kind of reading is to encourage *12* criticism. Many young people, at school and at college, are given books called The Classics, and are merely told to read them, as though they were expected to admire every single word in them. This is a mistake.

Walter Scott (1771–1832)—Scottish novelist and poet.   Ernest Hemingway (1899–1961)—American novelist.

No books are perfect. I remember still what a revelation it was to me at school when the master who taught us English literature poured scorn on Shakespeare's vulgar and corny jokes: those terrible puns, those cheap witticisms about sex—true marks (he told us) of the brilliant but half-educated man catering to the groundlings.° We were relieved to know that we did not *have* to laugh. But then (he went on), then the play of fancy when Shakespeare really gets off the ground, as in the Queen Mab speech in *Romeo and Juliet*, ah, *there*. . . . Thus we were taught to distinguish, even in the work of a great writer, between bad and good. A valuable lesson.

In the same way, I suffered a good deal from Walter Scott, and a **13** certain amount from Charles Dickens. I ought to have been told the obvious facts, which I know now—that Scott was writing in a tearing hurry in order to make money, and often obeying conventions for which he did not particularly care; but that when he wrote what he liked best, battle scenes and moments of tense drama and bold speeches by peasants and simple folk, he was a great imaginative writer. Dickens's° more complicated plots worried me to death, although *Oliver Twist* gripped me then as it grips me to this day. I should have been told that Dickens wrote them not as books, but as serials for magazines, and therefore committed faults of construction which I would have to overlook. A few hints like that would have made me ignore the bad parts of such books, and appreciate the good parts much more sincerely.

The third essential in encouraging the young to read is to explain, to **14** analyze, to dissect without killing. Young men and women, boys and girls, are short-sighted. They cannot without guidance carry a whole book in their head, so as to see its structure and its entire meaning. Listen to them describing a motion picture—you will hear that they do it all in sequence: 'And then she comes in, and she has a gun, and he takes it out of her pocket while he's kissing her, but she doesn't know that, and then the light suddenly goes out and the door opens. . . .' They seem to have very little idea that anyone wrote the entire picture as a single work with a plan—what Hollywood calls 'continuity.' Therefore, one of the things best worth teaching them is to see a piece of history, or a motion picture, or a book, or the plan of their own lives, as a large continuous whole, with a structure which can be taken in by the mind and analyzed.

But it is useless simply to tell youngsters to read A Book. It is like **15** telling them to go away and live for A Year. They should be told what to expect—week by week, section by section; they should be shown how to break down a big work into smaller parts, how to appreciate each part, and how to admire the skill with which the parts grow

---

Groundlings—audience of commoners.   **Charles Dickens (1812–1870)**—English novelist.

together into a single work of art. I am still grateful to the man who made me read Shakespeare's *Julius Caesar* when I was sixteen or so. I had scarcely even realized that all the men in the play were different, until he made me analyze the characters of Brutus and Cassius and Mark Antony, and how to find out—from their speeches alone—what made them tick. I had scarcely even realized that the play (and every play) had a measured movement, until he showed me how each act said something different in quality from all the others. At the end of that class, I not only understood the play of *Julius Caesar* better; I knew more about Shakespeare, I knew a little about the theater, and I was beginning to take an interest in psychology.

These are lessons which I have never forgotten. I have been trying to   *16* improve on them ever since.

Perhaps the lessons began with a little of the stick; but they ended   *17* with a delicious and nourishing carrot. And that is one of the main secrets of education—to hint at the stick, but to make sure the carrot is juicy. In the Book of Proverbs° there is a fine poem in which Wisdom speaks to mankind. She does not say she is compulsory. She says she is attractive and valuable:

> Receive my instruction, and not silver; and knowledge rather than choice gold. For wisdom is better than rubies; and all the things that may be desired are not to be compared to it.

Rhetorical Analysis Through Annotation

To carry his message to a nonspecialist audience, Highet uses personal experiences, common knowledge, and everyday language. After some introduction, he raises a problem, puzzles over it in a common sense way, and then offers several suggestions for solving the problem.

In the margin, note where Highet uses anecdotes from his own life and common experiences of his audience. Then note where he identifies the problem of getting students to enjoy compulsory reading and where he begins giving his three recommendations.

Discuss who exactly his audience seems to be (their age, socioeconomic background, interests, etc.) and what techniques he uses to appeal to that specific audience. On what clues in the text do you base your audience profile? What would be motivating this audience to be listening to this radio talk?

Finally, how does Highet broaden his discussion at the end of his talk? Underline what you take to be his main message. How much does Highet's talk focus on compulsory reading done in school by young people and how much on voluntary reading done outside of school by anyone?

Book of Proverbs—from the Old Testament.

Discussion Questions

Interpreting the Text

1. When Highet suggests choosing for students books that are "not only good, but appealing," he implies that there will be natural, widespread agreement on what those books are. Does he specify how one is to choose this type of book out of the larger canon? Does he mention specific, objective qualities, or is he being subjective?

2. Why does Highet think students should be encouraged to criticize books? Were you encouraged to? Do you think encouraging criticism will lead to negative or positive attitudes toward literature?

3. What does Highet mean by the structure of a book? Why does he think teachers should help students analyze the structure? What books have you read where understanding the structure helped you appreciate the book more? Which books had easy to understand structures and which books had difficult structures? Were there any books where you did not need to pay attention to the structure?

4. What are Highet's essentials for getting students to enjoy reading? How do these match with your own experience in and out of school? Would you agree with his recommendations? Would you change or add any recommendations?

Considering the Issues

5. What is your reaction to being told a book is great and you must read it? What were your reactions to assigned literature in school? Do your reactions fit the pattern described by Highet? Do you think you should be required to read certain books even if you do not find them interesting?

6. Have you read any of the books mentioned by Highet? Do you agree with his judgments about which books are deadly boring and which are endlessly fascinating? What were the most fascinating books you have read and what were their effects on you? Were any of these assigned books in school? If so, did their being assigned change the effect?

7. Highet concludes that students' lessons should begin "with a little of the stick," but end with a "delicious and nourishing carrot." What does he mean by the stick and the carrot? Do you feel that in school you are being hit with a stick and lured by a carrot, like a donkey? Do you agree with this description of education?

8. Compare Highet's essay to Eliot's. In what ways are both trying to achieve similar purposes before general educated audiences? In what ways are their audiences and purposes different? What different relationships do the two authors establish with their audiences? How do the similarities and differences of purpose, audience, and authorial stance account for the styles of the two essays?

9. This talk was given in 1957. What elements in it, if any, make it seem dated, and what makes it seem still fresh and relevant?

Writing Suggestions

1. To share your experiences of reading with the members of this course, write an autobiographical account either of your experiences with compulsory reading in school or of your reading on your own.

2. Imagine you were hired to teach a private course in literature for a younger brother, sister, cousin, nephew, niece, or friend whom you know well. For the parents of this student write up your plan for the course and your reasons, based both on general principles and your personal knowledge of the student. Include the books you would have the student read, what activities you would have the student do, and how you would teach.

3. For a course on radio and television broadcasting write an essay describing how Highet manages to appeal to a general audience while talking about a cultural topic. Point out any lessons that may be applied to contemporary radio and television. Discuss, as well, any drawbacks or difficulties you find in his approach.

4. Highet is dealing with a serious subject, how students can be taught to love literature, yet he uses humor to get his points across. As part of this course's concern for the techniques of writing, analyze his use of humor. What methods does he use? Who does he make fun of and how? When does he back off humor and switch to a serious tone?

5. A feminist may object to Highet's assumption that no one enjoys reading George Eliot, the famous female novelist, and that everyone enjoys reading boys' adventure stories and Hemingway. Write a condensed version of Highet's talk from a woman's point of view, altering his stories, examples, and anything else you feel reveals unconscious bias.

Shakespeare in the Bush

Laura Bohannan

Through her Western education, Laura Bohannan, professor of anthropology at the University of Illinois at Chicago, came to appreciate deeply the classics of Western literature. But when she did fieldwork with the Tiv tribe in Africa, she became aware how culture-bound her reactions to literature were. In describing her experiences of telling a Shakespearean story to the Tiv, she raises fundamental questions about the universality and wisdom of the great works of literature— the kind that Highet said would attract any student.

Because Bohannan considers people's responses to literature as part of broad cultural questions of the type raised by anthropology, this article appeared first in *Natural History* magazine rather than in a literary journal. It has been of interest to literary theorists, however, because it so strikingly calls into question the supposition that great literature speaks deeply to all and expresses universally held beliefs about the human condition.

JUST BEFORE I LEFT Oxford for the Tiv in West Africa, conversation   1
turned to the season at Stratford. "You Americans," said a friend, "often have difficulty with Shakespeare. He was, after all, a very English poet, and one can easily misinterpret the universal by misunderstanding the particular."

I protested that human nature is pretty much the same the whole   2
world over; at least the general plot and motivation of the greater tragedies would always be clear—everywhere—although some details of custom might have to be explained and difficulties of translation might produce other slight changes. To end an argument we could not conclude, my friend gave me a copy of *Hamlet* to study in the African bush: it would, he hoped, lift my mind above its primitive surroundings, and possibly I might, by prolonged meditation, achieve the grace of correct interpretation.

It was my second field trip to that African tribe, and I thought myself   3
ready to live in one of its remote sections—an area difficult to cross even on foot. I eventually settled on the hillock of a very knowledgeable old man, the head of a homestead of some hundred and forty people, all of whom were either his close relatives or their wives and children. Like the other elders of the vicinity, the old man spent most of his time performing ceremonies seldom seen these days in the more accessible parts of the tribe. I was delighted. Soon there would be three months of enforced isolation and leisure, between the harvest that takes place just before the rising of the swamps and the clearing of new farms when the water goes down. Then, I thought, they would have even more time to perform ceremonies and explain them to me.

I was quite mistaken. Most of the ceremonies demanded the presence   4
of elders from several homesteads. As the swamps rose, the old men found it too difficult to walk from one homestead to the next, and the ceremonies gradually ceased. As the swamps rose even higher, all activities but one came to an end. The women brewed beer from maize and millet. Men, women, and children sat on their hillocks and drank it.

People began to drink at dawn. By midmorning the whole homestead   5
was singing, dancing, and drumming. When it rained, people had to sit inside their huts: there they drank and sang or they drank and told stories. In any case, by noon or before, I either had to join the party or retire to my own hut and my books. "One does not discuss serious matters when there is beer. Come, drink with us." Since I lacked their capacity for the thick native beer, I spent more and more time with

Hamlet. Before the end of the second month, grace descended on me. I was quite sure that *Hamlet* had only one possible interpretation, and that one universally obvious.

Early every morning, in the hope of having some serious talk before *6* the beer party, I used to call on the old man at his reception hut—a circle of posts supporting a thatched roof above a low mud wall to keep out wind and rain. One day I crawled through the low doorway and found most of the men of the homestead sitting huddled in their ragged cloths on stools, low plank beds, and reclining chairs, warming themselves against the chill of the rain around a smoky fire. In the center were three pots of beer. The party had started.

The old man greeted me cordially. "Sit down and drink." I accepted *7* a large calabash° full of beer, poured some into a small drinking gourd, and tossed it down. Then I poured some more into the same gourd for the man second in seniority to my host before I handed my calabash over to a young man for further distribution. Important people shouldn't ladle beer themselves.

"It is better like this," the old man said, looking at me approvingly *8* and plucking at the thatch that had caught in my hair. "You should sit and drink with us more often. Your servants tell me that when you are not with us, you sit inside your hut looking at a paper."

The old man was acquainted with four kinds of "papers": tax receipts, *9* bride price receipts, court fee receipts, and letters. The messenger who brought him letters from the chief used them mainly as a badge of office, for he always knew what was in them and told the old man. Personal letters for the few who had relatives in the government or mission stations were kept until someone went to a large market where there was a letter writer and reader. Since my arrival, letters were brought to me to be read. A few men also brought me bride price receipts, privately, with requests to change the figures to a higher sum. I found moral arguments were of no avail, since in-laws are fair game, and the technical hazards of forgery difficult to explain to an illiterate people. I did not wish them to think me silly enough to look at any such papers for days on end, and I hastily explained that my "paper" was one of the "things of long ago" of my country.

"Ah," said the old man. "Tell us." *10*

I protested that I was not a storyteller. Storytelling is a skilled art *11* among them; their standards are high, and the audiences critical—and vocal in their criticism. I protested in vain. This morning they wanted to hear a story while they drank. They threatened to tell me no more stories until I told them one of mine. Finally, the old man promised that no one would criticize my style "for we know you are struggling with our language." "But," put in one of the elders, "you must explain what

---

Calabash—a gourd, used here as a bowl or cup.

we do not understand, as we do when we tell you our stories." Realizing that here was my chance to prove *Hamlet* universally intelligible, I agreed.

The old man handed me some more beer to help me on with my storytelling. Men filled their long wooden pipes and knocked coals from the fire to place in the pipe bowls; then, puffing contentedly, they sat back to listen. I began in the proper style, "Not yesterday, not yesterday, but long ago, a thing occurred. One night three men were keeping watch outside the homestead of the great chief, when suddenly they saw the former chief approach them." 12

"Why was he no longer their chief?" 13

"He was dead," I explained. "That is why they were troubled and afraid when they saw him." 14

"Impossible," began one of the elders, handing his pipe on to his neighbor, who interrupted, "Of course it wasn't the dead chief. It was an omen sent by a witch. Go on." 15

Slightly shaken, I continued. "One of these three was a man who knew things"—the closest translation for scholar, but unfortunately it also meant witch. The second elder looked triumphantly at the first. "So he spoke to the dead chief saying, 'Tell us what we must do so you may rest in your grave,' but the dead chief did not answer. He vanished, and they could see him no more. Then the man who knew things—his name was Horatio—said this event was the affair of the dead chief's son, Hamlet." 16

There was a general shaking of heads round the circle. "Had the dead chief no living brothers? Or was this son the chief?" 17

"No," I replied. "That is, he had one living brother who became the chief when the elder brother died." 18

The old men muttered: such omens were matters for chiefs and elders, not for youngsters; no good could come of going behind a chief's back; clearly Horatio was not a man who knew things. 19

"Yes, he was," I insisted, shooing a chicken away from my beer. "In our country the son is next to the father. The dead chief's younger brother had become the great chief. He had also married his elder brother's widow only about a month after the funeral." 20

"He did well," the old man beamed and announced to the others, "I told you that if we knew more about Europeans, we would find they really were very like us. In our country also," he added to me, "the younger brother marries the elder brother's widow and becomes the father of his children. Now, if your uncle, who married your widowed mother, is your father's full brother, then he will be a real father to you. Did Hamlet's father and uncle have one mother?" 21

His question barely penetrated my mind; I was too upset and thrown too far off balance by having one of the most important elements of 22

Hamlet knocked straight out of the picture. Rather uncertainly I said that I thought they had the same mother, but I wasn't sure—the story didn't say. The old man told me severely that these genealogical° details made all the difference and that when I got home I must ask the elders about it. He shouted out the door to one of his younger wives to bring his goatskin bag.

Determined to save what I could of the mother motif, I took a deep *23* breath and began again. "The son Hamlet was very sad because his mother had married again so quickly. There was no need for her to do so, and it is our custom for a widow not to go to her next husband until she has mourned for two years."

"Two years is too long," objected the wife, who had appeared with *24* the old man's battered goatskin bag. "Who will hoe your farms for you while you have no husband?"

"Hamlet," I retorted without thinking, "was old enough to hoe his *25* mother's farms himself. There was no need for her to remarry." No one looked convinced. I gave up. "His mother and the great chief told Hamlet not to be sad, for the great chief himself would be a father to Hamlet. Furthermore, Hamlet would be the next chief: therefore he must stay to learn the things of a chief. Hamlet agreed to remain, and all the rest went off to drink beer."

While I paused, perplexed at how to render Hamlet's disgusted solil- *26* oquy to an audience convinced that Claudius and Gertrude had behaved in the best possible manner, one of the younger men asked me who had married the other wives of the dead chief.

"He had no other wives," I told him. *27*

"But a chief must have many wives! How else can he brew beer and *28* prepare food for all his guests?"

I said firmly that in our country even chiefs had only one wife, that *29* they had servants to do their work, and that they paid them from tax money.

It was better, they returned, for a chief to have many wives and sons *30* who would help him hoe his farms and feed his people; then everyone loved the chief who gave much and took nothing—taxes were a bad thing.

I agreed with the last comment, but for the rest fell back on their *31* favorite way of fobbing off my questions: "That is the way it is done, so that is how we do it."

I decided to skip the soliloquy.° Even if Claudius was here thought *32* quite right to marry his brother's widow, there remained the poison motif,° and I knew they would disapprove of fratricide.° More hopefully I resumed, "That night Hamlet kept watch with the three who had seen

---

Genealogical—relating to ancestry.   **Soliloquy**—Hamlet's speech to himself, beginning "To be or not to be."   **Motif**—theme.   **Fratricide**—murder of one's brother.

his dead father. The dead chief again appeared, and although the others were afraid, Hamlet followed his dead father off to one side. When they were alone, Hamlet's dead father spoke."

"Omens can't talk!" The old man was emphatic.   33

"Hamlet's dead father wasn't an omen. Seeing him might have been   34
an omen, but he was not." My audience looked as confused as I sounded. "It *was* Hamlet's dead father. It was a thing we call a 'ghost.'" I had to use the English word, for unlike many of the neighboring tribes, these people didn't believe in the survival after death of any individuating° part of the personality.

"What is a 'ghost?' An omen?"   35

"No, a 'ghost' is someone who is dead but who walks around and   36
can talk, and people can hear him and see him but not touch him."

They objected. "One can touch zombis."   37

"No, no! It was not a dead body the witches had animated to sacrifice   38
and eat. No one else made Hamlet's dead father walk. He did it himself."

"Dead men can't walk," protested my audience as one man.   39

I was quite willing to compromise. "A 'ghost' is the dead man's   40
shadow."

But again they objected. "Dead men cast no shadows."   41

"They do in my country," I snapped.   42

The old man quelled the babble of disbelief that arose immediately   43
and told me with that insincere, but courteous, agreement one extends to the fancies of the young, ignorant, and superstitious, "No doubt in your country the dead can also walk without being zombis." From the depths of his bag he produced a withered fragment of kola nut, bit off one end to show it wasn't poisoned, and handed me the rest as a peace offering.

"Anyhow," I resumed, "Hamlet's dead father said that his own   44
brother, the one who became chief, had poisoned him. He wanted Hamlet to avenge him. Hamlet believed this in his heart, for he did not like his father's brother." I took another swallow of beer. "In the country of the great chief, living in the same homestead, for it was a very large one, was an important elder who was often with the chief to advise and help him. His name was Polonius. Hamlet was courting his daughter, but her father and her brother . . . [I cast hastily about for some tribal analogy] warned her not to let Hamlet visit her when she was alone on her farm, for he would be a great chief and so could not marry her."

"Why not?" asked the wife, who had settled down on the edge of the   45
old man's chair. He frowned at her for asking stupid questions and growled, "They lived in the same homestead."

"That was not the reason," I informed them. "Polonius was a stranger   46
who lived in the homestead because he helped the chief, not because he was a relative."

Individuating—giving individuality.

"Then why couldn't Hamlet marry her?" 47

"He could have," I explained, "but Polonius didn't think he would. 48
After all, Hamlet was a man of great importance who ought to marry
a chief's daughter, for in his country a man could have only one wife.
Polonius was afraid that if Hamlet made love to his daughter, then no
one else would give a high price for her."

"That might be true," remarked one of the shrewder elders, "but a 49
chief's son would give his mistress's father enough presents and patronage to more than make up the difference. Polonius sounds like a fool to
me."

"Many people think he was," I agreed. "Meanwhile Polonius sent his 50
son Laertes off to Paris to learn the things of that country, for it was
the homestead of a very great chief indeed. Because he was afraid that
Laertes might waste a lot of money on beer and women and gambling,
or get into trouble by fighting, he sent one of his servants to Paris
secretly, to spy out what Laertes was doing. One day Hamlet came
upon Polonius's daughter Ophelia. He behaved so oddly he frightened
her. Indeed"—I was fumbling for words to express the dubious quality
of Hamlet's madness—"the chief and many others had also noticed that
when Hamlet talked one could understand the words but not what they
meant. Many people thought that he had become mad." My audience
suddenly became much more attentive. "The great chief wanted to know
what was wrong with Hamlet, so he sent for two of Hamlet's age mates
[school friends would have taken long explanation] to talk to Hamlet
and find out what troubled his heart. Hamlet, seeing that they had been
bribed by the chief to betray him, told them nothing. Polonius, however, insisted that Hamlet was mad because he had been forbidden to
see Ophelia, whom he loved."

"Why," inquired a bewildered voice, "should anyone bewitch Hamlet 51
on that account?"

"Bewitch him?" 52

"Yes, only witchcraft can make anyone mad, unless, of course, one 53
sees the beings that lurk in the forest."

I stopped being a storyteller, took out my notebook and demanded to 54
be told more about these two causes of madness. Even while they spoke
and I jotted notes, I tried to calculate the effect of this new factor on the
plot. Hamlet had not been exposed to the beings that lurk in the forests.
Only his relatives in the male line could bewitch him. Barring relatives
not mentioned by Shakespeare, it had to be Claudius who was attempting to harm him. And, of course, it was.

For the moment I staved off questions by saying that the great chief 55
also refused to believe that Hamlet was mad for the love of Ophelia and
nothing else. "He was sure that something much more important was
troubling Hamlet's heart."

"Now Hamlet's age mates," I continued, "had brought with them a 56 famous storyteller. Hamlet decided to have this man tell the chief and all his homestead a story about a man who had poisoned his brother because he desired his brother's wife and wished to be chief himself. Hamlet was sure the great chief could not hear the story without making a sign if he was indeed guilty, and then he would discover whether his dead father had told him the truth."

The old man interrupted, with deep cunning, "Why should a father 57 lie to his son?" he asked.

I hedged: "Hamlet wasn't sure that it really was his dead father." It 58 was impossible to say anything, in that language, about devil-inspired visions.

"You mean," he said, "it actually was an omen, and he knew witches 59 sometimes send false ones. Hamlet was a fool not to go to one skilled in reading omens and divining the truth in the first place. A man-who-sees-the-truth could have told him how his father died, if he really had been poisoned, and if there was witchcraft in it; then Hamlet could have called the elders to settle the matter."

The shrewd elder ventured to disagree. "Because his father's brother 60 was a great chief, one-who-sees-the-truth might therefore have been afraid to tell it. I think it was for that reason that a friend of Hamlet's father—a witch and an elder—sent an omen so his friend's son would know. Was the omen true?"

"Yes," I said, abandoning ghosts and the devil; a witch-sent omen it 61 would have to be. "It was true, for when the storyteller was telling his tale before all the homestead, the great chief rose in fear. Afraid that Hamlet knew his secret he planned to have him killed."

The stage set of the next bit presented some difficulties of translation. 62 I began cautiously. "The great chief told Hamlet's mother to find out from her son what he knew. But because a woman's children are always first in her heart, he had the important elder Polonius hide behind a cloth that hung against the wall of Hamlet's mother's sleeping hut. Hamlet started to scold his mother for what she had done."

There was a shocked murmur from everyone. A man should never 63 scold his mother.

"She called out in fear, and Polonius moved behind the cloth. Shout- 64 ing, 'A rat!' Hamlet took his machete and slashed through the cloth." I paused for dramatic effect. "He had killed Polonius!"

The old men looked at each other in supreme disgust. "That Polonius 65 truly was a fool and a man who knew nothing! What child would not know enough to shout, 'It's me!'" With a pang, I remembered that these people are ardent hunters, always armed with bow, arrow, and machete; at the first rustle in the grass an arrow is aimed and ready, and the hunter shouts "Game!" If no human voice answers immediately, the arrow speeds on its way. Like a good hunter Hamlet had shouted, "A rat!"

I rushed in to save Polonius's reputation. "Polonius did speak. Hamlet *66*
heard him. But he thought it was the chief and wished to kill him to
avenge his father. He had meant to kill him earlier that evening. . . ." I
broke down, unable to describe to these pagans, who had no belief in
individual afterlife, the difference between dying at one's prayers and
dying "unhousell'd, disappointed, unaneled."°

This time I had shocked my audience seriously. "For a man to raise *67*
his hand against his father's brother and the one who has become his
father—that is a terrible thing. The elders ought to let such a man be
bewitched."

I nibbled at my kola nut in some perplexity, then pointed out that *68*
after all the man had killed Hamlet's father.

"No," pronounced the old man, speaking less to me than to the young *69*
men sitting behind the elders. "If your father's brother has killed your
father, you must appeal to your father's age mates; *they* may avenge
him. No man may use violence against his senior relatives." Another
thought struck him. "But if his father's brother had indeed been wicked
enough to bewitch Hamlet and make him mad that would be a good
story indeed, for it would be his fault that Hamlet, being mad, no longer
had any sense and thus was ready to kill his father's brother."

There was a murmur of applause. *Hamlet* was again a good story to *70*
them, but it no longer seemed quite the same story to me. As I thought
over the coming complications of plot and motive, I lost courage and
decided to skim over dangerous ground quickly.

"The great chief," I went on, "was not sorry that Hamlet had killed *71*
Polonius. It gave him a reason to send Hamlet away, with his two
treacherous age mates, with letters to a chief of a far country, saying
that Hamlet should be killed. But Hamlet changed the writing on their
papers, so that the chief killed his age mates instead." I encountered a
reproachful glare from one of the men whom I had told undetectable
forgery was not merely immoral but beyond human skill. I looked the
other way.

"Before Hamlet could return, Laertes came back for his father's fu- *72*
neral. The great chief told him Hamlet had killed Polonius. Laertes
swore to kill Hamlet because of this, and because his sister Ophelia,
hearing her father had been killed by the man she loved, went mad and
drowned in the river."

"Have you already forgotten what we told you?" The old man was *73*
reproachful. "One cannot take vengeance on a madman; Hamlet killed
Polonius in his madness. As for the girl, she not only went mad, she
was drowned. Only witches can make people drown. Water itself can't
hurt anything. It is merely something one drinks and bathes in."

°"unhousell'd, disappointed, unaneled"—without benefit of last rites.

I began to get cross. "If you don't like the story, I'll stop." 74

The old man made soothing noises and himself poured me some more 75 beer. "You tell the story well, and we are listening. But it is clear that the elders of your country have never told you what the story really means. No, don't interrupt! We believe you when you say your marriage customs are different, or your clothes and weapons. But people are the same everywhere; therefore, there are always witches and it is we, the elders, who know how witches work. We told you it was the great chief who wished to kill Hamlet, and now your own words have proved us right. Who were Ophelia's male relatives?"

"There were only her father and her brother." Hamlet was clearly out 76 of my hands.

"There must have been many more; this also you must ask of your 77 elders when you get back to your country. From what you tell us, since Polonius was dead, it must have been Laertes who killed Ophelia, although I do not see the reason for it."

We had emptied one pot of beer, and the old men argued the point 78 with slightly tipsy interest. Finally one of them demanded of me, "What did the servant of Polonius say on his return?"

With difficulty I recollected Reynaldo and his mission. "I don't think 79 he did return before Polonius was killed."

"Listen," said the elder, "and I will tell you how it was and how your 80 story will go, then you may tell me if I am right. Polonius knew his son would get into trouble, and so he did. He had many fines to pay for fighting, and debts from gambling. But he had only two ways of getting money quickly. One was to marry off his sister at once, but it is difficult to find a man who will marry a woman desired by the son of a chief. For if the chief's heir commits adultery with your wife, what can you do? Only a fool calls a case against a man who will someday be his judge. Therefore Laertes had to take the second way: he killed his sister by witchcraft, drowning her so he could secretly sell her body to the witches."

I raised an objection. "They found her body and buried it. Indeed, 81 Laertes jumped into the grave to see his sister once more—so, you see, the body was truly there. Hamlet, who had just come back, jumped in after him."

"What did I tell you?" The elder appealed to the others. "Laertes was 82 up to no good with his sister's body. Hamlet prevented him, because the chief's heir, like a chief, does not wish any other man to grow rich and powerful. Laertes would be angry, because he would have killed his sister without benefit to himself. In our country he would try to kill Hamlet for that reason. Is this not what happened?"

"More or less," I admitted. "When the great chief found Hamlet was 83 still alive, he encouraged Laertes to try to kill Hamlet and arranged a fight with machetes between them. In the fight both the young men

were wounded to death. Hamlet's mother drank the poisoned beer that
the chief meant for Hamlet in case he won the fight. When he saw his
mother die of poison, Hamlet, dying, managed to kill his father's brother
with his machete."

"You see, I was right!" exclaimed the elder.   *84*

"That was a very good story," added the old man, "and you told it *85*
with very few mistakes. There was just one more error, at the very end.
The poison Hamlet's mother drank was obviously meant for the sur-
vivor of the fight, whichever it was. If Laertes had won, the great chief
would have poisoned him, for no one would know that he arranged
Hamlet's death. Then, too, he need not fear Laertes' witchcraft; it takes
a strong heart to kill one's only sister by witchcraft.

"Sometime," concluded the old man, gathering his ragged toga about *86*
him, "you must tell us some more stories of your country. We, who
are elders, will instruct you in their true meaning, so that when you
return to your own land your elders will see that you have not been
sitting in the bush, but among those who know things and who have
taught you wisdom."

Rhetorical Analysis Through Annotation

Laura Bohannan tells her story as a chronological narrative of her experiences.
Part of that narrative is her change in thinking as she goes through her experience. That change of thinking conveys the main argumentative message of this
essay, that no universal meaning is embedded in a classic. What she had thought
was a universal interpretation of *Hamlet* turned out to be merely a Western one.

Underline all statements about her thinking or state of mind. Also note
particular experiences in the text that may have influenced her thinking or
feeling. In particular note those events that seemed to challenge or change her
state of mind.

Discuss how Bohannan manages to argue her point without ever presenting
it directly.

Discussion Questions

Interpreting the Text

1. In what ways does Bohannan rely on you the reader being familiar with
Hamlet? If you are not familiar with the play, what difficulties did you have in
following the narrative? Those members of the class who are familiar with the
play should then explain the necessary background for you to understand the
essay more fully.

2. Bohannan also assumes you know something about witchcraft. The tribespeople mention witches and witchcraft several times. What beliefs do they seem
to have about witchcraft? What other aspects of the belief system of the Tiv
tribespeople can you figure out from the narrative? Have you heard of any

similar beliefs elsewhere? Which seem strange and which seem understandable within the context of the tribal culture and experience?

3. Identify the specific misunderstandings and disagreements about the meaning of *Hamlet* that occur between Bohannan and the tribespeople. What differences of ideas lead to these differences of interpretation? How did Bohannan deal with the differences? How did the tribespeople? What, if anything, do they agree on?

4. What attitudes do the tribal elders have toward Bohannan, and what sort of relationship do they establish with her? How do those attitudes and that relationship affect her ability to communicate with the elders?

Considering the Issues

5. Based on your knowledge of the play and the description of *Hamlet* presented by Bohannan, what beliefs and customs expressed in the play strike you as different from our current beliefs and practices? Do you find any of these particularly strange?

6. In what way could Bohannan's experience telling the story of *Hamlet* to the tribespeople be described as an experiment? How could you describe her hypothesis, methods, results, and conclusions?

7. Why does Bohannan choose to make her point about culture through telling a personal experience narrative? What kinds of striking and persuasive incidents does the narrative let her present that may be more difficult to convey in other forms?

8. How does humor help Bohannan make her point? What points of the narrative are humorous and why? What attitudes does the humor make fun of?

9. If Bohannan had had an arrogant, closed-minded point of view, she could have written this story ridiculing the Tiv elders. Instead one gets a sense of her respect and affection for them, even though she does become exasperated and defensive at times. How exactly does she convey to us her positive attitude toward the subjects of her study?

Writing Suggestions

1. For a friend who finds the meaning of Bohannan's essay confusing, write a summary of the narrative, but bring out the main ideas more explicitly than Bohannan does.

2. Write a letter to your parents describing some part of your life that they may not understand or may find strange (such as a new style of rock music or some of your actions). Describe it so as to overcome their misunderstandings or bewilderment and to help them appreciate why it is important to you.

3. For a course in recent American culture, write a review of an older movie or television show that you have seen recently in a rerun. In the review, discuss how the movie or show reflects beliefs, attitudes, and values of the period when it was made. Do these dated cultural elements make the work harder or less

enjoyable to appreciate? Do your current beliefs, values, and attitudes lead you to see the story in a new or different way?

The Canon in Africa: Imperialism and Racism

Ngugi Wa Thiong'o

If the great works of literature convey the cultural beliefs of the society that calls those works great, then imposing the literature of one society upon another is a form of cultural oppression. According to this line of reasoning, each culture or group of people should have its own canon as part of its own culture, a canon that will represent local feeling and values.

In recent decades such thinking emerged most clearly in the newly independent countries of Africa, Asia, and the Caribbean. Until the middle of this century these areas were still largely colonies of European countries. The children who went to school were taught the literature of their European masters. Schoolchildren in Nigeria, India, and the Bahamas all read the great works of British literature. In Senegal, Algeria, and Vietnam French literature was the ideal.

Ngugi Wa Thiong'o (b. 1938) is a novelist and professor of literature at the University of Nairobi, Kenya. Here he describes the literary situation in Kenya in the 1970s, a decade after independence from Britain in 1963. He writes about the persistence of romantic British nature poetry and racism in the literary landscape of a tropical black African nation. He argues for the importance of a country developing its own sense of literature and not being the victims of foreigners' beliefs. The canon taught in school is crucial to cultural identity.

Ngugi originally presented this argument in 1973 to a conference of teachers of literature in Nairobi. He spoke not just of literary analysis and theory, but of what the audience must do. Although much writing on literature is academic and nonpolitical, critics and writers at times use their understanding of literature to analyze cultural issues and urge public action. Because literature conveys important understandings about the way we live, feel, and think, literary specialists are often accepted as authorities on social, cultural, and spiritual issues. Ngugi shares this belief about the social importance of literature, even though he rejects the literature of Europe.

> *Ignorant of their country, some people can only*
> *relate tales of ancient Greece and other*
> *foreign lands.*
>
> MAO TSE-TUNG

> *If we want to turn Africa into a new Europe, then*
> *let us leave the destiny of our countries to*
> *Europeans. They will know how to do it better*
> *than the most gifted among us.*
>
> FRANTZ FANON

THE SUBJECT OF OUR three days gathering and discussion is the 1
place and the teaching of African literature in our schools. I hope that
the very title will provoke us to anger and protest: how come that it
has taken ten whole years after constitutional independence, Uhuru wa
Bendera°, for us native sons and daughters to meet and to debate for
the first time on the subject—the place of our literature in our education
system? And why do we find it necessary to qualify this literature with
the word 'African', for what else should it be?

A Russian child grows under the influence of his native imaginative 2
literature: a Chinese, a Frenchman, a German or an Englishman first
imbibes his national literature before attempting to take in other worlds.
That the central taproot of his cultural nourishment should lie deep in
his native soil is taken for granted. This A B C of education is followed
in most societies because it is demanded by the practice and the experience of living and growing.

Not so in Africa, the West Indies and the colonized world as a whole, 3
despite the crucial role of the twin fields of literature and culture in
making a child aware of, and rediscover his environment.

Let me give you three examples: 4

The other day I found my own son trying to memorize a poem by 5
William Wordsworth.° I contained my disappointment and held the
book for him while, with a face tortured with the effort, he recited:

> I wander'd lonely as a cloud
> That floats on high o'er vales and hills,
> When all at once I saw a crowd,
> A host, of golden daffodils
> Beside the lake, beneath the trees,
> Fluttering and dancing in the breeze.

Uhuru Wa Bendera—literally, "freedom of the flag"; figuratively, nominal political independence without spiritual independence.   **William Wordsworth (1770–1850)**—English poet.

I asked him: What are daffodils? He looked at the illustration book: Oh, *6*
they are just little fishes in a lake!

Three years ago on a sunny hot afternoon, Okot p'Bitek and I went *7*
to a school where one of our former students was teaching. The children
hated poetry, she told us: Couldn't we convince them that though poetry
was difficult it was a distillation of human wisdom and thought? A
gigantic request since we had only one hour between us, but we would
do our best. For a start we asked them what poems they had already
learnt. Thereupon they told us about a poem of fourteen lines called a
sonnet written by one William Shakespeare comparing old age to Winter!

I know of a leading school in Kenya where, on top of Sheridan's *8*
School for Scandal°, Paul Gallico's *The Snow Goose*° and other literary
vintages in the same vein, (not a single African writer, though they had
possibly heard of Chinua Achebe's *Things Fall Apart*° and no doubt of
Charles Mangua's *Son of Woman*°—the latter through the girls' own
initiative) they have a text whose title I cannot recall which tells the
story of Queen Victoria and how she used to cough and sneeze and eat
pudding, and pull her dog's ears and of course anglicize (or is it civilize?)
her German husband.

These would be fit cases for jokes and laughter were they not the *9*
general practice in our schools. Indeed until a few years ago, the departments of literature (then called English departments) in Nairobi,
Dar-es-Salaam and Makerere Universities° would only teach British
authors from Chaucer through Oliver Goldsmith to Graham Greene.
That is how most of us were brought up under the old colonial system
administered from the University of London: but is there any reason
why our children in this day and age should be brought up on the same
impoverished diet administered in the so-called English departments,
often headed by some retired biology teachers or retired army majors
or men of God, whose main qualifications for the posts are a white skin,
long residence in the country, and of course an acquaintance with *The
London Book of English Verse*, or *A Penguin Book of English Verse*?

Why was this pattern so in our time? Why does it still persist? Has it *10*
all been an accident of content, time, place and persons?

Let us not mince words. The truth is that the content of our syllabi, *11*
the approach to and presentation of the literature, the persons and the
machinery for determining the choice of texts and their interpretation,
were all an integral part of imperialism in its classical colonial phase,
and they are today an integral part of the same imperialism but now in
its neo-colonial phase. Cultural imperialism, which during colonialism

---

Sheridan's *School for Scandal*—English comic play (1777).   **Paul Gallico's** *The Snow
Goose*—American novel (1941).   **Chinua Achebe's** *Things Fall Apart*—Nigerian novel
(1959).   **Charles Mangua's** *Son of Woman*—Kenyan novel (1971).   **Nairobi, Dar-es
Salaam, Makerere Universities**—in Kenya, Tanzania, and Tanganyika, respectively.

often affected the population and the country unevenly depending on the colonial policies of the marauding powers and the degree of resistance in each country and in different parts of the country, becomes the major agency of control during neo-colonialism. . . .

In [novels by people like Rudyard Kipling and Rider Haggard,° the] *12* European emerges as the hero, the superman, Batman, Tarzan, who can wipe a thousand thick-lipped, big-nosed, curly-haired blacks. The blacks, especially in Rider Haggard, are always of two kinds: the evil ones who are so described that a picture of a devil forms in a reader's mind,[1] and whose one characteristic is an insane hatred of white bene-factors out of sheer spite and motiveless envy; or the good ones who are always described in terms of grinning teeth and who always run errands for the white man, tremble in fear when the white man frowns in anger, or show an 'Uncle Tom' face of humility and gratitude for any favour bestowed on them by the European master.[2]

You get a variation of Haggard's two types in the novels of the racist *13* apologist for European settlerism in Kenya—Elspeth Huxley—especially in her two novels, *The Red Strangers* and *A Thing to Love*. Only now her bad evil Africans are those educated in western schools and instead of thanking the Lord for small mercies, actually demand political rights and urge the simple-souled African to violence and sabotage.

Karen Blixen° is another writer in the racist tradition. An aristocrat *14* from Denmark she came to Kenya at the beginning of this century and acquired a farm in the now fashionable district of Nairobi still bearing her name. She enjoyed wild animals and naked rugged nature. Later in her book, *Out of Africa*, she was to write:

> When you have caught the rhythm of Africa,
> You find that it is the same in all her music.
> What I learnt from the game of the country was useful
> to me in my dealings with Africans.[3]

She protests her love for natives and animals in the same breath: *15*

> As for me, from my first week in Africa, I had felt a great affection
> for the natives. It was a strong feeling that embraced all ages and both
> sexes. The discovery of the dark races was to me a magnificent en-
> largement of all my world. If a person with an inborn sympathy for
> animals had come into contact with animals late in life: or if a person
> with an instinctive taste for woods and forest had entered a forest for
> the first time at the age of twenty; or if someone with an ear for music
> had happened to hear music for the first time when he was already
> grown up; their cases might have been similar to mine.[4]

Rider Haggard (1856–1925)—English writer of adventure novels. **Karen Blixen** (1885–1962)—Danish writer, used the pen name Isak Dinesen.

In all her descriptions of African characters she resorts to animal imagery.   *16*
The African was really part of the woods and animals, part of Hegel's
unconscious nature. She gives medicine to Kamante and after he is cured
he becomes her very good cook.

> Kamante could have no idea as to how a dish of ours ought to taste,
> and he was, in spite of his conversion, and his connexion with civiliza-
> tion, at heart an arrant Kikuyu, rooted in the traditions of his tribe and
> his faith in them, as in the only way of living worthy of a human
> being. He did at times taste the food that he cooked, but then with a
> distrustful face, like a witch who takes a sip out of her cauldron. *He
> stuck to the maizecobs of his fathers.* Here even his intelligence sometimes
> failed him, and he came and offered me a Kikuyu delicacy a roasted
> sweet potato or a lump of sheep's fat—*as even a civilized dog, that has
> lived for a long time with people, will place a bone on the floor before you, as
> a present.*[5] (italics mine)

When she goes back to Denmark, her African characters keep on   *17*
visiting her in her dreams—but in the form of animals.

> It was then that my old companions began to put in an appearance in
> my dreams at night, and by such behaviour managed to deeply upset
> and trouble me. For till then no living people had ever found their
> way into those dreams. They came in disguise, it is true, and as in a
> mirror darkly, so that I would at times meet Kamante in the shape of a
> dwarf-elephant or a bat, Farah as a watchful leopard snarling lowly
> round the house, and Sirunga as a small jackal, yapping—such as the
> natives tell you that jackals will do in times of disaster with one fore-
> paw behind his ear. But the disguise did not deceive me, I recognised
> each of them every time and in the mornings I knew that we had been
> together, for a short meeting on a forest path or for a journey. So I
> could no longer feel sure that they did still actually exist, or indeed
> that they had ever actually existed, outside of my dreams.[6]

Her cosmos is hierarchically ordered with God at the top followed by   *18*
the white aristocracy, ordinary whites, domestic animals, wild animals
who are all in 'direct contact' with God. Africans don't figure anywhere
in this cosmic picture except as parts of wood and stones, different only
because occasionally they exhibit impulses towards animals.

Karen Blixen was once proposed by Hemingway for the Nobel prize   *19*
in Literature.

I quoted from Blixen liberally because she was no ordinary drunken   *20*
soldier or an uncouth frustrated missionary spinster come to Africa to
fulfil herself in lording it over schoolgirls and terrorizing timid African
teachers but a refined lady of some discrimination and learning. She
belongs to the same tradition of great racists like Hume°, Trollope°,

---

David Hume (1711–1776)—Scottish philosopher.   **Anthony Trollope (1815–1882)**—
English novelist.

Hegel°, Trevor-Roper° and all other arch-priests of privilege, racism and class snobbery.

The last group of writers I want to mention are those who set out to *21* sympathetically treat the African world either to appeal to the European liberal conscience or simply to interpret Africa for the Africans. But even among these, the African image is still in negative terms. For Joseph Conrad°, the African characters in *Heart of Darkness* are part of that primitive savagery that lay below the skin of every civilized being. He was telling his fellow Europeans: You go to Africa to civilize, to enlighten a heathen people; scratch that thin veneer of civilization and you will find the savagery of Africa in you too. For Joyce Cary°, the positive creative African in *Mister Johnson* is a clowning idiot whose desire and final fulfilment is having to be shot dead by an Englishman whom we are led to believe loves him well. We all love our horses and dogs and cats and we often shoot them to put them out of pain. So much for *Mister Johnson* and Master Joyce Cary. For William Blake°, the little black boy, cries thus:

> My mother bore me in the southern wild,
> And I am black, but O, my soul is white
> White as an angel is the English child,
> But I am black as if bereaved of light.[7]

He longs for the day he will die and be freed from the burden of his *22* skin colour, then he and the white boy will 'lean in joy upon our Father's knee':

> And then I'll stand and stroke his silver hair,
> And be like him, and he will then love me.[8]

This is the white liberal's dream of a day when black and white can *23* love one another without going through the agony of violent reckoning. Liberalism has always been the sugary ideology of imperialism: it fosters the illusion in the exploited of the possibilities of peaceful settlement and painless escape from imperialist violence which anyway is not called violence but law and order. Liberalism blurs all antagonistic class contradictions, all the contradictions between imperialist domination and the struggle for national liberation, seeing in the revolutionary violence of the former, the degradation of humanity:

Georg Wilhelm Friedrich Hegel (1170–1831)—German philosopher.   **Hugh Trevor-Roper (b. 1914)**—English historian.   **Joseph Conrad (1857–1924)**—Polish-born English novelist.   **Joyce Cary (1888–1957)**—English novelist.   **William Blake (1757–1827)**—English poet.

> Liberalism rejects ideological struggle and stands for unprincipled
> peace, thus giving rise to a decadent, philistine, attitude and bringing
> about political degeneration in certain units and individuals (among the
> oppressed) . . . and objectively has the effect of helping the enemy [i.e.
> imperialism].[9]

And nowhere is liberalism so clearly manifested as in imaginative liter- 24
ature.

A written literature also develops alongside people's oral fighting 25
literature again as part of the cultural struggle and cultural assertion. In
the case of Africa, the very act of writing was itself a testimony of the
creative capacity of the African and the first tottering but still important
steps by the 'educated' elite towards self-definition and the acceptance
of the environment from which they had been alienated by western,
Eurocentric imperialist education. But the literature produced, because
of its critical realism, also reflected the reality of the African struggle
against colonial domination.

Chinua Achebe is a case in point. His novels taken as a whole beau- 26
tifully delineate the origins, growth and development of a neo-colonial
native ruling class. This class has roots in the early Christian converts,
the early *asomi* who learnt to read and write; the court messengers; the
policemen; the road overseers, in *Things Fall Apart* and *Arrow of God*.
This class later becomes the backbone of the business and civil service
'been to's' in *No Longer at Ease*. In *A Man of the People*, the class inherits
power and begins to fulfil its historical mission of a messenger class, in
the process looting the people. Where the individual messenger was
bribed by individual families in *Things Fall Apart*; where the same individual messenger played one clan against another to confuse them
about his messenger role and cloud it with nepotism and hence eat the
bribe in peace in *Things Fall Apart* and *Arrow of God*, the same class now
extorts bribes from the whole country in *A Man of the People* and plays
one ethnic community against others on a national scale, again to mystify
its true role and character as a messenger class. In *Girls at War*, the class
involves the whole country in bloodshed in its intraclass warfare for a
share of the cake, the left-overs, given to it by the master.

Such a literature, again at its critical best and most committed, defines 27
a people not in terms of always being acted on but in terms of actors.
Okonkwo and Ezeulu as representatives of the people and people's spirit
of resistance make their own history. Okonkwo commits suicide rather
than submit and live in a world where he is denied the right to make
his own history through his control and development of the productive
forces. His act of killing an imperialist messenger is as symbolic as it is
prophetic. It is the new messenger class, the new errand boys of international monopoly capitalism that make total liberation difficult, for on
the surface they do look like one of Okonkwo's own people.

I believe that we as teachers of literature can help in this collective 28 struggle to seize back our creative initiative in history. For this it is essential that we grasp the true function and role of literature in our society. We can help principally in three ways:

1. In all our schools, teacher training colleges and community centres we must insist on the primacy and centrality of African literature and the literature of African people in the West Indies and America. Central to this is the oral literature of our people, including their contemporary compositions.

2. Where we import literature from outside, it should be relevant to our situation. It should be the literature that treats of historical situations, historical struggles, similar to our own. It should be the kind of literature that rejects oppressive social-economic systems, that rejects all those forces that dwarf the creative development of man. In this case anti-imperialist literatures from Asia and Latin America and literature from socialist countries are very important. But anti-imperialist, anti-bourgeois literature and the pro-people literature of struggle from writers in imperialist countries can add a considerable contribution to our own struggles for a better world.

3. While not rejecting the critical demands of the more formal elements and needs of any art, we must subject literature whether oral, African or from other lands to a most rigorous criticism from the point of view of the struggling masses. We must detect what is positive, revolutionary, humanistic in a work of art, support it, strengthen it; and reject what is negative and anti-humanistic in the same or other works.

All this is not easy for it calls upon us to re-examine ourselves, our 29 values, our own world outlook, our own assumptions and prejudices. Above all, it demands of us to re-examine our own stand and attitude to the struggle that still goes on in our continent: the struggle of our people against economic, political, and cultural imperialism of western European and Japanese capitalism, whose most ugly deformation is seen in South Africa, Rhodesia, Angola and Mozambique. It demands of us to adopt a scientific materialistic world outlook on nature, human society and human thought, and assume the standpoint of the most progressive and revolutionary classes (i.e. workers and peasants) in our society, for they are at the forefront in the struggle against imperialism and foreign domination, indeed against the suffocating alliance between the imperialist bourgeoisie° and the local pro-foreigner *comprador*° class.

In his last days in Conakry, Kwame Nkrumah° wrote that the spectre 30 of Black Power was haunting the world. Black Power here does not

---

Bourgeoisie—middle class of small merchants. *Comprador*—consumer. **Kwame Nkrumah** (1909–1972)—Ghanaian statesman.

mean a glorification of an ossified° past. Rather it means the true creative power of African people through a people's control of their forces of production and equitable distribution of the products of their sweat to enhance the quality of all their lives. Seen in this light, Black Power is impossible outside a socialist context and a total liberation of the African genius at all the levels we have been talking about. Literature, and our attitudes to literature, can help or else hinder in the creation of a united socialist Black Power in Africa based on the just continuing struggle of peasants and workers for a total control of their productive forces.

We writers and critics of African literature should form an essential *31* intellectual part of the anti-imperialist cultural army of African peoples for total economic and political liberation from imperialism and foreign domination.

Notes

[1] Note the description of Gagool in *King Solomon's Mines* haunted Graham Greene all his life, at least so he says in his collected Essays. And Micere Githae Mugo has written: 'I can never forget *King Solomon's Mines* nor the weird portrait of Gagool which for a long time epitomized in my childish mind the figure of an African woman in old age. It is only recently that I have got over my dread and fear of old black women.' See her article, *Written Literature and Black Image*, in Gachukia and Akivaga's *Teaching of African Literature in Schools*.

[2] See the description of this in *King Solomon's Mines*.

[3] Karen Blixen: *Out of Africa*, Penguin edition, p. 24.

[4] Ibid., p. 25.

[5] Ibid., p. 44.

[6] Isak Dinesen: *Shadows on the Grass* (John Murray, London, 1960), p. 45.

[7] William Blake: 'The Little Black Boy' (*The Complete Poems*, Longman, p. 58).

[8] Ibid., p. 58.

[9] Mao Tse-Tung: 'Combat Liberalism'.

Rhetorical Analysis Through Annotation

In examining attitudes in both Western and African literature, Ngugi considers the work of many authors. Some authors are mentioned only as passing references, as symbols of their work or ideas. Such passing mentions help establish the extent of racist attitudes and the existence of alternatives. Ngugi discusses the work of other authors at length to develop his argument in detail.

Underline any mention of an author and his or her works. Then, in the margin, note whether such reference is only in passing or is followed by detailed analysis. If the reference is brief, indicate the attitude or idea being symbolized

---

Ossified—become rigid.

and how Ngugi feels about it. If the reference is subject to detailed analysis, write down the main point being made by the analysis.

Discuss how the passing references and the detailed analyses fit in with the overall argument made by Ngugi.

Discussion Questions

Interpreting the Text

1. Exactly what aspects of the Wordsworth poem and Shakespeare sonnet strike Ngugi as inappropriate to be taught to Kenyan schoolchildren?

2. Ngugi discusses several categories of European writers. What are the categories and what are their defining characteristics? What are Ngugi's criticisms of them?

3. In a number of places Ngugi uses the language and concepts of Marxist socialism. At what spots can you find this? How does he use this language and these concepts? Why do you think he holds such views?

Considering the Issues

4. What does Ngugi recommend? In your opinion, are his recommendations realistic and workable? What would the effect of his recommendations be?

5. Ngugi objects to the European canon on two levels. Some is irrelevant to the African situation and some is racist. Are his criticisms fair? Have you encountered any literature that you felt was objectionable on either of these points?

6. How familiar should peoples be with each others' literature? Should Americans be required to read literature by Canadians, British, French, Latin Americans, Africans, or Chinese? What about Afro-American literature or native American literature?

7. How do the author's criticisms in the first part of the essay relate to his call for action in the last section? How do the sentences and style change as Ngugi moves from an account of the attitudes in European literature (the way those books *are*) to his desires for the future (what his audience *should* do)? In what other ways would you describe the differences between the first and second halves of the essay? Do the two different types of writing belong together in a single essay? If so, why and in what way?

8. Compare and contrast Ngugi's three recommendations and Gilbert Highet's three recommendations. How do they differ in their approaches to literature? How do they differ in their understanding of the relationship between form and content? How does each man say that literature should be taught and evaluated?

9. Do Ngugi's recommendations imply the use of censorship by allowing only literature with the correct point of view? If so, is the censorship justified by the social and political needs of the new African countries?

Writing Suggestions

1. Imagine you have a pen pal in Asia, Africa, or the Caribbean. The pen pal is curious about American life and literature. Write a letter recommending an American book you have enjoyed reading that also gives a scene of American culture. Explain what your pen pal must know about American life to understand the book and how the book will increase the pen pal's insight into American culture.

2. For a college political magazine, write a criticism of a book you have read that expresses racist, sexist, or otherwise bigoted attitudes you find offensive. Or write a positive review about a book with a social message that you approve of.

3. For a meeting of a college organization devoted to developing international understanding, write a talk about a movie, television show, book, work of art, or other creation from a South American, Caribbean, African, or Asian country that helped you understand that country better. Share your increased understanding with the members of the organization.

"In the Realm of the Imagination": Afro-American Literature and the American Canon

Richard Yarborough

Within the United States, groups of people have felt that their cultures have been left out of the canon, dominated by works by white males. Women, blacks, Hispanics, native Americans, Asian-Americans, and members of other minority groups have called for a reevaluation of the American canon so that it will reflect the cultural diversity of this country. The desire is not to throw out the old canon, but to open it up; not to get rid of William Shakespeare and Walt Whitman, but to add Adrienne Rich, Toni Morrison, Ralph Ellison, and N. Scott Momaday.

Richard Yarborough (b. 1951), a professor at UCLA, argues here that the works of black writers are, in many respects, similar to works already recognized in the canon. As Ngugi does, Yarborough sees literature as part of cultural struggle. This article (which appeared in the bulletin of the Association of Departments of English in 1984) was originally addressed to chairpersons of university departments of English, the people who have some power to influence what books shall be taught. It makes clear, however, that the canon issue goes beyond the classroom.

As do many literary essays, this essay relies on frequent references to prior literary works, which it is assumed the reader is familiar with. The traditional canon is a constant reference point and an assumed shared cultural knowledge. However, Yarborough matches every familiar work of the canon with a less familiar work from Afro-American literature which he feels should be recognized.

AS DARWIN T. TURNER has observed, "Afro-Americans have been   *1* writing literature in English since 1746 and publishing books in English since 1773" ("Teaching" 666). Nonetheless, it was not until almost a century after the first collegiate course in American literature was taught in 1872 (Jones 41) that the writings of blacks in the United States began to find their way to any significant extent into college curricula.[1] A decade ago, one might have found cause for optimism in the rush of publishers and educators to get on the black studies bandwagon. Today, however, it is evident that the struggle to broaden the canon has still not been won.

In fact, as we enter the last decades of the twentieth century, resistance   *2* to substantive change seems to have solidified. Fiscal problems, as well as the pedagogical and critical shift to the right, have provided sufficient rationalizations for those inclined to dismiss the validity of certain allegedly peripheral literatures. The eagerness to return to the "basics" and to safeguard primarily those courses judged by time-honored standards to be the most intellectually cost-effective frequently entails a reaffirmation of the canon's sanctity and the excommunication of all but those few works whose pagan roots can be tastefully ignored.[2] Ironically, perhaps the most famous work, Ellison's *Invisible Man* (the Saint Martin de Porres° of American fiction, as it were), argues desperately and powerfully that in order to be saved, the United States must not only acknowledge its cultural diversity but embrace and celebrate it. Nathan A. Scott suggests that Afro-American literature in particular can play an important role in our society:

> [I]n a period in which the literary imagination begins to suffer a great crisis of confidence in the dignity of *l'ecriture°* and in the capacity of the Word to deal with the realities of "postmodern" experience, it [the body of writing by Afro-Americans] is a literature not least remarkable in its assurance about the value of the verbal arts—and this is so, of course, because its practitioners are, most of them, rhetoricians who believe it to be within the power of a disciplined language to alter consciousness and thus to redeem the human reality. ("Literature" 340)

Saint Martin de Porres—The patron saint of France.   *L'écriture*—the act of writing.

By undervaluing the contributions of black authors, America is stunting   *3*
its artistic and spiritual growth.

In an article entitled "Cultural Consciousness in a Multi-Cultural   *4*
Society: The Uses of Literature," Wayne C. Miller points out that "the
United States, considered in a broader cultural perspective, is a com-
posite of peoples—red, white, black, brown, and yellow—still in the
process of self-definition" (29). The formation of an American canon
must be seen as a parallel evolutionary process. Further, one should keep
in mind that the development of an American literary history did not
begin until the late nineteenth and early twentieth centuries and that the
canon that resulted was in a state of considerable flux for some time. A
list of American "classics" compiled in 1918, for example, would have
differed radically from such a list drawn up just ten or fifteen years later.
To put it another way, when European settlers arrived in this country,
they did not find a five-foot shelf of Anglo-American masterpieces
waiting for them. Accordingly, "our first duty," as Benjamin T. Spencer
observed in 1949, "is semantic° contrition. If we are helpless to fix a
single meaning for the term [American literature], we can at least refrain
from a sharp orthodoxy which would impale on the stake of official
Americanism much that has been sensitively and maturely written
within our borders." He continues, "[To] enforce nationality on the
level of concepts is to narrow and impoverish American literature and
to lead it to an ironic betrayal of its own national tradition by making
it the ideological lackey of forces to which it should play the imaginative
tutor" (450). To the extent that radical change has become anathema° in
the study of American literature, the "betrayal" that Spencer mentions
is still taking place.[3]

The very concept of a literary canon as static, as something to be   *5*
revised only after much consideration and with the greatest reluctance,
must be called into question. Further, the challenge to this notion must
be mounted first in the college classroom, for that is where the sacredness
of the canon is maintained and where conventional views of American
literary history are reinforced. The content of most American literature
courses shows appallingly few signs of the progress that many assumed
would be a lasting result of the cultural upheaval of the 1960s. Recent
studies of popular anthologies reveal that while some constructive
changes have taken place, they are frequently token and hardly outbal-
ance the glaring omissions and editorial biases. Judith Fetterley and Joan
Schulz note that in a 1980 anthology published by Macmillan, for example, "fewer than 100 pages out of nearly 4000 are given to Black
writers, male *and* female" (5). Obviously, if the literature is not readily
available, it will not get taught.

Semantic—concerning meanings of words.   **Anathema**—to be shunned.

Particularly frustrating is the neglect accorded the wealth of writing   6
by Afro-Americans that can be incorporated quite effectively into most
American literature courses. A survey of twentieth-century American
experimental fiction might include *The System of Dante's Hell* by Amiri
Baraka (LeRoi Jones), *The Messenger* by Charles Wright, any of six
novels by Ishmael Reed, *The Flagellants* by Carlene H. Polite, *dem* or *A
Different Drummer* by William Melvin Kelley, or *Reflex and Bone Structure*
by Clarence Major. A course on realism and naturalism might include
The Marrow of Tradition or *The Colonel's Dream* by Charles W. Chesnutt
or *The Sport of the Gods* by Paul Laurence Dunbar; a course on literature
of the American South, fiction by Alice Walker, Ernest J. Gaines, or
Richard Wright; a course on poem sequences, *God's Trombones* by James
Weldon Johnson, *Annie Allen* by Gwendolyn Brooks, *Harlem Gallery* by
Melvin Tolson, or *Ask Your Mama: Twelve Moods for Jazz* by Langston
Hughes; a science fiction course, novels by Octavia Butler or Samuel
Delany; a survey of women's fiction in America, works by Gayl Jones,
Sarah Wright, Jesse Fauset, Pauline Hopkins, Toni Morrison, Dorothy
West, Harriet Wilson, or Margaret Walker. Finally, in a course on the
American bildungsroman,° one could teach *The Learning Tree* by Gor-
don Parks, *Not without Laughter* by Langston Hughes, *Train Whistle
Guitar* by Albert Murray, *Ruby* by Rosa Guy, *Beetlecreek* by William
Demby, *Daddy Was a Numbers Runner* by Louise Meriwether, *Snakes* by
Al Young, or *Brown Girl, Brownstones* by Paule Marshall. Courses in
other genres can be readily reconstructed as well. For instance, a survey
of American nonfiction might include works by David Walker, Frederick
Douglass, Mary Church Terrell, James Baldwin, Anna Julia Cooper,
Maya Angelou, George Schuyler, or W. E. B. DuBois.

While it is crucial to respect the integrity of the Afro-American literary   7
tradition, one must also realize that the works of most black authors
can be discussed in terms of the themes, motifs, and stylistic developments viewed as characteristically American.[4] That is, if there is room
in the syllabus for Mailer's *Barbary Shore*, then there is room for Richard
Wright's *The Outsider*; if for Miller's *Death of a Salesman*, then for
Lorraine Hansberry's *A Raisin in the Sun*; if for Robert Lowell's "For
the Union Dead," then for Robert Hayden's "Runagate, Runagate"; if
for Anderson's *Winesburg, Ohio*, then for Jean Toomer's *Cane*. Referring
to the concept of the "American Adam" in particular, Nathan A. Scott
writes:

> [O]ne of the significant bodies of evidence to be adduced° in this con-
> nection is that which is comprised by the work of Negro writers. . . .
> Knowing so intimately as they do the world of the insulted and the
> rejected, theirs is an experience of life in the United States that has

---

Bildungsroman—novel about a character's education and spiritual growing up.   **Adduced**—used as evidence.

bred in them a habit of reflection whose natural fulcrum is the dialec-
tic° of innocence and experience: the "wounded Adam" is bone of their
bone and flesh of their flesh.   ("Judgment" 830–31)

Other thematic links come readily to mind. The individual's quest for **8**
meaning in his or her past is just as central to Toni Morrison's *Song of
Solomon* or David Bradley's *The Chaneysville Incident* as it is to Faulkner's
Absalom, Absalom! and *The Bear*. Nick Carraway's painful encounter
with the futility of one ambitious American Dreamer's attempt to recreate himself in the image of success in Fitzgerald's *The Great Gatsby*
corresponds to Irene Redfield's experience as she witnesses the tragedy
of her friend Clare Kendry, who masquerades as white in search of
happiness and security in Nella Larsen's *Passing*. Steinbeck's *The Grapes
of Wrath* and Attaway's *Blood on the Forge* are both gritty dramatizations
of people uprooted from their land and forced to survive in a dehuman-
izing environment marked by physical hardship and economic exploitation. Dreiser's *Sister Carrie* and Ann Petry's *The Street* depict the lives
of single young women against the backdrop of a harsh, oppressive
urban landscape. Finally, Edna's uncertain struggling against the stric-
tures of male-dominated Creole society in Chopin's *The Awakening* and
Janie's painful growth from acquiescence to rebellion in Zora Neale
Hurston's *Their Eyes Were Watching God* are but two battles in the same
revolutionary war.

There are many explanations for why Afro-American literature has **9**
yet to be granted the place it deserves in literature textbooks and college
curricula. Perhaps the most important involves the training of those
who teach the literature. Canonicity is determined not only by election
to the major anthologies but by scholarly imprimatur° as well, and the
ethnocentrism° and sexism that plague most of the anthologies unfortunately extend to the dominant literary studies. If the important theorists and commentators in American literature rarely mention works by
Afro-American writers, what is the average graduate student to think
but that no such works exist or, if they do exist, that they are peripheral
and unworthy of serious analysis?

Hyatt Waggoner's famous *American Poets from the Puritans to the Present* **10**
is a particularly useful example because it suggests a connection between
the critic's basic assumptions about American literature and his or her
choice of writers to discuss. In the preface, Waggoner contends, "Our
poetry has been, and continues to be, more concerned with nature than
with society or culture, and more concerned with the eternal than with
the temporal" (xv). Further, he locates the fountainhead of the American
poetic tradition in Puritan thought. Is it then coincidental that in the
index of this 740-page volume we find the names of only two minority

---

Dialectic—two-sided relationship.   **Imprimatur**—official approval.   **Ethnocentrism**—
belief in the superiority of one's own ethnic group.

writers—W. S. Braithwaite, mentioned in a note on Pound, and N. Scott Momaday, cited for his introduction to a collection of poems by Frederick G. Tuckerman? I am hardly suggesting that black writers are not concerned with "nature" or "the eternal." (Indeed, one would think that Waggoner could have found at least one Afro-American author whose work met his criteria.) Rather, my point is that by defining the American poetic mainstream as he does—in terms of both cultural origins and dominant themes—he is necessarily defining *out* of that mainstream whole bodies of literature.

Then there is Richard Howard's *Alone with America: Essays on the Art*   11 *of Poetry in the U.S. since 1950*, which includes essays on forty-one contemporary poets, not one of whom is black. And why is it that in *American Free Verse*, Walter Sutton mentions Langston Hughes only briefly in conjunction with a discussion of Vachel Lindsay and treats the poetry of Amiri Baraka in one sentence? And why do Ihab Hassan's *Radical Innocence: The Contemporary American Novel* and Tony Tanner's *City of Words: American Fiction 1950–1970* deal thoroughly with only one Afro-American writer—predictably, Ralph Ellison?

The omission of works by black authors can often reflect the con-   12 tinuing refusal to acknowledge Afro-American literature as a valid field of study. Darwin Turner responds directly to this argument:

> [I]t is both absurd and hypocritical to raise the question of academic respectability about the study of the literature of an ethnic group composed of people who have been publishing literary works in America for more than 200 years, who have created some of the best-known folktales in America, and who include among their number such distinguished writers as Jean Toomer, Countee Cullen, Richard Wright, Gwendolyn Brooks, Ralph Ellison, James Baldwin, Lorraine Hansberry, and LeRoi Jones.   ("Teaching" 667)

In other cases, however, what we are confronting is ignorance, if not   13 of the works themselves then certainly of their cultural contexts. As Evan Watkins writes, "While it is true that a poem [or any other work of literature] can tell us nothing unless we listen, it is equally true that unless criticism is conceded to be a massively solipsistic° enterprise, the critic must be able to hear in the voice of the poem someone other than himself" (4). Before critics can accurately "hear" and fairly judge what the voice is saying in many works now considered to lie beyond the American literary pale, not only must they be exposed to the material but they must be taught ways to approach it. An effective presentation of Afro-American literature requires a firm grasp of the historical and cultural forces that shape it. Given the deficiencies and blind spots of

---

Solipsistic—of the view that the self is the only reality.

the American educational system, one cannot assume that either students or instructors have this background.[5]

The tremendous remedial education effort that must be undertaken   *14* will not be easy, however. First, pressure on teacher-scholars to specialize and to publish discourages the indulgence in the discursive reading that can often be a key to intellectual growth. Other factors include shrinking extramural° support for research in the humanities generally, limited job security of many scholars working in ethnic literatures, and the exceedingly small number of graduate students specializing in the field.

Then there is the sheer inertia of academic institutions. An excellent   *15* example that would seem to have little to do with Afro-American literature involves the course entitled Contemporary American Literature. Rarely counted among the average department's more crucial offerings, it often covers nearly forty years, from 1945 to the present. In the year 2000, this catchall course might well include works published between World War II and the end of the century. This forecast might sound ludicrous; but unless American literature is assigned the status it deserves and unless the training of scholars and teachers begins to encompass the multiplicity and diversity of American culture, it may well come to pass. I would further suggest that the reluctance of many English departments to acknowledge American literature as a living field—one that reflects not just a valued past but a vital and ever changing present—is directly related to their refusal to take the growing body of literature by minorities and women seriously.

Even if these obstacles are overcome, some difficult theoretical issues   *16* will remain, for we must acknowledge that the problem of broadening the canon is not merely pedagogical but essentially critical. Attempts to change the American canon from within, to integrate black writers into anthologies, course syllabi, and even works of criticism are steps in the right direction. But making room in the canon for ethnic and other overlooked authors entails reevaluating "mainstream" American literature. What then are the consequences of the attempt to "'place' the various American literatures in their cultural contexts," which Wayne Miller rightly claims is "the key to the next literary history of this nation" (33)? For example, after incorporating Afro-American texts, is it still possible to teach nineteenth-century American literature as if the enslavement of blacks and the Civil War virtually never took place (or as if they affected only a handful of American writers, and certainly in no enduring way)? How will the addition of *Twelve Years a Slave: Narrative of Solomon Northup* or *Narrative of William Wells Brown, a Fugitive Slave* to a book list change the teaching of Thoreau's *Walden*, Dana's *Two Years before the Mast*, or Melville's *Moby Dick*? To what

---

Extramural—from outside sources.

extent does one do a serious disservice not only to the Afro-American literary tradition but to American literature generally by failing to expose students to the rich body of oral expression in the United States? Further, is it feasible or even desirable to speak of a single literary tradition in this country? Can we say that Langston Hughes fits neatly into "the" American literary tradition when his work shows the influence not only of "Old Walt," as Hughes calls Whitman in a poem, but also of black folk expression? Is it possible to find one set of critical terms with which to discuss the works of both Wallace Stevens and Sterling Brown, Tennessee Williams and Douglas Turner Ward, Henry Adams and W. E. B. DuBois, Denise Levertov and Lucille Clifton, E. L. Doctorow and John A. Williams—terms that do not favor one author over another?

Seconding a contention that underlies the work of Raymond Williams,   17
Alan Wald argues that "virtually all of our received Euro-American literary categories—not only literary traditions, genres and conventions, but also the very notions of 'aesthetics' and 'imaginative literature'— serve hegemonic° functions in the sense of inculcating us with attitudes toward cultural phenomena that serve the interest of the status quo" (26–27). If this is true, one must ask whether certain critical methods are more suitable than others for evaluating and analyzing the works of black writers or of minority writers in general. Wald contends that "the most appropriate framework for analyzing the literary practice of blacks, Chicanos, Native American Indians, Asian Americans, and Puerto Ricans remains a politico-cultural notion of 'internal colonialism'" (18). To Werner Sollors, studies in ethnicity and cultural anthropology provide the most useful methodological models. Dorothy Ritsuko McDonald suggests that "the major problem . . . is in aesthetics. There is [in the work of many ethnic American writers] a firm rejection of the Western aesthetic yet no clearly defined ethnic one." What exactly is the "Western" aesthetic, and can one totally reject it? Can there be a "clearly defined ethnic" aesthetic? Can one formulate an aesthetic based on a shared sense of oppression and suffering at the hands of Western Europeans? These are some of the issues that must be addressed as we reconstruct the American literary canon.

Ultimately, however, the canon is just the tip of the iceberg, just one   18
step in a far more massive and daunting job—the need to enlarge the concept of American culture generally and thereby to achieve what Wald terms "genuine cultural equality." This goal cannot be reached "without a complementary struggle for social equality," since the literary contributions of blacks and other outsiders in this country are ignored or dismissed largely because to acknowledge their worth would entail acknowledging the humanity and worth of their authors (22). It would also entail a disquieting confrontation with the radical critique of Amer-

---

Hegemonic—dominant.

ican society that informs so much of the literature written by those who have been found wanting by the American cultural establishment. I would further suggest that the willful blindness of the institutions that define the American literary canon is directly related to the urge in this society to deny historical and cultural realities and to refuse to see any real connection between past actions and decisions and present conditions and obligations. This tendency finds its parallel in the propagation of a popular mythology that not only obscures and distorts history but also helps to alleviate this nation's deep and abiding sense of cultural insecurity.

If the striving for representation in the field of American literature *19* corresponds to a similar effort by minorities and women in the political and broader cultural spheres, where does that leave those of us in the academic profession? This question has been raised before, and we in the university balk at confronting it directly—perhaps to avoid revealing just how much (or how little) power we truly wield. Further, pursuing this issue lands us in the brier patch of extraliterary concerns into which, our training tells us, we have scant business getting ourselves. Nonetheless, America has "a documented history of cultural conflict and the uses of literature within that conflict," and we must become aware of how this strife affects our teaching, our research, and our critical statements (Miller 31; see also Gayle). This awareness, in turn, must shape how we define our professional functions and responsibilities. Seeking answers couched in solely pedagogical or critical terms represents a crucial stage in the attempt to effect change. In the final analysis, however, without our conceptualizing and engaging the task before us on a far broader scale, any solution we find will likely prove vulnerable to the same political and economic forces that currently plague the humanities in this country.

In the introduction to the Modern Library's *Anthology of American* *20* *Negro Literature*, published in 1944, John T. Frederick writes:

> In recent years our literature has been enriched by the work of writers of various large ethnic groups not characteristically expressed in previous decades. It is increasingly clear that our American literature of the future will be most strikingly characterized by the vitality and the substantial value of these new contributions.   (xv)

If we broaden Frederick's statement to include the work of American *21* women, growing numbers of scholars and teachers would today agree with this insightful prophecy. Nonetheless, it is disconcerting to realize that forty years after this statement was made, many Americans remain ignorant of the voices of their fellows. It is especially difficult these days to be sanguine° regarding the immediate future. Still, the attention these

---

Sanguine—optimistic.

issues have begun to receive might suggest some thawing of the iceberg, some indication that many are coming to share Ellison's idealistic conviction that "in the realm of the imagination all people and their ambitions and interests could meet" (12).

Notes

[1]Howard Mumford Jones also points out that there was only one professor of American literature in the country until 1917 (161).

[2]Robert Hemenway locates the origins of the concept of a literary canon in "ancient ecclesiastical scholarship"; "Just as the church canonizes saints, scholars and teachers elevate texts to the canon" (26). The notion of an established canon is also directly related to the commercialization of literary production in American society. See Richard Kostelanetz and Thomas Whiteside.

[3]Another bitter irony underlying the literary history of this country is that, as Blanche H. Gelfant notes, "[t]hose who now devalue ethnic literature repeat early accusations against American Literature in general" (766).

[4]Darwin Turner presents an excellent, concise argument in favor of the existence of a coherent Afro-American literary tradition ("Introductory Remarks").

[5]Hemenway addresses this same issue:

> You might conclude from the 1979 edition [of the *Norton Anthology of American Literature*] that the black part of the American literature canon has increased thirty-five-fold, even though those seventy pages constitute only 3.6% of the anthology's total. But the more relevant questions are: Do the black selections get taught? Do they get taught sensitively and well? And does their inclusion in the anthology, given our notions of a sacred canon, mean that they have now been accepted? I rather suspect not. (28)

Works Cited

Ellison, Ralph. *Shadow and Act*. New York: Random, 1964.

Fetterley, Judith, and Joan Schulz. "A MELUS Dialogue: The Status of Women Authors in American Literature Anthologies." *MELUS* 9.3 (1982): 3–17.

Frederick, John T. Introd. *Anthology of American Negro Literature*. Ed. Sylvestre C. Watkins. New York: Modern Library-Random, 1944.

Gayle, Addison, Jr. "Cultural Hegemony: The Southern White Writer and American Letters." In his *The Black Situation*. New York: Delta-Dell, 1970, 168–85.

Gelfant, Blanche H. "Mingling and Sharing in American Literature: Teaching Ethnic Fiction." *College English* 43 (1981): 763–72.

Hassan, Ihab. *Radical Innocence: The Contemporary American Novel*. Princeton, N.J.: Princeton Univ. Press, 1961.

Hemenway, Robert. "The Sacred Canon and Brazzle's Mule." *ADE Bulletin* 73 (Winter 1982): 26–32.

Howard, Richard. *Alone with America: Essays on the Art of Poetry in the U.S. since 1950*. New York: Atheneum, 1971.

Jones, Howard Mumford. *The Theory of American Literature.* Ithaca: Cornell Univ. Press, 1965.

Kostelanetz, Richard. *The End of Intelligent Writing: Literary Politics in America.* New York: Sheed, 1974.

McDonald, Dorothy Ritsuko. "Beyond Protest and Explanation." *MELUS* 8.3 (1981): 2.

Miller, Wayne Charles. "Cultural Consciousness in a Multi-Cultural Society: The Uses of Literature." *MELUS* 8.5 (1981): 29–44.

Scott, Nathan A. "Black Literature." In *Harvard Guide to Contemporary American Writing.* Ed. Daniel Hoffman. Cambridge: Belknap-Harvard, 1979, 287–341.

————. "Judgment Marked by a Cellar: The American Negro Writer and the Dialectic of Despair." *Denver Quarterly* 2.2 (1967). Rpt. in *Cavalcade: Negro American Writing from 1760 to the Present.* Ed. Arthur P. Davis and Saunders Redding. Boston: Houghton, 1971, 821–42.

Sollors, Werner. "Theory and Ethnic Message." *MELUS* 8.3 (1981): 15–17.

Spencer, Benjamin T. "An American Literature Again." *Sewanee Review* 47 (1949): 56–72. Rpt. in *A Storied Land.* Vol. 2. of *Theories of American Literature.* New York: Dutton, 1976, 439–50.

Sutton, Walter. *American Free Verse: The Modern Revolution in Poetry.* New York: New Directions, 1973.

Tanner, Tony. *City of Words: American Fiction 1950–1970.* New York: Harper, 1971.

Turner, Darwin T. "Introductory Remarks about the Black Literary Tradition in the United States of America." *Black American Literary Forum* 12 (1970): 140–47.

————. "The Teaching of Afro-American Literature." *College English* 31 (1970): 666–70.

Waggoner, Hyatt H. *American Poets from the Puritans to the Present.* New York: Dell, 1968.

Wald, Alan. "The Culture of 'Internal Colonialism': A Marxist Perspective." *MELUS* 8.3 (1981): 18–27.

Watkins, Evan. *The Critical Act: Criticism and Community.* New Haven: Yale Univ. Press, 1978.

Whiteside, Thomas. *The Blockbuster Complex.* Middletown, Conn.: Wesleyan Univ. Press, 1981.

Rhetorical Analysis Through Annotation

Each of Yarborough's paragraphs presents a step in his argument. Each has a slightly different focus than the previous one, moving the argument forward.

In the margin next to each paragraph, note the focus of the paragraph and the direction in which it moves the argument.

Discuss how the argument moves through the separate paragraphs to its conclusion. Does the argument form a unified whole, and if so, how is this accomplished? What is the overall structure of the argument?

Discussion Questions

Interpreting the Text

1. In the opening four paragraphs, Yarborough implies there are two possible views of the canon and canon change. What are they? Which does he prefer? Why? Which does he currently find dominant in current literature departments? What problem does that dominance present, and how is that problem related to the main argument of Yarborough's essay?

2. Yarborough argues that Afro-American literature is in some ways similar to canonical American literature and in some ways different. What specifically are the points of similarity and difference? What point is he trying to make by showing the similarities? By showing the differences? Why does he discuss the similarities before the differences? Overall, does he find similarities outweighing the differences or vice versa?

3. Which, if any, of the works mentioned by Yarborough are you familiar with? How does what he says about each of the works fit with your experience of reading that work? Do you need to be familiar with the works to understand his argument?

Considering the Issues

4. Yarborough argues that there is a long, rich history of Afro-American writing, dating back to before the American Revolution. Were you previously aware of this history or did you think that black writing was only a recent phenomenon in the United States? How do you account for your impressions of Afro-American literature? How do your impressions relate to the argument Yarborough makes about the exclusion of Afro-American literature from the American canon?

5. Do you think the argument Yarborough makes about the exclusion of Afro-American literature also applies to the literary work of other groups you may be familiar with? Can you support your opinion with some specific examples of works either excluded or included?

6. Yarborough links the literary canon with larger issues of cultural equality. How does he do this? Do you believe he is right? In what ways have blacks and other groups been excluded from "official" or "unofficial" American culture? In what ways have black culture and the cultures of other previously excluded groups started to change mainstream American culture? You may consider examples from language, family, fashion, popular dance, humor, or any other aspect of American life. Do you think American society is moving toward "genuine cultural equality" or is it still largely exclusionary?

Writing Suggestions

1. For a class in contemporary American culture, write an essay about a book, movie, television show, piece of music, or other work created by a black artist. Discuss ways the work is uniquely based in the black experience and ways it is indistinguishable from the work of other races. Use your comparison of this one work to discuss the larger issue of the degree to which black culture has influenced or become part of shared American culture and to what degree it remains separate or excluded.

2. Imagine a leader of your home community made a speech quoted in the newspaper arguing that the cultures of different groups should remain separate, with each group enjoying only its own culture. Write a letter to the editor of the local newspaper objecting to or supporting the leader's belief in cultural separatism.

3. Imagine you were on a panel with Richard Yarborough at a conference of teachers of literature. You were invited to give the reactions of a student to Yarborough's thoughts. Write a short talk giving your responses.

4. As part of this course's discussion of the forms of argument, compare the techniques Yarborough uses to argue for inclusion to the techniques Ngugi uses to argue for separatism. Discuss how the different rhetorical techniques each writer uses are appropriate to the stance they take toward the traditional canon, the audiences they are appealing to, and the actions they wish their audiences to take.

The Contents of English Literature

E. D. Hirsch, Jr.

In the 1980s some literary critics are again defending the canon, even though they concede that its contents may need changing. We need a canon, the argument goes, so that writers and readers share a common body of information, including names, images, concepts, proverbs, idioms, historical characters and events, and terms. Intelligent reading and writing depend on a common culture that establishes shared information and understandings. If we wish to have a literate culture, we must choose a set of texts and a body of knowledge to base that literacy on. Literacy has been declining in America, some argue, because there is no standard list of books that everyone has read.

E. D. Hirsch (b. 1928), a professor of English and literary critic at the University of Virginia, has made this argument most vigorously and publicly, for general as well as professional audiences. His concept of cultural literacy includes knowledge of all subjects, from geography to music to mathematics, but, as he says, English is "the subject most profoundly connected with the formation of a common culture." In the following article from the British *Times Literary Supplement* in 1982, he speaks directly to the issue of the literary canon. His audience is educated and academically oriented, but not limited to people specializing in literary studies.

In this article Hirsch recognizes the difficulties implicit in accepting a canon and the presumption of any group of people deciding what that canon should be. He attempts to overcome his audience's opposition through self-deflating ironies at the beginning and end, a carefully constructed history showing that canon formation has always involved self-conscious choice, arguments for the necessity of having a canon, mention of the dangers of *not* having a canon, and explicit recognition of the value of cultural pluralism.

THOSE WHO URGE US to preserve a canon of English literature are 1 on dangerous ground, since our literature has no canon of the biblical kind established once and for all by a council. The only council we have in the United States is The National Council of the Teachers of English, which its Secretary has rightly called "a body without a head." Nor have we anything resembling the academy that Arnold° wished us to cultivate within ourselves. By tradition, what correspond to the Five Books of Moses in Eng Lit are the Big Four of Chaucer, Shakespeare, Spenser, and Milton. But even that short list is not accepted by all the priestly preservers of the tradition. Spenser seems expendable to some. Nor is the purely *English* Tetrateuch° the sacred national literature of every nation where English is spoken and literature is taught. Where Spenser was, there shall Hawthorne be; and other substitutions will be made elsewhere: in Canada, India, and so on. When Hazlitt proposed the Big Four as our canon, he was making a novel, not a traditional, proposal since English Literature then as now was always in process. It is not a limited and fixed distillation from the past as was the literature of classical antiquity. Later in Hazlitt's° century, when Churton Collins succeeded in his campaign to offer students the literature of England as well as that of Greece and Rome, he introduced a subject that could not be completely analogous with any fixed corpus° of the classical heritage. In the century after that of Hazlitt and Collins, the body of literature written in English has continued to grow, and that same process which in Collins's day traded Virgil for Milton, once begun, may later trade Milton for Melville. As years pass, and excellent works keep appearing, the earlier part of the canon may shrink, the later expand; for students do not have infinite time in an infinite curriculum, and they have other texts to read and study besides poems, plays, and novels.

In mentioning students I have deliberately equated the literary canon 2 with the literary curriculum as it exists in schools and universities. There is, of course, another canon of English Literature—that long list of authors and works accepted as fit subjects for the ever expanding *Bib-*

Matthew Arnold (1822–1888)—English poet and critic.   **Tetrateuch**—four major authors.   **William Hazlitt (1778–1830)**—English critic and essayist.   **Corpus**—collection of works.

liography of the Modern Language Association. From that enormous catalogue have been extracted more serviceable canons, like the two-volume *Norton Anthology*. All of these canons have some reality for small parts of our culture, and a few undergraduates studying English may read even most of the works in the *Norton*. But the canon that chiefly concerns me is the one that is shared by a reasonably large part of our literate society. It consists of those works and authors that are widely taught in "English" (a required subject in our schools and often in our universities), and which can thereby become a widely shared part of our culture. This actual canon will exist only in so far as a shared curriculum exists.

In the United States we have always had to confront the task of self- *3* conscious culture-making with the help of the schools. Our parent cultures were diverse, and we being rebellious children were determined to establish our own cultural identity—witness Noah Webster's dictionary and Melville's prophecy that we shall make our own Shakespeares. This self-conscious culture-making created a special atmosphere for the teaching of literature in our schools. American teachers knew early that they were helping to form rather than merely preserve a culture. In this formative task, literature and literacy went together. Within the subject of "English," the two aspects were conceived as mutually supportive. For we could not take for granted either our literature or our literacy. A similar double purpose also guided literary teaching in those outlying provinces of Britain where culture-making rather than culture-inheriting became a conscious goal even in the universities. The first professor of English was Hugh Blair in Edinburgh, and his chair carried a double title which reflected the double aim of teaching both literature and literacy; it was called the chair of "Rhetoric and Belles Lettres." Similarly, Dowden's chair in Dublin was in "Oratory and English Literature." And in this country, English began as a course of instruction in literature along with oral and written composition. This duality of purpose had an influence on the texts chosen for the curriculum. For they often served both as literature and as subjects for composition.

The union of literature and literacy was reflected in the statement of *4* aims produced by our first national conference on the teaching of English. It took place in 1892, and the author of the statement was the Secretary of the conference, G. L. Kittredge, the celebrated Chaucerian and Shakespearian scholar of Harvard University. "The main objects" (he wrote on behalf of the conference) "of the teaching of English in schools seem to be two: (1) to enable the pupil to understand the expressed thoughts of others and to give expression to thoughts of his own; and (2) to cultivate a taste for reading, to give the pupil some acquaintance with good literature, and to furnish him with a means for extending that acquaintance." This duality in the very concept of "English" led no doubt to the following literary curriculum in American schools before 1900, which I list in order of decreasing frequency of use:

The Merchant of Venice, Julius Caesar, "First Bunker Hill Oration," "The Sketch Book," "Evangeline," "The Vision of Sir Launfal," "Snowbound," *Macbeth,* "The Lady of the Lake," *Hamlet,* "The Deserted Village," Gray's "Elegy," "Thanatopsis," *As You Like It,* "The Courtship of Miles Standish," "Il Penseroso," *Paradise Lost,* "L'Allegro," "Lycidas," *David Copperfield, Silas Marner.* And another two hundred titles were listed at least once in the schools surveyed. (The historical information in this paragraph was gleaned from the excellent book by Arthur Applebee, *Tradition and Reform in the Teaching of English,* Urbana, Ill. 1974).

While we might scorn such a hodge-podge for its incoherence and 5 unevenness, we must also concede that school canons will always tend to be random, confused, and short. They arise from diverse cultural and pedagogical purposes, and they are bound to be as arbitrary as they are heterogeneous°—arbitrary in the sense that any item on so short a list will surely have some worthy substitute. No text is inherently canonical; only a conscious cultural purpose can make it so; estimable cultures exist that are ignorant of Shakespeare. Our current American culture was not handed down intact from various parents. The contents of our actual canon must be partly the result of conscious and arbitrary choice.

In recent years, especially since the 1940s, we have evaded the neces- 6 sity for such choice. While maths and chemistry and physics are subjects that have an acknowledged canonical core and a widespread common curriculum, English, the subject most profoundly connected with the formation of a common culture, has none. There is in the State of California an official curriculum guide to the study of English in the schools. I was unable to find in it the title of a single work. *De minimis non curat praetor!*° It was not always thus, even in California. The whole period of English teaching in the United States from 1901 to the 1930s was dominated by the "uniform lists" put out by the College Entrance Examination Board. (They contained such works as *Julius Caesar, Macbeth, Silas Marner,* Milton's minor poems, and seven or eight more.) Justified complaint against the narrowness of these lists did not, however, result finally in richer and more diverse lists. It resulted in no lists at all. Now, in response to this vacuum, and to the lack of any common literary knowledge among students entering university, American colleges have started programs of "core curricula." But these will be futile gestures unless they are accompanied by more fundamental conceptual changes in our approach to the teaching of Eng Lit.

Today, the dominant theory behind the teaching of "English" can be 7 characterized by the term "educational formalism." This theory holds that what is really being taught in our schools, and particularly in our English courses, is a set of formal, transferable skills that can be applied

---

Heterogeneous—of mixed kinds.   **De minimis non curat praetor**—small things are not of interest to magistrates.

to later tasks of life. What is being taught is how to read, how to write, how to think. Of course, it is conceded that the materials used for developing these skills should be "appropriate" and "of high quality," but their specific content can be left to local choice. Such educational formalism is thought to be especially appropriate in the American context, because it harmonizes well with the American traditions of pluralism, federalism, and diversity. Formal skills, after all, apply to the most diverse materials. Another convenience of educational formalism, therefore, is that it insulates educators from the political danger of recommending particular texts—especially in the domain of literature, where such choices may carry powerful cultural and ideological implications.

In 1938, this how-to educational theory attached itself to another   8 formalism—literary formalism. The two doctrines were made for each other. From that moment began a new era—our era—in the teaching of Eng Lit. The doctrine of *literary* formalism holds that the essence of literature lies in its organic structure, in its formal system of relationships. Consequently, the task of teaching students how to read literature would be to teach the skills of identifying and describing those formal relationships. The inculcation of formal reading skills would thus be neatly correlated with the identification of the recurrent characteristics of literature. And best of all, content would not be altogether neglected in such a formal approach, since in literature (as opposed to technical writing or propaganda) the content is included in and expressed by the form. Thus students would learn how to read *any* literature, yet through this formal approach they would also acquire the valuable content of literature, which was inseparable from the form. Because of this principle of inseparability, the content that students got from literature would of course be quite different from the content absorbed from propaganda. Hence the teaching of Eng Lit was exempt from the fury and the mire of cultural politics, and even from the dilemmas of large-scale curricular decisions. Needless to say, this has been an attractive educational programme. . . .

I wish that the principles of educational and literary formalism were   9 in fact sound and workable. I admire and agree with the pluralistic and democratic values that have sponsored their use in the schools. But formalism has not worked, and the reason for its failure is, paradoxically, a formal one. It is this: the formal skills of reading and writing are not analogous to the formal skills of hitting a tennis-ball or swimming a breaststroke, skills that can be transferred, *mutatis mutandis*°, to different environments. It is true that significant elements of reading and writing skills are transferable in that way; but many elements are not. The skills of literacy depend significantly upon domains of specific tacit knowledge° that are not and could not be written down. Specialists in reading

---

Mutatis mutandis—the necessary things being changed.   **Tacit knowledge**—those things we know without being aware of them.

and sociolinguists have shown that explicit written features are often the smallest part of the literary transaction. The rest is background knowledge tacitly shared between writer and reader. This relevant background knowledge is *formally* necessary to the skills of reading and writing. (I develop this point with greater detail and fuller documentation in "Culture and Literacy," *Journal of Basic Writing*, Winter 1980).

Recently in the United States, where the extent of widely shared   10
cultural knowledge has diminished, the level of literacy has also declined. The two facts are causally related. Even among the white middle class, the literacy level has dropped, as we know from the declining scores of that group over the past decade in the Verbal Scholastic Aptitude Test. (The verbal SAT is essentially a vocabulary test, hence a literacy test too. It shows a high correlation with other measurements of reading and writing ability.) This decline in shared knowledge and in the shared vocabularies that accompany it is certainly not due entirely to deficiencies in Eng Lit, or even deficiencies in the schools alone. But the disappearance of a shared school curriculum must have something to do with the narrowing of the shared contents of our culture. And in this narrowing, our recent teaching of English has played a perhaps not trivial role. Consider the implications of the following experiment with an "inverse" SAT test. Robert A. Williams devised a test called the "Black Intelligence Scale of Cultural Homogeneity" (BITCH). According to Jay Amberg in an article in *The American Scholar* (51, 1982) "All of the items for the BITCH were drawn exclusively from black experience. When Williams administered the test to blacks and whites, the scoring pattern was the reverse of the SAT—blacks had higher scores." Similar pieces of evidence can be adduced° to show that formal skills of reading and writing vary directly with the reader's relevant knowledge.

This truth is implicitly familiar to every writer. The complexity and   11
subtlety of what can be expressed by the written word will depend upon the amount of shared knowledge that can be assumed among readers. Literacy is a continuum from poverty to affluence, in which the chief determinant is the quality of shared knowledge. For big cultures this shared background is vague at the edges. . . .

If we want a pluralist curriculum in the United States, the way to get   12
one is to appoint a pluralistic national body and ask them to hammer out curricular compromises, and give us curricular guides that actually name authors and works. If teachers then paid heed to such suggestions (and the teachers I know are eager for such guidance), we would begin to have a current canon of Eng Lit. The canon would be revised; it would change; but it might also attain a certain stability over the years. Any such nation-wide recommendations could then serve another important function. These canonical materials could be used in composition as well as in literary courses; for composition is also a subject that has

---

Adduced—used as support.

succumbed to the perils of formalism. The use of the canon would carry the additional advantage of once more linking Eng Lit and composition together as in the days of Blair, Dowden, and Kittredge.° The double job of teaching literature and literacy continues to be our authentic as well as our original task. If these suggestions, or something like them, were followed, the professing of literature might regain its usefulness, sense of purpose, and self-esteem. More important, SAT scores would rise.

Rhetorical Analysis Through Annotation

In this essay Hirsch refers to the ideas of other writers and critics who both support and oppose his argument. Other references serve to establish the history of the problem, and a final set of references give examples of works considered canonical at one time or another.

Underline each reference or set of references. In the margin, note whether the reference or set of references is to establish history, give examples of canonical works, support Hirsch's point of view, or provide him with a target for attack. Also note whether the reference is by name only, by summary or paraphrase, or by full quotation, and whether Hirsch then discusses the reference at any length.

Discuss how Hirsch uses each of the supporting references to build his argument and how he attacks each of the opposing references.

Discussion Questions

Interpreting the Text

1. What does Hirsch mean by educational formalism? In what subjects, if any, have you learned formal skills without much attention to content? Do you feel such formal skills learning was useful? Do you agree or disagree with Hirsch's attack on educational formalism?

2. How, according to Hirsch, are educational formalism and literary formalism related? How is formalism a response to cultural diversity? Why does he have mixed feelings about formalism?

3. What do SAT scores indicate? How important are they? Why does Hirsch discuss them at length and come back to them in his final line?

Considering the Issues

4. Does your college have a core curriculum, establishing certain knowledge as necessary for all students? What knowledge is defined as necessary by this core curriculum? What are the specific requirements in literature and the arts? If you have not yet taken these courses, you may examine the catalogue descriptions or the syllabi of the courses. How does this core curriculum fit in with Hirsch's

---

Blair, Dowden, Kittredge—educationists of the last two centuries.

ideas? How well do you think this core curriculum works to establish shared knowledge and common culture among the students and in society?

5. Hirsch asserts that to read and comprehend a piece of writing, the writer and the reader must share a large body of background knowledge. In your experience, which texts are hardest to read: those with complex sentences, those with long words, or those discussing subjects that you are not familiar with? How does your reading ability in areas you know well compare with your ability in areas you are less familiar with? Similarly, does your knowledge of a subject have any effect on your ability to write on that subject? Use examples from your experience.

6. How does Hirsch attempt to persuade readers of his position? What resistances and opposing arguments must he overcome, and how does he attempt to do so? Do you believe he succeeds?

Writing Suggestions

1. As part of this course's concern for communication, write a paper about a personal experience that shows what makes reading easy or difficult for you. You may write about a seemingly easy book that you found impossible to understand or a book that other people find difficult that you found not particularly troublesome. Explain why you think you did or did not have difficulty with the book.

2. Imagine the curriculum committee of your college was considering developing a new core curriculum. The committee, wishing for student input, has asked for position papers from interested students. Write a position paper arguing for your opinions as to whether there should be a core curriculum, whether it should differ from current requirements, and what such a core curriculum should contain, if anything.

3. Your local newspaper is running a series of articles on "What ever became of the classics?" Write a column for this series, exploring your reading and the reading of your friends, in school and out. Consider whether literary classics have any impact on your generation's reading. You may also wish to consider whether new classics have emerged to influence your generation.

The Dispossessing Eye: Reading Wordsworth on the Equatorial Line
Shirley Lim

Whatever the ultimate rights and wrongs of canon formation may be, the canon is a fact for each child discovering literature. The books we encounter as we grow up influence our vision of our selves, our lives,

and the world around us. Books may bind us more closely to the
immediate world around us or may lead us away from the world to
new worlds. Usually some of both happens.

The family of writer Shirley Lim (b. 1944) originally came from
the Hokkien region in southern China, but for many generations had
lived in Malaya, now called Malaysia. Her culture was a mixture of
Chinese and Malay elements, known as Nonya/Baba culture. However, in her childhood, Malaya was a British colony: education was
in English and transmitted British culture. Popular British books introduced her to the joys of language, and the classics of British literature helped shape her fundamental sense of herself. Her engagement
with the canon of another culture distanced her from the daily Asian
life that surrounded her, even while it introduced her to a new world.
She now lives in the United States and teaches at the State University
of New York. Here in a personal essay written for a book published
in 1986 on the literary canon she explores the meaning of those sep-
arations and discoveries, and finds there is no simple answer.

Although the contrast between the literature we discover and the
daily life around us may not be nearly as striking as it was for Shirley
Lim, perhaps we all share some of her sense of dispossession. It has
been said that literature is another country. In it we find feelings,
perceptions, observations not available in the supermarket or on the
ball field. The canon of literature, however and by whomever chosen,
defines the boundaries of that other country.

MY CHILDHOOD WORLD BEFORE the age of six is a blank tape. *1*
I can recall a few incidents, mostly nasty and scatological, having to do
with bouts of constipation and forced enemas, or bullying episodes by
brothers, uncles and cousins. My Hokkien/Nonya Malaysian family had
been fortunate in the number of males produced over two generations;
my paternal grandfather had one daughter and seven sons, my father
two daughters and eight sons. I remember life before six as a dishevelled,
miserable thing, swinging between rare treats (grapes, three-tiered ruf-
fled crinoline frocks, wicker doll furniture) and pervasive boredom and
sadness, that peculiar mixture of self-pity and outrage at finding oneself
alone before a locked door behind which all the others are having fun.
These remembrances, overflowing with still-fresh rancour, are scenes
from a silent movie. The emotions are heart-felt; they rumble and
thunder, but they are tongue-tied. I have no memory of how I must
have expressed them aloud.

My first true memory of spoken language occurs when I am six. I *2*
am lying on the upper bunk bed, pushing at the yellow painted iron
railings with my feet. My brothers are off somewhere shooting with
catapults and hard green berries or scavenging the garbage from neigh-

boring shops for dented tins of food (no one told them about botulism). The radio in the shoe store which my father manages downstairs is on. It is Children's Storytime on BBC. Even now, I hear the distinct flavour of the strongly accented British voice: "NOW, children when the PRINCESS discovered the DRAGON was sleeping, she CRRREPT down the stairs and. . . ." Into my dank sniffling mind, over my entire body of unvoiced sensations, creeps an intensity of pleasure: a slow tingle at first as the modulated voice takes me down the ancient road of Suspense, followed by deep satisfaction as we conclude in the fore-ordained destination of Happily Ever After. Gone, for the moment, is the loud disorienting buzz of unhappiness. In the jumble of feelings, impressions, and impulses, a flashlight shines and renders the confusion invisible. I hear a voice and see the world it said is beautiful.

Now, in hindsight, it is clear my first memory of spoken language is 3 also my first memory of the English language. If, by language, we mean those resources of sounds by which humans make sense of their world and themselves, sense being the (de)formation of sensations into pattern and order, then, for me, if not for other Malaysians of my generation, English was my mother tongue.

The psychological, sociological, and inherently political ramifications 4 of this childhood experience are beyond my abilities to uncover. Still, the nature of my initiation into the world of spoken language (its strong dramatic content; emotional satisfaction of resolution; mellifluous voice; artificial rhythms—"music"—of the narrative delivery; the visual content in the fairytale) must have influenced my burgeoning taste in literature; perhaps, even, to some extent, shaped a "literary" personality. But I would have probably remained a fervid reader of British romances and mysteries (by then I was reading every Denise Robbins, Barbara Cartland, and Agatha Christie° paperback in town) if Wordsworth had not come along.

I found William Wordsworth among schooltext anthologies: pieces of 5 the *Lyrical Ballads* stashed in among John Masefield ("Quinquireme of Nineveh . . ."), Walter De La Mare ("The moon was a ghostly galleon . . ."), Rupert Brooke ("That is forever England . . ."), and other early twentieth-century Georgian poets. My brothers' book-bags, which I pried into at the start of every school year for their prizes of large, shiny-paged texts on World Geography, History, and Poetry For Schools, carried substantial cloth-covered poetry collections usually divided into sections with titles such as "Nature," "Animals," "Melancholy," and "Narratives." My teachers, most of whom wore the heavy black habit of the Convent, were delighted to find a budding orator in among my untidy bundle of furies and nurtured my pretensions for competitive elocution performances. I was trained to pace the stage in

---

Denise Robbins, Barbara Cartland, and Agatha Christie—popular English writers of romances and mysteries.

a round of no more than four steps, to lift high my right hand at a peak of declamation, to whisper loudly at moments of dramatic stress, to defy the air around as the narrative rushed along. "The Inchcape Rock" could send shivers of hopelessness down any restless hall of schoolchildren; "the Highwayman," trotting in the moonlight, especially affected the moony girls. But "I Wandered Lonely as a Cloud," incorrectly titled in my stolen anthologies "The Daffodils," was my favourite poem.

I never recited it for an audience, unless you count my presence *6* audience enough. It was insufficiently thrilling to the scores of critical pupils who knew exactly what they liked, too brief to persuade the high judges of my skills in moving listeners to a pitch of excitement. At ten, I did not think of Wordsworth as a poet; I only experienced his poem as poetry,—perhaps, if not the purest response to literature, at least the simplest and most artless. And it was this poem I meant, at twenty-three, when I meant to reject the whole of the dead hand of British literary tradition and left for the United States to discover something new. "You British," I said, in the calloused manner of youth sneering at the mistakes of the past, "made us look for daffodils, so we never saw the *bunga raya* (hibiscus) growing everywhere in Malaysia."

The idea makes for a pretty statement, but grown older, I am perhaps *7* able to untangle the plot in a fairer manner. For it was not the British (whoever they were!) who "made" the poem's vision of golden daffodils compelling, but the poem itself. Its compulsion for me lay not so much in the imagery of plant life, (for, even at that early age, I knew the image was not central to the poem; had never felt the need to look up picture books to visualise the dancing host or to interlocute° those Malaysians who had been to England "in spring-time, in spring-time" and returned with precious nylons and woollens), but in its expression of the condition of absence, the mental state of vacuity in which images are involuntarily recreated.

Reciting the poem solemnly alone in the afternoons when my brothers *8* were out playing hockey or badminton or soccer and only the hot glaring streets awaited me, I read further and further into the lines: "For oft, when on my couch I lie/ In vacant or in pensive mood,/ They flash upon the inward eye/ Which is the bliss of solitude." They formed a mantra° confirming my moodiness and affirming its other-self; the ocean of interiority in which, left to my own lonely devices, I sank, mastered as the inward eye/I and transformed by poetic statement into "the bliss of solitude." The mantra taught me compensation. Where a mother would have urged her child to go out and play, Wordsworth's poem spoke of the wealth, the pleasure, to be attained in staying "inward." The poem taught me a way to value my experience, which judged socially then in my Asian context must be seen as a miserable failure, an only girl among six brothers, mother-abandoned, without resources:

Interlocute—converse.   **Mantra**—a Hindu sacred formula to be repeated to oneself.

it taught me the sovereignty of the subject. Not the mindless claims of "Invictus"° but the powers of imagination are appealed to here, a poet's eye which transforms vacancy to bliss.

Initially, such "day-dreaming" is escapist. It allows the ill-fitting psy- *9* che to turn away from vacancy, boredom, emptiness, discomfort, poverty, deprivation, loneliness, moodiness, misery, nothingness, outsiderness, external reality to pleasant fantasies, fanciful dreams, wishful thoughts, romantic yearnings, erotic musings, interior landscapes, internal meaning. But the escape is never passive. The imagination as a partner in the crime with the will actively conspires to break away, and, not much later, grown confident, returns to the world to take its revenge. For the imagination never stops loving the world. Thus the strange paradox that writers and artists who seem the most removed from the real world, as it is claimed by business, law, and science, continue to claim to show that world (as it is always being formed in humanity's imagination) to others. The subjective eye, while it is not non-ego, is truly itself in the act of looking at something. Moving from dreaminess to penetration, the Malaysian writer must look at his tropical world, the white noon and black early-falling night, the wind's rough soughing in the coarse coconut fronds, singing mosquitoes, the delicious decay of *blachan*,° and, more problematically, the movements of people eating, working, fighting, meeting, and not meeting. The eye is adult observer and analyser, creating illusions of depth and dimension which correspond in some satisfying way with meaning.

Still, subjectivity is a dirty word in intellectual circles. Among men, *10* it is associated with excessive feminisation and hysteria; among scientists with tainted observations; and in some literary schools with decadent personalistic styles. T.S. Eliot, in promulgating an "Impersonal theory of poetry" (*Tradition and the Individual Talent*), placed a permanent ban on subjectivity as a value in poetry. Discoursing on "the mind of the poet," he calls it "the shred of platinum"; "a more finely perfected medium in which special, or very varied, feelings are at liberty to enter into new combinations"; "a receptacle for seizing and stirring up numberless feelings, phrases, images, which remain there until all the particles which can unite to form a new compound are present together." How strange this disjuncture in definitions between the Romantic poet's "inward eye/ Which is the bliss of solitude" and the modern poet's "medium"; "receptacle"; "shred of platinum."

How much stranger the disjunctures in the Asian child struggling to *11* make meaning of British Romanticism and a transplanted American's idea of European Classicism! At sixteen I read "Prufrock" for the first time and dimly understood it, giving three cheers for the poet's adolescent self-consciousness and ironic-comic poses. But when, finally, in the

---

"Invictus"—An inspirational poem of the Victorian period.   **Blachan**—a fragrant shrimp-paste used in cooking.

University of Malaya, guided by Oxbridge° men who made gentle fun
of romances and feelings, I re-read both Wordsworth and Eliot in full,
I found that while Wordsworth's poetry deepened for me, I held off
from Eliot's influence, suspecting his work, at some level, of unconscious bad faith. I recognise now that it is not Eliot's bad faith I rejected
but Wordsworth's faith in the supremacy of the subject that I could not
give up. And although I have attempted at many turns to "de-subjec-
tivise" my themes, the influencing authority cannot be shaken.

What is more unfortunate than this Wordsworthian shape of my   12
sensibility is its un-Asian cast. For the child who turns from social misery
to private power, from public activities to solitary musings, is choosing
to be an individual. The concept of the individual in society is so familiar
in Western countries as to be banal; in an Asian country like the Malaysia
of my childhood, it was a term prickly with disapproval. While we
were all different, the differences being not only in short and tall or
quick and slow but in radical definitions of race, color, and religion, we
were all bound by social obligations: respect for elders and teachers;
filial obedience and loyalty; physical modesty and restraint; and many
other unstated social laws which ruled every aspect of our lives: what
we may wear; when we may eat; how and when we should talk; our
manner of walking; how to greet various members of our family; when
and how the dead should be buried; rituals for various holidays; how to
behave among men (women); how children should be raised: a host of
unquestioned lore concerning the behaviour of every member of that
particular social group, whether Malay, Chinese, Indian or Eurasian. In
all these prescribed modes, the individual was not a person who feels,
acts, and wants from within, rather a person who is directed by the
traditions and values of his society. An individual who expresses a feeling
or desire not contained within the social matrix is not merely odd but
dangerous, disrupting the values which allow the rest of his social group
to organize itself efficiently.

Perhaps it was the very variety of social organisation in Malaysia then   13
which made the idea of the individual ludicrous and shameful. What a
plentitude of types were available for observation: the *jaga*° lying on his
rope bed, his Sikh° beard and turban like a logo for every respectable
bank in the country; the Chinese shop-keeper in singlets° and short pants
beset on all sides by boxes and shelves of merchandise; the *towkay neo*,°
wrists adorned with half-a-dozen gold bangles, perched on a trishaw°
to a mahjong table; the Malay in his white haj° clothing and blue velvet
cap taking his shoes off before a mosque; the Tamil,° sleek, black, and
lithe, who sounds like a rattle of consonants as he talks to his companions

---

Oxbridge—from Oxford and Cambridge Universities in England.   **Jaga**—a janitor.
Sikh—member of a religious sect from India.   **Singlets**—undershirts.   **Towkay neo**—
wife of a rich man.   **Trishaw**—a hand-pulled travelling cart; a rickshaw.   **Haj**—a Mos-
lem who has made the pilgrimage to Mecca.   **Tamil**—a person from southern India.

at the coffee stall. Concentrated in the urban pockets of Malaysia in the fifties was half of Asia, and each racial/national group resisted assimilation. I ate *chappatis°* in Begum's house, *kutupat°* in Ahmad's home, chicken soup with the Gomez family; *pow°* in the Tans' bungalow.

Perhaps the riches were embarrassing because they were forced. In a multiracial society you could not avoid rubbing shoulders with "demons" and "barbarians" in schools, shops, and playing-fields. At the same time, in all that variety, you could not choose your identity—it was given to you. You were Chinese or Malay or Indian or Ceylonese or Eurasian. And then, if Chinese, you were Hokkien or Cantonese or Hakka or Hailam or Shanghainese. Perhaps a vision of *E Pluribus Unum* from the West could and may still fuse these types into a national identity in which the individual can find legitimisation, validation, protection, and structural resources. But as a child I was constantly confused by what I was told I was or should be and what I felt as the flow of my experiences. Because my family was Straits Settlements Nonya/Baba, I was considered Chinese by some groups; but because I could not read Mandarin and spoke very little Hokkien, I was called a Malay ghost by some Chinese. And all the time I was having a British education. Reading about glacial detritus° and glacial-formed lakes and then about Wordsworth's and Coleridge's inspiring walks in the Lake Country, I tried hiking through patches of laterite° wasteland, suffered numerous *lallang°* cuts on my bare legs, and learned that, like Malaysian social custom, British education was not easily transferable to actual subjective experience.   14

As a young woman, I observed that interracial marriages were rare. A few University students infected by Western notions of romantic love and freedom might experiment with interracial dating, but cases of attempted or successful suicide rising from the pain of family disapproval were reported in the *Straits Times* and passed along as common teenage wisdom. An individual examining her subjective condition outside such controlling social frames of racial and religious distinctions can justly be seen as examining a Western vapour. In a sociological argument, "solitude" becomes "alienation"; "the inward eye," the aesthete blind to social concerns.   15

As a young girl, in involuntarily choosing a certain "poetic" stance which empowered the subjective in my experiences, I did not realize I was also choosing a social statement. The authoritative voice which first made me conscious of "waters, rolling from their mountain-springs/ With a sweet inland murmur" also closed my ears to the babble of tongues in the eastern bazaar. As an excuse, I could say it is hard to listen to the self within in the noise of family reunions, but for a writer   16

Chappati—an Indian whole wheat bread. **Kutupat**—a Malay rice cake. **Pow**—a Chinese meat dumpling. **Detritus**—remains, garbage. **Laterite**—a red soil, not good for vegetation. **Lallang**—a tall, sharp-edged tropical grass.

of fiction that is a poor excuse. Between poetry and fiction falls the shadow of the world.

Tired though I am of Wordsworthian sublimity, I still find in it those 17 ancestral springs which lead me to write poetry in English. The very act itself is a statement of dispossession, and as Malaysia progresses further and further into its nationalistic future, claiming its own language, its own history, its own literary traditions, I am in danger of further losing possession of a national self, my public, my social traditions. That is as should be. Writing purposefully for a national literature, I suspect, is a distinctly anti-subjective act, although as a part-time critic I also wonder if Objectivism is part of "nationalistic" literature. A party of politicians seeks literature to reflect and express its vision of reality, either utilitarian or utopian; it is literature with a public mission, aimed like a cargo plane towards a not too distant future. The writer who ignores or denies the forces of history, the impersonal influence of materialism on his work is either deceiving himself or stupid. But while history teaches us what politicians instinctively know, that the past and the future are cemented in the material being of the present, to learn this is not always to attend the death of Art for Art's Sake. Art for the Masses or Art for Morality or Art for the Nation are finally slogans that are meaningless without the prior assumption that there is such a thing as art.

As someone who grew up in one world and found herself in another, 18 I wonder about the younger poets from the country. What eye will they turn upon themselves? If the power of imagination is not to be from within, from where will they seek that power? If a sense of self cuts the writer off from her society, can a sensitivity to social place give resources for expression? Or can the interaction of opposites—of self and other, inward and outward, individual and society—fuel a literary birth?

Finally, it is in this drama of opposition I place my faith. The past 19 with its offerings of a colonized consciousness, foster traditions, a transplanted language, does not engender nostalgia and sentimentality. But if the individual is to make meaning of the present, she must make meaning of those values which attached themselves, electrical neuron by electrical neuron, within a colonized past. A sociological critic may see individual consciousness as the product of material forces; the Wordsworthian-influenced reader on the equatorial line, however, must also acknowledge the mysterious value of the subjective self.

Observation and imagination are two weights of a dialectic,° as are 20 exile and nationhood, material and ideational, dispossession and possession. The world of the solitary reaper° is crowded out by the realities of high-rise flats and public housing; but modern urban housing creates conditions for greater isolation and loneliness. The value of the individ-

---

Dialectic—relationship of opposites.   Solitary reaper—referring to a poem by Wordsworth.

ual expands in response to its portended° extinction. Western technology and systems for creating wealth lead to a condition of comfort in which the need for philosophical and spiritual consolation can be felt. While the artist is not solitary, neither need he be a part of a binary system which feeds itself on opposition: self/society; feeling/mind; personal/impersonal; alienation/belonging. The individual acts within and upon a social structure and history is the unfolding drama encompassing the single and the multitude. In the dialectical movements of history, art is not merely the reflection nor expression of society but a re-integrative act, combining past and present, value and change, in the making of a viable culture.

Rhetorical Analysis Through Annotation

To give us a sense of her life, Shirley Lim describes the things that surrounded her. Many of the people and objects of daily life she describes are typically Asian, while her mental life was filled with British books and stories. She tends to associate the objects of Asian life with objectivity and the ideas of British literature with subjectivity, although more complex associations develop as the essay continues.

In the essay, underline passages that mention Asian things and circle descriptions of British things. In the margin note whether these things are associated with everyday life or with mental life and whether they are associated with objectivity or subjectivity.

Discuss why Lim makes the associations she does, where the associations become more complicated, and what Lim ultimately makes of the associations. At the end of the essay, does she value more Asian things or British things? Daily life or mental life? Objectivity or subjectivity? Or does she see all these opposites drawn together in a more complex pattern?

Discussion Questions

Interpreting the Text

1. Why does Lim call her early childhood experiences a blank tape? Why does she consider the earliest memories of language important? Why does she say that we make sense of our world through language?

2. What does Lim mean by subjectivity, imagination, and individuality? How does she see the three terms as being associated? In what way did British literature introduce her to these values? In what way did these values seem alien to the world she grew up in? What connection does she see between them and moodiness?

Portended—predicted, warned by omens.

3. According to Lim, in what ways is the imaginative writer constantly drawn back to the world? How does reality excite and constrain imagination? In what way does imagination help shape our sense of reality?

4. Does Lim regret being taught the British literary canon? Does she feel students should be taught only their own national literatures and writers write only to build the national identity? Does she feel, on the other hand, that writers and readers can divorce themselves from their native cultures and the worlds that surround them?

Considering the Issues

5. How does Lim's childhood life compare to yours? How does her childhood reading compare to yours? In what ways might her childhood have been similar if she grew up in the United States? In what ways different?

6. How important are the values of subjectivity, imagination, and individuality to American culture? How do you see them expressed in the life around us? How are American children introduced to them?

7. In what ways is your life defined by group identities and obligations? Do these group identities encourage or discourage your individuality and sense of private imagination? Is the group experience described by Lim as typically Asian similar to or different from your group experience? Do you believe one can maintain group loyalties and identifications while still developing an individual sense of the self? If so, how?

8. How does Lim use her own personal experience to raise larger issues of culture? At what points and in what ways does she switch from the personal to the general? How does she use herself as the meeting point for various concepts of culture? How does this personal view give a special perspective to the issues of canon and culture?

9. Compare Lim's concluding paragraph to that of T. S. Elliot's essay, "What Is a Classic?" How do the two writers' observations on the nature and function of art overlap and differ?

Writing Suggestions

1. Imagine you have achieved all your ambitions in life, and are now being interviewed about the early influences on your life. Write an answer to the question, "Which books have had the greatest influence on you?"

2. For a special issue of a college magazine devoted to the ethnic diversity of the students on campus, write an article describing the culture you grew up in. Consider whether you felt totally part of it or in any ways at odds with it. Try to describe in detail your specific identifications and alienations and their causes.

3. As part of your discussion about the ideas presented in the readings of this course, write an essay on whether literature draws you closer to the world around you or sets you apart in a world of individuality and subjectivity.

The Canon as Cultural Evaluation

Barbara Herrnstein Smith

In recent years, theory has become increasingly important in literary studies. This theory tries to explain the general principles and processes that underlie all literary activity. Barbara Herrnstein Smith (b. 1932), a professor of literary theory at Duke University, considers here the basic processes of canon formation. She addresses such fundamental questions as how we evaluate literary works, how we are influenced by others' evaluations, how these evaluations get turned into socially enduring judgments about which ones are classics, and what happens to a work once it enters into a canon. The selection here is excerpted from a longer essay entitled "Contingencies of Value." The essay appeared in 1983 in *Critical Inquiry*, a scholarly journal whose audience is largely literature professors.

Many people find reading theoretical articles like this one difficult. This selection, however, has little unusual vocabulary and does not rely on your familiarity with many works of literature or philosophical concepts. Rather the difficulty comes from the continuously abstract nature of the discussion. Ideas pile up, one on another. The same quality that may slow you down as you read, however, also makes this essay rich and stimulating.

TO EXIST IS TO evaluate. We are always calculating how things 1 "figure" for us—always pricing them, so to speak, in relation to the total economy of our personal universe. Throughout our lives, we perform a continuous succession of rapid-fire cost-benefit analyses, estimating the probable "worthwhileness" of alternate courses of action in relation to our always limited resources of time and energy, assessing, re-assessing, and classifying entities with respect to their probable capacity to satisfy our current needs and desires and to serve our emergent interests and long-range plans and purposes. We tend to become most conscious of our own evaluative behavior when the need to select among an array of alternate "goods" and/or to resolve an internal "contest of sentiments" moves us to specifically verbal or other symbolic forms of cost accounting; thus we draw up our lists of pros and cons, lose sleep, and bore our friends by overtly rehearsing our options, estimating the risks and probable outcomes of various actions, and so forth. Most of these calculations, however, are performed intuitively and inarticulately, and many of them are so recurrent that the habitual arithmetic becomes part of our personality and comprises the very style of our being and behavior, forming what we may call our principles or tastes—and what others may call our biases and prejudices.

I have been speaking up to this point of the evaluations we make for *2* ourselves. As social creatures, however, we also evaluate for one another through various kinds of individual acts and also through various institutional practices. . . .

Evaluations are among the most fundamental forms of social com- *3* munication and probably among the most primitive benefits of social interaction. (Animals—insects and birds as well as mammals—evaluate *for* one another, that is, signal to other members of their group the "quality" of a food supply or territory by some form of specialized overt behavior.)[1] We not only produce but also solicit and seek out both "expressions of personal sentiment" and "objective judgments of value" because, although neither will (for nothing can) give us "knowledge" of *the* value of an object, both may let us know other things we could find useful. For example, other people's reports of how well certain objects have gratified them, though "mere expressions of subjective likes and dislikes," may nevertheless be useful to us if we ourselves have produced those objects or if—as lovers, say, or parents or potential associates—we have an independently motivated interest in the current states, specific responses, or general structure of tastes and preferences of those people. Also, an assertion that some object (for example, some artwork) is good, great, bad, or middling can, no matter how magisterially delivered or with what attendant claims or convictions of absoluteness, usually be unpacked as a judgment of its *contingent*° value: specifically, as the evaluator's observation and/or estimate of how well that object, relative to others of the same implied category, has performed and/or is likely to perform certain particular (though taken-for-granted) functions for some particular (though only implicitly defined) set of subjects under some particular (unspecified but assumed) set or range of conditions. Any evaluation, therefore, is "cognitively° substantial" in the sense of being potentially informative about *something*. The actual interest of that information, however, and hence the value of that evaluation to *us* (and "we" are always heterogeneous°) will vary, depending on, among other things, the extent to which we have any interest in the object evaluated, believe that we take for granted the same taken-for-granted functions and assume the same assumed conditions, and also think that we (or others whose interests are of interest to us) are among that implicitly defined set of subjects—or, of course, the extent to which we have an interest in the evaluator's sentiments by reason of our independently motivated interest in him or her. . . .

The value of an explicit verbal evaluation—that is, its utility to those *4* who produce and receive it—will, like that of any other type of utterance, always be a function of specific features of the various transactions of which it may be a part, including the relevant interests of the speaker

---

Contingent—depending on circumstances.   **Cognitively**—relating to thought.   **Heterogeneous**—made up of different kinds.

and any of those who, at any time, become members of his or her de facto audience. It follows that the value of a value judgment may also be quite minimal or negative. For example, depending on specific (and readily imaginable) contextual features, an aesthetic judgment may be excruciatingly *un*interesting to the listener or elicited from the speaker at considerable expense to himself or herself. Also, aesthetic judgments, like any other use of language, may be intimidating, coercive, and otherwise socially and politically oppressive. If they are so, however, it is not because of any characteristic frailty of their propositional status° (and "justifying" them—that is, giving a show of justice to their claims of objectivity or universal validity—will not eliminate the oppression) but, once again, because of the nature of the transactions of which they are a part, particularly the social or political relationship between the evaluator and his or her audience (professor and student, for example, or censor and citizen) and the structure of power that governs that relationship.[2] We may return now from the discussion of individual overt value judgments to the more general consideration of evaluative behavior, normative° institutions, and the social mechanisms by which literary and aesthetic value are produced.

The Cultural Re-Production of Value

We do not move about in a raw universe. Not only are the objects we 5 encounter always to some extent pre-interpreted and preclassified for us by our particular cultures and languages, but also pre-evaluated, bearing the marks and signs of their prior valuings and evaluations by our fellow creatures. Indeed, preclassification is itself a form of pre-evaluation, for the labels or category names under which we encounter objects not only, as was suggested earlier, foreground certain of their possible functions but also operate as signs—in effect, as culturally certified endorsements— of their more or less effective performance of those functions.

Like all other objects, works of art and literature bear the marks of 6 their own evaluational history, signs of value that acquire their force by virtue of various social and cultural practices and, in this case, certain highly specialized and elaborated institutions. The labels "art" and "lit- erature" are, of course, commonly signs of membership in distinctly honorific categories. The particular functions that may be endorsed by these labels, however, are, unlike those of "doorstops" and "clocks," neither narrowly confined nor readily specifiable but, on the contrary, exceptionally heterogeneous, mutable,° and elusive. To the extent— always limited—that the relation between these labels and a particular set of expected and desired functions is stabilized within a community, it is largely through the normative activities of various institutions: most

---

Propositional status—value as true claims.   **Normative**—following or asserting social norms.   **Mutable**—changing.

significantly, the literary and aesthetic academy which, among other things, develops pedagogic° and other acculturative° mechanisms directed at maintaining at least (and, commonly, at most) a *sub*population of the community whose members "appreciate the value" of works of art and literature "as such." That is, by providing them with "necessary backgrounds," teaching them "appropriate skills," "cultivating their interests," and, generally, "developing their tastes," the academy produces generation after generation of subjects for whom the objects and texts thus labeled do indeed perform the functions thus privileged, thereby insuring the continuity of mutually defining canonical works, canonical functions, and canonical audiences.[3]

It will be instructive at this point to consider the very beginning of a 7 work's valuational history, namely, its initial evaluation by the artist (here, the author); for it is not only a prefiguration of all the subsequent acts of evaluation of which the work will become the subject but also a model or paradigm of all evaluative activity generally. I refer here not merely to that ultimate gesture of authorial judgment that must exhibit itself negatively—that is, in the author's either letting the work stand or ripping it up—but to the thousand individual acts of approval and rejection, preference and assessment, trial and revision that constitute the entire process of literary composition. The work we receive is not so much the achieved consummation of that process as its enforced abandonment: "abandonment" not because the author's techniques are inadequate to his or her goals but because the goals themselves are inevitably multiple, mixed, mutually competing, and thus mutually constraining, and also because they are inevitably unstable, changing their nature and relative potency and priority during the very course of composition. The completed work is thus always, in a sense, a temporary truce among contending forces, achieved at the point of exhaustion, that is, the literal depletion of the author's current resources or, given the most fundamental principle of the economics of existence, at the point when the author simply has something else—more worthwhile— to do: when, in other words, the time and energy s/he would have to give to further tinkering, testing, and adjustment are no longer compensated for by an adequately rewarding sense of continuing interest in the process or increased satisfaction in the product.

It is for comparable reasons that we, as readers of the work, will later 8 let our own experience of it stand: not because we have fully "appreciated" the work, not because we have exhausted all its possible sources of interest and hence of value, but because we, too, ultimately have something else—more worthwhile—to do. The reader's experience of the work is pre-figured—that is, both calculated and pre-enacted—by the author in other ways as well: for, in selecting this word, adjusting that turn of phrase, preferring this rhyme to that, the author is all the

---

Pedagogic—teaching.   **Acculturative**—passing culture on.

while testing the local and global effectiveness of each decision by im-
personating in advance his or her various presumptive° audiences, who
thereby themselves participate in shaping the work they will later read.
Every literary work—and, more generally, artwork—is thus the product
of a complex evaluative feedback loop that embraces not only the ever-
shifting economy of the artist's own interests and resources as they
evolve during and in reaction to the process of composition, but also all
the shifting economies of his or her assumed and imagined audiences,
including those who do not yet exist but whose emergent interests,
variable conditions of encounter, and rival sources of gratification the
artist will attempt to predict—or will intuitively surmise—and to which,
among other things, his or her own sense of the fittingness of each
decision will be responsive.[4]

But this also describes all the other diverse forms of evaluation by
which the work will be subsequently marked and its value reproduced
and transmitted: that is, the innumerable implicit acts of evaluation
performed by those who, as may happen, publish the work, purchase,
preserve, display, quote, cite, translate, perform, allude to, and imitate
it; the more explicit but casual judgments made, debated, and negotiated
in informal contexts by readers and by all those others in whose personal
economies the work, in some way, "figures"; and the highly specialized
institutionalized forms of evaluation exhibited in the more or less professional activities of scholars, teachers, and academic or journalistic critics—not only their full-dress reviews and explicit rank-orderings, evaluations, and revaluations, but also such activities as the awarding of
literary prizes, the commissioning and publishing of articles about certain works, the compiling of anthologies, the writing of introductions,
the construction of department curricula, and the drawing up of class
reading lists. All these forms of evaluation, whether overt or covert,
verbal or inarticulate, and whether performed by the common reader,
professional reviewer, big-time bookseller, or small-town librarian, have
functions and effects that are significant in the production and maintenance or destruction of literary value, both reflecting and contributing
to the various economies in relation to which a work acquires value.
And each of the evaluative acts mentioned, like those of the author,
represents a set of individual economic decisions, an adjudication° among
competing claims for limited resources of time, space, energy, attention—or, of course, money—and also, insofar as the evaluation in a
socially responsive act or part of a social transaction, a set of surmises,
assumptions, or predictions regarding the personal economies of other
people.

Although, as I have emphasized, the evaluation of texts is not confined
to the formal critical judgments issued within the rooms of the literary

9

10

Presumptive—imagined or assumed.   **Adjudication**—judgment.

academy or upon the pages of its associated publications, the activities of the academy certainly figure significantly in the production of literary value. For example, the repeated inclusion of a particular work in literary anthologies not only promotes the value of that work but goes some distance toward creating its value, as does also its repeated appearance on reading lists or its frequent citation or quotation by professors, scholars, and academic critics. For all these acts, at the least, have the effect of drawing the work into the orbit of attention of a population of potential readers; and, by making it more accessible to the interests of those readers (while, as indicated above, at the same time shaping and supplying the very interests in relation to which they will experience the work), they make it more likely both that the work will be experienced at all and also that it will be experienced as valuable.

The converse side to this process is well known. Those who are in *11* positions to edit anthologies and prepare reading lists are obviously those who occupy positions of some cultural power; and their acts of evaluation—represented in what they exclude as well as in what they include—constitute not merely recommendations of value but, for the reasons just mentioned, also determinants of value. Moreover, since they will usually exclude not only what they take to be inferior literature but also what they take to be nonliterary, subliterary, or paraliterary, their selections not only imply certain "criteria" of literary value, which may in fact be made explicit, but, more significantly, they produce and maintain certain definitions of "literature" and, thereby, certain assumptions about the desired and expected functions of the texts so classified and about the interests of their appropriate audiences, all of which are usually not explicit and, for that reason, less likely to be questioned, challenged, or even noticed. Thus the privileging power of evaluative authority may be very great, even when it is manifested inarticulately.[5] The academic activities described here, however, are only a small part of the complex process of literary canonization.

When we consider the cultural re-production of value on a larger time *12* scale, the model of evaluative dynamics outlined above suggests that the "survival" or "endurance" of a text—and, it may be, its achievement of high canonical status not only as a "work of literature" but as a "classic"—is the product neither of the objectively (in the Marxist sense) conspiratorial force of establishment institutions nor of the continuous appreciation of the timeless virtues of a fixed object by succeeding generations of isolated readers, but, rather, of a series of continuous interactions among a variably constituted object, emergent conditions, and mechanisms of cultural selection and transmission. These interactions are, in certain respects, analogous to those by virtue of which biological species evolve and survive and also analogous to those through which artistic choices evolve and are found fit or fitting by the individual artist. . . .

[What happens when a work enters into the canon?]   *13*

First, when the value of a work is seen as unquestionable, those of its   *14*
features that would, in a noncanonical work, be found alienating—for
example, technically crude, philosophically naive, or narrowly topical—
will be glozed over or backgrounded. In particular, features that conflict
intolerably with the interests and ideologies of subsequent subjects (and,
in the West, with those generally benign "humanistic" values for which
canonical works are commonly celebrated)—for example, incidents or
sentiments of brutality, bigotry, and racial, sexual, or national chauvinism—will be represented or rationalized, and there will be a tendency
among humanistic scholars and academic critics to "save the text" by
transferring the locus of its interest to more formal or structural features
and/or allegorizing its potentially alienating ideology to some more
general ("universal") level where it becomes more tolerable and also
more readily interpretable in terms of contemporary ideologies. Thus
we make texts timeless by suppressing their temporality. (It may be
added that to those scholars and critics for whom those features are not
only palatable but for whom the value of the canonical works consists
precisely in their "embodying" and "preserving" such "traditional values," the transfer of the locus of value to formal properties will be seen
as a descent into formalism and "aestheticism," and the tendency to
allegorize it too generally or to interpret it too readily in terms of
"modern values" will be seen not as saving the text but as betraying it.)

Second, in addition to whatever various and perhaps continuously   *15*
differing functions a work performs for succeeding generations of individual subjects, it will also begin to perform certain characteristic
cultural functions by virtue of the very fact that it *has* endured—that is,
the functions of a canonical work as such—and will be valued and
preserved accordingly: as a witness to lost innocence, former glory, and/
or apparently persistent communal interests and "values" and thus a
banner of communal identity; as a reservoir of images, archtypes, and
topoi°—characters and episodes, passages and verbal tags—repeatedly
invoked and recurrently applied to new situations and circumstances;
and as a stylistic and generic exemplar that will energize the production
of subsequent works and texts (upon which the latter will be modeled
and by which, as a normative "touchstone," they will be measured). In
these ways, the canonical work begins increasingly not merely to survive
within but to shape and create the culture in which its value is produced
and transmitted and, for that very reason, to perpetuate the conditions
of its own flourishing. Nothing endures like endurance.

As the preceding discussion suggests, the value of a literary work is   *16*
continuously produced and re-produced by the very acts of implicit and
explicit evaluation that are frequently invoked as "reflecting" its value
and therefore as being evidence of it. In other words, what are com-

---

Topoi—standard arguments or themes.

monly taken to be the *signs* of literary value are, in effect, also its *springs*. The endurance of a classic canonical author such as Homer, then, owes not to the alleged transcultural or universal value of his works but, on the contrary, to the continuity of their circulation in a particular culture. Repeatedly cited and recited, translated, taught and imitated, and thoroughly enmeshed in the network of intertextuality° that continuously *constitutes* the high culture of the orthodoxly educated population of the West (and the Western-educated population of the rest of the world), that highly variable entity we refer to as "Homer" recurrently enters our experience in relation to a large number and variety of our interests and thus can perform a large number of various functions for us and obviously has performed them for many of us over a good bit of the history of our culture. It is well to recall, however, that there are many people in the world who are not—or are not yet, or choose not to be—among the orthodoxly educated population of the West: people who do not encounter Western classics at all or who encounter them under cultural and institutional conditions very different from those of American and European college professors and their students. The fact that Homer, Dante, and Shakespeare do not figure significantly in the personal economies of these people, do not perform individual or social functions that gratify their interests, *do not have value for them*, might properly be taken as qualifying the claims of transcendent universal value made for such works. As we know, however, it is routinely taken instead as evidence or confirmation of the cultural deficiency—or, more piously, "deprivation"—of such people. The fact that other verbal artifacts (not necessarily "works of literature" or even "texts") and other objects and events (not necessarily "works of art" or even artifacts) have performed and do perform for them the various functions that Homer, Dante, and Shakespeare perform for us and, moreover, that the possibility of performing the totality of such functions is always distributed over the totality of texts, artifacts, objects, and events—a possibility continuously realized and thus a value continuously "appreciated"—commonly cannot be grasped or acknowledged by the custodians of the Western canon.

Notes

[1] To the extent that such forms of behavior are under the control of innate mechanisms that respond directly to—or, in effect, "register"—the conditions in question, they are not, strictly speaking, verbal or symbolic. For this reason, such evaluations may be "objective" in a way that, for better or worse, no human value judgment can be.

[2] I discuss these and related aspects of verbal transactions in *On the Margins of Discourse*, pp. 15–24 and 82–106, and in "Narrative Versions, Narrative Theories," *Critical Inquiry* 7 (Autumn 1980): 225–26 and 231–36.

Intertextuality—connections among related texts.

[3]Pierre Macherey and Etienne Balibar analyze some aspects of this process in "Literature as an Ideological Form: Some Marxist Propositions," trans. James Kavanagh, *Praxis* 5 (1981): 43–58.

[4]See Howard Becker, *Art Worlds* (Berkeley, Los Angeles, and London, 1982), pp. 198–209, for a description of some of the specific constraints that shape both the process and its termination and, more generally, for a useful account of the ways in which artworks are produced by "social networks."

[5]For a well-documented illustration of the point, see Nina Baym, "Melodramas of Beset Manhood: How Theories of American Fiction Exclude Women Authors," *American Quarterly* 33 (Summer 1981): 125–39. In addition to anthologies, Baym mentions historical studies, psychological and sociological theories of literary production, and particular methods of literary interpretation.

Rhetorical Analysis Through Annotation

In this article ordinary words such as *evaluation* are given special meaning by being discussed in depth and from several angles. These ordinary words then come to embody important concepts for the theory being presented.

Underline all uses of evaluation and related words (such as *value* and *valuational*) in the article. At each point you think the word is used in such a way or in such a context so as to add to the meaning, write in the margin how you think the meaning is being enriched or modified.

Circle any other words you find that gain added meaning in a similar way through the article.

Discuss how concepts are built up through the extended discussion of the essay.

Discussion Questions

Interpreting the Text

1. What does Smith mean by saying "To exist is to evaluate"?

2. How do objects, including works of art and literature, "bear the marks of their own evaluational history"?

3. How does the endurance of a classic help give it more value and help ensure a more positive response? How is this process related to how we respond to the "top of the charts" and the "oldies but goodies" of popular music?

4. How does Smith evaluate the fact that some cultures do not have the same literary canon shared by educated Westerners or any literary canon at all?

Considering the Issues

5. What are some evaluations you make in the course of the day? Why do you make these evaluations and how do they help you carry on with daily living?

6. What are some evaluations made by others that you have received recently? What effects did these socially communicated evaluations have on you? How did you feel about them and how did they influence your behavior?

7. Would you think any differently of the same story if you discovered it on a television program, in a comic book, or in a college literature anthology? What are your feelings if you are told the words to a song are by William Shakespeare? Bruce Springsteen? The advertising agency for Coca-Cola? Why do you get those different feelings?

8. What are some of the functions that the literary canon has for us? What are other cultural objects in our own culture that serve similar functions to the literary canon? In what ways are there canons of popular culture? How do these canons of popular culture influence the ways we feel, think, and perceive? Consider examples of how some popular songs, shows, celebrities, or consumer products encourage or discourage certain attitudes and actions.

9. How do film classics like *The Wizard of Oz, Gone with the Wind, Psycho*, or *Star Wars* get used as "a reservoir of images, archetypes, and topoi—characters and episodes, passages and verbal tags"? Can you think of another classic that has entered into our culture and continues "not merely to survive within but to shape and create the culture in which its value is produced"?

10. Does Smith ever shift out of general, abstract discussion to discuss any specific cases? If so, when and how? If not, how does she maintain clarity and specificity in her abstractions? How is each part of the abstract argument related to each other part?

Writing Suggestions

1. To clarify the meaning of Smith's argument for yourself, summarize her argument. Try to capture the main idea of each paragraph in a straightforward sentence in simple language.

2. For a class in philosophy, write a personal essay describing how you have come to evaluate a television show. Base this essay on your observations of yourself evaluating the show as you watch it. As you watch the show take notes on the different valuational thoughts you have. You may also use a tape recorder to keep track of your thoughts as you watch the show.

3. As part of your class discussion of this essay, write an essay describing the social meaning and impact of some cultural figure, from either popular or high culture. For example, you may write on how Elvis Presley came to be considered "the King" or what it means to our culture that he is held in such high regard. Or you may write on Robert Redford, Vanna White, Toni Morrison, George Bernard Shaw, Darryl Strawberry, Gloria Steinem, Rudolf Nureyev, or any other celebrity.

4. Smith describes how a writer is always evaluating as he or she writes, "tinkering" until it makes no sense to tinker further. As part of this course's concern for the writing process, write an essay examining whether and in what way this statement is true in your own writing. Use specific experiences you have had in writing to develop your argument.

Male Critics and Female Readers

Deborah Pope

If creating a canon is a process of cultural evaluation, as Barbara Herrnstein Smith argues, we may wish to reevaluate not only what works we include in the canon, but the very process by which the canon is formed. There may be cultural biases in the critical system by which we make judgments. Feminist literary criticism has raised fundamental issues about the kinds of literary criticism that have given rise to our current canon, suggesting that the enterprise of literary criticism is itself pervaded with sexist gender assumptions.

In this selection, Deborah Pope, professor of English at Duke University, characterizes the history and structure of literary studies to argue that the field is based on male gender assumptions that subordinate reading (perceived as a female activity) to criticism (perceived as a male activity). The development of a literary canon itself was part of a process of separating literary studies from the daily activity of reading. Pope's analysis suggests that women must break through these gender assumptions built into the structure of the discipline to redefine their relation to literature and its study. In this selection you will see echoes of many of the arguments and developments traced in this unit, but given a particular interpretation related to Pope's feminist perspective. This selection is excerpted from an essay appearing in a 1988 book of critical essays by many different scholars writing for other scholars, entitled *The Politics of Knowledge*.

In reading feminist criticism it is important to recognize that the discussion of male and female gender roles deals with how we have culturally defined what it means to be male or female, not with the biological or psychological realities of any individual. Gender roles are a matter of cultural perception, the cultural stereotypes that we use to think about roles. These gender roles are only real in the sense that they become self-fulfilling prophecies; one function of essays like this one is to help us gain perspective on these roles so that we are no longer constrained by their artificial limitations.

───────────────────

I AM AWARE THAT literature may bear a dubious reputation among   *1* academic disciplines of seeming the least connected with any real world, as having the most dependence on the rarefied air of the university, the least to gain from any movement outward to considerations of the marketplace. I am more than mournfully aware that some even see literary study as relegated to the level of pretentious competitions in personal taste and unseemly gossip about writers' lives, or as an extravagantly useless indulgence in the pursuit of arcane meanings and allusions whose ultimate purpose is the self-flattering exercise of a certain type of anal mind and the erecting of further barriers between those who know and those who do not. In either case, literary critics, to outsiders and even many insiders, can appear all too wrapped in the emperor's cloak of elitism and self-referential terminology, while literature itself has an unfortunate public posture of being defined as whatever it is nobody else is reading; indeed, as whatever it is nobody *can* read, except the handful of elect.[1] After all, what is readily available subverts the role and the expertise of the professional critic. It is no mystery why critics, out of self-preservation if nothing else, should tend to elevate the complex, the dense, the formal in their valuation of texts. This sense of literature as both disembodied and enclosed has been its curse, isolating it from any wide audience, and its self-justification as the dwindling, but noble preserve of what Matthew Arnold called "the best that has been thought and said."

What seems to many, however, an exaggerated retreat into the hieratic° is arguably a defensive posture arising out of literature's ironic proximity to popular "taint." That is, people as a matter of course do not just sit down and "do" economics, anthropology and Biblical archeology, but they do sit down and read—even, horrors, write. There is an interesting historical and psychological context for examining why literature and literary study in their present form carry the connotations they do, and it is directly related to feminist concerns. For in fact the distinctions between popular and trained readers, accessible and privileged° material, emotive and intellectual stances, carry gender inflections. An explanation may be sought in two factors: the historical origins of English literature as an academic field; and the corollary development that the critic is implicitly, if not always actually, male, and the reader is implicitly female. Scholars have located the origins of literature as a special field of academic study in the Victorian need for a spiritually uplifting and socially unifying body of national myth that would replace a religion devastated by Darwin, the Higher Criticism°, and the operations of utilitarian capitalism; and in the unprecedented entry of women into institutions of higher learning. Over the strenuous objections to its frivolity, lack of rigor, analytical substantiveness, dominance of mere taste and affectiveness, English studies were allowed into the universities when it was pointed out that these qualities made it the very thing to teach to the young women gaining increasing access to the universities. Eagleton's trenchant° analysis of literature's academic rise offers this rationale: "since English was an untaxing sort of affair, concerned with

2

Hieratic—sacred or rarefied.   **Privileged**—bearing higher status, only for an elite.
Higher Criticism—the attempt to analyze the Bible using historical and archeological evidence and methods of modern literary scholarship; the project of Higher Criticism began in late eighteenth-century Germany.   **Trenchant**—forceful and cutting.

finer feelings rather than with the more virile topics of *bona fide* academic 'disciplines,' it seemed a convenient sort of nonsubject to palm off on the ladies, who were in any case excluded from sciences and the professions."[2] But literary study came into its own with the nationalism of World War I and the rise of Anglo-American New Criticism° with its reaction against 'feminine' taste-mongering and impressionism, and its emphasis on a proselytizing zeal for masculine analysis, the rigorous intellectual scrutiny of highly technical formal properties of texts and their mind-bending, multiple ambiguities.

Yet the essential gender markings remained intact. Armed with the principles of New Criticism and the moral mandates of F. R. Leavis, the image of the literary critic has come down to us as "implicitly male," "cool," "magisterial," judgmental, Olympian, the "museum-guide" to tradition's artifacts; while the Reader is implicitly female, "hot," eager, emotional, immediate, the perennial student in need of perennial instruction from the male critic, who has "mastered" his subject.[3] That women are the primary consumers of literature—whether "popular" or great— is easily evidenced by the grocery store checkout or the gender profile of any undergraduate English department. Yet at the level of our culture's designations of value and significance in art, they remain the least enfranchised, the least included. For a woman to study literature seriously is to study texts that are written by male authors, enshrining masculine experience, and delivered under the authority of male professors and critics. Little wonder, then, Showalter's classic observation: "a woman studying English literature is also studying a different culture to which she must bring the adaptability of the anthropologist."[4] **3**

Feminist criticism began in this awareness of the need to address the invisibility of women's experience and significance in the way the dominant culture imagined itself. Women as writers, women as characters, women as symbols, women as readers have been kept invisible, unexpressed, or crucially distorted in the literary enterprise. As Adrienne Rich so eloquently asserts, for women to undertake the process of visioning and revisioning the whole of our literary heritage is "more than a chapter in cultural history; it is an act of survival."[5] **4**

Notes

[1]Jane Marcus makes the provocative point that there may be a relation in recent years between the inroads of feminist criticism in the academy and the increasing resort of male critics to the tenuously abstract in theory and language. Marcus suggests that feminist critics recovered the tools male critics

---

New Criticism—a form of literary criticism that pays close attention to the text and eliminates all concern for the cultural, historical, or biographical background of the literary work; this approach gained popularity in England and America in the decades following World War II.

had moved away from—i.e., textual criticism, recovery of manuscripts, biography, history, bibliography. "The more material and particular the labor of feminist critics became, the more abstract and antimaterial became the work of men. . . . The more we spoke in moral indignation and anger, the more Parnassian were the whispers of male theorists." Marcus, "Storming the Toolshed," in *Feminist Theory: A Critique of Ideology*, eds. Nannerl Keohane, Michelle Rosaldo, and Barbara Gelpi (Chicago: University of Chicago Press, 1982) 218.

[2]Terry Eagleton, *Literary Theory: An Introduction* (Minneapolis: University of Minnesota Press, 1983) 28.

[3]Sandra M. Gilbert, "Life Studies, or, Speech After Long Silence: Feminist Critics Today," *College English* 40 (1979): 853, 854, rpt. in *The New Feminist Criticism: Essays on Women, Language, and Theory*, ed. Elaine Showalter (New York: Pantheon, 1985).

[4]Elaine Showalter, "Women and the Literary Curriculum," *College English* 32 (1971): 856–57.

[5]Adrienne Rich, "When We Dead Awaken: Writing as Revision," in *Adrienne Rich's Poetry*, eds. Gelpi and Gelpi (New York: Norton, 1977) 92.

Rhetorical Analysis Through Annotation

Pope presents her argument concerning the exclusion of women from the discipline of literature by presenting an analysis of the social structure and history of the discipline in such a way as to reveal the subordinate role granted to women. This analysis and history is presented in general terms, based on general characterizations of groups and people, such as critics, readers, students, and people who view the discipline from the outside. Each of these groups is presented as having an attitude toward or relationship with one or more of the other groups.

Circle all words referring to groups or categories of people, or if there is an implied unstated group—as in the opening sentence (who perceives the reputation?)—define that group in the margin. Then in the margin identify the major characteristics that Pope attributes to each group. Also, if relevant, note whether that group represents disciplinary insiders (I) or outsiders (O), whether the group is perceived as masculine (M) or feminine (F), and whether the group is in fact predominantly male (m) or female (f).

The characterizations of the various groups also include terms that are directly evaluative or have positive or negative connotations. Put a box around all words that have an evaluative effect. Which groups are characterized positively and which negatively? Do the characterizations of any of the groups change as the article progresses? If so, why?

Discuss what opinion or relationship each group has toward other groups. Which of these attitudes or relationships are presented as positive and which as negative? How is Pope suggesting a change in attitude and relationship for women engaged in the discipline of literature? How may these changed attitudes and relationships change the character of the disciplines?

Discuss how convincing these general characterizations seem to you. Do these characterizations serve to reveal an underlying truth or do they distort the situation by exaggeration?

Discussion Questions

Interpreting the Text

1. Why do some people see literary studies as having little connection with the real world? Does Pope agree with that perception and why? Does she believe that literary studies should make a greater connection with the real world? If so, what would the specific kinds of connection be? How would her feminist proposals make literary studies more real?

2. To what historical and psychological causes does Pope attribute the rise of modern literary studies? Why has literary criticism become technical and cool? How has this history resulted in a distinction between the critic and the reader and how do the two differ?

3. How has the history of literary studies relied on male and female gender stereotypes in creating roles for men and women? How have these roles led to male domination of the profession? What aspects of the female experience have been excluded in this process?

Considering the Issues

4. In your experience has the study of literature been distant from the real world, or have your literature classes helped you see the connections between the real world and the literature you read? How may the teaching of literature be related to or different from the scholarly study of literature?

5. In what ways has the literature you have read in school been different from or similar to the reading you do on your own? In addition to considering whether the works themselves are different, consider whether you read those works in a different way because you are reading them inside or out of a school context. Have you ever read the same book on your own and in school? If so, was there any difference in the way you read it or in the experience you had with the book? To what would you attribute any difference you do find?

6. Do you find the works that you read in school expressed predominantly male viewpoints? If so, discuss specific examples. Do you find literary analysis to fit better with male gender roles than with female gender roles? Do males who are successful critics (students or teachers) appear more masculine; do female critics appear less feminine? Similarly, do people who read a lot on their own appear less masculine and more feminine? To what extent do you agree with Pope's analysis of gender roles in literary studies?

Writing Suggestions

1. For a course in literature, write an analysis of the gender roles you have found expressed in any work you have read. Consider the roles and personalities attributed to males and females as well as whether these roles establish relationships that grant greater power for one group or repress some aspect of either for both men and women.

2. For a course in literature that is attempting to raise fundamental issues of what it means to study literature as an academic discipline, write an essay comparing your experience of reading in school and outside of it. You may refer to the experiences of reading both canonical and noncanonical texts and of being obliged to analyze the texts versus not having to analyze them. You may use ideas you have gained from Pope's essay or any other selection in this unit.

3. Have you taken any course where you have found some sexist, racist, or other cultural bias in the subject as a whole or in some particular work you have read? If so, write an essay explaining exactly where you found this bias in the subject and what the effects of this bias have been. This essay may be in the form of a letter to the instructor to share your thoughts and gain the instructor's response if you think the instructor would be sympathetic to your concerns. Or this essay may be for an antibias study group, as is formed in some student organizations. In either situation your aim is to increase understanding rather than accuse people you disagree with of being biased.

Unit Writing Suggestions

1. Based on your readings in this unit, write a letter to the editor of the *New York Times* in response to the article "In Dispute on Bias . . ." which leads off this unit. State how you see the issues and what you see as the important considerations and arguments that should be taken into account in this and similar situations.

2. As part of the discussion in this course about the styles of writing in different disciplines, write an essay discussing whether there is a special literary style. Describe features of style and argument that appear in a number of essays in this unit and discuss whether these features differ from those of other disciplines. You may draw comparisons with selections from other units of this anthology.

3. As part of the professional discussion of the canon, write an essay on how the writing of literary criticism relies on knowledge of the literary canon. By analyzing selections from this unit, show how literary critics use the readers' knowledge of a range of literary works.

4. Several selections in this unit refer to the history of the term *canon* in religion, both in the selection of the official books of the Bible and in the designation of saints. What comparisons can you see between religious canonization of holy texts and holy people and the formation of the literary canon? Write your thoughts on this subject for the arts and society page of your college newspaper.

5. Imagine you are a member of a radical student organization (either right-wing or left-wing), calling for major changes in the university. Write a position paper setting forth your demands concerning what literature should be taught and your reasons. Direct this position paper at the faculty members of the English department and the university administration.

UNIT
2

HISTORY

Upward Mobility in America: How Much and for Whom?

Americans like to dream of instant wealth—whether from finding buried treasure, winning the lottery, or by inheriting a fortune from a long-lost relative. We are fascinated by glamorous celebrities and sports figures who have risen up from humble beginnings and now live among the super rich. Even those who come by their wealth through illegal methods command a certain fascination for their ability to make "easy money." This desire for money through some extraordinary luck, talent, or greed is a recurrent theme in our popular literature and movies.

An older version of the American Dream is based on the virtues of hard work, honesty, and perseverance. Our educational and religious institutions taught us that it was possible to go from rags to riches and become a right-minded, steady, and productive pillar of the community. One of the best-known promoters of the doctrine of industriousness was the circus man Phineas T. Barnum. During the 1880s his lecture, "The Art of Money-Getting," was in great demand. In this lecture Barnum blends his business and moral advice, always seeing the two as interrelated. Politeness, sobriety, and honesty, in addition to being the "correct" virtues to develop, were also viewed as the necessary tools for success in business.

Barnum followed a long line of moralizers, starting with the Puritan preacher Cotton Mather in the seventeenth century, Benjamin Franklin in the eighteenth century, Horatio Alger in the nineteenth century, and Bill Cosby in our own time. Franklin, perhaps the most famous self-made man in American history, wrote proverbial maxims that are familiar to all of us such as: "Laziness travels so slowly, that poverty soon overtakes him. . . . Early to bed, and early to rise, makes a man healthy, wealthy, and wise." The historian Irvin Wyllie pays special attention to Franklin in his 1954 book *The Self-Made Man in America*, excerpted in this unit. In particular, Wyllie considers the inspirational effect that Franklin's autobiography had on people in the early 1800s.

The doctrine of rags-to-riches through hard work is a moral imperative urged on each American from birth. The belief in a real chance for success has lured millions of immigrants to this country since the colonial period. Even when we attempt to reject such values, they form part of our attitudes and behavior, but what we believe in is not necessarily what actually exists. How many people have been able to rise above their position in life through their own efforts? How many more have stayed at or near the same level despite a lifetime of work? And how many have been crushed by inescapable poverty? Until recently, few historians asked these questions in any systematic way, and chose to assume instead that a few highly visible examples such as Abraham Lincoln, Andrew Carnegie, or Thomas Mellon were extreme examples of the mobility experienced by large numbers of newly prosperous, hard-working Americans. In the last thirty years, historians have done more extensive research to try to determine who has gotten richer and who has not.

Dispassionate historical examination requires looking at more than a few famous culture heroes; it requires finding general trends in large groups of people. The discipline of history has had to borrow concepts and methods from sociology and other social sciences. Historians became familiar with concepts like social stratification and social mobility, as defined, for example, in the book *Social Mobility in Industrial Society*, published in 1959 by sociologists Seymour Martin Lipset and Reinhard Bendix. An excerpt from this book appears here as well. Lipset and Bendix examine how the wealthy and powerful in any country will try to exclude newcomers from their ranks and thus make social mobility more difficult.

While sociologists were studying contemporary mobility patterns, historians started looking back to assess the reality of the rags-to-riches myth in the nineteenth century and the first half of the twentieth century. Stephan Thernstrom's 1964 study of mobility in nineteenth-century Newburyport, Massachusetts, marked the beginning of a series of similar studies, including investigations of Paterson, New Jersey, by Herbert Gutman, and of New York City by Thomas Kessner, all represented in this unit. Overall, these studies suggest that mobility was slower and more subtle than previously thought. Nonetheless, individuals of many groups have been able to move upward into more comfortable lives, especially in industrial centers like Paterson.

These same studies also underline the virtual lack of mobility for some groups, particularly blacks, who remain economically worse off than more recent immigrants. In the twentieth century social reformers have hoped that finding the precise reasons for this disparity might lead to changes so that blacks could share in the mobility opportunities America seems to be offering to everyone else. Daniel Patrick Moynihan, then an assistant secretary of labor and now a United States senator from New York, argued in 1965 that the black family had suffered serious deterioration from factors going back to the period of slavery. Moynihan recommends social programs aimed at rebuilding the black family structure. Herbert Gutman presented a different position in his 1976 book *The Black Family in Slavery and Freedom, 1750–1925*. He argues that problems with the black family structure are not so deep and result only from recent economic conditions. Thus, Gutman proposes improving conditions but not meddling in the social life of any group.

The Moynihan–Gutman debate shows how our understanding of history affects our current attempts to improve our lives. Current public policy depends on what we think has happened in the past to get us into our current situation. This unit ends with a 1985 magazine article by a former government official giving her recommendations for the black family. In Eleanor Holmes Norton's argument we can see reflected all the issues about social mobility raised by the historians.

In the past generation or two the federal government has made new efforts to assure all ethnic and racial groups access to routes of advancement in military service, higher education, vocational job training, and public office. Yet many problems remain. If all workers truly believed that they could move up the ladder of success by hard work, honesty, and perseverance, the many get-rich-quick schemes and dreams would not have such powerful appeal.

The Art of Money-Getting

Phineas T. Barnum

Phineas T. Barnum (1810–1891) was, in Horatio Alger fashion, poor at birth and rich at death, and in between achieved much as a showman in the circus. In true showman-like fashion Barnum extolled his own career as a model for others to follow. By selling the spectacle of his own life he became even richer. His autobiography sold almost half a million copies, and he collected lecture fees for over a hundred performances of "The Art of Money-Getting."

The lecture, written in 1882, urges the audience to follow the path of honesty, prudence, moderation, thrift, politeness, and hard work as a guaranteed way to success. Simple rules of behavior are put forth through maxims, personal experiences, homey examples, and further upright advice. In his good-natured but relentless exhortatory tone, Barnum creates an optimistic energy that makes the listener want to go right out and conquer the world.

Although not the writing of a historian, the following selection is typical of the primary materials historians and students of history must work with. The study of history is based on a careful reading of the statements and records of people from the past.

THE FOUNDATION OF SUCCESS in life is good health; that is the 1 substratum of fortune; it is also the basis of happiness. A person cannot accumulate a fortune very well when he is sick. He has no ambitions, no incentive; no force. Of course, there are those who have bad health and cannot help it; you cannot expect that such persons can accumulate wealth; but there are a great many in poor health who need not be so.

Many persons knowingly violate the laws of nature against their better 2 impulses, for the sake of fashion. For instance, there is one thing that nothing living except a vile worm ever naturally loved, and that is tobacco; yet how many persons there are who deliberately train an unnatural appetite, and overcome this implanted aversion for tobacco, to such a degree that they get to love it. They have got hold of a poisonous, filthy weed, or rather that takes a firm hold of them. Here are married men who run about spitting tobacco juice on the carpet and floors, and sometimes even upon their wives besides. They do not kick their wives out of doors like drunken men, but their wives, I have no doubt, often wish they were outside of the house.

These remarks apply with ten-fold force to the use of intoxicating 3 drinks. To make money, requires a clear brain. A man has got to see that two and two make four; he must lay all his plans with reflection and forethought, and closely examine all the details and the ins and outs of business. As no man can succeed in business unless he has a brain to enable him to lay his plans, and reason to guide him in their execution, so, no matter how bountifully a man may be blessed with intelligence, if the brain is muddled, and his judgment warped by intoxicating drinks, it is impossible for him to carry on business successfully. How many good opportunities have passed, never to return, while a man was sipping a "social glass" with his friend! How many foolish bargains have been made under the influence of the "nervine" which temporarily makes its victim think he is rich. How many important chances have been put off until to-morrow, and then forever, because the wine cup has thrown the system into a state of lassitude°, neutralizing the energies so essential to success in business. . . .

DON'T MISTAKE YOUR VOCATION.—The safest plan, and the one most 4 sure of success for the young man starting in life, is to select the vocation which is most congenial to his tastes.

We are all, no doubt, born for a wise purpose. There is as much 5 diversity in our brains as in our countenances. Some are born natural mechanics, while some have great aversion to machinery. Let a dozen boys of ten years get together and you will soon observe two or three are "whittling" out some ingenious device; working with locks or complicated machinery. When they were but five years old, their father could find no toy to please them like a puzzle. They are natural mechanics; but the other eight or nine boys have different aptitudes. I belong to the latter class; I never had the slightest love for mechanism; on the contrary, I have a sort of abhorrence for complicated machinery. I never had ingenuity enough to whittle a cider tap so it would not leak. I never could make a pen that I could write with, or understand the principle of a steam engine. If a man was to take such a boy as I was and attempt to make a watchmaker of him, the boy might, after an apprenticeship of five or seven years, be able to take apart and put together a watch; but all through life he would be working uphill and seizing every excuse for leaving his work and idling away his time. Watch-making is repulsive to him. . . .

SELECT THE RIGHT LOCATION. . . .   6

AVOID DEBT.—Young men starting in life should avoid running into 7 debt. There is scarcely anything that drags a person down like debt. It is a slavish position to get in, yet we find many a young man hardly out of his "teens" running in debt. He meets a chum and says, "Look at this; I have got trusted° for a new suit of clothes." He seems to look upon the clothes as so much given to him. Well, it frequently is so, but, if he succeeds in paying and then gets trusted again, he is adopting a habit which will keep him in poverty through life. Debt robs a man of his self-respect, and makes him almost despise himself. Grunting and groaning and working for what he has eaten up or worn out, and now

---

Lassitude—weakness, exhaustion.   **Trusted**—given credit.

when he is called upon to pay up, he has nothing to show for his money: this is properly termed "working for a dead horse." I do not speak of merchants buying and selling on credit, or of those who buy on credit in order to turn the purchase to a profit. The old Quaker said to his farmer son, "John, never get trusted; but if thee gets trusted for anything, let it be for manure, because that will help thee pay it back again."

PERSEVERE.—When a man is in the right path, he must persevere. I 8 speak of this because there are some persons who are "born tired"; naturally lazy and possessing no self-reliance and no perseverance. . . .

It is this go-aheaditiveness, this determination not to let the "horrors" 9 or the "blues" take possession of you, so as to make you relax your energies in the struggle for independence, which you must cultivate.

How many have almost reached the goal of their ambition, but losing 10 faith in themselves have relaxed their energies, and the golden prize has been lost forever. . . .

WHATEVER YOU DO, DO WITH ALL YOUR MIGHT.—Work at it, if neces- 11 sary, early and late, in season and out of season, not leaving a stone unturned, and never deferring for a single hour that which can be done just as well *now*. The old proverb is full of truth and meaning, "Whatever is worth doing at all, is worth doing well." Many a man acquires a fortune by doing his business thoroughly, while his neighbor remains poor for life because he only half does it. Ambition, energy, industry, perseverance, are indispensable requisites for success in business.

Fortune always favors the brave, and never helps a man who does 12 not help himself. It won't do to spend your time like Mr. Micawber in waiting for something to "turn up." To such men one of two things usually "turns up": the poor-house or the jail; for idleness breeds bad habits, and clothes a man in rags.

DEPEND UPON YOUR OWN PERSONAL EXERTIONS. . . .　　　　　　　　　　13

USE THE BEST TOOLS.—Men in engaging employees should be careful 14 to get the best. Understand, you cannot have too good tools to work with, and there is no tool you should be so particular about as living tools. If you get a good one, it is better to keep him, than keep changing. He learns something every day, and you are benefited by the experience he acquires. He is worth more to you this year than last and he is the last man to part with, provided his habits are good and he continues faithful. If, as he gets more valuable, he demands an exorbitant increase of salary on the supposition that you can't do without him, let him go. Whenever I have such an employee, I always discharge him; first, to convince him that his place may be supplied, and second, because he is good for nothing if he thinks he is invaluable and cannot be spared. . . .

BE SYSTEMATIC.—Men should be systematic in their business. A person 15 who does business by rule, having a time and place for everything, doing his work promptly, will accomplish twice as much and with half the trouble of him who does it carelessly and slipshod. By introducing system into all your transactions, doing one thing at a time, always meeting appointments with punctuality, you find leisure for pastime and recreation; whereas the man who only half does one thing, and then turns to something else and half does that, will have his business at loose ends, and will never know when his day's work is done, for it never will be done.

ADVERTISE YOUR BUSINESS. . . .   *16*

BE POLITE AND KIND TO YOUR CUSTOMERS.—Politeness and civility are *17* the best capital ever invested in business. Large stores, gilt signs, flaming advertisements, will all prove unavailing if you or your employees treat your patrons abruptly. The truth is, the more kind and liberal a man is, the more generous will be the patronage° bestowed upon him. "Like begets like." The man who gives the greatest amount of goods of a corresponding quality for the least sum (still reserving to himself a profit) will generally succeed best in the long run. This brings us to the golden rule, "As ye would that men should do to you, do ye also to them"; and they will do better by you than if you always treated them as if you wanted to get the most you could out of them for the least return. Men who drive sharp bargains with their customers, acting as if they never expected to see them again, will not be mistaken. They never will see them again as customers. People don't like to pay and get kicked also.

BE CHARITABLE.—Of course men should be charitable, because it is a *18* duty and a pleasure. But even as a matter of policy, if you possess no higher incentive, you will find that the liberal man will command patronage, while the sordid, uncharitable miser will be avoided. . . .

The best kind of charity is to help those who are willing to help *19* themselves. Promiscuous almsgiving, without inquiring into the worthiness of the applicant, is bad in every sense. But to search out and quietly assist those who are struggling for themselves, is the kind that "scattereth and yet increaseth." But don't fall into the idea that some persons practise, of giving a prayer instead of a potatoe, and a benediction instead of bread, to the hungry. It is easier to make Christians with full stomachs than empty.

DON'T BLAB.—Some men have a foolish habit of telling their business *20* secrets. If they make money they like to tell their neighbors how it was done. Nothing is gained by this, and ofttimes much is lost. Say nothing about your profits, your hopes, your expectations, your intentions. And this should apply to letters as well as to conversation. If you are losing money, be specially cautious and not tell of it, or you will lose your reputation.

PRESERVE YOUR INTEGRITY.—It is more precious than diamonds or *21* rubies. The old miser said to his sons: "Get money; get it honestly, if you can, but get money." This advice was not only atrociously wicked, but it was the very essence of stupidity. It was as much as to say, "If

---

Patronage—support from a richer or more powerful person.

you find it difficult to obtain money honestly, you can easily get it dishonestly. Get it in that way." Poor fool, not to know that the most difficult thing in life is to make money dishonestly; not to know that our prisons are full of men who attempted to follow this advice; not to understand that no man can be dishonest without soon being found out, and that when his lack of principle is discovered, nearly every avenue to success is closed against him forever. The public very properly shun all whose integrity is doubted. No matter how polite and pleasant and accommodating a man may be, none of us dare to deal with him if we suspect "false weights and measures." Strict honesty not only lies at the foundation of all success in life financially, but in every other respect. Uncompromising integrity of character is invaluable. It secures to its possessor a peace and joy which cannot be attained without it—which no amount of money, or houses and lands can purchase. A man who is known to be strictly honest, may be ever so poor, but he has the purses of all the community at his disposal;—for all know that if he promises to return what he borrows, he will never disappoint them. As a mere matter of selfishness, therefore, if a man had no higher motive for being honest, all will find that the maxim of Dr. Franklin can never fail to be true, that "honesty is the best policy."

The inordinate° love of money, no doubt, may be and is "the root of all evil," but money itself, when properly used, is not only a "handy thing to have in the house," but affords the gratification of blessing our race by enabling its possessor to enlarge the scope of human happiness and human influence. The desire for wealth is nearly universal, and none can say it is not laudable, provided the possessor of it accepts its responsibilities, and uses it as a friend to humanity. 22

The history of money-getting, which is commerce, is a history of civilization, and wherever trade has flourished most, there, too, have art and science produced the noblest fruits. In fact, as a general thing, money-getters are the benefactors of our race. To them, in a great measure, are we indebted for our institutions of learning and of art, our academies, colleges, and churches. It is no argument against the desire for, or the possession of wealth, to say that there are sometimes misers who hoard money only for the sake of hoarding, and who have no higher aspiration than to grasp everything which comes within their reach. As we have sometimes hypocrites in religion, and demagogues in politics, so there are occasionally misers among money-getters. These, however, are only exceptions to the general rule. But when, in this country, we find such a nuisance and stumbling block as a miser, we remember with gratitude that in America we have no laws of primogeniture°, and that in the due course of nature the time will come when the hoarded dust will be scattered for the benefit of mankind. To all 23

Inordinate—exceeding reasonable limits. **Primogeniture**—the system whereby the eldest son inherits the main part of the parents' estate.

men and women, therefore, do I conscientiously say, make money honestly, and not otherwise, for Shakespeare has truly said, "He that wants money, means, and content, is without three good friends."

Rhetorical Analysis Through Annotation

Maxims are brief, memorable statements of principle or rules of conduct. Barnum uses many traditional maxims and new sentences written to sound like traditional maxims.

Underline each sentence or phrase that you recognize as a traditional maxim and circle other sentences and phrases that sound like traditional maxims.

Discuss why Barnum uses so many maxim-like statements and what effect they have on the readers. Also, discuss the characteristics of such sentences and how to construct new ones.

Discussion Questions

Considering the Issues

1. What type of person would emerge from following all Barnum's prescriptions? Are the values Barnum proposed being espoused by any individuals or groups today? Does his advice remind you of particular individuals?

2. Which parts of Barnum's advice make sense to you, and which seem wrong, inappropriate, or unpalatable? Why?

3. In addition to maxims, what other techniques does Barnum use to make his advice appealing and memorable?

Writing Suggestions

1. Imagine you are Howard Hughes, Mother Theresa, Albert Einstein, Ronald Reagan, Jane Fonda, or another famous person. Write a speech directed at students entering college, giving them your rules for success. (You can be serious or comic in your approach to this assignment.)

2. Write an autobiographical account for your classmates of an occasion when you tried to follow a set of rules to improve yourself. Discuss how successful the attempt was and any morals that may be drawn from the experience.

3. For a creative writing class write a character sketch of one of the wealthier people you know. In your sketch you may want to compare the person's traits with those recommended by Barnum. If the person gives advice, you may wish to compare what they say to what they practice.

4. Barnum assumes that not only is a conventionally moral life compatible with business success, it is the best path to business success. Analyze the way Barnum blends moral advice ("be honest") and business advice ("don't blab"). In an essay for a college writing course, examine how he blends the two and uses

each type to reinforce the other. Does one or the other type of advice predominate?

5. For a school or church newspaper create five original maxims for the modern age. They may be serious, satiric, or comic.

The Self-Made Man in America
Irvin G. Wyllie

It is the historian's job to reconstruct the events, attitudes, and lifestyles of other eras largely by examining the words and records left behind by the people who lived at that time. Primary documents, such as Barnum's speech, can be pieced together in the secondary literature of the historians to create an accurate picture of former times.

In his book *The Self-Made Man in America* (1954), the cultural historian Irvin G. Wyllie traces the growth of the ideals that are expressed in Barnum's speech. In the excerpt that follows, Wyllie looks at how the concept of the self-made man arrived and grew in early America. In particular, he explores how Benjamin Franklin came to symbolize this concept.

The selection here relies on the chief literary tool of the historian: chronological narrative. He tells the story from the beginning, mentioning major events and important characters. Sometimes the narrative travels rapidly across many years in general terms, and sometimes it slows down to take a closer look at a particularly significant character or event.

THOUGH IT WAS AN American conceit that the self-made man was 1
peculiar to our shores, he had been known in other lands. Since virtually all societies provided some channels for vertical social circulation, men of this type had been common to all. In the older nations of Europe such institutions as the army, the church, the school, and the political party served as agencies for testing, sifting, and distributing individuals within various social strata. Even in associating the self-made man with wealth America enjoyed no special distinction, for in ancient Greece and Rome successful moneymakers often rose into the ruling class, regardless of social origin. And in the Italian city-states and the commercial centers of Western Europe at the close of the Middle Ages moneymaking was one of the most common and omnipotent means of social promotion.[1]

Seventeenth-century England was especially familiar with the eco- 2
nomic definition applied to this class of men, for as the English merchant

classes rose to power they inspired a substantial literature of justification. Publicists associated with the English business community turned out many pamphlets, sermons, and guidebooks which pointed out the way to wealth. One of these English classics was Richard Johnson's *Nine Worthies of London* (1592), an account of nine apprentices who rose to positions of honor through the exercise of personal virtue. Another of these handbooks, *A Treatise of the Vocations* (1603), written by William Perkins, a learned Cambridge theologian, was held in special regard by Americans. In the seventeenth century success-minded immigrants sometimes carried Perkins' book with them to the New World, and read it for guidance and inspiration.[2] Of course the great majority who came to America had no room for books, but they doubtless carried in their heads an ample store of self-help homilies°, for such maxims were common coin in England.

It is a commonplace of American colonial history that most immi- 3 grants came to the New World in the hope of improving their economic status. The agricultural laborer knew that land here was plentiful, and easily acquired, while tradesmen and day laborers built their hopes around the prospect of the high wages which were a natural consequence of the scarcity of labor. On every side American opportunities damaged class patterns inherited from Europe, and altered old orders of caste and custom. In a land where achievement was more important than titles of nobility there was always the possibility that a nobody could become a man of consequence if he worked hard and kept his eye on the main chance. Ralph Barton Perry put it very well when, speaking of colonial artisans and tradesmen, he observed that "They were neither so unfortunate as to be imbued with a sense of helplessness, nor so privileged as to be satisfied with their present status. They possessed just enough to whet their appetites for more and to feel confident of their power to attain it."[3]

After the starving time had passed and commercial towns had sprung 4 up along the Atlantic seaboard, urban dwellers could dream not just of competence but of wealth. Cadwallader Colden, reporting on New York City in 1748, asserted that "The only principle of life propagated among the young people is to get money, and men are only esteemed according to what they are worth—that is, the money they are possessed of."[4] This passion for wealth was one which enjoyed the sanction of religion, especially in New England, where Puritan clergymen assured their congregations that God approved business callings, and rewarded virtue with wealth. Cotton Mather, for example, in *Two Brief Discourses, one Directing a Christian in his General Calling; another Directing him in his Personal Calling* (1701) taught that in addition to serving Christ, which was man's general calling, all men were obliged to succeed in some useful secular employment, in order to win salvation in this life as well

---

Homilies—moralizing sermons and speeches.

as in the next. In *Essays To Do Good* (1710) he argued that prosperity was the gift of God, and that men of wealth were God's stewards, charged with the responsibility of doing good to their fellows.[5] Such doctrines as these, inherited from seventeenth-century England, occupied a central place in the American success rationale.

It was no accident that the best-known colonial self-made man was [5] Benjamin Franklin, a product of Puritan Boston. At a tender age he read Cotton Mather's *Essays To Do Good*, later crediting them with having had a profound and lifelong influence on his thought and conduct. He also received advice from his father, a humble Puritan candle-maker, who drummed into his head the meaning of the ancient proverb: "Seest thou a man diligent in his business? He shall stand before kings." Fortified by these principles of self-help Franklin migrated to Philadelphia, the Quaker commercial metropolis, to begin his rise in the printing trade. The story of his upward climb has always enjoyed a prominent place in the folklore of success. Through *Poor Richard's Almanack* (1732–1757) he publicized prosperity maxims which have probably exerted as much practical influence on Americans as the combined teachings of all the formal philosophers. Certainly in the nineteenth century the alleged virtues of the American people closely resembled the virtues of Poor Richard.[6]

During the American Revolution Franklin's energies were diverted [6] into other channels, and it was the third decade of the nineteenth century before his self-help themes were revived by a new generation of success propagandists. In the troubled years after 1763 publicists were too busy framing assertions of political independence, too busy contriving Federalist and Republican polemics, to be diverted to the writing of maxims of trade. And despite the gains made in industry, commerce, and finance between the Revolution and the period of Jackson's rise to power, few prophets arose to call young men to action in these spheres. By 1830, however, the impacts of the Industrial Revolution could no longer be ignored; in the great cities of the North and East, journalists, clergymen, lawyers and other spokesmen began to lay the foundations for the powerful nineteenth-century cult of the self-made man.

III

Appropriately Benjamin Franklin became the first object of adoration in [7] this cult, the convenient symbol which linked the success traditions of the two centuries. In 1826 Simeon Ide, a Vermont printer, dedicated a new edition of Franklin's *The Way to Wealth* and *Advice to Young Tradesmen* to the mechanics and farmers of New England. He urged every workingman to reflect on his own advantages, and to compare them with the disadvantages that Franklin had encountered, observing that "Perhaps he may, from a comparison, draw the conclusion, that he has greater advantages in his favour, and fewer discouragements to encounter, than had the persevering Franklin. If this be really the case, what other impediment can there be in his way . . . but the want of a resolute determination to merit, by a similar conduct, the good fortune which attended him?"[7] Ide urged any youth who aspired to wealth or station to lean on the counsel and example of Franklin where he might hope to find an almost infallible passport to the ultimatum of his wishes.

At Boston in 1831 a series of Franklin Lectures was begun with the avowed object of inspiring the young men of that city to make the most of their opportunities. Edward Everett inaugurated the series, proclaiming that the story of Franklin's rise could not be told too often. The most successful men in history, he declared, had been men "of humble origin, narrow fortunes, small advantages, and self-taught."[8] Twenty-six years later, when a statue of Franklin was unveiled in Boston, Robert C. Winthrop again used the occasion to arouse the working class from their lethargy:

> Behold him, Mechanics and Mechanics' Apprentices, holding out to you an example of diligence, economy and virtue, and personifying the triumphant success which may await those who follow it! Behold him, ye that are humblest and poorest in present condition or in future prospect,—lift up your heads and look at the image of a man who rose from nothing, who owed nothing to parentage or patronage, who enjoyed no advantages of early education which are not open,—a hundred fold open,—to yourselves, who performed the most menial services in the business in which his early life was employed, but who lived to stand before Kings, and died to leave a name which the world will never forget.[9]

Probably the number of poor boys who were actually inspired to great deeds by the example of Franklin was never large, but at least one, Thomas Mellon, founder of a great banking fortune, has testified to the influence of Franklin on his life. In the year 1828 young Mellon, then fourteen years old, was living on a farm outside the rising industrial city of Pittsburgh. After had had read a battered copy of Franklin's *Autobiography* which he had picked up at a neighbor's house, he found himself aflame with a new ambition. "I had not before imagined," he said, "any other course of life superior to farming, but the reading of Franklin's life led me to question this view. For so poor and friendless a boy to be able to become a merchant or a professional man had before seemed an impossibility; but here was Franklin, poorer than myself, who by industry, thrift and frugality had become learned and wise, and elevated to wealth and fame. The maxims of 'Poor Richard' exactly suited my sentiments. . . . I regard the reading of Franklin's *Autobiography* as the turning point of my life."[10] Abandoning the family farm at Poverty Point young Mellon migrated to Pittsburgh, where he made his way as a lawyer and money lender. Later when he had founded his own bank it was Franklin's statue that he placed at the front of the building as a symbol of his inspiration, and in the last years of his life he bought a thousand copies of Franklin's *Autobiography*, which he distributed to young men who came seeking advice and money.

Notes

[1]For a discussion of social promotion under European conditions, consult Pitirim Sorokin, *Social Mobility* (New York, 1927), pp. 139, 164–183.

[2]Louis B. Wright analyzes English success literature in *Middle Class Culture in Elizabethan England* (Chapel Hill, 1935), pp. 165–200.

[3]Ralph Barton Perry, *Puritanism and Democracy* (New York, 1944), p. 298. See also Arthur M. Schlesinger, "What Then Is the American, This New Man?" *American Historical Review*, XLVIII (1943), 227, 237, 239.

[4]Quoted in T. J. Wertenbaker, *The Golden Age of Colonial Culture* (New York, 1942), p. 48.

[5]The best analysis of Cotton Mather's ideas on business success is in Alfred W. Griswold, "Three Puritans on Prosperity," *New England Quarterly*, VII (1934), 475–493.

[6]For Franklin's influence on the nineteenth-century success ideology, see Louis B. Wright, "Franklin's Legacy to the Gilded Age," *Virginia Quarterly Review*, XXII (1946), 268–279.

[7]Simeon Ide, ed., *Benjamin Franklin, The Way to Wealth, Advice to Young Tradesmen, and Sketches of His Life and Character* (Windsor, Vt., 1826), p. 39.

[8]Edward Everett, *Orations and Speeches on Various Occasions by Edward Everett* (Boston, 1836), pp. 298–299.

[9]Robert C. Winthrop, *Oration at the Inauguration of the Statue of Benjamin Franklin* (Boston, 1856), p. 25.

[10]Quoted in Harvey O'Connor, *Mellon's Millions* (New York, 1933), p. 4.

Rhetorical Analysis Through Annotation

To show the full set of interconnected cultural associations surrounding the concept of the self-made man, Wyllie builds up his story piece by piece. Ideas first introduced earlier recur later in the story. Similarly books, statements, and characters keep recurring as later characters attach new meanings to them.

Underline the original mention and each recurrence of chief concepts that run through the story. Similarly circle the names of characters and books that recur later in the story. In the margin note which new meanings are being added in each recurrence of the idea, book, or character.

Discuss how this technique turns a chronological sequence of events into the story of a growing web of ideas and associations. Also consider how people and books come to be associated with certain ideas and in fact become symbols of those ideas.

Discussion Questions

Interpreting the Text

1. In what ways did the American concept of the self-made man rely on earlier history? In what ways did America provide a particularly ripe climate for this

concept to flourish? Does this climate continue today, or have conditions changed? Is the ideal of the self-made man still flourishing?

2. In what ways did religion and politics influence the growth of the ideal of the self-made man? Was religion or politics more influential? Do the same relationships between the ideal of the self-made man and religion and politics still hold today?

Considering the Issues

3. Does Benjamin Franklin still have the same symbolic meaning that he did in the nineteenth century? What were you told as you grew up about Benjamin Franklin? What did you feel about him as a model for behavior?

4. Has the ideal of the self-made man influenced the ideals of American feminism? Is there an ideal of the self-made woman? How important to the feminist movement is economic advancement through personal effort? Have any feminist heroines taken over the symbolic role that Franklin had?

5. In this selection, is more space devoted to Franklin's actual beliefs and accomplishments or to the way these beliefs and accomplishments were presented to the people and the way people perceived them? How important is it that Franklin was a writer and printer? Is Franklin mentioned more in this narrative in relationship to events during his life or after his death in 1790? What significance can you find in that?

6. What generalizations can you make based on this selection about the growth of cultural ideals and the development of associated symbols? Can you compare the story presented here with the rise of other cultural ideals in recent history and the emergence of symbolic heroes? Who are some of the major symbolic heroes of our culture and what do they represent? What institutions arise around these heroes, and what impact do these heroes have on individuals?

7. In his introductory overview of the self-made man, Wyllie mentions that in Europe, the army, church, school, and political realm had long "served as agencies for testing, sifting, and distributing individuals within various social strata." Is this the case here in America today? How does each institution sift people into classes and serve as an instrument for social mobility?

Writing Suggestions

1. For an American history class do some research on Franklin's life and write an essay comparing the facts of his life with the myth of Franklin's life as described by Wyllie.

2. For a course in business organization write a paper on the influence of large organizations on the ideals of self-advancement. Consider what types of opportunities are available in large organizations versus the benefits of self-employment. Also consider how choosing to enter a large organization may affect the career, ideals, and behavior of a young person on the rise.

3. As part of your own personal examination of your values write an essay on the importance of economic success as a goal in your life.

4. Imagine you have been invited to your former high school to give an inspirational speech to a student assembly. Write a speech about a great person you consider to be your model and what that model has meant to you.

5. For a course in contemporary American social problems write a paper about the possibility that the lives of many young people may be no better economically, if not worse, than that of their parents. Consider whether this new lack of mobility will cause strains on the traditional ideal of the self-made career, and whether new ideals may be needed.

Social Mobility

Seymour Martin Lipset and Reinhard Bendix

Although prior to 1960 a few historians attempted to study the social origins of selected business leaders, comprehensive studies of who became rich and who did not required mass statistical techniques and sociological concepts of social stratification and social mobility. Both these changes ran counter to the narrative specificity of traditional history. Historical studies tended to present great amounts of information about separate incidents or individuals, with each study presented as a separate narrative story. This familiarity with the specific details of each incident generally led historians to believe that each event had its own special features. Historians tended to be suspicious of theoretical generalizations and were reluctant to consider large numbers of individuals or incidents as similar.

In the past few decades, however, historians have paid more attention to the fate of the large numbers of ordinary people and, thus, have had to borrow much from other social sciences. The concept of social mobility was first introduced by the German sociologist Karl Mannheim in 1929, but became a major topic of sociological study in the 1950s. The following discussion of social mobility is from an important book on the subject by Seymour Martin Lipset of Stanford University and Reinhard Bendix of the University of California at Berkeley. Published in 1959, *Social Mobility in Industrial Society* came out just about the time when historians were getting interested in the concept.

This excerpt is from the introduction, where Lipset and Bendix establish the basic concepts they are going to use in the book. Their nontechnical explanation relies on the ideas of a number of classic authors, from Plato to Aldous Huxley, discussed in passing. They describe not only what social mobility is, but why it is important for the successful functioning of a society. In discussing what happens when adequate mobility opportunities do not exist, they point to the consequences for political stability.

IN EVERY COMPLEX SOCIETY there is a division of labor and a *1* hierarchy of prestige. Positions of leadership and social responsibility are usually ranked at the top, and positions requiring long training and superior intelligence are ranked just below. The number of leaders and highly educated individuals constitutes everywhere a small minority. On the other hand, the great majority is made up of persons in the lower strata° who perform manual and routine work of every sort and who command scant rewards and little prestige. In keeping with this division between "the few" and "the many" the stratification of society has often been pictured as a pyramid or a diamond; in the first analogy, society consists of a series of strata that become larger and more populous as we move down the hierarchy of reward and prestige, and in the second, to have small numbers at the top and bottom, with the mass of the population concentrated between. However it may be depicted, the point is that men grapple with the problems of determining the number of people at each rank in their society, and that through history various methods for doing this have been devised.[1]

The term "social mobility" refers to the process by which individuals *2* move from one position to another in society—positions which by general consent have been given specific hierarchical values. When we study social mobility we analyze the movement of individuals from positions possessing a certain rank to positions either higher or lower in the social system. It is possible to conceive of the result of this process as a distribution of talent and training such that privileges and perquisites° accrue° to each position in proportion to its difficulty and responsibility. An ideal ratio between the distribution of talents and the distribution of rewards can obviously never occur in society, but the approximation to this ideal, or the failure to approximate it, lends fascination to the study of social mobility.

Men and women occupying positions of high status generally en- *3* deavor to preserve their privileges for their kin and heirs; indeed, a "good" father is one who tries to pass the status he enjoys on to his children, and in many societies he will try to extend it to near and distant relatives as well. Hence, in every stratified, complex society there is, as Plato suggested, a straining towards aristocracy and a limitation of mobility. This tendency never runs its full course. To see why, it is sufficient to think of the kinds of society in which there would be no

---

Strata—levels in a hierarchy. **Perquisites**—benefits. **Accrue**—to come to someone as a benefit.

mobility: either a completely closed caste° system in which each variation of rank was entirely determined by the status of the family into which one was born; or a society wherein each individual would be assigned a position commensurate with his genetically determined talents, and moreover, one in which this scheme of distribution would be adequate for all social needs—such a society as Aldous Huxley depicted in his *Brave New World*, where manufactured fetuses were so treated as to produce laborers, technicians, slaves, or intellectuals. Neither of these extreme conditions is plausible.

There are two basic reasons why social mobility exists in every so-   4
ciety:

1. *Changes in demands for performance.* Complex societies change, and whether social change is slow or rapid it leads sooner or later to a change in the demands which different positions make on those who occupy them. The few who have inherited their high positions may not have the competence to meet the responsibilities which these positions entail. Yet in a society dominated by a hereditary ruling class these few exclude able individuals from lower ranks from positions of leadership. And their failure to lead, together with their exclusion of those capable of doing so, may cause tensions which will eventuate in the rise of a new social group and a subsequent attack upon the traditional prestige of the hierarchy.

2. *Changes in supplies of talent.* Just as there are changes in the demand for various kinds of talent, there are constant shifts in the supply. No elite or ruling class controls the natural distribution of talent, intelligence, or other abilities, though it may monopolize the opportunities for education and training. As long as many of those with high abilities belong to the lower strata (and many contemporary studies suggest that this is so), there will be leaders who come from those strata. The chance for potential leaders to develop the skills which will take them up from the ranks may be small, but sooner or later some will break through. Since those who do are usually people who can adapt themselves to new ways easily, they often become the core of a new group which challenges the dominant older one.

As Karl Mannheim pointed out, every ruling class faces certain dilem-   5
mas. In what ways and to what extent will it admit to leadership those lacking the proper social background? How many qualified newcomers (who may be dangerous if they are not absorbed) will, or rather, can, the elite accept without undermining its legitimate prestige? Under what conditions can an old elite refuse to learn new roles, and yet retain its monopoly on high status? These questions indicate the important relationship between a society's internal mobility and the stability of its

---

Caste—a strictly defined social class that is difficult to move out of, as in Hindu society.

political regime. Alexis de Tocqueville° attributed the French Revolution to the attempt of a hereditary aristocracy to maintain its privilege after its responsibilities had been assumed by other groups. On the other hand, a ruling class may admit into its ranks those from lower strata who perform key functions. The English aristocracy thus remained at the top despite a transformation of society because, though it continued its emphasis on inheritance of social status, it not only met new responsibilities but also shared its privileges with those who threatened its position. The United States supplies another good example of an open, flexible upper class. Though it never had a "blooded" aristocracy, America's old business families provided the basis for an elite group—but a group that was never strong enough to exclude the new class of financial magnates° and large corporation managers. (Of course, lack of traditional caste symbols made possible easy acceptance of newcomers into the elite.) In an expanding, dynamic society, such barriers to mobility as inherited rank can be a fundamental cause of instability, since expansion calls for an increase in the number of qualified leaders. As long as the ruling group is flexible it will allow ambitious and talented individuals to rise from the lower strata; yet an ever-present tendency toward the formation of an aristocracy tends to restrict such individual mobility in any society. If the restriction is sufficiently tight, it can provoke discontent, which may result in efforts by members of deprived groups to achieve *collective or group mobility*, sometimes through a struggle to supplant the dominant group.

Notes

[1]Kingsley Davis and W. E. Moore, "Some Principles of Stratification," *American Sociological Review*, 10 (1945): 242–249. Talcott Parsons, "A Revised Analytical Approach to the Theory of Social Stratification," *in* Reinhard Bendix and S. M. Lipset, eds., *Class, Status and Power: A Reader in Social Stratification* (Glencoe: The Free Press, 1953), pp. 92–128. Both contain general discussions of the subject.

Rhetorical Analysis Through Annotation

The definition and discussion of mobility here characterize social phenomena in three ways: the way things are, the process by which things develop and change, and how things become the object of study by social scientists. These three ways of discussing the phenomena can be associated with three different types of verbs: verbs of existence (such as *be*), verbs of action and change (such as *move* and *break through*), and verbs of intellectual activity (such as *analyze* and *represent*).

Alexis de Tocqueville (1805–1859)—French traveler, political commentator, and historian.
Magnates—powerful or influential people, especially in business.

In the text, underline verbs of existence, circle verbs of action and change, and box verbs of intellectual activity.

Discuss how these verbs help to define the kind of discussion taking place. Then consider how the three types of discussion fit together to form a unified whole. How does the combination of the three modes of discussion affect the overall meaning and shape of the selection?

Discussion Questions

Interpreting the Text

1. Does the concept of social stratification add anything to the notion that some people are rich and others are not? Does the term social mobility add anything to the notion that some people get richer and others get poorer?

2. According to the authors, what forces lead to stable class systems and what forces lead to social mobility?

3. What is the relation between political stability and mobility?

4. What do the authors mean by "traditional caste symbols" as a way of the elite governing newcomers' acceptance?

Considering the Issues

5. To what degree in our society does the distribution of talent and training correspond to the distribution of rewards? What features of our society help or hinder that correspondence? In this regard, how fair do you think our society is? How would you compare it to other societies you know about?

6. Is it important for parents to be able to pass on their advantages to their children? Consider the benefits and costs of inherited status from the perspective of both the individual and society.

7. Discuss as examples people you know that have undergone social mobility. What caused their change of status? How well do those causes fit with the two causes proposed by the authors: changed demand for talents and changed supply of talent?

8. How does the mobility system in America work to maintain or disrupt political stability?

Writing Suggestions

1. For an introduction to sociology course, answer the following examination question: Define in your own words the terms social stratification and social mobility. Give examples.

2. Imagine that the ideas you have learned about social mobility have caused you to think about your own family's history. In order to share your insights, write a letter to a sibling or friend discussing how and why your parents or grandparents have or have not had much social mobility.

3. You have been invited to participate in a panel on "America's Youth: What They See in Their Own Futures" for a television talk show. Prepare a short statement about how you see your mobility prospects.

4. For a political science course write an essay considering how social mobility or the lack of it has influenced political stability in any case in recent history you wish to discuss. To answer the question you may look at the political choices made by minorities in relation to how those minorities have seen their chances for mobility. Or, if you are aware of the politics of another country, such as in Asia or Latin America, you may discuss that.

5. Lipset and Bendix write, "No elite or ruling class controls the natural distribution of talent, intelligence, or other abilities." For a sociology course, write an essay on sports or artistic talent as an avenue for mobility for people who are poor but gifted. Consider the effects of channeling the energies of these people into these very visible but nonmainline professions that potentially offer great rewards but entail high risks and personal costs.

Poverty and Progress: Social Mobility in a Nineteenth Century City

Stephan Thernstrom

In 1964 Stephan Thernstrom, now of Harvard University, took up the challenge of social mobility in American history. His book, which is excerpted here, is written for historians but it takes its cue from sociological studies like those of Lipset and Bendix. By drawing a large-scale statistical picture of a sizable group of people who would otherwise be invisible to historians, Thernstrom attempts to change how historians view history. Because the rich and famous often leave extensive documentary records behind them, they tend to gain a disproportionate share of historical attention. It is far more difficult to get information and draw conclusions about ordinary people of the past.

The first excerpt is from the book's introduction. In it Thernstrom discusses the limitations of previous historical studies of social mobility and presents his method for gaining a more complete picture. The second excerpt is from the latter part of the book; it summarizes and discusses the conclusions drawn from the statistical analyses that form the bulk of the book.

> *Men of literary taste . . . are always apt to*
> *overlook the working-classes, and to confine the*
> *records they make of their own times, in great*
> *degree, to the habits and fortunes of their own*
> *associates, and to those of people of superior rank to*
> *themselves, of whose sayings and doings their*
> *vanity, as well as their curiosity, leads them most*
> *carefully to inform themselves. The dumb masses*
> *have often been so lost in this shadow of egotism,*
> *that, in later days, it has been impossible to discern*
> *the very real influence their character and condition*
> *has had on the fortune and fate of the nation.*
>
> FREDERICK LAW OLMSTED (1859)

AMERICAN LEGEND HAS IT that the United States has long been *1*
"the land of opportunity" for the common man. No other society has
so often celebrated social mobility, none has made a folk hero of the
self-made man to quite the same degree. The idea of the distinctive
fluidity of our social order has been a national obsession for more than
a century.

This has been the myth. How has it squared with social reality? The *2*
literature on social mobility in contemporary America is abundant, but
social scientists have made few efforts to examine the problem in historical depth. One of the most glaring gaps in our knowledge of nineteenth century America is the absence of reliable information about the
social mobility of its population, particularly at the lower and middle
levels of society. It was this gap which made recent discussions of the
question "are social classes in America becoming more rigid?" so incon-
clusive and superficial. A satisfactory verdict could hardly be arrived at
when so little was known about the actual extent of social mobility in
the United States prior to 1900.

This study of the social mobility of working class families in a nine- *3*
teenth century city thus ventures into unexplored territory. Virtually the
only systematic mobility research in America which extends back into
the nineteenth century has dealt with the social origins of members of
the American business elite.[1] Valuable as this research has been, it does
not provide a satisfactory basis for estimating the openness of the nineteenth century class structure. What is an "open" society? A society of
five millionaires and ten million paupers, for instance, cannot be so
described merely because the former are recruited from the ranks of the
poor by some process of free competition which selects individuals
purely on merit. As Americans have understood the term, an open
society is one with room at the middle as well as at the top; a society
in which mobility opportunities are widespread.

The business elite studies deal with social advances which were, if *4*
often dramatic, necessarily atypical. Almost nothing can be learned
about the range of mobility opportunities at the great base of the social
pyramid from a survey of the class origins of the elect few who climbed

to its very pinnacle. It is by now well established that the great majority of American millionaires, Wall Street bankers, and corporation presidents in both the nineteenth and twentieth centuries have come from middle class homes, but surely these are dubious grounds on which to assert that the American social structure as a whole has been relatively closed. A more relevant question for research is whether it was easy, difficult, or impossible for a laborer or a laborer's son to become a grocer, a foreman, or a farm owner in the United States a century ago. About opportunities at this social level we know dismayingly little. The plea that American history be written "from the bottom up" has been often voiced but rarely heeded.[2]

This volume deals with the lives of hundreds of obscure men who 5 resided in a New England community in the latter half of the nineteenth century. It traces the changing social position of unskilled manual laborers and their families, and suggests some hypotheses about working-class social mobility in other American cities of the period. These families stood at the very bottom of the social ladder by almost any criterion.° Living at the margin of subsistence, they suffered from the classic disabilities of the depressed social group: unemployment, illiteracy, bad housing, poor diets. It would be impressive testimony to the fluidity of the social structure if many of these unskilled workmen and their sons actually climbed to a higher social level. Certainly they represent the least favorable case with which to test the validity of popular American beliefs about widespread opportunities. . . .

Fortunately there is one source of information about the economic 6 and social situation of ordinary, unorganized laborers: original manuscript schedules of the United States Census. Starting in 1850, when a new method of census-taking was initiated, manuscript census schedules° provide the historian with a primitive social survey of the entire population of a community; occupation, place of birth, property holdings, literacy, and other useful information about every inhabitant is listed. These skeletal facts, supplemented by data from contemporary newspapers and other sources, made it possible to fix the social position of the unskilled laboring families of Newburyport at decade intervals, and to measure how much social mobility they experienced in the period 1850–1880. . . .[3]

The limits of the evidence upon which this book is based, it must be 7 repeated, are severe and inescapable. The task of the historian who takes as his subject the common citizens of a nineteenth century community seems at times to resemble that of the archaeologist, who seeks to breathe life into scattered artifacts from a long-dead civilization. This exercise in reconstruction was often painfully uncertain, and my interpretations are open to challenge at many points. But I hope that it will be

---

Criterion—principle for judgment.   **Manuscript census schedules**—handwritten notes made by census takers.

suggestive, and that it will convince some readers of the potentialities of history written "from the bottom up."

The Meaning of Mobility: A Trial Balance

If nineteenth century Newburyport was to develop a permanent prole-   8
tarian° class, the families dealt with in this study should have formed it. These unskilled workmen began at the very bottom of the community occupational ladder in the 1850–1880 period. Their situation seemed anything but promising. They lacked both vocational skills and financial resources. Many were illiterate, and few had the means to see that their children received more than a primitive education. Most were relative strangers in the city, migrants from New England farms or Irish villages. Few inhabitants of Newburyport at mid-century were more likely candidates for membership in a permanently depressed caste.

That these working class families did not remain in a uniformly   9
degraded social position throughout the 1850–1880 period is by now abundantly clear. If the Newburyport laboring class gave birth to no self-made millionaires during these years, the social advances registered by many of its members were nonetheless impressive. A brief review of the findings on geographical, occupational, and property mobility° will clarify the significance of these social gains and provide a fresh perspective on social stratification in the nineteenth century city.

By 1880 the undifferentiated mass of poverty-stricken laboring fam-   10
ilies, the "lack-alls" who seemed at mid-century to be forming a permanent class, had separated into three layers. On top was a small but significant elite of laboring families who had gained a foothold in the lower fringes of the middle class occupational world. Below them was the large body of families who had attained property mobility while remaining in manual occupations, most often of the unskilled or semi-skilled variety; these families constituted the stable, respectable, home-owning stratum of the Newburyport working class. At the very bottom of the social ladder was the impoverished, floating lower class, large in number but so transient° as to be formless and powerless.

The composition of the Newburyport manual labor force in the latter   11
half of the nineteenth century, we have seen, was extraordinarily volatile.° A minority of the laboring families who came to the city in those years settled for as long as a decade. Most did not, and it was these floating families whose depressed position most resembled the classic European proletariat. Recurrently unemployed, often on relief, they rarely accumulated property or advanced themselves occupationally. Substantial numbers of these impoverished unskilled workmen, men

---

Proletarian—of the working class.   **Property mobility**—social mobility through gain or loss of real estate and other valuable possessions.   **Transient**—changing.   **Volatile**—liable to sudden change.

who "had no interest in the country except the interest of breathing," were always to be found in Newburyport during this period, but this stratum had remarkably little continuity of membership.[4] Members of this floating group naturally had no capacity to act in concert against an employer or to assert themselves politically; stable organization based on a consciousness of common grievances was obviously impossible. The pressure to migrate operated selectively to remove the least successful from the community; a mere 5 percent of the laboring families present in Newburyport throughout this entire thirty-year period found both occupational mobility and property mobility beyond their grasp.

The floating laborers who made up this large, ever renewed transient *12* class occupied the lowest social stratum in nineteenth century Newburyport. A notch above it was the settled, property-owning sector of the working class; above that was the lower middle class, the highest social level attained by members of any of these laboring families. To obtain middle class status required entry into a nonmanual occupation and the adoption of a new style of life; this was an uncommon feat for either unskilled laborers or their children. Five sixths of the laboring families resident in Newburyport for a decade or more during this period found the middle class occupational world completely closed to them. And among the remaining sixth, the high mobility families, were many which remained partially dependent on manual employment for their support. It is doubtful that many of the elite high mobility families developed the attitudes and behavior patterns associated with the middle class style of life. This seems particularly unlikely in the case of laborers who became the operators of small farms, whose sons rarely entered middle class occupations. Nor did a marginal business or a menial clerkship necessarily provide the economic security and inspire the commitment to education needed to insure the transmission of middle class status to the next generation. The importance of the small group of laborers and laborers' sons who purchased shops and farms or found white collar jobs should not be minimized: these men did provide proof to their less successful brethren that class barriers could be hurdled by men of talent, however lowly their origin. But it should be emphasized that many of these upwardly mobile workmen obtained only a precarious hold on middle class status, and that their social milieu° often differed little from the milieu of the propertied sector of the working class.

By far the most common form of social advance for members of *13* laboring families in Newburyport in this period was upward movement *within* the working class, mobility into the stratum between the lower middle class and the floating group of destitute unskilled families. A few men from these intermediate mobility families became skilled craftsmen; this was extremely rare for the older generation but less unusual as an

---

Milieu—surroundings.

inter-generational move. Most often, however, these families advanced themselves by accumulating significant amounts of property while remaining in unskilled or semiskilled occupations. Here were men who offered the market little more than two hands and a strong back, but who succeeded in becoming respectable home owners and savings bank depositors.

What was the social significance of these modest advances? Nineteenth   **14** century propagandists took a simple view. The property-owned laborer was "a capitalist." If there was a working class in America, as soon as "a man has saved something he ceases to belong to this class"; "the laborers have become the capitalists in this new world." Accumulated funds, however small, were capital, and the possession of capital determined the psychological orientation of the workman. It was the nature of capital to multiply itself; he who possessed capital necessarily hungered for further expansion of his holdings. To save and to invest was the first step in the process of mobility; investment inspired a risk-taking, speculative mentality conducive to further mobility. The distinction between the "petty capitalist" workman and the rich merchant was one of degree. To move from the former status to the latter was natural; it happened "every day." Similar assumptions lie behind the still-popular view that "the typical American worker" has been "an expectant entrepreneur."[50]

This was sheer fantasy. A mere handful of the property-owning la-   **15** borers of Newburyport ventured into business for themselves. More surprising, the property mobility of a laboring man did not even heighten his children's prospects for mobility into a business or professional calling. Indeed, the working class family which abided by the injunction° "spend less than you earn" could usually do so only by sacrificing the children's education for an extra paycheck, and thereby restricting their opportunities for inter-generational occupational mobility.

Furthermore, the use these laborers made of their savings testifies to   **16** their search for maximum security rather than for mobility out of the working class. An economically rational investor in nineteenth century Newburyport would not have let his precious stock of capital languish in a savings bank for long, and he certainly would not have tied it up in the kind of real estate purchased by these laborers. The social environment of the middle class American encouraged such investment for rising profits, but the working class social milieu did not. The earning capacity of the merchant, professional, or entrepreneur rose steadily as his career unfolded—the very term "career" connotes this. The middle class family head was ordinarily its sole source of support, and the family was able both to accumulate wealth and to improve its standard of living

---

Entrepreneur—risk-taking businessperson.   **Injunction**—negative rule, prohibition.

out of normal increments° in the salary (or net profits) accruing to him over the years.

Ordinary workmen did not have "careers" in this sense. Their earning *17*
capacity did not increase with age; in unskilled and semiskilled occupations a forty-year-old man was paid no more than a boy of 17. Substantial saving by a working class family thus tended to be confined to the years when the children were old enough to bring in a supplementary income but too young to have married and established households of their own.

The tiny lots, the humble homes, and the painfully accumulated *18*
savings accounts were the fruits of those years. They gave a man dignity, and a slender margin of security against unpredictable, uncontrollable economic forces which could deprive him of his job at any time. Once the mortgage was finally discharged, home ownership reduced the family's necessary expenses by $60 to $100 a year, and a few hundred dollars in the savings bank meant some protection against illness, old age, or a sluggish labor market. A cynical observer would have noted the possibility that home ownership served also to confine the workman to the local labor market and to stengthen the hand of local employers, who were thus assured of a docile permanent work force, but few laborers of nineteenth century Newburyport were disposed to think in these terms.

Families belonging to the propertied stratum of the working class, in *19*
short, were socially mobile in the sense that they had climbed a rung higher on the social ladder, and had established themselves as decent, respectable, hard-working, churchgoing members of the community. They had not, however, set their feet upon an escalator which was to draw them up into the class of merchants, professionals, and entrepreneurs.[6]

The contrast between the literal claims of the rags-to-riches mythol- *20*
ogy and the actual social experience of these families thus appears glaring. A few dozen farmers, small shopkeepers, and clerks, a large body of home-owning families unable to escape a grinding regimen of manual labor: this was the sum of the social mobility achieved by Newburyport's unskilled laborers by 1880. Could men like these have felt that the mobility ideology was at all relevant to their lives?

I think so. True, many of the optimistic assertions of popular writers *21*
and speakers were demonstrably false. Class differences in opportunities were deep and pervasive; a large majority of the unskilled laborers in Newburyport and a large majority of their sons remained in the working class throughout the 1850–1880 period. Not one rose from rags to genuine riches. Whoever seeks a Newburyport version of Andrew Carnegie must settle for Joseph Greenough, keeper of a livery stable worth $15,000, and Stephen Fowle, proprietor of a small newsstand. But we

---

Increments—increases by steps.

err if we take the mobility creed too literally. The rapt attention nineteenth century Americans gave Russell Conwell° did not mean that his listeners literally believed that they soon would acquire riches equivalent to "an acre of diamonds." One ingredient of the appeal of mobility literature and oratory was that pleasant fantasies of sudden wealth and a vicarious° sharing in the spectacular successes of other ordinary men provided a means of escaping the tedious realities of daily existence. Fantasies of this sort are not likely to flourish among men who have no hope at all of individual economic or social betterment. And indeed the laborers of Newburyport had abundant evidence that self-improvement was possible. To practice the virtues exalted by the mobility creed rarely brought middle class status to the laborer, or even to his children. But hard work and incessant economy did bring tangible rewards—money in the bank, a house to call his own, a new sense of security and dignity. "The man who owns the roof that is over his head and the earth under his dwelling can't help thinking that he's more of a man than though he had nothing, with poverty upon his back and want at home; and if he don't think so, other people will."[7]

The ordinary workmen of Newburyport, in short, could view Amer- 22 ica as a land of opportunity despite the fact that the class realities which governed their life chances confined most of them to the working class. These newcomers to urban life arrived with a low horizon of expectations, it seems likely. If it is true that "in the last analysis the status of the worker is not a physical but a mental one, and is affected as much by comparisons with past conditions and with the status of other groups in the community as by the facts in themselves," the typical unskilled laborer who settled in Newburyport could feel proud of his achievements and optimistic about the future.[8] Most of the social gains registered by laborers and their sons during these years were decidedly modest—a move one notch up the occupational scale, the acquisition of a small amount of property. Yet *in their eyes* these accomplishments must have loomed large. The contradiction between an ideology of limitless opportunity and the realities of working class existence is unlikely to have dismayed men whose aspirations and expectations were shaped in the Irish village or the New England subsistence farm. The "dream of success" certainly affected these laboring families, but the personal measure of success was modest. By this measure, the great majority of them had indeed "gotten ahead."[9]

Notes

[1]See particularly F. W. Taussig and C. S. Joslyn, *American Business Leaders* (New York, 1932); C. Wright Mills, "The American Business Elite: A Collec-

---

Russell Conwell (1843–1925)—Massachusetts clergyman. Conwell gave his lecture "Acres of Diamonds" over six thousand times and used the proceeds to further the education of many young men of his time. **Vicarious**—experienced by imaginative sympathy with someone else.

tive Portrait," *The Tasks of Economic History*, suppl. V of the *Journal of Economic History* (Dec. 1945), pp. 20–44; Frances W. Gregory and Irene D. Neu, "The American Industrial Elite in the 1870's," in William Miller, ed., *Men in Business: Essays in the History of Entrepreneurship* (Cambridge, 1952), pp. 193–211; William Miller, "American Historians and the American Business Elite," *Journal of Economic History*, 9 (1949): 184–200; Mabel Newcomer, *The Big Business Executive* (New York, 1955). Chapter four of Seymour Lipset and Reinhard Bendix, *Social Mobility in Industrial Society* (Berkeley, 1959), analyzes this literature in detail and reports the findings of another empirical study of the question.

[2]The case for "writing history from the bottom up" is well stated by Caroline Ware and Constance M. Green in C. F. Ware, ed., *The Cultural Approach to History* (New York, 1940), pp. 273–286.

[3]Oscar Handlin, to whom I am indebted for the original suggestion to look into the manuscript schedules, made extensive use of them in *Boston's Immigrants: A Study in Acculturation* (rev. ed., Cambridge, Mass., 1959). Much of F. L. Owsley's *Plain Folk of the Old South* (Baton Rouge, 1949) is similarly based on data from original census schedules. The chief objective of both of these volumes was quite different from that of the present study; neither author, accordingly, traced individuals from census to census. The only work closely comparable to this one in its use of census materials is Merle E. Curti, *The Making of an American Community: a Case Study of Democracy in a Frontier County* (Stanford, 1959), a history of Trempealeau County, Wisconsin, in the period 1850–1880.

Manuscript census schedules, unhappily, are essentially confined to the 1850–1880 period. The first six United States Censuses (1790–1840) aimed at little more than a simple enumeration of the population. Individual inhabitants of a community were not listed by name, and there was no effort to compile the economic and social data which make the later censuses so valuable a source for the historian. Most of the 1890 schedules, including all of those for Massachusetts, were destroyed by fire. The 1900 and subsequent censuses are presently classified "confidential" by law; thus only aggregated data, on which it is impossible to trace individuals, are available to the historian. Manuscript schedules for the communities of Essex County for the years 1850, 1860, and 1870 are available at the Essex Institute, Salem, Mass. Duplicates of these, plus the schedules for 1880, may be found in the Massachusetts State Archives, Boston.

[4]The quoted phrase is Ireton's famous characterization of the English lower class during the Puritan Revolution; quoted from J. L. and Barbara Hammond, *The Town Labourer, 1760–1832: The New Civilization* (London, 1949), I, 68.

[5]For a recent elaboration of the familiar view that the psychology of the American working class has been entrepreneurial, see Gerald N. Grob, *Workers and Utopia: A Study of Ideological Conflict in the American Labor Movement, 1865–1900* (Evanston, 1961), pp. 165–166n, 189. The classic expressions of this approach are to be found in the writings of "the Wisconsin school" of labor history; see John R. Commons, et al., *History of Labor in the United States*, 4 vols. (New York, 1918–1935), and Selig Perlman, *A Theory of the Labor Movement* (New York, 1928).

[6]The growing contemporary literature on the sociology of working class life demonstrates the falsity of the simplistic assumption that increased material

security is rapidly making the working class indistinguishable from the middle class. See particularly, Richard Hoggart, *The Uses of Literacy: Aspects of Working Class Life, With Special Reference to Publications and Entertainments* (London, 1957); Berger, *Working Class Suburb*; Chinoy, *Automobile Workers and the American Dream*; S. M. Miller and Frank Riessman, "Are Workers Middle Class?" *Dissent*, 8 (1961): 507–513 and the works cited there; Miller and Riessman, "The Working Class Subculture: A New View," *Social Problems*, 9 (1961): 86–97; Herbert J. Gans, *The Urban Villagers: Group and Class in the Life of Italo-Americans* (Glencoe, Ill., 1962).

[7]*Herald*, May 10, 1856.

[8]This observation about status is from Norman J. Ware's *The Industrial Worker, 1840–1860* (Boston, 1924), p. 26. Ware employed what later came to be known as "reference group" theory in an effort to show that the American working class was losing status in these years. Centering his attention on artisan groups which were suffering from changes in technology and market organization during this period, Ware implied that the ordinary workman of the 1840's and 1850's judged his present circumstances against the ideal of the independent craftsman of old. My point here is just the opposite. For further critical comments on the dangers of equating the entire working class with the displaced artisan, see the discussion of Lloyd Warner and the Lynds.

[9]A number of recent studies support this line of argument. See Chinoy, *Automobile Workers*, chap. x; Lamar T. Empey, "Social Class and Occupational Ambition: A Comparison of Absolute and Relative Measures," *American Sociological Review*, 21 (1956): 703–709; J. Kenneth Morland, "Educational and Occupational Aspirations of Mill and Town School Children in a Southern Community," *Social Forces*, 39 (1960): 169–175.

Rhetorical Analysis Through Annotation

Footnotes can serve many functions other than giving the source of a quotation.

Next to each of Thernstrom's footnotes, briefly characterize the type of information and discussion in it. Does, for example, the note discuss a concept at greater length through quotations from other authors?

Then, using the footnote reference numbers, determine where in the main text the footnote refers to. Underline the specific item in the main text being commented on in the footnote. In the margin then briefly characterize the topic or argument in the sentences surrounding the footnote reference.

Discuss why in each case Thernstrom decides to supplement the discussion with the information in the footnote. Why doesn't he include this information in the main text? Does one kind of information get placed in the main text and another kind in the footnotes? How does Thernstrom use footnotes to organize his information and overall argument?

Discussion Questions

Interpreting the Text

1. What deficiencies does Thernstrom find in previous historical studies? How does he redefine the essential questions to be asked? How does his study fit in with his redefined questions?

2. Thernstrom lists the type of information available in census schedules as follows: "occupation, place of birth, property holdings, literacy." What types of questions do you think can be answered by such data and what questions cannot be answered? Why does Thernstrom call this data severely limited?

3. In what ways was there mobility for the people studied by Thernstrom? In what ways was the mobility limited?

Considering the Issues

4. What were the mobility opportunities that were in fact available to unskilled workmen in Newburyport between 1850 and 1880? Do you consider these substantial? Did they seem sufficient for the workers at that time? In light of Lipset and Bendix's discussion of mobility and political stability, what attitude and degree of commitment do you feel these workers had to the social system that offered them that degree of mobility?

5. Thernstrom suggests that although the rags-to-riches preaching of that time was not literally true, it was true in a limited way and served a positive psychological function. Explain how this may have been the case. Discuss whether you agree with Thernstrom about the overall positive influence of this less than true teaching. Are there any similar myths we tend to believe today that although not completely true are partly true and have a positive psychological function for us?

6. Thernstrom moves between generalizations, large statistical statements, and specifics about individuals' lives. Identify passages where he does each of these things and discuss how he ties them together in a coherent presentation.

Writing Suggestions

1. Imagine you have read this selection for an American history course you are taking. Answer the following essay question the teacher gives you in the form of a fifteen minute in-class quiz: According to Thernstrom, what degree of mobility was there for workers of mid-nineteenth century Newburyport?

2. Imagine you are an editor for a political magazine needing a short filler article of about two hundred words. You frequently fill such spaces with summaries of politically relevant books, such as Thernstrom's. Prepare a summary of Thernstrom's book assuming your magazine is left-wing. Then write another, assuming your magazine is right-wing.

3. From Thernstrom's description of the attitudes, ambitions, and lives of the people he studied, write a character sketch of a typical worker of that place and time. The sketch, written for a creative writing workshop, can be either descriptive or narrative.

4. For a writing proficiency examination imagine you must write an essay on the theme, "People Should Reject Half-truths and Face the Truth: Agree or Disagree." In order to give this dull topic some life, you decide to approach the assignment by discussing the role of the rags-to-riches myth in the lives of the workers Thernstrom studied. Write that essay.

5. For your personal reading journal discuss whether you found Thernstrom's conclusions surprising or interesting in any way or whether they were exactly what you expected them to be. Explain your reaction.

Rags-to-Riches in Paterson, New Jersey
Herbert G. Gutman

Following Thernstrom's study more regional studies began to fill out the patterns of mobility in different areas and among different classes. In fact, the following essay appeared in a collection of a dozen such studies on nineteenth century cities by various historians, and was edited by Thernstrom himself and Richard Sennett. Researchers who open up new areas of investigation often encourage others to do similar work, because the work is seen as far too large and important to be left to a single individual. For original ideas to thrive, other researchers need to actively use the ideas. Although the fear of intellectual theft may result in occasional hesitancies, most researchers find that intellectual generosity is by far the most successful policy.

Herbert Gutman, professor of history at City University of New York, goes beyond merely repeating Thernstrom's work here with a different town and a different class. He goes beyond a statistical approach to gain a sense of the lives of the people studied. He combines traditional historical methods of research and particularistic narratives with Thernstrom's sociological overview techniques. To do this he looks at different types of source materials and shapes his argument in a different way. His different approach also leads to somewhat different conclusions. Notice how in the early part of the article Gutman reviews the work of others in order to establish the significance of his own unique approach.

IN RECENT DECADES, HISTORIANS have vigorously disputed the   *1*
validity of the belief that nineteenth-century American industrialists rose from "rags to riches." A popular literature has been subjected to critical textual analysis, and the promises of popular ideology have been measured by empirical head-counting that involves the collection of data about the social origins of "business leaders." These studies share a common conclusion: very few workers—day laborers, unskilled workers, and skilled artisans—became successful manufacturers. After studying nearly two hundred leaders of the largest early twentieth-century corporations, William Miller convincingly concluded that to look for

men of "working class or foreign origins" among the most powerful financiers, public utility and railroad executives, and mining and manufacturing corporation officials was "to look almost in vain." Fully 95% came from families of upper- or middle-class status. Not more than 3% started as poor immigrant boys or even as poor American farm boys. Andrew Carnegie was an important American in 1900, but hardly any men of his economic class or social position shared with him a common career pattern. . . .[1]

The most detailed study of the early post–Civil War "industrial elite" [2] has been conducted by Frances W. Gregory and Irene D. Neu, who generally confirmed the earlier findings.[2] Gregory and Neu examined the careers of 303 leaders of the railroad, textile (mostly cotton), and steel industries in the 1870s by studying the place of birth, the occupation of the father, the religious affiliation, the educational level attained, and the age on first starting work of the executives of seventy-seven large firms. . . . For the men they studied, Gregory and Neu found little evidence that "the top-level businessman" of the 1870s was "but a generation removed from poverty and anonymity."[3]

More recently, Stephan Thernstrom has brought significant and orig-[3] inal insight to the patterns of social mobility in mid-nineteenth-century industrializing America. *Poverty and Progress: Social Mobility in a Nineteenth Century City* breaks with older studies of social mobility by focusing in close detail on one community: it treats the career patterns of nearly three hundred unskilled day laborers in Newburyport, Massachusetts, between 1850 and 1880.[4] Thernstrom finds among them a good deal of geographic mobility out of the city, but for those immigrant and native workers and their sons who remained, substantial material improvement ("property mobility" or the acquisition of personal and real estate) and occupational mobility (from unskilled to semiskilled and skilled work). Their most common form of social advancement was "upward mobility *within* the working class." Thernstrom finds no evidence of spectacular upward mobility: "In the substantial sample of workers and their sons studied for the 1850–1880 period not a single instance of mobility into the ranks of management or even into a foremanship position was discovered." Many workers and their sons improved in these thirty years, some even as small shopkeepers and white-collar workers. But not one met the test of the rags-to-riches ideology. "Few of these men and few of their children," Thernstrom concludes, "rose very far on the social scale; most of the upward occupational shifts they made left them manual workers still, and their property mobility, though strikingly widespread, rarely involved the accumulation of anything approaching real wealth."

The findings of Thernstrom, Gregory and Neu, and Miller, among [4] others, are the work of serious scholars, careful in their methods, deep in their research, and modest in their conclusions. But there is question about the larger inferences to be drawn from these studies about the social origins of the industrial manufacturing class in the decades of prime American industrialization. Hundreds, even thousands, of successful manufacturers—often members of particular elites in their particular communities but rarely memorialized on the national level—did not meet the criteria for admission to the *Dictionary of American Biography* or the *National Cyclopedia of American Biography*. Gregory and Neu reveal in detail the social origins of "the industrial elite" of the 1870s, but draw heavily in their narrow sample on a well-developed industry (cotton textile manufacturing) and an industry that attracted as its leaders lawyers, merchants, and financiers (the railroads). Thernstrom tells much that is new and significant about the life style and aspirations of mid-nineteenth-century workers, but Newburyport had developed as a manufacturing city before 1850; and although the composition of its population changed between 1855 and 1880, the city underwent little development in the years studied.

What of the manufacturers who founded new firms that involved   5 small outlays of capital at the start? What of the workers, skilled as well as unskilled, who lived in rapidly expanding cities? In these pages, we shall examine a select group of successful local manufacturers in one such city—the locomotive, machinery, tool, and iron manufacturers of Paterson, New Jersey, between 1830 and 1880. Were they as a group a lesser mirror image of the archetypal° industrialist described by Gregory and Neu? If there were workers among them, were they unusual and atypical? Information is available only on their occupational careers and their places of birth, but it is sufficient to test the reality of the promise of rags to riches in one important industrial city. . . .

Although the Paterson iron and machine industries have not yet found   6 their historian, a quick glance suggests their importance to the city's development and even to the national economy. In the mid-1850s, Paterson had four locomotive factories: Rogers, Ketchum & Grosvenor (probably the second largest such factory in the country, outdistanced only by the Philadelphia Baldwin Locomotive Works); the New Jersey Locomotive and Machine Company; the Danforth Locomotive and Machine Works; and William Swinburne's Locomotive Works. Swinburne's enterprise failed in 1857–58, but the three that survived had an annual capacity of 135 locomotives in 1859. Eighteen years later, their combined capacity had risen to 554, sixty-four more than the Baldwin Works. In 1837–38, Rogers, Ketchum & Grosvenor (renamed the Rogers Locomotive Works in 1858 after Rogers' death) completed its first five locomotives. In the great burst of railroad construction between 1869 and 1873, the factories filled orders for no less than 1,683 locomotives. Overall, between 1837 and 1879, Paterson locomotive workers built 5,167 locomotives and contributed much to the "transportation revolution."

Archetypal—original model or pattern.

The growth of the Paterson iron, tool, and machinery manufacturers 7 may have been less spectacular than the locomotive manufacture but was just as substantial in different ways. Textile machinery and tools formed an important part of the local manufactured product. The market for Paterson firms after 1850 reached across the continent and even stretched around the globe. The J. C. Todd Machine Works (later Todd & Rafferty) marketed its hemp and twine machinery as far away as England and even in Russia, Latin America, and Asia in the late 1850s. After 1857, the Paterson Iron Works, which specialized in rolling large bars of iron, built heavy forgings used by transoceanic steamships and even sent iron shafts across the continent on order to the Pacific Mail Steamship Company. The Watson Manufacturing Company exported its millwright work and machinery to Mexico and South America, and gained wide attention for its turbine wheels and Corliss steam engines. The huge bevel wheels° it constructed helped make the Higgins Carpet Factory one of New York City's great manufacturing establishments. The manufacture of structural iron later allowed the Watson firm to contract to build iron bridges in and near New York City, and its finished iron found place in the city's Museum of Natural History, Metropolitan Museum of Art, Equitable Building, and Lenox Library. In the 1870s and 1880s, the Passaic Rolling Mill also found important customers in the great metropolis nearby: the iron beams that built New York's first elevated trains came from it as did the iron for such projects as the Harlem River bridge, the *New York Post* building, and the massive Seventh Regiment Armory. Finished iron from the Passaic Rolling Mill also helped build the new state capitol in Albany, a widely acclaimed drawbridge over the Mississippi River at St. Paul, an elevated cable car in Hoboken, and the 1876 Centennial Exposition buildings in Philadelphia. These examples are cited merely to illustrate the importance of the Paterson locomotive, iron, and machine factories in the development of industry and transportation and in the building of Victorian American cities.

What were the social origins and career patterns of the men who 8 founded and developed these particular firms between 1830 and 1880? These men or their firms persevered in the turbulent early decades of industrialization. In 1880, some of the pioneer manufacturers were dead, others at the height of their careers, and a few still relatively new to enterprise. Many had failed in comparison to the number that succeeded. Although the printed sources tell little about those who started unsuccessful manufacturing enterprises, there is no reason to doubt that these men differed in social origin from their more favored contemporaries. For the group that succeeded, useful biographical information has been found for nearly all of them. What follows therefore is *not a sample* but

---

Bevel wheels—gear wheels with the gear teeth cut at an angle.

a description of the social origins of the most successful Paterson iron, locomotive, and machinery manufacturers.[5]

Scientific American, groping for a simple sociological generalization   9 about these men, praised Paterson's early enterprisers in these words: "In the eastern States [New England], flourishing cities have been built up by corporations of wealthy capitalists. . . . In Paterson, it was different. With few exceptions, almost every manufacturer started, financially, at zero, enlarging his establishment as the quicksilver expanded in his purse." *Scientific American* was not guilty of mouthing abstract rhetoric or just putting forth a paean° of traditional tribute to an invisible hero, the "self-made man." Instead, it accurately described the successful locomotive, iron, and machinery manufacturers of the era, and what it wrote applied as well to the group in 1840 and 1880 as in 1859.

One Paterson manufacturer started as a clerk. A second, the son of a   10 farmer, made his way first in railroad construction before turning to iron manufacture. Two others had fathers who were manufacturers. George Van Riper took over a bobbin-pin factory in 1866 that had been started by his grandfather in 1795 as a small shop and then run by his father for thirty-five years. Patrick Maguinnis was the son of an Irish cotton manufacturer who left Dublin after the failure of revolutionary anti-British agitation and manufactured cotton and velveteen first in Baltimore and then in Hudson, New York.

But the social origin of these four manufacturers was not characteristic   11 of the thirty-odd men studied. The typical successful Paterson manufacturer arrived in the city as a skilled ironworker or a skilled craftsman or as a young man who learned his skill by apprenticing in a Paterson machinery works. Individual proprietorship or copartnership allowed him to escape from dependence and start his own firm. Only a small number of Paterson apprentices became manufacturers between 1830 and 1880, but most successful Paterson iron, machinery, and locomotive manufacturers started their careers as workers, apprenticed to learn a skill, and then opened small shops or factories of their own.

With only a few important exceptions, the men who were either   12 Paterson-born or migrants to Paterson before 1830 played an insignificant role in the subsequent development of these industries. In 1825, the Rev. Dr. Samuel Fischer counted seventy-seven ironworkers in eleven blacksmith shops, two millwright shops, and a single iron foundry. Some repaired and built textile machinery. Trumbull lists at least ten machine shops that lasted only a few years. Biographical information is lacking for the men who started these faulted firms, but information is available for four men who pioneered in the development of the Paterson machinery and locomotive industries: John Clark, his son John Clark, Jr., Thomas Rogers, and Charles Danforth. Not one was native to the

---

Paean—an expression of joy and praise.

city. John Clark, Sr., settled there first. Born in Paisley, Scotland, the elder Clark, then aged twenty-one, migrated to Paterson in 1794 with his wife and two children to build machinery for the S. E. U. M. After the society failed, Clark, first with his partner and then alone, used a portion of the idle mill to manufacture textile machinery. One son, John, Jr., followed in his footsteps, and in the early 1820s took two partners, Abram Godwin (a local resident, Godwin's father had served on George Washington's military staff) and Thomas Rogers. A hotel and storekeeper and the father of Parke Godwin, noted later as a journalist and as editor of the *New York Evening Post,* Abram Godwin supplied Clark with capital. Rogers' contribution was of another order.

Born in 1792 in Groton, Connecticut, and, according to Trumbull, *13* descended from a Mayflower Pilgrim, Thomas Rogers apprenticed himself at the age of sixteen to a Connecticut house carpenter. He settled in Paterson as a journeyman house carpenter and built several dwelling houses before a cotton-duck manufacturer hired him to construct wooden loom patterns. Soon Rogers was building wooden looms for John Clark, Sr. After the elder Clark retired, Rogers joined with Godwin and young Clark to expand the firm. The three partners bought an empty cotton mill, purchased a small foundry and a molding shop, and managed, for the first time in Paterson, a machine shop with all branches of the trade under "one roof." The partners prospered in the 1820s, but in 1831 Rogers left the firm to start his own machine works, the Jefferson Works, and to spin cotton yarn. Rogers' early triumphs as a machine builder attracted the attention of Morris Ketchum and Jasper Grosvenor, two New York City merchant capitalists and financiers active as railroad developers. A partnership was founded, called Rogers, Ketchum & Grosvenor. A house carpenter turned skilled machinist and then machine manufacturer thus had as business associates two men whom *Scientific American* called "men of abundant means and decided financial ability."

Charles Danforth replaced Rogers in the machine works of Clark and *14* Godwin. The evidence concerning Danforth's background is unclear. Trumbull records that his father was a Norton, Massachusetts, "cotton manufacturer," but a more detailed biographical sketch in *The History of Bergen and Passaic Counties* notes that Danforth's father was "engaged in agricultural pursuits" and that in 1811, then fourteen, Danforth worked as a throstle-piercer before engaging as an ordinary seaman. After the War of 1812, he taught school near Rochester, New York, and in 1824 superintended a cotton carding room in a Matteawan, New York, factory. Hired to help set up a new cotton mill in Hohokus, New Jersey, he invented an improved spinning frame and settled in Paterson in 1828 to manufacture it as a partner with Godwin and Clark. Financial troubles in the late 1830s caused the dissolution of the partnership, and in 1840 Danforth bought out the entire machine-shop interest and in 1848 formed Charles Danforth and Company. His partner was John Edwards, his foreman. Born in England, Edwards moved to Paterson as a young man and worked in a hotel; he later apprenticed to John Clark and became his foreman, keeping the same supervisory position under Rogers and Danforth. Danforth so valued Edwards' abilities that he gave him a one-tenth interest in the firm.

The career of another workman, William Swinburne, illustrates this 15 same mobility through the possession of technological skills. . . .

As a group, the developers of the Paterson locomotive industry, 16 except for Ketchum and Grosvenor (and they lived in New York City), experienced enormous occupational mobility in their lives. In one generation—often in a few years—men jumped class lines and rose rapidly in prestige and status. One can argue about Danforth, but Prall had been an orphan and a clerk as a boy, and the others—Clark, Rogers, Swinburne, Watts Cooke, Sr., his sons William, John, and Watts, Jr.—had all started in life as skilled artisans and risen to become factory foreman or superintendents and owners of large, new manufacturing enterprises. The triumphs of these men were only part of the Paterson story. Their locomotive factories became workshops that trained machinists and other skilled ironworkers. Most did not all stay within the firm. They struck out on their own as small manufacturers to be swept up and tested by the surge of industrial development after 1843. A few became manufacturers of great wealth; most succeeded in a more modest fashion. All were closely identified with the development of Paterson's iron and machinery and tool industries between 1843 and 1880—a process shaped by the efforts of self-made men entirely different in social origin from the archetypal members of Gregory and Neu's "industrial elite" in the 1870s. None came from professional, mercantile,° or manufacturing backgrounds. Only one was born in New England, and almost all of them were British immigrants. These were not "princes" prepared by training and education to become "kings" of industry. Instead, they rose from the lower classes and achieved substantial material rewards in their lifetimes. For those of their contemporaries who sought "proof" about the promise of rags to riches, these men served as model, day-to-day evidence.

Paterson's two most successful machinery works were started by 17 apprentice machinists, one who labored as a child in a cotton factory and the other who grew up on a farm and worked first as a carpenter. William Watson and Joseph Todd learned their machinist skills in the Paterson machine and locomotive shops. . . . *[A series of detailed biographies of machine manufacturers follows and then a similar presentation of iron manufacturers.]*

Much remains to be written about the Paterson iron, locomotive, and 18 machinery manufacturers who started in life as workers, but their social status, their political role (many held public office), and their labor policies cannot be briefly summarized.[6] What matters for purposes of

---

Mercantile—merchant or trade.

this study is the fact that the rags-to-riches promise was not a mere myth in Paterson, New Jersey, between 1830 and 1880. So many successful manufacturers who had begun as workers walked the streets of that city then that it is not hard to believe that others less successful or just starting out on the lower rungs of the occupational mobility ladder could be convinced by personal knowledge that "hard work" resulted in spectacular material and social improvement. Thernstrom has argued convincingly that small improvements in material circumstances counted for much in explaining the social stability of Newburyport between 1850 and 1880. What role did the frequent examples of spectacular upward mobility in developing industrial Paterson play vis-à-vis its social structure? Whether the social origin of the Paterson manufacturers was typical of other manufacturers of that era cannot yet be known, but their career pattern was quite different from the one uncovered by other students of the nineteenth-century American "business elite."

Detailed research, however, has not yet been done on the manufac- [19] turers of other new industrial cities such as Buffalo, Pittsburgh, Cincinnati, and Chicago. Developing industrial cities and new manufacturing industries offered unusual opportunities to skilled craftsmen and mechanics in the early phases of American industrialization. Such was the case in Paterson, and surely such opportunities existed in other cities. Who took advantage of such opportunities, however, is still a subject for careful inquiry. The detailed examination of other local industrial "elites" will make it possible to learn whether the Paterson manufacturers were a mutant group or mere examples of a pattern of occupational mobility common to early industrializing America. Whatever the final findings, such community-oriented studies will shed unusually important light on one of the many dark corners of the mid-nineteenth-century American economic and social structure.

Notes

[1] William Miller, "American Historians and the Business Elite," in William Miller, ed., *Men in Business. Essays on the Historical Role of the Entrepreneur* (New York, 1962), pp. 309–28.

[2] Frances W. Gregory and Irene D. Neu, "The American Industrial Elite in the 1870's: Their Social Origins," in Miller, *Men in Business*, pp. 193–211.

[3] See Miller, ed., *Men in Business*, p. 149.

[4] Stephan Thernstrom, *Poverty and Progress: Social Mobility in a Nineteenth Century City* (Cambridge, 1964), passim but especially pp. 114, 161–65, 213, 223.

[5] Several sources supply the salient data, but the most important is L. R. Trumbull, *A History of Industrial Paterson, Being a Compendium of the Establishment, Growth, and Present Status in Paterson, N.J.., of the Silk, Cotton, Flax, Locomotive, Iron and Miscellaneous Industries; Together with Outlines of State, County and Local History, Corporate Records, Biographical Sketches, Incidents of Manufacture, Interesting Facts and Valuable Statistics.* Published in Paterson in 1882, the Trumbull volume is just what its title suggests: an ill-digested but rich and invaluable collection of local firm histories interspersed with

biographical accounts of early Paterson industrialists. Supplementary biographical information is found in Charles Shriner, *Paterson, New Jersey. Its Advantages for Manufacturing and Residence: Its Industries, Prominent Men, Banks, Schools, Churches, etc., Published Under the Auspices of the [Paterson] Board of Trade* (Paterson, 1890); Edward B. Haines, ed., *Paterson, New Jersey, 1792–1892. [The] Centennial Edition of the Paterson Evening News* (Paterson, 1892); William Nelson and Charles Shriner, *History of Paterson and Its Environs. The Silk City* (New York and Chicago, 1920). These books share a common weakness in celebrating uncritically the triumphs of local enterprise, but it is unwise to dismiss them as no more than primitive public relations works. Buried among adjectives of pious praise are rich morsels of data that tell much about these local "heroes" and their firms. Additional information has been culled from Paterson city directories published in 1859, 1871–72, and 1880–81, and from a detailed survey of Paterson manufacturers that appeared in the first volume of *Scientific American* in 1859 under the dates October 29 and November 5, 12, and 19.

[6]Some evidence of the social and political role played by the Paterson manufacturers in the 1870s is found in H. G. Gutman, "Class, Status, and Community Power in Nineteenth-Century American Industrial Cities—Paterson, New Jersey: A Case Study," in Frederic C. Jaher, ed., *The Age of Industrialism in America: Essays in Social Structure and Cultural Values* (New York, 1968), pp. 263–87.

Rhetorical Analysis Through Annotation

Although Gutman presents many details about Paterson's industries and industrialists, these details are always related to argumentative points he is making.

Identify passages of historical details by drawing lines down the margin next to such passages. Then underline the ideas or argumentative points being made or supported through the details.

Discuss how the detailed passages support or develop the points made by Gutman. What devices does he use to make sure you see the connection between ideas and details? What connections are left only implicit? What overall impression or effect does Gutman achieve by this combination of historical detail and general points?

Discussion Questions

Interpreting the Text

1. Compare the summary of Thernstrom's book with the excerpt you have read. What points made by Thernstrom does Gutman emphasize and what does Gutman minimize or overlook? Given Gutman's overall line of argument, why does he summarize as he does? Although you have not read the other historians he summarizes, can you identify themes that Gutman emphasizes and how these themes relate to his argument?

2. In what particular ways does Gutman's study differ in design from the previous studies summarized? What clues in the discussion of the summaries and the lead-in to the new study help make you aware of those differences?

3. What sources does Gutman use to find out about Paterson industrialists? Where are these sources identified? What does Gutman say about these sources and why? What types of information are such sources likely to reveal? What are the advantages and disadvantages of such sources?

4. What conclusions about mobility of Paterson industrialists does Gutman draw? What evidence does he have for the conclusions?

Considering the Issues

5. How do Gutman's conclusions vary from Thernstrom's and from the conclusions of the other writers that were summarized? What implications for our view of American society do these differences have?

6. Why does Gutman suggest that further study is needed? Why does he suggest the particular lines for study that he does? What distinguishes the particular cities he pinpoints for further study?

Writing Suggestions

1. Imagine you are taking a course in American urban history and are assigned Gutman's article to read. Prepare a two hundred word summary of the article for your study group.

2. Are the kinds of opportunities that were available to the men described by Gutman available to enterprising people today? Has the age of opportunity passed, or have the opportunities changed? Write an essay on this subject to share your views about your future with your classmates in this course.

3. For your local historical society's newsletter, research and write a short essay about the background and career of one of the important people in the economic development of your town or city.

4. Imagine you are producing a series of half-hour shows for educational TV on the "Makers of Industrial America." Prepare an outline of your plan for an episode about any one or two of the Paterson industrialists described here. Indicate the scenes and visuals you will use. Alternatively, imagine the series is fictionalized historical melodrama, called "The Money Merchants," and prepare an appropriate story outline.

The Golden Door: Italian and Jewish Immigrant Mobility in New York City, 1880–1915

Thomas Kessner

As the picture of mobility in different cities and among different classes was filled in, questions arose about how different groups fared, particularly immigrant groups. Immigrants, drawn to a new country by a desire to improve their lives, seemed to share an especially deep belief in the rags-to-riches vision of America. Social mobility for immigrant groups meant joining the American mainstream, making a new home. Historians, now attuned to the issues of mobility, wanted indeed to see if the streets were paved with gold for the different waves of immigrants who made America their home. In a sense the historians began examining whether the middle-class, melting-pot vision of America was really working.

In 1977 Thomas Kessner of City University of New York published the most impressive of the immigrant studies, a comparison of Italian and Jewish immigrant mobility in New York City at the turn of the twentieth century. Although he found variation in how rapidly the mobility occurred, within a short period both groups seemed to move into the economic mainstream.

In a number of ways, Kessner's study is quite ambitious. In making a comparison between two groups, he, of course, doubles his research, and in picking New York as his research site he takes on not only the nation's largest city, but also the center of twentieth-century immigration. The numbers of people Kessner had to study and make generalizations about far exceeded limited groups of workers or industrialists in small cities like Newburyport or Paterson. Moreover, Kessner combines the statistical studies based on census data, as used by Thernstrom, with the detailed historical narratives about the lives of individuals used by Gutman. The following passage from Kessner's book discusses the core issue, how long it took for poor immigrants to move into better paying occupations. Kessner's audience is intended to be fellow historians.

AT HEART, THE ISSUE of mobility concerns the effect of time on   1
occupational status; not time in general, for that becomes a simple query into the bearing of age on achievement, but rather "American time." This chapter focuses on the correlation° between occupational status and time spent in the United States. The central hypothesis is that in a mobile society longer exposure to its opportunities will result in gradually escalating° status.

The traditional approach has been to choose a sample of individuals   2
at one point in time and trace the group over a period of years, usually a decade, while holding a finger to its occupational pulse. This methodology presents formidable obstacles, however. The most important problem stems from the difficulty of tracing individuals. Too many subjects are lost sight of along the way and sometimes this wreaks havoc

---

Correlation—connection.   Escalating—increasing.

on the sample's credibility. Nevertheless, the trace method remains important and necessary in the study of mobility.[1]

Fortunately it is possible in the present study to supplement the con- *3* ventional methodology with another approach. For every individual that it listed, the New York State Census provided information on both occupation and length of residence in the United States, permitting us to explore the connection between American time and occupation level, the nub of the mobility issue. Thus in this chapter two methods of mobility analysis are applied to the census data, first the more general probing of the relationship between economic status and years in the United States, and then the tracing of individual immigrants over time.

A sample drawn from the 1905 Census was divided into four co- *4* horts°—0–6 years, 7–14 years, 15–25 years, and 26 years or more— representing length of residence in the United States. The resulting distribution for New York Italians is presented in Table 1, and points to a certain ambivalence° in their patterns of progress. Two status levels, low white-collar and skilled blue-collar, were quite active, one waxing and the other waning in direct relation to American time. But the other three strata were far more sluggish, maintaining a regular percentage of the total, regardless of length of residence.[2]

Whether he had been in the country for two, three or twenty-five *5* years, the likelihood that an Italian immigrant would land in the upper white-collar category did not exceed 2 per cent. Disdain for education and the large proportion originally anchored to unskilled jobs made it

	1–6 Years	7–14 Years	15–25 Years	26 to 99 Years	Total
I	.5	1.9	1.9	13.5	1.5
II	8.1	14.3	21.6	25.0	13.1
III	29.5	27.4	18.9	11.5	26.2
IV	20.0	20.4	21.4	11.5	20.0
V	42.0	35.9	38.3	38.5	39.2
Sample Size	881	565	378	52	1,876
Per Cent of Total Sample	47.0	30.1	20.1	2.8	100

Table 1.   Occupational distribution for New York City Italians by length of residence in the United States.

Table Key: I — Upper white collar   IV — Semiskilled
II — Lower white collar   V — Unskilled
III — Skilled blue collar

Source: Sample Data from New York State Census for 1905.

Cohorts—age groups.   Ambivalence—having conflicting impulses.

unlikely that even after 25 years a significant number of Italians could soar to the highest occupational levels.

Only in the last grouping, composed of Italians who had lived in the *6* United States over 26 years, did the upper white-collar fragment climb sharply. Indeed, this entire cohort differed markedly from the three others. The anomaly stems from the fact that these Italians, who arrived in the country before 1879, were mostly from the more advanced northern part of the kingdom. Northerners coming to the United States brought along more money, were more literate, and included more professionals than the later-arriving southerners. Hence their occupational history differed from the stolid pattern of their southern compatriots.[3]

The one occupation stratum showing consistent time-related expansion *7* was the lower white-collar grouping. It grew from 8 per cent of those in the United States less than six years, to 22 per cent of the 15–25 cohort, and 25 per cent of the northern-dominated old-timers who settled before 1879. A close analysis of this class's progress reveals the sector responsible for this headway. While office and sales-related occupations did not increase in step with the American-time variable, and peddling did so only slightly, the number of blue-collar Italians crossing into white-collar retailing neatly correlated with length of residence.

The Italian built his progress slowly. He saved his blue-collar earnings *8* until he could invest them in a store and then worked for the best. Such shorter routes to the white collar as the professions and office work were closed to him. His way of moving up was by a hand-over-hand climb out of manual labor into a grocery store, a barber shop, or a saloon. "For we must remember," noted a contemporary commentator on the Italian condition, "that many general laborers, miners, and others are tempted to enter 'bisinesse,' and that they can do so by learning fifty words of English and buying a fruit stand. . . . In New York many men have begun with a pushcart, then got the privilege of a stand, then a concession to sell garden produce . . . and finally have set up a shop of their own." Of the 22 per cent of the 15–25 cohort who achieved lower white-collar status, all but 5 per cent did so as shopkeepers.[4]

In sketching a design for immigrant advancement one might outline *9* a neat process of mobility where classes move up step by step, over time. As length of residence rises, concentrations increase at the higher echelons° with corresponding decreases at the lower levels. Ideally the bottom class would deplete itself first, then the next lowest and on. As Table 1 demonstrates, this was not true of New York Italians. The only blue-collar "feeder" class that declined in rhythm with upper-class increase was the skilled category. Levels four and five show no appreciable decline over the first three age brackets (the over 26 group which

---

Echelons—levels.

accounted for less than 3 per cent of the total again offers an exception; its semiskilled class was considerably smaller than either of the previous cohorts).

To account for this we must turn back to the historical particulars of 10 the Italian experience in New York. Until after the 1890s Italians had not yet penetrated most skilled trades. Those who arrived earlier, therefore, primarily settled into unskilled and semiskilled occupations. When skilled jobs did become available, longer settled Italians had no special advantage in landing these jobs. And if they were already employed they generally stuck to familiar patterns. Therefore, newly arrived Italians often found it possible to be trained into skilled jobs, with little competition from their longer tenured compatriots. Consequently the lower blue-collar classes did not feed the skilled class.

One example that illustrates this point is the larger number of barbers 11 among earlier settlers. Apparently later immigrants found a wider range of options and avoided this occupation, but those who had landed earlier and taken to barbering originally did not choose to give it up and move into another field which might rate higher status on some objective scale of occupations.

Moreover, the persistent significance of the large unskilled class across 12 all cohorts is a very significant factor in Italian sluggishness. All laborers, skilled and less skilled alike, had problems making ends meet, witness the numerous descriptions of working-class poverty in this era. But no group had it harder than the unskilled laborer. Not only was his type plentiful, but he compounded his weakness by being illiterate and an easy mark for preying bosses and middlemen. Thus he had to rely on a working wife and children to make ends meet, especially, as often happened, when he was out of work. It was seldom possible for such a laborer to string together a sufficient number of work days to save money and invest it in a business.[5]

Patterns of Jewish progress over American time contrast with the 13 Italian experience, as Table 2 shows. The changes are far more dramatic and activity is apparent on a wider scale, affecting four of the five classes. Only the unskilled class languished as if it bore no relation to the issue, which is precisely the case.

Jewish expansion in both upper and lower white-collar classes corre- 14 lates neatly with the amount of time spent in the United States. The upper class increased by a steady increment of 5 or 6 per cent in passing from cohort to cohort, starting as 4 per cent of the most recent settlers and finally swelling to 21 per cent of the longest-resident group.

Jews produced a larger professional class than did the Italians. With 15 the passage of time in America, Jewish attorneys, physicians, and teachers proliferated, as they translated this time into schooling and professional training. The major thrust for upper white-collar expansion, however, came from rapid strides in upper-level enterprise, as Jews moved into garment manufacture, real estate, and the building industry.[6]

	1–6 Years	7–14 Years	15–25 Years	26 to 99 Years	Total
I	4.0	10.7	14.8	21.4	8.9
II	15.2	32.1	39.5	46.4	26.8
III	46.7	31.5	29.1	17.9	37.3
IV	32.6	24.1	15.3	10.7	25.4
V	1.5	1.6	1.2	3.6	1.5
Sample Size	854	619	481	28	1,982
Per Cent of Total Sample	43.1	31.2	24.3	1.4	100

Table 2. Occupational distribution for New York City Russian Jews by length of residence in the United States.
Source: Sample Data from New York State Census for 1905.

The low white-collar series exhibited even greater growth. The role **16** played by this class doubled to 30 per cent in going from the first cohort to the second. Of the recent settlers in such positions most worked as peddlers and shopkeepers, with a smaller number in sales and clerical work. But peddling declined sharply over the four groupings, while sales and clerical work increased slightly. Retailing was the major factor in lower white-collar growth, which eventually amounted to 46 per cent after 26 years. As with the Italians, such enterprise served as the mainspring for rapid white-collar progress. The Industrial Commission commented on this:

> Economic advancement comes to . . . poverty stricken Hebrews with surprising rapidity. There is no way of telling definitely what proportion of the very poor eventually rise out of that condition, or how long it takes for them to do so. General observation, however, seems to indicate that the proportion is considerable and the rate rapid.[7]

Italian mobility was confined to an interplay of only two neighboring **17** status levels and therefore limited in range. Jewish mobility proved broader because it involved all four of the occupational levels. Both skilled and semiskilled sectors declined as the two upper divisions expanded. Of the most recent settlers, 47 per cent were skilled laborers. For the next cohort, skilled labor decreased in concentration to 32 per cent *at the same time* that semiskilled labor decreased from 33 to 24 per cent. "Every year," observed one scholar, "large numbers [of Jews] desert the clothing industry to go into such occupations as small shopkeepers, insurance agents and clerks." Jewish tailors often found themselves replaced by other nationalities, but this seldom provided cause for despair, as they moved up to contracting or manufacturing and small business.[8]

Both New Immigrant groups redeemed the American promise of *18* mobility. Progress *was* a function of time. But it was also a function of ethnicity. Jews experienced more progress than Italians. It was not that Jews came with more money, or even that they saved more money— both groups were thrifty—but rather that the "middlemen of Europe" brought more entrepreneurial savvy° and "middle class" values. More- over, they did not suffer the sharp braking force of stagnant low-skill sectors which held back Italian progress. . . . [*A second analysis based on career tracing leads to similar conclusions.*]

Whatever method is used to measure mobility there is convincing *19* proof that America's promise was fulfilled in the dynamic immigrant city. As a 1920 study of New York business leaders concluded: "Very few of New York's optimistic philanthropists°, much less the landlords, saw in the procession of prospective Italian citizens the many prosperous merchants, mechanics, professional men and bankers who now consti- tute so important a part of the City's life."[9]

One such success story was written by Giuseppe Tuoti, who opened *20* a real estate office on Grand Street in 1885. Within the decade the number of Italians owning real estate went from fewer than 100 to 3,000, while leaseholders increased from 50 to 1,000, and Mr. Tuoti's activities in housing properties expanded and prospered. In 1887, he formed a com- pany to develop the town of Woodridge in New Jersey, which provided suburban housing for his slum-dwelling countrymen. Soon thereafter he turned to colonization operations in other New Jersey areas, on Staten Island, and on Coney Island. He also helped erect modern tenements in the Bronx. In 1906, in recognition of his exhibit at the Milan Exposition which portrayed the progress of Italians in New York from 1885 on, Tuoti received a commendation from the Italian Government. By 1924, "million dollar transfers of property . . . [were] daily occurrences," for this leading realtor.[10]

Over a short span of time many Italians found economic success. *21* "The tradespeople prosper rapidly," concluded a 1902 report on New York's Italians. "The Italian barber enlarges his shop, perhaps sells out, becomes a banker; the fruit peddler expands and may eventually become an importer." Having escaped the static world of absentee-owned *lati- fundia*° where years followed each other in regular patterns of peasant poverty, Italians took advantage of a New World economy where pat- terns were far more dynamic and progessive.[11]

Jews made their move into business earlier than the Italians and as a *22* result attained higher concentrations in the white-collar sector. To suc- ceed they had to cut prices and costs, introduce new techniques and machinery. This helped them take control of the clothing business, and

---

Savvy—practical skill, cleverness.   **Philanthropists**—charity-givers.   *Latifundia*—large landed estates.

as the case of Isaac Goldman illustrates, it was put to use in other areas as well.

In 1876 Isaac Goldman was discharged from his position as a com-   23 positor in a printing shop. Opening a two-man printing shop on William Street, he experimented with the latest machinery. By 1888 the shop had moved three times, each time to larger and more modern quarters. In 1895 the Goldman Company boasted the first linotype° machines in New York. Each of these machines could turn out more work in one day than four experienced printers. Goldman did not allow himself to rest on these innovations or settle for a stable business. In 1905 he sold all of his machinery, moved to a new factory, and installed new equip- ment, a process he repeated a decade later. By this time, Goldman's press was producing highly profitable business catalogues and a long list of periodicals.[12]

Notes

[1]For a discussion of some problems that mobility researchers encounter, and the liberties one such scholar took, see Stephan Thernstrom, *The Other Bostonians* (Cambridge, 1973), 46, 265–88.

[2]Of New York's gainfully employed Italians in 1905, over 47 per cent lived in the country less than six years and only 3 per cent were in America before 1879, reinforcing the earlier point that the status of Italians in 1905 tells us little about the progress of the 1880 colony.

[3]The professional fragment alone in the 26–99 cohort accounted for 6 per cent. Among the other cohorts the proportion of professionals never exceeded .9 per cent. Aside from the data in Table 1, this much-noted difference can be studied in the figures presented by the Immig. Comm., *Reports*, I–II, passim.

[4]Robert Foerster, *Italian Emigration of Our Times*, 338; Indust. Comm., XV, 474.

[5]On the laboring class see Robert Coit Chapin, *The Standard of Living Among Workingmen's Families in New York City* (New York, 1909); Eli Ginsberg and Hyman Berman, eds., *The American Worker in the Twentieth Century* (New York, 1963); Clarence D. Long, *Wages and Earnings in the United States: 1850–1890* (Princeton, 1960); United States Industrial Commission, *Reports* (19 vols., Washington, 1901–2); United States Senate, *Report on the Relations Between Capital and Labor* (4 vols., Washington, 1885); Robert H. Bremner, *From the Depths: The Discovery of Poverty in the United States* (New York, 1956); John A. Garraty, *The New Commonwealth: 1877–1890* (New York, 1968), 128–78; John A. Garraty, ed., *Capital and Labor in the Gilded Age* (Boston, 1968); Walter E. Weyl, "The Italian Who Lived on 26¢ a Day," *Outlook*, XCIII (Dec. 1909), 966–75.

[6]Both Samuel P. Abelow, *History of Brooklyn Jewry* (Brooklyn, 1937), and Alter F. Landesman, *Brownsville: The Birth, Development and Passing of a Jewish Community in New York* (New York, 1969), devote considerable space to the Jewish building industry. See also Abraham Schepper, "The Jew as Builder and Landlord," *The Jewish Forum*, I (June 1918), 272–77.

[7]Indust. Comm., XV, 477.

Linotype—a typesetting machine invented in the late nineteenth century.

[8]Jesse Pope, *The Clothing Industry*, 106.
[9]William Thompson Bonner, *New York, The World's Metropolis* (New York, 1924), 380.
[10]*Ibid.*
[11]Indust. Comm., XV, 474.
[12]Bonner, *New York, The World's Metropolis*, 601.

Rhetorical Analysis Through Annotation

The first part of this excerpt is organized around the two statistical tables presented in it.

Underline each direct reference to the tables or data contained in them. Circle each indirect reference, elaborating ideas developed from the table. In the margin, note which table is referred to, and how the direct or indirect reference is related to the table.

Discuss how Kessner structures his discussion around these tables. Also consider how the last section containing success stories relates to the data tables.

Discussion Questions

Interpreting the Text

1. Compare the two statistical methods discussed by Kessner: tracing career paths and correlating economic status with time in America. How is each done? What is the difference between the two? What are the advantages and disadvantages of each? Why does Kessner carry out both methods in his book? How and why does he supplement the two with traditional historical narratives in this selection?

2. Look carefully at the two tables in the article. First, determine what the numbers mean. Next, describe what occupational distribution patterns you find among recent immigrants of each group. Do the patterns change with time and how? Which categories change the most and where is there most stability? Then see how the mobility patterns of the two groups compare. Finally, compare your conclusions based on the examination of the tables with Kessner's conclusions stated in the body of the text.

3. What are Kessner's overall conclusions about mobility of Italian and Jewish immigrants? What similarities and differences appeared in the mobility patterns of the two groups?

Considering the Issues

4. How do Kessner's conclusions fit in with your previous knowledge and beliefs about immigrant groups? How do the mobility patterns presented here compare with your impression of the mobility patterns of more recent immigrant groups such as those from Latin America and Asia?

5. By now most members of the two groups Kessner has studied have been in the United States for over fifty years. To what degree do you believe they remain economically separate groups, with different paths for mobility? Or do

you feel members of these groups have merged into an economic mainstream and share a style of economic advancement?

6. Some people may object to the kind of ethnic comparisons made in this selection because these comparisons may make some groups seem less successful and reinforce ethnic stereotypes. Do you think this selection does either? If so, what unfavorable comparisons and unfair stereotypes do you find? If not, how does Kessner avoid these effects? Do you think worries over stereotyping should lead researchers to avoid such investigations?

Writing Suggestions

1. Using Kessner's data and views, write a short essay for a contemporary American history class on what role ethnicity plays in mobility in contemporary American life. You may also add your own impressions of the mobility of ethnic groups not discussed by Kessner.

2. Kessner suggests that Jews and Italians moved into different industries and occupations. In your experience and observations of contemporary American life, do you find that particular industries and occupations still often have a disproportionate number of workers from one or another ethnic group? You may base your discussion on one or two occupations or industries that you are familiar with. Discuss why the pattern of ethnic separation or mixing that you notice has emerged. The essay is for a sociology class.

3. For the feature page of a local newspaper write a human interest story about how a recent immigrant family you know of has been making its way in the American economy.

4. For a magazine or newsletter of political commentary, write an article describing how discrimination held back a particular group's advancement or how discrimination did not provide an overwhelming obstacle. Use this discussion in support of a position for or against affirmative action by employers.

5. Using information, examples, or ideas from this selection, write the script for a sixty-second "Liberty Moment" for television. Include ideas for the visual part of the presentation.

The Negro Family: The Case for National Action

Daniel Patrick Moynihan

Throughout history, people have been aware that some groups were better off than others, that economic success seemed to come more easily to some while others seemed to be stuck at the bottom of the economic ladder. But such observations are too easily ignored as "facts" of life that are beyond our control. The scholarly studies of mobility have made it clear that some groups have been seriously excluded and, moreover, that intelligible factors appear to have determined success of certain groups. As the problem of excluded groups became something that could be understood and dealt with, the problem was certainly no longer something that could be ignored. In particular, the long-standing problem of the inability of the majority of American blacks to join the economic mainstream troubled the nation's conscience. Even after the overt barriers of open discrimination were removed by the civil rights laws of the 1960s, only part of the black community seemed to be able to take advantage of any new opportunities.

In 1965, Daniel Patrick Moynihan, then assistant secretary of labor (now U.S. Senator from New York), proposed that the lack of mobility among blacks was due to problems in the black family structure caused by years of slavery, discrimination, and poverty. In the publicly distributed report, excerpted here, he argued that blacks could be brought into the mainstream of American life only if the government actively worked at rebuilding the black family. This report became the basis of a major speech by President Johnson and the rationale for a number of Great Society programs, which attempted to alleviate poverty and social inequality.

The report is a political document, and as such is filled with action-oriented, emotional language, and makes forceful arguments with boldly displayed statistics. However, the report draws its strength from the fact that it is based on a scholarly, historical argument. The simplified charts and statistics are drawn from the same sources used in the more academic essays in this unit. The essential analysis, moreover, rests on historical claims about what happened to blacks economically and socially. The excerpts here are from all sections of the report to give the reader a sense of the total argument.

THE FUNDAMENTAL PROBLEM HERE is that the Negro revo- *1* lution, like the industrial upheaval of the 1930's, is a movement for equality as well as for liberty. . . .

But by and large, the programs that have been enacted in the first *2* phase of the Negro revolution—Manpower Retraining, the Job Corps, Community Action, et al.—only make opportunities available. They cannot insure the outcome.

The principal challenge of the next phase of the Negro revolution is *3* to make certain that equality of results will now follow. If we do not, there will be no social peace in the United States for generations. . . .

There is a considerable body of evidence to support the conclusion that Negro *4* *social structure, in particular the Negro family, battered and harassed by discrimination, injustice, and uprooting, is in the deepest trouble. While many young Negroes are moving ahead to unprecedented levels of achievement, many more are falling further and further behind.*

The Negro American Family

At the heart of the deterioration of the fabric of Negro society is the 5
deterioration of the Negro family.

It is the fundamental source of the weakness of the Negro community 6
at the present time.

There is probably no single fact of Negro American life so little 7
understood by whites. The Negro situation is commonly perceived by
whites in terms of the visible manifestations of discrimination and poverty, in part because Negro protest is directed against such obstacles,
and in part, no doubt, because these are facts which involve the actions
and attitudes of the white community as well. It is more difficult,
however, for whites to perceive the effect that three centuries of exploitation have had on the fabric of Negro society itself. Here the
consequences of the historic injustices done to Negro Americans are
silent and hidden from view. But here is where the true injury has
occurred: unless this damage is repaired, all the effort to end discrimination and poverty and injustice will come to little.

The role of the family in shaping character and ability is so pervasive 8
as to be easily overlooked. The family is the basic social unit of American
life; it is the basic socializing unit. By and large, adult conduct in society
is learned as a child. . . .

The white family has achieved a high degree of stability and is main- 9
taining that stability.

By contrast, the family structure of lower class Negroes is highly 10
unstable, and in many urban centers is approaching complete breakdown.

N.b. There is considerable evidence that the Negro community is in 11
fact dividing between a stable middle-class group that is steadily growing
stronger and more successful, and an increasingly disorganized and disadvantaged lower-class group. There are indications, for example, that
the middle-class Negro family puts a higher premium on family stability
and the conserving of family resources than does the white middle-class
family. The discussion of this paper is not, obviously, directed to the
first group excepting as it is affected by the experiences of the second—
an important exception. . . .

*Nearly a Quarter of Urban Negro Marriages Are
Dissolved.*

Nearly a quarter of Negro women living in cities who have ever married 12
are divorced, separated, or are living apart from their husbands. . . .

	Urban		Rural nonfarm		Rural farm	
	Nonwhite	White	Nonwhite	White	Nonwhite	White
Total, husbands absent or divorced	22.9	7.9	14.7	5.7	9.6	3.0
Total, husbands absent	17.3	3.9	12.6	3.6	8.6	2.0
Separated	12.7	1.8	7.8	1.2	5.6	0.5
Husbands absent for other reasons	4.6	2.1	4.8	2.4	3.0	1.5
Total, divorced	5.6	4.0	2.1	2.1	1.0	1.0

Table 1.   Percent distribution of ever-married females with husbands absent or divorced, rural-urban, 1960.
Source: U.S. Census of Population, 1960, Nonwhite Population by Race, *PC (2) 1c, table 9, pp. 9–10.*

Nearly One-Quarter of Negro Births Are Now Illegitimate.

Both white and Negro illegitimacy rates have been increasing, although 13
from dramatically different bases. The white rate was 2 percent in 1940;
it was 3.07 percent in 1963. In that period, the Negro rate went from
16.8 percent to 23.6 percent. . . .

Almost One-Fourth of Negro Families Are Headed by Females.

As a direct result of this high rate of divorce, separation, and desertion, 14
a very large percent of Negro families are headed by females. While the
percentage of such families among whites has been dropping since 1940,
it has been rising among Negroes.
   The percent of nonwhite families headed by a female is more than 15
double the percent for whites. Fatherless nonwhite families increased by
a sixth between 1950 and 1960, but held constant for white families.
   It has been estimated that only a minority of Negro children reach 16
the age of 18 having lived all their lives with both their parents. . . .

The Breakdown of the Negro Family Has Led to a Startling Increase in Welfare Dependency.

The majority of Negro children receive public assistance under the 17
AFDC program at one point or another in their childhood.
   At present, 14 percent of Negro children are receiving AFDC° assis- 18
tance, as against 2 percent of white children. Eight percent of white

---

AFDC—Aid to Families with Dependent Children.

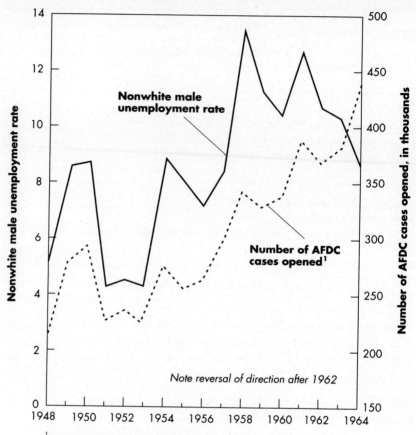

Figure 1 shows two curves. Left axis: "Nonwhite male unemployment rate" from 0 to 14. Right axis: "Number of AFDC cases opened, in thousands" from 150 to 500. X axis: years 1948 to 1964.

Labels on chart:
Nonwhite male unemployment rate
Number of AFDC cases opened[1]
Note reversal of direction after 1962

[1] Does not include cases opened under program which commenced in some states in 1961 of assistance to children whose fathers are present but unemployed.

Figure 1. Cases opened under AFDC compared with unemployed rate for nonwhite males.
Source: AFDC cases opened from HEW; nonwhite male unemployment rates from Department of Labor.

children receive such assistance at some time, as against 56 percent of nonwhites, according to an extrapolation based on HEW° data.

The Roots of the Problem

Slavery

American slavery was profoundly different from, and in its lasting effects on individuals and their children, indescribably worse than, any recorded   *19*

HEW—Health, Education, and Welfare (now Health and Human Services).

servitude, ancient or modern. The peculiar nature of American slavery was noted by Alexis de Tocqueville and others, but it was not until 1948 that Frank Tannenbaum, a South American specialist, pointed to the striking differences between Brazilian and American slavery. The feudal, Catholic society of Brazil had a legal and religious tradition which accorded the slave a place as a human being in the hierarchy of society— a luckless, miserable place, to be sure, but a place withal. In contrast, there was nothing in the tradition of English law or Protestant theology which could accommodate to the fact of human bondage—the slaves were therefore reduced to the status of chattels°—often, no doubt, well cared for, even privileged chattels, but chattels nevertheless. . . .

The Reconstruction

With the emancipation of the slaves, the Negro American family began *20* to form in the United States on a widespread scale. But it did so in an atmosphere markedly different from that which has produced the white American family.

The Negro was given liberty, but not equality. Life remained hazard- *21* ous and marginal. Of the greatest importance, the Negro male, particularly in the South, became an object of intense hostility, an attitude unquestionably based in some measure on fear.

When Jim Crow° made its appearance towards the end of the 19th *22* century, it may be speculated that it was the Negro male who was most humiliated thereby; the male was more likely to use public facilities, which rapidly became segregated once the process began, and just as important, segregation, and the submissiveness it exacts, is surely more destructive to the male than to the female personality. Keeping the Negro "in his place" can be translated as keeping the Negro male in his place: the female was not a threat to anyone.

Unquestionably, these events worked against the emergence of a *23* strong father figure. The very essence of the male animal, from the bantam rooster to the four-star general, is to strut. Indeed, in 19th century America, a particular type of exaggerated male boastfulness became almost a national style. Not for the Negro male. The "sassy nigger" was lynched. . . .

Urbanization

Country life and city life are profoundly different. The gradual shift of *24* American society from a rural to an urban basis over the past century and a half has caused abundant strains, many of which are still much in evidence. When this shift occurs suddenly, drastically, in one or two

---

Chattels—articles of personal property.   **Jim Crow**—the system of racial segregation against blacks.

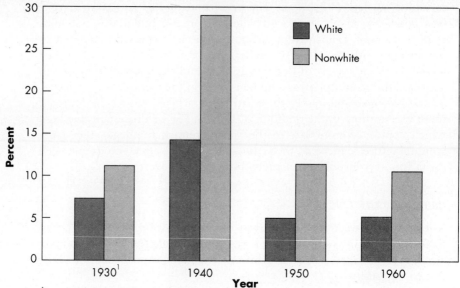

[1] Based on gainful worker concept. Includes persons 10 years of age and over.

Figure 2.   Unemployment among Negroes outside the South has persisted at catastrophic levels since the first statistics were gathered in 1930.
Source: Bureau of Labor Statistics, computed from decennial census of population.

generations, the effect is immensely disruptive of traditional social patterns. . . .

In every index of family pathology—divorce, separation, and deser-   *25* tion, female family head, children in broken homes, and illegitimacy— the contrast between the urban and rural environment for Negro families is unmistakable. . . .

Unemployment and Poverty

The fundamental, overwhelming fact is that *Negro unemployment*, with   *26* the exception of a few years during World War II and the Korean War, *has continued at disaster levels for 35 years.*

The Tangle of Pathology

In essence, the Negro community has been forced into a matriarchal   *27* structure which, because it is so out of line with the rest of the American society, seriously retards the progress of the group as a whole, and imposes a crushing burden on the Negro male and, in consequence, on a great many Negro women as well.

There is, presumably, no special reason why a society in which males   *28* are dominant in family relationships is to be preferred to a matriarchal arrangement. However, it is clearly a disadvantage for a minority group to be operating on one principle, while the great majority of the population, and the one with the most advantages to begin with, is operating on another. This is the present situation of the Negro. Ours is a society which presumes male leadership in private and public affairs. The arrangements of society facilitate such leadership and reward it. A subculture, such as that of the Negro American, in which this is not the pattern, is placed at a distinct disadvantage. . . .

The Case for National Action

In a word, a national effort towards the problems of Negro Americans *29* must be directed towards the question of family structure. The object should be to strengthen the Negro family so as to enable it to raise and support its members as do other families. After that, how this group of Americans chooses to run its affairs, take advantage of its opportunities, or fail to do so, is none of the nation's business.

Rhetorical Analysis Through Annotation

This political report contains much emotional and value-loaded language, unlike the usually dispassionate language of history and the social sciences.

Underline any words or phrases that appear to carry emotions or judgments.

Discuss where such words tend to appear and how more dispassionate language and statistics are used in relation to the emotional words. Consider the impact of such language on the readers of the report and evaluate its appropriateness for a political document; that is, does the language match the purpose of the document?

Discussion Questions

Interpreting the Text

1. What are the main points in Moynihan's argument? How are these points highlighted through organization, wording, and graphic design?

Considering the Issues

2. How does the fact that this is a public report to urge government action influence the kind of argument made, the organization, and the manner of presentation? In what ways does this report still retain some features of academic writing? What further comparisons can you make with the previous few selections by academic historians and sociologists?

3. Which parts of Moynihan's argument do you find persuasive and which parts unpersuasive? Overall, would you agree with his conclusions and support a national policy to reconstruct the black family?

4. Based on your impressions gained from the news media and your experiences, how does the situation today compare with the situation described by Moynihan?

Did Great Society programs have any impact on the problems he described? Has the black middle class grown? Has the gap between the black middle class and the poor blacks gotten wider? Are the poor blacks better or worse off today? What is the present condition of the black family? Have the problems associated with broken homes, illegitimacy, and absentee fathers gotten worse for blacks? For members of other racial and ethnic groups? Have these changes had any economic impact?

5. Does the government have the right or responsibility to concern itself with the family life of any group? How do you feel about having one particular group targeted for government attention? Is it possible for a government to have any impact on a group's social life? Will changes in a group's social life have any impact on economic problems?

Writing Suggestions

1. As part of this course's discussion about how different types of texts work, write an essay analyzing how Moynihan combines several different types of writing (political, sociological, historical, and economic) to create a public policy argument. Consider how he uses the different types of discourse in different parts of his report and how he ties the different parts together into a coherent statement.

2. Imagine a magazine such as *Reader's Digest* has a regular series of articles called "Struggling Against Odds." For this series write a narrative about how someone you know overcame family difficulties to become a great success.

3. One of the arguments Moynihan makes rests on the psychological effects of employment and unemployment. For a course in personal psychology write an essay on this topic, based on your experiences and feelings surrounding your first job or being fired or being unemployed.

4. Write an editorial for your local newspaper either supporting or opposing the continuation of funding for a government-sponsored family counseling service for households suffering unemployment or receiving welfare.

Like It Was

Herbert G. Gutman

The Moynihan report generated a lot of controversy from all parts of the political spectrum. The right opposed in principle government social programs; the left saw the report as diverting attention away from needed economic redevelopment; and the center felt the report was an insult to black life and history.

The most incisive criticisms, however, came not from the political front, but from academic historians who questioned the basis of Moynihan's analysis. Herbert Gutman's book *The Black Family in Slavery and Freedom, 1750–1925* (1976) in particular finds in the historical record little indication of the deep-seated deterioration of the black family that Moynihan claims. Gutman finds that even through the difficulties of slavery and then relentless discrimination and poverty, the black family remained a flexible and creative response to difficult situations, binding blacks together in a supportive social network. Through 1925 (where Gutman's study ends), the husband/father remained an important and regular feature of most black families. Gutman concludes that the current difficulties of the black family identified by Moynihan are the result of rather specific economic and political policies of the mid-twentieth century that have forced blacks off the land and into urban unemployment and a demoralizing welfare system. Gutman believes the way to solve the problems is to repair the damage these policies have caused rather than to attempt to meddle in black family life. Most of all, we must avoid making judgments based on incorrect stereotypes rather than historically accurate information.

The excerpt presented here examines the adaptations of the black family to reconstruction and urbanization of the early twentieth century. Through census figures Gutman draws a picture of a generally organized black family life that successfully adapted to the changing pressures placed on it.

BLACK AMERICANS WERE ALMOST all poor in the period covered *1* by this study, whether they lived in the North or the South, in cities or on farms. But poverty did not entail household disorganization. The adaptive capacities disclosed by Afro-American slaves in the century and a half preceding the general emancipation also revealed themselves in the nearly three-quarters of a century that separated the general emancipation from the onset of the Great Depression. That is made clear from an examination of state and federal manuscript censuses in 1880, 1900, 1905, and 1925. It permits some inferences about a few pertinent questions: the composition of the typical *lower-class* Afro-American household, the differences and similarities in households among "privileged" and "ordinary" Afro-Americans, the differences and similarities between urban and rural black and white lower-class households, and the impact of early twentieth-century northern migration on the black household. Such statistical evidence describes the household, not the family, tells nothing about the roles played by adult men and women within such households, and tells nothing about the relationships between persons living in different households. Kin networks, for example, cannot be reconstructed from these census data. Despite these limitations, the data nevertheless disprove conventional beliefs about the lower-class black family. It did not disintegrate following emancipation, and it did not disintegrate as a consequence of the great migration to northern cities prior to 1930. . . .

1880 . . . .

The Southern Urban and Rural Afro-American Household

Examination of the internal composition of 14,345 southern rural and *2* urban Afro-American households and 2050 subfamilies° discloses that nine in ten blacks lived in households that had at their core two or more members of a black nuclear family: a husband and wife, two parents and their children, or a single parent (usually a mother) with one or more children. Single-person households were few and so were irregular households (those in which neither marital nor blood ties connected two or more persons). Black households usually contained between two and seven persons.[1] The typical black household everywhere contained only the members of a core nuclear family.° Such households were more common in rural than in urban settings. When a black "nuclear household" expanded to include lodgers who were not kin, such a household became an "augmented household." Most augmented households had a single lodger. Very few had more than two lodgers. Nuclear households expanded in yet another way by making place for relatives. Such households are called "extended households." Most black subfamilies lived in extended households, but the typical extended black household usually included the core nuclear family and one or two relatives. It was more common for an urban than a rural extended black household to contain a mother or a mother-in-law. But the typical kin living in extended black households were not elderly persons. They were grandchildren, nephews and nieces, and brothers and sisters of the adult family heads. Grandchildren were more common in extended rural households. Brothers and sisters were found most frequently in extended urban households.[2]

By combining all types of households and subfamilies, we find that a *3* husband or father was present in most households and subfamilies. The husband-father household was more common in rural (ranging from 82 to 86 percent) than in urban (ranging from 69 to 74 percent) settings. *Fathers* with unskilled occupations headed families just as regularly as *fathers* with either artisan skills or middle-class occupations. If the slaves had been without a norm that prized the completed immediate family, large numbers of southern blacks in 1880 should have lived in disorga-

---

Subfamilies—either a husband and wife, two parents and their children, or a single parent and children living with another nuclear family in the same household. **Core nuclear family**—the basic family unit of parents and children.

nized households. That was not the case. The manuscript pages of the 1880 federal census reveal with unfailing regularity that urban and rural ex-slaves had retained powerful familial connections and that nearly all households had at their core a nuclear family. The typical southern black household, moreover, had at its head a male who was either a farm laborer, a tenant farmer, a sharecropper, an urban service worker, or an urban day laborer. . . .

1900 . . . .

Unlike earlier censuses, the 1900 census revealed invaluable information [4] about marriage, family, childbearing, and sexual behavior. It asked women how many children had been born to them and still lived either inside or outside the household, and it asked men and women about the length of their marriages. As in 1880, a small percentage of mothers under forty described themselves as "single." A significant number everywhere but especially in the rural places reported the birth of a child either prior to marriage or during the first year of marriage. Such evidence indicated the prevalence° of prenuptial° intercourse, childbirth out of wedlock, and bridal pregnancy. But the small number of single women aged thirty and older shows that marriage usually followed either pregnancy or the birth of a child.

Long marriages were common among these rural and urban blacks, [5] and so was the attachment of parent to child. The disorder that accompanied the Reconstruction and Redemption years had not caused casual marriages to occur among women born between 1866 and 1875. Half of the married St. Helena's° women in this age group had lived with the same spouse for between ten and nineteen years. Nearly the same percentage of Jackson° women had marriages of that length, as did a lesser but still-significant percentage of Issaquena° women. Women born between 1846 and 1855 had even longer marriages. Two of three married Issaquena women had lived with the same spouse for at least twenty years, and the percentage was higher among the Jackson Ward women (80 percent) and still higher among the St. Helena's women (85 percent). The length of marriages reported by the St. Helena's and Jackson Ward blacks but not by the Issaquena blacks hardly differed at each age level from the length of marriage reported by Jones County, Mississippi, whites in 1900. In all places studied, furthermore, more than nine in ten children whose mother was not yet thirty years old lived with their parents. If a mother lived alone, the percentage hardly differed. These data, however, are no reason to idealize the condition of the late-nineteenth-century southern black family. The 1900 federal census disclosed

---

Prevalence—dominance.   **Prenuptial**—prior to marriage.   **St. Helena**—a rural, sea-island community in South Carolina.   **Jackson**—a ward in Richmond, Virginia.   **Issaquena**—a county in Mississippi.

how many children were born to women and how many had died by 1900. The median number of children born to rural black women aged forty to forty-nine in 1900 was nearly the same among St. Helena's and Issaquena women and somewhat lower among the Jackson Ward women. Three in ten children born to these St. Helena's women were dead by 1900, and the number increased to nearly one in two among the Issaquena and Jackson Ward women. The comparable figure among poor white Jones County women was one in five. It cost a great deal to be a parent of a southern rural or urban black child in the decades following emancipation and preceding the great migration to the North. . . .°

1905

New York City Afro-American Households

Early twentieth-century migration from the rural South to the urban North did not shatter the black family. That is disclosed by a study of the 1905 New York State manuscript census. By 1905, New York City was already attracting black migrants, and the occupational and household status of 14,368 black residents in the San Juan Hill and Tenderloin districts is examined next. Perhaps as many as three-fourths of this population's adults had been born in the South Atlantic states, especially Virginia.[3] About two-thirds were between the ages of fifteen and thirty-nine.[4] Adult women significantly outnumbered adult men, and about one in four women aged fifteen and older was a lodger or lived alone. The occupational status of black men could not have been worse by early-twentieth-century standards. About 5 percent (more than half of these clerks) were not unskilled laborers, service workers, or skilled workmen. Nine percent were skilled workers, and one in four of them either an actor or a musician. Fewer blacks with skills worked in the building trades than as actors and musicians. If these Tenderloin and San Juan Hill men typified the range of occupations held by other 1905 New York City blacks, the scarcity of skilled workers meant that migrant blacks did not threaten the occupational status of skilled white workers. Instead, these men had been bypassed by the industrial advances identified with development of capitalism in nineteenth- and early-twentieth-century America. They either carried few skills with them from the South (a possibility strongly suggested by the deteriorating status of Richmond and Mobile skilled black workers in 1880) or were excluded from many unskilled occupations open to native and immigrant white New Yorkers. . . . 6

Largely a young adult population, the economically depressed San Juan Hill and Tenderloin blacks did not live in disorganized households. Less than 10 percent lived alone or in boarding houses. Slightly more 7

The great migration to the North—the migration of blacks from the rural southern communities to northern cities during the period between the two world wars.

than four in five lived in households of between two and seven persons. About 10 percent of households with two or more persons had no residents related by either blood or marriage.[5] Overall, about six in seven New York blacks lived in a household that had at its core two or more persons related by either blood or marriage. Nearly half of these households contained just members of a nuclear family, and two in five were augmented households. Most families took in one or two lodgers; relatively few took in more than three. About one in six households contained kin other than members of the immediate family, a high percentage given the population's migrant character. Except where subfamilies were present, the extended household usually included one relative and rarely more than two. These were most often members of the family of origin: mothers and mothers-in-law, adult siblings, and adult nephews and nieces.[6]

Migration and the changing composition of the Afro-American house-   8
hold (especially the relative decline of the nuclear household) among New York City blacks in 1905 are not evidence that husbands and fathers were less frequently within the family than in the South in 1880 or 1900. A husband or father was present in slightly more than four in five (83 percent) San Juan Hill and Tenderloin households and subfamilies. Nine of ten adult women did not head either households or subfamilies. Among those that did, more than half were elderly women. Women under thirty headed about one in five male-absent households and subfamilies. Most of these (three in four) had one child. One woman under thirty among these nearly fifteen thousand blacks headed a male-absent household that had in it more than two children. Young black women heading households and subfamilies were far less important in New York City in 1905 than in Richmond in 1880. One of every eleven Richmond women aged twenty to twenty-nine headed such a household or subfamily in 1880. In New York City in 1905, the proportion was one of every twenty-five similarly aged women. The typical New York City black household in 1905 had at its head a poor male unskilled laborer or service worker. Six in seven adult New York City black men were either laborers or service workers. And six in seven *fathers* (men living with a wife and children or just their children) were either laborers or service workers. A man's age did not affect the father's place in the family. Eighty-four percent of men aged forty-five and older were either laborers or service workers, and 88 percent of similarly aged *fathers* had similar occupations. . . .

1925

Black Manhattan and Its Households in 1925—
Neither Sodom Nor Mecca

Important changes in the composition of the New York City black   9
households also occurred between 1905 and 1925. The single-person and

irregular household declined slightly in importance compared with the household with a nuclear core. The shape of irregular households, however, hardly changed over the two decades.[7] Households containing just members of an immediate family declined in importance. In 1925, just one in three West Indian and two in five native black households were nuclear in composition. About half of all black households had one or more lodgers in them, and about one in five households had one or more relatives other than members of the immediate family. Just as the household expanded, so, too, did the relative importance of the subfamily. In 1905, there had been one subfamily for every eight households. Twenty years later, there was one subfamily for every three (native blacks) or four (West Indian) households. The composition of the typical Harlem household in 1925 was very different from the typical southern rural or urban household in 1880. Over this half century, the simple nuclear household declined in importance, and extended and augmented households as well as subfamilies increased in importance. . . .

The changing composition of the household, a fact of great impor- *10* tance in describing the adaptive behavior of early-twentieth-century southern black migrants to New York City, was not accompanied by any increase in the male-absent household or subfamily. About five in six 1905 New York City black households and subfamilies contained either a husband or a father. That was so in six of seven 1925 households and subfamilies. A father was present in seven in ten families. That happened more frequently in West Indian than in native black families. Despite the low economic status of most males, the adverse over-all sex ratio, the great number of unattached lodgers, the decline of the nuclear household, and the increased importance of the augmented household and the subfamily, the percentage of black women in all age-specific groups heading male-absent households and subfamilies either remained constant or declined between 1905 and 1925. The male-absent household and subfamily changed in one important way over these two decades: the subfamily without a resident father became more important than the household without a resident father.[8] But the age distribution of the mothers involved remained nearly the same. Slightly more than half of the women heading either households or subfamilies were at least forty years old. Insignificant differences distinguished the native black from the West Indian women. Despite their disadvantaged sex ratio, nearly the same percentage of native black women aged twenty to twenty-nine (4.2 percent) as similarly aged West Indian women (4 percent) headed either households or subfamilies. Overall, the male-absent household and subfamily headed by a young black woman and filled with numerous children was relatively insignificant in 1925. Three percent of all households and subfamilies were male-absent and headed by women under thirty. One percent of all households and subfamilies were male-absent and had in them three or more children. The population studied contained 13,922 households and subfamilies. Just thirty-two—0.3 percent—were male-absent, headed by a woman not yet thirty, and contained three or more children. Not surprisingly, five in six black children under the age of six lived with both parents. Only 124 children in this community of more than fifty thousand men, women, and children lived with a nonrelative. Fathers, once again, in these and other families were overwhelmingly unskilled laborers and service workers. And fathers with these occupations matched in number the percentage of adult males with these occupations. That was just as true for the native black father as for the West Indian father. Age did not matter. Three in four native black men aged forty-five and older were either laborers or service workers, and 74 percent of native black fathers aged forty-five and older had similar occupations. . . .

Central Harlem may not have been Mecca in the middle 1920s. But *11* neither was it Sodom. No evidence whatsoever sustains the assertion in Gilbert Osofsky's *Harlem: The Making of a Ghetto* that "the slave heritage, bulwarked by economic conditions, continued into the twentieth century to make family instability a common factor in Negro life."[9] And that is so because such large numbers of lower-class southern black migrants had adapted familial and kin ties—rooted in their prior historical experiences first as slaves and afterward as free rural southern workers and farmers—to life in the emerging ghetto.

At all moments in time between 1880 and 1925—that is, from an adult *12* generation born in slavery to an adult generation about to be devastated by the Great Depression of the 1930s and the modernization of southern agriculture afterward—the typical Afro-American family was lower-class in status and headed by two parents. That was so in the urban and rural South in 1880 and in 1900 and in New York City in 1905 and 1925. The two-parent household was not limited to better-advantaged Afro-Americans (rural landowners, artisans and skilled workers, and members of the tiny black middle-class elite). It was just as common among farm laborers, sharecroppers, tenants, and northern and southern urban unskilled laborers and service workers. It accompanied the southern blacks in the great migration to the North that has so reshaped the United States in the twentieth century.

Harlem in 1925 differed from rural South Carolina and Mississippi in *13* 1880. So did black residents in both settings. The typical lower-class Afro-American household also changed over that half century. It expanded and grew more complex. That process apparently started in the South between 1880 and 1900 and was greatly accelerated by the migration of vast numbers of poor southern blacks to northern cities prior to 1930. Just how this changing household and the family (or families) within it related to larger Afro-American kinship patterns and just how those kin networks changed between 1880 and 1925 cannot be learned from data drawn from manuscript censuses. Such sources, however, reveal enough about the interior composition of Afro-American households to confound a vast and ill-informed popular and academic mythology that so misrepresented the diverse capacities of the descendants of enslaved Afro-Americans to adapt to changing external circumstances in the century following the general emancipation.

Notes

[1]Everywhere, more than half of the households contained between two and four persons. If the household size reported in 1880 in four Paterson, New Jersey, census enumeration districts typified that common among northern white workers, then the urban and rural southern black household did not differ in size from the white working-class household. Large numbers of immigrant (especially Irish, English, German, and Dutch by birth) and native white workers lived in these four districts. Fewer households with between two and seven residents existed in this predominantly working-class white community (87 percent) than in any of the rural and urban southern black communities studied.

[2]Most subfamilies in black households lived with kin in extended households. About half of all Richmond subfamilies had an affinal or a consanguinal tie to the host family, but the percentage was higher in the other places: Mobile (61 percent), Natchez (75 percent), rural Adams County (75 percent), Mount Albium (80 percent), Beaufort (82 percent), Lane's Schoolhouse (89 percent), and St. Helena's Island and Township (98 percent). Although most black subfamilies lived in extended households and not among strangers, most extended black households did not contain related subfamilies. Except for St. Helena's Island and Township, about one in three extended households included a subfamily. The rest usually comprised an immediate family and one or two relatives. Between half and three-fifths of all single relatives in extended rural households were women of all ages, a percentage that increased to between two-thirds and four-fifths in the cities. A mother or mother-in-law was more common in the urban extended households: about one of four Natchez, Mobile, and Richmond single relatives in extended households were elderly mothers. The typical single relatives in extended households, however, were not elderly women but grandchildren, nieces and nephews, and brothers and sisters. This fact hints at significant continuities between an immediate family and the two families of origin. Grandchildren were more common in extended rural households; brothers and sisters were more common in extended urban households. Together, these three sets of blood kin made up between two-thirds (Beaufort) and three-fourths (St. Helena's Island and Township) of all single relatives in extended households. Apart from pointing to connections between an immediate family and a family of origin, such patterns suggest the rarity of matrifocal authority.

[3]Because the 1905 census listed only the place of birth for foreign residents, nothing can be learned from it about migration patterns by native blacks. The published 1900 and 1910 federal censuses revealed such information, as did a 1905 survey of New York City black tenement dwellers conducted by Mary White Ovington and summarized in her classic study, *Half A Man: The Status of the Negro in New York* (1911). The percentage of New York-born blacks fell between 1900 (45 percent) and 1910 (37 percent) as migrants from other northern states, from foreign places and especially from the Caribbean islands, and from the American South and especially from the South Atlantic states made it to the great metropolis. In 1910, 45 percent of the state's black residents had been born in the South, and of this number more than nine of ten

came from the South Atlantic states, Maryland, and the District of Columbia. Foreign-born blacks also increased in importance between 1900 (3.6 percent) and 1910 (9.6 percent). All of these percentages included young children born in New York State to southern or foreign-born black parents, so that these over-all figures greatly underestimated the proportion of adult migrants. Demographic and social data has been gathered on all blacks living in the following Tenderloin streets: Twenty-first, Twenty-fourth to Forty-third, Forty-sixth to Forty-eighth, and Fifty-first to Fifty-third streets between Sixth and Eighth avenues. In addition, similar information was collected about San Juan Hill blacks living west of Tenth Avenue on Fifty-ninth to Sixty-third, Sixty-seventh, and Sixty-eighth streets.

[4]See W. E. B. Du Bois, "The Negroes of Farmville, Virginia, A Social Study," *Bulletin in the Department of Labor*, XIV (January 1898), 9, in which Du Bois pointed out how the pattern of migration to northern cities largely involved "persons in the twenties and thirties, leaving an excess of children and old people." "The proportion of children under 15," Du Bois explained of these village Prince Edward County, Virginia, blacks, "is also increased by the habit which married couples and widowed persons have of going to cities and leaving their children with grandparents. This also accounts for the small proportion of colored children in a city like Philadelphia."

[5]About 10 percent of the total population lived in 476 irregular households. Not all such households contained unrelated residents. One in four had in them two or more persons related to one another. Of these 122 households, ninety-one included brothers and sisters (usually young adults), and another twenty-five had in them an aunt or uncle with that person's nephews or nieces. The typical migrant kin-related irregular household had in it persons related to one another in a family of origin. Neither these irregular kin-related households nor those with only unrelated members were large in size. Two of every five had just two inhabitants, and another two of five had either three or four residents. Only 6 percent of these irregular households had six or more residents. Hardly any contained young children: in all, the 476 irregular households had thirty-four children under the age of fifteen in them. It seems clear therefore that these irregular households had very few complete or broken nuclear families. Some probably included men and women living together as husband and wife in common-law relationships. Such marriages were then legal in New York State. A common-law marriage, however, was not possible in two of five of the 476 households because these contained only either men or women. In nearly three of four of remaining households (6 percent of all households with two or more residents) men and women were close enough in age to suggest the possibility of either casual sexual ties or common-law marriages among some of them.

[6]The percentage of extended households hardly differed between 1880 and 1905. Urban New York City blacks in 1905 were mostly migrants. It is striking evidence of the tenacity of kin ties among these lower-class blacks that extended households were just as common among New York City blacks in 1905 as among rural Mississippi and South Carolina blacks in 1880. But the extended household was less common among New York City blacks in 1905 than among southern rural and urban blacks in 1900. Leaving aside related subfamilies (most often a woman with her children), the typical New York City extended black household in 1905 contained either a mother (or mother-in-law) or an adult sibling (a brother or sister to either parent in the house-

hold and usually aged between fifteen and twenty-nine). Nephews and nieces followed in importance and were also usually between the ages of fifteen and twenty-nine. Hardly any grandchildren lived in the extended urban black household in 1905.

Yet another pattern observed in the 1880 black households appeared among the 1905 New York City black households. The female-headed nuclear household—that is, a mother and just her children—was unusual: 6 percent of all kin-related households. Three in ten male-absent households and subfamilies were simple nuclear households (31 percent); the rest were extended (14 percent) and augmented (37 percent) households or subfamilies (22 percent). Most black male-absent households and subfamilies were not isolated family units. Instead, a mother and her children lived with either boarders or relatives. Men of approximately the same age as the mother lived in three in ten of the 222 female-headed augmented households, and if some of these men and women lived together as husband and wife these were not "male-absent households." Very few boarders were unrelated children. At least half (52 percent) of the 135 female-headed subfamilies belong to an extended household; related by blood and less frequently by marriage to a second family in the household. Some were mothers with young children who lived with a married son or daughter. Others were widowed, single, or divorced women who lived with their parents or, occasionally, with another relative. Very few of these extended households were three-generation female-headed households. About one in twenty female-headed households was a three-generation household, and only 0.9 percent of all kin-related black Tenderloin and San Juan Hill households were three-generation female-headed households. The migration of rural and urban southern blacks to New York City in the late nineteenth and early twentieth centuries had not increased the importance of the male-absent black household or subfamily. Poor New York City blacks incorporated women cut off from a spouse into larger households. That was so in 1880, and migration to the North had not given these poor blacks reason to abandon such women.

[7]The composition and size of irregular households hardly changed between 1905 and 1925. In 1925, 45 percent of such households contained two persons, as contrasted with 42 percent in 1905. The number with six or more people increased 0.4 percent. In the 1382 irregular 1925 households, there lived seventy-nine children under the age of fifteen. A larger percentage in 1925 (32 percent) than in 1905 (26 percent) had related persons in them, and once again brothers and sisters predominated. Nearly seven in ten kin-related irregular households had a sibling core. The percentage of irregular households with persons of the same sex also remained constant: 40 percent in 1925, as compared with 41 percent in 1905. The Manhattan black population had increased at a staggering rate between 1905 and 1925, but the place of the irregular household in this larger black community had not become more important in these twenty years.

[8]Dramatic changes occurred in the types of male-absent units between 1905 and 1925. As a percentage of all female-headed households and subfamilies, the simple nuclear and augmented household dropped from 67 percent in 1905 to 53 percent in 1925. The female-headed extended household increased slightly, but the greatest increase occurred in the percentage of male-absent subfamilies, increasing from 22 percent (1905) to 35 percent (1925). *For the first*

time, the typical male-absent domestic arrangement was the subfamily. Although the three-generation matrifocal household still remained quite uncommon, its frequency increased slightly over this twenty-year period from 0.9 percent to 1.1 percent. The percentage of augmented father-absent households with male lodgers near the same age as the mother increased between 1905 (31 percent) and 1925 (37 percent). Despite these changes and especially the increased importance of the subfamily, the ages of women in male-absent households and subfamilies together with the number of children in such domestic units followed the 1905 pattern.

[9]Gilbert Osofsky, *Harlem: The Making of a Ghetto* (1963), 133–34.

Rhetorical Analysis Through Annotation

Although organized chronologically, this selection is not simply an historical narrative of a series of events. A comparison is set up among conditions at four different times, and in two different types of setting.

Underline all statements that explicitly draw comparisons among the conditions at various times or places. In the margin note any implicit comparisons established through parallel statements or data, even though the comparison is not specifically mentioned.

Discuss how the various comparisons are drawn together to establish Gutman's overall point.

Discussion Questions

Interpreting the Text

1. What are the major features of black family life at each point in time examined by Gutman? What conclusions can you draw about the black family based on this data?

2. What indications of family disorganization do come through in the statistics? How do these compare with normal levels of disorganization among other groups and in other periods? What explicit comparisons are made with equivalent white populations and what conclusions can be drawn from these comparisons?

3. What indications appear in these pages of the economic status and particular hardships of blacks during this period? How does this information fit with the information on family structure? What does putting these two kinds of information together do to the overall conclusions to be drawn from the selection?

Considering the Issues

4. Why are the notes so extensive in this selection? What kind of information is placed in the notes? How does this information support the main text? Why isn't this information placed within the main text?

5. How important do you think Gutman's findings are for thinking about current problems? What are the implications?

6. What other examples of adaptation of family structure among other groups and during other periods are you aware of? How many different models of family structure can you think of? Which do you think would be most successful under which conditions?

Writing Suggestions

1. Imagine you are studying this selection in order to prepare for a class discussion for a course in American social history. Draw up a comparative chart to find similarities and differences among the family structures described in each of the four periods. Underneath the chart write out in note form your comparative observations and then the interpretations or ideas suggested by your observations.

2. Imagine you were a newspaper reporter when Gutman's study was released. You are assigned to write a three-hundred word story under the headline, "History Professor Explodes Racist Myths about the Black Family." Write the article, including easy-to-understand summaries of the major points that undercut false stereotypes about the black family.

3. As an articulate member of a college political organization of your choice, you are asked to give a speech on a campus-wide political forum on "Family Values and Economics: Where Does the Government Fit In?" Write a five-minute statement outlining your position, your reasons, and major evidence.

4. A close friend of yours, now married and living in another city, has been depressed about the impact of economic hardships on his or her own family. Write a letter of advice or support. As part of this letter you may wish to discuss whether economic hardship necessarily means family troubles.

Restoring the Traditional Black Family
Eleanor Holmes Norton

Fundamental historical issues continue to shape our daily lives. The problem of equal mobility opportunities for all is not just a dry academic abstraction. As Lipset and Bendix suggest, citing de Tocqueville, any group that finds itself excluded becomes a threat to political stability. The problem of an underclass, uncommitted to and resentful toward the society around it, has increasingly threatened a breakdown in urban order in recent years.

Eleanor Holmes Norton, chairman of the Equal Employment Opportunity Commission in President Carter's administration and now a professor of law at Georgetown University, examines the problem of poor blacks, alienated and unable to enter the economic mainstream.

The article, from a 1985 Sunday magazine section of the *New York Times*, uses the work of historians to untangle the problem and pinpoint potential solutions. In this article we see reflected directly and indirectly all the readings in this unit. As a popular article for a general educated audience, this selection presents a more straightforward analysis with less detailed evidence than some of the previous selections; nonetheless, the article argues carefully and thoughtfully to make a serious contribution to public policy.

WHAT WOULD SOCIETY BE like if the family found it difficult to *1* perform its most basic functions? We are beginning to find out. Half of all marriages in this country end in divorce, and half of all children will spend a significant period with only one parent.

Startling and unsettling changes have already occurred in black family *2* life, especially among the poor. Since the 1960's, birth rates among blacks have fallen dramatically, but two out of every three black women having a first child are single, compared to one out of every six white women. Today, well over half of black children in this country are born to single women. Why are female-headed households multiplying now, when there is less discrimination and poverty than a couple of generations ago, when black family life was stronger?

The disruption of the black family today is, in exaggerated micro- *3* cosm°, a reflection of what has happened to American family life in general. Public anxiety has mounted with the near-doubling of the proportion of white children living with one parent (from 9 percent to 17 percent) since 1970. Single parents of all backgrounds are feeling the pressures—the sheer economics of raising children primarily on the depressed income of the mother (a large component of the so-called "feminization of poverty"); the psychological and physical toll when one person, however advantaged, must be both mother and father, and the effects on children.

The stress on American family life was recently addressed by Senator *4* Daniel P. Moynihan, Democrat of New York, on the 20th anniversary of his controversial "Moynihan Report." The original report confined its analysis to the black family. Moynihan, who in April delivered a series of lectures at Harvard on the family, said, "I want to make clear this is not a black issue." Indeed, just last month, the problem of increasing poverty among all the nation's children was underscored in a major report from two Federal agencies.

Yet until recently, many blacks have had an almost visceral° reaction *5* to mention of black family problems. Wounds to the family were seen

---

Microcosm—a small system symbolizing a larger system.   **Visceral**—intensely emotional.

as the most painful effect of American racism. Many blacks and their supporters have regarded talk of black family weaknesses as tantamount° to insult and smear. Some conservatives have taken signs of trouble in the black family as proof that the remaining problems of race are internal and have announced the equivalent of "Physician, heal thyself."

At the heart of the crisis lies the self-perpetuating culture of the ghetto. 6 This destructive ethos° began to surface 40 years ago with the appearance of permanent joblessness and the devaluation of working-class black men. As this nation's post-World War II economy has helped produce a black middle class, it has also, ironically, been destroying the black working class and its family structure. Today, the process has advanced so far that renewal of the black family goes beyond the indispensable economic ingredients. The family's return to its historic strength will require the overthrow of the complicated, predatory° ghetto subculture, a feat demanding not only new Government approaches but active black leadership and community participation and commitment.

While this crisis was building, it received almost no public attention, in 7 part because of the notorious sensitivity of the subject. Yet 20 years ago, Martin Luther King Jr. spoke candidly about the black family, spelling out the "alarming" statistics on "the rate of illegitimacy," the increase in female-headed households and the rise in families on welfare. The black family, King asserted, had become "fragile, deprived and often psychopathic."

King relied in part on the Moynihan report, written when the Senator 8 was an Assistant Secretary of Labor. Many were stunned by what one critic called the report's "salacious 'discovery'"—its discussion of illegitimacy, matriarchy and welfare and its view that black family structure had become, in its own words, a "tangle of pathology" capable of perpetuating itself without assistance from the white world. As a result, the report's concern with remedies, including jobs, and its call for a national family policy were eclipsed.

The delay has been costly to blacks and to the country. When King 9 spoke out, the statistics he characterized as alarming showed that two-and-a-half times as many black families as white ones were headed by women. Today, it is almost three-and-a-half times as many—43 percent of black families compared with 13 percent of white families. Since 1970, out-of-wedlock births have become more prevalent throughout society, almost doubling among whites to 11 percent. But among blacks, births to single women have risen from 38 percent in 1970 to 57 percent in 1982.

While families headed by women have often proved just as effective 10 as two-parent families in raising children, the most critical danger facing

---

Tantamount—equal. **Ethos**—the disposition or character of a group of people. **Predatory**—living by preying on others.

female-headed households is poverty. Seventy percent of black children under the age of 18 who live in female-headed families are being brought up in poverty. In 1983, the median income for such households was $7,999, compared to almost $32,107 for two-parent families of all races, in which both spouses worked. Without the large increase in female-headed households, black family income would have *increased* by 11 percent in the 1970's. Instead, it fell by 5 percent.

As last month's report from the Congressional Research Service and *11* the Congressional Budget Office pointed out, "The average black child can expect to spend more than five years of his childhood in poverty; the average white child, 10 months."

Buried beneath the statistics is a world of complexity originating in *12* the historic atrocity of slavery and linked to modern discrimination and its continuing effects. What has obscured the problem is its delicacy and its uniqueness. The black family has been an issue in search of leadership. Discussion of problems in the black family has been qualitatively different from debates on voting rights or job discrimination. Fear of generating a new racism has foreclosed whatever opportunity there may have been to search for relief, driving the issue from the public agenda and delaying for a generation the search for workable solutions. Today, when nearly half of all black children are being raised in poverty, further delay is unthinkable.

Blacks themselves have been stunned by recent disclosures of the *13* extent of the growth of poor, alienated female-headed households. The phenomenon is outside the personal experience of many black adults. Many have overcome deep poverty and discrimination only because of the protection and care of stable traditional and extended families. As recently as the early 1960's, 75 percent of black households were husband-and-wife families. The figure represents remarkable continuity— it is about the same as those reported in census records from the late 19th century. Indeed, the evidence suggests that most slaves grew up in two-parent families reinforced by ties to large extended families.

The sharp rise in female-headed households involves mostly those *14* with young children and began in the mid-1960's. The phenomenon— while by no means a trend that permeates the entire black community— affects a significant portion of young people today, many of whom are separated economically, culturally and socially from the black mainstream. They have been raised in the worst of the rapidly deteriorating ghettos of the 1960's, 1970's and 1980's, in cities or neighborhoods that lost first the white and then the black middle and working classes. Drugs, crime and pimps took over many of the old communities. Blacks remaining were often trapped and isolated, cut off from the values of the black working poor and middle class—where husbands often work two jobs, wives return to work almost immediately after childbirth and extended families of interdependent kin are still more prevalent than among whites.

A complete explanation of black family disruption does not emerge 15
from a roundup of the usual suspects, including the many factors that
make American family life generally less stable these days: the ease and
relative acceptance of separation, divorce and childbirth outside of marriage; the decline of religion and other traditional family-reinforcing
institutions, and welfare rules that discourage family unity and penalize
economic initiative. Anecdotal explanations—the girl-mothers are said
to want to love and receive affection from a baby; the boy-fathers
reportedly brag about making babies—are also inadequate. Such anecdotes do not explain how the strong presumption in favor of marriage
before childbearing has been overcome so often.

The emergence of single women as the primary guardians of the 16
majority of black children is a pronounced departure that began to take
shape following World War II. Ironically, the women and children—the
most visible manifestations of the change—do not provide the key to
the transformation. The breakdown begins with working-class black
men, whose loss of function in the post-World War II economy has led
directly to their loss of function in the family.

In the booming post-World War I economy, black men with few skills 17
could find work. Even the white South, which denied the black man a
place in its wage economy, could not deprive him of an economic role
in the farm family. The poorest, most meanly treated sharecropper was
at the center of the work it took to produce the annual crop.

As refugees from the South, the generation of World War I migrants 18
differed in crucial respects from the World War II generation. The World
War I arrivals were enthusiastic, voluntary migrants, poor in resources
but frequently middle class in aspiration. They were at the bottom of a
society that denied them the right to move up very far, but they got a
foothold in a burgeoning economy.

Family stability was the rule. According to a 1925 study in New York 19
City, five out of six children under the age of six lived with both parents.
Nationally, a small middle class emerged, later augmented by the jobs
generated by World War II, service in the armed forces and the postwar
prosperity that sometimes filtered down to urban blacks.

Today's inner-city blacks were not a part of these historical processes. 20
Some are the victims of the flight of manufacturing jobs. Others were
part of the last wave of Southern migrants or their offspring, arriving
in the 1950's and 1960's. They often migrated not because of new
opportunities but because of the evaporation of old ones. Mechanized
farming made their labor superfluous in agriculture, but unlike the blacks
of earlier generations and European immigrants, later black migrants
were also superfluous in the postwar cities as manufacturing work for
the less-skilled and poorly educated declined. Today's postindustrial
society, demanding sophisticated preparation and training, has only ex-
acerbated° these problems.

Exacerbated—made worse.

This permanent, generational joblessness is at the core of the meaning *21*
of the American ghetto. The resulting, powerful aberration° transforms
life in poor black communities and forces everything else to adapt to it.
The female-headed household is only one consequence. The underground economy, the drug culture, epidemic crime and even a highly
unusual disparity between the actual number of men and women—all
owe their existence to the cumulative effect of chronic joblessness among
men. Over time, deep structural changes have taken hold and created a
different ethos.

An entire stratum of black men, many of them young, no longer *22*
performs its historic role in supporting a family. Many are unemployed
because of the absence of jobs, or unemployable because their ghetto
origins leave them unprepared for the job market. Others have adapted
to the demands of the ghetto—the hustle, the crime, the drugs. But the
skills necessary to survive in the streets are those least acceptable in the
outside world.

The macho role cultivated in the ghetto makes it difficult for many *23*
black men, unable to earn a respectable living, to form households and
assume the roles of husband and father. Generationally entrenched joblessness joined with the predatory underground economy form the bases
of a marginal life style. Relationships without the commitments of
husband and father result.

This qualitative change in fundamental family relationships could have *24*
occurred only under extreme and unrelentingly destructive conditions.
Neither poverty nor cyclical unemployment° alone could have had this
impact. After all, poverty afflicts most of the world's people. If economic
and social hardships could in themselves destroy family life, the family
could not have survived as the basic human unit throughout the world.

The transformation in poor black communities goes beyond poverty. *25*
These deep changes are anchored in a pervasively middle-class society
that associates manhood with money. Shocking figures show a long,
steep and apparently permanent decline in black men's participation in
the labor force, even at peak earning ages. In 1948, before the erosion
of unskilled and semiskilled city and rural jobs had become pronounced,
black male participation in the labor force was 87 percent, almost a full
point higher than that of white males.

In the generation since 1960, however, black men have experienced a *26*
dramatic loss of jobs—dropping from an employment rate of 74 percent
to 55 percent in 1982, according to the Center for the Study of Social
Policy in Washington. While white male employment slipped in that
period, much of the white decline, unlike that of the blacks, is attributed
to early retirement. Since 1960, the black male population over the age
of 18 has doubled, but the number employed has lagged badly.

Aberration—unusual variation from a norm.   Cyclical unemployment—temporary unemployment during an economic downturn.

These figures tell a story not only of structural unemployment°, but   *27*
of structural changes in low-income black families. The unemployment
rates of young blacks have been the most devastating and militate against
the establishment of stable marriages. This year, for instance, black teen-
agers overall had an unemployment rate of 39 percent, two-and-a-half
times that of white teen-agers. The loss of roles as workers has led to
the acceptance of other roles for financial gain, many of them antisocial.
Aside from the fact that large numbers of young men are imprisoned,
disabled by drugs or otherwise marginal or unavailable as marriage
partners, there is an unusual disparity between the sheer numbers of
black men and black women. Among whites, the ratio of men to women
does not change significantly until age 50, when men's shorter life
expectancy creates a gap. But among blacks, beginning at age 20,
women outnumber men significantly enough to have a major impact
upon the possibility of marriage.

Some argue persuasively that the female-headed family is an adapta-   *28*
tion that facilitates coping with hardship and demographics. This seems
undeniable as an explanation, but unsatisfactory as a response. Are we
willing to accept an adaptation that leaves the majority of black children
under the age of 6—the crucial foundation years of life—living in poverty? Given a real choice, poor blacks, like everybody else, would hardly
choose coping mechanisms over jobs, educational opportunity and family stability.

Yet, the remedy for ghetto conditions is not as simple as providing   *29*
necessities and opportunities. The ghetto is not simply a place. It has
become a way of life. Just as it took a complex of social forces to
produce ghetto conditions, it will take a range of remedies to dissolve
them. The primary actors unavoidably are the Government and the
black community itself.

The Government is deeply implicated in black family problems. Its   *30*
laws enforced slavery before the Civil War and afterward created and
sanctioned pervasive public and private discrimination. The effects on
the black family continue to this day. Given the same opportunities as
others, blacks would almost certainly have sustained the powerful family
traditions they brought with them from Africa, where society itself is
organized around family.

Quite apart from its historical role, the Government cannot avoid   *31*
present responsibility. It can choose, as it now does, to ignore and delay
the search for ways to break the hold of the ghetto, such as early
intervention with young children and training and education for the
hard-core poor. Although programs capable of penetrating ghetto conditions have proved elusive, the current Government posture of disen-
gagement is folly. With the poor growing at a faster rate than the middle

---

Structural unemployment—permanent unemployment built into the economic system.

class, the prospect is that succeeding generations will yield more, not fewer, disadvantaged blacks. An American version of a *lumpenproletariat* (the so-called underclass), without work and without hope, existing at the margins of society, could bring down the great cities, sap resources and strength from the entire society and, lacking the usual means to survive, prey upon those who possess them.

Perhaps the greatest gap in corrective strategies has been the failure *32* to focus on prevention. Remedies for deep-rooted problems—from teen-age pregnancy to functional illiteracy—are bound to fail when we leave the water running while we struggle to check the overflow. A primary incubator for ghetto problems is the poor, female-headed household. Stopping its proliferation would prevent a spectrum of often-intractable social and economic problems.

Remedies often focus at opposite ends—either on the provision of *33* income or of services. Neither seems wholly applicable to entrenched ghetto conditions. Public assistance alone, leaving people in the same defeatist environment, may reinforce the status quo. The service orientation has been criticized for using a disproportionate amount of the available resources relative to the results obtained.

More appropriate solutions may lie between income and service strat- *34* egies. Programs are likely to be more successful if they provide a rigorous progression through a series of steps leading to "graduation." This process, including a period of weaning from public assistance, might prove more successful in achieving personal independence. Such programs would be far more disciplined than services to the poor generally have been. They would concentrate on changing life styles as well as imparting skills and education. The test of their effectiveness would be the recipients' progress in achieving economic self-sufficiency.

To reach boys and men, especially the hard-core unemployed, more *35* work needs to be done to cull the successful aspects of training and job programs. Effective training models need to be systematically replicated. It is untenable to abandon the hard-core unemployed, as the Reagan Administration has done, by moving to a jobs program that focuses on the most, rather than the least, trainable. Ghetto males will not simply go away. As we now see, they will multiply themselves.

The welfare program—a brilliant New Deal invention now stretched *36* to respond to a range of problems never envisioned for it—often deepens dependence and lowers self-esteem. Although welfare enjoys little support anywhere along the political spectrum, it continues for lack of an alternative.

Reconceived, a public-assistance program could reach single mothers *37* and offer them vehicles to self-sufficiency. The counterparts of young women on welfare are working downtown or attending high school or junior college on grants to low-income students. Far from foreclosing such opportunities because a woman has a child, public assistance should be converted from the present model of passive maintenance to a program built around education or work and prospective graduation.

Studies of the hard-core unemployed have shown women on welfare *38*
to be the most desirous of, open to and successful with training and
work. Some, especially with young children, will remain at home, but
most want work or training because it is the only way out of the welfare
life. Some promising experiments in work and welfare are underway in
such cities as San Diego and Baltimore. But the old "workfare" approach, when administered as another form of welfare with no attempt
to break the cycle of dependency, is self-defeating. Gainful employment,
even if in public jobs for those unaccommodated by the private sector,
would have beneficial effects beyond earning a living. Jobs and training
would augment self-esteem by exposing women to the values and discipline associated with work, allowing them to pass on to their children
more than their own disadvantages.

The ghetto, more than most circumscribed cultures, seeks to perpet- *39*
uate itself and is ruthless in its demand for conformity. However, it
contains institutions of the larger society—schools, churches, community groups. With minor additional resources, schools, for example,
could incorporate more vigorous and focused ways to prevent teen-age
pregnancy. If pregnancy occurs, girls could be motivated to remain in
school, even after childbirth, thus allowing an existing institution to
accomplish what training programs in later life do more expensively
and with greater difficulty.

Schools and other community institutions also need to become much *40*
more aggressive with boys on the true meaning and responsibilities of
manhood, and the link between manhood and family. Otherwise, many
boys meet little resistance to the ghetto message that associates manhood
with sex but not responsibility.

Most important, nothing can substitute for or have a greater impact *41*
than the full-scale involvement of the black community. Respect for the
black family tradition compels black initiative. Today, blacks are responding. Many black organizations are already involved, including the
National Urban League, the National Association for the Advancement
of Colored People, the National Council of Negro Women and the
National Urban Coalition. In 1983, the country's major black leaders
endorsed a frank statement of the problems of the black family and a
call for solutions. The statement, published by the Joint Center for
Political Studies, a black research center in Washington, represented the
first consensus view by black leadership on the problems of the black
family. Significantly, it went beyond a call for Government help, stress-
ing the need for black leadership and community efforts.

With the increase in the number of black public officials, many black *42*
mayors, legislators and appointed officials control some of the resources
that could help shape change. Although they cannot redesign the welfare
system by themselves, for example, some are in a position to experiment
with model projects that could lead to more workable programs—such
as supplementing welfare grants with training or work opportunities for

single mothers; promoting family responsibility and pregnancy prevention for boys and girls through local institutions, and encouraging the
completion of school for single teen-aged parents.

The new black middle class, a product of the same period that saw *43*
the weakening of the black family, still has roots in the ghetto through
relatives and friends. From churches, Girl Scout troops and settlement
houses to civil-rights organizations, Boys' Clubs and athletic teams, the
work of family reinforcement can be shared widely. The possibilities
for creative community intervention are many—from family planning
and counseling and various roles as surrogate parents and grandparents,
to sex education, community day care and simple, but crucial, con-
sciousness-raising. Most important is passing on the enduring values
that form the central content of the black American heritage: hard work,
education, respect for family, and, notwithstanding the denial of personal opportunity, achieving a better life for one's children.

Rhetorical Analysis Through Annotation

Although discussing current problems, Norton uses much historical information
and makes predictions and proposals for the future.

Identify direct discussions of current problems by drawing a line in the margin
next to such discussions. Next to discussions of historical materials write a few
words indicating their relevance to current issues, and underline phrases and
sentences where Norton connects the historical materials to the current situation.
Mark discussions of the future by double lines in the margin.

Discuss how Norton structures her argument to tie together past, present,
and future to encourage action about a current problem.

Discussion Questions

Interpreting the Text

1. The historical analysis in this article takes advantage of both Moynihan's and
Gutman's analyses. Where and to what extent does the author follow Moynihan's
analysis, and where and to what extent does she follow Gutman's? How does
she combine the two in an overall point of view? What ideas and findings does
she add that neither Moynihan nor Gutman presented? What is her overall picture
of the history and current state of the black family?

2. What comparisons does Norton make between white and black social structure? To what extent are the types of problems she identifies in the black
community also becoming growing problems for parts of the white community?

Considering the Issues

3. Compare the black urban immigrants in the early part of this century with
the working class poor of Newburyport examined by Thernstrom. In what
ways are they similar? Now compare both groups with the new industrialists

of Paterson examined in Gutman's earlier article. What conclusions can you draw about social structure, race, and class at that period in America?

4. How do the post-World War II poor blacks compare with the post-World War I group? What accounts for the differences?

5. What proposals does the author offer? How successful do you think these proposals will be in solving the problems she identifies? Are such programs likely to be implemented?

6. What does Norton find wrong with the welfare program and how would she change it? Do you agree with her?

7. In what ways does this presentation for a Sunday magazine differ from the scholarly academic presentations of Gutman and the political presentation of Moynihan?

Writing Suggestions

1. Imagine you have a summer job working as an assistant to a member of Congress. You have read the article and been impressed with it. In order to call the article to the congressperson's attention write a short note telling what impresses you, followed by a three hundred word summary of the article.

2. Write a letter to the editor of the magazine in which this article appeared to agree or disagree with any point made by Norton.

3. You are a member of a political action group. Write up a short list of specific proposals on an issue of importance to your group. Then write a covering letter to a specific government official explaining why your proposals should be enacted. Alternatively, you may write your proposals and rationale in the form of a position paper for the general voter.

Unit Writing Suggestions

1. After class your economics professor makes an offhand comment that all we have to do to alleviate problems of black poverty is to strengthen the overall economy. Having read the material in this unit, you are bothered by your professor's simplistic view. Write the professor a lengthy letter arguing for a more subtle view of the problem.

2. Imagine you are taking an examination in a course on American history since 1850. Answer the exam essay question, "Based on your reading for this course, describe and evaluate the extent, character, and limitations on social mobility in America since 1850."

3. For a course in American myths, write an essay evaluating the excerpt of Barnum's speech on the "Art of Money-Getting" in light of the other materials presented in this unit.

4. Your cousin in high school has written you a letter describing his problems with history. He complains that history is just a list of dates and names to remember, "a dull story of dead kings and long-ago wars" that has nothing to do with life today. Write him a letter to convince him that historians are concerned with important arguments about the forces that shape our lives. Use examples from the historians in this unit.

5. As part of your discussion in this course about the interaction of reading and writing, write an essay discussing how the different authors represented in this unit use and respond to the writings of the earlier authors. Discuss the way that history is not only a conversation among historians, but also includes the voices of the people historians study as well as, in an important sense, the voices of society contemporary with the historians.

6. Imagine your parents have written you a serious letter inquiring about whether what you have been learning at college has influenced your goals and values in life. Write them a letter in answer, particularly discussing how your goals for economic advancement have been affected by your better understanding of the realities and processes of social mobility in this country.

UNIT
3

SOCIAL SCIENCES
Memory: The World We Carry with Us

The problem of how memory works lies at the heart of psychology, for beyond genetically programmed instructions or instincts, all that we know is stored in memory. Our memories hold what we have seen, learned, done, enjoyed, and suffered. Success at various endeavors, from hunting and farming to education, depends on remembering facts and procedures. Out of our memories we construct our very sense of ourselves.

Yet memory remains elusive. It seems to come and go with a will of its own. We may have a hard time remembering what we need at the store, and then suddenly our minds are flooded with spontaneous recollections of events years past. If only we could control our memories, having everything we needed at our fingertips when we need it, we could go through life (not to speak of school) so much more easily.

When we consider the human nervous system it is hard to know where memories reside. In the brain there is lots of folded grey matter but there are no diskettes labeled "Summer of '83" or "Ancient History of China." We know very little about how memory traces are stored as chemical signals and then how those chemical codes are translated into the form of memory we consciously experience, such as a visual image of our grandfather or a number associated with the world population. Nothing taunts the mind–body distinction quite as much as the problem of memory, for memory is as impressionistic and subjective as the smell of a loved one and so crudely physical as a chemical sitting on the end of a neuron.

Psychology developed as a separate discipline out of philosophy and natural history in the nineteenth century. One of the field's early practitioners was Hermann Ebbinghaus, who did experimental work on memory in the 1880s. Memory has been a subject of inquiry for much longer, however. The ancient Greek and Roman philosophers considered memory an important puzzle. In the ancient world, improving memory was a significant practical matter, for written language was still relatively new, and books were rare. A person could only have access to the knowledge carried in his or her own mind or in the minds of acquaintances who could be consulted. In particular, orators, who had to be able to speak fluently, eloquently, and knowledgeably before large groups, would be helped by expanded memories. Ancient rhetoricians like Quintilian developed several techniques for enhancing memory.

Quintilian first describes the importance of memory in terms that would be familiar to anyone of that time. He then sets forth a well-known method for improving the memory, the method of places. This method requires you to imagine a space such as a room. As you mentally walk around the room you visualize at various spots the items to be remembered. When you need to remember the items you mentally walk through the room again in the same order and notice the same items you left there. Quintilian's concept of memory, however, is already influenced by the appearance of written language. He finds the method of places inadequate to the new literate task of memorizing a written speech verbatim, and he suggests improvements to take advantge of writing as a memory aid. In finding writing an aid to memory, Quintilian disagrees with Plato, who lived five centuries earlier, when writing was much newer. And, of course, Quintilian presented his advice on memorization in writing.

Modern psychologists have approached memory in different ways. Sigmund Freud, in attempting to understand unusual behavior, became interested in the complex emotions he considered to make up the subconscious mind. These complex feelings, for him, explained the elusiveness of personal memory. Spontaneous memories and their retelling became doorways into the darkness of the subconscious. Thus Freud sees in Goethe's retelling of a childhood memory an indication of the writer's extreme attachment to his mother and jealousy towards a newborn sibling. Current clinical psychoanalysis has developed out of the Freudian tradition.

A tradition contrary to the Freudian one developed out of experimental psychology. Experimental psychology, rather than looking into the unconscious processes of the mind, looks at the structure and function of memory. For Ebbinghaus, memory could best be studied by seeing what people, including himself, could remember under controlled laboratory conditions. Other experimentalists, such as Frederick C. Bartlett in the 1930s, thought that through experiments we could also gain some understanding of how material was organized in memory. Most academic psychology has developed within the experimental tradition, and is represented here by a review essay and an experimental report.

In his review essay, Cofer describes the work of Ebbinghaus, Bartlett, and other researchers, and their findings on memory processes, retention, span, the effect of repetition, differences among people, and different types of memory (short term, long term, episodic, semantic). In "Long-Term Memory for a Common Object" Nickerson and Adams report the results of experiments testing subjects' ability to (1) draw accurately a penny and (2) recognize a correctly drawn one. "Performance was surprisingly poor on all tasks," they write, and yet clearly people can distinguish a penny from other coins and objects in their pockets and purses. Thus the authors conclude that recognition tasks do not put a large demand on memory. In other words, we do not have to remember much about the exact details of a penny's appearance to recognize one when we need one.

Some academic psychologists have recently criticized the laboratory's experimental approach as missing the social reality of memory. Ulric Neisser argues that memory is no single thing that can be isolated in the laboratory. Rather he calls for studies of memory in real-life contexts. He examines the ways in which people actually use memories in their lives: to define themselves through childhood and other memories; for self-improvement; for testimony in trials; to learn from other people's past experiences and history; in everyday life for practical purposes such as remembering a planned activity and recognizing a friend; for reciting songs, prayers, or poems; and to do any activity that requires a skill. Neisser feels that each of these areas deserves further study, even though such study of real life will be more difficult than laboratory work.

Finally, physiology, through the physical study of the brain and its chemistry, has offered another approch to understanding memory. A textbook selection presents the current state of knowledge about the brain and its functions with regard to memory.

Whatever psychology takes as its subject—brain, subconscious mind, chemistry, behavior, actions in everyday life—the aim of the discipline is to understand human beings more fully. This unit ends with clinical accounts of the effects of unusual memory capacities on two people. The first man, described by Aleksandr Luria, has the gift of a remarkably powerful memory; the other, described by Oliver Sacks, has suffered extensive amnesia through alcoholic deterioration.

Just as the psychological approaches vary in the selections here, so do the modes and styles of presentation. The ancient author Quintilian offers advice though anecdotes and procedural directions; Freud interprets a text; academic psychologists review the literature and describe experiments with a minimum of personal intrusion. Physiology textbook authors summarize and clarify the signficance of a range of studies. The clinical accounts offer detailed portraits of individuals. It is appropriate for a field that studies patterns and variations in the way people think and act that these selections represent a variety of styles and authorial voices.

The Art of Memory

Quintilian

Today, most things we need to know are recorded in books and magazines, on computer and videotape. If our memory fails us on some important fact, we can always look it up in some reference. In fact, with computers, we can let the computer search for what we need. Only in specific circumstances is it important to have a highly developed memory—such as learning a part in a play, remembering all the names of your business clients, preparing for an examination, or reminiscing about your past. Before electronics, newspapers, and books, however, memory was exceedingly important, because people only had access to the knowledge remembered by the people around them. The ability to remember many details, retell long stories, or deliver speeches from memory was highly prized.

Quintilian, a Roman rhetorician of the first century A.D., lived after the advent of books, but literacy still had not totally transformed the culture; speech making from memory was still of great importance.

The following excerpts are from his *Institutio Oratoria*, which sets out a course of training for orators. He describes the "method of places" for improving memory and methods for using writing to aid memorization. Although like a textbook in recommending procedures and presenting useful information, Quintilian's Institutes depend more on persuasion than textbooks now tend to do. Perhaps because he was teaching adults, he devoted much energy to persuading his readers that his advice is good advice and worth following. Modern textbooks have a much more take-it-or-leave-it attitude.

SOME REGARD MEMORY AS being no more than one of nature's 1 gifts; and this view is no doubt true to a great extent; but, like everything else, memory may be improved by cultivation. . . . Our whole education depends upon memory, and we shall receive instruction all in vain if all we hear slips from us, while it is the power of memory alone that brings before us all the store of precedents, laws, rulings, sayings and facts which the orator must possess in abundance and which he must always hold ready for immediate use. Indeed it is not without good reason that memory has been called the treasure-house of eloquence. But pleaders need not only to be able to retain a number of facts in their 2 minds, but also to be quick to take them in; it is not enough to learn what you have written by dint of repeated reading; it is just as necessary to follow the order both of matter and words when you have merely thought out what you are going to say, while you must also remember what has been said by your opponents, and must not be content merely with refuting their arguments in the order in which they were advanced, but must be in a position to deal with each in its appropriate place. Nay, even extempore° eloquence, in my opinion, depends on no mental activity so much as memory. For while we are saying one thing, we must be considering something else that we are going to say: consequently, *3* since the mind is always looking ahead, it is continually in search of something which is more remote: on the other hand, whatever it discovers, it deposits by some mysterious process in the safe-keeping of memory, which acts as a transmitting agent and hands on to the delivery what it has received from the imagination. I do not conceive, however, that I need dwell upon the question of the precise function of memory. . . . My inclination is rather to marvel at its powers of reproducing and presenting a number of remote facts after so long an interval, and, what is more, of so doing not merely when we seek for such facts, but even at times of its own accord, and not only in our waking moments, but *4* even when we are sunk in sleep. And my wonder is increased by the fact that even beasts, which seem to be devoid of reason, yet remember and recognise things, and will return to their old home, however far they have been taken from it. Again, is it not an extraordinary inconsistency that we forget recent and remember distant events, that we cannot recall what happened yesterday and yet retain a vivid impression of the acts of our childhood? And what, again, shall we say of the fact that the things we search for frequently refuse to present themselves and then occur to us by chance, or that memory does not always remain with us, but will even sometimes return to us after it has been lost? But *5* we should never have realised the fullness of its power nor its supernatural capacities, but for the fact that it is memory which has brought oratory to its present position of glory. For it provides the orator not merely with the order of his thoughts, but even of his words, nor is its power limited to stringing merely a few words together; its capacity for endurance is inexhaustible, and even in the longest pleadings the patience of the audience flags long before the memory of the speaker. This fact may even be advanced as an argument that there must be some art of memory and that the natural gift can be helped by reason, since training enables us to do things which we cannot do before we have had any *6* training or practice. On the other hand, I find that Plato asserts that the use of written characters is a hindrance to memory, on the ground, that is, that once we have committed a thing to writing, we cease to guard it in our memory and lose it out of sheer carelessness. And there can be no doubt that concentration of mind is of the utmost importance in this connexion; it is, in fact, like the eyesight, which turns to, and not away from, the objects which it contemplates. Thus it results that after writing for several days with a view to acquiring by heart what we have written,

---

Extempore—spontaneous, impromptu.

we find that our mental effort has of itself imprinted it on our memory. . . .   7

It is an assistance to the memory if localities are sharply impressed upon the mind, a view the truth of which everyone may realise by practical experiment. For when we return to a place after considerable absence, we not merely recognise the place itself, but remember things that we did there, and recall the persons whom we met and even the unuttered thoughts which passed through our minds when we were there before. Thus, as in most cases, art originates in experiment. Some place is chosen of the largest possible extent and characterized by the utmost possible variety, such as a spacious house divided into a number of rooms. Everything of note therein is carefully committed to the   8 memory, in order that the thought may be enabled to run through all the details without let or hindrance. And undoubtedly the first task is to secure that there shall be no delay in finding any single detail, since an idea which is to lead by association to some other idea requires to be fixed in the mind with more than ordinary certitude. The next step is to distinguish something which has been written down or merely thought of by some particular symbol which will serve to jog the memory; this symbol may have reference to the subject as a whole, it may, for example, be drawn from navigation, warfare, etc., or it may, on the other hand, be found in some particular word. (For even in cases   9 of forgetfulness one single word will serve to restore the memory.) However, let us suppose that the symbol is drawn from navigation, as, for instance, an anchor; or from warfare, as, for example, some weapon. These symbols are then arranged as follows. The first thought is placed, as it were, in the forecourt; the second, let us say, in the living-room; the remainder are placed in due order all round the *impluvium*° and entrusted not merely to bedrooms and parlours, but even to the care of statues and the like. This done, as soon as the memory of the facts requires to be revived, all these places are visited in turn and the various deposits are demanded from their custodians, as the sight of each recalls   10 the respective details. Consequently, however large the number of these which it is required to remember, all are linked one to the other like dancers hand in hand, and there can be no mistake since they join what precedes to what follows, no trouble being required except the preliminary labour of committing the various points to memory. What I have spoken of as being done in a house, can equally well be done in connexion with public buildings, a long journey, the ramparts of a city, or even pictures. . . .

I am far from denying that those devices may be useful for certain purposes, as, for example, if we have to reproduce a number of names   11 in the order in which we heard them. For those who use such aids place the things which have to be remembered in localities which they have

---

Impluvium—open courtyard of a Roman house.

previously fixed in the memory; they put a table, for instance, in the forecourt, a platform in the hall and so on with the rest, and then, when they retrace their steps, they find the objects where they had placed them. Such a practice may perhaps have been of use to those who, after an auction, have succeeded in stating what object they had sold to each buyer, their statements being checked by the books of the moneytakers; a feat which it is alleged was performed by Hortensius.° It will, however, be of less service in learning the various parts of a set speech. For *12* thoughts do not call up the same images as material things, and a symbol requires to be specially invented for them, although even here a particular place may serve to remind us, as, for example, of some conversation that may have been held there. But how can such a method grasp a whole series of connected words? . . .

If a speech of some length has to be committed to memory, it will be well to learn it piecemeal, since there is nothing so bad for the memory as being overburdened. But the sections into which we divide it for this purpose should not be very short: otherwise they will be too many in number, and will break up and distract the memory. . . .   *13*

There is one thing which will be of assistance to everyone, namely, to learn a passage by heart from the same tablets on which he has committed it to writing. For he will have certain tracks to guide him in his pursuit of memory, and the mind's eye will be fixed not merely on the pages on which the words were written, but on individual lines, and at times he will speak as though he were reading aloud. Further, if the writing should be interrupted by some erasure, addition or alteration, there are certain symbols available, the sight of which will prevent us from wandering from the track. This device bears some resemblance to the mnemonic° system which I mentioned above, but if my experience *14* is worth anything, is at once more expeditious° and more effective.

Rhetorical Analysis Through Annotation

Quintilian offers his advice through attempting to persuade the reader of a series of claims.

By underlining or rephrasing in your own words in the margin, identify the main claims Quintilian tries to persuade us of. Then in the margin next to each claim briefly note the kinds of argument used to bolster that claim, such as praising the special values of memory or reminding us of our various needs for good memory.

Discuss whether and in what ways persuasion aids the transmission of advice. Consider what differences may exist between Quintilian's relationship with his readers and a modern textbook writer's relationship with his or her students.

Hortensius Hortalus 114–50 B.C.—Roman orator.   **Mnemonic**—memory-improving.
Expeditious—speedy and efficient.

Discussion Questions

Interpreting the Text

1. What importance does Quintilian find for memory? How much is that importance related to the specific tasks of an orator and how much is generally relevant?

2. In what ways does Quintilian agree and disagree with Plato?

3. What methods does Quintilian offer for the improvement of memory? What are the advantages and limitations of each?

4. How is the memorization of speeches by studying your own transcription related to the method of places? In what ways is it an improvement?

Considering the Issues

5. Does memory have the same importance in our lives as Quintilian attributes to it? In what ways is memory important for us? In what ways do we no longer rely so heavily on it?

6. How good is your memory? Do you think memory can be improved through learned techniques? Do you have any specific techniques for improving your memory?

7. What method do you use if you are trying to remember where you left a book or your keys? Is your method related in any way to the method of places?

8. What is the role of visualization in the various memory methods discussed? How do the methods described here relate to the methods you use to study for tests, learn a part for a play, or memorize a piece of music? To what extent does visualization help your memory?

Writing Suggestions

1. Write a set of instructions for anyone wishing to learn the method of places. Use a specific example to make the method clearer.

2. For this course, as part of the discussion of the effect of writing on knowledge, write an essay discussing the influence of writing on memory. You may consider whether writing has changed our need for memory, our concept of it, or our techniques of memory. As background you may wish to consult Plato's *Phaedrus* to explore the argument between Plato and Quintilian on whether writing has diminished our capacity for memory.

3. Write a self-help column for your local paper offering some piece of advice (on any subject) you think generally useful. Persuade your readers that the advice is good and that they should follow it, using some of the techniques of persuasion that Quintilian does.

An Early Memory from Goethe's Autobiography

Sigmund Freud

Many would date the beginning of modern clinical psychology from Freud's investigation of the unconscious mind at the turn of the twentieth century. Freud's work with disturbed people convinced him that seemingly irrational behavior, speech, and thoughts reflected deep processes in the mind of which we were not consciously aware. Through talks with his patients, he explored the inner distresses that led to disturbed behavior. He took great interest in dreams, slips of the tongue, jokes, and verbal associations that might reflect unconscious concerns of the mind. Memories he thought similar to these other associative verbal reports, because we only remember certain details and not others, and we retell these memories with particular emphases and distortions. He found memories to be projective; that is, we project ourselves into them.

His only data was the speech or writings of individuals; from these reports he would attempt to read out or interpret their minds. Psychoanalysis depends on this interpretation of meaning. In this case, written in 1917 for a scholarly journal, Freud interprets a memory reported by the famous eighteenth-century German writer, Johann Wolfgang von Goethe, as described in the author's autobiography, *Poetry and Truth*. By relating this memory to Goethe's particular family relationships and to general patterns of emotional stress, Freud reconstructs Goethe's psychological make-up. Freud then uses this one case to discuss the general issue of the relationship of psychological attitudes and life success.

"WHEN WE TRY TO remember what happened to us in early child- 1
hood, we often confuse what others have told us with our own directly perceived experiences." The poet Goethe makes this remark near the beginning of his account of his own life, an account which he began to write when he was 60 years old. It is preceded only by a brief description of his birth ". . . on August 28, 1749, at noon as the clock struck twelve." A favorable constellation of the stars may have been responsible for his survival: he was almost given up for dead at birth, and strenuous efforts were required before he saw the light of day. After the remark about memory, there is a brief description of the house he grew up in, and especially of an enclosed area that opened on to the street, which the children—he and his younger sister—liked best. But then Goethe really describes only a single event that can be assigned to his "earliest

childhood" (before the age of four?), an event of which he seemed to have retained a personal memory. His account of this episode is as follows:

> Across the street lived the three brothers von Ochsenstein, sons of the late Village Mayor. They grew fond of me, and busied themselves with me and teased me in many ways.
>
> My family loved to tell all sorts of stories about the mischievous tricks to which those otherwise solemn and lonely men encouraged me. I will recount only one of these pranks here. There had been a pottery sale; not only had the kitchen been supplied for some time to come, but miniature crockery of the same sort had been bought for us children to play with. One fine afternoon, when there was nothing doing in the house, I played with my dishes and pots in the rooms (mentioned above) that fronted on the street. Since this didn't come to much, I tossed a piece of crockery out into the street and was delighted by its cheerful crash. The brothers saw how much this amused me, so that I clapped my hands with delight, and called out "another!" I did not hesitate to fling the next pot, and—encouraged by repeated shouts of "another"—a whole assortment of little dishes, saucepans, and jugs onto the pavement. My neighbors continued to signal their approval, and I was more than glad to amuse them. My supplies ran out, but they continued to shout "another!" I hurried straight to the kitchen and fetched the earthenware plates, which of course made an even jollier show as they broke. So I ran back and forth with one plate after another, as I could get them down from the shelf, and when the brothers still claimed to be unsatisfied I hurled every bit of crockery within my reach to ruin in the same way. Only later did someone appear to thwart me and put a stop to it. The damage was done, and in return for all that broken crockery there was at least a wonderful story, which amused the rogues who had been its prime movers till the end of their days.

In preanalytic times this passage would not have been disturbing and   *2* could be read without hesitation, but now the analytic conscience has come to life. We have formed definite opinions and have definite expectations about early childhood memories, and would like to suppose that they apply quite generally. It is not a meaningless or insignificant matter when some one particular of a child's life escapes the general forgetting of childhood. On the contrary, one must suppose that what has been retained in memory is also what was most significant for that period of life: either it already had great importance at the time or else it acquired that importance through the effect of later experiences.

It is true that the great significance of such childhood memories is   *3* rarely obvious. Most of them appear unimportant or even trivial, and at first it seemed incomprehensible that just these could defy the amnesia of childhood. The individual who had preserved them through long years as his personal memories could no more do them justice than the stranger to whom he related them. Recognition of their significance required a certain amount of interpretive work—work that either showed how their contents should be replaced by something else, or demonstrated their connection to other unmistakably important experiences for which they had substituted as so-called "screen memories."°

Whenever one works through a life history psychoanalytically, one *4* always succeeds in clarifying the meaning of the earliest recollections in this way. As a rule it turns out that the very memory to which the analysand° gives primacy, which he tells first as he begins his life story, is the most important and holds the key to the secret chambers of his mental life. But in the case of the little incident related by Goethe, we do not have enough to work with. The ways and means that we use to reach interpretations with our own patients are naturally unavailable here, and it does not seem possible to link the incident itself in any clear way with important experiences of his later life. A prank that damaged some household goods, carried out under the influence of outsiders, is surely not a suitable vignette to stand for everything Goethe tells us about his rich life experience. The impression of complete innocence and irrelevance seems to be confirmed for this childhood memory, which may thus teach us not to push the claims of psychoanalysis too far or to apply them on inappropriate occasions.

I had long since put this small problem out of my mind when chance *5* brought me a patient who presented a similar childhood memory, but in a more comprehensible context. The patient was a highly cultured and intelligent man, twenty-seven years old, whose whole life was consumed by a conflict with his mother that reached into nearly every aspect of his existence, severely impairing the development of his capacity to love and to lead an independent life. The conflict went far back into his childhood, apparently to his fourth year. Before that time he had been a weak and always sickly child, but his memory had turned that difficult time into a paradise because he then possessed the unrestricted affection of his mother, not divided with anyone else. When he was not yet four his brother was born, a brother who is still living today. In reacting to this intrusion, he transformed himself into a headstrong and unmanageable lad who constantly provoked his mother's strictness. He never again got on the right track.

When he became my patient—not least because his bigoted mother *6* detested psychoanalysis—he had long since forgotten his jealousy of his brother, a jealousy which in its time had even led him to try to kill the baby in its cradle. He now treated his younger brother with great respect. Nevertheless certain apparently unmotivated actions, in which he suddenly caused severe injury to animals that he otherwise loved—

Screen memories—condensed, symbolic memories that show some displacement from the original events.   **Analysand**—person under analysis.

his hunting dog, and birds that he had carefully tended—were probably best understood as echoes of the hostile impulse once directed against his little brother.

This patient reported that on one occasion, around the time when he 7 tried to kill his hated brother, he had thrown all the crockery he could reach out of the window of his house into the street. The very same thing that Goethe describes in his personal recollections! It is worth noting that my patient was a foreigner who had not had a German education; he had never read Goethe's autobiography.

This piece of information necessarily suggested to me that Goethe's 8 childhood recollection might be interpreted in the way that my patient's story had made irresistible. But could the conditions necessary to support this interpretation be found in the poet's childhood? Goethe himself lays the responsibility for his childhood prank on the urgings of the von Ochsensteins, but his account actually indicates that his neighbors had only cheered him on to continue his own activity. He had begun quite spontaneously. When he gives "Since this (his playing) didn't come to much" as his reason for beginning, we can safely conclude that he was unaware of the real motive of his action at the time he wrote the autobiography, and probably for many years before.

It is known that Johann Wolfgang Goethe and his sister Cornelia were 9 the oldest survivors of a larger set of rather sickly children. Dr. Hanns Sachs has been kind enough to provide me with the dates pertaining to those of Goethe's siblings who died young:

a. Hermann Jakob, christened on Monday, November 27, 1752, reached the age of six years and six weeks; buried on January 13, 1759.

b. Katharina Elisabetha, christened on Monday, September 9, 1754; buried on Thursday, December 22, 1755 (one year and four months old).

c. Johanna Maria, christened on Tuesday, March 29, 1757; buried on Saturday, August 11, 1759 (two years and four months old). This was certainly the very charming and pretty young girl described by her brother.

d. Georg Adolph, christened on Sunday, June 15, 1760; buried, eight months old, on Wednesday, February 18, 1761.

Goethe's closest sister, Cornelia Friederica Christiana, was born on 10 December 7, 1750, when he was one-and-a-quarter years old. The very small difference in their ages virtually excludes her as an object of jealousy. It is known that when children's emotional life is awakened, they never react so strongly against the siblings who are already there; they rather direct their antipathy toward the new arrivals. Then, too, it would be impossible to reconcile the scene we are trying to interpret with Goethe's tender age at the time of (and just after) Cornelia's birth.

Goethe was three-and-a-quarter years old when his first brother, Her- *11* mann Jakob, was born. About two years later, when he was about five, his second sister arrived. Both ages must be considered in trying to date the crockery-smashing incident. The first may be more likely; it also corresponds more closely with the case of my patient, who was about three-and-three-quarters when his brother was born.

It is worth noting that brother Hermann Jakob, to whom this attempt *12* at interpretation seems to lead, was not such a fleeting guest in Goethe's nursery as the later siblings. Surprisingly, there is not a single word about him in his elder brother's life story.[1] He attained more than six years of age, and when he died Johann Wolfgang was nearly ten years old. Dr. Ed. Hitschmann, who was kind enough to make his notes on this matter available to me, has expressed this opinion:

> Young Goethe was also not unhappy at a younger brother's death. At least his mother gave the following account, reported by Bettina Brentano: "It seemed strange to his mother that he shed no tears at the death of his brother Jakob, who was his playmate; indeed, he seemed somewhat irritated at the lamentations of his parents and sisters. When the mother later asked the obstinate boy if he hadn't loved his brother, he ran to his room and brought out a pile of papers from under his bed. They were covered with lessons and stories, and he told her that he had done all this to teach it to his brother." Thus it seems that the older brother had at least enjoyed playing father to the younger, showing off his own superiority.

We can conclude that the throwing out of the crockery was a sym- *13* bolic, or more precisely a magical act. By this act the child (Goethe as well as my patient) gives vigorous expression to his wish that the disturbing intruder be eliminated. We do not need to deny the delight that the child takes in the crashing objects. The fact that an action is pleasurable in itself does not prevent—indeed, it invites—repetition in the service of other motives. But we do not believe that delight in jingling and smashing could have assured these childish pranks a permanent place in the memories of grown men. We do not even hesitate to introduce an additional complication into our account of the motivation for this act. The child who breaks the crockery knows perfectly well that he is being naughty, and that the adults will scold him for it. If this knowledge does not restrain him, he probably has some grudge against his parents; he wants to show how bad he is.

Taking delight in breaking and in broken things would also be possible *14* if the child just threw the fragile objects on the floor. On this basis, throwing them out the window into the street would remain unexplained. But "out" seems to be an essential component of the magical act, which stems from its hidden meaning. The new baby is to be removed through the window, perhaps because it came through the window in the first place. The whole affair would then be equivalent to what we are told was the response of one child when he was informed that the stork had brought him a little sister. "Let him take her away again" was his suggestion.

However, we are fully aware how dubious it is—apart from any **15** internal uncertainties—to base the interpretation of a childhood event on a single analogy. For this reason I withheld my interpretation of the little scene from Goethe's autobiography for many years. Then one day I had a patient who began his analysis with the following sentences, which I reproduce verbatim:

> I am the oldest of eight or nine brothers and sisters.[2] One of my first memories is of my father sitting on his bed in his nightclothes, laughingly telling me that I had acquired a brother. I was then three-and-three-quarters years old; that is the difference in age between me and my closest brother. Then I know that shortly afterwards (or was it the year before?)[3] I threw various objects—brushes, or maybe just one brush, and shoes and other things—out the window into the street. I also have a still earlier memory. When I was two years old I spent the night with my parents in a hotel room in Linz when we were traveling to Salzkammergut. I was so restless during the night and cried so much that my father had to hit me.

In the face of this testimony I had to abandon all doubt. When a **16** patient in the analytic setting produces two ideas one after the other, almost in a single breath, we must interpret their proximity as a causal connection. So it was as if the patient had said "Because I learned that I had acquired a brother, I threw those things into the street soon thereafter." The throwing out of the brushes, shoes, etc. is recognizable as a reaction to the birth of the brother. It is also helpful that this time the thrown objects were not crockery but other things, probably just those that happened to be within reach. In this way the throwing out itself is revealed as the essential element of the action. The delight in jingling and breaking, and the nature of the objects on which the "execution is carried out" are revealed as variable and inessential.

Naturally the principle of relatedness must also be valid for the pa- **17** tient's third memory, which was placed at the end of the sequence although it is actually the earliest. It is easily applied. We understand that the two-year-old child was restless because he couldn't stand his father and mother being together in bed. On the journey it was probably impossible to prevent the child from witnessing this intimacy. Of the feelings that were aroused in the tiny jealous child at that time, a bitterness against women remained as a continuing source of disturbance in the development of his later life.

After these two experiences, I suggested to a meeting of the Psycho-   *18*
analytic Society that behavior of this sort in young children might not
be so rare. In response, Dr. von Hug-Hellmuth has made two further
observations available to me. Here are her reports:

I

At about three-and-a-half years, little Erich "very suddenly" acquired
the habit of throwing everything that didn't suit him out the window.
But he also did it to things that weren't in his way and had nothing to
do with him. On his father's birthday, when he was three years, four-
and-a-half-months old, he hauled a heavy rolling pin from the kitchen
into another room and flung it out of a window of the third-floor
apartment onto the street. A few days later the mortar-pestle went the
same way, followed by a pair of his father's heavy mountaineering
boots that he first had to take out of their storage box.[4]

At that time his mother had a miscarriage; she had been seven or
eight months pregnant. After that the little boy "seemed to have been
transformed, he was so good and so quietly gentle." In the fifth or
sixth month he had repeatedly said to his mother, "Mommy, I'm
going to jump on your stomach," or "Mommy, I'll squash your stomach flat." In October, a few days before the miscarriage, he said, "If I
really have to have a brother, let it at least not be till after Christmas."

II

A young woman of nineteen spontaneously offered the following as
her earliest recollection:

I see myself sitting under the table in the dining room, ready to
creep out, feeling terribly disobedient. On the table is my coffee-
mug—I can see the pattern of the porcelain clearly, even now—which I
had just been going to throw out the window when my grandmother
happened to come into the room.

The fact was that nobody had been concerning themselves with me,
and as a result a "skin" had formed on the coffee—which I always
found loathsome and still do.

My brother, who is two-and-a-half years younger than I am, was
born that day; that was why nobody had time for me.

They still talk about how unbearable I was that day. Around noon I
threw my father's favorite glass off the table; I soiled my dress several
times; I was in the foulest possible mood all day long. I also smashed
one of my bathtub toys in my rage.

It is hardly necessary to comment on these two cases. They confirm,   *19*
without any additional analysis, that the child's bitterness about the
expected or actual appearance of a competitor expresses itself in the act
of throwing things out the window as well as by other naughty and
destructive deeds. The "heavy objects" in the first case probably symbolize the mother herself, at whom the child's anger is directed so long

as the new baby has not yet actually appeared. The three-and-a-half-year-old boy knows that his mother is pregnant, and is quite sure that she is sheltering the baby in her body. . . .

If we now return to Goethe's early memory, and put what we think   *20* we have learned from the cases of these other children in its place, we find a perfectly comprehensible connection that would otherwise have remained undiscovered. It runs as follows: "I was a child of fortune; fate kept me alive although I had been given up for dead when I came into the world. The same fate got rid of my brother, so that I did not have to share my mother's love with him." From there the train of his thoughts goes on to another person who died in that early period of his life: his grandmother, who lived like a quiet and friendly ghost in another room of his home.

As I have already said elsewhere, he who has been the unquestioned   *21* darling of his mother will keep that feeling of victory, that certainty of success, for the rest of his life. It is a feeling that not infrequently brings real success in its wake. And a remark like "My strength is rooted in my relationship with my mother" would have been an entirely appropriate way for Goethe to begin the story of his life.

Notes

[1][*Freud added the following footnote to the article when it was published in 1924.*] I will use this opportunity to retract an incorrect statement that never should have occurred. Later on in the first volume, the younger brother *is* mentioned and described. This is done in the course of Goethe's recollections of the burdensome illness of childhood, which afflicted his brother "not a little." "He was of a delicate constitution, quiet and self-willed; we never had a real relationship with one another. Also he did not really survive the years of childhood." [*Apparently Freud himself made a Freudian slip in his eagerness to establish what he thought was a Freudian slip on Goethe's part.*]

[2]A striking momentary lapse. Unquestionably it was already produced by the wish to get rid of the brother. (cf. Ferenczi, On the formation of transient symptoms during analysis, *Zentralblat für Psychoanalyse*, 1912, 2.)

[3]This expression of doubt, attached to the most essential part of the patient's statement, is a form of resistance. The patient himself retracted it shortly thereafter.

[4]He always chose heavy objects.

Rhetorical Analysis Through Annotation

The core of this selection is a memory narrative, repeated several times for different people. In the margin next to each narrative of an expulsion incident, place a single line and identify the person telling the incident.

Each memory narrative is then placed in the context of the person's family relationships as a child. In the margin, mark each account of family relationships with double lines.

The feeling individual stands in between each narrative and the family circumstances. Circle each statement of a child's attitude toward the family relationship and the incident and any supporting details confirming this attitude.

These separate analyses are then connected in a general pattern. Underline all Freud's attempts to discuss the connection of these separate incidents, and put a double underline under all generalizations developed from the repeated pattern.

Discuss how Freud develops general conclusions out of a pattern of separate cases, and then uses that pattern to help support individual interpretations. How would you evaluate his use of evidence, the completeness of his reasoning, and the certainty of Freud's conclusions? On what does he rest his attempt to persuade?

Discussion Questions

Interpreting the Text

1. What conclusions does Freud draw about this one incident in Goethe's life? About Goethe's personality? About this type of memory in many people? About tensions individuals feel about their family relationships? About memory and the unconscious? About interpretation?

2. How are these different conclusions related? Which was Freud most interested in? Which do you find most significant?

3. Why does Freud note that the patient had not read Goethe's autobiography? Why is it important to Freudian theory that these actions and thoughts occur spontaneously to individuals?

Considering the Issues

4. Why does this document make statements on so many different levels? What makes this text so complex? Is that complexity a strength or a weakness of the text?

5. Do the interpretations offered here seem plausible, persuasive, or far-fetched? Do you think people's memories, feelings, and behaviors really are shaped by early childhood experiences and thoughts?

6. Have you ever witnessed a child's behavior or emotions similar to those described here? Have the incidents you witnessed involved jealousy over a new brother or sister? How do children tend to react to new siblings? Do you think our views of such situations have been influenced by Freud's view?

7. Do you agree with Freud's assessment of the relationship between success and feeling oneself to be mother's darling? How does this idea relate to the experience of people you know?

Writing Suggestions

1. Imagine you are undergoing analysis. Describe a childhood memory and then discuss what it may mean. Or, describe your attitude toward some member of your family and then any memories that arise. Or, more casually, just start writing about your childhood. In all cases your purpose will be psychoanalytic, to help understand yourself better and to share that understanding with a trusted person. These notes need not be shared with classmates if you do not wish them to be. Associate freely. Do not worry about writing a well-structured essay.

2. Pretend you are a psychologist, giving an interpretation of some memory of a friend, family member, teacher, or boss. You may fabricate the memory as well as the psychological principles in order to develop your own view of what is going on in this person's mind. You may wish to do this as a comic parody of psychological interpretations.

3. As part of the class's discussion of ideas raised by the reading, write an essay about family relationships and success. Base your essay on an interview with someone you consider successful. Ask the person interviewed about childhood, family life, and to what he or she attributes success. Use the evidence of the interview to support or counter Freud's claim.

4. For a class in psychology, describe the Freudian method based on this example.

5. For a course in literary criticism, write an essay comparing Freudian interpretation to literary interpretation. Consider the methods and purpose as well as how they handle a specific text. You may wish to compare how Freud handles the passage from Goethe's autobiography with how a literary critic might handle it.

Two Experimental Traditions in the Study of Memory

Charles N. Cofer

At the same time that medically trained Freud was talking with patients in Vienna, philosophically trained professors in Germany, England, and the United States were attempting to understand the mind through experiments. Most modern university departments of psychology grew out of this tradition of experimental psychology. Instead of interpreting what people say about themselves, experimental psychologists watch what people (and animals) do under controlled, experimental conditions. Thus, experimental psychology tends to emphasize behavior rather than thinking. Extreme behaviorists tend to be totally uninterested in thinking, while the less extreme ones think that behavior can give important clues about the structure of thought.

The following selection, written in 1975, reviews how experimental psychology has approached memory. The earliest attempts were to describe the human capacity for memory as exhibited in carefully controlled experimental conditions, separated from the complicating factors of daily life. Cofer, professor of psychology at Pennsylvania State University, calls this the Ebbinghaus tradition, after one of the earliest experimental psychologists. The more recent attempts to use experiments to develop theories about the structure of mind, Cofer calls the Bartlett tradition.

This review of the literature originally appeared as an introduction to a volume of studies by various researchers. In the social sciences and natural sciences, such reviews are commonly placed at the beginning of books and articles to show how the new work fits in and addresses important current issues. Such reviews establish that findings are part of a focused disciplinary discussion. Review articles are sometimes published as independent essays to sum up work in a field and point to new directions. Each review, although drawing on the literature of the field, presents the author's particular synthesis, and thus offers a personal view.

THE STUDY OF MEMORY by psychologists has a long history of *1* experimental work, dating from the publication in 1885 of Hermann Ebbinghaus' monograph, *Memory*. However, consideration of memory has not been solely the province of psychologists. Memory has been a topic of interest to philosophy as early as the time of Plato and Aristotle; to psychiatry and neurology as part of the diagnostic examination; to psychoanalysis as represented in Freud's theory of forgetting as a consequence of repression; to literature as seen in Proust's *Remembrance of Things Past*; and, recently, to computer scientists and students of artificial intelligence, who must provide a "memory" or storage of facts, principles, and operations in order to write programs for complex processing by computer.

It is beyond the scope of this book to deal with memory as it concerns *2* psychiatry, psychoanalysis, and literature. Philosophy does not enter directly either, although the thoughtful reader will discern in these pages a number of philosophical issues, largely in the form of implicit assumptions about memory and the ways in which human beings deal with and represent experience. Representations that endure after an actual experience has ended are, of course, the essence of memory. Memory is the name we give to our ability, good or poor, to hold in mind both recent experiences and those which constitute our pasts. We remember what we learned in school, what we have read, what people have said, where we live and work, what we did yesterday and what we must do today or tomorrow. Of course, a common complaint is that we do not remember things well; this is one of the reasons for our interest in memory. Were our memories perfect, never failing us in time of need, we should probably not concern ourselves with memory at all.

The assumption that memorial processes can be studied . . . has un- **3** derlain all experimental work on memory since it was initiated by Ebbinghaus in the years 1879–1880 (see Ebbinghaus, 1885, p. 33). Yet, in the last quarter century, the problems to which experimentation has been directed have shifted from those that concerned Ebbinghaus. While his emphasis on careful laboratory procedures and quantitative methods remains, recent investigators have identified new problems and devised new techniques for their study. The chapters in this book represent some of these conceptual and methodological developments. It will be instructive to discuss, in summary form, the concerns of students of memory throughout the history of its experimental study, the methods they have used in experimentation, and how both those concerns and those methods have altered as the decades have passed.

The Ebbinghaus Tradition

Ebbinghaus, in the introduction to his monograph (pp. 1–2), referred **4** to certain effects of memory, which presumably spurred him to study memory. He pointed out three effects of memory: (a) we can "by an exertion of the will" recover lost states (i.e., reproduce them); (b) prior states can occur to us involuntarily (i.e., spontaneously); (c) even without the reproduction of "lost states," the states continue to have influence—they may govern "a certain range of thought" and they represent "the boundless domain of the effect of accumulated experiences. . . ." Ebbinghaus also spoke of the conditions on which memory depends, referring to differences among individuals and to differences in the contents to be regained. He suggested roles for attentiveness and interest, as well as for repetition, as conditions of memory. He pointed out how little was known about memory, and he saw a value in applying the methods of natural science to its study. Yet, he realized the difficulties. How, he asked, can we keep "constant the bewildering mass of causal conditions which, insofar as they are of mental nature, almost completely elude our control, and which, moreover, are subject to endless and incessant change?" Further, how can we "measure numerically the mental processes which flit by so quickly and which on introspection are so hard to analyze?" (pp. 7–8).

Ebbinghaus solved these methodological difficulties by setting up **5** laboratory studies of memory on himself. He standardized conditions, invented materials to be studied, devised a procedure of investigation, and found ways of measuring his results in quantitative form.

The study of memory, as Ebbinghaus realized, is difficult, and he **6** thought to circumvent these difficulties by the means just listed. It is not clear whether he felt that his studies contributed to the solution of the problems he raised in his introductory chapter. At any rate, he did not discuss his findings in relation to those problems.

How did he solve the problems of method he had set forth? Basically, 7 he solved them by studying the retention of associations he acquired under strictly controlled conditions. First, he invented the nonsense syllable, a unit composed of a vowel surrounded by two consonants which was not a three-letter word. He made up over 2300 of these syllables and, for an experiment, assembled some of the syllables into a list to be learned in order from beginning to end. He used lists of varying lengths (e.g., 8 items or 32 items), read through each list a number of times, tested his ability to recite the items in order from memory, and concluded his study of a list when he could recite the items in order without error either once or twice.

As a measure of performance, Ebbinghaus simply counted the number 8 of repetitions it took him to be able to recite the list without error; he also measured the time in seconds required for him to learn lists to this criterion of mastery. With this measure he could compare for difficulty lists of different lengths and could measure their retention over time. To assess retention, he relearned lists; if after a time interval he could relearn a list in fewer repetitions or in less time than had been required for original learning then there was a saving. He used the savings method to study retention or forgetting as well as to examine certain other problems (e.g., the formation of remote associations).

The methods introduced by Ebbinghaus dominated the study of mem- 9 ory (called verbal learning by Meumann as early as 1913) for 65 to 70 years. A basic feature of his methods is that material is presented *de novo*° to a person who is to learn or remember it. As Meyer and Schvaneveldt point out, some recent investigations of memory omit this step and use procedures to gain access to what a person already knows. However, before the developments to which Meyer and Schvaneveldt refer occurred, even investigators not sympathetic to the use of nonsense syllables, rote memory, or repetition in studies of memory (such as Bartlett, 1932) presented the to-be-remembered material to their subjects.

We cannot review here all of the work that was conducted in the 10 Ebbinghaus tradition (see McGeoch and Irion, 1952). But the bulk of it was concerned with five main problems: (a) the conditions governing economy in learning; (b) the differences in acquisition and retention occasioned by different sorts of materials, for example poems versus lists of nonsense syllables; (c) differences among people in learning and retention; (d) the conditions and the theory of forgetting; (e) the transfer of training, that is, the extent to which and the conditions under which learning one thing (e.g., one language) affects the learning of another

---

De novo—for the first time.

thing (e.g., another language) either positively or negatively. Numerous variations in methods, procedures, and materials were introduced in the course of these various studies but their general tenor remained close to that of Ebbinghaus' work.

The Bartlett Tradition

In 1932 Frederick C. Bartlett reported experiments that deviated in   *11* several ways from those of the Ebbinghaus tradition. He did present a passage—a story—but usually only once. He tested for recall of the passage over substantial time intervals. Bartlett opposed the use of repetition and meaningless materials, although his famous story, "The War of the Ghosts," was a version of an Eskimo folk tale and contained a number of unfamiliar elements, such as unusual sequences, supernatural ideas, and actions (e.g., hunting for seals) not common in the experience of his experimental subjects, who were British. He published some of the "recalls" he obtained, and they displayed a great deal of error when compared with the original. They were abbreviated for one thing, but, more dramatically, they contained normalizations of the original content in the direction of making that content more compatible with the subject's knowledge and cultural experience. From these recalls, Bartlett concluded that memory is a schematic process—people remember a general impression of a passage they have read and a few details; out of these components they construct or reconstruct a version which they believe is a fair representation of the original.

Bartlett's findings have received a good deal of citation, but until   *12* recently they were not followed up very much by further studies or by theoretical analysis. Most of the work reported in this book is, however, more in his tradition than in the tradition of Ebbinghaus.

Structural Analyses of Memory

That memory may be viewed as a system of interrelated components is   *13* a structural idea. It is not an entirely new idea, as William James (1890, 1, pp. 643–648) distinguished between *primary memory*, one that endured for a very brief period of time, and *secondary memory*, "the knowledge of a former state of mind after it has already once dropped from consciousness . . ." (p. 648). Meumann (1913, p. 317) made a similar distinction. Further, there have long been tests of an individual's *memory span*, that is, of the maximum number of digits, letters, isolated words, or words in sentences one can report in order after a single presentation. James' distinction, however, was essentially a phenomenal° one, and the

---

Phenomenal—based on perceived experience.

concept of memory span has been used mainly to test intelligence, compare the abilities of people of different ages, and study psychological and neurological disorders.

The recent development of structural models of memory was fore- *14* shadowed in Miller's (1956) paper. Miller used data from memory-span experiments to show that normal, adult, educated people can repeat back in order an average of only seven digits, letters, or words, despite the different informational loads that these kinds of material carry. He recognized, of course, that we are capable of much better memorial performances than this, and he suggested that the capacity of memory is augmented by coding or recoding devices. For example, we can perhaps remember 25 words rather than 7 if, say, the 25 words include 5 words from each of 5 categories, such as animals, weapons, articles of clothing, names of countries, and names of cities. As we listen to or read the list of words we can recode this input into the category names and, at recall, remembering the category names, produce the instances to which they are related.

In his paper Miller developed the notion of the organism as an infor- *15* mation-processing device, with a limited capacity for handling information but with procedures for overcoming, at least to some extent, this limited capacity. Broadbent (1958) introduced an information-processing approach that contained explicitly a short-term memory (STM) of limited capacity. While information resided in this memory, it could be rehearsed and transferred to a more permanent store; alternatively, without rehearsal, it would be lost.

At about this time, Brown (1958), Peterson and Peterson (1959), and *16* Sperling (1960) reported investigations of short-term memory. Peterson and Peterson showed that under certain conditions there is rapid forgetting of subspan° items (like nonsense syllables), and Sperling suggested that after very brief visual presentation the information in the visual image is lost very rapidly. It seemed obvious to various writers that these observations required that there be not one but several memories in the human system, a very short-term memory as suggested by Sperling's findings, a short-term memory according to the Brown-Peterson experiments, and a long-term memory (LTM) to accommodate the obvious fact that all of us can and do retain enormous amounts of information over very long time intervals. . . .

Structural models of memory represent a departure from simple as- *17* sociative models of memory. The latter, seemingly present in the works of such writers as Hobbes, Locke, Hume, and Ebbinghaus, represent the memorial process as a system of paths or chains of association that lead us from a question or some other cue to the answer or fact which memory contains. . . .

Subspan—less than the standard memory span.

Structural accounts of memory can be more complex than those we **18** have considered so far. For example, it may be desirable to subdivide the long-term-memory component already mentioned. Tulving (1972) made such a suggestion, pointing out that in our long-term memories we have available to us knowledge of the episodes in our pasts as well as knowledge of rules, facts, principles, and the like which have an existence independent of our own personal pasts. He suggested the terms *episodic memory* and *semantic°* memory for these two classes of knowledge. One might distinguish them in the following way. My knowledge of how to take the square root of a number is representative of knowledge that is independent of me as an individual; it is part of arithmetic, a system of rules which anyone can learn. However, my memory or knowledge of having learned this skill—where and by whom it was taught to me or in what book I studied it—is more or less unique; it is a memory of an event or events that occurred in a time or place in my past. The rules for finding a square root are part of semantic memory; the remembrance of where, when, and how I learned those rules is part of episodic memory.

Tulving stressed differences between these two sorts of memories. **19** One difference is that semantic memory is productive or generative, whereas episodic memory is not. Thus, I can apply the rules for taking a square root to any number, or my knowledge of the rules for alpha-betizing words to any words. Memory for episodes does not have this character. There are, no doubt, parts of semantic memory which are not productive or generative° either, like knowledge I may have of the succession of Presidents of the United States or of the sequence of the Kings and Queens of England. But much knowledge in semantic mem-ory is potentially generative.

References

Bartlett, F. C. *Remembering*. Cambridge: Cambridge University Press, 1932.
Broadbent, D. E. *Perception and communication*. London: Pergamon, 1958.
Brown, J. Some tests of the decay theory of immediate memory. *Quarterly Journal of Experimental Psychology*, 1958, *10*, 12–21.
Ebbinghaus, H. *Memory* (H. A. Ruger and C. E. Bussenius, trans.). New York: Teachers College, 1913. Reprint. New York: Dover, 1964. (Originally published in 1885.)
James, W. *The principles of psychology* (2 vols.). New York: Henry Holt, 1890.
Jarvella, R. J. Syntactic processing of connected speech. *Journal of Verbal Learning and Verbal Behavior*, 1971, *10*, 409–416.
McGeoch, J. A., and Irion, A. L. *The psychology of human learning*. New York: Longmans, Green, 1952.

Semantic—relating to word meanings.   **Generative**—able to generate new behaviors or knowledge.

Meumann, E. [*The psychology of learning: An experimental investigation of the economy and technique of learning*] (J. W. Baird, trans.) New York: D. Appleton, 1913. (Originally published in 1912.)

Miller, G. A. The magical number seven, plus or minus two: Some limits on our capacity for processing information. *Psychological Review*, 1956, *63*, 81–97.

Peterson, L. R., and Peterson, M. J. Short-term retention of individual items. *Journal of Experimental Psychology*, 1959, *58*, 193–198.

Sperling, G. The information available in brief visual presentations. *Psychological Monographs*, 1960, *74*, No. 11.

Tulving, E. Episodic and semantic memory. In E. Tulving and W. Donaldson (Eds.), *Organization of memory*. New York: Academic Press, 1972.

Rhetorical Analysis Through Annotation

The review tells a three-level story about researchers, research, and ideas. Circle the names of researchers and statements about them as individuals. Mark with a line in the margin each narrative describing the research they did. Underline statements about the meaning of what they did, or the major ideas derived from their work. Discuss how these three separate levels of accounts are organized and related to each other. Discuss what is the most significant message at each level and how these various messages are related.

These three levels are then connected to make an overall narrative. Put the letters "tr" next to each transitional sentence or phrase. Discuss how each transition makes a connection beween the levels of researchers, research, and ideas.

Finally look at the opening and closing of the entire selection. Discuss which of the three levels are emphasized in these framing sections and how all three levels are united.

Discussion Questions

Interpreting the Text

1. Cofer quotes Ebbinghaus about the "bewildering mass of causal connections" that make the study of memory difficult. What do you think Ebbinghaus meant by this? What are some of the things you think may affect memory? How do the laboratory experiments of Ebbinghaus attempt to simplify matters? What complex causal factors are left out? Which are not? Do you think the method was likely to prove successful? In what way? What were the strong and weak points of his method?

2. Why might have Bartlett objected to the use of artificial rote memory tasks as the way to study memory? How were these objections related to his theory that people remember general impressions more than details?

3. What does the connected narrative of this review of the literature tell you that would not be told by a series of separate summaries of the same research discussed here?

4. What is the difference between semantic and episodic memories? Give additional examples of the difference, other than the one provided by Cofer.

Considering the Issues

5. Are the study and theory of forgetting the same as the study and theory of remembering? In what ways may they be similar and connected and in what ways different?

6. How do the various studies described here compare to your experience of memory? You may think about rote memory in school, memory of impressions, and differences between short- and long-term memory.

Writing Suggestions

1. As part of this class's discussion of the meaning of specialized studies for nonspecialists, write a personal account of your experience of memory. Relate your experiences to concepts discussed in this chapter, such as short- and long-term memory, gist versus detail, and rote learning.

2. Imagine you are taking an examination in a course in psychology. Use the material in this section to respond to the assignment, "Review the major trends in the psychological study of memory."

3. Write a letter to a former teacher about the effectiveness of how the teacher fostered learning and memory. Use the research reported here to praise, complain, or make suggestions.

4. Imagine that you are the official historian of ideas for one of your classes. Choose a meeting of the class in which you are discussing concepts and take careful notes. Then review the discussion in an essay, describing the important issues that emerged, the major ideas, and how individuals developed different lines of thinking.

Long-Term Memory for a Common Object

Raymond S. Nickerson and Marilyn Jager Adams

In the following article from the research journal *Cognitive Psychology*, Raymond S. Nickerson and Marilyn Adams, psychologists working under a Defense Department contract for the private research company Bolt Beranek and Newman, suggest that our memories are not nearly as good as we think. But their results, published in 1979, suggest that our memories are good enough for our purposes; our need to know, they conclude, conditions what we remember.

The simple results of the experiments gain additional meaning when they are compared to findings of other researchers. Apparent contradictions among findings lead to deeper insights and a sense of how a wide range of results may fit together. The extensive consideration of the literature in the discussion section shows how the various findings presented in this article and in others illuminate each other.

Abstract   A series of experiments was done to determine how completely and accurately people remember the visual details of a common object, a United States penny. People were asked to: draw a penny from unaided recall; draw a penny given a list of its visual features; choose from among a list of possible features those which do appear on a penny; indicate what was wrong with an erroneous drawing of a penny; and select the correct representation of a penny from among a set of incorrect drawings. Performance was surprisingly poor on all tasks. On balance, the results were consistent with the idea that the visual details of an object, even a very familiar object, are typically available from memory only to the extent that they are useful in everyday life. It was also suggested that recognition tasks may make much smaller demands on memory than is commonly assumed.

MANY THINGS CAN BE recognized on the basis of their visual *1* characteristics. Moreover, laboratory studies have shown that people are quite adept at discriminating between complex pictures they have seen a short time before and those they have not, even when given hundreds (Nickerson, 1965; Shepard, 1967) or thousands (Standing, 1973; Standing, Conezio, & Haber, 1970) of pictures to remember and allowed to inspect each for only a few seconds. Both of these observations are consistent with the idea of a visual memory that readily assimilates and retains an abundance of information about the stimuli to which it is exposed.

In fact neither introspection nor the results of picture recognition *2* studies tells us how much information regarding any particular visual pattern has been stored. When people demonstrate the ability to recognize something, they may be demonstrating only that they can place that thing in an appropriate conceptual category. And the category may be more or less broadly defined, depending on one's purpose—as when an object is recognized as an automobile, as opposed to being recognized as a Volkswagen, or as the specific Volkswagen that belongs to John Doe. Similarly, when people show that they can distinguish a picture they have seen before from one they are looking at for the first time, they show only that they have retained enough information about the "old" picture to distinguish it from the new one. Given that one typically cannot say how much information *must be* retained in order to permit such categorizations and distinctions, one cannot rule out the possibility that they may be made on the basis of a small portion of the information that the patterns contain.

The experiments reported in this paper are addressed to the question *3* of how accurately and completely the visual details of a common object, a United States penny, are represented in people's memories. We chose to study people's knowledge of a common object rather than of laboratory stimuli because we are interested in the nature of the information that normally accrues in memory. As a stimulus, a penny has the advantage of being complex enough to be interesting but simple enough to be analyzed and manipulated. And it is an object that all of our subjects would have seen frequently.

Experiment I

The purpose of the first experiment was to see how accurately people *4* could reproduce a penny through unaided recall.

Method

The subjects were 20 adult United States citizens. Each was given a set *5* of empty circles, 2 in. in diameter, and asked to draw from memory what is on each side of a U.S. penny. Subjects were asked to include all the pictorial and alphanumeric detail they could, and they were allowed to draw as many versions of each side as they wanted.

For purposes of scoring the drawings, we focused on the eight features *6* listed in Table 1. Each subject's drawing was scored according to: (a) whether each of these eight features was present; (b) whether each was located on the correct side of the coin; and (c) whether it was drawn in the correct position in the circular area. The head was scored as being in the correct position only if it was drawn as an east-facing profile.

Top side
  Head
  "IN GOD WE TRUST"
  "LIBERTY"
  Date

Bottom side
  Building
  "UNITED STATES OF AMERICA"
  "E PLURIBUS UNUM"
  "ONE CENT"

Table 1.   Features identified for scoring purposes in Experiment I.

Results

In general, performance was remarkably poor. Figure 1 shows some 7
examples of the drawings we obtained. Of the eight critical features,
the median number recalled and located correctly was three. Not counting the Lincoln head and the Lincoln Memorial, the median number of
recalled and correctly located features was one. Only 4 of our 20 subjects
got as many as half of them. Only 1 subject (an active penny collector)
accurately recalled and located all eight.

   Figure 2 shows an analysis of the errors with respect to each feature. 8
The overall probability that a feature would be either omitted or mislocated was .61. The probability that a feature would be omitted was
.33; excluding the Lincoln head and the Lincoln Memorial, this probability was .43. The only features that all our subjects produced were a
head and a date. All but one subject also recalled a building as the central
figure on the bottom side. The feature most frequently omitted was
LIBERTY; only two of our subjects remembered that this is on the
coin, and one of them located it on the wrong side. UNITED STATES
OF AMERICA, E PLURIBUS UNUM, and ONE CENT were also
omitted by about half of our subjects. It is interesting to note that with
the exception of Lincoln's head, the Memorial, and ONE CENT, all of
these items occur on every current U.S. coin.

   Figure 2 also shows that subjects were quite poor at locating those 9
features they did recall. The probability of mislocating a correctly recalled feature was .42. The only feature that was consistently located
correctly was the building, which would be difficult to position incorrectly if it were recalled at all. Excluding the building, the probability

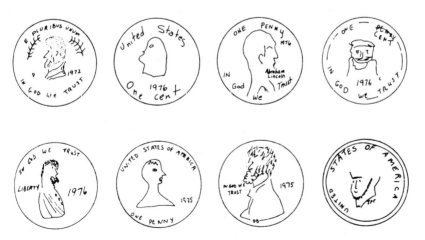

Figure 1.   Examples of drawings obtained from people who tried
to reproduce a penny from memory.
*Source: Cognitive Psychology. Copyright © 1979 Academic Press, Inc. Re-
printed with permission.*

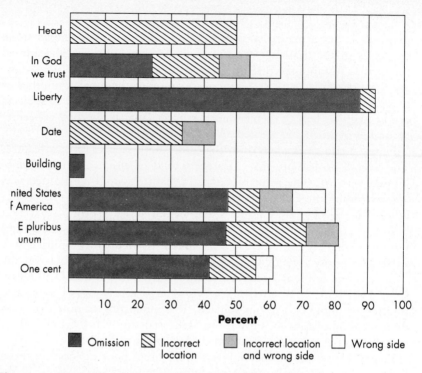

Figure 2. Types of errors produced when subjects attempted to draw a penny from memory.
Source: Cognitive Psychology. *Copyright © 1979 Academic Press, Inc. Reprinted with permission.*

of mislocating a feature was .50. Exactly half of our subjects faced the Lincoln head in the wrong direction.

Ten subjects exercised the option of drawing more than one version   10
of the coin, although one of them redrew the top side only. Across the 19 cases in which multiple versions of a side of the coin were drawn, the final choice was the most accurate version in six cases, equivalent to the other(s) in eight cases, and worse than at least one of the rejected versions in five cases. We had suggested this option partly because we suspected that subjects would do better if they could draw several versions and then decide which looked best; evidently we were wrong.

Subjects' memories for the coin also appeared uneven in that they   11
often recalled minor details while omitting or confusing more conspicuous ones. For example, every one of the 19 subjects who drew a building on the bottom side of the coin drew it with a colonnade, and 5 of them even drew a tiny figure of Lincoln inside; on the other hand, 7 subjects drew the building with a peaked roof, 1 with a dome, and 2 with chimneys. Eleven subjects finished their drawings of Lincoln at the neck; of those who drew any part of the torso, only 4 extended it to

the edge of the coin. Eleven subjects indicated that the coin could or should have a mint mark, but several of them had incorrect ideas about what letters were appropriate, and only 5 of them located the mark under the date. Three subjects indicated that the designer's initials should be on the head of the coin, but only 1 of them correctly specified what or where those initials should be.

There were relatively few intrusion errors: Three subjects thought *12* that "PENNY" was imprinted on the coin; two thought "ABRAHAM LINCOLN" was. Eight subjects drew sheaves or wreaths. Perhaps that should not be surprising inasmuch as pre-1959 pennies did have wreaths; but that was over 20 years ago and today it is very difficult to find pre-1959 pennies in circulation. In any case, one of these subjects was the one who forgot the building: on the tail of the coin he drew a wreath with the words "ONE CENT" inside, similar to how the old pennies look. Of the others, four drew the sheaves on the tail of the coin and three drew them on the top side encircling Lincoln's bust. . . .

Experiment IV

On the basis of Experiments I, II, and III, one might conclude that our *13* knowledge of the way pennies look is in general quite vague and incomplete. Yet, given our familiarity with pennies, this conclusion seems incredible. An alternate explanation is that we generally do have in memory a relatively complete and accurate representation of a penny, but that this representation is holistic° and unanalyzable. Under this hypothesis people might be expected to be inept at reproducing or recognizing a penny feature by feature. However, they should be good at judging whether or not a facsimile is accurate.

Experiment IV was designed to assess this hypothesis. Each subject *14* was given a drawing of the head of a penny. The task was to decide whether or not the drawing was accurate and, if not, to specify what was wrong with it. If the holistic-representation hypothesis is correct, subjects should be good at determining whether a drawing is accurate, but not necessarily so good at specifying what is wrong with it if it is not accurate.

Method

The stimuli were 15 different drawings of the head of a U.S. penny. *15* These are shown in Fig. 3. One of the versions (A) was accurate; the others were inaccurate in that at least one feature was omitted, mislocated, or added. These inaccuracies are specified in the second column of Table 3. The subjects were 127 U.S. citizens in a Psychology I lecture at Brown University. Each subject was given one of the drawings and

---

Holistic—perceived as an integrated whole.

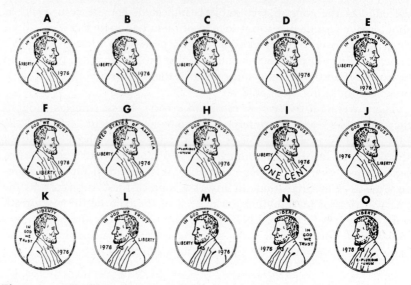

Figure 3.   The fifteen drawings of the top side of a penny that
were used in Experiments IV and V. A brief characterization of
each drawing is given in Table 2.
Source: Cognitive Psychology. *Copyright © 1979 Academic Press, Inc. Reprinted with permission.*

asked to decide whether it was an accurate reproduction of a penny,
and, if not, to describe what was wrong with it. Each drawing was
evaluated by 8 or 9 subjects.

Results

The results are summarized in Table 2. The third column gives the
number of subjects who examined each version, and the fourth gives
the number of those who accepted that version as correct. The first
thing to note is that our predictions were off again. Only four of the
eight subjects who saw the accurate version, accepted it as such. Moreover, the accurate drawing was not a clear favorite. Versions G and I
were respectively accepted by four and six of the nine subjects who saw
them, and five others were accepted by at least one subject. The incorrect
reproductions that were judged to be correct seem to have little in
common: for version D a feature was missing; for G a feature was
substituted; for I an extra feature was added; for J and K the positions
of two of the features were switched; for M, the bust was reversed; and
N was thoroughly mixed up. On the basis of these data, then, we can
point to no particular configural or featural properties that were controlling subjects' responses.

16

		Experiment IV		
Drawing	Characterization	No. of subjects	No. who thought drawing accurate	No. who identified error(s)
A	Correct	8	4	—
B	1 Omission	9	0	6(2)
C	1 Omission	9	0	9(1)
D	1 Omission	8	2	3(1)
E	1 Mislocation	9	0	8(0)
F	1 Mislocation	8	0	5(0)
G	1 Substitution	9	4	1(0)
H	1 Substitution	8	0	2(0)
I	1 Addition	9	6	2(1)
J	2 Features interchanged	8	2	4(2)
K	2 Features interchanged	8	3	3(1)
L	Mirror image	9	0	4(3)
M	Reversed face	8	3	3(1)
N	Mirror with 2 features interchanged	9	1	1(1)
O	Mirror with 1 omission, 1 mislocation, and 1 addition	8	0	0(0)

Table 2. Characterizations of the drawings shown in figure 3 and results from Experiment IV.

The fifth column in Table 2 gives the number of subjects who correctly indicated which features were in error for each drawing. The number who identified only these features as incorrect and specified exactly what was wrong with them is given in parentheses; the balance includes subjects who incompletely or incorrectly specified what was wrong with the erroneous feature(s) as well as those who cited other, correct features as erroneous. . . .

Discussion

The results of these experiments suggest that our memory representations of the details of a penny's characteristics are very incomplete and imprecise. Our subjects were not able to draw a penny from memory; indeed, their attempts to do so were, for the most part, grossly inaccurate. Nor were they able to position features correctly, even when told what the features are. They were somewhat better able to indicate which of several listed features are on a penny; however, even in this case, performance was far from perfect, and confidence was not uniformly high. They were unable to specify what was wrong with erroneous facsimiles of a penny, and two of those facsimiles were accepted as bona fide representations as frequently as was the correct drawing. In a forced-choice situation, less than half of our subjects selected the correct representation from among a set of incorrect drawings, and almost all of them found several of the incorrect drawings to be plausible possibilities. Even such a prominent feature as the orientation of the Lincoln head seemed not to be encoded well at all.

These results violate our intuitions regarding what we know about 19
the way things look. Most people, we suspect, would be willing to say that they know what a penny looks like or at least that they would have no trouble recognizing one when they saw it. A typical reaction of our subjects after participating in this study was one of surprise, and sometimes embarrassment, at how difficult their tasks, which initially sounded so simple, turned out to be. Certainly, all of our subjects had seen pennies many thousands of times during their lives; some had collected them as a hobby. And we had, after all, selected a penny as our stimulus because we thought it would be at least as familiar to most people as any other object we might have used. The results may also seem surprising in view of the findings of several other studies of visual memory. How are they to be reconciled, for example, with the fact that people can distinguish with a high degree of accuracy between complex pictures they have seen briefly and those they have not, even after having seen a large number of pictures? Our discussion of these results, and our attempt to reconcile them with studies of visual memory that have yielded more impressive findings, will draw upon the notions of cue redundancy, meaningfulness, interference, and inference.

As was noted in the introductory passage, it is not clear what sorts 20
of information regarding pictures must be retained in order to permit the kind of performance reported in such studies as those of Nickerson (1965, 1968), Shepard (1967), and Standing et al. (1970). The pictures that were used in those studies were complex and diverse. On the average, they probably differed from each other with respect to a very large number of details, and it may be that the distinction between "old" and "new" stimuli could be made on the basis of any of a number of small subsets of those details. Similar suggestions have been made by Goldstein and Chance (1970) and by Green and Purohit (1976).

To the extent that this notion of a multiplicity of cues on which 21
distinctions might be based is taken as at least a partial explanation of recognition-memory performance with complex pictures, it also helps to explain the poorer performance of our subjects on our recognition tasks. The incorrect drawings of pennies that were used in these tasks did not always differ from the correct drawing with respect to a large number of features. Indeed, in many instances the difference involved only a single feature. It cannot be said of these stimuli, therefore, as it

can of those in the cited studies, that the necessary distinctions could be made on the basis of any of a large variety of distinguishing cues.

While the idea of cue redundancy does help, we believe, to account *22* for the ability of people to distinguish between pictures they have seen before and those they have not, it cannot be the whole story. Meaningfulness must also be implicated in some way. Recognition performance is much poorer with relatively abstract complex visual patterns, such as snowflakes and inkblots, than with random photographs of real-life scenes (Goldstein & Chance, 1970). Moreover, support for the idea that it is not their abundance of details alone that makes pictures memorable comes from an experiment in which recognition memory was tested for (a) photographs, (b) one-sentence verbal descriptions of the photographs, (c) line drawings of the main themes of the photographs, and (d) those same line drawings embellished with details not essential to the main themes (Nelson, Metzler, & Reed, 1974). The unembellished line drawings were recognized as well as the photographs and embellished line drawings, both immediately and after 7 days.

Recognition of the importance of meaningfulness also helps to rec- *23* oncile our results with those of picture-memory experiments. While a penny is certainly a meaningful object, the particular details that appear on it, and the spatial relationships among those details, are relatively arbitrary. The visual components of a penny do not play the same role in determining the meaning of the whole, as do the components of many real-life scenes.

The importance of meaningfulness is illustrated by our subjects' poor *24* memory for orientation. The conclusion that people tend to have little, if any, remembrance of the direction in which the Lincoln head faces is supported by the results of all these experiments. Our explanation of why people do not remember the orientation of the profile on a coin is because it has no significance: One orientation will do quite as well as the other, and neither is incongruous in the context of the other components of the coin.

There is other evidence that memory for orientation is often poor. *25* For example, Bartlett (1932) noted that subjects were unable to remember the orientation of faces on pictures shortly after having seen them. Other investigators have found subjects in picture-recognition experiments to be about as likely to recognize the mirror image of a picture as the original picture itself (Dallet, Wilcox, & D'Andrea, 1968; Standing et al., 1970). Standing et al. also tested subjects' ability to discern whether or not a picture had been reversed. Eighty-six percent accuracy on this task following a 30-min retention interval fell to 71% after 24 hr; in contrast, after 24 hr recognition accuracy, ignoring orientation, was at 94%. Finally, Blount, Holmes, Rodger, and Coltheart (1975) found that the ability of subjects to discriminate original from mirror-image views of art masterpieces that they had seen before was not greatly above chance (62%).

There is also evidence that orientation is more likely to be remembered   26
if it is meaningful than if it is not. Kraft and Jenkins (1977), for example,
have shown that how well a person remembers the orientation of the
elements of a visual scene may depend on whether orientation is significant or incidental in the context in which the elements occur. Thus, if
a sequence of pictures represents a meaningful sequence of events such
as a story, and, in particular, one in which the meaningfulness of the
story would not be preserved if the orientation of the pictures were
changed, then orientation information may be retained with a relatively
high degree of accuracy. If the pictures of the sequence are independent
of one another, however, such information tends not to be retained.

In addition to cue redundancy and meaningfulness, a third factor that   27
relates to the performance of our subjects is interference. There was
some evidence in our results that some subjects may have confused
features of current pennies with those of pennies that are no longer in
circulation. There is also the possibility of interference from memory
for features on other coins. For example, subjects who drew a dome on
the Lincoln Memorial may have been experiencing interference from
their memories of the back of a nickel, which has a relief of Monticello.
With respect to the orientation of the Lincoln head, it is worth noting
that on all other current U.S. coins that show busts, the head faces in
the other direction. Indeed, there is a preponderance of left over right
cheeks in art work in general (McManus & Humphrey, 1973). We are
inclined to attribute the confusion over the orientation of Lincoln's head
to its lack of significance, as indicated above. However, for some of our
subjects, this confusion may be less indicative of poor memory for this
aspect of a penny than of interference from memories of so many other
profiles.

So far, we have focused on reconciling our results with those of some   28
other studies of visual memory. We have attributed the differences between our results and those of several picture-memory experiments in
part to differences in the multiplicity of distinctive cues on which performance could depend and in the degree of meaningfulness of stimulus
features and the relationships among them. We have also noted the
possibility of interference between memory representations of pennies
and those of other visual patterns, especially other U.S. coins. These
considerations seem to fall short, however, of explaining why we are so
poor at specifying, or even recognizing, what a penny looks like. Why
are our memory representations for so familiar an object not more
complete and precise?

One plausible explanation is that there is no need for them to be any   29
better. Perhaps what we mean when we say that we know what a penny
looks like is that we can distinguish a penny from other things from
which we normally have to distinguish it, for example, from other
coins. This does not require that we know what a penny looks like in
any detail. The features that are salient for distinguishing a penny from
other U.S. coins are probably its color and size. And even when one

has occasion to distinguish a penny from a foreign coin of similar color and size, a gross comparison of their features will generally suffice. (In view of our subjects' relatively good memory for the date, it is noteworthy that of the features considered in this study, it is the only one that many of us find valuable for distinguishing among pennies.) What is interesting about this explanation is that it suggests that many of the numerous things we all can "recognize," we may recognize on the basis of memory representations that are as incomplete and imprecise as our representations of pennies appear to be. Skeptics are invited to try to draw from memory a telephone dial or their watch face or any other thing at which they frequently look.

We should note that our subjects' underlying memory representations *30* may have been even more vague than our results suggest. The fact that a subject drew a particular feature in the first of our experiments does not prove that he or she relied on stored information about pennies in particular to do so. All current U.S. coins have a head on one side. Moreover, they all contain a date and the words LIBERTY, E PLU-RIBUS UNUM and UNITED STATES OF AMERICA. Even if one were not aware of this fact, one might expect any coin to display its denomination, the name of the country of coinage, and the year of mint. Remembering, or being able to guess, that the building on the back side of the penny is the Lincoln Memorial, coupled with a memory representation—from some source other than a penny—of what that looks like, could provide a basis for an accurate drawing. More generally, many correct responses may have been derived from memories for different but related information. Inference may be seen as the productive counterpart of interference. These considerations illustrate a methodological difficulty that characterizes much long-term memory research: namely, the difficulty (perhaps impossibility) of distinguishing between what is remembered and what is inferred.

There is, finally, one possible explanation of our results that puts them *31* in a quite different light. Perhaps it is not that we only know about the grosser or more salient aspects of our visual worlds, but that that is all we are conscious of knowing. Haber and Erdelyi (Erdelyi & Becker, 1974; Haber, 1970 Haber & Erdelyi, 1969) have reported some provocative indications that visual memories may be quite elaborate but stubbornly inaccessible for purposes of recall or reconstruction. There is also the older literature on introspection and imageless thought. In summarizing his review of this literature, Woodworth quotes Book (1910): "conscious attitude seems to represent a stage in a process of development which begins with vivid, imaginal thought, and slowly and gradually passes downward to a stage of automatic or instinctive control" (Woodworth, 1938, p. 790). As an everyday illustration that we may know at some level more than we are aware of knowing: People often note when a friend wears new clothes, although they probably could not begin to describe their friend's wardrobe.

It may be adaptive for the details of our visual experiences to be *32* inaccessible. One is reminded of Luria's mnemonist who had so much trouble recognizing people's faces because, as he put it, they are "constantly changing" (Luria, 1968, p. 64). If we do indeed have such deep and elaborate knowledge, it may play a critical role in our abilities to navigate about our worlds. On the other hand, it may be that when we understand better the process of navigation, we may find that it requires less elaborate information about the world than we would have thought. In any case, in many situations it matters little how much a person knows unless that knowledge can somehow be made public. The results from these experiments should at least give us pause about the accuracy of testimonies on topics that we know like the "backs of our hands."

Concluding Comment

On balance, the results from these experiments demonstrate that fre- *33* quent exposure to an object and the ability to "recognize" that object for practical purposes do not guarantee that the object is represented accurately in memory in any great detail. To the contrary, they raise the question of whether visual long-term memory is much less rich and elaborate than has often been supposed.

The results also lead us to the following conjecture: Typically, the *34* details of visual stimuli are not retained in memory—or at least they are not available from memory—unless there is some functional reason for them to be. In other words, what one is most likely to remember about the visual properties of objects is what one needs to remember in order to distinguish those objects in everyday life. In general, investigators of human memory have not focused on the question of sufficiency. As one aspect of the study of what is stored in memory, it might be useful to give more thought to the question of what information *must* be retained in order to permit one to identify common objects or to distinguish them from each other. It may turn out that because of the multiplicity of features with respect to which most objects of interest differ from each other, the constraining effects of the contexts in which objects are typically encountered, and the role of inferential processes, recognition may make much smaller demands on memory than has commonly been believed.

References

Anisfeld, M., & Knapp, M. Association, synonymity, and directionality in false recognition. *Journal of Experimental Psychology*, 1968, **77**, 171–179.

Bartlett, F. C. *Remembering*. Cambridge: Cambridge Univ. Press, 1932.

Blount, P., Holmes, J., Rodger, J., & Coltheart, M. On the ability to discriminate original from mirror-image reproductions of works of art. *Perception*, 1975, **4**, 385–389.

Dallett, K., Wilcox, S. G., & D'Andrea, L. Picture memory experiments. *Journal of Experimental Psychology*, 1968, **76**, 312–320.

Erdelyi, M. H., & Becker, J. Hypermnesia for pictures. Incremental memory for pictures but not words in multiple recall trials. *Cognitive Psychology*, 1974, **6**, 159–171.

Goldstein, A. G., & Chance, J. E. Visual recognition memory for complex configurations. *Perception and Psychophysics*, 1970,**9**, 237–241.

Green, D. M., & Purohit, A. K. Visual recognition memory for large and small binary pictures. *Journal of Experimental Psychology: Human Learning and Memory*, 1976, **2**, 32–37.

Haber, R. N. How we remember what we see. *Scientific American*, 1970, **222**, 104–112.

Haber, R. N., & Erdelyi, M. H. Emergence and recovery of initially unavailable perceptual material. *Journal of Verbal Learning and Verbal Behavior*, 1967, **6**, 618–628.

Kintsch, W. *Learning, memory, and conceptual processes*. New York: Wiley, 1970(a).

Kintsch, W. Models for free recall and recognition. In D. A. Norman (Ed.), *Models of human memory*. New York: Academic Press, 1970(b).

Kraft, R. N., & Jenkins, J. J. Memory for lateral orientation of slides in picture stories. *Memory & Cognition*, 1977, **5**, 397–403.

Luria, A. R. *The mind of a mnemonist*. New York: Basic Books, 1968.

McManus, I. C., & Humphrey, N. K. Turning the left cheek. *Nature (London)*, 1973, **243**, 271–272.

Nelson, T. O., Metzler, J., & Reed, D. A. Role of details in the long-term recognition of pictures and verbal descriptions. *Journal of Experimental Psychology*, 1974, **102**, 184–186.

Nickerson, R. S. Short-term memory for complex meaningful visual configurations: A demonstration of capactiy. *Canadian Journal of Psychology*, 1965. **19**, 155–160.

Nickerson, R. S. A note on long-term recognition memory for pictorial material. *Psychonomic Science*, 1968, 11, 58.

Shepard, R. N. Recognition memory for words, sentences, and pictures. *Journal of Verbal Learning and Learning Behavior*, 1967, **6**, 156–163.

Standing, L. Learning 10,000 pictures. *Quarterly Journal of Experimental Psychology*, 1973, **25**, 207–222.

Standing, L., Conezio, J., & Haber, R. N. Perception and memory for pictures: Single-trial learning of 2500 visual stimuli. *Psychonomic Science,* 1970, **19**, 73–74.

Underwood, B. J. Are we overloading memory? In A. W. Melton & E. Martin (Eds.), *Coding processes in human memory*. Washington DC: Winston, 1972.

Woodworth, R. S. *Experimental psychology*. New York: Holt, 1938.

Rhetorical Analysis Through Annotation

The abstract at the beginning of the article summarizes some major points but does not reflect all the reasoning that goes on in the article. Next to each sentence (or phrase, where appropriate) in the abstract indicate which section of the article is referred to. Then in the article itself note what types of material are included in each section that are not mentioned in the abstract. Consider, for example, what type of material is hidden behind the phrase "on balance" in the abstract. Similarly, consider what happens to evaluation of the literature.

Discuss the differences between the way the experimental sections are reduced for the abstract and the way the introduction, discussion, and conclusion are treated. Consider which major elements and issues are simplified or vanish and which elements are emphasized. Discuss how these differences between full text and abstract may indicate different functions for the two.

Discussion Questions

Interpreting the Text

1. In what way do people have good visual memories, according to studies mentioned by the authors? How do the two experiments presented here show that people have poor memory for visual details? Why should such results appear surprising?

2. What possible explanations are offered to reconcile the results here with other experiments that show good visual memory? How much of the difference may be attributable to each of the explanations? How do the other experimental results that are brought in support each explanation?

3. Why do redundancy, meaningfulness, and interference not add up to a sufficient explanation of the results here? What further explanations do Nickerson and Adams offer?

Considering the Issues

4. What are some situations in which you are called on to discriminate objects that look similar, such as finding your car in a parking lot? In such cases, how do you distinguish the objects? For example, how do you know which of two 1984 red Plymouth Horizons is yours?

5. How may the concept of meaningfulness explain the difference between how much and what things different people remember? What may a car mechanic remember about a look at an engine compared to what a metallurgist may remember? How may psychiatrists, artists, and writers have different memories for faces?

6. How may the concept of memory interference apply to other tasks, such as learning a new language, learning about several different wars, or recognizing acquaintances?

7. How is the concept of meaningfulness related to, but different than, the concept of need to remember? What differences in cloth may be meaningful to a clothes designer? What differences may the designer need to remember? How may the concepts of meaningfulness and need to remember explain differences between teachers' expectations of what students should be able to remember and students' actual memory of the material?

8. In what ways are the ideas or meanings developed for the experiments on memory for the penny dependent on ideas developed through the literature?

What conclusions do the authors draw that receive most of their justification through the literature? What conclusions could they draw just on the experiments alone, without the literature? Could the experiments originally have been imagined without the existence of the prior literature? If yes, how might the experimental design have been different?

9. How broadly do you think the conclusions of the article should be generalized? Does the need to know determine just what details we remember of certain familiar objects like pennies or does the need to know seem to characterize large parts of our memory? In your experience, do you tend to remember what you need to know and to forget what you do not need to know?

10. Following the authors' suggestion, draw from memory the face of your watch, then compare the drawing to the actual object. How do the results of this little experiment compare with the findings of the article? Or try to describe a friend's wardrobe from memory and relate the results to the authors' discussion of conscious and unconscious visual memories.

Writing Suggestions

1. Imagine you are a psychologist attempting to reproduce the results reported by Nickerson and Adams. Using all members of the class as your subjects, run an experiment similar to experiment 1, except using a nickel as the coin to be drawn. Write up the results of the experiment for a psychological journal. Follow the structure of abstract, background, description of experiment, etc., used by Nickerson and Adams. The data set may be photocopied so that all members of the class can write up the same experiment. (Note that this experimental replication is technically contaminated by the subjects' familiarity with the original experiment.)

2. For a psychology course explore the implications of the conclusions of Nickerson and Adams for your own memory. Describe the face of someone close to you (or anything else that you think you know very well) in as great detail as you can using only your memory. Then discuss possible reasons for the degree and selection of details you were able to recollect.

3. Write a letter to one of your teachers explaining the difficulties you and your classmates have in remembering material for the exam. Use the concepts of meaningfulness and need to know in order to analyze the material to be remembered and to make suggestions to the teacher for more appropriate requirements.

4. For a psychology course write a brief essay placing Nickerson and Adams's study in either the Ebbinghaus or Bartlett tradition of experimental psychology, as described by Cofer.

Everyday Memory in Natural Contexts

Ulric Neisser

Despite the enormous growth of academic experimental psychology in this century (*Psychological Abstracts* currently lists, for example, over 30,000 studies a year), not all academic psychologists believe that experiments are the only or best way to understand the human mind. They believe the laboratory setting may strip away important elements of context and that the behavior itself may lose its motivation and meaning when taken out of context. Memory in the laboratory, in short, is not the same thing as memory in everyday life. Ulric Neisser, professor of psychology at Cornell, argues that a new type of study is needed, one that addresses a whole new set of questions. He argues in an informal, personal style but shows unquestionable command of the ideas and knowledge of the field. The informal style also reflects that this was first written as a speech, before Neisser converted it into an article, published in 1978.

The first half of the article (not presented here) reviews the history of experimental work on memory. The excerpt here begins with the summary of the first part and continues with Neisser's proposals.

IN SHORT, THE RESULTS of a hundred years of the psychological *1* study of memory are somewhat discouraging. We have established firm empirical generalizations, but most of them are so obvious that every ten-year-old knows them anyway. We have made discoveries, but they are only marginally about memory; in many cases we don't know what to do with them, and wear them out with endless experimental variations. We have an intellectually impressive group of theories, but history offers little confidence that they will provide any meaningful insight into natural behavior. Of course, I could be wrong: perhaps this is the exceptional case where the lessons of history do not apply, and the new theories will stand the test of time better than the old ones did. Let me be frank: I have not pinpointed any fatal flaw in Hunt's distributed memory model (Hunt, 1971), Tulving's conception of encoding specificity (Tulving, 1974), Anderson's ACT (1976), or the others. I cannot prove that they are misguided. But because they say so little about the everyday uses of memory, they seem ripe for the same fate that overtook learning theory not long ago.

The psychologists who have spent a century studying esoteric forms *2* of memory in the laboratory are not really uninterested in its more ordinary manifestations, and have always hoped that their work would have wide applicability sooner or later. Their preference for artificial tasks has a rational basis: one can control variables and manipulate conditions more easily in the lab than in natural settings. Why not work under the best possible conditions? Memory is memory, or so it would seem. This methodological assumption resembles the assumptions made by the learning theorists in their study of "learning." Unfortunately, it turned out that "learning" in general does not exist: wasps and songbirds and rats integrate past experiences into their lives in very different ways. I think that "memory" in general does not exist either. It is a concept left over from a medieval psychology that partitioned the mind into independent faculties: "thought" and "will" and "emotion" and many others, with "memory" among them. Let's give it up, and begin to ask our questions in different ways. Those questions need not be uninformed by theory, or by a vision of human nature, but perhaps they can be more closely driven by the characteristics of ordinary human experience.

What we want to know, I think, is how people use their own past   *3* experiences in meeting the present and the future. We would like to understand how this happens under natural conditions: the circumstances in which it occurs, the forms it takes, the variables on which it depends, the differences between individuals in their uses of the past. "Natural conditions" does not mean in the jungle or on the desert, unless that happens to be where our subjects live. It means in school and at home, on the job and in the course of thought, as carefree children and as reflective old men and women. Because changes in the social and cultural environment can change the uses of the past, we will have to study many settings. The psychological laboratory is the easiest of these settings in which to work, but it is also among the least interesting; we ourselves are the only people who spend much time there voluntarily. . . .

Although I am far from sure how to classify the phenomena of   *4* memory, I must put them in some kind of order to discuss them at all. Science cannot proceed without some way of defining things so we can set out to study them. The organization I will use is based on the functions of memory. What do we use the past *for*? Happily, when the question is put in this way, it turns out that the sum total of relevant psychological work is not zero after all. There has been some valuable research and thinking about the natural uses of memory, usually by individuals outside the mainstream of contemporary theory. These beginnings offer promising leads for further work; I will mention some of them below.

First of all, everyone uses the past to define themselves. Who am I? I   *5* have a name, a family, a home, a job. I know a great deal about myself: what I have done, how I have felt, where I have been, whom I have known, how I have been treated. My past defines me, together with my present and the future that the past leads me to expect. What would I be without it? Much of that formative past is now tacit rather than explicit knowledge: I do not dwell on it, and I cannot recall it as such. The specifics are beyond recall, although their resultant is here in person.

Some things, however, I can remember very explicitly when I choose. I think back on my childhood, or my youth, or on something that happened this morning. Typically I do this alone, silently, without telling anybody. I often do it deliberately and voluntarily, but memories may also come unbidden—"involuntary memories," as Salaman (1970) calls them—either in waking life or in sleep. All these are cases where the past becomes present to me, and to me alone.

Many questions suggest themselves about such personal evocations. **6** Some were asked long ago by Freud and the psychoanalysts. Why do just these memories come, and not others? When are they trustworthy, and when fabricated? Why do I have so few from my very early child-hood? Do some people have more of them than others, and if so why? What function do they serve? How does the nature and incidence of personal recollection vary with age, culture, sex, and situation? What happens when whole sections of the past become inaccessible, as in functional amnesias?

Work has been done on some of these questions, but not much. Freud **7** (1905) drew attention to the phenomenon of infantile amnesia and tried to explain it by repression; Schachtel (1947) later proposed a cognitive account which seems more plausible (cf. Neisser, 1962). Freud also wrote two papers on early memories (1899, 1917), a topic which has been studied sporadically over the years by many psychologists (Dudycha and Dudycha, 1941) recently including Douglas Herrmann and me. Our questionnaire study (Herrmann and Neisser, 1978) suggests that women college students may have slightly better memory of childhood experi-ences than men do. Others have noticed the same sex difference in early memories; I wish I understood it. We still know very little about these questions, and what we do know mostly concerns deliberate, voluntary remembering. Spontaneous recall may be quite a different matter. Esther Salaman's fascinating autobiographical book *A Collection of Moments* (1970), which describes many images of early childhood that came to her unbidden and unexpected, may be a useful source of hypotheses about spontaneous memory.

One frequently recalls past experiences in search of some sort of self- **8** improvement. Where did I go wrong? Could I have done things differ-ently? What were my alternatives? How did all this start? These ques-tions can be asked privately or with a listener. "Going public," even to a single individual, makes a difference. Both private and shared recol-lection can have profound consequences for that sense of self which is so dependent on what one remembers. Psychoanalysis and psychother-apy are obvious examples of this use of the past, but they are by no means the only ones. Something similar probably happens in the Cath-olic confessional, of which I know very little. Some Communist coun-tries have institutionalized confession as a way of strengthening social unity and reforming individual behavior. To be sure, those who confess in political settings must be quite careful about what they say. Is that selectivity exhibited only in their public statements, or does it extend to what they remember privately? According to recent experimental evidence, people's memory of their own prior attitudes can change dramatically when the attitudes themselves have shifted (Goethals and Reckman, 1973).

There are other occasions when one's personal memories achieve a kind of public importance. A familiar example occurs in legal testimony, where an exact account of the past can be critical in determining a defendant's future. Psychologists have been interested in this issue for many years. At the beginning of the century William Stern published several volumes of a scholarly journal devoted exclusively to the psychology of testimony (*Beiträge zur Psychologie der Aussage*) and Münsterburg wrote a widely cited book about it called *On the Witness Stand* (1909). Unfortunately, this early work produced few insights except that the testimony of eyewitnesses is often inaccurate. A series of ingenious experiments by Elizabeth Loftus (e.g., Loftus and Palmer, 1974; Loftus, 1975) has revived interest in the problem, and begun to define the kinds of distortions that can occur as well as their sources.

One does not remember only events that one has personally experienced, but also those known at secondhand—things that have happened to other people. We learn from the experiences of our friends and acquaintances, and also from historical figures whose lives are somehow relevant to our own. In a literate society, we do not often think of history as something remembered; it is usually something written down. In many parts of the world, however, history has long been the responsibility of memory specialists, or oral historians, whose knowledge of ancient deeds and agreements exerts a controlling influence on contemporary events. D'Azevedo (1962) has described the role of oral historians among one African tribe, the Gola; it seems clear that this cultural practice is widespread in Africa and elsewhere. The history that is passed on through generations in this way is surprisingly accurate. The historians do not learn it by rote, but in an integrated and intelligent way. Whether this requires special gifts and special training, or whether anyone could remember any amount of oral history if it were appropriate to do so, is an open question.

In general, the relation between literacy and memory is poorly understood. It is one of those issues where every possible position can be and has been plausibly argued. Perhaps unschooled individuals from traditional societies have particularly *good* memories, because they must rely on those memories so heavily where nothing can be written down (Riesman, 1956). Perhaps, however, they have relatively *poor* memories because they lack the general mnemonic skills and strategies that come with literacy and schooling (Scribner and Cole, 1973). Certainly they perform badly in standard psychological memory experiments (Cole, Gay, Glick, and Sharp, 1971). Or maybe they are just like us: good at remembering what interests them. That is what Bartlett (1932) thought, though he could not resist endowing nonliterate Africans with a special facility for low-level "rote recapitulation" as well. In my own view, it may be a mistake to treat culture and literacy as overriding variables: individual differences and individual experience are more important. If the experimental task is remembering oral stories, then experience in listening to stories will make a big difference. That is probably why E. F. Dube (1977) recently found that both schooled and unschooled young people from Botswana were far better at story recall than American school children of the same age. However, he also found enormous individual differences correlated with estimates of the subjects' intelligence, made by tribal elders for the nonliterate children and on the basis of school grades for the others. The best of the unschooled subjects exhibited remarkably high levels of recall.

12 Memory is also involved in many activities of daily life. We make a plan and have to remember to carry it out, put something down and have to recall where it is, are given directions and must remember them if we are to reach our destination, encounter a prior acquaintance and want to pick up the relationship where it left off. Our access to the past is probably better when remembering is embedded in these natural activities than when it occurs in isolation. At least this is true for young children, as Istomina (1975) has shown in an elegant series of experiments. Different individuals are unequally skilled in different kinds of everyday memory, according to questionnaire data that Herrmann and I have recently collected (Herrmann and Neisser, 1979). But we still know almost nothing about these practical uses of memory, important as they are.

13 In most instances of daily remembering, it is meanings and not surface details that we must recall. Just as the oral historian remembers what happened instead of memorizing some formula of words that describes it, so too we recall the substance of what we heard or read rather than its verbatim form. This is now generally acknowledged, even in laboratory research. The new wave of enthusiasm for Bartlett's ideas and for the use of stories as memory materials has led us to devalue the study of rote memorization almost completely. This is entirely appropriate, if "rote memory" means the learning of arbitrary lists of words or syllables for experimental purposes. The fact is, however, that many cultural institutions depend heavily on exact and literal recall. When we speak of remembering a song or a poem, for example, we do not mean that we have the gist of it but that we know the words. Rubin (1977) has recently shown that literal memory for the National Anthem, the Lord's Prayer, and similar texts is widespread among Americans. Verbatim memory is even more important in other societies, I think; some memorize the Koran where others study the Bible and still others learn long speeches from Shakespeare. This happens whenever it is the text itself, and not just its meaning, that is important. A text can be important for many reasons: patriotic, religious, esthetic, or personal. For singers

and actors, the reason can even be professional. Whatever the reason, people's ability to recite appropriate texts verbatim at appropriate times ought to be deeply interesting to the psychology of memory. The fact that we have not studied it is another particularly striking example of my original proposition: If X is an interesting memory phenomenon, psychologists avoid it like the plague. Hundreds of experimentalists have spent their lives working on rote memory, without ever examining the rote memorization that goes on around them every day.

The last use of the past that I will discuss concerns intellectual activity *14* itself. Although I have little talent for recalling the sources of quotations, I am not too bad at remembering experiments; if it were otherwise, I could not have prepared this address. However, this ability certainly does not make me unique. Everybody who is skilled at anything necessarily has a good memory for whatever information that activity demands. Physicists can remember what they need to know to do physics, and fishermen what they need for fishing; musicians remember music, art critics recall paintings, historians know history. Every person is a prodigy to his neighbors, remembering so much that other people do not know. We should be careful in what we say about memory in general until we know more about these many memories in particular.

These are some of the important questions, and we must seek the *15* answers as best we can. Our search need not be entirely haphazard; I am not recommending an aimless accumulation of ecological minutiae. We will surely be guided by our general conceptions of human nature and human social life, as well as by more particular hypotheses about the phenomena we study. Without such conceptions and hypotheses, we can make little progress. The challenge will be to shift from testing hypotheses for their own sake to using them as tools for the exploration of reality.

It is a challenge that will not be easy to meet. The realistic study of *16* memory is much harder than the work we have been accustomed to— so much harder that one can easily forgive those who have been reluctant to undertake it. After all, we bear no malice toward that legendary drunk who kept looking for his money under the streetlamp although he had dropped it ten yards away in the dark. As he correctly pointed out, the light was better where he was looking. But what we want to find *is* in the dark, out there where real people make use of their pasts in complicated ways. If we are to find it, we must look there.

References

Anderson, J. R. *Language, Memory, and Thought*. Hillsdale, N.J.: Lawrence Erlbaum, 1976.

Bartlett, F. C. *Remembering*. Cambridge: Cambridge University Press, 1932.

Cole, M., Gay, J., Glick, J. A., and Sharp, D. W. *The Cultural Context of Learning and Thinking*. New York: Basic Books, 1971.

D'Azevedo, W. L. Uses of the past in Gola discourse. *Journal of African History*, 1962, *3*, 11–34.

Dube, E. F. *A Cross-Cultural Study of the Relationship Between "Intelligence" Level and Story Recall*. Doctoral Dissertation, Cornell University, Ithaca, N.Y., 1977.

Dudycha, G., and Dudycha, M. Childhood memories: A review of the literature. *Psychological Bulletin*, 1941, *38*, 668–682.

Freud, S. Three contributions to the theory of sex. In A. A. Brill (ed.), *The Basic Writings of Sigmund Freud*. New York: Random House, 1905; republished 1938.

Freud, S. Screen memories. In J. Strachey (ed.), *Collected Papers of Sigmund Freud* (Vol. 5). London: Hogarth Press, 1899; republished 1956.

Freud, S. Eine Kindheitserinnerung aus 'Dichtung und Wahrheit'. *Imago*, 1917, *5*.

Goethals, G. R., and Reckman, R. F. The perception of consistency in attitudes. *Journal of Experimental Social Psychology*, 1973, *9*, 491–501.

Herrmann, D. J., and Neisser, U. An inventory of everyday memory experiences. In M. M. Gruneberg, P. E. Morris, and R. N. Sykes (eds.), *Practical Aspects of Memory*. London: Academic Press, 1978.

Hunt, E. What kind of a computer is man? *Cognitive Psychology*, 1971, *2*, 57–98.

Istomina, Z. M. The development of voluntary memory in preschool-age children. *Soviet Psychology*, 1975, *13*, 5–64.

Loftus, E. G. Leading questions and the eye-witness report. *Cognitive Psychology*, 1975, *7*, 560–572.

Loftus, E. G., and Palmer, J. C. Reconstruction of automobile destruction: An example of the interaction between language and memory. *Journal of Verbal Learning and Verbal Behavior*, 1974, *13*, 585–589.

Münsterburg, H. *On the Witness Stand*. New York: Doubleday, 1909.

Neisser, U. Cultural and cognitive discontinuity. In T. E. Gladwin and W. Sturtevant (eds.), *Anthropology and Human Behavior*. Washington, D.C.: Anthropological Society of Washington, D.C., 1962.

Riesman, D. *The Oral Tradition, the Written Word, the Screen Image*. Yellow Springs, Ohio: Antioch Press, 1956.

Rubin, D. C. Very long-term memory for prose and verse. *Journal of Verbal Learning and Verbal Behavior*, 1977, *16*, 611–622.

Salaman, E. *A Collection of Moments*. London: Longman Group, 1970.

Schachtel, E. G. On memory and childhood amnesia. *Psychiatry*, 1947, *10*, 1–26.

Scribner, S., and Cole, M. Cognitive consequences of formal and informal education. *Science*, 1973, *182*, 553–559.

Tulving, E. Recall and recognition of semantically encoded words. *Journal of Experimental Psychology*, 1974, *102*, 778–787.

Rhetorical Analysis Through Annotation

Neisser argues for a new view of memory by setting traditional experimental studies against everyday experience represented in a variety of ways.

In the margin, identify by the letter *p* where Neisser describes his *personal* experience, by the letters *gr* where he describes the experience of particular *groups* of people, by the letters *gen* where he describes the *generalized* experience of humanity, and by the letter *r* where he describes the *research* experience reported in the literature. Also note on what basis or evidence he cites each.

Discuss how he uses each of these kinds of experience in his argument and how he combines them in contrasting or mutually supporting ways.

Discussion Questions

Interpreting the Text

1. What does Neisser mean by suggesting that memory does not exist? How does this compare with the claim that learning does not exist? Does this mean that people do not learn or remember?

2. What does Neisser mean by rats, songbirds, and other animals integrating past experience into their lives in different ways? What are some ways you use your own past experiences in meeting the present and the future?

3. What are the various ways memory enters into everyday life, according to Neisser? Do these correspond to your experience or the experience of people around you?

4. What connection may there be between literacy and memory?

5. What does Neisser mean by fishermen remembering what is necessary for fishing? What are some of those things? How does memory being part of an activity give a somewhat different view of memory than that of a fixed faculty, a memory box in the head? What types of things do you remember in this sense?

6. What is the meaning of the story of the drunk? How does it apply here?

Considering the Issues

7. Neisser says that he is suggesting a new approach, but then he cites much relevant literature. In what way does he use this literature? Is his approach new or not? In what sense may it be considered new?

8. What exactly is Neisser advocating as a new kind of research? How, specifically, will this be different from previous experimental work?

9. How does Neisser use the first person here? How does this compare to the use of the first person in the article by Nickerson and Adams?

Writing Suggestions

1. For a psychology class write an essay describing and evaluating Neisser's argument and proposals.

2. For a school magazine write a personal, philosophic essay describing how your past defines you, according to Neisser's discussion. Or disagree with Neisser's assertion, describing your difficulty in defining yourself in this way.

3. Neisser accuses many psychological studies of proving things that "every ten-year-old knows anyway" and of avoiding interesting topics. For a psychol-

ogy course write a critique of Nickerson and Adams's study (pp. 218–230) in which you either use it to support Neisser's opinion or refute it.

4. Neisser discusses how many people are able to recite texts word-for-word for patriotic, religious, esthetic, or personal reasons. To help you explore and evaluate the personal truth of Neisser's claim, complete the following exercise, the results of which you will share with your classmates in this course. Write down the words to a song, prayer, or other text that you think you remember. Then compare your version against a printed version of the original. How close are your versions? Write a brief essay about why the text that you remembered is important to you and why you happen to know it by heart; make reference to Neisser's discussion of this phenomenon.

Brain Systems and Memory

*Floyd E. Bloom, Arlyne Lazerson, and
Laura Hofstadter*

Yet another way to attempt to understand psychology is through physiology, the study of bodily function. Speculations about the brain and behavior have a long tradition dating back to the ancient civilizations, but the rise of modern neural physiology corresponds approximately with those of clinical and experimental psychology in the last part of the nineteenth century.

The following is from an undergraduate textbook in physiological psychology. The title of the book, published in 1985, indicates the fundamental concept of physiological psychology that all mental activity and behavior have a biological basis: *Brain, Mind, and Behavior.* In order to make the connection between biology and psychology, the scientific investigations described here entail studying what happens to thinking and behavior when the biological equipment of the nervous system is somehow altered. Although current standards of experimental ethics permit tampering with the brains of living animals, such experiments with humans are clearly out of the question, so human studies have relied on examining people with naturally occurring brain damage.

In standard textbook fashion, the various studies of humans and animals are summarized and organized as illustrations of general principles which are now largely agreed upon as reliable knowledge by researchers in the field. The presentation is organized around the various parts of the brain and the physiological processes within it.

FOR ANIMALS WITH BRAINS, we want to know more than which *1* cellular changes may constitute memory storage; we want to know how memory is organized in the brain. Which regions of the brain are important? Which brain systems participate in learning and memory? Recent research has been able to provide some important clues.

The Cerebellum

The cerebellum functions in the control of all kinds of movement (see *2* Figure 1). It "programs" the coordination of the many individual movements that go to make up the action of, say, lifting an apple to your mouth to bite on it. Patients who have sustained injuries to the cerebellum report that they must consciously perform each step of a complex movement that they had performed "automatically" before their injury—bringing the apple up and stopping its movement before it makes contact with their lips, for example.

Recent work (McCormick et al., 1982) suggests that a wide variety *3* of classically conditioned learned responses may be stored in the cerebellum. For example, in one experiment, rabbits were conditioned to blink an eyelid in response to a tone. A puff of air directed at the rabbit's eye (US)° was repeatedly associated with the sound of a tone (CS)°. Like people, rabbits show the reflex response of blinking (UR)° when an irritating stimulus, such as a puff of air, hits the eye. After a number of pairings of air puffs with the tone, the rabbits learned to blink just at the sound (CR)°.

With the conditioning process complete, the researchers removed a *4* very small part of the rabbits' cerebellum on the left side, the same side as the eye that had been trained. The conditioned response completely disappeared, but the unconditioned response—blinking in response to a puff of air—remained normal. In addition, the right eyelid could be conditioned to the tone, but the left eyelid could never relearn the response. The memory trace for eyelid conditioning seems to develop in this one particular region of the cerebellum—the deep cerebellar nuclei—and destruction of that region also destroys that trace. Other neural changes may also contribute to the learned response, but the changes in the cerebellum are obviously essential.

The Hippocampus

The hippocampus (see Figure 1) has been the subject of much research *5* over the past three decades, but we still cannot say precisely what functions it performs in learning and memory. Studies conducted from various points of departure have discovered several roles that it may play. The few human patients who are known to have suffered severe damage in both left and right hippocampi show serious learning prob-

---

US—unconditioned stimulus.   CS—conditioned stimulus.   UR—unconditioned response.   CR—conditioned response.

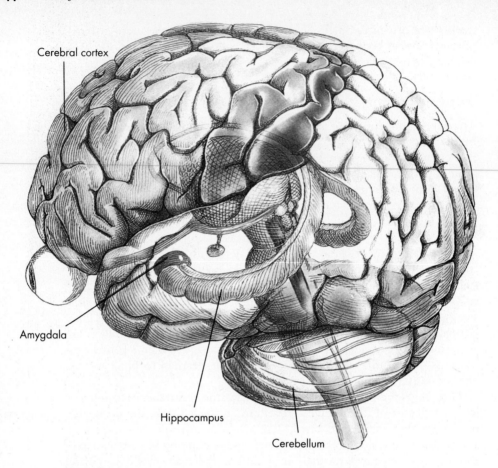

Cerebral cortex

Amygdala

Hippocampus

Cerebellum

Figure 1.   The brain structures most likely to be involved in memory functions.
Source: From Brain, Mind, and Behavior *by Floyd E. Bloom et al. Copyright © 1985 Educational Broadcasting Company. Used with the permission of W. H. Freeman and Company.*

lems. After the damage occurs they are unable to store memories of anything they learn; they cannot even remember the name or the face of someone they encountered only minutes before. Their memory of events that occurred before their brain damage, however, appears to be unimpaired.

By implanting electrodes in single neurons of rats' brains, researchers 6
have learned that some neurons in the hippocampus seem to respond only when the animal is at a certain place in a familiar environment (O'Keefe & Nadel, 1978). The monitored cell remains quiet until the animal reaches a certain point. At that point, and only at that point, the neuron begins firing rapidly. As soon as the rat moves past this place, the neuron quiets down (see Figure 2). In rats, at least, the hippocampus apparently plays an important role in the learning of a "spatial map."

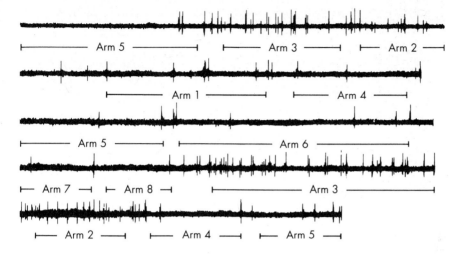

Figure 2. Oscilloscope records of activity in one neuron of a rat's hippocampus as the rat runs freely through the maze.
Source: From D. S. Olton, M. Branch, and P. Best, "Spacial Correlates of Hippocampal Unit Activity," Experimental Neurology *1978, 58, 87. Copyright © 1978 by Academic Press, Inc. Reprinted with permission.*

This spatial map is not analogous to a road map, however. Rather, it 7 is a kind of filter for sensory events that have already been processed by the cerebral cortex. The rat's hippocampus is, in a sense, "recognizing" a space that the rat has traveled before. If the hippocampus is damaged, the rat's ability to learn a maze at all is severely damaged.

Another study (Olton et al., 1980) used a maze modeled after the 8 way rats forage in the wild (see Figure 3). Every arm of the maze had food at its end, as would many routes in a natural setting. The rat's problem was to remember where it had already been in order to run to a place where it had not yet eaten the food. After only a few runs, normal rats learned the maze so well that they never retraced their steps. When these rats' hippocampi were removed, however, they often retraced their paths, apparently unable to remember where they had been and where they had not. It was as though the rat had lost its "working memory."

That the hippocampus operates somehow in "working memory," or 9 short-term memory, is indicated by its differing levels of activity during classical conditioning. Little, if any, neuronal activity goes on in the hippocampus during conditioning of the eyelid blink in rabbits, for example. Even rabbits without a hippocampus can be conditioned to blink an eyelid. But if a rabbit's hippocampus is subjected to enough electrical stimulation to produce the abnormal neuronal activity of epileptic-like seizures, the rabbit is unable to learn the response, as Richard Thompson and his colleagues have found. (In this matter, at least, an

Figure 3.   The radial-arm maze created by Olton to test memory in rats (Olton, 1977).
Source: Ben Rose. © Miriam Rose. Courtesy, Center for Creative Photography, University of Arizona.

abnormal hippocampus is worse than no hippocampus at all.) If a pause is introduced between presentation of the tone and the puff of air, neurons in the hippocampus start to fire during that pause, as if the hippocampus kept the tone in working memory until the puff of air arrived. When Thompson made training tasks more complex, reversing the rules on an animal trained to respond to one stimulus and not to respond to another, he recorded massive neuronal activity in the hippocampus. The added complexity seemed to require more neural activity. Nevertheless, the role of the hippocampus in simple eyelid conditioning and its role as a "spatial mapmaker," or "working memory," are two very different things.

Recent research has revealed that cells in the hippocampus, when   10
stimulated repeatedly by electrodes, continue firing for as long as weeks

after the stimulation stops. This technique, called *long-term potentiation°*, produces neuronal firing resembling that found in an animal going about the ordinary business of learning something.

You will recall that many neurons, after repeated stimulation, become 11 less active. Researchers believe that the increased excitability of hippocampal neurons after repeated stimulation may represent long-lasting changes taking place at the synapses there, changes that underlie learning. And it does appear that after long-term potentiation, the neurons involved do show structural changes. Some researchers have provided evidence that the heads of dendritic° spines swell. Others have shown that the number of synapses° onto dendritic shafts increases. Such changes in neuron structure and in the quality and quantity of connectivity between them might be the neural basis for certain kinds of learning and memory. No conclusions are possible yet, but research is continuing.

The hippocampus receives very indirect neural input from all the 12 senses. Messages traveling along neural pathways from the brainstem and cortex undergo considerable sensory processing, but eventually they reach the hippocampus, the amygdala, or the hypothalamus, or all of these structures. Pathways down from the cortex also pass through these structures. A study using monkeys as subjects showed that both the hippocampus and the amygdala had to be removed to destroy previous learning and prevent new learning. Before the operation, the monkeys learned relatively quickly to choose the novel object of a pair—one that they had not seen before. After their operations, monkeys minus only amygdala or those minus only hippocampus relearned the novelty task only a little less successfully than normal monkeys did: 91 percent versus 97 percent correct. The monkeys who had lost both their hippocampus and their amygdala, however, had only a 60 percent success rate, almost the level of chance. Either they could not learn the criterion for making a choice, or they could not remember and recognize objects they had already seen.

It is clear that the hippocampus plays a role in learning and memory, 13 even if its exact function cannot yet be described. Now let us look at a structure even more certainly responsible for learning but whose functions are even less well understood.

The Cortex

There is no doubt that the cerebral cortex in the human brain is vital to 14 learning and memory, but its complexity makes it difficult to study.

Potentiation—the state of holding an electrical charge, which enhances the response of a system.   **Dendritic**—belonging to the nerve fiber which projects off the nerve cell body.   **Synapse**—junction between two neurons; a gap across which neurotransmitters, such as epinephrine, pass.

Because human thinking and problem-solving usually employ language, animal experiments can offer only the roughest analogies. The simple learning involved in habituation, sensitization, and classical conditioning does not seem to require higher cortical functions.

Monkeys can learn to solve several kinds of problems that involve *15* complex learning. The animals are trained on a number of discrimination problems, and if, as a result of the earlier training, they are able to learn later problems more quickly, they are said to have formed a *learning set*. For example, in the *oddity problem* devised by Harry Harlow, the primate psychologist, monkeys are shown a set of three objects, two of which are identical—two toy cars and a truck, for example. They are rewarded for picking the odd object. After a monkey picks the truck in a number of trials, it is shown three entirely different objects—two oranges and an apple, for example. Eventually, the monkey apparently forms the concept of "oddness," and picks the odd object of a set every time on the first trial (see Figure 4). Loss of large parts of the temporal lobes of the cortex destroys the ability to form such concepts.

The fact that animals raised in enriched environments have slightly *16* thicker cortical layers and more elaborated neuronal structures than animals raised in deprived environments shows that experience—learning—affects the cortex in animals. It must be that in human beings, in whom the cortex is so prominent, the same sorts of changes occur. In

Figure 4. A monkey at Harry Harlow's primate laboratory at the University of Wisconsin solves an oddity problem.
Source: Harlow Primate Laboratory University of Wisconsin. Reprinted with permission.

conjunction with the other brain structures that help us process information, the human cortex stores our experience, and it must change as we learn and remember. But it is not yet possible to say precisely what those changes are.

Transmitter Systems

An animal's survival depends on its remembering which events predict 17
pleasure and which predict pain. Therefore the value of information to an animal—that is, whether or not a piece of information should be stored in memory—depends in part on what occurs after it has initially registered the information. Several hormones and neurotransmitters have been suggested as the agents that influence, or modulate, this initial learning.

A prime candidate for this role is the hormone *norepinephrine*, secreted 18
by the adrenal medulla° during states of emotional arousal. If pain is used as punishment in training animals to perform a behavior—a strong electrical shock to the foot, for example—and the animals are then given a small dose of norepinephrine, they later show much better memory for the correct behavior than animals not given the chemical. A weak electrical shock does not mobilize as much of the body's natural norepinephrine, and animals so trained require much more injected norepinephrine to produce the same improvement in memory. Amphetamine, a stimulant drug known to facilitate memory, also works by activating the body's norepinephrine and dopamine systems. . . . Because circulating norepinephrine cannot cross the blood/brain barrier°, the precise physiological mechanism that would mediate its role in learning is not known.

Protein Synthesis

All the molecules in our bodies are continuously being broken down 19
and reformed. In the brain, too, 90 percent of its proteins are broken down and replaced within no more than two weeks. The structures made up of proteins do not change, of course: the process is more like that of individual bricks in a brick house being replaced here and there.

The template on which protein is made in the cell is RNA. A number 20
of studies have suggested that the rate of RNA production of protein seems to increase in animals during learning. The problem with such findings is that everything a neuron does involves protein synthesis, so there is really no way to know exactly what the increased rate reflects.

Adrenal medulla—an endocrine gland near the kidneys which secretes adrenalin.
Blood/brain barrier—a barrier between the blood system and the brain that prevents many chemicals from passing into the brain.

Figure 5. These ducklings imprinted on Nobel-prize-winning ethologist Konrad Lorenz because he was the first moving object they saw after hatching.
Source: Thomas McAvoy, Life Magazine © Time, Inc. Reprinted with permission.

In one series of experiments on baby chicks, Steven Rose and his colleagues made every effort to control outside influences. All chicks show the natural species-specific learning behavior of *imprinting*. They become attached to and follow—that is, they learn to recognize—the first moving object they encounter as soon after hatching as they can walk, usually in about 16 hours. The moving object is usually their mother, although some researchers of animal behavior have had chicks following balls, mechanical toys, and even themselves. **21**

Increased production of protein can be detected in the chick's brain within 2 hours of its exposure to an imprinting stimulus. To rule out any possible effects not related to this learning, researchers cut the pathway that transfers visual information between the two halves of the chick's brain. In effect, they used one-half of the chick's brain as a control for the other (experimental) half. When they covered one eye so **22** that the chick saw the imprinting stimulus with just one eye, the rate of protein synthesis was greater in the half of the brain that learned to recognize the imprinting stimulus.

The role of these newly manufactured proteins in memory, it is *23* conjectured, would be to travel down the axon° to the synapse and change the synapse structure in ways that would, at least temporarily, make it more effective. This modification, then, would be the physical basis of the learning.

References

Harlow, H. F. 1949. The formation of learning sets. *Psychological Review*, 56:51–56.

McCormick, D. A., G. A. Clark, D. G. Lavord, and R. F. Thompson. 1982. Initial localization of the memory trace for a basic form of learning. *Proceedings of the National Academy of Science USA*, 79:2731–2735.

O'Keefe, J., and L. Nadel. 1978. *The Hippocampus as a Cognitive Map*. London: Oxford University Press.

Olton, D. S., J. T. Becker, and G. E. Handelmann. 1980. Hippocampal function: Working memory or cognitive mapping. *Physiological Psychology*, 8: 239–246.

Rose, S. P. R., P. P. G. Bateson, and G. Horn. 1973. Experience and plasticity in the nervous system. *Science*, 181: 506–514.

Thompson, R. F., T. Berger, and J. Madden. 1983. Cellular processes of learning and memory in the mammalian CNS. *Annual Review of Neuroscience*, 6: 447–491.

Rhetorical Analysis Through Annotation

The task of this selection is to associate brain locations (identified in the illustration on page 244) with memory functions and processes. Next to the heading of each section note whether the subtitle names a location, a functioning system, or a process.

At the opening of each section and at several other points, explicit associations are made between brain locations and memory functions or processes. Underline each such statement. Circle words that qualify the association or indicate the level of certainty. Discuss the certainty and generality of the association made between location and function or process in each case.

The associations are then elaborated through experiments. In the margin place a bracket next to each experiment and note what aspect of the association the experiment elaborates.

Finally, discuss what the difficulties are in associating a location with an activity and how the text overcomes the difficulties.

Axon—core of the nerve fiber along which nerve impulses pass from the cell body to the synaptic junction.

Discussion Questions

Interpreting the Text

1. What parts of the brain are discussed? What do we know about their functions?

2. How have surgical (physiological) procedures been combined with experimental (psychological) procedures to learn more about the functions of parts of the brain. Why is it necessary or useful to combine methods of investigation?

3. What is imprinting? How is it related to memory? What do the experiments described here show about how the brain may store memories?

4. Overall, how much have physiological investigations been able to tell us about memory? How detailed is our picture of how memory functions relate to brain structure? How much can physical structure tell us about psychological function? What are the difficulties in connecting a physical organ with mental operations?

5. Do any of the investigations here relate to any of the concepts presented in other selections in this unit? How do the issues of memory become changed when treated from a physiological point of view?

6. How does the form of a textbook summary of current knowledge lead to a different kind of synthesis of the literature than appears in reviews of the literature, such as that by Cofer on pages 211–217? How do the roles of evaluation differ? How do the overall structures of the narratives differ?

7. In recent years protests have arisen about the use of animals in the type of experiments described here. Protesters have made a strong case that animals should have rights and be treated ethically by scientists. Do you believe the animals in the experiments described here have been treated ethically? Do you think researchers are justified in experimenting on rabbits, rats, monkeys, and chicks, as described in this textbook selection, in order to learn where functions of memory reside in the brain?

Writing Suggestions

1. For an exam in biology write a short essay answering the question: What do we currently know about the role of various brain areas in memory and the chemical processes by which memory is stored?

2. Prepare a short textbook selection describing the parts of a simple machine (such as a hammer, a lever, or a kite) and their function. As the selection does, use a diagram as a central element in your description.

3. For a course in biology, write an essay on the degree to which memory is adaptive, that is, useful to animals (including humans) in their survival in nature. Use relevant sections of this textbook selection as a source to back up your points.

The Mind of a Mnemonist

A. R. Luria

People with extremely good memories and people with impaired memories have offered special insights to psychologists. The most famous study of a person with an eidetic, or photographic, memory was done by the Soviet psychologist A. R. Luria in 1968. Luria details the extent of a man's amazing memory, and gains some fascinating clues as to how that memory is structured. Particularly fascinating is the role of synesthesia, the conversion of one sense impression into another, in allowing the man (known as S.) to create mental pictures. Even more, Luria helps us see the personal implications of having such a memory. Luria's account reminds us that to a large extent memory defines a person and greatly affects the quality of life.

Luria, in an excerpt from his book *The Mind of a Mnemonist*, mixes experimental accounts with personal narrative. The basic story is of one person learning about another, with the experiments being only focused moments of inquiry within the larger process of increasing mutual familiarity.

THE ACTUAL BEGINNING OF this account dates back to the 1920's, 1 when I had only recently begun to do work in psychology. It was then that a man came to my laboratory who asked me to test his memory.

At the time the man (let us designate him S.) was a newspaper reporter 2 who had come to my laboratory at the suggestion of the paper's editor. Each morning the editor would meet with the staff and hand out assignments for the day—lists of places he wanted covered, information to be obtained in each. The list of addresses and instructions was usually fairly long, and the editor noted with some surprise that S. never took any notes. He was about to reproach the reporter for being inattentive when, at his urging, S. repeated the entire assignment word for word. Curious to learn more about how the man operated, the editor began questioning S. about his memory. But S. merely countered with amazement: Was there really anything unusual about his remembering everything he'd been told? Wasn't that the way other people operated? The idea that he possessed certain particular qualities of memory which distinguished him from others struck him as incomprehensible.

The editor sent him to the psychology laboratory to have some studies 3 done on his memory, and thus it was that I found myself confronted with the man.

At the time S. was just under thirty. The information I got on his 4 family background was that his father owned a bookstore, that his mother, an elderly Jewish woman, was quite well-read, and that of his numerous brothers and sisters (all of them conventional, well-balanced types) some were gifted individuals. There was no incidence of mental illness in the family.

S. had grown up in a small Jewish community and had attended 5 elementary school there. Later, when it was discovered that he had musical ability, he was enrolled in a music school, where he studied in the hope that he might some day become a professional violinist. However, after an ear disease had left his hearing somewhat impaired, he realized he could hardly expect to have a successful career as a musician. During the time he spent looking for the sort of work that would best suit him he happened to visit the newspaper, where he subsequently began work as a reporter.

S. had no clear idea what he wanted out of life, and his plans were 6 fairly indefinite. The impression he gave was of a rather ponderous and at times timid person who was puzzled at having been sent to the psychology laboratory. As I mentioned, he wasn't aware of any peculiarities in himself and couldn't conceive of the idea that his memory differed in some way from other people's. He passed on his editor's request to me with some degree of confusion and waited curiously to see what, if anything, the research might turn up. Thus began a relationship of almost thirty years, filled with experiments, discussions, and correspondence.

When I began my study of S. it was with much the same degree of 7 curiosity psychologists generally have at the outset of research, hardly with the hope that the experiments would offer anything of particular note. However, the results of the first tests were enough to change my attitude and to leave me, the experimenter, rather than my subject, both embarrassed and perplexed.

I gave S. a series of words, then numbers, then letters, reading them 8 to him slowly or presenting them in written form. He read or listened attentively and then repeated the material exactly as it had been presented. I increased the number of elements in each series, giving him as many as thirty, fifty, or even seventy words or numbers, but this, too, presented no problem for him. He did not need to commit any of the material to memory; if I gave him a series of words or numbers, which I read slowly and distinctly, he would listen attentively, sometimes ask me to stop and enunciate a word more clearly, or, if in doubt whether he had heard a word correctly, would ask me to repeat it. Usually during an experiment he would close his eyes or stare into space, fixing his gaze on one point; when the experiment was over, he would ask that we pause while he went over the material in his mind to see if he had retained it. Thereupon, without another moment's pause, he would reproduce the series that had been read to him.

The experiment indicated that he could reproduce a series in reverse 9 order—from the beginning to the end—just as simply as from start to finish; that he could readily tell me which word followed another in a series, or reproduce the word which happened to precede one I'd name. He would pause for a minute, as though searching for the word, but immediately after would be able to answer my questions and generally made no mistakes.

It was of no consequence to him whether the series I gave him 10 contained meaningful words or nonsense syllables, numbers or sounds; whether they were presented orally or in writing. All he required was that there be a three-to-four-second pause between each element in the series, and he had no difficulty reproducing whatever I gave him.

As the experimenter, I soon found myself in a state verging on utter 11 confusion. An increase in the length of a series led to no noticeable increase in difficulty for S., and I simply had to admit that the capacity of his memory *had no distinct limits;* that I had been unable to perform what one would think was the simplest task a psychologist can do: measure the capacity of an individual's memory. I arranged a second and then a third session with S.; these were followed by a series of sessions, some of them days and weeks apart, others separated by a period of several years.

But these later sessions only further complicated my position as ex- 12 perimenter, for it appeared that there was no limit either to the *capacity* of S.'s memory or to the *durability of the traces he retained.* Experiments indicated that he had no difficulty reproducing any lengthy series of words whatever, even though these had originally been presented to him a week, a month, a year, or even many years earlier. In fact, some of these experiments designed to test his retention were performed (without his being given any warning) fifteen or sixteen years after the session in which he had originally recalled the words. Yet invariably they were successful. During these test sessions S. would sit with his eyes closed, pause, then comment: "Yes, yes . . . This was a series you gave me once when we were in your apartment . . . You were sitting at the table and I in the rocking chair . . . You were wearing a gray suit and you looked at me like this . . . Now, then, I can see you saying . . ." And with that he would reel off the series precisely as I had given it to him at the earlier session. If one takes into account that S. had by then become a well-known mnemonist, who had to remember hundreds and thousands of series, the feat seems even more remarkable.

All this meant that I had to alter my plan and concentrate less on any 13 attempt to *measure* the man's memory than on some way to provide a *qualitative analysis* of it, to describe the *psychological aspects of its structure.* Subsequently I undertook to explore another problem, as I said, to do a close study of the peculiarities that seemed an inherent part of the psychology of this exceptional mnemonist.

I devoted the balance of my research to these two tasks, the results 14 of which I will try to present systematically here, though many years have passed since my work with S.

The Initial Facts

Throughout the course of our research S.'s recall was always of a 15
spontaneous nature. The only mechanisms he employed were one of the
following: either he continued to *see* series of words or numbers which
had been presented to him, or he converted these elements into *visual
images.*

The simplest structure was one S. used to recall *tables of numbers* 16
written on a blackboard. S. would study the material on the board,
close his eyes, open them again for a moment, turn aside, and, at a
signal, reproduce one series from the board. Then he would fill in the
empty squares of the next table, rapidly calling off the numbers. It was
a simple matter for him to fill in the numbers for the empty squares of
the table either when asked to do this for certain squares I chose at
random, or when asked to fill in a series of numbers successively in
reverse order. He could easily tell me which numbers formed one or
another of the vertical columns in the table and could "read off" to me
numbers that formed the diagonals; finally, he was able to compose a
multi-digit number out of the one-digit numbers in the entire table.

In order to imprint an impression of a table consisting of twenty 17
numbers, S. needed only 35–40 seconds, during which he would examine the chart closely several times. A table of fifty numbers required
somewhat more time, but he could easily fix an impression of it in his
mind in 2.5–3 minutes, staring at the chart a few times, then closing his
eyes as he tested himself on the material in his mind.

The following is a typical example of one of dozens of experiments 18
that were carried out with him (Experiment of May 10, 1939):

He spent three minutes examining the table I had drawn on a piece 19
of paper (Table 1), stopping intermittently to go over what he had seen
in his mind. It took him 40 seconds to reproduce this table (that is, to
call off all the numbers in succession). He did this at a rhythmic pace,
scarcely pausing between numbers. His reproduction of the numbers in

Table 1

6	6	8	0
5	4	3	2
1	6	8	4
7	9	3	5
4	2	3	7
3	8	9	1
1	0	0	2
3	4	5	1
2	7	6	8
1	9	2	6
2	9	6	7
5	5	2	0
x	0	1	x

the third vertical column took somewhat longer—1 minute, 20 seconds—whereas he reproduced those in the second vertical column in 25 seconds, and took 30 seconds to reproduce this column in reverse order. He read off the numbers which formed the diagonals (the groups of four numbers running zigzag through the chart) in 35 seconds, and within 50 seconds ran through the numbers that formed the horizontal rows. Altogether he required 1 minute, 30 seconds to convert all fifty numbers into a single fifty-digit number and read this off. . . .

At first glance the explanation seems quite simple. He told us that he 20 continued *to see* the table which had been written on a blackboard or a sheet of paper, that he merely had to "read it off," successively enumerating the numbers or letters it contained. Hence, it generally made no difference to him whether he "read" the table from the beginning or the end, whether he listed the elements that formed the vertical or the diagonal groups, or "read off" numbers that formed the horizontal rows. The task of converting the individual numbers into a single, multi-digit number appeared to be no more difficult for him than it would be for others of us were we asked to perform this operation visually and given a considerably longer time to study the table.

S. continued to see the numbers he had "imprinted" in his memory 21 just as they had appeared on the board or the sheet of paper: the numbers presented exactly the same configuration they had as written, so that if one of the numbers had not been written distinctly, S. was liable to "misread" it, to take a 3 for an 8, for example, or a 4 for a 9. However, even at this stage of the report our attention had been drawn to certain peculiarities in S.'s account which indicated that his process of recall was not at all simple.

Synesthesia

Our curiosity had been aroused by a small and seemingly unimportant 22 observation. S. had remarked on a number of occasions that if the examiner said something during the experiment—if, for example, he said "yes" to confirm that S. had reproduced the material correctly or "no" to indicate he had made a mistake—a blur would appear on the table and would spread and block off the numbers, so that S. in his mind would be forced to "shift" the table over, away from the blurred section that was covering it. The same thing happened if he heard noise in the auditorium; this was immediately converted into "puffs of steam" or "splashes" which made it more difficult for him to read the table.

This led us to believe that the process by which he retained material 23 did not consist merely of his having preserved spontaneous traces of visual impressions; there were certain additional elements at work. I suggested that S. possessed a marked degree of *synesthesia*. If we can trust S.'s recollections of his early childhood (which we will deal with in a special section later in this account), these synesthetic reactions could be traced back to a very early age. As he described it:

When I was about two or three years old I was taught the words of a
Hebrew prayer. I didn't understand them, and what happened was that
the words settled in my mind as puffs of steam or splashes . . . Even
now I *see* these puffs or splashes when I hear certain sounds.

Synesthetic reactions of this type occurred whenever S. was asked to 24
listen to *tones*. The same reactions, though somewhat more complicated,
occurred with his perception of *voices* and with speech sounds.

The following is the record of experiments that were carried out with 25
S. in the Laboratory on the Physiology of Hearing at the Neurological
Institute, Academy of Medical Sciences.

Presented with a tone pitched at 30 cycles per second and having an
amplitude of 100 decibels, S. stated that at first he saw a strip 12–15
cm. in width the color of old, tarnished silver. Gradually this strip
narrowed and seemed to recede; then it was converted into an object
that glistened like steel. Then the tone gradually took on a color one
associates with twilight, the sound continuing to dazzle because of the
silvery gleam it shed.

Presented with a tone pitched at 50 cycles per second and an amplitude of 100 decibels, S. saw a brown strip against a dark background
that had red, tongue-like edges. The sense of taste he experienced was
like that of sweet and sour borscht, a sensation that gripped his entire
tongue.

Presented with a tone pitched at 100 cycles per second and having an
amplitude of 86 decibels, he saw a wide strip that appeared to have a
reddish-orange hue in the center; from the center outwards the bright-
ness faded with light gradations so that the edges of the strip appeared
pink.

Presented with a tone pitched at 250 cycles per second and having an
amplitude of 64 decibels, S. saw a velvet cord with fibers jutting out
on all sides. The cord was tinged with a delicate, pleasant pink-orange
hue.

Presented with a tone pitched at 500 cycles per second and having an
amplitude of 100 decibels, he saw a streak of lightning splitting the
heavens in two. When the intensity of the sound was lowered to 74
decibels, he saw a dense orange color which made him feel as though a
needle had been thrust into his spine. Gradually this sensation diminished.

Presented with a tone pitched at 2,000 cycles per second and having
an amplitude of 113 decibels, S. said: "It looks something like fire-
works tinged with a pink-red hue. The strip of color feels rough and
unpleasant, and it has an ugly taste—rather like that of a briny pickle
. . . You could hurt your hand on this."

Presented with a tone pitched at 3,000 cycles per second and having
an amplitude of 128 decibels, he saw a whisk broom that was of a
fiery color, while the rod attached to the whisks seemed to be scatter-
ing off into fiery points.

The experiments were repeated during several days and invariably the   *26*
same stimuli produced identical experiences.

What this meant was that S. was one of a remarkable group of people,   *27*
among them the composer Scriabin, who have retained in an especially
vivid form a "complex" synesthetic type of sensitivity. In S.'s case every
sound he heard immediately produced an experience of light and color
and, as we shall see later in this account, a sense of taste and touch as
well.

S. also experienced synesthetic reactions when he listened to some-   *28*
one's *voice*. "What a crumbly, yellow voice you have," he once told
L. S. Vygotsky° while conversing with him. At a later date he elaborated
on the subject of voices as follows:

> You know there are people who seem to have many voices, whose
> voices seem to be an entire composition, a bouquet. The late S. M.
> Eisenstein° had just such a voice: listening to him, it was as though a
> flame with fibers protruding from it was advancing right toward me.
> I got so interested in his voice, I couldn't follow what he was say-
> ing. . . .
>   But there are people whose voices change constantly. I frequently
> have trouble recognizing someone's voice over the phone, and it isn't
> merely because of a bad connection. It's because the person happens to
> be someone whose voice changes twenty to thirty times in the course
> of a day. Other people don't notice this, but I do.
>   (Record of November 1951.)

> To this day I can't escape from seeing colors when I hear sounds.
> What first strikes me is the color of someone's voice. Then it fades off
> . . . for it does interfere. If, say, a person says something, I see the
> word; but should another person's voice break in, blurs appear. These
> creep into the syllables of the words and I can't make out what is
> being said.
>   (Record of June 1953.)

The Art of Forgetting

Many of us are anxious to find ways to improve our memories; none   *29*
of us have to deal with the problem of how to forget. In S.'s case,
however, precisely the reverse was true. The big question for him, and
the most troublesome, was how he could learn to forget.

In the passages quoted above, we had our first glimpse of the problems   *30*
S. ran into, trying to understand and recall a text. There were numerous
details in the text, each of which gave rise to new images that led him
far afield; further details produced still more details, until his mind was

---

L. S. Vygotsky—a well-known Russian psychologist.   **S. M. Eisenstein**—a famous film
director.

a virtual chaos. How could he avoid these images, prevent himself from seeing details which kept him from understanding a simple story? This was the way he formulated the problem.

Moreover, in his work as a professional mnemonist° he had run into *31* another problem. How could he learn *to forget* or *to erase* images he no longer needed? The solution to the first problem proved to be simple enough, for as S. continued to work on his technique of using images for recall, he tended to make increasingly greater use of shorthand versions of them, which automatically cut out many superfluous details.

The second problem, however, was more difficult to solve. S. fre- *32* quently gave several performances an evening, sometimes in the same hall, where the charts of numbers he had to recall were written on the one blackboard there and then erased before the next performance. This led to certain problems, which he described as follows:

> I'm afraid I may begin to confuse the individual performances. So in my mind I erase the blackboard and cover it, as it were, with a film that's completely opaque and impenetrable. I take this off the board and listen to it crunch as I gather it into a ball. That is, after each performance is over, I erase the board, walk away from it, and mentally gather up the film I had used to cover the board. As I go on talking to the audience, I feel myself crumpling this film into a ball in my hands. Even so, when the next performance starts and I walk over to that blackboard, the numbers I had erased are liable to turn up again. If they alternate in a way that's even vaguely like the order in one of the previous performances, I might not catch myself in time and would read off the chart of numbers that had been written there before.
>
> (From a letter of 1939.)

How was S. to deal with this? During the early stages, his attempts *33* to work out a technique of forgetting were of an extremely simple nature. Why, he reasoned, couldn't he use some external means to help him forget—write down what he no longer wished to remember. This may strike others as odd, but it was a natural enough conclusion for S. "People jot things down so they'll remember them," he said. "This seemed ridiculous to me, so I decided to tackle the problem my own way." As he saw it, once he had written a thing down, he would have no need to remember it; but if he were without means of writing it down, he'd commit it to memory.

> Writing something down means I'll know I won't have to remember it. . . . So I started doing this with small matters like phone numbers, last names, errands of one sort or another. But I got nowhere, for in

---

Mnemonist—a performer of memory tricks.

my mind I continued to see what I'd written . . . Then I tried writing all the notes on identical kinds of paper, using the same pencil each time. But it still didn't work.

He went further and started to discard and then burn the slips of *34* paper on which he had jotted down things he wished to forget. Here for the first time we have evidence of something we shall have occasion to return to later in this account: that S.'s richly figurative imagination was not sharply cut off from reality; rather, he turned to objects in the external world when he needed a means to work out some mental operation.

The "magical act of burning" he tried proved of no use to him. And *35* after he had burned a piece of paper with some numbers he wanted to forget and discovered he could still see traces of the numbers on the charred embers, he was desperate. Not even fire could wipe out the traces he wanted to obliterate!

The problem of forgetting, which had not been solved by his naïve *36* attempt to burn his notes, became a torment for him. Just when he thought a solution was unattainable, however, something occurred which proved effective, though it remained as unfathomable to him as it did to those of us who were studying him.

> One evening—it was the 23rd of April—I was quite exhausted from having given three performances and was wondering how I'd ever get through the fourth. There before me I could see the charts of numbers appearing from the first three performances. It was a terrible problem. I thought: I'll just take a quick look and see if the first chart of numbers is still there. I was afraid somehow that it wouldn't be. I both did and didn't want it to appear . . . And then I thought: the chart of numbers isn't turning up now and it's clear why—it's because I don't want it to! Aha! That means if I don't want the chart to show up it won't. And all it took was for me to realize this!

Odd as it may seem, this brought results. It may very well be that S. *37* had become fixated on an *absence of images*, and that had something to do with it. Possibly, too, his attention had been diverted, or the image was inhibited, and the added effect of autosuggestion was enough to destroy it. It seems pointless to conjecture about a phenomenon that has remained inexplicable. What we do have is evidence of the results it achieved.

> At that moment I felt I was free. The realization that I had some guarantee against making mistakes gave me more confidence. I began to speak more freely, could even permit myself the luxury of pausing when I felt like it, for I knew that if I didn't want an image to appear, it wouldn't. I felt simply wonderful. . . .

Rhetorical Analysis Through Annotation

Luria creates a strong sense of people's individuality by portraying himself, the mnemonist, and others as confronted by unusual events or problems, which they then need to figure out or overcome.

Mark each statement where someone is represented as facing something unusual, puzzling, or troublesome. Note in the margin what that individual does to address the situation.

Discuss what kind of picture this creates of people. In this light, of what consequence is it that Luria mentions continued contact with the subject for thirty years? Of what importance is the biographical portrait presented of the mnemonist (253–254). How does the portrayal of people here compare with the pictures of subjects and investigator presented in the previous experimental articles (see pp. 210–217 and 219–231)? How does the portrayal compare to Neisser's portrayal of individuals (pp. 234–240)? To the portrayal of experimental animals and brain-damaged humans in the textbook account of the brain-damaged (pp. 243–244)?

Discussion Questions

Interpreting the Text

1. What was S.'s method for memorizing a list? How does this compare with your study methods?

2. What is synesthesia? What role did it play in S.'s memory? How did S.'s attempts to forget use his synesthetic faculties?

3. In what way was forgetting a problem for S.? How did he solve this problem? What does this solution reveal about his memory?

4. How did S.'s knowledge of his special talent develop? How did knowledge of it change his life? How did he deal with his talent? Can you compare his case with any other people with special talents you may be aware of?

Considering the Issues

5. Have you ever experienced synesthesia? How is synesthesia used in art, music, literature, cooking, and perfume making?

6. Are there any similarities between the way S.'s memory works and the method of loci for enhancing memory (described by Quintilian on p. 198)?

7. Are you ever haunted by memories that clutter up your mind? Do they tend to be personal or academic (such as facts you crammed for an exam that will not go away)? Do you have any desire or way to control these excess memories?

8. How does this account fit in with some of the other presentations of memory in this unit? For example, does S. seem to have a distinction between short- and

long-term memory? Where or how does the concept of gist enter into S.'s memory? In S.'s memory more like the type Ebbinghaus studied or that Bartlett studied? Does synesthesia or photographic qualities enter in elsewhere in the main line of research?

9. Does S.'s memory seem like ours, only better, or does his memory work differently than ours does? Do you see any similarities between his memory and yours, or are they just totally different?

Writing Suggestions

1. For a psychology class write an essay on how S.'s memory is typical or atypical of other people's memories, based on the research you have read, your own experience, and your knowledge of others.

2. For a local newspaper write a story about someone you have known for several years who has a special talent. In your account try to get at exactly what the talent consists of, how it operates, and how the person relates to the talent.

3. For a literature class, write an essay analyzing Luria's view of character and skill in character portrayal (see Rhetorical Analysis Through Annotation questions).

4. Write a letter to a psychologically trained academic counselor. Describe your experience trying to remember material for exam, part for a play, or other rote material. Ask for the counselor's evaluation and advice to improve your memory.

5. Nickerson and Adams quote Luria in their discussion of how it may be a good thing that people do not keep too many details in their minds about visual experiences: "One is reminded of Luria's mnemonist who had so much trouble recognizing people's faces because, as he put it, they are 'constantly changing'" (p. 230). For a psychology class write an essay about the ways in which S.'s memory made his life difficult and what we can learn about the benefits of an average memory from him.

The Lost Mariner

Oliver Sacks

How much memory means to our life is strikingly represented by people who lack memory. Oliver Sacks, a neurologist at a home for people with severe neurological disorders, records the case of a man stuck in time. His loss of memory erases his life as he lives it. Yet there seems to remain an essential enduring humanity, a part of him that lives beyond his memory.

Sacks goes even beyond Luria in exploring what the subject's psychological state means for the subject's life. It is not surprising that Sacks finds Luria's work important, and in fact writes to the Soviet psychologist concerning this case. A bit more surprising is the neurologist's affinity for philosophers; his concern for what it means for a person to live without memory inevitably draws him to philosophical thoughts about life. Sacks interest in the human meaning of psychological disorders has led him to write for the general public. This essay first appeared in 1985 in the *New York Review of Books*, a general circulation periodical.

You have to begin to lose your memory, if only in bits and pieces, to realise that memory is what makes our lives. Life without memory is no life at all . . . Our memory is our coherence, our reason, our feeling, even our action. Without it, we are nothing . . . (I can only wait for the final amnesia, the one that can erase an entire life, as it did my mother's . . .)
—LUIS BUÑUEL°

THIS MOVING AND FRIGHTENING segment in Buñuel's recently 1 translated memoirs raises fundamental questions—clinical, practical, existential, philosophical: what sort of a life (if any), what sort of a world, what sort of a self, can be preserved in a man who has lost the greater part of his memory and, with this, his past, and his moorings in time?

It immediately made me think of a patient of mine in whom these 2 questions are precisely exemplified: charming, intelligent, memoryless Jimmie G., who was admitted to our Home for the Aged near New York City early in 1975, with a cryptic transfer note saying, 'Helpless, demented, confused and disoriented.'

Jimmie was a fine-looking man, with a curly bush of grey hair, a 3 healthy and handsome forty-nine-year-old. He was cheerful, friendly, and warm.

'Hiya, Doc!' he said. 'Nice morning! Do I take this chair here?' He 4 was a genial soul, very ready to talk and to answer any questions I asked him. He told me his name and birth date, and the name of the little town in Connecticut where he was born. He described it in affectionate detail, even drew me a map. He spoke of the houses where his family had lived—he remembered their phone numbers still. He spoke of school and school days, the friends he'd had, and his special fondness for

---

Luis Buñuel—Spanish filmmaker.

mathematics and science. He talked with enthusiasm of his days in the navy—he was seventeen, had just graduated from high school when he was drafted in 1943. With his good engineering mind he was a 'natural' for radio and electronics, and after a crash course in Texas found himself assistant radio operator on a submarine. He remembered the names of various submarines on which he had served, their missions, where they were stationed, the names of his shipmates. He remembered Morse code, and was still fluent in Morse tapping and touch-typing.

A full and interesting early life, remembered vividly, in detail, with *5* affection. But there, for some reason, his reminiscences stopped. He recalled, and almost relived, his war days and service, the end of the war, and his thoughts for the future. He had come to love the navy, thought he might stay in it. But with the GI Bill, and support, he felt he might do best to go to college. His older brother was in accountancy school and engaged to a girl, a 'real beauty,' from Oregon.

With recalling, reliving, Jimmie was full of animation; he did not *6* seem to be speaking of the past but of the present, and I was very struck by the change of tense in his recollections as he passed from his school days to his days in the navy. He had been using the past tense, but now used the present—and (it seemed to me) not just the formal or fictitious present tense of recall, but the actual present tense of immediate experience.

A sudden, improbable suspicion seized me.   *7*

'What year is this, Mr. G.?' I asked, concealing my perplexity under *8* a casual manner.

'Forty-five, man. What do you mean?' He went on, 'We've won the *9* war, FDR's dead, Truman's at the helm. There are great times ahead.'

'And you, Jimmie, how old would you be?'   *10*

Oddly, uncertainly, he hesitated a moment, as if engaged in calcula- *11* tion.

'Why, I guess I'm nineteen, Doc. I'll be twenty next birthday.'   *12*

Looking at the grey-haired man before me, I had an impulse for *13* which I have never forgiven myself—it was, or would have been, the height of cruelty had there been any possibility of Jimmie's remembering it.

'Here,' I said, and thrust a mirror toward him. 'Look in the mirror *14* and tell me what you see. Is that a nineteen-year-old looking out from the mirror?'

He suddenly turned ashen and gripped the sides of the chair. 'Jesus *15* Christ,' he whispered. 'Christ, what's going on? What's happened to me? Is this a nightmare? Am I crazy? Is this a joke?'—and he became frantic, panicked.

'It's okay, Jimmie,' I said soothingly. 'It's just a mistake. Nothing to *16* worry about. Hey!' I took him to the window. 'Isn't this a lovely spring day. See the kids there playing baseball?' He regained his colour and started to smile, and I stole away, taking the hateful mirror with me.

Two minutes later I re-entered the room. Jimmie was still standing 17
by the window, gazing with pleasure at the kids playing baseball below.
He wheeled around as I opened the door, and his face assumed a cheery
expression.

'Hiya, Doc!' he said. 'Nice morning! You want to talk to me—do I 18
take this chair here?' There was no sign of recognition on his frank,
open face.

'Haven't we met before, Mr G.?' I asked casually. 19

'No, I can't say we have. Quite a beard you got there. I wouldn't 20
forget *you*, Doc!'

'Why do you call me "Doc"?' 21

'Well, you are a doc, ain't you?' 22

'Yes, but if you haven't met me, how do you know what I am?' 23

'You *talk* like a doc. I can *see* you're a doc.' 24

'Well, you're right, I am. I'm the neurologist here.' 25

'Neurologist? Hey, there's something wrong with my nerves? And 26
"here"—where's "here"? What is this place anyhow?'

'I was just going to ask you—where do you think you are?' 27

'I see these beds, and these patients everywhere. Looks like a sort of 28
hospital to me. But hell, what would I be doing in a hospital—and with
all these old people, years older than me. I feel good, I'm strong as a
bull. Maybe I *work* here . . . Do I work? What's my job? . . . No,
you're shaking your head, I see in your eyes I don't work here. If I
don't work here, I've been *put* here. Am I a patient, am I sick and don't
know it, Doc? It's crazy, it's scary . . . Is it some sort of joke?'

'You don't know what the matter is? You really don't know? You 29
remember telling me about your childhood, growing up in Connecticut,
working as a radio operator on submarines? And how your brother is
engaged to a girl from Oregon?'

'Hey, you're right. But I didn't tell you that, I never met you before 30
in my life. You must have read all about me in my chart.'

'Okay,' I said. 'I'll tell you a story. A man went to his doctor com- 31
plaining of memory lapses. The doctor asked him some routine questions, and then said, "These lapses. What about them?" "What lapses?"
the patient replied.'

'So that's my problem,' Jimmie laughed. 'I kinda thought it was. I 32
do find myself forgetting things, once in a while—things that have just
happened. The past is clear, though.'

'Will you allow me to examine you, to run over some tests?' 33

'Sure,' he said genially. 'Whatever you want.' 34

On intelligence testing he showed excellent ability. He was quick- 35
witted, observant, and logical, and had no difficulty solving complex
problems and puzzles—no difficulty, that is, if they could be done
quickly. If much time was required, he forgot what he was doing. He
was quick and good at tic-tac-toe and checkers, and cunning and aggressive—he easily beat me. But he got lost at chess—the moves were
too slow.

Homing in on his memory, I found an extreme and extraordinary *36* loss of recent memory—so that whatever was said or shown to him was apt to be forgotten in a few seconds' time. Thus I laid out my watch, my tie, and my glasses on the desk, covered them, and asked him to remember these. Then, after a minute's chat, I asked him what I had put under the cover. He remembered none of them—or indeed that I had even asked him to remember. I repeated the test, this time getting him to write down the names of the three objects; again he forgot, and when I showed him the paper with his writing on it he was astounded, and said he had no recollection of writing anything down, though he acknowledged that it was his own writing, and then got a faint 'echo' of the fact that he had written them down.

He sometimes retained faint memories, some dim echo or sense of *37* familiarity. Thus five minutes after I had played tic-tac-toe with him, he recollected that 'some doctor' had played this with him 'a while back'—whether the 'while back' was minutes or months ago he had no idea. He then paused and said, 'It could have been you?' When I said it *was* me, he seemed amused. This faint amusement and indifference were very characteristic, as were the involved cogitations to which he was driven by being so disoriented and lost in time. When I asked Jimmie the time of the year, he would immediately look around for some clue— I was careful to remove the calendar from my desk—and would work out the time of year, roughly, by looking through the window.

It was not, apparently, that he failed to register in memory, but that *38* the memory traces were fugitive in the extreme, and were apt to be effaced within a minute, often less, especially if there were distracting or competing stimuli, while his intellectual and perceptual powers were preserved, and highly superior.

Jimmie's scientific knowledge was that of a bright high school grad- *39* uate with a penchant for mathematics and science. He was superb at arithmetical (and also algebraic) calculations, but only if they could be done with lightning speed. If there were many steps, too much time, involved, he would forget where he was, and even the question. He knew the elements, compared them, and drew the periodic table—but omitted the transuranic elements.°

'Is that complete?' I asked when he'd finished.   *40*

'It's complete and up-to-date, sir, as far as I know.'   *41*

'You wouldn't know any elements beyond uranium?'   *42*

'You kidding? There's ninety-two elements, and uranium's the last.' *43*

I paused and flipped through a *National Geographic* on the table. 'Tell *44* me the planets,' I said, 'and something about them.' Unhesitatingly, confidently, he gave me the planets—their names, their discovery, their distance from the sun, their estimated mass, character, and gravity.

Transuranic elements—elements with greater atomic number than uranium, all first identified after 1950.

'What is this?' I asked, showing him a photo in the magazine I was 45
holding.

'It's the moon,' he replied. 46

'No, it's not,' I answered. 'It's a picture of the earth taken from the 47
moon.'

'Doc, you're kidding! Someone would've had to get a camera up 48
there!'

'Naturally.' 49

'Hell! You're joking—how the hell would you do that?' 50

Unless he was a consummate actor, a fraud simulating an astonish- 51
ment he did not feel, this was an utterly convincing demonstration that
he was still in the past. His words, his feelings, his innocent wonder,
his struggle to make sense of what he saw, were precisely those of an
intelligent young man in the forties faced with the future, with what
had not yet happened, and what was scarcely imaginable. 'This more
than anything else,' I wrote in my notes, 'persuades me that his cut-off
around 1945 is genuine . . . What I showed him, and told him, produced
the authentic amazement which it would have done in an intelligent
young man of the pre-Sputnik era.'

I found another photo in the magazine and pushed it over to him. 52

'That's an aircraft carrier,' he said. 'Real ultramodern design. I never 53
saw one quite like that.'

'What's it called? I asked. 54

He glanced down, looked baffled, and said, 'The *Nimitz*!' 55

'Something the matter?' 56

'The hell there is!' he replied hotly. 'I know 'em all by name, and I 57
don't know a Nimitz . . . Of course there's an Admiral Nimitz, but I
never heard they named a carrier after him.'

Angrily he threw the magazine down. 58

He was becoming fatigued, and somewhat irritable and anxious, under 59
the continuing pressure of anomaly and contradiction, and their fearful
implications, to which he could not be entirely oblivious. I had already,
unthinkingly, pushed him into panic, and felt it was time to end our
session. We wandered over to the window again, and looked down at
the sunlit baseball diamond; as he looked his face relaxed, he forgot the
Nimitz, the satellite photo, the other horrors and hints, and became
absorbed in the game below. Then, as a savoury smell drifted up from
the dining room, he smacked his lips, said 'Lunch!', smiled, and took
his leave.

And I myself was wrung with emotion—it was heartbreaking, it was 60
absurd, it was deeply perplexing, to think of his life lost in limbo,
dissolving.

'He is, as it were,' I wrote in my notes, 'isolated in a single moment 61
of being, with a moat or lacuna° of forgetting all round him . . . He is

---

Lacuna—a gap.

man without a past (or future), stuck in a constantly changing, mean-ingless moment.' And then, more prosaically, 'The remainder of the neurological examination is entirely normal. Impression: probably Kor-sakov's syndrome°, due to alcoholic degeneration of the mammillary bodies°.' My note was a strange mixture of facts and observations, carefully noted and itemised, with irrepressible meditations on what such problems might 'mean', in regard to who and what and where this poor man was—whether, indeed, one could speak of an 'existence', given so absolute a privation of memory or continuity.

I kept wondering, in this and later notes—unscientifically—about 'a 62 lost soul', and how one might establish some continuity, some roots, for he was a man without roots, or rooted only in the remote past.

'Only connect'—but how could he connect, and how could we help 63 him to connect? What was life without connection? 'I may venture to affirm,' Hume° wrote, 'that we are nothing but a bundle or collection of different sensations, which succeed each other with an inconceivable rapidity, and are in a perpetual flux and movement.' In some sense, he had been reduced to a 'Humean' being—I could not help thinking how fascinated Hume would have been at seeing in Jimmie his own philo-sophical 'chimaera'° incarnate, a gruesome reduction of a man to mere disconnected, incoherent flux and change.

Perhaps I could find advice or help in the medical literature—a liter- 64 ature which, for some reason, was largely Russian, from Korsakov's original thesis (Moscow, 1887) about such cases of memory loss, which are still called 'Korsakov's syndrome', to Luria's *Neuropsychology of Memory* (which appeared in translation only a year after I first saw Jimmie). Korsakov wrote in 1887:

> Memory of recent events is disturbed almost exclusively; recent impressions apparently disappear soonest, whereas impressions of long ago are recalled properly, so that the patient's ingenuity, his sharpness of wit, and his resourcefulness remain largely unaffected.

To Korsakov's brilliant but spare observations, almost a century of 65 further research has been added—the richest and deepest, by far, being Luria's. And in Luria's account science became poetry, and the pathos of radical lostness was evoked. 'Gross disturbances of the organization of impressions of events and their sequence in time can always be observed in such patients,' he wrote. 'In consequence, they lose their integral experience of time and begin to live in a world of isolated

---

Korsakov's syndrome—a set of symptoms resulting from alcohol-caused neurological damage. **Mammillary bodies**—either of two small, round masses of grey matter in the hypothalamus, located close to one another. **David Hume (1711–1776)**—Scottish phi-losopher. **Chimaera**—an imaginary monster.

impressions.' Further, as Luria noted, the eradication of impressions (and their disorder) might spread backward in time—'in the most serious cases—even to relatively distant events.' . . .

At this point, persuaded that this was, indeed, 'pure' Korsakov's, 66 uncomplicated by other factors, emotional or organic, I wrote to Luria and asked his opinion. He spoke in his reply of his patient Bel, whose amnesia had retroactively eradicated ten years. He said he saw no reason why such a retrograde amnesia should not thrust backward decades, or almost a whole lifetime. . . .

What could we do? What should we do? 'There are no prescriptions,' 67 Luria wrote, 'in a case like this. Do whatever your ingenuity and your heart suggest. There is little or no hope of any recovery in his memory. But a man does not consist of memory alone. He has feeling, will, sensibilities, moral being—matters of which neuropsychology cannot speak. And it is here, beyond the realm of an impersonal psychology, that you may find ways to touch him, and change him. And the circumstances of your work especially allow this, for you work in a Home, which is like a little world, quite different from the clinics and institutions where I work. Neuropsychologically, there is little or nothing you can do; but in the realm of the Individual, there may be much you can do.'

Luria mentioned his patient Kur as manifesting a rare self-awareness, 68 in which hopelessness was mixed with an odd equanimity. 'I have no memory of the present,' Kur would say. 'I do not know what I have just done or from where I have just come . . . I can recall my past very well, but I have no memory of my present.' When asked whether he had ever seen the person testing him, he said, 'I cannot say yes or no, I can neither affirm nor deny that I have seen you.' This was sometimes the case with Jimmie; and, like Kur, who stayed many months in the same hospital, Jimmie began to form 'a sense of familiarity'; he slowly learned his way around the home—the whereabouts of the dining room, his own room, the elevators, the stairs, and in some sense recognised some of the staff, although he confused them, and perhaps had to do so, with people from the past. He soon became fond of the nursing sister in the Home; he recognised her voice, her footfalls, immediately, but would always say that she had been a fellow pupil at his high school, and was greatly surprised when I addressed her as 'Sister'.

'Gee!' he exclaimed, 'the damnedest things happen. I'd never have 69 guessed you'd become a religious, Sister!'

Since he's been at our Home—that is, since early 1975—Jimmie has 70 never been able to identify anyone in it consistently. The only person he truly recognises is his brother, whenever he visits from Oregon. These meetings are deeply emotional and moving to observe—the only truly emotional meetings Jimmie has. He loves his brother, he recognises him, but he cannot understand why he looks so old: 'Guess some people age fast,' he says. Actually his brother looks much younger than his age, and has the sort of face and build that change little with the years. These are true meetings, Jimmie's only connection of past and present, yet they do nothing to provide any sense of history or continuity. If anything they emphasise—at least to his brother, and to others who see them together—that Jimmie still lives, is fossilised, in the past.

All of us, at first, had high hopes of helping Jimmie—he was so 71 personable, so likable, so quick and intelligent, it was difficult to believe that he might be beyond help. But none of us had ever encountered, even imagined, such a power of amnesia, the possibility of a pit into which everything, every experience, every event, would fathomlessly drop, a bottomless memory-hole that would engulf the whole world. . . .

One tended to speak of him, instinctively, as a spiritual casualty—a 72 'lost soul': was it possible that he had really been 'desouled' by a disease? 'Do you think he *has* a soul?' I once asked the Sisters. They were outraged by my question, but could see why I asked it. 'Watch Jimmie in chapel,' they said, 'and judge for yourself.'

I did, and I was moved, profoundly moved and impressed, because I 73 saw here an intensity and steadiness of attention and concentration that I had never seen before in him or conceived him capable of. I watched him kneel and take the Sacrament on his tongue, and could not doubt the fullness and totality of Communion, the perfect alignment of his spirit with the spirit of the Mass. Fully, intensely, quietly, in the quietude of absolute concentration and attention, he entered and partook of the Holy Communion. He was wholly held, absorbed, by a feeling. There was no forgetting, no Korsakov's then, nor did it seem possible or imaginable that there should be; for he was no longer at the mercy of a faulty and fallible mechanism—that of meaningless sequences and memory traces—but was absorbed in an act, an act of his whole being, which carried feeling and meaning in an organic continuity and unity, a continuity and unity so seamless it could not permit any break.

Clearly Jimmie found himself, found continuity and reality, in the 74 absoluteness of spiritual attention and act. The Sisters were right—he did find his soul here. And so was Luria, whose words now came back to me: 'A man does not consist of memory alone. He has feeling, will, sensibility, moral being . . . It is here . . . you may touch him, and see a profound change.' Memory, mental activity, mind alone, could not hold him; but moral attention and action could hold him completely.

But perhaps 'moral' was too narrow a word—for the aesthetic and 75 dramatic were equally involved. Seeing Jim in the chapel opened my eyes to other realms where the soul is called on, and held, and stilled, in attention and communion. The same depth of absorption and attention was to be seen in relation to music and art: he had no difficulty, I noticed, 'following' music or simple dramas, for every moment in music and art refers to, contains, other moments. He liked gardening, and had taken over some of the work in our garden. At first he greeted the garden each day as new, but for some reason this had become more familiar to him than the inside of the Home. He almost never got lost or disoriented in the garden now; he patterned it, I think, on loved and remembered gardens from his youth in Connecticut.

Jimmie, who was so lost in extensional 'spatial' time°, was perfectly 76 organised in Bergsonian° 'intentional' time°, what was fugitive, unsustainable, as formal structure, was perfectly stable, perfectly held, as art or will. Moreover, there was something that endured and survived. If Jimmie was briefly 'held' by a task or puzzle or game or calculation, held in the purely mental challenge of these, he would fall apart as soon as they were done, into the abyss of his nothingness, his amnesia. But if he was held in emotional and spiritual attention—in the contemplation of nature or art, in listening to music, in taking part in the Mass in chapel—the attention, its 'mood', its quietude, would persist for a while, and there would be in him a pensiveness and peace we rarely, if ever, saw during the rest of his life at the Home.

I have known Jimmie now for nine years—and neuropsychologically, 77 he has not changed in the least. He still has the severest, most devastating Korsakov's, cannot remember isolated items for more than a few seconds, and has a dense amnesia going back to 1945. But humanly, spiritually, he is at times a different man altogether—no longer fluttering, restless, bored, and lost, but deeply attentive to the beauty and soul of the world, rich in all the Kierkegaardian° categories—the aesthetic, the moral, the religious, the dramatic. I had wondered, when I first met him, if he was not condemned to a sort of 'Humean' froth, a meaningless fluttering on the surface of life, and whether there was any way of transcending the incoherence of his Humean disease. Empirical science told me there was not—but empirical science, empiricism, takes no account of the soul, no account of what constitutes and determines personal being. Perhaps there is a philosophical as well as a clinical lesson here: that in Korsakov's, or dementia, or other such catastrophes, however great the organic damage and Humean dissolution, there remains the undiminished possibility of reintegration by art, by communion, by touching the human spirit: and this can be preserved in what seems at first a hopeless state of neurological devastation.

Rhetorical Analysis Through Annotation

This is a study of character, employing many of the techniques used in fiction, such as character description° and development, dramatic narratives, dialogue,

---

Extensional "spatial" time—time as experienced in the physical world. **Henri Bergson (1859–1941)**—French philosopher.   **"Intentional" time**—time as felt internally.
Sören Kierkegaard (1813–1855)—Danish philosopher and theologian.

climactic descriptions, and finely noticed concrete detail. Yet all Sacks's vividly retold incidents serve specific purposes in the overall philosophic narrative.

Look at the passage beginning "With recalling, reliving . . ." (p. 265) and ending "Whatever you want" (p. 266). Circle each characterization of emotions. In the margin write the attitude or emotion displayed in each line of dialogue. Also comment on the changing relationship of the two characters. Place an arrow at the climax of the sequence. Place a second arrow where there is a change in mood. Underline features that help maintain the new mood.

Discuss the dramatic techniques and structure of this passage. Then discuss how the dramatization of this sequence helps support the various ideas being developed at this point in the essay.

Are other parts of the essay equally dramatic? How does the dramatic quality of this case study compare with the case study recounted by Luria (pp. 253–261)? Does the degree of drama in this study ever affect the plausibility or persuasiveness of the writing?

Discussion Questions

Interpreting the Text

1. In what ways was Jimmie G.'s sense of himself dependent on his memories?

2. How did the lack of memory interfere with his current activities? Which activities could he carry out and which could he not?

3. What does Luria mean by the distinction between the neuropsychological and the individual? How does this distinction apply to Jimmie G.? How does it also apply to Sacks?

4. What does Sacks mean by spiritual attention? In what activities does Jimmie G. show spiritual attention?

5. What do the quotations from various philosophers mean? How do they relate to Jimmie G.'s life? What insight does Jimmie G.'s life shed on these statements? Do these statements shed light on our more typical lives?

Considering the Issues

6. How is the ability to carry on different activities dependent on immediate and longer-term memory? Consider, for example, the ability to participate in a class discussion, the ability to cook a meal, and the ability to play a baseball game.

7. How dependent is your own sense of yourself on your memory? Imagine you lost your memory for a particular part of your life, such as your relationship with one individual or your activities for one summer; how would your sense of self be changed, if at all? Is there part of your sense of self that may not be dependent on memory?

8. What types of activities other than those mentioned by Sacks may involve spiritual attention? How would you explain spiritual attention in your own terms? Have you ever experienced it? Do you doubt its existence?

Writing Suggestions

1. Imagine you are a doctor writing a brief report on Jimmie G.'s condition for your files. Write a hundred-word description of his neurological problem.

2. Imagine you are Sacks and you receive a letter from Jimmie's closest war buddy, who wanted to know how Jimmie's life had been, whether he had been happy. Write a letter in response.

3. For the feature page of your local newspaper, write a personal interest story about how one handicapped person you know copes with the handicap and how that handicap has affected the person's course of life. Use dramatic scenes to bring out the personal meaning of the handicap, like Sacks does for Jimmie G.

Unit Writing Suggestions

1. For an examination in a psychology course, write an essay in answer to the question, "What are some of the different approaches psychologists have taken to the study of memory and what have these approaches discovered?"

2. For a literary magazine, write a personal essay on "Understanding My Own Memory." You may refer to concepts and details cited in the articles of this unit, but only in the context of exploring how your own memory works and how it relates to your life and identity.

3. Imagine someone close to you is beginning to lose his or her memory from Alzheimer's disease or some other neurological damage. Write a long letter to a philosophically inclined friend reflecting on the importance of memory to life, identity, and activity, using insights gained from this unit.

4. Several selections in this unit recount experiments while several others narrate individual case studies. Textbook and review articles in this unit offer second hand accounts of both types of investigation as well. As part of this class's discussion of the influence of types of writing on knowledge, write an essay comparing the kind of knowledge produced by both experiments and case studies. Consider which type of investigation each encourages and which type of knowledge statement results.

5. Using the readings in this unit, write an essay in which you discuss whether these articles suggest differences exist between memory as it applies to intentional learning of specific material (as in school) and as it applies to recollection of life experiences. What are those differences and how significant are they?

UNIT

4

BUSINESS

Productivity: Organizing Work, Motives, and Goals

Business-minded people like to talk about "the bottom line"—the final profit or loss of any venture. But in practice, the bottom line comes only after many other items: product ideas and design, factory and equipment, materials and labor, motivation and supervision of workers, coordination of work, sales, transport, bookkeeping, payroll, and financing. If business were just the bottom line, more people would be rich and fewer would have to work long hours.

In part because of the complexity of modern business, work has increasingly become the means by which we organize our lives. The company has displaced the traditional organizing units of the tribe, the extended family, or the village. Where we live, what we do most of the day, the people we meet, our career goals, our personal obsessions, the products we use are all influenced by the businesses or other organizations we work for and those supplying our community.

The academic study of business and public administration attempts to help us understand, gain control of, and improve those economic organizations that so powerfully shape our lives. Because the purpose of the academic study of business is largely to train people who want to work in business, its primary focus is on teaching those factors that help a business succeed and be more profitable. But understanding the most advisable business procedures is necessarily intertwined with understanding the ways of life created by different organizations.

Productivity is one of the topics of continuing interest to people in business, for if you can get workers to produce more goods, the labor cost of each unit will be less and the owners can keep more of the sales price or they can choose to lower the price to increase the number of units sold. But productivity influences more than just the profits of company owners, as Richard Kopelman discusses in the first selection in this unit. Jobs and wages for workers depend on the workers' ability to produce; even the way of life and economic health of our country can depend on the productivity of its workers.

The opening selection discusses some reasons productivity is an important issue. The unit then presents several approaches to improving worker productivity. Frederick Taylor, the founder of scientific business management, long ago advised that work tasks be organized more efficiently; that approach is still alive today, as may be seen in the case study of Burger King. Another approach to productivity is through the reward system of wages; Rosabeth Kanter's article describes some recent attempts to change the wage system to improve output. A third approach—goal-setting—is presented through a series of four articles: Edwin Locke's study and a follow-up by Latham and Baldes show the way an idea develops through research and then works its way into textbooks, and finally becomes practical advice for working businesspeople. Other approaches to productivity not represented here include selection and training of personnel, leadership and organizational structure, feedback, and work scheduling. The unit ends with a case study of how the management of Burger King thinks about productivity in its own organization.

The selections in this unit fall into a variety of styles. There are two academic essays (Locke; and Latham and Baldes), written by academics to academics, offering focused evidence for specific claims. These essays follow closely the styles and formats of writing in the social sciences. Two textbook selections (the Kopelman and the Latham and Wexley) summarize academic research for students entering the practical world of business. Four selections (Taylor, Kanter, Foster, and Swart) are addressed directly to working businesspeople, offering advice for immediate use. These selections tend to offer clear explanations, direct advice, concrete examples, and down-to-earth language; however, one author's (Swart) special role in representing himself and his company leads to a more complex style.

Understanding productivity can be of interest to us in personal ways, even if we do not aspire to be business managers. The principles of productivity derived from business situations can help us consider our own personal productivity, what we accomplish and what we do not, and how we can accomplish more. Perhaps even more significantly, by seeing the ways productivity can be controlled, we can consider how they may influence our way of life. We can consider what it means to think about ourselves as producers.

Why Productivity Is Important

Richard E. Kopelman

The concept of productivity is likely to conjure up images of bosses taking advantage of workers: a slave driver with a whip, or Charlie Chaplin frantically trying to keep up with a speeding assembly line that eventually swallows him up into the machinery. Although managers and owners certainly do have a direct economic interest in getting more work out of their employees, workers also have an interest in productivity, as Richard Kopelman, professor of management at Baruch College, explains in this excerpt from a textbook published in 1986.

By bringing together an array of economic statistics, theories, and examples, Kopelman offers a concise but compelling case for the stake we all have in increased productivity.

BETWEEN 1947 AND 1967 productivity increases in the private busi- *1* ness sector averaged 3.2 percent per year; between 1967 and 1977 the average annual increase was 1.6 percent; and from 1977 to 1984 the average annual increase was 1.1 percent.[1] But why should we concern ourselves with productivity, a concept difficult to define and a phenomenon complex to measure? Because lagging productivity growth threatens our standard of living and national well-being in three ways.

Real Income.   Growth in real income is dependent upon the produc- *2* tion of more goods and the provision of more services, given available resources. We cannot, after all, consume more than we produce, unless we are willing to exhaust our savings and deplete capital.[2] Increased productivity, therefore, means more goods and services available for consumption (hence a higher standard of living) and/or increased capital formation, through greater savings.

National Competitiveness.   In competitive markets, where prices re- *3* flect costs, scarcity, and values, productivity translates into jobs. If the United States fails to increase productivity as rapidly as other countries, domestically produced goods will become less and less competitive. Consequently, efficient foreign producers will win ever-increasing shares of domestic and foreign markets. Obviously, if we cannot sell, we cannot employ: the loss of competitiveness means loss of jobs.

Quality of Life.   Increased productivity provides the means for an *4* improved quality of life. Without productivity growth the economic pie is necessarily of fixed size, and attention naturally turns to divvying up the pie—i.e., the "zero-sum society" described by Lester Thurow.[3] One consequence is that various social programs (e.g., Social Security and

Medicaid) must be contained or taxes increased. More generally, the result is a host of battles: between workers and retirees, between minorities and the majority, between city dwellers and suburbanites, between rich and poor, and on and on. But this need not be the case. Productivity growth creates the wherewithal to finance social programs, to improve education, to protect employees, consumers, and the environment, to support leisure-time pursuits—in short, to enhance the quality of life.

The relationship between productivity growth and real income, na- 5 tional competitiveness, and quality of life has been addressed in broad terms. A more detailed discussion follows.

Real Income

There is much evidence that real income is tied to productivity. Figure 6 1 shows the strong correlation between real wages and productivity, and Figure 2 shows the other side of the coin, the correlation between labor costs and prices. As one commentator put it: Can a man run faster than his shadow?

Of course, some industries have shown strong rates of productivity 7 growth, while others have lagged far behind. Average annual productivity growth rates for selected industries are shown in Table 1. Not surprisingly, in industries with high productivity growth during the

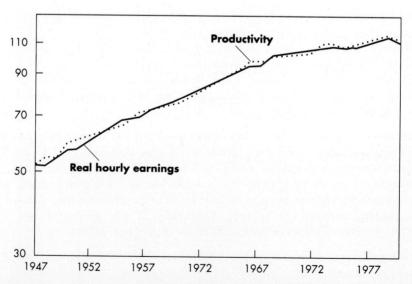

Figure 1. Real earnings and labor productivity (output per hour) in the United States, 1947 to 1979 (1967 = 100).
Source: U.S. Bureau of Labor Statistics.

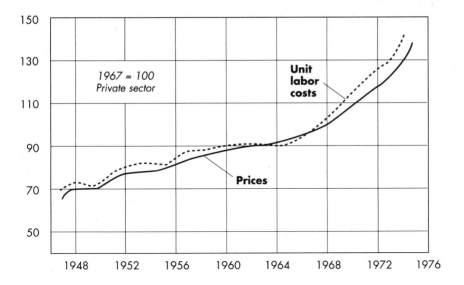

Figure 2. Prices and unit labor costs in the United States, 1947
to 1974 (1967 = 100).
Source: Reprinted from December 6, 1976 issue of Business Week *by special
permission, copyright © 1976 by McGraw-Hill, Inc.*

Industry	Percent average annual change in productivity (output per hour)
Synthetic fibers	7.96
Malt beverages	7.05
Telecommunications	6.64
Hosiery	4.86
Air transportation	4.05
Pharmaceuticals	3.76
Farm machinery	2.44
Steel	1.62
Concrete products	0.26
Footwear	0.09
Restaurants	−0.65
Laundry and cleaning	−0.85
Retail food stores	−0.96
Coal mining	−2.24

Table 1. Average annual growth in selected U.S. industries,
1970 to 1980.
Source: U.S. Department of Commerce, Statistical Abstract of the United
States *(Washington, D.C.: GPO, 1982–83), p. 399.*

| Countries | Percent average annual increase | |
	Manufacturing productivity	Real hourly compensation
Japan	7.40	4.14
Belgium	7.21	6.25
Netherlands	5.97	4.63
Denmark	5.79	3.95
West Germany	4.86	5.60
Italy	4.86	4.98
France	4.75	4.58
Sweden	3.30	3.58
United Kingdom	2.91	3.81
Canada	2.78	2.46
United States	2.54	0.84

Table 2.   Average annual growth in eleven industrialized countries, 1970 to 1980.
Source: U.S. Department of Commerce, Statistical Abstract of the United States *(Washington, D.C.: GPO, 1982–83), p. 874.*

1970s, real wages rose: 50 percent in transportation and utilities and 25 percent in manufacturing. In industries with low productivity growth, real wages declined: 18 percent in service industries and 35 percent in retail trade.[4]

An examination of productivity growth rates across eleven industrial- 8 ized countries reveals a similar relationship (see Table 2). Between 1970 and 1980 the U.S. productivity growth rate in manufacturing was 2.54 percent, far below the 4.86 percent median growth rate of the other countries. Concomitantly, the average annual increase in real hourly compensation was 0.84 percent in the United States, less than one-fifth of the 4.36 percent median increase in the other ten countries. And this finding is not an aberration. The four countries with the highest productivity growth rates experienced growth in real compensation that was 78 percent higher than that experienced by the four countries with the lowest productivity growth rates.[5]

Real wages are inherently linked to the value of goods and services 9 produced per hour worked. Moreover, according to what is often called Bowley's law, the return to labor (wages and salaries) relative to the return to capital (rent, interest, profit) shows remarkable constancy, averaging 75 percent of the economic pie. In *A Century of Pay*, Brown and Browne reported that in five countries, labor's share of national income consistently averaged 75 percent between 1860 and 1960.[6] Had the United States maintained an average productivity growth rate of 3 percent during the 1970s, the average household would have had $4000 more personal income by 1980 and an estimated $7700 more by 1985.[7]

The relationship between productivity and standard of living has been *10* known for some time. Seventy years ago Frederick W. Taylor observed:

> There is fully twenty times the output per man now than there was three hundred years ago. That marks the increase in the real wealth of the world; that marks the increase in the happiness of the world, that gives us the opportunity for shorter hours, for better education, for amusement, for art, for music, for everything that is worthwhile in this world—goes right straight back to this increase in the output of the individual. . . . From what does the progress the world has made come? Simply from the increase in the output of the individual all over the world.[8]

The connection between productivity and numerous desiderata (a *11* higher standard of living, lower inflation, increased investment, more jobs, greater leisure, etc.) is inexorable, regardless of the economic system. Consider the following: Labor productivity in East Germany in 1960 was 71 percent of that in West Germany, and the standard of living, 78 percent of that in West Germany; labor productivity in East Germany in 1980 was 46 percent of that in West Germany, and the standard of living, 43 percent of that in West Germany.[9]

Certainly the relationship between productivity and various social *12* goals did not escape Yuri Andropov, the late Soviet leader. In his words (to factory workers):

> Miracles, as they say, don't happen. You understand yourselves that the Government can only give so many goods as are produced. The growth of wages—if it is not accompanied by needed wares, of good quality, if, finally, services are suffering—cannot give a real improvement in material well-being. . . . Everything we do and produce must be done and produced, to the degree possible, at minimum cost, high quality, quickly and durably. It is necessary to produce more goods, so shelves will not be empty any longer.[10]

National Competitiveness

The evidence we have examined pertinent to real income growth across *13* industrialized countries is, perhaps, disconcerting, but results are even grimmer in industries with low productivity (see Table 1). In steel, for example, or in footwear, we see the dramatic effects of low productivity growth on competitiveness, and the consequent loss of jobs. In 1970 the iron and steel industry employed 531,000 people and imports were 80 percent higher than exports. By 1981, employment had dropped to 391,000 and imports were 495 percent greater than exports. While net imports rose from 4 percent to 14 percent of domestic consumption, employment declined by 26 percent.[11] The decline in the footwear industry was even more pronounced: from 233,000 workers in 1965 to 144,000 workers in 1981, a reduction of 38 percent. During the same period, imports increased from $160 million to over $3 billion.[12] Of course, all U.S. industries have not fared as badly as the two cited, yet lagging productivity is certainly one of the reasons why imports have grown more rapidly than exports. Although many factors influence the merchandise balance of trade, clearly, economic competitiveness is contributory. In 1960, the United States showed a surplus of $5 billion, by 1981 a deficit of more than $25 billion.[13]

Quality of Life

Besides raising the standard of living, productivity growth allows for   14
alternative uses of all means of production: leisure in place of labor, consumption in place of capital formation, and conservation of natural resources in place of depletion.[14] Further, productivity growth allows for the transfer of income to insure that human wants do not go unmet. In this regard the United States has made admirable strides: expenditures on social programs increased from $62 billion in 1970 to almost $300 billion in 1982.[15] As Felix Rohatyn put it, "Fairness and wealth have to go hand in hand. . . . Without the capacity to create wealth, it is impossible to deal with the issue of fairness."[16] In the absence of productivity growth, society is faced with the painful dilemma of program cuts vs. tax increases.

Notes

[1]Paradoxically, the dramatic slowdown in productivity growth in recent years may prove beneficial: surely there would currently be far less interest in productivity had increases continued at around 1.5 percent annually.

[2]And, of course, capital is needed to replace and modernize plant and equipment, the nonhuman means of production.

[3]Lester C. Thurow, *The Zero-Sum Society* (New York: Basic Books, 1980).

[4]U.S Department of Commerce, *Statistical Abstract of the United States* (Washington, D.C.: GPO, 1979), pp. 414, 420. These data pertain to real 1978 wages in constant 1967 dollars.

[5]U.S. Department of Commerce, *Statistical Abstract of the United States* (Washington, D.C.: GPO, 1982–83), p. 874. It should be noted that U.S. productivity growth in manufacturing was higher than for the private business sector as a whole.

[6]E. H. Phelps Brown and Margaret Browne, *A Century of Pay* (New York: St. Martin's Press, 1968).

[7]*New York Times*, 23 Jan. 1980, p. D3.

[8]Frederick W. Taylor, "The Principles of Scientific Management," *Advanced Management Journal* (Sept. 1963), p. 31; originally published in the Dec. 1916

Bulletin of the Taylor Society, based on an address given by Taylor in Mar. 1915.

[9]Werner Obst, "Growing Economic Gap between the Two Germanies," *Wall Street Journal*, 10 Nov. 1982, p. 29.

[10]*New York Times*, 1 Feb. 1983, pp. A1, 4. Copyright © 1983 by the New York Times Company. Reprinted by permission.

[11]*Statistical Abstract of the United States*, (1982–83), pp. 724, 791. With respect to steel alone, imports amounted to 22 percent of domestic consumption by 1983, despite "voluntary restraints"—i.e., protectionist agreements. *Wall Street Journal*, 16 Feb. 1983, p. 34.

[12]*Statistical Abstract of the United States* (1982–83), pp. 397, 843; also U.S. Department of Commerce, *Statistical Abstract of the United States* (Washington, D.C.: GPO, 1966), p. 224.

[13]U.S. Department of Commerce, *Statistical Abstract of the United States* (Washington, D.C.: GPO, 1982–83), p. 833.

[14]John W. Kendrick, *Understanding Productivity: An Introduction to the Dynamics of Productivity Change* (Baltimore: Johns Hopkins Univ. Press, 1977), pp. 6–7, 108.

[15]Daniel Yankelovich, *New Rules: Searching for Self-Fulfillment in a World Turned Upside Down* (New York: Bantam, 1982), p. 200.

[16]*The Economist*, 19 Sept. 1981, p. 32.

Rhetorical Analysis Through Annotation

Kopelman uses many statistics, presented numerically in the text and in tables, and graphically in figures. Despite the amount of statistics he uses, the argument does not get bogged down in numbers. Rather, all the statistics serve the main line of verbal reasoning. Each set of statistics is chosen, organized, and displayed to support a specific idea expressed in words.

Circle each set of statistics. In the margin note how the statistics are organized and displayed. Then underline the statement that each set of statistics supports or develops.

Discuss how the selection, organization, and display of statistics help support verbally framed arguments. Also discuss how the way the statistics are discussed in the text helps bring out their significance for the various points being made.

Discussion Questions

Interpreting the Text

1. What has been the trend in U.S. productivity over the last forty years? Why should this concern us?

2. What is the relationship between real wages and productivity? Between labor cost and productivity? Why are these relations important?

3. What is Bowley's law? How does this law link the fate of workers to the fate of business?

4. How has U.S. productivity compared with that of other countries in recent history? In what industries have we had a particularly poor productivity record? What effect has low productivity had on our international trade?

5. How does low productivity affect social programs and national lifestyle?

Considering the Issues

6. Do you think the state of the national economy influences your life and the lives of the people around you? If so, in what way? If not, why not? Consider influences more subtle than the direct impact on the family paycheck.

7. Do you agree that the national quality of life is improved by increased productivity and prosperity? Are there aspects of the quality of life that are not influenced or even hurt by economic problems?

8. Does Kopelman's presentation convince you that workers as well as owners have an interest in increased productivity? Is there any way in which increased productivity may not be a total benefit for workers?

9. In addition to the statistics he quotes from sources, Kopelman quotes the ideas of four other people at length: Lester Thurow (a contemporary political economist), Frederick Taylor (the originator of scientific management), Yuri Andropov (the late Soviet leader), and Felix Rohatyn (a financier who has been concerned with civic causes). What kind of information does Kopelman use from each? How does this information help his argument? How is the identity of each person used by Kopelman to strengthen his point?

Writing Suggestions

1. For an examination in management, write a two-hundred-word essay using material from this selection to answer this question: "Does the rate of increase in U.S. productivity present any problems for the health of our economy?"

2. Imagine you were an executive of a manufacturing company negotiating a new contract with your factory workers' union. You are trying to include workload increases in the contract, but the union representatives are resisting this demand. Using information from this chapter, write a statement of a few paragraphs explaining to the union members why a productivity increase is in the workers' interest.

3. Imagine you are a union representative in the situation described in the previous question. Offer your response to the executive's statement.

4. As part of this course's discussion of rhetorical techniques, write an essay on how to use statistics effectively, using this selection as your main example.

The Art of Shoveling

Frederick Taylor

Frederick Winslow Taylor (1856–1915) learned about productivity as a laborer at the Midvale Steel Company. He worked his way up to foreman before returning to college to complete a degree in mechanical engineering. At Bethlehem Steel he originated the study of scientific management and became a consultant to many major American manufacturing companies. The following, based on a speech, is excerpted from his book, *Principles of Scientific Management* (1911).

Taylor's method was direct and practical. He would walk out on the shop floor with a tape measure and stopwatch and calculate which way of working produced the most results in the least time. His blunt recommendations had to be easily understood and persuasive to self-taught managers in the days before the M.B.A. In the passage that follows he demonstrates his general approach by turning to a specific problem: how best to shovel coal. He shows us the solution to that problem by means of a chronological narrative, embedding several small, easily understood stories within it. As well, he identifies himself with his audience and answers the objections he expects they will have. Note that Taylor assumes, in his day, all managers will be "gentlemen."

NOW, GENTLEMEN, SHOVELING IS a great science compared with   *1*
pig-iron° handling. I dare say that most of you gentlemen know that a good many pig-iron handlers can never learn to shove right; the ordinary pig-iron handler is not the type of man well suited to shoveling. He is too stupid; there is too much mental strain, too much knack required of a shoveler for the pig-iron handler to take kindly to shoveling.

You gentlemen may laugh, but that is true, all right; it sounds ridic-   *2*
ulous, I know, but it is a fact. Now, if the problem were put up to any of you men to develop the science of shoveling as it was put up to us, that is, to a group of men who had deliberately set out to develop the science of doing all kinds of laboring work, where do you think you would begin? When you started to study the science of shoveling I make the assertion that you would be within two days—just as we were within two days—well on the way toward development of the science of shoveling. At least you would have outlined in your minds those elements which required careful, scientific study in order to understand the science of shoveling. I do not want to go into all of the details of shoveling, but I will give you some of the elements, one or two of the most

---

Pig-iron handling—carrying large blocks of crude iron.

important elements of the science of shoveling; that is, the elements that reach further and have more serious consequences than any other. Probably the most important element in the science of shoveling is this: There must be some shovel load at which a first-class shoveler will do his biggest day's work. What is that load? To illustrate: When we went to the Bethlehem Steel Works and observed the shovelers in the yard of that company, we found that each of the good shovelers in that yard owned his own shovel; they preferred to buy their own shovels rather than to have the company furnish them. There was a larger tonnage of ore shoveled in that works than of any other material and rice coal came next in tonnage. We would see a first-class shoveler go from shoveling rice coal with a load of 3½ pounds to the shovel to handling ore from the Massaba Range, with 38 pounds to the shovel. Now, is 3½ pounds the proper shovel load or is 38 pounds the proper shovel load? They cannot both be right. Under scientific management the answer to this question is not a matter of anyone's opinion; it is a question for accurate, careful, scientific investigation.

Under the old system you would call in a first-rate shoveler and say, 3 'See here, Pat, how much ought you to take on at one shovel load?' And if a couple of fellows agreed, you would say that's about the right load and let it go at that. But under scientific management absolutely every element in the work of every man in your establishment, sooner or later, becomes the subject of exact, precise, scientific investigation and knowledge to replace the old, 'I believe so', and 'I guess so'. Every motion, every small fact becomes the subject of careful, scientific investigation.

What we did was to call in a number of men to pick from, and from 4 these we selected two first-class shovelers. Gentlemen, the words I used were 'first-class shovelers'. I want to emphasize that. Not poor shovelers. Not men unsuited to their work, but first-class shovelers. These men were then talked to in about this way, 'See here, Pat and Mike, you fellows understand your job all right; both of you fellows are first-class men; you know what we think of you; you are all right now; but we want to pay you fellows double wages. We are going to ask you to do a lot of damn fool things, and when you are doing them there is going to be someone out alongside of you all the time, a young chap with a piece of paper and a stop watch and pencil, and all day long he will tell you to do these fool things, and he will be writing down what you are doing and snapping the watch on you and all that sort of business. Now, we just want to know whether you fellows want to go into that bargain or not? If you want double wages while that is going on all right, we will pay you double; if you don't, all right, you needn't take the job unless you want to; we just called you in to see whether you want to work this way or not.

'Let me tell you fellows just one thing: If you go into this bargain, if 5 you go at it, just remember that on your side we want no monkey business of any kind; you fellows will have to play square; you fellows will have to do just what you are supposed to be doing; not a damn bit of soldiering° on your part; you must do a fair day's work; we don't want any rushing, only a fair day's work and you know what that is as well as we do. Now, don't take this job unless you agree to these conditions, because if you start to try to fool this same young chap with the pencil and paper he will be onto you in fifteen minutes from the time you try to fool him, and just as surely as he reports you fellows as soldiering you will go out of this works and you will never get in again. Now, don't take this job unless you want to accept these conditions; you need not do it unless you want to; but if you do, play fair.'

Well, these fellows agreed to it, and, as I have found almost universally 6 to be the case, they kept their word absolutely and faithfully. My experience with workmen has been that their word is just as good as the word of any other set of men that I know of, and all you have to do is to have a clear, straight, square understanding with them and you will get just as straight and fair a deal from them as from any other set of men. In this way the shoveling experiment was started. My remembrance is that we first started them on work that was very heavy, work requiring a very heavy shovel load. What we did was to give them a certain kind of heavy material ore, I think, to handle with a certain size of shovel. We sent these two men into different parts of the yard, with two different men to time and study them, both sets of men being engaged on the same class of work. We made all the conditions the same for both pairs of men, so as to be sure that there was no error in judgement on the part of either of the observers and that they were normal, first-class men.

The number of shovel loads which each man handled in the course 7 of the day was counted and written down. At the end of the day the total tonnage of the material handled by each man was weighed and this weight was divided by the number of shovel loads handled, and in that way, my remembrance is, our first experiment showed that the average shovel load handled was 38 pounds, and that with this load on the shovel the man handled, say, about 25 tons per day. We then cut the shovel off, making it somewhat shorter, so that instead of shoveling a load of 38 pounds it held a load of approximately 34 pounds. The average, then, with the 34 pound load, of each man went up, and instead of handling 25 he had handled thirty tons per day. These figures are merely relative, used to illustrate the general principles, and I do not mean that they were the exact figures. The shovel was again cut off, and the load made approximately 30 pounds, and again the tonnage ran up, and again the shovel load was reduced, and the tonnage handled per day increased, until at about 21 or 22 pounds per shovel we found that these men were

---

Soldiering—slacking off, malingering.

doing their largest day's work. If you cut the shovel load off still more, say until it averages 18 pounds instead of 21½, the tonnage handled per day will begin to fall off, and at 16 pounds it will be still lower, and so on right down. Very well; we now have developed the scientific fact that a workman well suited to his job, what we call a first-class shoveler, will do his largest day's work when he has a shovel load of 21½ pounds.

Now, what does that fact amount to? At first it may not look to be   8 a fact of much importance, but let us see what it amounted to right there in the yard of the Bethlehem Steel Co. Under the old system, as I said before, the workmen owned their shovels, and the shovel was the same size whatever the kind of work. Now, as a matter of common sense, we saw at once that it was necessary to furnish each workman each day with a shovel which would hold just 21½ pounds of the particular material which he was called upon to shovel. A small shovel for the heavy material, such as ore, and a large scoop for light material, such as ashes. That meant, also, the building of a large shovel room, where all kinds of laborers' implements were stored. It meant having an ample supply of each type of shovel, so that all the men who might be called upon to use a certain type in any one day could be supplied with a shovel of the size desired that would hold just 21½ pounds. It meant, further, that each day each laborer should be given a particular kind of work to which he was suited, and that he must be provided with a particular shovel suited to that kind of work, whereas in the past all the laborers in the yard of the Bethlehem Steel Co. had been handled in masses, or in great groups of men, by the old-fashioned foreman, who had from twenty-five to one hundred men under him and walked them from one part of the yard to another. You must realize that the yard of the Bethlehem Steel Co. at that time was a very large yard. I should say that it was at least 1½ or 2 miles long and, we will say, a quarter to a half mile wide, so it was a good large yard; and in that yard at all times an immense variety of shoveling was going on.

There was comparatively little standard shoveling which went on   9 uniformly from day to day. Each man was likely to be moved from place to place about the yard several times in the course of the day. All of this involved keeping in the shovel room ten or fifteen kinds of shovels, ranging from a very small flat shovel for handling ore up to immense scoops for handling rice coal, and forks with which to handle the coke, which, as you know, is very light. It meant the study and development of the implement best suited to each type of material to be shoveled, and assigning, with the minimum of trouble, the proper shovel to each one of the four to six hundred laborers at work in that yard. Now, that meant mechanism, human mechanism. It meant organizing and planning work at least a day in advance. And, gentlemen, here is an important fact, that the greatest difficulty which we met with in this planning did not come from the workmen. It came from the management's side. Our greatest difficulty was to get the heads of the various departments each day to inform the men in the labor office what kind of work and how much of it was to be done on the following day.

This planning the work one day ahead involved the building of a 10 labor office where before there was no such thing. It also involved the equipping of that office with large maps showing the layout of the yards so that the movements of the men from one part of the yard to another could be laid out in advance, so that we could assign to this little spot in the yard a certain number of men and to another part of the yard another set of men, each group to do a certain kind of work. It was practically like playing a game of chess in which four to six hundred men were moved about so as to be in the right place at the right time. And all this, gentlemen, follows from the one idea of developing the science of shoveling; the idea that you must give each workman each day a job to which he is well suited and provide him with just that implement which will enable him to do his biggest day's work. All this, as I have tried to make clear to you, is the result that followed from the one act of developing the science of shoveling.

In order that our workmen should get their share of the good that 11 came from the development of the science of shoveling and that we should do what we set out to do with our laborers—namely, pay them 60 per cent higher wages than were paid to any similar workmen around that whole district. Before we could pay them these extra high wages it was necessary for us to be sure that we had first-class men and that each laborer was well suited to his job, because the only way in which you can pay wages 60 per cent higher than other people pay and not overwork your men is by having each man properly suited and well trained to his job. Therefore, it became necessary to carefully select these yard laborers; and in order that the men should join with us heartily and help us in their selection it became necessary for us to make it possible for each man to know each morning as he came in to work that on the previous day he had earned his 60 per cent premium, or that he had failed to do so. So here again comes in a lot of work to be done by the management that had not been done before. The first thing each workman did when he came into the yard in the morning—and I may say that a good many of them could not read and write—was to take two pieces of paper out of his pigeonhole; if they were both white slips of paper, the workman knew he was all right. One of those slips of paper informed the man in charge of the tool room what implement the workman was to use on his first job and also in what part of the yard he was to work. It was in this way that each one of the 600 men in that yard received his orders for the kind of work he was to do and the implement with which he was to do it, and he was also sent right to the part of the yard where he was to work, without any delay whatever. The old-fashioned way was for the workmen to wait until the foreman got good and ready and had found out by asking some of the heads of departments what work he was to do, and then he would lead the gang off to some part of the yard and go to work. Under the new method each man gets his orders almost automatically; he goes right to the tool room, gets the proper implement for the work he is to do, and goes right to the spot where he is to work without any delay.

The second piece of paper, if it was a white piece of paper, showed   12 this man that he had earned his 60 per cent higher wages; if it was a yellow piece of paper the workman knew that he had not earned enough to be a first-class man, and that within two or three days something would happen, and he was absolutely certain what this something would be. Every one of them knew that after he had received three or four yellow slips a teacher would be sent down to him from the labor office. Now, gentlemen, this teacher was no college professor. He was a teacher of shoveling; he understood the science of shoveling; he was a good shoveler himself, and he knew how to teach other men to be good shovelers. This is the sort of man who was sent out of the labor office. I want to emphasize the following point, gentlemen: The workman, instead of hating the teacher who came to him . . . looked upon him as one of the best friends he had around there. He knew that he came out there to help him. . . . Now, let me show you what happens. The teacher comes, in every case, not to bulldoze the man, not to drive him to harder work than he can do, but to try in a friendly, brotherly way to help him, so he says, 'Now, Pat, something has gone wrong with you. You know no workman who is not a high-priced workman can stay on this gang, and you will have to get off of it if we can't find out what is the matter with you. I believe you have forgotten how to shovel right. I think that's all there is the matter with you. Go ahead and let me watch you awhile. I want to see if you know how to do the damn thing, anyway.'

Now, gentlemen, I know you will laugh when I talk again about the science of shoveling. I dare say some of you have done some shoveling. Whether you have or not, I am going to try to show you something about the science of shoveling, and if any of you have done much shoveling, you will understand that there is a good deal of science about it.

There is a good deal of refractory° stuff to shovel around a steel   13 works; take ore, or ordinary bituminous coal, for instance. It takes a good deal of effort to force the shovel down into either of these materials from the top of the pile, as you have to when you are unloading a car. There is one right way of forcing the shovel into materials of this sort, and many wrong ways. Now, the way to shovel refractory stuff is to press the forearm hard against the upper part of the right leg just below the thigh, like this (indicating), take the end of the shovel in your right hand and when you push the shovel into the pile, instead of using the muscular effort of your arms, which is tiresome, throw the weight of

---

Refractory—difficult to handle.

your body on the shovel like this (indicating); that pushes your shovel in the pile with hardly any exertion and without tiring the arms in the least. Nine out of ten workmen who try to push a shovel in a pile of that sort will use the strength of their arms, which involves more than twice the necessary exertion. Any of you men who don't know this fact just try it. This is one illustration of what I mean when I speak of the science of shoveling, and there are many similar elements of this science. Now, this teacher would find, time and time again, that the shoveler had simply forgotten how to shovel; that he had drifted back to his old wrong and inefficient way of shoveling, which prevented him from earning his 60 per cent higher wages. So he would say to him, 'I see all that is the matter with you is that you have forgotten how to shovel; you have forgotten what I showed you about shoveling some time ago. Now, watch me,' he says, 'this is the way to do the thing.' And the teacher would stay by him two, three, four or five days, if necessary, until he got the man back again into the habit of shoveling right.

Rhetorical Analysis Through Annotation

Taylor uses several techniques to create a sense of close camaraderie with his audience of businessmen.

Circle all the times he directly addresses the audience as gentlemen, or you, or some equivalent form of address.

Underline some examples of down-to-earth workplace language.

Mark in the margin some examples of Taylor using his own experiences and feelings as an example.

Mark in the margin other uses of shop floor examples.

Mark in the margin other techniques that help build a close rapport with the audience.

Discuss the overall effect of these various techniques. Do you think Taylor has successfully established trust and equality with his audience? Or does he appear to be condescending?

Discussion Questions

Interpreting the Text

1. What were the most significant ideas that Taylor was trying to get across to his audience? What is the point of each of the stories? How do these small points add up into an overall argument?

2. Taylor describes the way in which efficient shoveling was rewarded by higher pay. How did Bethlehem Steel combine several approaches to increase productivity? How did the company need to change to institute Taylor's system?

3. In what way does Taylor try to appeal to the business instincts of his audience? In what ways does his advice contradict business instincts? How does Taylor try to soften or resolve the contradictions?

Considering the Issues

4. Imagine you were a worker being studied by Taylor. How would you react to his studying you? Why?

5. Does Taylor's advice seem more applicable to certain types of business? If so, which? Are there any businesses for which Taylor's principles seem inappropriate? To what degree do you feel his principles are followed in businesses today?

6. Have you ever worked in an office or factory organized according to Taylor's principles? If so, did those principles benefit you, the management, or no one? Alternately, have you ever worked in an office or factory that would have gained by greater awareness of Taylor's principles? How?

Writing Suggestions

1. Imagine you are telling a friend how to do a task you regularly do on the job or at home, whether making a grilled cheese sandwich or keeping office receipts. Describe both less effective and more effective methods, so that your friend will understand the difference between them and will choose the better alternative.

2. Discuss how Taylor's approach may be applied to your studying for college. Write your essay for a self-help seminar on study skills.

3. Write a comic piece for your school newspaper adopting Taylor's approach and style to describe a study of some task totally inappropriate for efficiency study, such as writing a poem, dancing, or general goofing off.

4. As part of this course's concern for the effective use of language, write an essay discussing how you can get other people to follow your advice, using the selection from Taylor as one of your primary examples of persuasive or unpersuasive advice giving.

The Attack on Pay

Rosabeth Moss Kanter

In the previous article, Frederick Taylor's main approach to increasing productivity is to improve workers' efficiency. He touches on another approach, however: getting workers to work harder by offering rewards, especially the reward of money. The idea of financial reward is as old as money itself, and is the basis of all nonbarter economies. Bonuses and pay for piecework have long been part of company finances, but the hierarchical structure of organizations and the desire for predictability have tended to establish stable wage and salary rates, insensitive to daily accomplishment. Recently corporations have attempted to break through the stagnation caused by fixed wages.

Rosabeth Kanter, professor of business administration at the Harvard Business School, describes the current attempts to make a more direct connection between productivity and individual earnings. She considers both the reasoning behind these attempts and difficulties that arise. She offers a broad review of current trends as well as specific advice and cautions about implementation. Such information would be most useful to working managers, who are the primary readers of the *Harvard Business Review*, where the article first appeared in 1987. In offering the latest trends for the consideration of working managers this article is similar to the previous selection by Taylor; in the seventy intervening years, however, managers themselves have changed, so Kanter must communicate with them in a strikingly different way.

———————————

STATUS, NOT CONTRIBUTION, HAS traditionally been the basis *1* for the numbers on employees' paychecks. Pay has reflected where jobs rank in the corporate hierarchy—not what comes out of them.

Today this system is under attack. More and more senior executives *2* are trying to turn their employees into entrepreneurs—people who earn a direct return on the value they help create, often in exchange for putting their pay at risk. In the process, changes are coming into play that will have revolutionary consequences for companies and their employees. To see what I have in mind, consider these actual examples:

• To control costs and stimulate improvements, a leading financial services company converts its information systems department into a venture that sells its services both inside and outside the corporation. In its first year, the department runs at a big profit and employees begin to wonder why they can't get a chunk of the profits they have generated instead of just a fixed salary defined by rank.

• In exchange for wage concessions, a manufacturer offers employees an ownership stake. Employee representatives begin to think about total company profitability and start asking why so many managers are on the payroll and why they are paid so much.

• To encourage initiative in reaching performance targets, a city government offers large salary increases to managers who can show major departmental improvements. After a few years, the amount in managers' paychecks bears little relationship to their levels in the organization.

In traditional compensation plans, each job comes with a pay level *3* that stays about the same regardless of how well the job is performed or what the real organizational value of that performance is. Pay scales reflect such estimated characteristics as decision-making responsibility, importance to the organization, and number of subordinates. If there is a merit component, it is usually very small. The surest way—often the only way—to increase one's pay is to change employers or get promoted. A mountain of tradition and industrial relations practice has built up to support this way of calculating pay.

Reward Performance You Want to Encourage

Proponents of this system customarily assert that the market ultimately   *4* determines pay, just as it determines the price of everything else that buyers wish to acquire. Compensation systems cannot be unfair or inappropriate, therefore, because they are incapable of causing anything. Actually, however, because it is so difficult to link people's compensation directly to their contributions, all the market really does is allow us to assume that people occupying equal positions tend to be paid equally and that people with similar experience and education tend to be worth about the same. So while the market works in macroeconomic° terms, the process at a microeconomic° level is circular: we know what people are worth because that's what they cost in the job market; but we also know that what people cost in the market is just what they're worth.

Given logic like this, it's not hard to see why such strange bedfellows   *5* as feminist activists and entrepreneurially minded managers both attack this traditional system as a manifestation of the paternalistic benefits offered across the board by Father Corporation. "We've got corporate socialism, not corporate capitalism," charged the manager of new ventures for a large industrial company. "We're so focused on consistent treatment internally that we destroy enterprise in the process."

These old arrangements are no longer supportable. For economic,   *6* social, and organizational reasons, the fundamental bases for determining pay are under attack. And while popular attention has focused on comparable worth—equalizing pay for those doing comparable work—the most important trend has been the loosening relationship between job assignment and pay level.

Four separate but closely related concerns are driving employers to   *7* rethink the meaning of worth and look beyond job assignments in determining pay—equity, cost, productivity, and the rewards of entrepreneurship.

It's Not Fair!

Every year, routine company surveys show fewer employees willing to   *8* say that traditional pay practices are fair. In particular, top management

---

Macroeconomic—relating to large economic changes which aggregate many individual economic choices.   Microeconomic—relating to individual economic choices.

compensation has been assailed as unjustifiably high, especially when executives get large bonuses while their companies suffer financial losses or are just recovering from them.

Despite economic data showing an association between executive 9 compensation and company performance, many professionals still argue that the amounts are excessive and reflect high status rather than good performance. Likewise, the existence of layers on layers of highly paid managers no longer seems entirely fair. Employees question why executives should be able to capture returns others actually produce. And they are beginning to resent compensation plans like the one in a leading well-run bank that gives managers bonuses of up to 30% of their pay for excellent branch performance, while branch employees get only a 6% to an 8% annual increase.

If executives get bonuses for raising profits, many urge, so should the 10 workers who contribute to those profits. Indeed, this is the theory behind profit sharing in general. Such programs, and there are several widely used variants, have in common the very appealing and well-accepted notion that all employees—not just management—should share in the gains from enhanced performance.

Profit sharing is ordinarily a straightforward arrangement in which a 11 fraction of the net profits from some period of operation are distributed to employees. The distribution may be either immediate or deferred, and the plan may not include all employees.

The plan at Lincoln Electric, the world's largest manufacturer of arc- 12 welding products, is particularly generous. Every year, Lincoln pays out 6% of net income in common stock dividends—the "wages of capital." The board determines another sum to be set aside as seed money for investment in the future. The balance, paid to all employees, ranges from 20% of wages and salary, already competitive, to more than 120%. The company has remained profitable even in the face of sales declines in the 1981–1983 recession, to the benefit of employees as well as stock-holders.

Overall, probably about a half million companies have some form of 13 profit sharing, if both deferred and cash payouts are included. In private enterprises other than those categorized as small businesses, government statistics show that by 1983 19% of all production employees, 27% of all technical and clerical employees, and 23% of all professional and administrative employees were covered by profit-sharing agreements.

The variant known as gain sharing takes profit sharing one giant step 14 further by attempting, usually with some elaborate formula, to calculate the contributions of specific groups of employees whose contingent pay depends on those varying results. Although the basis for calculation varies from one gain-sharing plan to another, the plans have two principles in common: first, the payout reflects the contribution of groups rather than individuals (on the theory that teams and collective effort are what count), and second, the rewards to be shared and the plan for their distribution are based on objective, measurable characteristics (so that everyone can see what is owed and when).

According to experts, several thousand companies have gain-sharing   *15* programs of some sort. These programs already involve millions of workers and seem to be growing in popularity. The Scanlon Plan, probably the oldest, best-known, and most elaborate gain-sharing system, usually distributes 75% of gains to employees and 25% to the company. In addition, this plan is organized around complex mechanisms and procedures that spell out how employees at various levels are to participate, not only in control of the process but also in opportunities to help improve performance and thereby their own shares. At Herman Miller, Inc., gain sharing is described not simply as a compensation system but rather as a way of life for the company.

Group or all-employee bonuses, especially when linked to fairly spe-   *16* cific indicators, provide another way to share some of the benefits of good performance more equitably. But evidence shows that their potential far exceeds their use. Although group performance bonuses are continuing to grow, top executives are much more likely to capture a portion of the benefits of increased profitability than employees are. In a recent Conference Board study of 491 companies, 58% had top executive bonus plans but only 11% had profit-sharing plans, 8% all-employee bonuses, 3% group productivity incentives, and fewer than 1% group cost-control incentives.

Performance-related compensation plans generally ignore employees   *17* other than top management and, to a lesser extent, some middle managers. And even in incentive-conscious high-technology companies, gain sharing is rare. While more than half the high-tech companies included in a recent Hay Associates compensation survey had cash or stock awards for individuals, only 6% had gain-sharing or group profit-sharing programs. Concerns about equity—including those framed in terms of comparable worth—are not altogether misplaced therefore.

Companies have long been concerned with one fundamental fairness   *18* issue—the relative compensation of employees in general. Now, however, they face two new issues that are complex, hard to resolve, and rapidly getting worse. The first, evident in the debate over gain sharing and profit sharing, sets up what employees get against what the organization gets from their efforts. The second, evident in the debate over comparable worth, is how groups in an organization fare in relation to each other. At the very least, these issues call for better measurement systems or new principles on which various constituencies can agree.

Let Them Eat Dividends

Facing challenges from competitors, companies in every field are seeking   *19* ways to reduce fixed labor costs. One sure way is to peg pay to performance—the company's as well as the individual's. Merit awards, bonuses, and profit-sharing plans hold out the promise of extra earnings for those who truly contribute. But it is their cost-reduction potential that really makes executives' eyes sparkle with dollar signs.

Making pay float to reflect company performance is the cornerstone *20* of MIT economist Martin L. Weitzman's proposal for a "share economy." If many companies can be induced to share profits or revenues with their employees, Weitzman argues, then the cure for stagflation° would be at hand. Among other things, companies would have an incentive to create jobs because more workers would be paid only in proportion to what they have brought in.[1]

For organizations struggling to compete, these macroeconomic im- *21* plications are a lot less tantalizing than the more immediate benefits to be gained by asking workers to take their lumps from business cycles— or, employees would add, poor management decisions—along with their companies. Moreover, a similar logic clearly accounts for some of the appeal of employee ownership, especially to companies in industries where deregulation has created enormous cost competitiveness.

According to one recent book about employee ownership, *Taking* *22* *Stock: Employee Ownership at Work*, at least 6 major airlines and 15 trucking companies have adopted employee ownership plans in response to deregulation.[2] Overall, the authors estimate that some 11 million employees in 8,000-plus businesses now own at least 15% of the companies employing them.

While many companies have found employee ownership attractive *23* primarily as a financing scheme, there is little doubt that, properly designed and managed, it can positively affect corporate success. Take Western Air Lines as an illustration. After losing $200 million over four years, this company created the Western Partnership by trading a 32.4% ownership stake, a meaningful profit-sharing plan, and four seats on the board of directors for wage cuts and productivity improvements of 22.5% to 30%. In 1985 Western distributed more than $10 million to its 10,000 employees—$100 each in cash and the rest in employees' accounts. Now employees are making about $75 million on Western's sale to Delta.

Such schemes have obvious advantages over another highly visible *24* alternative for fixed-labor-cost reduction—two-tier wage systems, which bring in new hires at a lower scale than current employees. Most of us can see the obvious inequity in paying two groups differently for doing exactly the same job. But pay pegged to actual performance? Earnings tied to company profits? What could be more fair?

The clear problems—that lower paid employees cannot afford income *25* swings as readily as the more highly paid and that employee efforts are not always directly related to company profitability—do not seem to

---

Stagflation—a combination of economic stagnation and price inflation.

deter the advocates. The fixed part of the paycheck is already shrinking in many American companies. Even the bonus is being used to supplement these efforts, especially among manufacturing companies. A recent study by the Bureau of National Affairs reveals that one-shot bonus payments, replacing general pay increases, were called for in almost 20% of all 1985 union contract settlements outside the construction industry, up from a mere 6% in 1984. Similarly, 20% of the 564 companies in Hewitt Associates' 1986 compensation survey gave one-time bonuses to white-collar workers, up from 7% in 1985.

These one-time payments do not raise base pay, nor do they affect 26 overtime calculations. In fact, just the opposite occurs: they reduce the cost of labor. More than two-thirds of the bonus provisions the BNA studied were accompanied by wage freezes or decreases.

Bucks for Behavior

The cost attack is one straightforward way for companies to become 27 more competitive, at least in the short run. In the long run, however, pay variations or rewards, contingent on specific and measurable achievements of individuals at every level, are likely to be even more effective in stimulating employee enterprise and channeling behavior. What better way could there be, proponents argue, to help employees recognize what is most useful and to guide their efforts appropriately?

Merrill Lynch's compensation system for its 10,400 brokers, intro- 28 duced in February 1986, is a good example. To encourage brokers to spend more time with larger, more active customers, the firm has cut commissions for most small trades and discounts and rewards the accumulation of assets under its management. The pay system was developed in direct response to new products like the firm's Cash Management Account because the old system wasn't adequate to reward performance in new and growing areas management wanted to stress.

Commissions and bonuses for sales personnel are standard practice in 29 most industries, of course. What seem to be changing are the amounts people can earn (for example, more than double one's salary at General Electric Medical Systems' Sales and Service Division), the number of people who can earn them, and the variety of productivity bonuses, especially in highly competitive new industries.

PSICOR is a small Michigan company supplying equipment and 30 professionals (called perfusionists) for open-heart surgery. Perfusionists are in great demand and frequently change employers, so founder Michael Dunaway searched for a way to give them immediate rewards because the standard 10% increase at the end of the year was too remote.

First he tried random bonuses of $100 to $500 for superior perfor- 31 mance, but tracking proved difficult. Then in 1982 he hit on the idea of continuous raises—increases in every paycheck—calculated to add up to at least a 5% annual raise over base salary, with up to 8% more in a lump sum at year-end based on overall performance. Employee response was positive, but the accounting department was soon drowning in paperwork.

PSICOR's latest system combines quarterly raises of up to 5% a year, *32* based solely on performance, with a series of additional bonuses to reward specific activities: higher caseloads, out-of-town assignments, professional certification, and the like. Turnover is less than 2% and drops to less than $\frac{1}{2}$% for those employed two years or more.

Of course, some companies are going in exactly the opposite direc- *33* tion—for seemingly good reason. As an ex-director of sales compensation for IBM confessed, "We used to give bonuses and awards for every imaginable action by the sales force. But the more complex it got, the more difficult it was to administer, and the results were not convincing. When we began to ask ourselves why Digital Equipment had salespeople, who are tough competitors, on straight salary, we decided perhaps we'd gone overboard a bit."

Even in commercial real estate leasing, long a highly performance- *34* oriented business, one major and very effective Boston company— Leggat, McCall & Werner, Inc.—has for years had its brokers on salary.

Nevertheless, the tide is moving in the other direction—toward more *35* varied individual compensation based on people's own efforts. This trend reaches its fullest expression, however, not in pay-for-performance systems like those just described but in the scramble to devise ways to reward people in organizations for acting as if they were running their own businesses.

A Piece of the Action

The prospect of running a part of a large corporation as though it were *36* an independent business is one of the hottest old-ideas-refurbished in American industry. Many companies are encouraging potential entrepreneurs to remain within the corporate fold by paying them like owners when they develop new businesses. And even very traditional organizations are looking carefully at the possibility of setting up new ventures with a piece of the action for the entrepreneurs. "If one of our employees came along with a proposition, I'm not sure how anxious we'd be to do it," one bank executive said. "But ten years ago, we wouldn't have listened at all. We'd have said, 'You've got rocks in your head.'"

Most of the new entrepreneurial schemes pay people base salaries, *37* generally equivalent to those of their former job levels, and ask them to put part of their compensation at risk, with their ownership percentage determined by their willingness to invest. This investment then substitutes for any other bonuses, perks, profit sharing, or special incentives they might have been able to earn in their former jobs. Sometimes the returns are based solely on percentages of the profits from their ventures; sometimes the returns come in the form of phantom stock pegged to the companies' public stock prices. Potential entrepreneurs cannot get as rich under this system as they could if they were full owners of independent businesses who shared ownership with other venture capitalists. But they are also taking much less risk.

AT&T's new venture development process, begun just before divestiture,° illustrates how large corporations are trying to capture entrepreneurship. Currently seven venture units are in operation, each sponsored by one of AT&T's lines of business. One started in 1983, three in 1984, and three more in 1985. The largest is now up to 90 employees. 38

William P. Stritzler, the AT&T executive responsible for overseeing this process, offers venture participants three compensation alternatives corresponding to three levels of risk. 39

Option one allows venture participants to stick with the standard corporate compensation and benefits plan and to keep the salaries associated with their previous jobs. Not surprisingly, none of the seven has chosen this option. 40

Under option two, participants agree to freeze their salaries at the levels of their last jobs and to forgo other contingent compensation until the venture begins to generate a positive cash flow and the AT&T investment is paid back (or, with the concurrence of the venture board, until the business passes certain milestones). At that point, venture participants can get one-time bonuses equal to a maximum of 150% of their salaries. Five of the seven venture teams have selected this option. 41

The third option, chosen by two self-confident bands of risk takers, comes closest to simulating the independent entrepreneur's situation. Participants can contribute to the venture's capitalization through paycheck deductions until the venture begins to make money and generate a positive cash flow. Investments are limited only by the requirement that salaries remain above the minimum wage—to avoid legal problems and prevent people from using personal funds. In exchange, participants can gain up to eight times their total investment. 42

To date, participants have put in from 12% to 25% of their salaries, and one of the two ventures has already paid several bonuses at a rate just below the maximum. The other, a computer-graphics-board venture housed outside Indianapolis, could return $890,000 to its 11 employee-investors in the near future. 43

The numbers show just how attractive AT&T employees find this program: ideas for new ventures began coming in before the program was announced, and in the planning year alone, 300 potential entrepreneurs developed proposals. Perhaps 2,000 ideas have been offered since, netting a venture formation rate of about 1 from every 250 ideas. People 44

Divestiture—selling off or otherwise getting rid of holdings or divisions. AT&T, under court order, divested itself of local telephone services, which are now controlled by regional telephone companies.

from every management level have been funded, including a first-line supervisor and a fifth-level manager (at AT&T, roughly equivalent to those just below officer rank), and in principle, management is even willing to offer this option to nonmanagers.

Entrepreneurial incentives are especially prevalent at high-technology *45* companies—not surprising given the importance and mobility of innovators. For example, a 1983 random sample of 105 Boston-area companies employing scientists and engineers compared the high-tech enterprises, dependent on R&D for product development, with their more traditional, established counterparts. The high-tech companies paid lower base salaries on average but offered more financial incentives, such as cash bonuses, stock options, and profit-sharing plans.[2]

The entrepreneurial paycheck is on the rise wherever management *46* thinks that people could do as well or better if they were in business for themselves—in high tech and no-tech alike. Au Bon Pain, a Boston-based chain of bakeries and restaurants, with $30 million in revenue from 40 stores nationwide, is launching a partnership program that will turn over a big piece of the action to store managers. Under the plan, annual revenues exceeding $170,000 per store will be shared fifty-fifty with the partners.

If business developers and revenue growers are getting a chance to *47* share in the returns, will inventors in the same companies be far behind? Probably not. The inventors' rights challenge is another nudge in the direction of entrepreneurial rewards.

Traditional practice has rewarded salaried inventors with small bo- *48* nuses (often $500 to $1,000) for each patent received and some non-monetary incentives to encourage their next inventions. Recognition ranges from special awards and promotion to master status entailing the use of special laboratories, freedom of project choice, sabbaticals, and the like. Cash awards are often given, but they are generally not tied to product returns. For outstanding innovation, IBM, for example, offers awards (which can be $10,000 or more) and invention achievement ($2,400 and up).

Increasingly, however, we are seeing strong competitive and legal *49* pressures to reward employed inventors as if they were entrepreneurs by tying their compensation to the market value of their output. They too want a piece of the action and a direct return on their contributions.

The Challenge to Hierarchy

If pay practices continue to move toward contribution as the basis for *50* earnings, as I believe they will, the change will unleash a set of forces that could transform work relationships as we know them now. To illustrate, let's look at what happens when organizations take modest steps to make pay more entrepreneurial.

In 1981, the city of Long Beach, California established a pay-for- *51* performance system for its management as part of a new budgeting process designed to upgrade the city government's performance against quantifiable fiscal and service delivery targets. Under the new system, managers can gain or lose up to 20% of their base salaries, so the pay of two managers at the same level can vary by up to $40,000. Job category and position in the hierarchy are far weaker determinants of earnings. In fact, at least two people are now paid more than the city manager.

While the impact of a system like this on productivity and entrepre- *52* neurship is noticeable, its effect on work relationships is more subtle. People don't wear their paychecks over their name badges in the office, after all. But word does get around, and some organizations are having to face the problem of envy head-on. In two different companies with new-venture units that offer equity participation, the units are being attacked as unfair and poorly conceived. The attackers are aggrieved that venture participants can earn so much money for seemingly modest or even trivial contributions to the corporation overall, while those who keep the mainstream businesses going must accept salary ceilings and insignificant bonuses.

The Iron Cage of Bureaucracy Is Being Rattled

In companies that establish new-enterprise units, this clash between two *53* different systems is self-inflicted. But sometimes the conflict comes as an unwelcome by-product of a company's efforts to expand into new businesses via acquisition. On buying a brokerage firm, a leading bank found that it had also acquired a very different compensation system: a generous commission arrangement means that employees often earn twice their salary in bonuses and, once in a while, five times. In 1985, six people made as much in salary and commissions as the chairman did in his base salary, or roughly $500,000 each. These people all made much more than their managers and their managers' managers and virtually everyone else in the corporation except the top three or four officers, a situation that would have been impossible a few years ago.

Now such discrepancies cannot be prevented or kept quiet. "People *54* in the trade know perfectly well what's happening," the bank's senior administration executive told me. "They know the formula, they see the proxy statements, and they are busy checking out the systems by which we and everybody else compensate these people."

To avoid the equivalent of an employee run on the bank—with every- *55* one trying to transfer to the brokerage operation—the corporation has felt forced to establish performance bonuses for branch managers and some piece-rate systems for clerical workers, though these are not nearly as generous as the managers' extra earning opportunities.

This system, though it solves some problems, creates others. The *56* executive responsible recognizes that although these new income-earning opportunities are pegged to individual performance, people do not work in isolation. Branch managers' results really depend on how well their employees perform, and so do the results of nearly everyone else except those in sales (and even there a team effort can make a difference). Yet instead of teamwork, the bank's practices may encourage competition, the hoarding of good leads, and the withholding of good ideas until one person can claim the credit. "We talk about teamwork at training sessions," this executive said, "and then we destroy it in the compensation system."

Team-based pay raises its own questions, however, and generates its *57* own set of prickly issues. There is the "free rider" problem, in which a few nonperforming members of the group benefit from the actions of the productive members. And problems can arise when people resent being dependent on team members, especially those with very different organizational status.

The New Bottom Line Is What You Contribute

There are also pressure problems. Gain-sharing plans, in particular, can *58* create very high peer pressure to do well, since the pay of all depends on everyone's efforts. Theodore Cohn, a compensation expert, likes to talk about the Dutch company, Philips, in which twice-yearly bonuses can run up to 40% of base pay. "Managers say that a paper clip never hits the floor—a hand will be there to catch it," Cohn recounts. "If a husband dies, the wake is at night so that no one misses work. If someone goes on vacation, somebody else is shown how to do the job. There is practically no turnover."

Similarly, Cohn claims that at Lincoln Electric, where performance- *59* related pay is twice the average factory wage, peer pressure can be so high that the first two years of employment are called purgatory.[4]

Another kind of pressure also emerges from equity-ownership and *60* profit-sharing systems—the pressure to open the books, to disclose managerial salaries, and to justify pay differentials. Concerns like these bubble up when employees who may never have thought much about other people's pay suddenly realize that "their" money is at stake.

These concerns and questions of distributional equity are all part of *61* making the system more fair as well as more effective. Perhaps the biggest issue, and the one most disturbing to traditionalists, is what happens to the chain of command when it does not match the progression of pay. If subordinates can out-earn their bosses, hierarchy begins to crumble.

Social psychologists have shown that authority relationships depend *62* on a degree of inequality. If the distance between boss and subordinate declines, so does automatic deference and respect. The key word here is *automatic*. Superiors can still gain respect through their competence and fair treatment of subordinates. But power shifts as relationships become more equal.

Once the measures of good performance are both clearly established 63 and clearly achieved, a subordinate no longer needs the goodwill of the boss quite so much. Proven achievement reflected in earnings higher than the boss's produces security, which produces risk taking, which produces speaking up and pushing back. As a result, the relationship between boss and subordinate changes from one based on authority to one based on mutual respect.

This change has positive implications for superiors as well as subor- 64 dinates. For example, if a subordinate can earn more than the boss and still stay in place, then one of the incentives to compete for the boss's job is removed. Gone, too, is the tension that can build when an ambitious subordinate covets the boss's job and will do anything to get it. In short, if some of the *authority* of hierarchy is eliminated, so is some of the *hostility*.

In most traditional organizations, however, the idea of earning more 65 than the boss seems insupportable and, to some people, clearly inequitable. There are, of course, organizational precedents for situations in which people in lower ranked jobs are paid more than those above. Field sales personnel paid on commission can often earn more than their managers; star scientists in R&D laboratories may earn more than the administrators nominally placed over them; and hourly workers can make more than their supervisors through overtime pay or union-negotiated wage settlements. But these situations are usually uncommon, or they're accepted because they're part of a dual-career ladder or the price of moving up in rank into management.

To get a feeling for the kinds of difficulties pay imbalances can create 66 in hierarchical organizations, let's look at a less extreme case in which the gap between adjacent pay levels diminishes but does not disappear. This is called pay compression, and it bothers executives who believe in maintaining hierarchy.

In response to an American Management Association survey of 613 67 organizations, of which 134 were corporations with more than $1 billion in sales, 76% reported problems with compression.[5] Yet only a few percentage points divide the organizations expressing concern from those that do not. For example, the average earnings difference between first-line production supervisors and the highest paid production workers was 15.5% for organizations reporting compression problems, and only a little higher, 20%, for those not reporting such problems. In the maintenance area, the difference was even less—15.1% average earnings difference for those who said they had a problem versus 18.2% for those who said they did not. Furthermore, for a large number of companies claiming a compression problem, the difference between levels is actually greater than their official guidelines stipulate.

What is most striking to me, however, is how great the gap between *68* adjacent levels still is—at least 15% difference in pay. Indeed, it is hard to avoid the conclusion that the executives concerned about compression are responding not to actual problems but to a perceived threat and the fear that hierarchy will crumble because of new pay practices.

What organizations say they will and won't do to solve compression *69* problems supports this interpretation. While 67.4% of those concerned agree than an instant-bonus program would help, 70.1% say their companies would never institute one. And while 47.9% say that profit sharing for all salaried supervisors would help, 64.7% say that their companies would never do that either. In fact, the solutions least likely to be acceptable were precisely those that would change the hierarchy most—for example, reducing the number of job classifications, establishing fewer wage levels, and granting overtime compensation for supervisors (in effect, equalizing their status with that of hourly workers). On the other hand, the most favored solutions involved aids to upward mobility like training and rapid advancement that would keep the *structure* of the hierarchy intact while helping individuals move within it.

Innovative Thoughts

The attacks on pay I've identified all push in the same direction. Indeed, *70* they overlap and reinforce each other as, for example, a decision to reward individual contributors makes otherwise latent concerns about equity much more visible and live. Without options, private concerns can look like utopian dreams. Once those dreams begin to appear plausible, however, what was "the way things have to be" becomes instead a deliberate withholding of fair treatment.

By creating new forms for identifying, recognizing, and ultimately *71* permitting contributions, the attack on pay goes beyond pay to color relationships throughout an organization. In the process, the iron cage of bureaucracy is being rattled in ways that will eventually change the nature, and the meaning, of hierarchy in ways we cannot yet imagine.

Wise executives, however, can prepare themselves and their compa- *72* nies for the revolutionary changes ahead. The shift toward contribution-based pay makes sense on grounds of equity, cost, productivity, and enterprise. And there are ways to manage that shift effectively. Here are some options to consider:

• Think strategically and systematically about the organizational implications of every change in compensation practices. If a venture unit offers an equity stake to participants, should a performance-based bonus with similar earning potential be offered to managers of mainstream businesses? If gain sharing is implemented on the shop floor, should it be extended to white-collar groups?

• Move toward reducing the fixed portion of pay and increasing the variable portion. Give business unit managers more discretion in distributing the variable pool, and make it a larger, more meaningful amount. Or allow more people to invest a portion of their salary in return for a greater share of the proceeds attributed to their own efforts later on.

• Manage the jealousy and conflict inherent in the more widely variable pay of nominal peers by making standards clear, giving everyone similar opportunities for growth in earnings, and reserving a portion of the earnings of stars or star sectors for distribution to others who have played a role in the success. Balance individual and group incentives in ways appropriate to the work unit and its tasks.

• Analyze—and, if necessary, rethink—the relationship between pay and value to the organization. Keep in mind that organizational levels defined for purposes of coordination do not necessarily reflect contributions to performance goals, and decouple pay from status or rank. And finally, be prepared to justify pay decisions in terms of clear contributions—and to offer these justifications more often, to more stakeholder groups.

Author's note: I thank Barry Stein, Cynthia Ingols, Paul Loranger, Carolyn Russell, Wendy Brown, and D. Quinn Mills for their valuable contributions.

Notes

[1] Martin Weitzman, *The Share Economy: Conquering Stagflation* (Cambridge: Harvard University Press, 1984).

[2] Michael Quarrey, Joseph Blasi, and Corey Rosen, *Taking Stock: Employee Ownership at Work* (Cambridge, Mass.: Ballinger, 1986).

[3] Jay R. Schuster, *Management Compensation in High Technology Companies: Assuring Corporate Excellence* (Lexington, Mass.: Lexington Books, 1984).

[4] Theodore H. Cohn, "Incentive Compensation in Smaller Companies," *Proceedings of the Annual Conference of the American Compensation Association* (Scottsdale, Ariz.: ACA, 1984), pp. 1–7.

[5] James W. Steele, *Paying for Performance and Position* (New York: AMA Membership Publishing Division, 1982).

Rhetorical Analysis Through Annotation

This article is built around a conflict between two sets of opposing desires or values. On one side are found stability, organization, hierarchy, and predictability; on the other side productivity, individuality, creativity, and risk. Traditional pay systems are associated with the former; the innovations described in the article are associated with the latter. At various points in the article one value system is presented more positively than the other, and at other times the evaluation switches. The ultimate viewpoint of the article about pay depends on the final balance achieved between the two value systems.

Underline once every word reflecting the organizational stability value system. Underline twice every word reflecting the individual risk value system. Next to each of these value words, place in the margin a + or a − to indicate whether the term is presented positively or negatively within the surrounding sentences. Note the explicit or implicit reasons for the evaluation.

Circle any passages where terms from the two value systems are explicitly placed in conflict. In the margin note whether either system is favored in the passage and why.

Discuss how the various proposals and the analysis of the benefits and difficulties are linked to the two value systems and their conflict. Also discuss how the author seems to switch allegiance from one system to another. Where does Kanter finally stand at the end of the article? Where is the burden of value choice ultimately placed? What role does history take in determining the value choice and how does that change our view of individual choices?

Discussion Questions

Interpreting the Text

1. What are the four concerns driving the reevaluation of pay systems? What is the effect of each concern, and what kinds of reward systems does Kanter associate with each?

2. What are profit sharing, gain sharing, employee ownership, performance bonuses and commissions, and venture development schemes? What are their similarities and differences? What benefits, effects, and difficulties does each have?

3. What kind of distortions, both internally and externally, can occur with bonus systems?

4. What is a two-tier pay system, and why does it create difficulties?

5. What is pay compression? How real is it? Why is it a problem, if it is one?

Considering the Issues

6. How does the traditional wage system destroy enterprise and create conservative attitudes?

7. Does giving workers a greater stake in the company undermine or strengthen the position of managers? Does it strengthen or weaken the organization?

8. Compare Kanter's style with Taylor's. In particular consider their use of examples, the comprehensiveness and depth of discussion, and the degree of direct advocacy versus analytical distance. How may the differences in style reflect the differences in the ways they perceive the audience? In what ways has the professionalization of managers over the last decades presented the two authors with different audiences?

Writing Suggestions

1. As part of class discussion of the issues raised in the readings, write an essay describing your experiences working in a fixed wage system or in a variable wage system, such as piecework, bonus, or partnership (in a lawn-care service, for example). Discuss your experience in relation to the ideas raised in the essay and use the experience to evaluate those ideas.

2. Imagine you are an executive running a division of a business of your choosing (for examples, a fast-food outlet, a computer sales and repair store, or an electronics components factory). The top management has asked you to consider adopting a profit-sharing scheme of any of the types discussed here. Write a memorandum back to the top management giving your recommendations and reasons.

3. Using the scenario in item 2 above, imagine the workers in your division have heard rumors of the possible change in pay system and have asked you about it. Write a response stating and justifying your intentions in a way that will satisfy them.

4. For a management course write an essay on the theme, "Every solution has a problem." Discuss this theme in relation to the pay plans presented in this article and any other experiences you may have had in organizations.

5. Kanter includes an analysis of "authority relationships" in her discussion, drawing on the work of social psychologists. She describes how the *automatic* deference and respect that a subordinate feels for a boss declines as pay becomes linked to performance rather than to the boss's goodwill. With this decline can come genuine mutual respect and a more relaxed, productive, less hostile relationship. For your college writing course, compare the teacher–student relationship with the boss–subordinate one described by Kanter. You may wish to consider how the teacher–student dynamic would change if somehow student papers were marked and graded not by your own teacher, but by another teacher.

The Relationship of Intentions to Level of Performance

Edwin A. Locke

In the following article from the *Journal of Applied Psychology*, Edwin Locke, a psychologist at the University of Maryland, presents another route to increased motivation and increased output. In this seminal article written in 1966, he suggests that specific goals, even without any specific reward attached, drive workers to produce more. Basing his argument on psychological research on intentions, Locke hypothesizes that goal setting positively affects workers' mental attitude and consequent productivity.

Although this idea seems little more than common sense—the kind of inspirational advice a parent or teacher might give you: "set high goals for yourself," "nothing ventured, nothing gained," etc.— Locke's establishing and refining the idea through experiment moves it out of the realm of folk wisdom and into the realm of reliable principle with defined limits. Through scholarly examination he finds out to what degree, under what conditions, and in what way the common sense principle is true, and when it is not. He also helps to establish human intentions as an important psychological variable, something that not all research psychologists have been willing to accept.

Locke tests this hypothesis in a way that is standard within the field of experimental psychology, reported as Experiment 1 below. Having shown the plausibility of the general hypothesis, he refines the idea through Experiments 2 and 3. The article follows the form of a typical experimental research article, trying to establish a general theoretical proposition on the basis of specific data generated by an experiment. The article begins with an introduction/review of the literature, then each of the three experiments follows the pattern of introduction, method, results and discussion; the article ends with an overall conclusion. Although the article follows a standard format, each part fits into a logically developing line of argument, beginning with the review of literature that develops a sequence of ideas, through each of the experiments, each of which is specifically designed to answer a question raised by the line of reasoning. The conclusion grows directly out of the sequentially developed reasoning of the article.

The influence of experimental psychology so evident in this article reflects the strong influence of the social sciences on the academic study of business. Taylor's concern for scientific management can be seen as the beginning of this change of style, but Taylor was still writing primarily for working managers. In the latter half of the twentieth century, academic disciplines studying business have developed as identifiable communities that communicate within themselves, concerned more with the validity of general propositions than with immediate practical advice. In later selections, we will see how the style of presentation of these ideas changes in relation to the more practically oriented audiences of business students and working managers.

Abstract Laboratory experiments are reported which stem from Ryan's approach to motivation. The fundamental unit is the "intention." The experiments examined the relationship between intended level of achievement and actual level of performance. A significant linear relationship was obtained in all 3 experiments: the higher the level of intention, the higher the level of performance. The findings held both between and within Ss° and across different tasks. The implications for the explanation of behavior are discussed.

THERE HAS BEEN CONSIDERABLE research on the relationship 1 of various demographic,° social, psychological, and personality variables to productivity or level of performance. Likert (1961) and Parker (1963) have emphasized human relations and supervisor variables. Katzell, Barrett, and Parker (1961) and Parker (1963) have examined the effects of situational (e.g., city size) variables on performance. Dunnette, Campbell, and Jaastad (1963) among others have studied the effects of group structure on output quantity. Atkinson (1958) and McClelland (1961) have explored the relationship between the need for achievement and quantity of output.

These approaches have in common the fact that they do not specify 2 what it is the individual is consciously trying to do in these situations. The process by which situational and supervisory variables affect performance is usually left unspecified or is assumed to involve some complex conscious or unconscious reasoning process on the part of the individual. The "need for achievement" is specifically acknowledged not to be a part of the individual's conscious experience in spite of its apparent influence on his behavior (McClelland, Atkinson, Clark, & Lowell, 1953).

Recently Ryan[1] has suggested that a considerable part of human be- 3 havior is controlled by the individual's conscious intentions,[2] that is, by what the individual is trying to do. As Ryan[3] notes "It is impossible to perform a psychological experiment upon a human subject without manipulating and controlling his intention. . . . In spite of this fact, the experimental study of . . . [intentions] has been relatively neglected in modern psychology."

Ryan (see note 3) expanding on earlier discussions of this topic (Ryan, 4 1958; Ryan & Smith, 1954) has suggested that a fruitful approach to the prediction and explanation of human behavior would be to examine the way in which intentions (see note 2) are related to actual behavior. Ryan argues that these lower level (immediate, specific) explanations should precede the more abstract (higher level) explanations (e.g., in terms of general needs, drives, and presses etc.).

The present research, a series of three laboratory experiments, will 5 examine the way in which intentions affect level of performance. More

---

S—subject.   **Demographic**—relating to the distribution and characteristics of different groups of people.

specifically the purpose will be to see how the level of intended achievement is related to actual level of achievement. The term "intended level of achievement" is very close in meaning to the term "level of aspiration" coined back in the 1930s, and means the future level of performance an individual will try for. Interestingly a close examination of the old level of aspiration literature reveals that almost in no case was it used as an *independent variable.*° Rather the effects of such variables as previous success and failure, amount of experience with the task, age, and selected personality variables on level of aspiration were the focus of interest (for reviews see Festinger, 1942; Frank, 1941; Lewin, 1958; Rotter, 1942).

However, a series of studies by Mace (1935), though not using the **6** level of aspiration terminology, did use it as an independent variable. On one complex arithmetic task he told one group of Ss to "do their best," another to try to get at least "70 correct answers" in 20 minutes, another to beat a score representative of their best previous performance, and a fourth group to beat a specific standard each day which was based on the skill of the individual S. In this experiment the last group learned much faster than the others. Unfortunately Mace did not vary the "intended level of achievement" along a single dimension so we have no means of making any predictions as to the shape of the relationship from his findings. We may conclude, however, that manipulating the intentions had a considerable effect on the learning rate of the Ss.

In a more recent experiment Eason and White (1961) found that when **7** Ss were instructed to stay on the target in a pursuit rotor task for 0%, 50%, or 100% of the time, respectively, their performance matched their intentions quite well. In a second experiment reported in the same article there was a less direct manipulation of intentions. The task was a pursuit rotor task, and the targets were a series of seven concentric copper rings mounted in a rotating turntable and separated from each other by gaps. The Ss in different conditions were told to try and stay within different rings. For instance, Ss would be told to stay within Ring X, and that all time spent within Ring X including rings inside this ring would be counted. (Ss were not told, however, to stay as close to the center ring as possible.) The amount of time spent on each of the rings was computed separately. A "performance quality" score was obtained by multiplying the distance of each ring from the center ring by the amount of time spent on that ring, summed over all rings and divided by the total time spent on all rings. The scores could thus be described as "average distance from center" scores. Eason and White found that the smaller the target complex (i.e., the smaller the diameter of the ring within which they were told to try to remain) the higher the performance quality, or the less the average distance from center score.

Independent variable—the factor allowed to change freely in an experiment, usually the variable which is the prime object of study of the experiment.

Eason (1963) replicated this finding with more *S*s and greater variation in target size.

Again there is little basis for making generalizations about the rela- 8 tionship between level of intended achievement and level of performance though the results of Eason and White and Eason at least suggest a linear function,° that is, the higher the level of control called for, the higher the level of control attained.

Experiment I

Method

The task in this experiment involved listing objects or things that could 9 be described by a given adjective (e.g., "heavy"). There were 15 trials and *S*s were given a different adjective on each trial and told to list things or objects that could be described by the adjective for 1 minute. The *E*° told *S*s how to score their own protocols. Generally any answer was acceptable that did not repeat things in the same category (e.g., for "hot," the responses "coffee," "tea," and "soup" would all be considered "beverages"). The *S*s were also told that *E* would check their answers at a later date. In scoring, however, *E* simply counted up the number of responses given by each *S* on each trial regardless of quality. The scores then are simply performance quantity scores.

The *S*s (paid summer school volunteers) were divided at random into 10 three groups. Each group had a different "standard of success" to beat

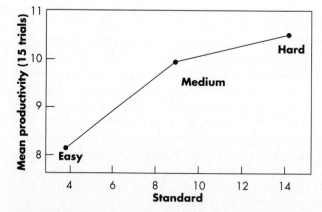

Figure 1. Mean productivity per trial by group—Experiment I.
Source: American Psychological Association. Reprinted with permission.

Linear function—a direct, proportional relationship, which appears as a straight line when represented on a standard two-dimensional graph.   *E*—experimenter.

on each trial. In the Easy group ($N°$ = 26) the standard of success was 4 things or objects on each trial. Thus to be "successful" on a trial Ss had to give at least 5 things or objects. In the Medium group (N = 22) the standard of success was 9 objects on each trial. In the Hard group (N = 23) the standard of success was 14 objects on each trial. A successful trial was defined as one on which a S beat his standard. The Ss in all groups were told that this was a test of creativity and that the standards were "what E considered to be a successful performance on the basis of his experience with the task" and represented "slightly above the average performance."

11   The "levels of intended achievement" in this experiment, therefore, were taken to be the standards of success set by the E.

12   The Ss kept track of their successes by counting up the number of acceptable responses given on each trial and indicating on a score sheet whether or not they had beaten their standard after each trial. Before each trial Ss indicated their subjective probability of beating the standard on the forthcoming trial by circling the appropriate number on a scale from .05 to 1.00 graded in steps of .05.

Results

13   As indicated previously the level of performance scores was simply the total number of responses given by each S on each trial. To check for equal ability all Ss began with a practice trial on which they were told to "do their best"; t tests on the mean scores for each group on this trial were computed. The Easy group had a significantly higher mean output than each of the other two groups on the practice trial; however, no corrections were made in the experimental data due to the substantial differences that emerged between the Easy groups and the other two anyway. Thus the differences between the Easy group and the other two are slight underestimates of the true differences.

14   Figure 1 shows the results for each group combined for all trials; mean output per trial is shown as a function of the standard. Table 1 shows the results of a trend analysis[4] and t tests performed on these data. There was a clear, significant linear trend, and it was accounted for almost entirely by the difference between the Easy group and the other two.

15   Lest these results seem in some way "obvious" (because the Ss were presumably trying to do what they were told), the number of trials (for all Ss in each group combined) on which the Easy, Medium, and Hard groups actually beat the *Easy group standard* (i.e., 4) was also computed. The Ss in the Easy group, whose task was to beat a standard of 4, actually beat it comparatively less often than did the Ss in the Medium and Hard groups whose standards were higher. The overall chi-square value for the frequency data was 10.75 (p < .01).

N—number.

Source	SS	df	F	p
Between	46.20	2	—	
Linear	43.50	1	10.82	.01
Quadratic	2.70	1	<1	ns
Within	273.07	68	—	

Comparison	df	t	p
Easy versus Hard	47	2.96	.01
Easy versus Medium	46	2.33	.05
Medium versus Hard	43	1.15	ns

Table 1.   Trend analysis and *t* test results for productivity: Experiment I.

Discussion

These results clearly support the notion of a linear function relating level **16** of intended achievement and level of performance. Due to limitations on the ability of the *S*s there is no exact correspondence between the two variables but the shape of the function is the important thing. This relationship held even though the Hard standard was so difficult to reach that the objective (proportion of successes) and subjective (mean ratings) probabilities of being successful at it were, respectively only .13 and .17.

Experiment II

The previous experiment was designed simply to determine the shape **17** of the relationship between level of intended achievement and level of performance. This experiment was designed with four additional considerations in mind: (*a*) How high a level of aspiration would *S*s set if allowed to set it themselves? (*b*) What would be the effect of changing the standards for some *S*s during the experiment? (*c*) Would the same difference between the Easy and Hard conditions emerge if the experiment were continued for an additional five trials? (*d*) Would the previous findings replicate using a slightly different task? . . .

Discussion

This experiment yielded the following answers to the questions posed **18** earlier: (*a*) *S*s set moderate (objective probability of success = .53) levels of intended achievement if given the choice and told to do "as well as possible." (*b*) Raising the standards within the same group resulted in a marked increase in output as the standards increase. (*c*) The Hard group continued their high output through 20 trials even though they were rarely able to beat the standard (objective probability of success = .07). (*d*) The difference between the Easy and Hard groups was replicated with a different though similar task.

Again the linear model relating level of intended achievement and *19* level of performance was supported, thus some basis was made for the generality of the original finding.

[*Experiment III explores in greater detail finding (b) of experiment II, that 20 output increased as standards increased.*]

Conclusion

On the basis of the experiments reported here we can make one major *21* generalization: the higher the level of intended achievement the higher the level of performance. This includes levels of intention so high that Ss can reach them less than 10% of the time.

If we were to take task difficulty or probability of success as the *22* independent variable (although in these experiments difficulty was clearly dependent upon the level of intended achievement) these short-term results do not support Atkinson's theory (1957) which predicts that a maximum level of performance will be obtained when the probability of success is moderate (.50) and will be uniformly low as the probabilities decrease from this in both directions. Although one experiment by Atkinson (1958) supports his theory, other data reported by McClelland (1961, p. 216) appear to support the linear model obtained here. The important difference between Ryan's (see Footnote 2) approach and theories such as those of Atkinson is that the latter attempt to go directly from aspects of the task or situation to behavior without taking account of the intentions of the Ss. Unless one assumes that man responds automatically, like a robot, to situational pressures, then it would seem unwise to expect theories which do not account for intentions to explain all of behavior. Although Atkinson's complete model uses an individual variable (need for achievement) even this is asserted *not* to be part of the individual's conscious experience.

References

Atkinson, J. W. Motivational determinants of risk-taking behavior. *Psychological Review*, 1957, 64, 359–372.

Atkinson, J. W. Towards experimental analysis of human motivation in terms of motives, expectancies, and incentives. In J. W. Atkinson (Ed.), *Motives in fantasy, action and society*. New York: Van Nostrand, 1958. Pp. 288–305.

Dunnette, M. D., Campbell, J., & Jaastad, K. The effects of group participation on brainstorming effectiveness for two industrial samples. *Journal of Applied Psychology*, 1963, 47, 30–37.

Eason, R. G. Relation between effort, tension level, skill, and performance efficiency in a perceptual motor task. *Perceptual & Motor Skills*, 1963, 16, 297–317.

Eason, R. G., & White, C. T. Muscular tension, effort, and tracking difficulty: Studies of parameters which affect tension levels and performance efficiency. *Perceptual & Motor Skills*, 1961, 12, 331–372.

Festinger, L. A theoretical interpretation of shifts of level of aspiration. *Psychological Review*, 1942, 49, 235–250.

Frank, J. D. Recent studies of the level of aspiration. *Psychological Bulletin*, 1941, 38, 218–226.

Katzell, R. A., Barrett, R. S., & Parker, T. C. Job satisfaction, job performance, and situational characteristics. *Journal of Applied Psychology*, 1961, 45, 65–72.

Lewin, K. Psychology of success and failure. In C. L. Stacey & M. F. DeMartino (Eds.), *Understanding human motivation*. Cleveland: Allen, 1958. Pp. 223–228.

Likert, R. *New patterns of management*. New York: McGraw-Hill, 1961.

Locke, E. A. The relationship of intentions to motivation and affect. Unpublished doctoral dissertation, Cornell University, 1964.

Mace, C. A. Incentives: Some experimental studies. *Industrial Health Research Board Report* (Great Britain), 1935, No. 72.

McClelland, D. C. *The achieving society*. New York: Van Nostrand, 1961.

McClelland, D. C., Atkinson, J. W., Clark, R. A., & Lowell, E. L. *The achievement motive*. New York: Appleton-Century-Crofts, 1953.

Parker, T. C. Relationships among measures of supervisory behavior, group behavior, and situational characteristics. *Personnel Psychology*, 1963, 16, 319–334.

Rotter, J. B. Level of aspiration as a method of studying personality: I. Critical review of methodology. *Psychological Review*, 1942, 49, 463–474.

Ryan, T. A. Drives, tasks and the initiation of behavior. *American Journal of Psychology*, 1958, 71, 74–93.

Ryan, T. A., & Smith, Patricia C. *Principles of industrial psychology*. New York: Ronald, 1954.

Tukey, J. W. The problem of multiple comparisons. Princeton: Princeton University, 1953. (Mimeo.)

Notes

[1]Unpublished mimeos, 1964. Chapter I: Explaining behavior; Chapter II: Explanatory concepts; Chapter V: Experiments on intention, task, and set; Chapter VI: Intentional learning; Chapter VII: Unintentional learning. Ithaca: Department of Psychology, Cornell University.

[2]Ryan actually uses the term "task" to designate what the writer means by "intention" (Ryan uses the latter as a synonym). To prevent confusion, the author will use "intention" as Ryan uses the word "task" and will reserve "task" for its traditional meaning as "a piece of work to be accomplished."

[3]Unpublished mimeos, 1964. Chapter V, p. 1.

[4]Equal intervals were assumed for the trend analysis. This assumption ap-

pears justified as the intervals were equal both in terms of the standards and the mean objective degrees of success.

Rhetorical Analysis Through Annotation

This article carries on a complex argument of several stages through the presentation of experiments.

For Experiment I and for the article as a whole, underline or highlight the sentences that announce the problems or questions to be addressed in the experiments, the most significant results in relation to those questions or problems, and the relevant conclusions. Then identify those sentences or phrases that link the sections together, either by overall synthesizing comments or by providing transitions. Use brackets in the margin to identify these connective passages. Finally outline the structure of the overall argument.

Discuss how the format of experimental report can be used to develop an argument. How is the hypothesis presented in the introduction related to the design of Experiment I? How do the results of Experiment I lead to the new questions of Experiment II? How does the conclusion draw together and extend the arguments presented through the several experiments?

Discussion Questions

Interpreting the Text

1. What are the different approaches taken to productivity described in Locke's review of the literature? What is his evaluation of each of these approaches? On what does he base these evaluations?

2. What previous work has been done on the relationship between intentions and performance? What are the limitations of this research? How do the experiments reported here attempt to make up for the shortcomings of previous work?

Considering the Issues

3. Based on your summary of the argument of the article (see Writing Suggestion 1 below), discuss how the different sections of the article contribute to its overall argumentative structure. Also compare your summaries with the abstract Locke provides at the beginning. How do you account for any differences?

4. Do you think the laboratory setting and the artificial task of word games provide an adequate test of real-world productivity? In what ways is naming objects similar or dissimilar to shoveling coal? What distortions may the task and the experimental setting produce in the results?

5. Why is human intention a difficult concept for experimental psychologists to work with and why do some psychologists consider it not a valid scientific concept? Why is it an important concept for psychologists to consider?

Writing Suggestions

1. Write a summary of the main steps of Locke's reasoning presented in the article. This summary is to be written for class discussion of the logic of the essay. (See discussion question 3 above.)

2. Describe one or more incidents when the presence or absence of goals for you affected your life and compare your experience with Locke's findings. Discuss whether your experience supports or does not support his findings. Consider this essay part of your classroom discussion of Locke's ideas.

3. Write a letter of advice to a younger friend about the importance of setting goals in life. You may refer to Locke's findings, but make them apply as closely as you can to the situation of this real or imagined friend.

The 'Practical Significance' of Locke's Theory of Goal Setting

Gary P. Latham and J. James Baldes

Once an idea—introduced by one researcher—is perceived as correct and powerful by other researchers, they will do follow-up work to refine and extend the idea. Gary P. Latham has written a number of articles and books developing Locke's theory. He did the research described below with J. James Baldes in 1975, while both were working for a large lumber company, Weyerhaeuser. Latham and Baldes apply Locke's ideas on the theory of productivity to the practical world of actual production. Unlike Locke, who argues for the general validity of a basic claim, Latham and Baldes argue only for the usefulness of a procedure in a particular kind of work setting. Applied research, like this, determines not whether a claim is true, but whether an idea works.

The article follows the standard experimental report format—abstract, introduction/review of literature, method, results, and discussion—but since it relies on Locke's article for the theory, it does not need to discuss extensively the background assumptions and fundamental ideas covered in Locke's articles.

Abstract   The practical significance of Locke's theory of goal setting was assessed using a time series design.° Data on the net weight of 36 logging trucks in six logging operations were collected for 12 consecutive months. Performance improved immediately upon the assignment of a specific hard goal. Company cost accounting procedures indicated that this same increase in performance without goal setting would have required an expenditure of a quarter of a million dollars on the purchase of additional trucks alone.

LOCKE'S (1968) THEORY OF goal setting has been questioned with *1* regard to its generality to industry (Campbell *et al.*, 1970; Heneman and Schwab, 1972). Survey data collected from 292 independent Southern pulpwood producers, however, have shown that goal setting accompanied by the presence of supervision results in high productivity and a low number of injuries (Ronan *et al.*, 1973). The results regarding productivity were corroborated through an analysis of variance of data collected from 892 additional procedures.

Latham and Kinne (1974) experimentally assessed the effects of a one- *2* day training program on goal setting over 12 consecutive weeks. The results showed that independent producers who set a specific production goal for their crew had higher productivity and lower absenteeism than those who were matched and randomly assigned to a control 'do your best' condition.

These studies would appear to support the external validity of goal *3* setting from a statistical standpoint. Statistical significance, however, is only one step in probing the external validity of a theory. The crucial consideration is whether or not the application of the theory changes behaviour enough to make a difference to an organisation's objectives (Campbell *et al.*, 1970).

The purpose of the present article is to describe a time series design *4* that assessed the utility or 'practical significance' of Locke's theory on the performance of company logging trucks. The problem investigated was that of increasing the net weight of trucks that transport logs from the woods to the mill. Normally, it takes 60–120 logs/trees for a truck to carry its maximum legal load. Because each tree differs in length and in diameter, it is a matter of judgment as to how many and what type should be carried in a given load.

The hypothesis tested was that the effects of goal setting would appear *5* in the form of an increase in the slope or level of the performance curve, as compared to the baseline performance. Further, it was hypothesized

---

Time series design—an experimental design using a series of events where conditions are changed over time.

that performance improvement would be evident after the first month of goal setting. This hypothesis was based on the earlier finding by Latham and Kinne (1974) that the effects of goal setting were immediate and consistent over time.

Method

Subjects

Six company logging operations in Oklahoma were studied. Each operation consisted of 6 to 10 people who performed one of the following operations: (a) felling a tree; (b) dragging the tree to a landing; (c) loading the tree into a truck; or (d) driving the truck to the mill where it is weighed and unloaded. There were approximately six trucks and six drivers assigned to each logging operation. The truck drivers differed from previous woods workers who had been studied (Latham and Kinne, 1974; Ronan et al., 1973) in that they were paid by the hour as opposed to piecerate, they were company employees as opposed to independent entrepreneurs, and they were members of a union. Data were collected on the net weights of 36 trucks. This number represented all the company's logging trucks in this area. **6**

Procedure

A detailed analysis of the performance of each logging operation revealed that the trucks were frequently falling far short of their maximum legal net weight. This finding, plus the results of the work previously cited on goal setting, were explained to the timberlands management and union leadership. **7**

A 94 per cent truck net weight was decided upon as a 'difficult' but attainable performance goal. This goal was assigned to the drivers whose job responsibilities include loading the truck to the maximum legal weight. Prior to establishing a specific goal, these workers had been urged to simply 'do their best' in this phase of the operation. **8**

At the onset of goal setting, the drivers were told that this was an experimental programme, that they would not be required to make more truck runs, and that there would be no retaliation if performance suddenly increased and then decreased. No monetary rewards or fringe benefits other than verbal praise were given for improving performance. No special training of any kind was given to the supervisors or the drivers. **9**

Results

The close geographical and working relationships of the six logging operations made it impossible to use a control group that would not **10** learn of the goal setting procedure. Thus, a time series design (Campbell and Stanley, 1966) was used to evaluate the results.

Measures of the net weight of all 36 logging trucks were collected for *11* three consecutive months prior to goal setting. In order to be certain that the fluctuations in weather and season would not bias the results favourably, these pre-measures were collected during the summer when logging conditions are optimal, that is, July, August and September. The results of the goal setting were monitored for nine consecutive months, i.e. October–June. The results are shown in Figure 1.

The immediate change in the slope and level of the performance curve° *12* supports the hypothesis that setting a specific hard goal versus a generalised goal of 'do your best' leads to a substantial increase in performance. Moreover, it is evident that this increase holds across time despite changes in season (fall, winter, and spring). Interviews with drivers concerning the slight decrease in performance during the second month of goal setting revealed that they were testing management's statement that no punitive steps would be taken against them if performance suddenly dropped. No such steps were taken and performance again increased.

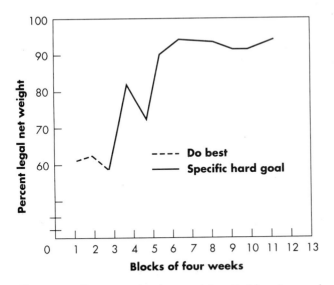

Figure 1.   Percentage legal net weight of 36 logging trucks across blocks as a function of a specific hard goal.
Source: American Psychological Association. Reprinted with permission.

Performance curve—the graphic representation of the amount of work accomplished.

Discussion

The results of this study, when viewed in conjunction with previous 13
work on independent wood producers (Latham and Kinne, 1974; Ronan
et al., 1973), lend strong support to the external validity of goal setting
theory for the logging industry. Corporate policy prevents a detailed
public discussion of the impact of this particular study on the company.
However, it can be said that without the increase in efficiency due to
goal setting it would have cost the company a quarter of a million
dollars for the purchase of additional trucks in order to deliver the same
quantity of logs to the mills. This figure does not include the cost for
the additional diesel fuel that would have been consumed or the expenses
for recruiting and hiring additional truck drivers.

The rival hypothesis that knowledge of results (KOR), rather than 14
goal setting, could have brought about the dramatic increase in performance was ruled out on the grounds that the truck weight had always
been available to each individual driver as soon as the truck was weighed
in the wood yard. This finding supports Locke's (1968) contention that
the mere presence of KOR does not increase performance unless it is
used by the individual to set a specific hard goal. It is interesting to
note, however, that subsequent to goal setting the drivers began to
record their truck weight on a 'trip sheet' that had previously been used
to record the particular logging site from which the wood had been
hauled. Thus, it would appear that goal setting may have led to an
increased awareness of KOR.

Similarly, the rival hypothesis that the improvement in performance 15
was due primarily to intergroup competition was ruled out because no
special prizes or formal recognition programmes were provided for those
groups who came closest to or exceeded the goal. No effort was made
by the company to single out one 'winner'. KOR was provided in terms
of how well the group, rather than the individual, was doing in terms
of meeting or exceeding the goal. More importantly, the opportunity
for competition to occur prior to goal setting had always been available
to the drivers through their knowledge of the daily and weekly truck
weights of each of the other drivers. However, anecdotal information
suggests that goal setting did lead to informal competition among drivers. This competition may very well explain why the drivers remained
committed to a very difficult goal over the nine-month period.

Finally, the rival hypothesis that the results of this study were due to 16
social facilitation or the pervasive Hawthorne effect° was ruled out since
the amount of attention and 'supervisory presence' given to the drivers
before and after goal setting were relatively equal. Latham and Kinne

---

Hawthorne effect—subjects change their behaviors because they are aware they are part
of an experiment.

(1974) have shown that woods workers who had a specific production goal had significantly higher productivity than those workers who received only attention and recognition. The only additional instructions given to the supervisors in the present study were to give specific verbal praise to the driver for meeting or exceeding the goal and to withhold negative comments when the goal was not met.

The setting of a goal that is both specific and challenging leads to an *17* increase in performance because it makes clear to the individual what he is supposed to do. This in turn may provide the worker with a sense of achievement, recognition, and commitment in that he can compare how well he is doing now versus how well he has done in the past and in some instances, how well he is doing in comparison to others. Thus, the worker is not only incited to expend greater effort, but he may devise better or more creative tactics for attaining the goal. In the present study, several drivers on their own initiative made recommendations for minor modifications on their trucks. These modifications included raising the forward stakes in the truck which, in some cases, appeared to enable the driver to increase the accuracy of his judgments as to the weight of the wood that he was carrying.

References

Campbell, D. T., and Stanley, J. C., *Experimental and Quasi-Experimental Designs for Research* (Chicago: Rand-McNally, 1966).

Campbell, J. P., Dunnett, M. D., Lawler, E. E., and Weick, K. E., *Managerial Behavior, Performance and Effectiveness* (New York: McGraw-Hill, 1970).

Heneman, H. G., and Schwab, D. P., 'Evaluation of Research on Expectancy Theory Prediction of Employee Performance', *Psychological Bulletin*, 78 (1972) 1–9.

Latham, G. P., and Kinne, S. B., III, 'Improving Job Performance Through Training in Goal Setting', *Journal of Applied Psychology*, 59 (1974) 187–91.

Locke, E. A., 'Towards a Theory of Task Motivation and Incentives', *Organizational Behavior and Human Performance*, 3 (1968) 157–89.

Ronan, W. W., Latham, G. P., and Kinne, S. B., III, 'Effects of Goal Setting and Supervision on Worker Behavior in an Industrial Situation', *Journal of Applied Psychology*, 58 (1973) 302–7.

Notes

Both authors are based at Weyerhaeuser Company, Tacoma, Washington.

The authors are grateful to E. E. Locke, T. M. Mitchell, and G. A. Yukl for their suggestions in preparing this manuscript.

The two previous studies of independent wood producers were conducted under the auspices of the American Pulpwood Association Harvesting Research Project. Association policy, coupled with the fact that these producers were noncompany employees, prevented the collection of data concerning profits.

Rhetorical Analysis Through Annotation

As many scholarly articles do, this article uses references to other articles to tie its thinking in to other work.

Circle each reference made in this article to other articles.

Discuss how Latham and Baldes use these references to build their own argument and tie their work in with the work of others.

Discussion Questions

Interpreting the Text

1. Consider the ways the impact of the workplace and the cost implications of different procedures are brought out in the article. From your conclusions, decide who this article is intended for. Is this purely for an academic audience? To what group of academics would the concern for practical applications and dollars appear important? What managers might find the academic style of this article to be important?

2. The opening sentence of the article raises a question about Locke's theory. How does this question provide a focus for the rest of the article? How does the review of literature relate to the question? How does the experiment address the question?

3. Once an experiment is moved out of the laboratory into a real-world situation, many uncontrolled variables may influence the results and invalidate possible conclusions. In this experiment, how are on-the-job conditions controlled enough to provide a valid experiment?

4. In the method section the subjects are described as nonentrepreneurs, union members, and employees paid on an hourly rate. Why are these important facts worth being mentioned? What other descriptions might be given of the subjects that are not given here? Why might these other descriptive facts be considered less relevant here?

Considering the Issues

5. In what ways do the conclusions here go beyond or extend Locke's original conclusions? How significant do you consider these extensions?

6. This experiment examines the effect of group goals of a work team rather than individual goals first examined by Locke. Do you think it makes a difference whether goals are individual or group goals? Do you personally find it easier to set and accept group or personal goals? How does group cooperation or individual discipline enter into meeting these goals?

Writing Suggestions

1. For a course in business management write a paragraph discussing the implications of the temporary second month drop in productivity.

2. Latham and Baldes suggest there may be a relationship between goal setting and knowledge of results (KOR). In order to satisfy yourself as to whether this accords with your own experience, write a paragraph discussing whether your knowledge of your own results and the results of others has influenced your ability to meet goals.

3. For a course in psychology, design and describe a personal experiment to test whether the conclusions presented here apply to your own work and productivity.

4. Remember a work situation you have been involved in. Imagine you are supervisor of that work situation. Write a memo to your boss describing your plan to use goal setting to improve the productivity of your work group.

Goal-Setting Research—A Textbook Presentation

Gary P. Latham and Kenneth N. Wexley

Goal-setting theory has had great success in the research literature. A review article from 1981, "Goal Setting and Improved Productivity (1969–1980)," reports over one hundred and fifty studies of goal setting, over 90 percent of which support Locke's findings. With such support from the research, the theory can be offered as reliably sound advice to businesspeople and students. The next selection is from a management textbook for M.B.A. students, written in 1981 by Latham (now teaching at the University of Washington) and a new collaborator, Kenneth N. Wexley, at Michigan State University. The authors summarize the basic theory, describe some major studies, and present principles to be drawn for management.

As part of a textbook presenting authoritative information, the selection docs not need to argue for the validity of the theory, nor need it present new and original experiments extending research knowledge. Rather it must only present the theory clearly and help the students understand the ideas and their importance. The research evidence is presented only as illustration of the concrete meaning of the theory and leads directly to the implications for successful management. These implications are stated as numbered rules to follow, practical guidance for the student on the way to a managerial job.

GOAL SETTING IS A technique that has received a great deal of *1* attention in the scientific literature within the past ten years. This is because it is a fundamental concept indigenous to most, if not all, motivation theory (Locke, 1978; Latham & Locke, 1979). Nevertheless, many people in industry have down played its importance because they believe there is nothing new in the concept, and that almost everyone sets goals. They are right in asserting that there is little that is novel in this approach. They are wrong in assuming that the concepts are systematically applied throughout most organizations. Whenever one group of employees is required to have specific production goals, they invariably increase their productivity substantially over that of groups who allegedly set goals, but actually do not. This is true regardless of whether the employees are engineers, typists, or loggers.

The Theory

The theory underlying goal setting began in a laboratory. In a series of 2 experiments (Locke, 1968), individuals were assigned different types of goals on a variety of simple tasks (e.g., addition, brainstorming, assembling toys). It was found repeatedly that individuals who were assigned *hard* goals performed better than individuals who were assigned moderate or easy goals. Furthermore, individuals who had *specific* challenging goals outperformed individuals who were trying to do their best. Finally, it was found that *incentives* such as praise, feedback, participation, and money lead to an improvement in performance only if they cause the individual to set specific hard goals.

There are three related reasons why goal setting affects performance. 3 Primarily, the setting of goals has a *directive* effect on what people think and do. Goals focus activity in one particular direction rather than others. Simultaneously, goals regulate energy expenditure, since people typically put forth *effort* in proportion to the difficulty of the goal, given that the goal is accepted. Finally, difficult goals lead to more *persistence* (which can be viewed as directed effort over time) than easy goals. These three dimensions, namely, direction (choice), effort, and persistence are three central aspects of the motivation/appraisal process.

The Evidence

The following studies illustrate the value of setting specific goals. Ronan, 4 Latham, and Kinne (1973) identified three supervisory styles used by independent logging supervisors in the South; (1) staying on the job with the crew, (2) setting specific production goals, but not staying with the crew, and (3) setting a specific production goal *and* staying on the job with the crew. The productivity of crews whose supervisors exhibited the first style was mediocre. Turnover was a problem in the crews whose supervisors set goals, but left the crew unsupervised. Productivity was highest and injury rates were lowest when the supervisor set a specific goal and closely supervised the crew.

Latham and Kinne (1974) located 20 independent logging crews who *5*
were all but identical in crew size, mechanization level, terrain on which
they worked, productivity, and attendance. The logging supervisors of
these crews were in the habit of staying on the job with their men, but
they did not set production goals. Half of the crews were randomly
selected to receive training in goal setting. In this way no one could be
accused of only teaching goal setting to those supervisors who were
already high performers.

The logging supervisors who were to set goals were told that a way *6*
had been found to increase their productivity at no financial expense to
anyone. They were given production tables that had been developed
through time and motion techniques by the company's industrial engineers. The tables enabled the supervisor to determine how much wood
should be harvested in a given number of man-hours. The 10 supervisors
in the training group were asked to use these tables as a guide for
determining a specific production goal to assign to their employees. In
addition, each sawhand was given a tally-meter (counter) that he could
wear on his belt. The sawhand was asked to punch the counter each
time he felled a tree. Permission was requested from the supervisor to
measure the crews' performance on a weekly basis.

The 10 supervisors in the control group (the people who were not *7*
asked to set goals) were told that the researchers were interested in
learning the extent to which productivity is affected by absenteeism and
injuries. Therefore, they were urged to do their best to maximize their
productivity and crew attendance, and to minimize injuries. It was
explained that the data would be used to find ways to increase productivity at little or no cost to the wood harvester.

To avoid the Hawthorne Effect (improvements due merely to atten- *8*
tion received) the control group was visited as frequently as the training
group. Performance was measured for 12 weeks. For all 12 weeks the
productivity of the goal-setting group was significantly higher than that
of the control group. Moreover, absenteeism was significantly lower in
the groups that set specific goals than in the groups who were simply
urged to do their best. Injury and turnover rates were low in both
groups. These were important findings because these people were considered marginal workers (Porter, 1973) in that their attendance, turnover, and productivity is unacceptable by conventional industry standards. They may work three days one week, one day a second week,
and no days a third week. Many have little or no education beyond
elementary school. They were not employed by pulp and paper companies; however, they were people on whom these companies in the
South were largely dependent for their wood supply.

Why should anything so simple and inexpensive as goal setting affect *9*
the work of these people so significantly? Anecdotal evidence from
conversations with both the loggers and the company woods managers
who visited them suggested several reasons.

Harvesting timber can be a monotonous, tiring job with little or no 10
meaning for most woods workers in the South. By introducing a goal
that is difficult but attainable, a challenge is provided. Moreover, a
specific goal makes it clear to the worker what is required. Goal feedback
via the tally-meter, and weekly record keeping provides the worker with
a sense of achievement, recognition, and accomplishment. The employee
can see how well he is doing now versus how well he has done in the
past, and, in some cases, how well he is doing in comparison with
others. Thus, the employee may not only expend greater effort, but
may also devise better or more creative tactics for attaining the goal
than he was previously using.

In a third study (Latham & Baldes, 1975), the problem that confronted 11
the organization was the loading of logging trucks. If the trucks were
overloaded, the unionized drivers could be fined by the Highway Department and ultimately lose their jobs. If the trucks were underloaded,
the company lost money. The drivers decided to underload the trucks.

For three months management tried to solve this problem by (1) 12
urging the drivers to try harder to fill the truck to its legal net weight,
and (2) developing weighing scales that could be attached to the truck.
The latter approach was not cost effective. The scales were unreliable
and continually broke down due to the rough terrain on which the
trucks travelled. The drivers all but ignored the first approach. For the
three months in which the problem was being examined, the trucks
were seldom loaded in excess of 60 percent of the truck's capacity.

At the end of the three month period, the results of previous goal 13
setting studies were explained to the union. They were told (1) that the
company would like to set a specific net weight goal for the drivers, (2)
that no monetary reward or fringe benefits other than verbal praise
could be expected for improved performance, and (3) that no one would
be criticized for failing to attain the goal. The idea that simply setting a
specific goal would solve a production problem seemed too incredible
to be taken seriously—by the union. Nevertheless, agreement was
reached that a difficult but attainable goal of 94 percent of truck net
weight would be assigned to the drivers providing that no one would
be reprimanded for failing to attain the goal. This latter point was
emphasized to the company's supervisors.

Within the first month performance improved to 80 percent of the 14
truck legal net weight. After the second month, however, performance
decreased to 70 percent. Interviews with the drivers revealed that they
were testing management's statement that no punitive steps would be
taken against them if their performance suddenly dropped. Fortunately,
no such steps were taken by supervisors; and, performance exceeded 90
percent of the truck's net weight after the third month. Their performance has remained at this level for six years.

The results over the nine month period in which this study was 15
conducted saved the company $250,000. This figure, determined by the

company's accountants, is based on the purchase of the extra trucks that would have been required to deliver the same quantity of logs to the mill if goal setting had not been implemented. This figure would have been even higher if it included the cost for the additional diesel fuel that would have been consumed, and the expenses that would have been necessary for recruiting and hiring the additional truck drivers.

Why could this procedure work without the union demanding an *16* increase in hourly wages? First, the drivers did not feel that they were really doing anything differently, which in a sense was true. They were not working harder; but they were working more efficiently than they had in the past. Moreover, the men began to record their truck weight in a pocket notebook, *and* they began to brag about their accomplishments to their peers. They viewed the goal setting as a challenging game, "It is great to beat the other guy."

Competition was a crucial variable for bringing about goal commit- *17* ment.[1] However, the hypothesis that the improvement in performance was due only to the competition can be rejected because no special prizes or formal recognition programs were provided for those individuals who came closest to or exceeded the goal. No effort was made by the company to single out one winner. More important, the opportunity for competition to occur prior to goal setting had always existed for the drivers through *their knowledge* of their truck's weight, and the truck weight of each of the 36 other drivers every time they hauled wood into the wood yard. In short, competition affected productivity in that it led to the acceptance of and commitment to the goal; but, it was the setting of the goal, and the working toward it that brought about the increase in performance and the decrease in costs.

Several investigators have examined the benefit of involving the em- *18* ployees in setting specific performance goals. At General Electric, Meyer (Meyer, Kay, & French, 1965) examined the results of allowing middle level managers to participate in setting specific performance goals during their performance appraisal. Meyer found that goals were attained more often when the employee had a say in the goals that were set than when the goals were assigned by a supervisor. However, this was true only for employees with a supervisor whose managerial style throughout the year encouraged employee participation in decision making. Employees with a supervisor who did not normally encourage participation performed better when the goals were assigned to them. Meyer concluded that the way a goal is set is not as important as it is to set a specific goal.

At Weyerhaeuser Company, Latham (Latham, Mitchell, & Dossett, *19* 1978) examined the results of involving engineers and scientists in the setting of goals during the performance appraisal. BOS° were used. The

---

BOS—behavioral objectives; goal defined by concrete outcomes.

major finding of this study was that participation in goal setting is important to the extent that it leads to higher goals being set than is the case where the goals are assigned unilaterally by a supervisor. And yet, employee perception of goal difficulty was the same among those with assigned and participatively set goals. Only individuals with participatively set goals performed significantly better than individuals who were either urged to do their best or received no feedback at all. Finally, as the theory states, giving employees specific feedback without setting specific goals on the basis of their feedback had little or no impact on employee performance.

In a subsequent study at Weyerhaeuser (Dossett, Latham, & Mitchell, 20 1979), female clerical personnel were randomly assigned to participative, assigned, or do-your-best goal conditions on a clerical test. With goal difficulty held constant, goal attainment in terms of test scores was higher in the assigned than it was in the participative condition. The performance appraisal results of these same people on BOS showed that assigned goals resulted in higher performance and greater goal acceptance than did participatively set goals.

In reviewing these results, Likert (personal communication, August 21 1977) commented that when assigned goals have been effective, the supervisor had always behaved in a highly supportive manner. Three key aspects of modern organizational theory (Likert, 1967) are supportive relationships with employees, participative decision making, and goal setting. Latham and Saari (1979b) tested this assumption in a laboratory setting where students were given a brainstorming task.

Goal difficulty was held constant between the participative and as- 22 signed goal setting groups. The supportiveness of the experimenter was varied by having him behave in either a supportive or a hostile manner. Supportiveness led to higher goals being set than was the case when the experimenter was nonsupportive. The setting of specific goals led to higher performance than urging people to do their best. Finally, participation increased performance by increasing the individual's understanding of how to attain the goals.

In summary, goal setting is effective because it clarifies exactly what 23 is expected of an individual. As several employees have commented, "by receiving a specific goal from the supervisor we are able to determine for the first time what that S.O.B. really expects from us." Moreover, the process of working for an explicit goal injects interest into the task. It provides challenge and meaning to a job. Through goal attainment, feelings of accomplishment and recognition (from self and/or supervisor) occur.

Effective goal setting in performance appraisal should take into ac- 24 count the following points:

1. Setting specific goals leads to higher performance than adopting an attitude of do your best. That is, a specific score on BOS should be

specified along with the key behaviors that the employee needs to work on to improve or maintain the score.

2. Participation in goal setting is important to the extent that it leads to the setting of higher goals than those that are assigned unilaterally by superiors. Participation does not necessarily lead to greater goal acceptance than when goals are assigned by a supportive manager. However, employee understanding of how to attain them may be increased as a result of participating in the goal setting process.

3. Given goal acceptance and ability, the higher the goal, the higher the performance. However, the goal should be reasonable. If the goals are unreasonable, employees will not accept them. Nor will employees get a sense of accomplishment from pursuing goals that are never attained. People with low self-confidence or ability should be given more easily attainable goals than those with high self-confidence and ability.

4. Performance feedback is critical for showing employees how they are doing relative to the goals, maintaining the employees' interest in the goals, revising goals, and prolonging effort to attain the goals.

5. If employees are evaluated on overall level of performance rather than goal attainment, they will continue to set high goals regardless of whether the goals are attained. High goals lead to higher performance levels than easy goals. If employees are evaluated on goal attainment regardless of the difficulty of the goal, they are likely to set low goals or reject hard goals imposed by supervisors.

6. There must be some latitude for the individual to influence performance. Where performance is rigidly controlled by technology or work flow (such as the typical assembly line) goal setting may have little effect on performance.

7. Workers must not feel threatened that they will lose their jobs if they increase their performance under the goal setting procedure. Most people have enough sense not to put themselves out of work by being too productive. Goal setting is most effective when the supervisor behaves in a supportive manner when interacting with subordinates.

Note

[1]A word of caution: We do not recommend setting up formal competition. As Latham and Locke (1979) noted, competition may lead employees to place individual goals ahead of company goals. The emphasis should be on accomplishing the task, getting the job done, not necessarily "beating" the other person.

Rhetorical Analysis Through Annotation

Narrative story telling is a main tool of presentation in this selection.
  Use lines drawn in the margin to identify which parts are told as stories.
  Discuss how the various ideas and experiments are turned into stories. Then discuss how these stories relate to the discussions around them.

Discussion Questions

Interpreting the Text

1. According to this selection, what qualifications or elaborations need to be made of the simple claim that setting goals improves productivity? Under what conditions and with what limitations is goal setting effective?

2. Do the various experiments described lead to exactly the same conclusions, or do they each develop some particular nuance of goal setting? How do all the descriptions add up to a total picture of what we know about goal setting?

3. What advice do the authors offer for implementing goal setting? Does this advice come directly from the experiments or elsewhere?

4. According to this selection, why does goal setting work?

5. In what ways (beyond the final set of numbered principles) do the authors emphasize the significance of the theory and point out the practical implications of it?

Considering the Issues

5. Compare the summaries of Locke (1968) and Latham and Baldes (1975) presented in this selection with the originals printed in this volume. How do the summaries differ from the originals beyond being shorter? Consider material selected for inclusion in the summary, emphases, structure of the presentation, tone, and level of technical language and detail. What do these differences suggest to you about the differences between research articles and textbooks?

6. What other aspects of this selection remind you of typical textbook presentations?

7. Does this article indicate any risks or disadvantages to goal setting or any moderating conditions that may limit efficacy? To what extent do you think this presentation is evenhanded and unbiased?

Writing Suggestions

1. Imagine you were taking a management course with this passage as part of your required textbook. Prepare a set of study notes for this selection.

2. Rewrite the set of seven principles of goal setting at the end of the selection as personal self-help rules presented in an advice column in a newspaper or popular magazine. Identify the newspaper or magazine you are writing for.

3. Write an essay evaluating the goal-setting procedures in your classes in the light of the theory, research, and principles discussed in this selection. In the course of this essay discuss whether any changes in goal-setting procedures may evoke better work from you. Consider this essay as part of your dialogue with your teachers over your education.

4. For a philosophy course on ethics, write a short essay discussing the ethical implications of the manipulation of goals by employers. You may consider such questions as: does goal setting increase or decrease human freedom and/or dignity? Does it matter who sets the goals?

Better Management for Better Productivity: The Role of Goal Setting

Lawrence W. Foster

Today the problem of reaching businesspersons with advice is different than in Frederick Taylor's day. Then, a few managerial experts, usually in a consultant role, spoke directly and almost exclusively to managers. Today, professional advice-givers may be closeted in universities, writing first for their academic colleagues, for they must first convince the other academics that their advice is sound to ensure that they have a legitimate product to pass on to industry. Their second audience is likely to be their students, who sit in front of them every day in class to receive an authoritative view of the best of current knowledge. The business audience is a distant third.

Business managers, because they have practical experience, concrete problems, and real worries about profits and losses, are likely to be skeptical of academic theorizing and complicated, abstract solutions. To reach these people, any academic advice-giver must present practical solutions to practical problems in a nontechnical way. The bottom-line meaning for increased profits must always be clearly spelled out. Practitioner journals like the *Harvard Business Review* and the *National Productivity Review* (the source of the following article from 1983) provide such readable advice.

In this article, Lawrence Foster, a professor of organizational behavior, strategy, and policy at Michigan State University, first demands the business reader's attention by showing how his subject relates to the well-known and disturbing problem of a decline in

American productivity. Only after showing that other approaches are inadequate to this fundamental business problem does Foster present principles of goal setting. The emphasis is on explanation and urging the importance of the ideas rather than on reporting research and giving detailed evidence.

IN THE 1980s THE rallying cry for American business clearly must be   1
more productivity. During the past three decades, the rate of U.S. productivity has been slowing. In 1950 it took more than seven Japanese workers to produce what was made by a single American worker. It took three West Germans to match the output of each American. Today, however, those ratios are significantly altered. The output of two Japanese workers equals that of a single American; the ratio of U.S. to West German productivity has halved, from three-to-one to three-to-two. If present projections by the American Productivity Center in Houston are correct, West German productivity (measured by total product per work hour) will surpass that of the U.S. in 1984. France is projected to pass us in 1985; Japan by 1991.

How do American managers reverse these disturbing trends? What   2
lies ahead for us? The comparative figures on productivity and its rate of change for the United States and its trading partners are sobering. But those numbers can be misleading as to the cause of the problem. By measuring productivity by output per worker, they imply that the American work force is less capable, less motivated, less dedicated to "good work" than are those of our economic competitors. The numbers seductively focus on the worker per se and on his or her inputs into the productive process even though individual workers have, in fact, limited power over their level of productivity. Increased productivity, if it is to come, must come from management, for it is American managers, not American workers, who have the power to influence productivity.

Barriers to Technological Innovation

As American managers turn their attention to enhancing productivity,   3
they are discovering that technology as a means of productivity improvement is less viable than before.

Rates of inflation and borrowing have pushed costs of capital expenditures for technological innovations to record levels.

Traditionally, technology and its applications have been the source of   4
greatest productivity increases. New machines, new materials, and new

processes can enable manufacturing labor to double or triple its rates of productivity virtually overnight. Using new ultrasonic cleaning technology, for example, Westinghouse has increased productivity in its iron molding facilities by 900 percent. Similarly, a single architect, using computer-aided design and a computer library of preengineered components, can produce all the plans needed for a $3 million structure in a single morning. Using CAD° systems, architectural design firms are reducing fees from 10 percent to 60 percent while simultaneously increasing their bottom-line numbers.

But the decade of the 1980s presents new and heretofore unexperi-   5 enced barriers to the continued increase of productivity through technology. One barrier is the recently constructed aggregate° of financial and labor market forces unique in U.S. industrial history. A record number of workers entered the U.S. labor force in the 1970s as the baby-boom generation grew to maturity. This expansion was further augmented by the record number of women who abandoned traditional roles outside the labor pool and moved into new and expanded roles within the labor force. During the years from 1965 to 1980, the labor pool grew by about twenty-eight million workers, an increase over twice that of the preceding fifteen-year period. This record influx of workers helped keep real wages relatively low for the manufacturing industries. When adjusted for inflation, the real hourly wage for non-manufacturing workers in the U.S. has actually declined by an average rate of over 0.5 percent per year since 1974.

At the same time, rates of inflation and borrowing have combined to   6 push costs of capital expenditures for technological innovations to record levels. As the record costs of capital work through the economic system, managers face longer payback periods° for technological investments than could have been imagined even a few years ago. The result is that technological decisions have become more dangerous, more expensive, and require larger payoffs than has been true in the past. When this occurs during a time of record labor availability, "rational" managers, particularly those in relatively labor-intensive industries, have enormous disincentives to utilize technology freely.

An additional barrier to the easy application of technology stems from   7 the shifting makeup of the labor force. For the first time, more than half of the workers in the U.S. are employed in service industries. Large gains in productivity accruing from technological advances have, historically, come not from service-sector industries but from manufacturing, where the nature of the tasks more readily lends itself to improved efficiencies. For example, productivity in retail food sales has remained relatively static since the mid-1930s, when the invention of the shopping cart provided a major increase in the dollar sales volume that could be

---

CAD—computer-aided design.   **Aggregate**—total.   **Payback period**—the time necessary to earn back the initial investment.

supported by each employee. Today, electronic checkout and volume pricing offer fewer productivity gains than did the shopping cart almost a half-century ago. Thousands of service industry jobs remain little changed from their early days. Nursing, retail clothing sales, stock and security brokering, cab driving, plumbing, surgery, topless dancing, and insurance sales all await major advances in productivity rates. In the meantime, employment in these and other service industries continues to expand each year, packing greater numbers of workers into areas of low productivity and thereby lowering national productivity averages.

If there is no change, the problem of sluggish productivity rates will *8* become even more acute toward the end of the 1980s. In 1983 the baby-boom effect will begin to dissipate. Fewer and fewer workers will enter the labor force. As the labor pool shrinks, wage rates, previously held in check by the abundance of potential employees, will rise. The mandate for managers will be to introduce ways of increasing individual produc-tion at a rate equal to or greater than the wage escalation. The mandate is a challenging but critical one; each incremental wage increase that remains unmatched by a production increase will reduce overall pro-ductivity rates in the economy.

Productivity Through Better Management

Faced with a shrinking labor pool and unprecedented barriers to tech- *9* nological innovation, American managers must look in new directions to gain increased productivity.

Better management is a clear alternative.   *10*

Fortunately, in the past decade and a half significant strides have been *11* made toward a fuller understanding of just what constitutes better man-agement. Through the work of Edwin A. Locke at the University of Maryland, Gary Latham at Washington University, and Edward E. Lawler at the University of Southern California, for example, it has become apparent that the setting of specific and concrete goals for employees plays a critical role in maintaining elevated levels of produc-tivity.

Standards define the level of efforts and outcomes required to avoid failure—not the levels required to achieve success.

Formal goal setting is the articulation to individual workers of a set *12* of specified objectives, the accomplishment of which ensures overall success for the organization. It offers organizations synergetic° benefits

---

Synergetic—having to do with the combination of several factors to produce an effect not resulting from any of the factors separately.

from its employee base by integrating the efforts of hundreds or thousands of people doing a myriad of tasks within the organizational setting.

For goal setting to succeed, there must be a set of performance criteria 13 by which the efforts of individual employees can be evaluated in the appraisal process.

Perhaps, though, the most important ingredient in the success of a 14 formal goal-setting program is the benefits such a program brings to the individual working man or woman. If better management is to bring about better performance, each worker must perceive that it is both possible and worth the effort to do a superior job. The establishment of strong links between level of organizational performance and the rewards—both intrinsic and extrinsic—accruing to the individual in exchange for that performance is critical to the achievement of productivity gains. Research data (along with case histories, anecdotal evidence, and common sense) provide clear empirical support for the importance of the link between performance and rewards.[1] When that link exists, individuals are assured that incremental efforts to increase productivity bring incremental rewards. Until it exists, managers have no impact on the performance levels of individuals, be they executives, bench press operators, product designers, sheet metal benders, or receptionists.

But performance can be neither defined, evaluated, nor rewarded in 15 the absence of goals. And, unfortunately, few organizations have developed a formal system that assigns to individual workers specific goals of an interrelated and mutually supportive nature. While it is true that most organizations keep before them objectives that serve to guide the efforts of the executive team and have a formal system of controls and budgets that set expected standards, these activities in and of themselves do not necessarily constitute effective management for productivity. Standards are by their very nature definitions of minimal performance levels. They define the level of efforts and outcomes required to avoid failure—not the levels required to achieve success. For managers seeking productivity gains the difference between goals and standards is more than mere semantics. Standards result in adequate performance; goals define and yield performance levels far beyond those necessary to avoid personal failure.

Increased Productivity Through Formal Goal Setting

Goal setting has three advantages to offer under the conditions of the 16 coming decade. First, it is a technique that promises significant payoffs for a relatively small investment of hard dollar resources. Second, making the rather heroic assumption that the direct benefits of goal setting can be accurately isolated and costed out, the payback period of investments, when compared to major capital projects, is virtually instantaneous. Third, goal setting is a technique that is equally applicable to both service and to manufacturing environments.

Goal Setting and Motivation

Specific individual goals define performance levels so as to differentiate 17 superior performance from the merely adequate. Establishing and managing from a clear set of goals is not just an academic exercise for a manager; it has far-reaching consequences for the way individuals within the organization perform tasks and in the way those tasks are perceived. Managers at all levels of the organization who employ goal setting can expect significant positive payoffs *provided* they understand the right ways to use goals for maximizing motivation.

Performance Payoffs from Goal Setting
- Difficult goals lead to better performance than do moderate or easy goals.
- Specific goals increase interest in a task.
- Imposed goals can improve productivity more than self-defined goals.

Difficult goals lead to better performance than do moderate or 18
easy goals   Most goals are met. "Rise to the challenge" has a great deal of appeal for high achievers within an organization. Often, placing a specific goal before an individual worker is sufficient in and of itself to increase motivation and effort. However, when targets remain undefined or are ambiguous, the job incumbent does not feel challenged. The employee needs a clear goal.

Specific goals act as a ceiling on individual efforts and aspirations. 19 Once met, the effort to go beyond what has been held up before the employee as a target is much reduced. But until a specific target is reached, employees strive hard for success. The greatest effort takes place when the individual perceives the target to be within reach, with the effort increasing until the accomplishment is attained. Since most goals are met, a difficult goal calling for greater effort will result in better performance by individuals at all levels of the organization than will goals that are less challenging.

Specific goals increase interest in a task   In 1975 the Department 20 of Health, Education and Welfare released the results of the largest, most complete, and most ambitious survey ever carried out within the U.S.

labor force. In interviews and questionnaires with over 375,000 workers, researchers found that interesting work was the most desired and sought after type of labor. More important than money, more important than recognition, more important than degree of participation in decision making, more important than rate or pace of work was the inherent interest of the work. Interesting work was number one.

All members of an organization derive to some degree a measure of 21 intrinsic motivation when challenged to successfully complete a task. A specific statement of goals increases intrinsic motivation, for it provides a target against which performers can compete. Competition increases not only interest in doing the task but increases motivation to do the job well. Weyerhaeuser Incorporated saved over a quarter of a million dollars of budgeted cost on a single job by setting specific goals for workers. After attaining a preset and clearly stated goal, the individuals felt successful and felt the self-enhancement that accompanies success.

Organizations that fail to provide specific goals for individuals cheat 22 those individuals of the opportunity to experience organizational success on a relatively frequent basis—one of the most satisfying feelings available to workers.

Imposed goals can improve productivity more than self-defined 23 **goals**   Motivation research has found an irony in the area of self-defined goals. Those individuals who are most concerned with accomplishment, those who have the highest need to achieve, are not the individuals who set the highest goals for themselves. Instead, it is the lower achievers who establish high goals. Low achievers have less aversion to failure than do high achievers. High achievers find failure to be a deep and painful experience—one to be avoided whenever possible. These individuals set goals that are neither high nor low but moderate in scope and, most of all, carry a high probability of attainment. Given that most goals are met, high achievers can usually do better than this. Therefore, managers who impose realistic but high goals on their employees will be rewarded with higher levels of productivity.

Managers who impose realistic but high goals on their employees will be rewarded with higher levels of productivity.

Put another way, participative goal setting, as opposed to top-down 24 goal setting, results in overall lower performance with other factors held equal. But the key to effective goal setting lies in the word "realistic." The goals must be attainable. When managers set goals at levels that are clearly unachievable, the net effect is frustration and surrender. Individual workers simply give up without making a genuine effort to reach the targets. For those workers who are high achievers, it is better never to have tried at all than to have tried and fallen short.

Managing a Formal Goal-Setting Program

When a manager sets out to bring greater productivity to an organization   *25*
via a formal goal-setting program, a number of guidelines must be kept
in mind as he or she begins to put the system into operation.

Guidelines for Goal Setting

- Managers should assign specific goals.
- Managers should set objectives as facets of the job as
  much as possible.
- Managers should concentrate on successful performance.
- Managers should understand the means of goal attain-
  ment.

While apparently simple, the decisions required by the guidelines take a   *26*
great deal of thought and an intimate familiarity with the organization
and its tasks. Without such effort and knowledge, the full payoff of a
goal-setting system cannot accrue. Implementing these guidelines presents the manager with the principal challenge of successful goal setting.

Managers Should Assign Specific Goals

Specific goals produce higher levels of performance than the instruction   *27*
to simply "do your best." Merely assuming that each individual will do
his or her best does not provide guidance. It offers no direction, no
identity with larger organizational efforts, no integration, and, finally,
no level of expected effort. Workers with no clear understanding of
goals are often left with feelings of ambiguity about their roles and of
their value to the organization. With this ambiguity come feelings of
frustration with an alienation from the organization.

At all organizational levels, an important part of the manager's job is   *28*
to ensure a feeling of belonging and integration in the work force.
Setting specific goals for individuals and relating those goals to the
overall objectives of the firm are principal methods of building integration while reducing ambiguity. One major Midwestern construction
firm specializing in a unique national market was able to reduce turnover
about 8 percent and cut its project costs over 15 percent, or $12 million,
annually after introducing a program of specific goal setting for individuals. Crew foremen were given specific goals expressed as budgets and
time schedules on a three-week basis. They, in turn, made specific
scheduling goals for team members on a weekly level. All crews and 80
percent of the individuals involved improved performance by an average
of almost 35 percent. Improvements for crew foremen ranged from 15
percent to 50 percent over prior performance with nonspecific goals.

Today the firm considers its goal-setting program as providing a major competitive advantage over its rivals, one translating directly to the bottom line of its project bid sheets.

Managers Should Set Objectives in as Many Facets of the Job as Possible

Individuals give greater emphasis to those aspects of their job where *29* goals are set than to those where no goals are established. Every job has certain facets which lend themselves better to measurement than do other facets. It is easy for an organization to focus attention on those parts of the task that can be easily measured by building a set of goals based on the quantifiable factors. It is, however, dangerous to exclude nonquantifiable factors. A mid-level manager of an engineering group, for example, may be given goals concerned with (1) running the group at or under budget for the year, (2) completing the equivalent of 25,000 hours of product design with the assigned personnel, and (3) completing the equivalent of three and one-half major design projects within the year. These goals, because they are visible and can be quantified and measured easily, focus the attention of the group manager on attainment. However, they simultaneously reduce the likelihood that he or she will work to develop creativity within the group or develop management talent for his or her eventual replacement. These activities are of great importance to the organization's ultimate health and success, but because they are not specified as goals, they may be left unaccomplished.

Managers Should Concentrate on Successful Performance

Emphasis on errors and performance deficiencies leads to avoidance of *30* risk-taking behavior and results in attempts by subordinates to establish easy objectives. An emphasis on negative performance with no concurrent attention to positive results has disastrous consequences for organizational performance. It is a recipe for organizational dry rot.

An emphasis on negative performance with no concurrent attention to positive results has disastrous consequences for organizational performance.

Effort and action in organizations inevitably carry with them some *31* degree of risk. All management decisions involve risk; all efforts to bring change, however infinitesimal, incur risk. When individuals who make decisions in organizations learn that successful gambles are treated simply as another expected part of the job, while unsuccessful gambles carry serious consequences for personal careers, they soon learn to avoid taking risks. Workers are taught to avoid making decisions, to avoid working for adaptation and change. They learn to maintain and protect the status quo at all costs. They learn that there is no payoff for innovative behavior. They learn that the boat shall not be rocked.

Under an organizational climate oriented toward the maintenance of   32
the status quo, employees have only a limited number of choices. Some—the dynamic, the caring, the achieving—will ultimately leave the organization for another organization whose philosophy of management they share. Others—the timid, the pedestrian, the politic—will remain behind and adjust their behaviors to the rewards offered. The long-term result is stagnation.

Managers Should Understand the Means of Goal Attainment

Considerable frustration and resentment can occur when individuals are   33
held responsible for attaining goals but do not control the means of achieving them. A pervasive problem in organizations is the difficulty of understanding the means of goal attainment, at least to a degree sufficient to allow accurate evaluation. Often the means of attaining traditional goals in organizations are so dependent on the efforts of others that specific goal setting can introduce frustration and resentment instead of productivity. Both the assembler on the line who is denied a production bonus because of faulty component parts and the executive who receives no recognition for superhuman efforts in the face of crippling economic conditions are likely to bear a good bit of hostility toward the organization. The assembler played no role in the purchase and acceptance of the faulty component parts; the executive had no influence over the delivered price of energy nor the level of the prime rate, nor over any factor that affected the economic climate.

Incongruence of goals with the means for attaining those goals serves   34
to frustrate instead of give impetus to productivity. It follows, then, that any goals set for individuals within an organization must provide for the means necessary to attain those goals. Organizations engaged in goal-setting activities have an obligation to develop a clear understanding of the means of goal attainment and to measure goal attainment according to criteria that reflect individual control.

The Effect of Participation in Goal Setting

It has been estimated that at one time or another over half of the Fortune   35
500 companies° have used a sysem of Management By Objectives. MBO

Fortune 500 companies—the 500 largest corporations in the United States, as identified by *Fortune* magazine.

is the most common participative goal-setting intervention in American companies. Users of MBO systems report that a number of unrelated factors often undermine the effectiveness of the system. It may be that reporting systems become so burdensome that the intention, and thus the integrity, of participation is sabotaged. It may be that the criteria for the measurement of goal attainment are meaningless for evaluating results. It may be that the disproportionate demands of an MBO system require its demise in order to free time and resources for tasks more central to the productive function of the organization. It may be that, in some organizations for some of the time, MBO aids the organization in achieving more effective and efficient production.

Whatever success a company has experienced with MBO, however, *36* it is clear that the success did not result from the participative aspects of goal setting. Edwin A. Locke argues persuasively that the salient difference in organizations is *goal setting per se*, not whether goals have been set participatively.[2] Whenever an organization introduces goal setting into an environment where no real attention has been directed toward the definition of its goals or the means of goal attainment, performance of individuals increases dramatically, regardless of the degree of participation involved.

Conclusion

The problem of productivity is not ephemeral. There will be no return *37* to the "normalcy" of a bygone era. For managers in the 1980s, today *is* normal. The challenge is a personal one—to manage better under the conditions of the new normalcy. It is a normalcy of shrinking and more expensive labor pools; a normalcy in which technological fixes will become more expensive and less immediately applicable to a majority of our economy's jobs. It is also one in which individual managers will make a far more important difference than in the past. An important step in making that difference is to teach individuals the worth of performing well. Goal-setting techniques help teach individuals that lesson. They define for individuals the difference between adequate and outstanding performance. For organizational survival in the 1980s, this distinction is critical.

Notes

[1] See, e.g., Edward E. Lawler, Jr., *Pay and Organizational Development* (Reading, Mass.: Addison-Wesley, 1981).

[2] Edwin A. Locke, "Participation in Decision-Making: One More Look," *Research in Organizational Behavior*, Vol. 1, ed. Barry A. Slaw (Greenwich, Conn.: JAI Press, 1979), pp. 265–339.

Rhetorical Analysis Through Annotation

Magazines frequently use graphic features such as different size print, boldface headlines, lists, and boxed sections to make the text more striking and easier to read.

Circle all special graphic features you can identify in this article.

Discuss the effect of each of these graphic features.

Discussion Questions

Interpreting the Text

1. What kind of problem is first presented in the article? Why would that be of interest to businesspeople? Why is so much space devoted to discussing technological solutions to productivity problems?

2. What kind of technological innovation is the shopping cart? Why did it provide great gains in food-selling productivity? Why are shopping carts mentioned in this article?

Considering the Issues

3. Which industries is the advice presented here most likely to apply to: the computer industry? automobile manufacturing? retailing? the restaurant industry? Discuss your reasons for thinking so.

4. Discuss the use of research materials in this article. Where is research mentioned? What points are the references to research making? Is the emphasis and presentation of the research changed from the original articles and textbook presentations? In what ways does the article rely on research that it does not mention? What things are added in this article beyond the research?

5. Among the four articles about goal setting presented here what differences have you noticed? Do they offer different accounts of the limitations and conditions under which goal setting works? Do they give different accounts of the reasons why it works? Do they treat the issue of who sets the goals differently?

6. Among the four goal-setting articles, what are the differences in emphasis and presentation between the two research articles and the two versions aimed at practical advice?

Writing Suggestions

1. How do you feel about the concept of productivity as a way of measuring your own work? Write a short personal essay to share your feelings with your class.

2. Write a letter of suggestion to a boss or supervisor you have had, urging the adoption of an improvement you explain in the letter.

3. As part of this course's discussion of the use of rhetorical techniques, write an essay analyzing the effect of the various graphic techniques in this selection.

The Burger King Corporation Productivity Program

William W. Swart

Case studies, such as the following, are of use to academics, students, and working businesspeople. For academic analyses, case studies provide concrete data about the factors that influence results and the effect of particular decisions. For students, textbook case studies illustrate theories and present practical problems for students to consider. For businesspeople case studies are a way of sharing experience and ideas. Writing a positive case study about your own company is also a way of boosting the image of your company and thereby improving your company's position in the marketplace. It is even a way of bragging about your own accomplishments.

The following case study written for a business audience combines a number of these functions. As part of a book called *Productivity Improvement: Case Studies of Proven Practice* (1981), this case study's most obvious purpose is to share practical ideas that have worked in real situations. When he wrote the article, William W. Swart was Director of Industrial Engineering and Operations Research at Burger King, so he had reasons to make Burger King and the productivity program he implemented look good. In reading this piece you must be careful to sort out the image building from the substantial information. Big words and near empty abstractions may make for less clarity, but they may work well for public relations.

The organization of this study differs from that of the other pieces in this section. Rather than being organized around advice or research, the article is based on the perception and solution of a problem. By giving you a glimpse of the inner workings of Burger King and a sense of how the managers perceive their own company, this study gives you a very different perspective of the company than presented by the television advertisements with singing cooks and dancing cashiers.

WHAT THE BURGER KING logo does for bringing customers into   *1*
the store and producing revenues, our productivity programs do for

decreasing our costs. We have grown substantially over the years in both size and image that is reflected in the changing facade of our units. All the changes in architectural properties that our stores have taken on over the years are made with one concept in mind: increasing productivity.

Let's contrast Burger King with other Fortune 500 corporations such 2 as Allegheny Ludlum Industries, with sales of $1.55 billion per year, or Grumman Aircraft, with 1979 sales of $1.49 billion. You might ask, what does this have to do with Burger King? Well, directly it doesn't, except that as a system, our sales are substantially higher. We sell more dollars worth of hamburgers, sandwiches, and french fries than either of those companies do in steel or aircraft. Specifically, we sell roughly 600 million "Whopper" sandwiches in one year and a like quantity of associated products such as french fries and drinks. So, in that sense, we are a large corporation. We are the second largest restaurant corporation in the world, second only to McDonald's.

Although we are bigger than Grumman or Allegheny Ludlum in unit 3 sales, we have more in common with them than one might think. You may think of us as a service industry or a restaurant industry. However, in terms of productivity, Burger King is really a manufacturing industry. Our philosophy allies us more closely to a General Motors assembly plant than to the typical restaurant.

Special Characteristics of the Burger King Corporation

As a corporation, Burger King has some interesting characteristics. Our 4 production facilities consist of what in effect constitutes a number of assembly lines. In terms of the size of our individual facilities, we are not large. What makes us large is that we have approximately 2,800 plants across the United States plus a few more in other countries of the world. We employ about 130,000 people. It is not unusual for our plants to manufacture more than 1,000 hamburgers an hour. This typically happens right after having sold only 50 in the previous hour—and may drop off to 50 in the subsequent hour. Furthermore, you cannot store the product for tomorrow, because the shelf life of the product is only 10 minutes. Consequently, you cannot take advantage of lulls in your demand to replenish your inventories. We must be able to produce whatever is demanded when it is demanded.

Burger King must deliver large volumes in short periods of time. We 5 originally organized our stores to take advantage of mass production efficiencies by organizing for assembly-line operations. Our product flow starts with raw material inventories and progresses through in-process storage and through various production processes. The production line involves the manufacturing process of grilling buns and broiling meat; preassembly into "undressed" sandwiches as output from the broiler; product transformation in the microwave oven; some more assembly to dress the sandwich; packaging; and, finally, end-product inventory.

We originally designed our stores to be efficient with this production *6* process in mind, but we have made some changes since then. We introduced a new product line, the specialty sandwich. When you introduce new products or an entirely new product line, the efficiencies that you originally enjoyed tend to become liabilities instead of assets. In order to accommodate these new products, we had to modify, augment, and redesign our original production facilities. This created many problems that had to be solved in order to maintain our productivity.

Not only did we introduce a new product line but we scored a classical *7* marketing coup when we introduced our "Have It Your Way" concept. This concept means, for example, that if you do not like onions, you can walk into one of our stores and ask for your product without onions. What does that do to productivity? All of a sudden you go from a mass-production, assembly-line operation to almost a customizing, job-shop operation. So by introducing the specialty sandwiches and various marketing campaigns, such as "Have It Your Way," we created severe production problems.

A review of the performance of Burger King Corporation for the past *8* several years shows that the demand for our products has increased dramatically. This growth is in part the result of the increased well-being of the American consumer. We are able to predict what people will spend on food away from home. This is closely correlated to their disposable income, which has gone up dramatically. The fast-food segment is the fastest growing part of the restaurant industry.

When we look at the future, even with the ongoing recession and the *9* continuing energy problems, we find that we are going to continue growing. In 1976, Burger King system sales were approximately $750 million; in 1980, we expect to top $2 billion. By 1983, we expect to continue that growth by increasing average sales per restaurant from $750,000 to $1 million. We expect to increase the number of restaurants from 2,800 to 3,700 in those three years. Also, we expect to have 250 restaurants abroad. So the future can be envisioned as one of constant growth.

What will that constant growth coupled with our increasingly com- *10* plex manufacturing environment do to us? We clearly cannot service a constantly increasing number of customers with our present methods and facilities. The first step in our plan to meet the future is to increase our productivity in everything that we do today and then to plan our capacity expansion in the most productive manner possible. This joint attention to current and future productivity will be the key to our future success.

Productivity Planning at Burger King

The foundations of our productivity planning and improvement ac- *11* tivities are the integration of the industrial engineering and operations research functions. The time study, methods, improvement, facility layout, work sampling, and human engineering aspects of the industrial engineering function are the grass roots of the productivity effort. The modeling and systems analysis aspects of the operations research function provide the overall framework used to coordinate, direct, and evaluate the industrial engineering efforts from a total systems point of view.

The crucial role of models in our efforts can perhaps best be under- *12* stood when you consider that our productive capacity is deployed over 2,800 restaurants. Consequently, it is impossible to focus individual attention on every manufacturing facility. We must bring our manufacturing facilities to a central location for analysis, as opposed to taking our expertise to each of our individual facilities. For this reason, we use simulation models to evaluate alternatives that will increase our productivity. We employ optimization models to minimize our cost. We use statistical models to detect the true effects of changes in procedures, equipment, layout, or manning on our ability to service customers better. When we look at the use of these types of models, we are concerned essentially with two levels of productivity analysis:

1. Increasing the productivity in our individual stores.
2. Increasing the productivity of the service functions that provide materials and other services to the stores.

In the area of increasing the productivity of our overall service func- *13* tions to the stores, we have, for example, developed models in our procurement function that optimize our meat-buying process. In one week we use approximately 3 million pounds of hamburger. By focusing on how that particular purchasing function is performed, we were able to save approximately one cent per pound. By this one application of what we call productivity analysis, we have been able to save the corporation more than $1 million a year.

Not only are we focusing on the individual product-buying optimi- *14* zation; we are also increasing our productivity through improving our distribution. We have our own distribution fleet, called Distron. We now have the ability to improve our productivity by optimizing our costs for transportation from our distribution centers to our individual warehouses. That activity adds another $200,000 per year savings.

When we think of the implementation of increasing productivity at *15* the store level, we think of increasing what we refer to as people productivity. As is generally acknowledged, there is a tremendous amount to be gained by soliciting input from people who are actually performing the work. We have developed an organized process in order to obtain franchisee° or store input about suggestions to increase productivity. Furthermore, through the use of our models it has been possible to test and evaluate productivity improvement suggestions. Two areas in which we have been particularly successful are labor productivity and drive-through operations.

In the area of labor productivity, it is important to realize that we are *16* at a point where labor threatens to become the largest cost element in our balance sheet. With the new labor laws, our wages have risen from just a couple dollars an hour a few years back to well over $3.25 an hour now, and wages continue to rise. We cannot pass on that labor cost to our customers and still maintain our leadership in this industry. Consequently, we are performing a substantial amount of work in improving our labor standards.

Industrial engineering efforts are continually employed in studying *17* methods and procedures for integrating the store layout and equipment characteristics with the most productive positioning and staffing strategy at every conceivable sales level. These results must also assure that our product quality and service standards are met. The way we go about that is through a systematic analysis of all types of stores. We have approximately ten different layouts in our 2,800 stores. In the past, these stores were staffed without a lot of attention to labor cost because labor was relatively cheap. Now, that has changed. We are examining and analyzing the integrated operation of each store through our store simulation models. This process starts out by simulating the least staffing possible and then systematically subjecting the simulated store to an increased sales level. At some point, we are then able to observe where the bottlenecks that impede productivity occur. We explore the alternatives of adding additional people at the various positions in our manufacturing facility or using different equipment. On the basis of the results of our models, we determine where the next person or equipment change should be added. By exploring each alternative, we can observe how the store operates by additional staffing or equipment improvement.

We are also able to observe the effects of these changes on our cashiers *18* and other parts in the sales area. We can also observe the effects on our production system and our customers, including how long it will take to obtain orders. This is the single most important determinant of our performance in the competitive marketplace. What we have accomplished so far indicates a savings of well over 1 percent of sales a year in labor productivity through systematic analysis and fine tuning of

---

Franchisee—the owner of a local outlet who pays a fee to the franchisor (e.g., Burger King, Carvel, or Midas Muffler) for the right to use the brand name and sell the standard product.

labor utilization. It has also resulted in improved customer service and product quality.

In another aspect of improving our labor productivity, models have 19 been used to develop a more effective crew scheduling system. This is an area of particular difficulty, since our demand can fluctuate as much as 1,000 percent within a half-hour. This demand fluctuation also has an impact on the amount of labor required in each of those half-hours. Unfortunately, it is not possible to hire someone to come in just for the half-hour you might need him. Most states have laws that require an employee to work for at least a certain number of hours. Our models allow us to improve labor productivity by matching actual people to our labor requirements during the day so as to minimize the amount of excess labor in the store.

The productivity of our drive-through operations has been consider- 20 ably enhanced with the aid of franchisee input together with corporate personnel. An early examination of Burger King's drive-through speed of service versus that of Wendy's and McDonald's revealed that all three corporations provided comparable speed of service. On the basis of this information, Burger King defined the drive-through area as one where a competitive advantage could be attained over our major competitors if the speed in which customers could be served could be increased without imperiling food quality.

Extensive method and procedure studies culminated in a list of 21 changes in the way the drive-through operated. Although none of the changes was revolutionary, the joint effect of all changes resulted in a 30 percent reduction of the time it took to service a customer. At the drive-through, this improvement in service capacity is tantamount to an increase in drive-through sales capacity. Since this was achieved without additional resources being required, it constituted a substantial net gain in productivity.

Aiming for Future Productivity Growth

After optimizing productivity within our store, the next step in our 22 productivity program focuses on future growth. Specifically, we concern ourselves with optimizing our capacity expansion over time to meet our growing needs. This is accomplished through a program we call Productivity Planning for Profit, which, like the rest of our productivity program, is based on the results of our industrial engineering and operations research efforts.

Our findings have been placed in a kit that is easily understandable at 23 the store level. The computer models have provided the foundations for improving the sales projections and for developing and evaluating productivity improvements at various stages of growth. The results have been embodied in easy-to-use kits that are obtainable by our franchisees. We provide training sessions in each of our ten regions for our district managers. These district managers, after being trained, play the role of productivity consultants.

The first phase of the productivity consultant–franchisee interface is a *24* productivity audit for the store during which diagnostic tools are made available and used to assess the productivity level of the store. As one example of the diagnostic tools, corporate service standards for stores suggest that, on the average, a customer should receive an order within three minutes from the time of entry. Furthermore, with our particular production capabilities, we should be able to service a car in 30 seconds or less after the car reaches our drive-through window. If any of these is not achieved at a particular store, then there is an indication that the store has productivity problems.

Our productivity planning-for-profit kit enables a store manager or *25* franchisee to diagnose why he may not be meeting company standards. It helps pinpoint the problem to a specific area of the store (such as the counter) or any of the production stations (such as the fry station, drink station, and so on).

Once we have analyzed the store's current productivity and have *26* provided suggestions for meeting standards, then we focus on the future. The productivity consultant works with the individual store operator to plan sales on a year-to-year basis. We project sales increases attributable to inflation and real growth. The resulting information is applied to an *improvement decision path*. This indicates to the store operator at what sales level he is likely to reach certain bottlenecks. It also indicates what investments will be needed to increase productivity. For example, we have found that when a particular type of store reaches approximately $700,000 a year in sales, the productivity can be significantly enhanced by introduction of kitchen read-out devices that are tied to the cash register. In most of our stores, orders are transmitted to the kitchen by a microphone. Once a store reaches a level of about $700,000 a year, there is so much confusion in the kitchen because of microphone message transmission during busy periods that productivity actually declines. We have developed a series of printers/CRT devices that can be tied to the cash register, which will communicate the order to the production facilities in the kitchen.

Thus, through the application of the improvement decision path, it *27* can be determined what has to be done at various sales levels in order to maintain the productivity of the store and prevent long waiting lines from occurring. For each suggested action, we provide an explanation of why the productivity improvement is needed, what the benefit will be in terms of the additional sales that can be realized, how long it will take that particular improvement to pay back its cost, and where these particular improvements can be purchased.

Given the special relationship that exists between a franchisor and *28* franchisee, it is preferable that our franchisee voluntarily adopt any programs that are developed. So we work hard to sell our productivity programs to them. They must be convinced that the sequence of productivity improvements and investments that result from the joint effort between the productivity consultant and the franchisee will yield an overall contribution to the store's operating profit.

Once we have performed this type of bottleneck analysis for one   29
particular year, we incorporate the investment into our overall profit analysis. We indicate how this particular productivity improvement will have an impact upon the net store operating profit for that particular year. We do this for the entire sequence of five years. On the basis of that, we develop what we refer to as a store operation plan, which is reviewed on a yearly basis.

Using these concepts, we expect that through productivity we can   30
become the industry leader. We expect to increase both our top-line and bottom-line dollars. Finally, we expect to be in a growth posture which will assure us of attaining that goal.

Rhetorical Analysis Through Annotation

This selection often uses long words and managerial jargon to describe simple events.

Underline passages that you think can be written more simply. In the margin rewrite these passages using simpler language.

Referring to specific passages, discuss why you think the author of the selection chose the more difficult wording. What would be the effect of the simpler wording? Which choice do you find more appropriate and effective?

Discussion Questions

Interpreting the Text

1. Swart writes, "When you introduce new products or an entirely new product line, the efficiencies that you originally enjoyed tend to become liabilities instead of assets." What exactly does that mean? What are the practical consequences of this idea for Burger King when they add specialty items to their traditional burger production? How may other kinds of fast food operations, such as pizza or soft ice cream franchises, be affected by new product lines? Can you think of examples from other industries?

2. What is meant by simulation models, optimization models, and statistical models? What are each of these models likely to tell you?

3. What general and specific improvements were implemented at Burger King? What specific problems were these intended to address? How does the essay make these improvements seem more broad ranging than they are?

Considering the Issues

4. Swart writes of "integrating the store layout and equipment characteristics with the most productive positioning and staffing strategy." Based on the dis-

cussion here and what you know about Burger King and other fast food outlets, discuss specific examples of this idea in operation. How may this idea apply to other types of business such as supermarkets, gas stations, or manufacturing plants? Compare the layouts of small mom-and-pop stores with chain-store outlets. What may account for the differences?

5. What parts of the improvements come from a Taylor efficiency approach, from a reward-motivation model, and from a Locke goal-setting approach? Which approach is relied on the most?

Writing Suggestions

1. Based on any experiences you may have had working at a Burger King or similar place, evaluate the effectiveness of the productivity approach suggested here. You may wish to discuss motivation and morale in such an environment. Imagine you are writing this evaluation for a productivity consultant who has just visited your workplace and has asked for your opinion.

2. As part of this class's discussion of rhetorical practices, analyze the ways in which Swart attempts to make himself and his company look good.

3. Write a lifestyles feature article for a local newspaper on a behind-the-scenes look at Burger King.

Unit Writing Suggestions

1. Write an essay comparing and evaluating the several different presentations of goal setting. What are the differences among them and why do these differences appear? For you as a reader, which was most informative, persuasive, enjoyable, or effective? Why? This essay is part of your own class discussion of what constitutes good writing.

2. What changes and elaborations occurred in the concept of goal setting as time passed? Write a short essay as part of your class discussion of how knowledge grows through a group process.

3. Based on the selections here, write an essay for a class in business management, discussing and evaluating different approaches to improving productivity: work efficiency, rewards, goal setting, and intrinsic accomplishment.

4. For a class discussion of the ideas raised in this unit, write a personal essay on "Raising My Productivity as a Student: What Works

for Me." Or write an essay on "Productivity—Is That What School (or Life) Is All About?"

5. Write a newspaper article on "How to Live a More Productive Life." The piece can be humorous or it can offer earnest advice.

6. For the editorial page of your school newspaper write a column on "Shoveling Coal, Hauling Logs, or Collecting Paychecks." The editorial should discuss what kinds of tasks, goals, and motivations the workplace will hold for students after graduation.

UNIT

5

NATURAL SCIENCES
The Greenhouse Effect: A Change in the Weather

The news media inform us daily of major scientific discoveries that may change our lives. New diseases and new cures, fundamental particles and recombined DNA, exploding galaxies and black holes, supercomputers and superconductors—all seem suddenly thrust on the public, simply on the word of some scientists. Scientists' words have great authority in our society and are rarely questioned by the lay public, but the scientific claims are not absolute truths that emerge spontaneously from the mouths of all-wise scientists. Such claims emerge from a process of exploration, data gathering, calculation, assertion, and argument, where any claim is open to criticism. Current scientific beliefs are only the best answers that the community of scientists can come up with and convince each other of, based on the best current theories and available evidence. New problems, new theories, and new evidence can change the understanding and beliefs held by the scientific community.

The warming of the Earth's atmosphere by what is popularly called the "greenhouse effect" is one of those newsworthy scientific findings that is likely to be of increasing importance to our lives over the next few decades. As the world industrializes, the increasing amount of carbon dioxide in our atmosphere resulting from the burning of coal, oil, and gas in large amounts creates a greenhouse-like atmosphere, letting in solar energy quite freely while at the same time absorbing heat radiating from the earth. In the coming years the warming of the atmosphere will affect climate, agriculture, sea level, and health; therefore it is of great interest to governments, corporations, farmers, and all the rest of us.

This section explores the greenhouse effect: what it is, why it occurs, and why it matters to us. More importantly, it explores how scientists gather ideas and evidence, form hypotheses, come to conclusions, argue with each other, and explore the consequences of their findings. We will see how and why scientists communicate with each other and with the general society.

First we look at how the idea gained public attention through news stories such as the report in the *New York Times*; we then trace the story back to the heart of the scientific community. The next article from a special interest magazine (the *EPA Journal*) offers a more detailed explanation but still does not require that you have any special scientific background to understand it. A selection from a college textbook illustrates how scientists communicate necessary background concepts to scientists in training, that is, students. With these explanations and background concepts, you will be able to examine some of the original scientific articles that present, argue over, and explore the consequences of the greenhouse effect. Selections from congressional testimony and a policy conference illustrate how scientists can and do dramatize their findings for nonspecialists to encourage appropriate social action. These calls to action become translated into government policy through political documents such as the final letter from forty-two senators to the president of the United States.

As you move through the different selections, you see not only a difference in the depth of the presentation but a difference in the very nature of the communication. For example, the newspaper report of a scientific announcement emphasizes the novelty of the information presented and elaborates on the unexpected consequences this is likely to have for our lives. The question and answer format of the magazine article allows a careful explanation of the greenhouse phenomenon. The congressional testimony, policy paper, and senatorial letter dramatize the importance of this phenomenon for the future of our country. The textbook develops the concepts necessary for a full understanding in a step-by-step exposition. Finally, the actual scientific papers engage in argument using evidence, theory, and the results of computer models to make their claims persuasive.

Curiously, the closer we move to the heart of scientific discussion, the less authority the scientists hold. In the newspaper and general-circulation magazine stories, the word of the scientist makes the reported claims seem true. Scientists are treated there as the ones who know, the ones who are sharing their knowledge with us. Before Congress, which is made up of specialists in public policy and which has its own science advisors, the scientists offer evidence of their findings and argue the seriousness of the situation. The textbook must present an orderly, logical construction that convinces students of the rationality of the knowledge and offers the students the possibility of command of the knowledge. Thus, the authority transfers to the students as they gain control of the knowledge. Finally, in the debate among scientific peers, claims only gain authority from convincing evidence and arguments that answer all criticisms and appear stronger than those that have been offered in support of all counterclaims. Scientists must earn their authority for each claim by convincing other scientists.

In looking at how scientists discuss issues you may be surprised by the variety of ways they communicate. Articles are not tightly tied to the narrow model of experimental report you may have learned in laboratory courses. Various kinds of evidence are brought to bear on each claim, including nonexperimental observations, approximations, and data from historical archives. Arguments crop up over the best ways to gather and interpret evidence. But perhaps the most unusual feature of this set of articles is the way generalizations are formed through modeling.

Most of the claims presented here are not based on a precise and complete account of what goes on in the atmosphere—a far too complicated task given our current tools and knowledge. Rather, the scientists develop their claims through the use of climate models that are mathematical representations of the relationships among elements of the climate system: air, winds, water, and solar radiation. Climate models include many simplifications, especially where processes, such as the physics of cloud formation, are poorly understood. The equations are then solved to simulate today's climate and the climate caused by an increase in carbon dioxide in the atmosphere. Rather than following the traditional approach of obtaining limited findings from a clean, controlled laboratory set-up, the model-builders try to achieve a grasp, albeit imperfect, of the whole messy world. The advent of computers has made such modeling more widespread in the sciences, as the computers become capable of rapidly making the extensive calculations required to gain results from the modeling equations.

Another feature of modern science that may surprise you is the importance of collaborative research groups. Several of the articles presented here come from a single group that has worked on this problem. This research group, sponsored by the United States government through NASA (the National Aeronautics and Space Administration), has developed a research program to study the greenhouse effect and its implications. The National Science Foundation and the National Oceanographic and Atmospheric Administration also sponsor major research groups working on climate models to study potential effects of climate change. Because the research is so expensive, requiring the cooperation of many scientists, massive amounts of computer power, and extensive data gathering (much of it through satellites), a few groups have tended to dominate the work. Centralization of research frequently occurs in modern science when large resources and massive undertakings are involved or when government interests are at stake. In this country much scientific research is funded or even directly run by government agencies. Thus congressional testimony by scientists serves not only to warn the government of the need for action but also to remind Congress of the need for continued funding of large scientific research projects.

The need to continue studying the global warming trend is great. One scientist, Wallace S. Broecker, put it this way in the research journal *Nature*:

The inhabitants of planet Earth are quietly conducting a gigantic environmental experiment. So vast and so sweeping will be the consequences that, were it brought before any responsible council for approval, it would be firmly rejected. Yet it goes on with little interference from any jurisdiction or nation. The experiment in question is the release of CO_2 and other so-called "greenhouse gases" to the atmosphere. Because these releases are largely by-products of energy and food production, we have little choice but to let the experiment continue. We can perhaps slow its pace by eliminating frivolous production and by making more efficient use of energy from fossil fuels. But beyond this we can only prepare ourselves to cope with its effects.

E.P.A. Report Says Earth Will Heat Up Beginning in 1990's

Philip Shabecoff

Most of us find out about scientific discoveries through the newspaper or television news, in between fast-breaking political stories, economic reports, and accounts of battles in distant countries. Science becomes part of the news, part of the turmoil and change of our daily world, even though scientific investigations are frequently slow processes, examining ancient or even timeless phenomena. Scientists have been looking at fundamental particles, rocks, our atmosphere, and viruses for many years; even more, these particles, gases, rocks, and viruses were around quite a while before scientists began looking at them.

Yet a new claim in science is news, for it brings some phenomenon to our attention, so that we can think and act on it. According to recent studies, the conditions that result in the heating of our atmosphere have been developing since the beginning of the industrial revolution, but until recent studies brought the climatic change to our attention we did not notice it and could not begin to think about its impact on us. Scientific awareness of such problems is the first step toward public awareness.

Thus news announcements often have a triple time scale: the immediate publicity time scale concerning the discovery and its announcement; the longer research time-scale; and the even longer time-scale of the phenomena being investigated. The publicity surrounding the announcement of a discovery turns slowly evolving nature into today's news. Scientists themselves help to create this sense of fast-breaking news through public reports, press conferences, and dramatic announcements at conferences. Scientists seek publicity for some of their findings both because they believe the findings require public action and because they need to garner additional resources to continue their work. Findings that do not need public action or funding are less likely to receive such wide publicity. In the case at hand, however, scientists at the Environmental Protection Agency created a dramatic report that did become news.

In order to transform the long-term climate change into a clear and immediate threat that makes news, Philip Shabecoff, science reporter for the *New York Times*, must explain scientific concepts and slower developing research projects to readers who may have little scientific training. In this article from October 18, 1983, diagrams, graphs, and explanatory paragraphs help make it clear why the quiet worlds of nature and research erupt into everyday affairs through the medium of the newspaper.

THE ENVIRONMENTAL PROTECTION AGENCY warned in a *1*
report made available today that the warming of the earth known as the
"greenhouse effect" will begin in the 1990's.

John S. Hoffman, director of strategic studies for the agency, said in *2*
an interview today: "We are trying to get people to realize that changes
are coming sooner than they expected. Major changes will be here by
the years 1990 to 2000, and we have to learn how to live with them."

The report, which was completed last month by Mr. Hoffman's *3*
office, said the warming trend, the result of a buildup of carbon dioxide
in the atmosphere, is both imminent and inevitable. In the next century,
it warns, the world will have to learn to deal with major changes in
climate patterns, with disrupted food production and with significantly
higher coastal waters.

The greenhouse effect, Mr. Hoffman said, "means a lot more than *4*
the temperature getting a little warmer." "There could be big changes,"
he said. "New York City could have a climate like Daytona Beach, Fla.,
by 2100."

Although private scientists have made similar predictions for years, *5*
this report is the first warning by the Federal Government that the
"greenhouse effect" is not a theoretical problem but a threat whose first
effects will be felt within a few years.

The report said that there was still considerable uncertainty about the *6*
speed and size of the temperature changes but that the best estimates
now suggested that global average temperatures could increase 2 degrees
centigrade, or 3.6 degrees Fahrenheit, by the year 2040.

By the year 2100, the increase could total 5 degrees centigrade, or 9 *7*
degrees Fahrenheit. Such increases in the average temperature of the
earth would be accompanied by increases up to three times as large in
the polar regions, which could cause the polar ice caps to melt rapidly.

After examining trends in atmospheric patterns and fuel uses, the *8*
agency said that no strategy for mitigating the problem, even a total
ban on the use of fossil fuels, could do more than delay the warming
effect a few years.

Fossil fuels are the major source of the carbon dioxide, which lets *9*
sunlight enter the atmosphere and heat the earth but inhibits the escape
of heat radiation into space. The report strongly recommended that
planning start now for dealing with the threat.

"A soberness and sense of urgency should underlie our response to a *10*
greenhouse warming," the report concluded.

The projected average temperature changes do not necessarily reflect *11*
the disruptive effects of wide seasonal swings that could bring extremes
of heat or drought or rainfall, Mr. Hoffman said.

He said the report, written by Stephen Seidel and Dale Keyes, was *12*
reviewed by about 100 scientists before publication and most of the
criticism was that the projections of the amount of warming were "too
conservative."

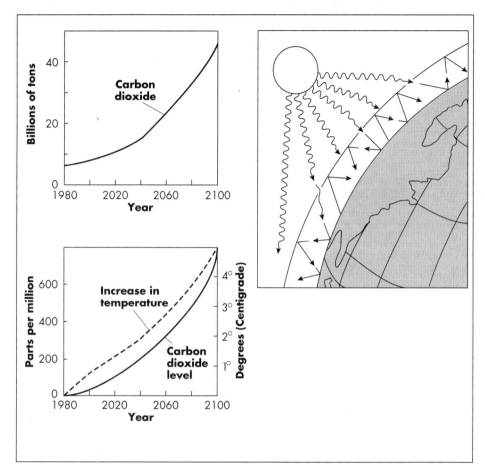

Figure 1. Atmospheric carbon dioxide and the "greenhouse effect," based on most likely (mid-range) scenario.
a. Projected emission of carbon dioxide in billions of tons.
b. Effect of carbon dioxide level on atmospheric temperature.
c. Carbon dioxide, mostly from fuel-burning, traps heat radiation from earth and atmosphere, preventing dissipation into space.
Source: Environmental Protection Agency. Rendering: Copyright © 1983 by The New York Times Company. Reprinted by permission.

Some Specifics Are Uncertain

The report, which examined computer projections of different ways of *13* dealing with the carbon dioxide problem, including the management of fuel use, said more research was needed. Uncertainties include the timing and size of the warming trend and where and how specific areas of the earth will be affected, the report said. More also needs to be found out about the impact of other "greenhouse gases," including methane° and nitrous oxide.°

But the report included this warning: "Our findings support the 14 conclusion that a global greenhouse warming is neither trivial nor just a long-range problem."

Noting that only a few decades remain to plan for and cope with the 15 full impact of the warming trend, the report said that "changes by the end of the 21st century could be catastrophic taken in the context of today's world."

"Innovative thinking and strategy-building are sorely needed," the 16 report said and added, "Means must be found to explore the advantages of climate change where they appear, and to minimize the adverse effects."

Mr. Hoffman said the change could benefit some areas, for example 17 by increasing rainfall for agriculture. But the adverse effects could cause economic disruptions costing billions of dollars, he said. Some of these effects could be mitigated with proper planning, he asserted.

Impact on Coastal Areas

Mr. Hoffman said another study by the environmental agency examined 18 the potential impact on coastal areas of a higher sea level caused by the melting of polar snow and ice. The study said that in Charleston, S.C., for example, an increase in the sea level of four to seven feet by the year 2100 was probable. By 2075, the study found, the rising sea level would cost the city $1.25 billion in lost residential and industrial buildings and lost land.

The report said that with proper planning and action, including plan- 19 ning of new building sites, building bulkheads, contouring the land and other measures, the total economic loss could be reduced to $440 million.

On Thursday, the National Research Council of the National Acad- 20 emy of Sciences is planning to make public a major study on the increase in carbon dioxide in the atmosphere.

Rhetorical Analysis Through Annotation

News reports usually identify the who, what, where, and when of the story in the opening sentence or paragraph, called the "lead." These items are then typically expanded one by one in the ensuing paragraphs. Because of the double time scale of the story (fast-breaking report and slower natural phenomenon), the lead contains two levels of who, what, where, and when. Both sets are then developed in each ensuing paragraph.

Methane—an odorless, colorless, flammable gas; a "greenhouse" gas.   Nitrous oxide— a colorless, organic gas, sometimes used as an anesthetic; a "greenhouse" gas.

Circle and label each who, what, where, and when in the lead. Identify whether it belongs to the fast-breaking report (*r*) part of the story—which tells of human actors and actions—or the slower natural phenomenon (*p*) part of the story—which tells of inanimate objects.

Label each ensuing paragraph as to which part of the lead paragraph it elaborates.

Discuss how the story fills out both levels of events, creating a news event out of a slowly unfolding process. Discuss what happens to the middle timescale of research in this story, and why it seems to drop out of sight.

Discussion Questions

Interpreting the Text

1. What is the greenhouse effect? On what does it have an impact? How big is that impact likely to be?

2. What do the graphs and illustrations demonstrate? Why are they included? How do they relate to the printed text?

3. What are the uncertainties concerning the greenhouse effect? Why do these uncertainties exist? Of what importance are they? Do they detract from the overall certainty that the phenomenon exists and is important?

4. Who are the individuals involved in presenting this report? What is their involvement in the issue? What is Hoffman's relationship to other scientists involved in this issue?

5. What are the implications of the greenhouse phenomenon for public planning and policy?

Considering the Issues

6. What impact do you think the greenhouse effect may have on your life? Were you aware of the greenhouse effect before reading this? How do you feel about the predictions presented here?

7. What might be the impact on your community of a four degree Fahrenheit mean annual temperature increase? Why might just a few degrees temperature increase make a serious difference?

8. Which groups or individuals in our society and in other countries might be particularly concerned about or interested in this report? Is there sufficient information in this report to meet their needs? Where can they go for further relevant details? Which groups or individuals might not be so concerned?

9. Why is it important that the Environmental Protection Agency has issued this report rather than individual scientists? What interest might the EPA have in publicizing these findings?

10. What other science stories in the recent past have had similar implications for our daily life? Were they reported in similar ways? Are there other findings that might have great impact but which are underreported? Are there other

significant findings you are aware of that have been ignored in the press because they have no impact on daily life? Have some insignificant, low-impact findings been overreported? How do you account for these differences in reporting?

Writing Suggestions

1. Rewrite this report for television news, then for radio news. Then write a short commentary for this course discussing the differences in the form of the report for the three different media.

2. Invent an outrageous, science fiction-type discovery made by scientists. Write a newspaper report announcing this discovery and making clear its consequences for the ordinary citizen.

3. For a regional magazine that describes life in your city, county, or state, write an article describing what life will be like in your area in a hundred years with the temperature increased by almost ten degrees Fahrenheit. Consider secondary effects as well, such as changes in health, vegetation, and sea level.

4. For a forum on environmental pollution, write a speech that describes the climatic change as a result of atmospheric pollution.

The Greenhouse Effect: An Explanation

Dr. David Rind

Nontechnical magazines such as the *EPA Journal* are more likely to explain issues of public concern than to report fast-breaking developments. While pursuing the issue in greater depth than daily or weekly periodicals, these monthly and quarterly journals still carefully define all terms and explain all ideas fully from the beginning. Because the articles wish to give a detailed and accurate picture of what we currently know, they are careful to qualify statements and not to exaggerate the threats or consequences of the scientific findings.

In such articles on scientific issues for the general educated reader, the scientist is often presented as an authority—the one who knows and can explain the facts, the one who can sort the certain out from the less certain, the one who can predict the consequences. The question and answer interview format used in the following article from 1986 helps bring out that authority. An anonymous journalist asks the questions while the authoritative Dr. David Rind provides the answers. David Rind is a scientist on a team that developed one of the climate models that predict the greenhouse effect. He also is a joint author of several of the more technical papers that follow.

THE GREENHOUSE EFFECT HAS caught the imagination of the 1
general populace in the last decade, and the respected, generally conservative scientific establishment has become associated with relatively dire
predictions of future climate change. How much is actually known about
the greenhouse effect? Can we really establish how climate will change,
and when? By separating "hard" science—that which can be verified and
is considered well understood—from scientific theory or estimate we
can investigate how likely a near-term alteration in climate really is. We
explore this subject through responses to a series of questions.

Do We Really Understand the "Greenhouse" Effect?

The greenhouse effect is the name for the physical process where energy 2
from the sun passes through the atmosphere relatively freely, while heat
radiating from the earth is absorbed by particular gases in the atmosphere. Although a few uncertainties remain, we can generally calculate
very accurately the radiation absorption° by different gases. When the
concentration of a gas changes, we know how much more energy is
being absorbed. This additional absorption by itself warms the planet;
for example, doubling the concentration of carbon dioxide in the atmosphere would eventually lead to an increase of the global air temperature by 1.2°C, without any other changes in the climate system. What
we do not know, however, is how the rest of the system will react.
Current models predict that the warming due to increased carbon dioxide will also increase the evaporation of water vapor from the ocean;
because water vapor is itself a greenhouse gas, this will warm the planet
further. In addition, as more snow and ice melt in the warming climate
less energy from the sun will be reflected back to space (snow and ice
are very good reflectors) which promotes further warming. These are
examples of "positive feedbacks," and both of these system responses
are very likely to occur, although we cannot be sure of the magnitude
of the changes. The models also predict that cloud cover will change in
such a way as to cause even more warming. Clouds are not yet well
understood, and the predicted changes are very uncertain. But the net
result of these different processes in the models is to amplify the direct
doubled CO_2 warming by more than a factor of three, producing a 4°C
temperature rise. Yet it is only the initial greenhouse effect due to
increased CO_2, or increases in other trace gases,° which we know with
great confidence.

Radiation absorption—the process whereby the atmosphere retains energy from the
sun's rays.   Trace gases—gases found only in small amounts in the atmosphere; a
number of these gases increase the greenhouse effect of the atmosphere.

Can We Use the Temperatures on Other Planets to Determine What the Feedback of the System Will Be?

The atmospheres of other nearby planets validate the general concept of   3
the greenhouse theory, especially in a qualitative° sense, but they cannot
tell us what the magnitude of the changes on Earth will be. Venus, with
a massive atmosphere composed essentially of carbon dioxide, has a
surface air temperature almost 500°C warmer than would be expected
without a greenhouse effect. Mars, with a very thin atmosphere and
thus little greenhouse capacity, has an observed temperature close to the
expected; and Earth, with intermediate amounts of greenhouse gases, is
about 30°C warmer than it would be otherwise. The differences among
the planets are very large, and cannot really be used to estimate sensitivity to small changes in greenhouse capacity. Furthermore, as noted
above, the big uncertainty lies in the magnitude of the system response,
or its "feedbacks"—the most important feedbacks all involve the reaction
of processes having to do with water, and the other planets have no
freestanding water.

Are Greenhouse Gases Increasing?

An atmospheric monitoring system established in 1958 has measured   4
systematically increasing concentrations of carbon dioxide over the last
28 years. We also believe that concentrations have increased since the
turn of the century, although we are less certain about the magnitude
of that change. Chlorofluorocarbons are artificially generated gases with
greenhouse capacity which are known to be increasing; they have no
natural sources, and probably did not exist in the atmosphere prior to
the last few decades. Recent measurements indicate that other greenhouse gases, such as methane and nitrous oxide, also are increasing,
although we are not sure how long this has been happening. As we are
not sure of the reason for their increase, we have less confidence in their
long-term trend. In addition, greenhouse gases of which we are only
now becoming aware may be increasing, such as some of the more
exotic man-made chlorine-fluorine compounds.

Is the Temperature Record of the Past Century Consistent with This Greenhouse Gas Increase?

Estimates are that the global average surface air temperature has in-   5
creased by about 0.6°C in the past 100 years; available records are
uneven. Temperature recording stations were much less abundant 100

Qualitative—describing characteristics in a general way, as opposed to quantitative.

years ago, and large portions of the globe were poorly sampled, especially in the Southern Hemisphere. Even today, full global coverage is
not available. The record, such as it is, does not indicate a ubiquitous°
warming since that time, since the Northern Hemisphere has apparently
cooled from the 1940s into the early 1970s. This cooling is inconsistent
with the concept of greenhouse warming, but it may be due to other
climate perturbations° (such as variations in the solar constant or volcanic
aerosols)° or simply represent internal variability within the system. The
overall warming for the past century is the right order of magnitude of
the expected greenhouse effect; however, due to uncertainties in the
actual temperature change, in the climate feedback factor, in the actual
CO_2 amount in 1880, and in the rate of ocean heat uptake (which slows
down the atmospheric warming), we cannot be more precise in determining what the expected warming should have been. Similarly, due to
the other uncertainties, we cannot use the record to establish what the
climate feedback factor really is.

Are Current Models Adequate to Allow Us to Forecast Climate Change?

Numerical models, called general circulation models, calculate the re- 6
sponse of the climate system to the increases in trace gases. The three
current models all estimate that the doubled CO_2 climate will have a
global average temperature 4°C warmer than today. They are thus all
calculating similar climate feedback factors, but as the different models
handle many processes similarly, the unanimity does not guarantee accuracy. The treatment of cloud cover in all the models represents a
major uncertainty. The models also show differences in the seasonal and
latitudinal distributions of the calculated warming. It is unlikely that the
models could be wrong by more than a factor of two, but this cannot
be proven.

In addition, a climate change forecast should indicate when the warm- 7
ing would be expected to be evident. Only one model (the Goddard
Institute for Space Studies [GISS] model) has been used in a time-
transgressive° mode to calculate the climate for the next 50 years. The
results indicate substantial warming in the next decade. This calculation
is affected to some extent by uncertainties in ocean heat uptake and the
true climate feedback factor. By providing an estimate of how much
warming should be observed in the relatively near future, we will have
a chance to test the accuracy of these models.

Ubiquitous—occurring everywhere.   **Perturbations**—changes or disturbances.   **Volcanic aerosols**—dust spewn into the atmosphere by volcanic eruptions.   **Time-trans-
gressive**—extending over different time periods.

How "Dire" Is the Forecast of Coming Climate Change?

Ice covered what is now New York City during an ice age climate 8 estimated to be some 4°C colder than today's. Considering that the doubled CO_2 climate is estimated to be warmer by the same amount, large changes in the climate system may well be expected if this comes to pass. The forecast for the next 50 years from the GISS model gives changes of 2°C by the year 2020, which would make the earth warmer than it is thought to have been at any point in historical time. Estimates for summer temperatures in the doubled CO_2 climate indicate that Washington, DC, which currently experiences 36 days of temperature above 90°F, would routinely have 87 such days; Dallas would go from 19 days with temperatures above 100°F to 78 days. Sea level rise due to thermal expansion of the oceans would cause severe problems in many coastal cities, and this effect would be exacerbated if additional glacial melting occurred. Rainfall patterns would likely be substantially altered, posing the threat of large scale disruptions of agricultural and economic productivity. The impact of the climate changes predicted by the current models would be immense, and, if the timing is correct, they will come quickly.

Is There Any Way to Prevent These Changes from Occurring?

The climate is being altered by the release of trace gases due to fossil 9 fuel° consumption and industrial processes. These are factors inherent to our current civilization. It is hard to visualize changes sufficient to influence the overall trace gas trend, short of a major catastrophe, although it may be possible to limit specific trace gas increases (such as the chlorofluorocarbons). Our ability to manipulate the climate system deliberately, so as to offset the warming by some other process, is nonexistent. It is likely that the additional greenhouse capacity which has been added during the past 50 years has already built considerable warming into the system, which has not yet been realized due to the slow response of the ocean.

The climate of the next century will very likely be substantially dif- 10 ferent from today's, and uncertainties in our knowledge of the true climate sensitivity prevent us from knowing exactly how different it will be. The consequences of the estimated climate change would be enormous. With that in mind, it is worthwhile for us to factor climatic changes into our decision-making process, while appreciating the uncertainties that still exist in our understanding.

Fossil fuel—fuel derived from carbon stored in the earth, such as coal, oil, and natural gas.

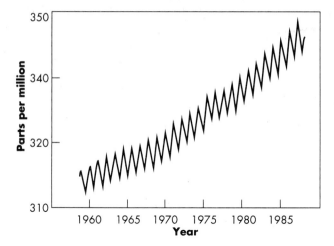

Figure 1.   Carbon dioxide concentrations. Measurements of atmospheric levels of CO_2 show a steady seasonal upward trend over the past 30 years. Chart shows levels measured in parts per million in volume.
Source: Environmental Protection Agency.

Rhetorical Analysis Through Annotation

In explaining what we know about the greenhouse effect, this article is very careful to identify how well or certain we know what we know.

Circle those questions that ask Rind to explain how we know something and how well we know it.

In the answers, underline all words or phrases that identify the level of certainty of the claim being made or qualify that certainty through a hedge.

Discuss the various techniques used to establish the level of certainty for various claims. Why is it important for the article to establish the level of certainty for the various claims?

Discussion Questions

Interpreting the Text

1. What is the greenhouse effect? What are the mechanisms by which it operates?

2. What claims are made about the greenhouse effect? How certain is each of these claims?

3. What factors make for uncertainty?

4. How do trace gases affect the greenhouse effect?

5. How has the greenhouse effect influenced the climate over the last century? What is the likely effect over the next century? What accounts for the differences

between the past and future predicted changes? How do the different results for the last century still help to confirm the predictions for the next?

Considering the Issues

6. How serious is the tone and the direness of the account here? What aspects of the article create the tone? Is the seriousness warranted? How does the tone compare with that of the preceding *New York Times* article?

7. What impact did reading this article have upon you? How might the claims here change your view of the future? Might they have any specific impact on your own life choices? Might they affect government and industry planning and economic choices?

8. Why is the author identified as a doctor? Is this common in other articles? How is this view of the author consistent with the role the author takes throughout the article? How does this role relate to the question and answer format? In what other kinds of documents have you seen the question and answer format used? How do the uses of this format in those other documents compare to the use here?

Writing Suggestions

1. Imagine the president of the United States has been handed a major report about the imminent climatic change. To calm public fears and to reassure Americans that he or she is in charge, the president must make a short statement at a press conference tomorrow. You are the presidential speech writer assigned the task of writing a five-minute statement explaining what the greenhouse effect is, what we know about it, and what the government intends to do about it. Write the statement for the president to deliver.

2. As part of this class's discussion of the use of rhetorical forms, write an essay on the uses and implications of the question and answer format. Use as your main examples this selection, an advertisement using this format, and an information pamphlet of the kind distributed by your bank, union, or dentist.

3. Imagine you are the registrar at your college. Write a question and answer pamphlet explaining to students about registration and registration procedures; or you can imagine any other role and situation that would require a question and answer pamphlet for you to write.

4. For a sensationalist newspaper (such as the kind sold at supermarket checkout counters) write a doom and gloom article about the greenhouse effect or about an astounding future that awaits us. Exaggerate rather than qualify, create a more active, attitude-laden voice for the journalist, and make sure you have a truly attention-getting headline.

The Atmospheric Temperature Balance:
A Textbook Account

Stanley David Gedzelman

Scientific textbooks introduce students to the fundamental concepts of science. Dramatic, specific cases or issues facing contemporary science and society may serve to enliven the presentation or demonstrate the consequences of the general principles, but they rarely form the main topic. Accordingly, the following presentation from an atmospheric science textbook is primarily concerned with the processes of radiation and absorption that determine planetary temperatures. The temperature of the earth's atmosphere is treated as a specific case of the general principles presented first. Similarly, the general characteristics of the atmospheric greenhouse effect take priority over the specific imbalances currently observed on earth.

Stanley David Gedzelman, a professor at College of the City of New York, begins with a dramatic question about life on other planets to introduce the basic physical laws and equations controlling planetary temperature. Students are taught to use these laws and equations through a series of problems. After a sufficient number of laws, concepts, and equations are presented, the greenhouse effect can then be presented as a special case, an interesting sidelight. Gedzelman's textbook was published in 1980.

IS LIFE POSSIBLE ON other planets? In the past, this might have been *1* regarded as a science fiction question, but now we have reached the point where it is possible to make reasonable guesses. Life as we know it is based on the chemistry of the carbon atom and requires liquid water. Liquid water exists under a narrow range of temperatures—from 0 to 100°C under normal atmospheric pressure. Of all the planets in our solar system only the earth has an average temperature within this range (Mars is close). Why does the earth have such equable temperatures?

It is easy to give a qualitative answer to this question. If the earth *2* were much closer to the sun, it would get more sunlight and therefore be warmer. On the other hand, if the earth were much farther from the sun than it is, the temperatures would be much colder. Thus, the earth is at just the right distance from the sun (for our purposes).

Unfortunately, a descriptive answer to such questions is not very *3* useful. We want to know what temperatures to expect on any planet, and we want to know why the temperature averages 15°C on earth. Fortunately, it is possible to get a quantitative answer. There is a law that can be used to determine the temperature of an object so long as you know how much radiation it receives from the sun.

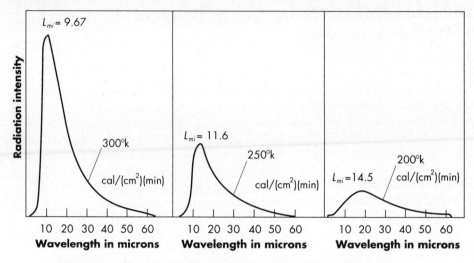

Figure 1. Planck's law of radiation for three different temperatures. The areas under the curves are proportional to the total rate at which heat is radiated (i.e., the intensity). Notice how the intensity of radiation increases rapidly as temperature increases (i.e., the Stefan-Boltzmann law), but the most intense wavelength gets shorter (i.e., Wien's law).
Source: From The Science and Wonders of the Atmosphere *by Stanley David Gedzelman. Copyright © 1980 John Wiley & Sons, Inc. Reprinted by permission of John Wiley & Sons, Inc.*

Planck's law is the fundamental law of radiation. It is the law you **4** read about near the beginning of Chapter 7—the law whose mathematical derivation helped in the birth of modern physics. Planck's law is too complicated to present mathematically in this book, but it is portrayed simply in Figure 1. Planck's law tells us both the total rate of radiation and the wavelengths of the radiation.

Planck's law refers only to objects said to be in thermal equilibrium°. **5** This means it does not apply to objects undergoing chemical reactions such as burning. Similarly, the light from fireflies or other phosphorescent objects is also not governed by Planck's law.

Planck's law gives the maximum amount of radiation that a body can **6** give off as a function of its temperature. An object that radiates heat at this maximum rate is called a **black body**, because such objects also absorb all the heat or light that shines on them (at the same wavelengths). Radiation rates of real substances are given in Table 1.

Thermal equilibrium—having the amount of heat in balance, with a stable temperature.

Substance	Emissivity (Percent)
Water	92 to 96
Snow	82 to 99.5
Sand	84 to 95
Forest	90
Grasslands	90
Human skin	95
Aluminum foil	1 to 5

Table 1.   Radiation rate (emissivity) of objects compared with black-body radiation rate.

This terminology may seem somewhat confusing because both the **7** sun and snow radiate as practically like black bodies. On the other hand, aluminum foil radiates heat at only 1 to 5% of the maximum (or black body) rate. This is why hot food wrapped in aluminum foil stays hot for a relatively long time.

Planck's rather complicated law can be broken down into two rather **8** simple laws. Both of these simpler laws were actually discovered before Planck's law. One part of Planck's genius was to realize and then prove that these two simpler laws are immediate consequences of the general radiation law.

The first of the two simpler laws is called **Wien's law**. Wien's law **9** states that as the temperature of an object increases, the wavelength of the most intense radiation that it emits decreases. It can be written

Wien's Law:

$$L_{mi} = \frac{2900}{T}$$

where L_{mi} stands for the *most intense* wavelength in microns°, and T is the absolute temperature°.

Wien's law has two very important and interesting consequences. The **10** first of these is very colorful. Take a piece of iron and throw it into a fire. As the iron gets hotter it begins to glow with a dull red color. As the iron continues to get even hotter, the color gradually changes to orange and eventually to white. At this point the iron would begin to melt but, if it could be heated further, it would glow blue!

This is true of all radiating objects. As they become hotter the color **11** changes from red to white to blue. The explanation is rather simple.

Micron—a unit of length equal to one millionth of a meter.   **Absolute temperature**—temperature measured or calculated on the absolute scale.

Since temperature is in the denominator of the equation for Wien's law, as the temperature increases the fraction decreases. This means that the wavelength decreases. Now you must recall that red is the color with the longest wavelength, while blue has a much shorter wavelength.

Therefore, when we look into space we can actually tell something 12 about the temperature of the stars (and our sun) by their color—blue stars are the hottest and red stars the coolest.

The second important consequence of Wien's law is that it leads to 13 the well-known "greenhouse effect." The greenhouse effect will be described shortly. Basically without the greenhouse effect, temperatures on earth would be considerably colder.

When the wavelengths of the sun's radiation are determined, it is 14 found that the most intense wavelength is $L_{mi} \cong 0.5$ microns. Now let's see how Wien's law can help us find the temperature of the sun.

Example 1
What is the temperature on the sun?

Information: The sun's most intense radiation has a wavelength of approximately 0.5 microns.

Equation:
  Wien's law

$$L_{mi} = \frac{2900}{T}$$

or, solving for the temperature,

$$T = \frac{2900}{L_{mi}}$$

Substitute:

$$T = \frac{2900}{0.5}$$

Solution

$$T = 5800° \text{ (absolute or Kelvin)}$$

Note: This is the temperature of the photosphere°, that is, the effective radiating surface and coldest part of the sun.

Example 2
The earth has an average temperature of 15°C or 288°K (Kelvin)°. Since the earth radiates almost like a black body all the time, why doesn't it glow at night?

Photosphere—the surface of the sun.   Kelvin (K)—288°K is about 59°F.

Equation:
  Wien's law

$$L_{mi} = \frac{2900}{T}$$

Substitute:
  Use $T = 290$ for computational ease

$$L_{mi} = \frac{2900}{290}$$

Solution

$$L_{mi} = 10 \text{ microns}$$

Ten microns corresponds to infrared radiation and our eyes are not sensitive to this. Otherwise, we actually would be able to "see" the earth glowing at night.

Keep these two examples in mind when the greenhouse effect is **15** discussed. The sun's radiation consists predominantly of radiation with wavelengths near 0.5 microns and is therefore called short-wave radiation, whereas the earth's radiation at 10 microns is called long-wave radiation.

The second simple law is known as the **Stefan-Boltzmann law**, **16** after its two discoverers, Joseph Stefan (1835–1893) and Ludwig Boltzmann (1844–1906). The Stefan-Boltzmann law states that the rate at which an object radiates heat is proportional to the fourth (4th) power of the absolute temperature. In equation form

Stefan-Boltzmann Law:

$$T^4 = (I)(123)(10)^8$$

where T is the absolute temperature and I is the *intensity* or radiation in units of calories° per square centimeter per minute.

The Stefan-Boltzmann law is of central importance in meteorology. **17** It is from this law that we can determine the average temperature of a planet (or any object) just by knowing the amount of heat it receives from the sun.

The Stefan-Boltzmann law actually tells how much heat a body ra- **18** diates away and not how much it receives. However, since the average temperature of the earth and the other planets does not change very much, this automatically implies that there is an almost exact balance between the incoming and outgoing radiation. Therefore, any time that the Stefan-Boltzmann law is used to tell the temperature of a planet, what is really being computed is an average *balance* temperature.

Calories—a unit of heat equal to the amount of heat necessary to raise the temperature of 1 gram of water 1°C.

Example 3

A planet receives an average of 0.5 calories per square centimeter per minute from the sun. What do you expect the average temperature of this planet to be?

Information: Under balanced conditions the average heat leaving a planet is equal to the average radiation that it receives. Thus

$$I = 0.5$$

Equation:

The Stefan-Boltzmann law

$$T^4 = (I)(123)(10)^8$$
$$= (0.5)(123)(10)^8$$
$$= (61.5)(10)^8$$

This is T^4, not T! To find T simply take the square root twice in a row. Thus,

$$\sqrt{T^4} = T^2 = \sqrt{61.5)(10)^8} = (7.85)(10)^4$$

and

$$\sqrt{T^2} = T = \sqrt{(7.85)(10)^4} = (2.80)(10)^2$$

Solution

$$T = 280°K$$

Note: If you haven't guessed it by now this example applies to the *earth*. What this means is that the Stefan-Boltzmann law provides a remarkably accurate estimate of the earth's average temperature (actually 288°K) without once referring to the properties of the atmosphere!

The Stefan-Boltzmann law can also be used to find out the intensity **19** of radiation if we already know the temperature of an object. For instance, since the sun is near 5800°K, we can use the law to find that the intensity of radiation on the sun is roughly 91,000 calories per square centimeter per minute. Then, multiplying by the number of square centimeters on the sun's surface, we find that the sun radiates $(56)(10)^{26}$ calories every minute. Heating at that rate would melt a one-cubic-kilometer iceberg in one-ten billionth of a second! . . .

Reflection of Sunlight (Albedo) and the Ice Ages

Benjamin Franklin once performed the following experiment. After a **20** snowfall he covered several patches of snow with differently colored cloth strips. Franklin found that the snow melted most rapidly under the black cloth and least rapidly under the white cloth. From this he correctly concluded that in a hot, sunny climate you stay cooler when you wear light-colored clothing. Europeans living in the tropics took over 100 years to discard fashion and to profit from Franklin's observation.

If you ever tried to run barefooted across a blacktop road during a *21* summer afternoon, you quickly realized how hot the ground can get. At the same time the white line in the middle of the road is far cooler than the asphalt.

When light is reflected from any object it does not contribute anything *22* to the heating of the object. Only that fraction of the light that is absorbed produces heat. Thus, dark objects absorb sunlight and heat up, while light-colored objects reflect much of the sunlight and remain cooler.

The **albedo** is the technical term for the reflectivity of an object. *23* For example, an object that reflects 30% of the light that strikes it has an albedo of 30. Typical albedos of objects and planets are listed in Table 2.

Most soils, plants, and even water have very low albedos, while snow, *24* ice, and clouds have high albedos. Thus, even though the sun is low in the sky in the polar lands, snow blindness has always been a problem to the hunting eskimos. Not only do the eskimos have to shield their eyes from the direct sunlight, but also from the reflected sunlight as well. Any eskimo and skier knows the value of sunglasses.

There is an even more important consequence of albedo. Since the *25* reflected fraction of the sunlight does not contribute to heating, light-colored objects have a cooling influence. It is actually possible to change

Substance or Planet	Albedo (Percent)
Water	
With sun's elevation 90°	3
With sun's elevation 30°	7
With sun's elevation 10°	24
Snow, fresh	75 to 95
Ice, sea	30 to 40
Sand, dry	35 to 45
Soil, dark	5 to 15
Forest	10 to 20
Grassland	15 to 20
Clouds, thick	70 to 90
Clouds, thin	35 to 50
Earth	30
Moon	6.7
Mercury	7
Jupiter	45
Mars	16
Venus	76

Table 2. Albedos of various surfaces.

the climate of the earth by changing its albedo. For instance, in the past 100 years because of industrialization the air has been filled with many more dust particles (called aerosols). These aerosols tend to increase the albedo of the earth and thus produce a cooling effect on earth. Some meteorologists believe that this effect is partially responsible for the global cooling° that has taken place since about 1940.

Large volcanic eruptions inject dust explosively into the stratosphere 26 where it remains suspended for months or even years. This volcanic dust also increases the earth's albedo, and there is some evidence to show that the great volcanic eruptions such as Krakatoa in 1883 and Tambora in 1815 were followed by a few years of significantly colder weather.

To some the most frightening prospect is the distinct possibility that 27 an ice age can start itself! It is possible that due to the natural variability of weather one particular winter may be exceptionally snowy. Since snow has a much higher albedo than bare ground, more sunlight striking the earth would be reflected than normal. Thus less sunlight than normal would be absorbed on earth and temperatures would drop.

It is conceivable that this could start a chain reaction. As world 28 temperatures begin to drop not only will it be easier for it to snow (rather than to rain), but some ocean water will start to freeze. Since ice also has a high albedo, even more sunlight will be reflected from the earth, and this in turn will produce a further cooling, and so on. This chain reaction is called a **positive feedback mechanism** (see Figure 2). In meteorology there are many other feedback mechanisms (both positive and negative) that can potentially affect the weather and climate.

The ice-albedo feedback mechanism constitutes an essential ingredient 29 of most ice age theories. Calculations using the Stefan-Boltzmann law, which take the effects of albedo into account, show that if the entire earth were covered with ice the temperatures would fall so low that the ice would not even melt at the equator! According to one theory, if the ice were to spread further toward the equator than 40° latitude, the chain reaction would begin, and the ice would continue spreading right to the equator.

On the other hand, we can also look forward to the possibility of a 30 much warmer climate. If the millions of square kilometers of polar ice were covered with a thin dark film, the albedo would decrease and more heat would be absorbed on earth. This would cause the temperatures to rise, thus melting some of the ice. This would lead to further decreases in the albedo and therefore further warming, and so on until all the ice melted. It now lies within our technological power to end the ice age in this way, but the millions of cubic kilometers of melted ice would then run into the oceans and cause sea level to rise. Most of the world's

---

Global cooling since 1940—cooling from 1940 to about 1965 has reversed in the last two decades as the greenhouse effect has been building. See Hansen *et al.*, p. 393.

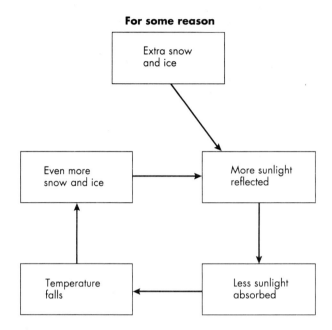

Figure 2. The albedo-climate feedback mechanism. If, for any reason, there is more snow and ice on earth, the feedback mechanism can begin to work like a chain reaction.
Source: From The Science and Wonders of the Atmosphere *by Stanley David Gedzelman. Copyright © 1980 John Wiley & Sons, Inc. Reprinted by permission of John Wiley & Sons, Inc.*

largest cities such as New York, London, Paris, Shanghai, Tokyo, Calcutta, Rio de Janeiro, Sao Paolo, Buenos Aires, and Statesboro would then be submerged.

This is the stuff that modern novels are made of. However, the issue *31* is not a joking one—the possible consequences are enormous. In Chapter 24 this issue will be examined further. Until then, "Remember the albedo."

The Greenhouse Effect

If we "remember the albedo" and recalculate the balance temperature *32* on earth (earth's albedo is 30%), the new answer is 255°K or −18°C. This result is less accurate than the simple balance temperature calculation that did not take the albedo into account (Example 3)! Actually, we are lucky that this new result is not accurate, since at −18°C the earth would have a perpetual ice age.

We must now answer the question, "Why does the realistic inclusion *33* of the effect of albedo produce such an inaccurate answer for the balance temperature of the earth?" By sheer coincidence, the cooling effect of the earth's albedo is almost exactly offset by the warming due to the greenhouse effect. Actually, the greenhouse effect is slightly more important than the influence of the albedo on earth; with the greenhouse effect the earth is warmed to 15°C.

The **greenhouse effect** is the property of the atmosphere that permits   34
sunlight in rather easily, but releases that heat back into space only with great difficulty. Because of the greenhouse effect, the atmosphere retains considerably more heat, and thus the temperature of the earth's surface is higher than otherwise (see Figure 3).

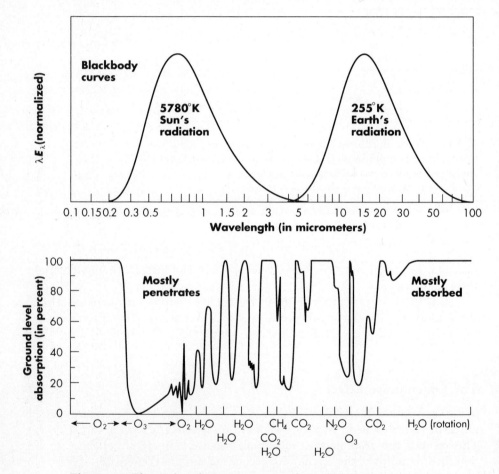

Figure 3.   The sun's radiation occurs mostly at short wavelengths, which easily penetrate the atmosphere. The earth's radiation occurs at long wavelengths and is largely absorbed by the atmosphere. This produces the greenhouse effect.

Source: From The Science and Wonders of the Atmosphere *by Stanley David Gedzelman. Copyright © 1980 John Wiley & Sons, Inc. Reprinted by permission of John Wiley & Sons, Inc.*

How does the greenhouse effect operate? This is where Wien's law is *35* important. The short-wave radiation from the sun largely penetrates the atmosphere and is absorbed at the ground. The ground then heats up and reradiates long-wave radiation from the ground which does not penetrate the atmosphere very well.

Now, recall Einstein's law which states that each different wavelength *36* of radiation corresponds to a different energy. Each molecule absorbs only those wavelengths with the appropriate energy. The fact is that wavelengths shorter than 0.3 or longer than 1.5 microns are readily absorbed by CO_2, H_2O, O_3, and cloud droplets. The intermediate range of wavelengths—from 0.3 to 1.5 microns—are hardly absorbed at all and easily penetrate to the ground. Most of the sun's radiation falls within this intermediate range of wavelengths so it easily penetrates the atmosphere. On the other hand, virtually all of the earth's radiation is longer than 1.5 microns and therefore is largely absorbed by the atmosphere.

The CO_2, H_2O, O_3, and cloud droplets heat up when they absorb *37* the long-wave radiation from the ground. These heated molecules then collide with the other air molecules, thus heating the rest of the atmosphere as well. Once these absorbing gases have heated up, they too radiate heat. Some of this radiation escapes to space, but some heads back toward the ground. *This extra radiation (in addition to the solar radiation) received at the earth's surface produces the greenhouse effect.* The greenhouse effect on earth produces a net warming of about 32°C[1] (see Figure 4).

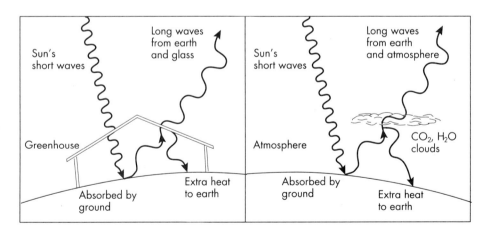

Figure 4.   The greenhouse effect. The atmosphere reradiates some of the heat it received back to the earth. This represents an extra source of heat for the ground, making it warmer than it otherwise would have been.

Source: From The Science and Wonders of the Atmosphere *by Stanley David Gedzelman. Copyright © 1980 John Wiley & Sons, Inc. Reprinted by permission of John Wiley & Sons, Inc.*

There are a number of interesting situations to which the greenhouse 38
effect applies. Consider the case of two nearby cities that have identical
temperature and humidity conditions at nightfall. The only difference is
that city *A* is cloudy and city *B* is clear. The question is, "Which city
will be colder by morning?"

The answer is simple. Since clouds strengthen the greenhouse effect 39
by absorbing the radiation from the ground and reradiating some of it
back to the ground, the air at city *A* cools slowly overnight. At city *B*,
there is a greater net loss of heat from the ground, since less heat is
reradiated back to ground level. Therefore, city *B* cools more rapidly at
night. In a manner of speaking, the clouds act like a blanket holding
heat in.

Rule: Clear nights get colder than cloudy nights (all other conditions
being the same).

There are even times when the temperature of the cloud base is 40
warmer than the ground temperature, and in such cases the air temperature will actually warm slightly overnight.

Another interesting consequence of the greenhouse effect is that fog 41
is more likely after a clear night than after a cloudy night (see Figure 5).
Since the air near the ground cools more on the clear night, there is a
greater chance that condensation will occur. Thus fog in the morning is
often a sign of a clear day to come. More will be said about this in
Chapter 11.

The greenhouse effect still exists without clouds, but it is then some- 42
what weaker. During clear conditions the strength of the greenhouse
effect varies with the amount of water vapor in the air. As a result, in
the desert or in the high mountains, temperatures fall rapidly at night,
and diurnal temperature variations tend to be quite large (at least $15°C$).

There are also feedback mechanisms that involve the greenhouse ef- 43
fect. For instance, the strength of the greenhouse effect depends on the
amount of water vapor in the atmosphere. As the air warms, its capacity
for holding water vapor increases. This potentially strengthens the
greenhouse effect and could lead to further warming.

It is conceivable, though quite unlikely, that the oceans could be boiled 44
away by such a chain reaction. It would be far more likely if the earth
were as close to the sun as Venus is. Such a chain reaction is known as
a **runaway greenhouse**. There is strong evidence that the greenhouse
effect on Venus is an example of just such a runaway-greenhouse effect.

Scientists believe that a runaway-greenhouse effect has caused tre- 45
mendous amounts of water to completely boil away from the planet
Venus. The theory goes something as follows. At first Venus had an
atmosphere with large quantities of water vapor, and it may even have
had something of an ocean. But the enormous quantities of water vapor
in the air caused the temperature to rise past a critical point. The vapor
molecules then moved fast enough to escape from the gravitational field

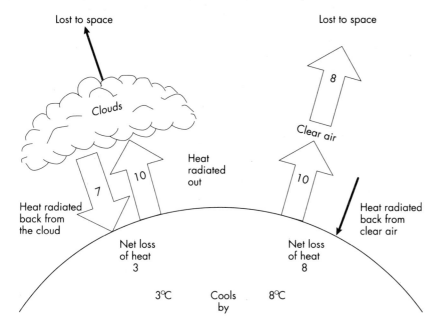

Figure 5.   Clear nights get colder than cloudy nights because clouds increase the greenhouse effect. Thus, clouds and the greenhouse effect act like blankets. Numbers are merely schematic.
Source: From The Science and Wonders of the Atmosphere *by Stanley David Gedzelman. Copyright © 1980 John Wiley & Sons, Inc. Reprinted by permission of John Wiley & Sons, Inc.*

of Venus, but the high temperature had another fundamental effect on the atmosphere of Venus.

You should recall that the atmosphere is 90 times more massive than our atmosphere and is composed almost entirely of CO_2. Theory indicates that the 15% increase of CO_2 in our atmosphere over the last century has produced a small global warming of about 0.25°C. Since Venus' atmosphere contains about 250,000 times as much CO_2 as the earth's, you can imagine how strong the greenhouse effect is there.   **46**

Once the temperature on Venus reached a certain critical point (as you have read in Chapter 6) the rocks composed of calcium carbonate, $CaCO_3$, began to degenerate into CaO and CO_2. The CO_2 which was then released into the atmosphere further increased the greenhouse effect, and this then caused even more $CaCO_3$ to decompose. As a result there is no longer a reasonable chance of finding life on Venus (see Figure 6).   **47**

Such a runaway-greenhouse effect is not expected to occur on earth, unless the sun suddenly begins to radiate more intensely. Fortunately, this is not expected to happen for about another 10 billion years.   **48**

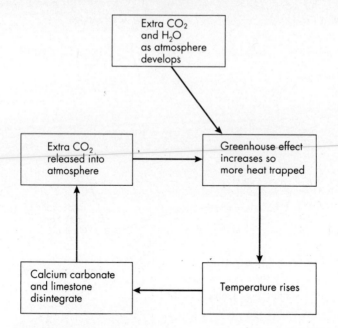

Figure 6.   The runaway-greenhouse effect. Such a chain reaction is unlikely on earth because of the distance to the sun.
Source: From The Science and Wonders of the Atmosphere *by Stanley David Gedzelman. Copyright © 1980 John Wiley & Sons, Inc. Reprinted by permission of John Wiley & Sons, Inc.*

Note

[1]It may now please you to read that, although the principle is correct, the term—greenhouse effect—is actually a misnomer. The main reason that greenhouses on earth are so hot is that the glass prevents the heated air from rising. Greenhouses made of rock salt (which allows infrared radiation to escape) are almost as hot as greenhouses made of glass. Furthermore, most of the heat lost by the greenhouse is lost by heat conduction (see Chapter 9) and not by radiation.

Rhetorical Analysis Through Annotation

This textbook selection builds advanced concepts on more basic ones. The fundamental concepts are emphasized through a variety of graphic and textual features, including being assigned a special name. They are later then referred to and combined with other concepts.

Underline the name of each fundamental concept where it is first introduced. In the margin, bracket the nearby passage where the concept is explained and elaborated. Circle every time later in the text that each of these fundamental concepts is referred to or used. Also circle concepts mentioned as being discussed in previous chapters.

Discuss how the meaning and importance of each concept is established, how it is given concrete application, and how it is fitted together with other concepts to build a complex model of atmospheric temperature. In particular consider the role of example problems, tables, and figures.

Discussion Questions

Interpreting the Text

1. What are Wien's law and the Stefan-Boltzmann law? How are they related to Planck's law?

2. Why is it useful to know the characteristics of any object's radiation? Of a planet's radiation? What characteristics does Wien's law let you know? The Stefan-Boltzmann law?

3. What is albedo? How does it help you calculate the amount of energy absorbed by a planet or any other object?

4. What factors may cause the atmosphere to cool? To heat up? Do these two factors balance each other? Under what conditions may they go out of balance? Does this author predict that they will go out of balance on earth? Do any of the other authors in this unit?

5. How does the greenhouse effect heat up the earth? How is the heating affected by cloud cover? What unusual situations arise from the greenhouse effect? How does a runaway effect come about?

Considering the Issues

6. Which concepts are the most difficult to follow? Can you explain why? Do difficulties result from the lack of required background knowledge, combination of concepts, use of mathematics, or other factors?

7. How do the explanations here differ from the explanations in earlier articles? What different topics are covered? What are the differences in order, structure of explanation, and purpose?

8. What light does this selection shed on the greenhouse effect problem? Does it discuss the problem directly? Is the greenhouse effect something new as a result of increasing CO_2? What is the difference between a process and a problem? Why is this process now considered a problem?

9. Why is the concept of a balanced system important to the maintenance of life on earth? What threat does a runaway greenhouse effect pose? Do you know of other examples of balanced and runaway systems? Are there any situations in which runaway systems are preferable to balanced systems?

10. Is this passage similar in structure and explanatory strategy to any textbooks for your current courses? How does it compare to textbooks in different disciplines? How do you account for the similarities or differences in structure?

Writing Suggestions

1. For a course in atmospheric science using Gedzelman's textbook, write a set of study notes to prepare for an examination.

2. Imagine that you are taking a course that uses Gedzelman's textbook, and that you are finding the textbook difficult to follow. Write a letter to your instructor explaining your difficulties and asking for clarification or elaboration. On the other hand, if you find the material intelligible and interesting, write a letter to the instructor explaining what you find exciting in the material and why.

3. (a) Imagine that you were the instructor of a course in atmospheric science using Gedzelman's textbook. Write a series of examination questions that would test your students' familiarity with and understanding of the main concepts of this selection. (b) Now, imagining that you are a student in the course, write your answers to the exam questions you just wrote.

4. Write a science fiction story about a science student waking up one day to discover that the earth's albedo, Wien's law, or any other concept or equation presented here had changed radically. Based on this premise, describe the difficulties or adventures that would result.

Climate Impact of Increasing Atmospheric Carbon Dioxide

J. Hansen, D. Johnson, A. Lacis, S. Lebedeff, P. Lee, D. Rind, G. Russell

Predictions about the impact of the greenhouse effect on the earth's climate are derived from an atmospheric model that was presented to the scientific world in the following article. A team of scientists under James Hansen at the NASA Goddard Space Flight Center in New York worked on this problem for several years before this key article was published.

In contemporary science, a model is a series of mathematical equations that describes the behavior of a complicated system. The equations are then built into a computer program that carries out the specific calculations. To construct the model's equations, scientists usually have to make some simplifying assumptions. That is, they have to pretend that the system is not as complicated or detailed as it is. But still they try to include all the factors they believe will significantly affect the overall outcome. In this case, in calculating the overall pattern of atmospheric temperatures, the research team does not worry about daily changes in temperature or the effects of a harsh winter.

Rather they look only at overall trends resulting from changes in absorption and radiation of solar energy. In collecting observed temperature data to compare with model computations, they look only at annual averages for large sections of the earth.

Because this article must convince other scientists of the validity of the model, the authors explain the assumptions and construction of the model carefully in a step-by-step fashion. Each of the general concepts is turned into a mathematical equation that can then be used as part of the model.

Because of the technical care and completeness, this article is difficult to read. Parts of it you may not be able to understand exactly. However, the concepts of radiation, absorption, and the greenhouse effect that you learned through the previous articles in this unit should make the overall reasoning familiar. Do not worry if you cannot follow every sentence in detail. Just try to get a general sense of the argument.

Scientists themselves often read only parts of articles, looking for important information and skipping over less immediately relevant sections. Even scientists find some articles hard to read carefully, and will work through in detail only those parts they really need. Often scientists "black-box" difficult, technical parts of the reading. That is, they just get the general idea of the section and skip over the detailed argument. Later, if they find they need to review the argument in detail, they can open up the black box through a careful reading. In order to help you read this article, some of the more technical parts have been "black-boxed" by replacing them with brief summaries.

The article begins by discussing how increased carbon dioxide can affect global temperature. This should be familiar to you from previous selections, even though the presentation here is more technical. The difficulties with this theory, however, are then presented. The introduction ends with an outline of the article, showing how the authors intend to overcome these objections by constructing a model whose results will be compared with observed data; the model will then be used to predict the future climate.

The model draws on the basic theory of radiation and absorption to which you were introduced in the previous textbook selection. The model is made more complicated by changing it from a zero-dimensional model to a one-dimensional model. This means that instead of looking at the planet and the atmosphere as a single whole unit, the model takes into account changes in the atmosphere as height above ground increases. A fully three-dimensional model would take into account changes over all places on the planet and in the atmosphere; 3-D models have since been constucted by Hansen's team and several other working groups in the U.S. and Europe. Here, the one-dimensional model is modified by considering the effects of atmospheric moisture, clouds, snow cover, and the ocean's slow response to temperature change. Other possible variables, such as the effects of solar warming, volcanic aerosols, changing vegetation patterns, changing cloud covers, and increasing trace gases, are examined and discounted.

The authors then need to compare the model against historical temperature data. But gathering these data also presents problems, because adequate temperaure records have not been kept for the whole planet and because adding up results from all over the planet is difficult to do coherently.

To test their model and their method for aggregating data, the authors examine the actual effects on global temperature of various recent events that have changed radiation and absorption in the atmosphere, such as the eruption of the Indonesian volcano Mount Agung in 1963. By comparing predictions from their model with the results, they find their model satisfactory. They similarly find their model consistent with global temperatures for the entire century. Future climate changes due to increasing CO_2 are then predicted and consequences are examined.

Summary   The global temperature rose by 0.2°C between the middle 1960's and 1980, yielding a warming of 0.4°C in the past century. This temperature increase is consistent with the calculated greenhouse effect due to measured increases of atmospheric carbon dioxide. Variations of volcanic aerosols and possibly solar luminosity appear to be primary causes of observed fluctuations about the mean trend of increasing temperature. It is shown that the anthropogenic° carbon dioxide warming should emerge from the noise level of natural climate variability by the end of the century, and there is a high probability of warming in the 1980's. Potential effects on climate in the 21st century include the creation of drought-prone regions in North America and central Asia as part of a shifting of climatic zones, erosion of the West Antarctic ice sheet with consequent worldwide rise in sea level, and opening of the fabled Northwest Passage.

ATMOSPHERIC CO_2 INCREASED FROM 280 to 300 parts per mil- 1
lion in 1880 to 335 to 340 ppm in 1980 (1, 2), mainly due to burning of fossil fuels. Deforestation and changes in biosphere° growth may also have contributed, but their net effect is probably limited in magnitude (2, 3). The CO_2 abundance is expected to reach 600 ppm in the next century, even if growth of fossil fuel use is slow (4).

Anthropogenic—caused by human beings.   **Biosphere**—all the regions on earth that support life.

Carbon dioxide absorbs in the atmospheric "window" from 7 to 14 *2* micrometers which transmits thermal radiation emitted by the earth's surface and lower atmosphere. Increased atmospheric CO_2 tends to close this window and cause outgoing radiation to emerge from higher, colder levels, thus warming the surface and lower atmosphere by the so-called greenhouse mechanism (5). The most sophisticated models suggest a mean warming of 2° to 3.5°C for doubling of the CO_2 concentration from 300 to 600 ppm (6–8).

The major difficulty in accepting this theory has been the absence of *3* observed warming coincident with the historic CO_2 increase. In fact, the temperature in the Northern Hemisphere decreased by about 0.5°C between 1940 and 1970 (9), a time of rapid CO_2 buildup. In addition, recent claims that climate models overestimate the impact of radiative perturbations° by an order of magnitude (*10, 11*) have raised the issue of whether the greenhouse effect is well understood.

We first describe the greenhouse mechanism and use a simple model *4* to compare potential radiative perturbations of climate. We construct the trend of observed global temperature for the past century and compare this with global climate model computations, providing a check on the ability of the model to simulate known climate change. Finally, we compute the CO_2 warming expected in the coming century and discuss its potential implications.

Greenhouse Effect

The effective radiating temperature of the earth, T_e, is determined by *5* the need for infrared emission from the planet to balance absorbed solar radiation:

$$\pi R^2(1 - A)S_0 = 4\pi R^2 \sigma T_e^4 \tag{1}$$

or

$$T_e = [S_0(1 - A)/4\sigma]^{1/4} \tag{2}$$

where R is the radius of the earth, A the albedo of the earth, S_0 the flux° of solar radiation, and σ the Stefan-Boltzmann constant. For $A \sim° 0.3$ and $S_0 = 1367$ watts per square meter, this yields $T_e \sim 255$ K.

The mean surface temperature is $T_s \sim 288$ K. The excess, $T_s - T_e$, *6* is the greenhouse effect of gases and clouds, which cause the mean radiating level to be above the surface. An estimate of the greenhouse warming is

$$T_s \sim T_e + \Gamma H \tag{3}$$

Perturbations—disturbances.   **Flux**—amount of radiant energy emitted, transmitted, or received per unit of time.   ~—approximately equals.

where H is the flux-weighted° mean altitude of the emission to space and Γ is the mean temperature gradient (lapse rate) between the surface and H. The earth's troposphere° is sufficiently opaque in the infrared that the purely radiative vertical temperature gradient is convectively unstable, giving rise to atmospheric motions that contribute to vertical transport of heat and result in $\Gamma \sim 5°$ to 6°C per kilometer. The mean lapse rate is less than the dry adiabatic° value because of latent heat release by condensation as moist air rises and cools and because the atmospheric motions that transport heat vertically include large-scale atmospheric dynamics as well as local convection. The value of H is ~5 km at midlatitudes (where $\Gamma \sim 6.5°C\ km^{-1}$) and ~6 km in the global mean ($\Gamma \sim 5.5°C\ km^{-1}$).

The surface temperature resulting from the greenhouse effect is anal-   7
ogous to the depth of water in a leaky bucket with constant inflow rate. If the holes in the bucket are reduced slightly in size, the water depth and water pressure will increase until the flow rate out of the holes again equals the inflow rate, Analogously, if the atmospheric infrared opacity increases, the temperature of the surface and atmosphere will increase until the emission of radiation from the planet again equals the absorbed solar energy.

The greenhouse theory can be tested by examination of several plan-   8
ets, which provide an ensemble of experiments over a wide range of conditions. The atmospheric composition of Mars, Earth, and Venus lead to mean radiating levels of about 1, 6, and 70 km, and lapse rates of $\Gamma \sim 5°$, 5.5°, and 7°C km^{-1}, respectively. Observed surface temperatures of these planets confirm the existence and order of magnitude of the predicted greenhouse effect (Eq. 3). Data now being collected by spacecraft at Venus and Mars (*12*) will permit more precise analyses of radiative and dynamical mechanisms that affect greenhouse warming.

One-Dimensional Model

A one-dimensional radiative-convective (1-D RC) model (*5, 13*), which   9
computes temperature as a function of altitude, can simulate planetary temperatures more realistically than the zero-dimensional model of Equation 1. The sensitivity of surface temperature in 1-D RC models to changes in CO_2 is similar to the sensitivity of mean surface temperature in global three-dimensional models (*6–8*). This agreement does not validate the models; it only suggests that one-dimensional models can simulate the effect of certain basic mechanisms and feedbacks. But the agreement does permit useful studies of global mean temperature change with a simple one-dimensional model.

Flux-weighted—taking flux differences into account.   Troposphere—the lowest layer of the atmosphere, extending ten to twenty kilometers above the earth; most weather phenomena occur in the troposphere.   Adiabatic—without change of heat.

The 1-D RC model uses a time-marching procedure to compute the **10** vertical temperature profile from the net radiative and convective energy fluxes:

$$T(h, t + \Delta t) = T(h, t) + \frac{\Delta t}{c_p \rho}\left(\frac{dF_r}{dh} + \frac{dF_c}{dh}\right) \qquad (4)$$

. . . .

[*This equation and assumptions behind it are explained. The model is then* **11** *modified by adding in conditions known to affect climate. The significance of various factors is calculated, and only the most significant are left in the model.*]

We conclude that study of global climate change on time scales of **12** decades and centuries must consider variability of stratospheric° aerosols and solar luminosity, in addition to CO_2 and trace gases. Tropospheric aerosols and ground albedo are potentially significant, but require better observations. Cloud variability will continue to cause uncertainty until accurate monitoring of global cloud properties provides a basis for realistic modeling of cloud feedback effects; however, global feedback is implicitly checked by comparison of climate model sensitivity to empirical climate variations, as done below.

Observed Temperature Trends

Data archives (*39*) contain surface air temperatures of several hundred **13** stations for the last century. Problems in obtaining a global temperature history are due to the uneven station distribution (*40*), with the Southern Hemisphere and ocean areas poorly represented, and the smaller number of stations for earlier times.

We combined these temperature records with a method designed to **14** extract mean temperature trends. The globe was divided by grids with a spacing not larger than the correlation distance for primary dynamical transports (*41*), but large enough that most boxes contained one or more stations. The results shown were obtained with 40 equal-area boxes in each hemisphere, but the conclusions are not sensitive to the exact spacing. Temperature trends for stations within a box were combined successively:

$$T_{1,n}(t) = \frac{(n^\star - 1)T_{1,n} + T_n - \overline{T_n} + \overline{T_{1,n}}}{n^\star} \qquad (8)$$

to obtain a single trend for each box, where the bar indicates a mean for the years in which there are records for both T_n and the cumulative $T_{1,n}$ and $n^\star(t)$ is the number of stations in $T_{1,n}(t)$. Trends for boxes in a latitude zone were combined with each box weighted equally, and the

---

Stratosphere—the layer of the atmosphere just above the troposphere, with a relatively constant temperature.

global trend was obtained by area-weighting the trends for all latitude zones. A meaningful result begins in the 1880's, since thereafter continuous records exist for at least two widely separated longitudes in seven of the eight latitude zones (continuous Antarctic temperatures begin in the 1950's). Results are least reliable for 1880 to 1900; by 1900, continuous records exist for more than half of the 80 boxes.

The temperature trends in Figure 1 are smoothed with a 5-year run-   15
ning mean to make the trends readily visible. Part of the noise in the unsmoothed data results from unpredictable weather fluctuations, which affect even 1-year means (42). None of our conclusions depends on the nature of the smoothing.

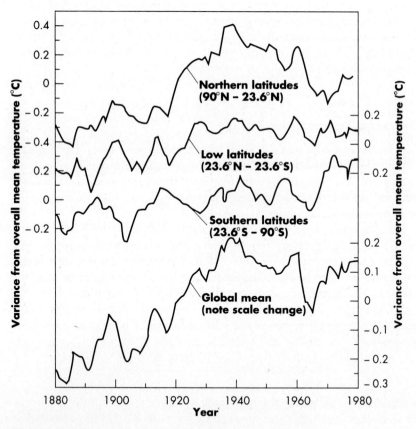

Figure 1. Observed surface air temperature trends for three latitude bands and the entire globe. Temperature scales for low latitudes and global mean are on the right.

Source: Adapted from J. Hansen et al., "Climate Impact of Increasing Atmospheric Carbon Dioxide," Science 213 (1981): p. 961. Copyright 1981 by the AAAS. Reprinted with permission.

Northern latitudes warmed ~ 0.8°C between the 1880's and 1940, *16* then cooled ~ 0.5°C between 1940 and 1970, in agreement with other analyses (*9, 43*). Low latitudes warmed ~0.3°C between 1880 and 1930, with little change thereafter. Southern latitudes warmed ~ 0.4°C in the past century; results agree with a prior analysis for the late 1950's to middle 1970's (*44*). The global mean temperature increased ~ 0.5°C between 1885 and 1940, with slight cooling thereafter.

A remarkable conclusion from Figure 1 is that the global temperature *17* is almost as high today as it was in 1940. The common misconception that the world is cooling is based on Northern Hemisphere experience to 1970.

Another conclusion is that global surface air temperature rose ~ 0.4°C *18* in the past century, roughly consistent with calculated CO_2 warming. The time history of the warming obviously does not follow the course of the CO_2 increase, . . . indicating that other factors must affect global mean temperature.

Model Verification

Natural radiative perturbations of the earth's climate, such as those due *19* to aerosols produced by large volcanic eruptions, permit a valuable test of model sensitivity. Previous study of the best-documented large volcanic eruption, Mount Agung in 1963, showed that tropical tropospheric and stratospheric temperature changes computed with a one-dimensional climate model were of the same sign and order of magnitude as observed changes (*45*). It was assumed that horizontal heat exchange with higher latitudes was not altered by the radiative perturbation.

We reexamined the Mount Agung case for comparison with the pres- *20* ent global temperature record, using our model with sensitivity ~ 2.8°C. The model, with a maximum global mean aerosol increase in the optical depth $\Delta\tau = 0.12$ (*45*), yields a maximum global cooling of 0.2°C when only the mixed-layer heat capacity is included and 0.1°C when heat exchange with the deeper ocean is included with $k = 1$ cm^2 sec^{-1}. Observations suggest a cooling of this magnitude with the expected time lag of 1 to 2 years. Noise or unexplained variability in the observations prevents more definitive conclusions, but similar cooling is indicated by statistical studies of temperature trends following other large volcanic eruptions (*46*). . . .

[*The implications of the Mount Agung case for the greenhouse effect are* *21* *examined in greater detail. Other phenomena affecting radiation patterns are also examined and found consistent with the model proposed here for greenhouse heating.*]

The test of the greenhouse theory provided by the extremes of equi- *22* librium climates on the planets and short-term radiative perturbations is reassuring, but inadequate. A crucial intermediate test is climate change on time scales from a few years to a century.

Model versus Observations for the Past Century

Simulations of global temperature change should begin with the known   *23*
forcings: variations of CO_2 and volcanic aerosols. Solar luminosity variations, which constitute another likely mechanism, are unknown, but
there are hypotheses consistent with observational constraints that variations not exceed a few tenths of 1 percent. . . .

   [*Detailed model calculations are described and results are compared to historical*   *24*
data. The calculation results and data are displayed and compared in Figure 2.]

   The general agreement between modeled and observed temperature   *25*
trends strongly suggests that CO_2 and volcanic aerosols are responsible
for much of the global temperature variation in the past century. Key
consequences are: (i) empirical evidence that much of the global climate

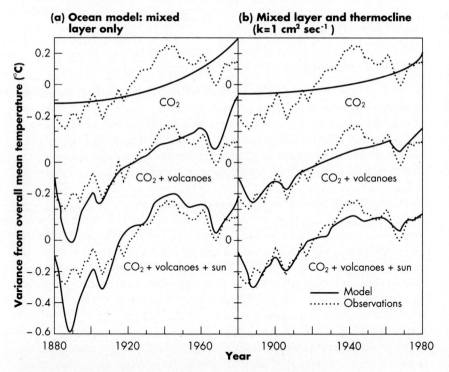

Figure 2.   Global temperature trend obtained from climate
model with sensitivity 2.8°C for doubled CO_2. The results in (a)
are based on a 100-m mixed-layer ocean for heat capacity; those
in (b) include diffusion of heat into the thermocline to 1000 m.
The forcings by CO_2, volcanoes, and the sun are based on
Broecker (25), Lamb (27), and Hoyt (48). Mean ΔT is zero for
observations and model.

Source: Adapted from J. Hansen et al., "Climate Impact of Increasing Atmos-
pheric Carbon Dioxide," Science 213 (1981): p. 963. Copyright 1981 by the
AAAS. Reprinted with permission.

variability on time scales of decades to centuries is deterministic and (ii) improved confidence in the ability of models to predict future CO_2 climate effects.

Projections into the 21st Century

Prediction of the climate effect of CO_2 requires projections of the amount of atmospheric CO_2, which we specify by (i) the energy growth rate and (ii) the fossil fuel proportion of energy use. We neglect other possible variables, such as changes in the amount of biomass° or the fraction of released CO_2 taken up by the ocean.   26

Energy growth has been 4 to 5 percent per year in the past century, but increasing costs will constrain future growth (*1, 4*). Thus we consider fast growth (~ 3 percent per year, specifically 4 percent per year in 1980 to 2020, 3 percent per year in 2020 to 2060, and 2 percent per year in 2060 to 2100), slow growth (half of fast growth), and no growth as representative energy growth rates.   27

Fossil fuel use will be limited by available resources (Table 1). Full use of oil and gas will increase CO_2 abundance by < 50 percent of the preindustrial amount. Oil and gas depletion are near the 25 percent level,   28

Fuel	Energy supplied in 1980* (10^{19} J)	(%)	CO_2 release per unit energy (oil = 1)	Airborne CO_2 added in 1980* (%)	(ppm)	CO_2 added through 1980 (ppm)	Potential airborne CO_2 in virgin reservoirs† (ppm)
Oil	12	40	1	50	0.7	11	70
Coal	7	24	5/4	35	0.5	26	1000
Gas	5	16	3/4	15	0.2	5	50
Oil shale, tar sands, heavy oil	0	0	7/4	0	0	0	100
Nuclear, solar, wood, hydroelectric	6	20	0	0	0	0	0
Total	30	100		100	1.4	42	1220

Table 1. Energy supplied and CO_2 released by fuels.
*Based on late 1970's.
†Reservoir estimates assume that half the coal above 3000 feet can be recovered and that oil recovery rates will increase from 25 to 30 percent to 40 percent. Estimate for unconventional fossil fuels may be low if techniques are developed for economic extraction of "synthetic oil" from deposits that are deep or of marginal energy content. It is assumed that the airborne fraction of released CO_2 is fixed.

Biomass—living matter.

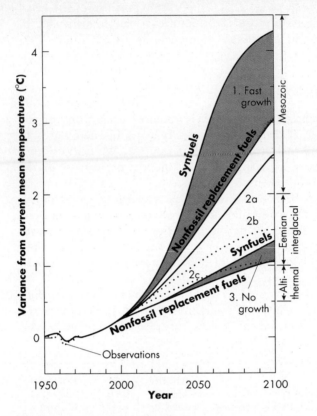

Figure 3. Projections of global temperature. The diffusion coefficient beneath the ocean mixed layer is $1.2 \text{ cm}^2 \text{ sec}^{-1}$, as required for best fit of the model and observations for the period 1880 to 1978. Estimated global mean warming in earlier warm periods is indicated on the right. 1 = fast growth; 2 = slow growth; 2a = no coal phaseout; 2b = coal phaseout beginning 2020; 2c = coal phaseout beginning 2000. 3 = no growth.
Source: Adapted from J. Hansen et al., "Climate Impact of Increasing Atmospheric Carbon Dioxide," Science 213 (1981): p. 965. Copyright 1981 by the AAAS. Reprinted with permission.

at which use of a resource normally begins to be limited by supply and demand forces (4). But coal, only 2 to 3 percent depleted, will not be so constrained for several decades.

The key fuel choice is between coal and alternatives that do not 29 increase atmospheric CO_2. We examine a synfuel option in which coal-derived synthetic fuels replace oil and gas as the latter are depleted, and a nuclear/renewable resources option in which the replacement fuels do not increase CO_2. We also examine a coal phaseout scenario: after a specific date coal and synfuel use are held constant for 20 years and then phased out linearly over 20 years.

Projected global warming for fast growth is 3° to 4.5°C at the end of *30* the next century, depending on the proportion of depleted oil and gas replaced by synfuels (Figure 3). Slow growth, with depleted oil and gas replaced equally by synfuels and nonfossil fuels, reduces the warming to ~ 2.5°C. The warming is only slightly more than 1°C for either (i) no energy growth, with depleted oil and gas replaced by nonfossil fuels, or (ii) slow energy growth, with coal and synfuels phased out beginning in 2000.

Other climate forcings may counteract or reinforce CO_2 warming. A *31* decrease of solar luminosity from 1980 to 2100 by 0.6 percent per century, large compared to measured variations, would decrease the warming ~ 0.7°C. Thus CO_2 growth as large as in the slow-growth scenario would overwhelm the effect of likely solar variability. The same is true of other radiative perturbations; for instance, volcanic aerosols may slow the rise in temperature, but even an optical thickness of 0.1 maintained for 120 years would reduce the warming by less than 1.0°C.

When should the CO_2 warming rise out of the noise level of natural *32* climate variability? An estimate can be obtained by comparing the predicted warming to the standard deviation, σ, of the observed global temperature trend of the past century (50). The standard deviation, which increases from 0.1°C for 10-year intervals to 0.2°C for the full century, is the total variability of global temperature; it thus includes variations due to any known radiative forcing, other variations of the true global temperature due to unidentified causes, and noise due to imperfect measurement of the global temperature. Thus if T_0 is the current 5-year smoothed global temperature, the 5-year smoothed global temperature in 10 years should be in the range $T_0 \pm 0.1$°C with probability ~ 70 percent, judging only from variability in the past century.

The predicted CO_2 warming rises out of the 1σ noise level in the *33* 1980's and the 2σ level in the 1990's (Figure 4). This is independent of the climate model's equilibrium sensitivity for the range of likely values, 1.4° to 5.6°C. Furthermore, it does not depend on the scenario for atmospheric CO_2 growth, because the amounts of CO_2 do not differ substantially until after year 2000. Volcanic eruptions of the size of Krakatoa or Agung may slow the warming, but barring an unusual coincidence of eruptions, the delay will not exceed several years.

Nominal confidence in the CO_2 theory will reach ~ 85 percent when *34* the temperature rises through the 1σ level and ~ 98 percent when it exceeds 2σ. However, a portion of σ may be accounted for in the future from accurate knowledge of some radiative forcings and more precise knowledge of global temperature. We conclude that CO_2 warming should rise above the noise level of natural climate variability in this century.

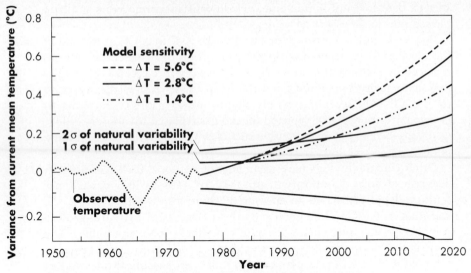

Figure 4.   CO₂ warming versus noise level of natural climate variability. Comparison of projected CO₂ warming to standard deviation (σ) of observed global temperature and to 2σ. The standard deviation was computed for the observed global temperatures in Figure 1. Carbon dioxide change is from the slow-growth scenario. The effect of other trace gases is not included. *Source: Adapted from J. Hansen et al., "Climate Impact of Increasing Atmospheric Carbon Dioxide," Science 213 (1981): p. 965. Copyright 1981 by the AAAS. Reprinted with permission.*

Potential Consequences of Global Warming

Practical implications of CO₂ warming can only be crudely estimated,   35 based on climate models and study of past climate. Models do not yet accurately simulate many parts of the climate system, especially the ocean, clouds, polar sea ice, and ice sheets. Evidence from past climate is also limited, since the few recent warm periods were not as extreme as the warming projected to accompany full use of fossil fuels, and the climate forcings and rate of climate change may have been different. However, if checked against our understanding of the physical processes and used with caution, the models and data on past climate provide useful indications of possible future climate effects (51).

Paleoclimatic° evidence suggests that surface warming at high latitudes   36 will be two to five times the global mean warming (52–55). Climate models predict the larger sensitivity at high latitudes and trace it to snow/ice albedo feedback and greater atmospheric stability, which mag-

---

Paleoclimate—climate during ancient times.

nifies the warming of near-surface layers (6–8). Since these mechanisms will operate even with the expected rapidity of CO_2 warming, it can be anticipated that average high-latitude warming will be a few times greater than the global mean effect.

Climate models indicate that large regional climate variations will *37* accompany global warming. Such shifting of climatic patterns has great practical significance, because the precipitation patterns determine the locations of deserts, fertile areas, and marginal lands. A major regional change in the double CO_2 experiment with our three-dimensional model (6, 8) was the creation of hot, dry conditions in much of the western two-thirds of the United States and Canada and in large parts of central Asia. The hot, dry summer of 1980 may be typical of the United States in the next century if the model results are correct. However, the model shows that many other places, especially coastal areas, are wetter with doubled CO_2.

Reconstructions of regional climate patterns in the altithermal° (53, *38* 54) show some similarity to these model results. The United States was drier than today during that warm period, but most regions were wetter than at present. For example, the climate in much of North Africa and the Middle East was more favorable for agriculture 8000 to 4000 years ago, at the time civilization dawned in that region.

Beneficial effects of CO_2 warming will include increased length of the *39* growing season. It is not obvious whether the world will be more or less able to feed its population. Major modifications of regional climate patterns will require efforts to readjust land use and crop characteristics and may cause large-scale human dislocations. Improved global climate models, reconstructions of past climate, and detailed analyses are needed before one can predict whether the net long-term impact will be beneficial or detrimental.

Melting of the world's ice sheets is another possible effect of CO_2 *40* warming. If they melted entirely, sea level would rise $\sim$ 70 m. However, their natural response time is thousands of years, and it is not certain whether CO_2 warming will cause the ice sheets to shrink or grow. For example, if the ocean warms but the air above the ice sheets remains below freezing, the effect could be increased snowfall, net ice sheet growth, and thus lowering of sea level.

Danger of rapid sea level rise is posed by the West Antarctic ice sheet, *41* which, unlike the land-based Greenland and East Antarctic ice sheets, is grounded below sea level, making it vulnerable to rapid disintegration and melting in case of general warming (55). The summer temperature in its vicinity is about -5°C. If this temperature rises $\sim$ 5°C, deglaciation could be rapid, requiring a century or less and causing a sea level rise

---

Altithermal—period of highest temperature.

of 5 to 6 m (55). If the West Antarctic ice sheet melts on such a time scale, it will temporarily overwhelm any sea level change due to growth or decay of land-based ice sheets. A sea level rise of 5 m would flood 25 percent of Louisiana and Florida, 10 percent of New Jersey, and many other lowlands throughout the world.

Climate models (7, 8) indicate that $\sim$ 2°C global warming is needed 42 to cause $\sim$ 5°C warming at the West Antarctic ice sheet. A 2°C global warming is exceeded in the 21st century in all the CO_2 scenarios we considered, except no growth and coal phaseout.

Floating polar sea ice responds rapidly to climate change. The 5° to 43 10°C warming expected at high northern latitudes for doubled CO_2 should open the Northwest and Northeast passages along the borders of the American and Eurasian continents. Preliminary experiments with sea ice models (56) suggest that all the sea ice may melt in summer, but part of it would refreeze in winter. Even a partially ice-free Arctic will modify neighboring continental climates.

Discussion

The global warming projected for the next century is of almost unprec- 44 edented magnitude. On the basis of our model calculations, we estimate it to be $\sim$ 2.5°C for a scenario with slow energy growth and a mixture of nonfossil and fossil fuels. This would exceed the temperature during the altithermal (6000 years ago) and the previous (Eemian) interglacial period 125,000 years ago (53), and would approach the warmth of the Mesozoic, the age of dinosaurs.

Many caveats must accompany the projected climate effects. First, the 45 increase of atmospheric CO_2 depends on the assumed energy growth rate, the proportion of energy derived from fossil fuels, and the assumption that about 50 percent of anthropogenic CO_2 emissions will remain airborne. Second, the predicted global warming for a given CO_2 increase is based on rudimentary abilities to model a complex climate system with many nonlinear processes. Tests of model sensitivity, ranging from the equilibrium climates on the planets to perturbations of the earth's climate, are encouraging, but more tests are needed. Third, only crude estimates exist for regional climate effects.

More observations and theoretical work are needed to permit firm 46 identification of the CO_2 warming and reliable prediction of larger climate effects farther in the future. It is necessary to monitor primary global radiative forcings: solar luminosity, cloud properties, aerosol properties, ground albedo, and trace gases. Exciting capabilities are within reach. For example, the NASA Solar Maximum Mission is monitoring solar output with a relative accuracy of $\sim$ 0.01 percent (57). Studies of certain components of the climate system are needed, especially heat storage and transport by the oceans and ice sheet dynamics. These studies will require global monitoring and local measurements of processes, guided by theoretical studies. Climate models must be developed to reliably simulate regional climate, including the transient response (*58*) to gradually increasing CO_2 amount.

Political and economic forces affecting energy use and fuel choice *47* make it unlikely that the CO_2 issue will have a major impact on energy policies until convincing observations of the global warming are in hand. In light of historical evidence that it takes several decades to complete a major change in fuel use, this makes large climate change almost inevitable. However, the degree of warming will depend strongly on the energy growth rate and choice of fuels for the next century. Thus, CO_2 effects on climate may make full exploitation of coal resources undesirable. An appropriate strategy may be to encourage energy conservation and develop alternative energy sources, while using fossil fuels as necessary during the next few decades.

The climate change induced by anthropogenic release of CO_2 is likely *48* to be the most fascinating global geophysical experiment that man will ever conduct. The scientific task is to help determine the nature of future climatic effects as early as possible. The required efforts in global observations and climate analysis are challenging, but the benefits from improved understanding of climate will surely warrant the work invested.

References and Notes

[1]National Academy of Sciences, *Energy and Climate* (Washington, D.C., 1977).

[2]U. Siegenthaler and H. Oeschger, *Science* **199**, 388 (1978).

[3]W. S. Broecker, T. Takahashi, H. J. Simpson, T.-H. Peng, *ibid.* **206**, 409 (1979).

[4]R. M. Rotty and G. Marland, *Oak Ridge Assoc. Univ. Rep. IEA-80-9(M)* (1980).

[5]W. C. Wang, Y. L. Yung, A. A. Lacis, T. Mo, J. E. Hansen, *Science* **194**, 685 (1976).

[6]National Academy of Sciences, *Carbon Dioxide and Climate: A Scientific Assessment* (Washington, D.C., 1979). This report relies heavily on simulations made with two three-dimensional climate models (*7, 8*) that include realistic global geography, seasonal insolation variations, and a 70-m mixed-layer ocean with heat capacity but no horizontal transport of heat.

[7]S. Manabe and R. J. Stouffer, *Nature (London)* **282**, 491 (1979); *J. Geophys. Res.* **85**, 5529 (1980).

[8]J. Hansen, A. Lacis, D. Rind, G. Russell, P. Stone, in preparation. Results of an initial CO_2 experiment with this model are summarized in (*6*).

[9]National Academy of Sciences, *Understanding Climate Change* (Washington, D.C., 1975).

[10]R. E. Newell and T. G. Dopplick, *J. Appl. Meteorol.* **18**, 822 (1979).

[11]S. B. Idso, *Science* **207**, 1462 (1980); *ibid.* **210**, 7 (1980).

[12]*J. Geophys. Res.* **82** (No. 28) (1977); *ibid.* **85** (No. A13) (1980).

[13]S. Manabe and R. T. Wetherald, *J. Atmos. Sci.* **24**, 241 (1967). . . .

[25]W. S. Broecker, *Science* **189**, 460 (1975). . . .

[27]H. H. Lamb, *Philos. Trans. R. Soc. London Ser. A* **255**, 425 (1970). . . .

[39]R. L. Jenne, *Data Sets for Meteorological Research* (NCAR-TN/IA-111, National Center for Atmospheric Research, Boulder, Colo., 1975); *Monthly Climate Data for the World* (National Oceanic and Atmospheric Administration, Asheville, N.C.).

[40]T. P. Barnett, *Mon. Weather Rev.* **106**, 1353 (1978).

[41]S. K. Kao and J. F. Sagendorf, *Tellus* **22**, 172 (1970).

[42]R. A. Madden, *Mon. Weather Rev.* **105**, 9 (1977).

[43]W. A. R. Brinkman, *Quart. Res. (N.Y.)* **6**, 335 (1976); I. I. Borzenkova, K. Ya. Vinnikov, L. P. Spirina, D. I. Stekhnovskiy, *Meteorol. Gidrol.* 7, 27 (1976); P. D. Jones and T. M. L. Wigley, *Clim. Monit.* **9**, 43 (1980).

[44]P. E. Damon and S. M. Kunen, *Science* **193**, 447 (1976).

[45]J. E. Hansen, W.-C. Wang, A. A. Lacis, *ibid.* **199**, 1065 (1978).

[46]R. Oliver, *J. Appl. Meteorol.* **15**, 933 (1976); C. Mass and S. Schneider, *J. Atmos. Sci.* **34**, 1995 (1977). . . .

[51]W. W. Kellogg and R. Schware, *Climate Change and Society* (Westview, Boulder, Colo., 1978).

[52]CLIMAP Project Members, *Science* **191**, 1131 (1976).

[53]H. H. Lamb, *Climate: Present, Past and Future* (Methuen, London, 1977), vol. 2.

[54]W. W. Kellogg, in *Climate Change*, J. Gribbin, Ed. (Cambridge Univ. Press, Cambridge, 1977), p. 205; *Annu. Rev. Earth Planet. Sci.* 7, 63 (1979).

[55]J. J. Mercer, *Nature (London)* **271**, 321 (1978); T. Hughes, *Rev. Geophys. Space Phys.* **15**, 1 (1977).

[56]C. L. Parkinson and W. W. Kellogg, *Clim. Change* **2**, 149 (1979).

[57]R. C. Willson, S. Gulkis, M. Janssen, H. S. Hudson, G. A. Chapman, *Science* **211**, 700 (1981).

[58]S. H. Schneider and S. L. Thompson, *J. Geophys. Res.*, in press.

[59]We thank J. Charney, R. Dickinson, W. Donn, D. Hoyt, H. Landsberg, M. McElroy, L. Ornstein, P. Stone, N. Untersteiner, and R. Weiss for helpful comments; I. Shifrin for several typings of the manuscript; and L. DelValle for drafting the figures.

Rhetorical Analysis Through Annotation

Several devices are used to help readers find their way through this article. These devices include the boxed summary in the beginning, a projective summary description of the argument in the fourth paragraph, section headings, section ending conclusions and summaries, strong paragraph topic sentences, analogies and simplified explanations, visual aids, and a final discussion.

Mark each device that helps the reader through the text.

Discuss how each of these devices orients the reader to the developing argument, helps highlight key points, and makes the overall shape and impact of the argument clear.

Discussion Questions

Interpreting the Text

1. What objections have been raised to the theory that increasing carbon dioxide should lead to atomspheric warming? How does this article address those objections?

2. Explain as best you can the meaning of equations one through three. How are these equations related to the concepts presented in the previous textbook selection (371–384)?

3. How does examination of other planets help confirm the greenhouse effect?

4. What are the advantages of a one-dimensional model over a zero-dimensional model? Why is a three-dimensional model not used?

5. How did the authors gather and put together historical temperature data? What have the general temperature trends been over the past century?

6. How do the model calculations correspond to the historical temperature trends? What factors were considered in the comparison between model and historical data? How were these factors considered? Which factors proved most significant? What do the authors mean by "noise"?

7. What projections were necessary to predict future climatic temperature? Under what assumptions were these projections made? How did predictions differ under various assumptions?

8. What factors limit our ability to estimate the consequences of global warming? What consequences are nonetheless likely? How does this warming compare with prehistoric periods?

9. What kind of social action do the authors suggest? What do they expect? Why?

Considering the Issues

10. In what ways does this article present an argument? Who are the authors trying to convince of what? How do various parts of the essay meet objections or argue for new points? At what points are different parts of the argument treated as being won so that the article can shift to a different type of argument? In this sense, does the article black-box its earlier parts as it goes on?

11. Compare the level of detail of diagrams, findings, and concepts with the level in previous selections in this unit. What makes the level consistently more difficult here? How did you go about attacking the difficulty? How did the knowledge you gained from the previous selections help you understand this article?

12. What are the effects of this kind of writing on people not trained in science or people trained in a different branch of science? Are these effects intentional or simply a consequence of the communication needs of the scientists? What communications barriers result from these effects? Are you familiar with any

area that uses technical arguments? What are the social and communication consequences of this technicality?

13. How does the model-building kind of argument presented here compare to the more traditional hypothesis-and-experiment form of scientific argument you may be familiar with? Have you seen the model-building approach used elsewhere in science? In any other branch of knowledge?

14. Compare the summary with the entire article. What does the comparison tell you about how the authors see the overall importance of the article versus the need for technical argument? In what ways may the readers of the entire article differ from the readers of just the abstract? Are there different groups who may just read different sections of the article?

Writing Suggestions

1. For a course in atmospheric science, write a brief summary of the article, particularly drawing attention to points that were not covered in the textbook assignment (see pages 371–384).

2. As part of this course's discussion of forms of communication in different disciplines, write an analysis of this article to demonstrate the role of argumentation in science.

3. For the editorial page of your local newspaper write a thought piece about how dependent our lives have become on incomprehensible findings of science or about how you can come to understand even difficult science if you think it important enough.

4. For a class in philosophy write an essay on model building as a way of thinking about the world. You may discuss either how philosophers have built world models in their theories or how you have built mental models of some parts of the world in order to understand your life and the people around you better.

Climatic Effects of Atmospheric Carbon Dioxide: An Exchange

Michael MacCracken; S. B. Idso; and J. Hansen et al.

Just because scientists develop a careful case for their claims does not mean that their arguments are ironclad or that all other scientists immediately agree with them. Long-range confirmation of the climate model developed by Hansen and his group depends on how closely the predictions generated by the model conform with future global temperature. Though the model may predict future temperatures fairly well, other scientists and the Hansen group are working to develop more powerful models, taking into account improved understanding of climate processes and more variables, thus giving more detailed and accurate predictions.

In the short range, other scientists may find reasons not to accept the claims of Hansen *et al.* Scientists are trained to be skeptical about each other's arguments and to question any weaknesses they may find in each other's reasoning. This questioning takes place in front of other scientists at conferences or in the pages of journals. The community of working scientists ultimately decides who has the more compelling arguments by the way in which they use each other's findings in their own future work. Work considered reliable and usable becomes the basis for future work and, therefore, becomes part of the shared knowledge. Work considered unreliable, uncertain, or unusable (and therefore ignored) does not enter into the shared knowledge.

The following exchange of letters over the Hansen *et al.* analysis appeared in the same journal as the original article, *Science*, but almost two years later, in 1983. If you notice the small dates at the end of each letter, however, you will see that the critical letters were written only four and nine months after the original article appeared. Science is fast moving, and publication delays are sometimes long, so it is important to note when articles and letters were actually written, and not just when they were published.

In looking at the criticisms and the reply by the original team, notice how the critics do not attempt to reject the complex model altogether. Nor in this case do they launch all-out negative arguments. Rather they tend to accept the reliability of most of the data and many of the conclusions of the article they criticize. They raise specific questions about particular points in the argument by pointing to uncertainties, details about the data, and other studies revealing complications in the data and argument. Rather than destroying the claims, the strategy appears to make the claims appear less reliable. Hansen *et al.* then try to repair the reliability by showing that their analysis takes into account the considerations raised by the critics MacCracken and Idso as much as current knowledge and technology would allow. They further suggest how future work might clarify uncertainties raised by the critics.

Each contribution to science is part of a conversation among scientists who share many common assumptions and mutual respect, even though they may disagree on specific points. Rarely does an article become immediately accepted knowledge in the exact form in which it was originally presented. Accepted scientific knowledge emerges only out of a process of negotiation and discussion within the scientific community.

HANSEN *ET AL.* (1) HAVE used numerical models to provide some 1
insight into why and how the climate will respond to increasing CO_2
concentrations. In addition, however, they argue that the consistency of
results from one-dimensional climate models and from observations of
global surface air temperature over the last 100 years indicates that the
climate is warming due to increasing CO_2 concentrations as global
models predict. I agree that the climatic record is not inconsistent with
the projected warming to be expected if there is to be an increase of 2
to 3 K° for a doubling of CO_2 concentrations and strongly agree that
first detection of such changes should be sought by analyses such as
done by Hansen *et al.* However, there are a number of limitations in
their analysis that must be resolved if we are to say with as much
confidence as their article conveys that the initial climatic response to
increasing CO_2 has been detected. Among the issues to be resolved are
the following.

Although observations [such as figure 3 in (1)] show a global cooling 2
from the late 1930's to the early 1960's, the results of Hansen *et al.* with
their best model show a much smaller decrease. Thus, while their curve
looks good, it chops off the peaks and valleys over the last 60 years. Is
that because of natural fluctuations or because of a serious omission in
the model? We do not yet know.

Even the very small decrease in temperature from 1930 to 1960 shown 3
by Hansen's model is strongly dependent on the physically untested
postulation° of Hoyt (2) concerning umbra/penumbra ratio. Hansen *et
al.* comment that Hoyt's hypothesis was the only one of three viable
contenders concerning solar activity that worked. This aspect of their
work is extremely uncertain. In addition, their analysis does not consistently apply in each of their three areas. For example, the 1935 to 1960
cooling takes place almost exclusively north of 23.6°N. They do not
explain why umbra/penumbra only works in that region (in an exaggerated way) and not over the other 70 percent of the globe.

Hansen *et al.* have not analyzed the volcanic results on a hemispheric 4
or regional basis. Why, for example, does the near-equatorial Mount
Agung eruption in 1963 have a larger effect in the Northern than the
Southern Hemisphere when observations show much more aerosol in
the Southern Hemisphere? The answer usually given is that the ocean's
thermal inertia is larger in the Southern Hemisphere, but in some other
cases—for example, around 1900 to 1910—the response was much larger

---

K—degrees on the Kelvin temperature scale. One degree change on the Kelvin scale is
equivalent to one degree change on the centigrade, or 1⅘ degrees on the Fahrenheit
scale.   **Physically untested postulation**—a hypothesis not tested by comparison to actual physical evidence.

in the Southern Hemisphere, yet many of the volcanic eruptions at that time were in the Northern Hemisphere.

The authors indicate that their results tend to confirm model results *5* for global climate change. Virtually all of these models also indicate an amplification of the temperature change in polar regions, yet recent data of Angell and Korshover (*3*) (and, I suspect, Hansen's data) do not show this. Hansen *et al.* should also say that the polar amplification—the largest regional effect predicted by models—is not confirmed. It is essential that a reasonable set of climatic parameters that are expected to respond to increasing CO_2 be determined and a coordinated search be initiated to find correlated changes among them all.

There are a number of uncertainties related to the size of the CO_2- *6* induced temperature change used by Hansen *et al.* (i) The history of CO_2 concentrations is known only back to 1957. Before that they rely on carbon cycle considerations that virtually ignore the suspected contribution of CO_2 to the atmosphere by the biosphere. If the biosphere played a role, their fit will change. (ii) Their climate model balances some simplifications against others in arriving at the expected temperature change. The 2.8 K temperature increase used for a doubling of CO_2 could be wrong by a factor of 2, which would affect the correlation. (iii) Their continent/ocean ratioing to increase the size of the climatic effect seems to assume that the continents cannot themselves cause heat to be transported to the upper atmosphere (for instance, by convection) and then radiated to space; instead, this heat must be transported upward by additional latent heat release after warming the ocean. The assumption needs to be tested. (iv) Their analysis begins in the 1880's, when the climate was apparently quite cool due to major volcanic injections during that decade. Stratospheric aerosol concentrations 100 years ago were not well measured. Extending the temperature data set back to 1850 may help reduce any bias introduced by the choice of time interval.

As an alternative analysis, one could estimate the climatic effect of *7* increasing CO_2 by comparing the minimum temperatures reached after Krakatoa° and after Agung, which were equatorial volcanoes. On a global basis the difference is about 0.25 K (the Agung minimum being warmer), with about 0.3 K north of 23.6°N, 0.15 K south of 23.6°S, and 0.25 K in tropical regions. Most data suggest that Krakatoa was bigger than Agung (25 percent larger Lamb dust veil index), so the maximum CO_2 effect from 1883 to 1963 must be less than 0.25 K, probably more like 0.2 K. This is not very different than Hansen's result. However, one might then ask why Agung, if it was smaller, appears to have caused a larger temperature decrease from prevailing values than did Krakatoa.

Krakatoa—an Indonesian volcano that erupted in 1883.

In summary, although Hansen *et al.* have probably carried out a 8 broader scale analysis than any previous investigators, I believe that they have understated many uncertainties that deserve careful consideration.

MICHAEL C. MACCRACKEN

Atmospheric and Geophysical Sciences Division, Lawrence Livermore National Laboratory, Livermore, California 94550

Notes

[1]J. Hansen, D. Johnson, A. Lacis, S. Lebedeff, P. Lee, D. Rind, G. Russell, *Science* **213**, 957 (1981).
[2]D. V. Hoyt, *Nature (London)* **282**, 388 (1979).
[3]J. K. Angell and J. Korshover, *Mon. Weather Rev.* **105**, 375 (1977).
[4]This work was performed under the auspices of the U.S. Department of Energy at Lawrence Livermore National Laboratory under contract W-7405-Eng-48.

30 December 1981

Hansen *et al.* (*1*) make much of an apparent increase in mean global 9 air temperature starting in the mid-1960's. However, this warming comes about as a result of their southern latitude data set, which represents far fewer stations than either their low latitude or northern latitude data sets; and when the latter measurements are studied, just the opposite is seen. For instance, a simple linear regression analysis° of their low latitude data shows an almost unchanging temperature for the last 55 years, while for northern latitudes the trend has been strongly negative at more than 0.1°C per decade since 1935. The latter result is especially significant, for general circulation models of the atmosphere all predict that the CO_2-induced warming should be most evident at high latitudes.

To give some feel for the magnitude of discrepancy, it can be derived 10 from the calculations of Hansen *et al.* that the "probable" global warming predicted by the models between 1935 and 1980 is about 0.25°C. Since they then suggest that high latitude warming should be two to five times the global mean warming, the models predict that northern latitude temperatures should have increased by 0.5° to 1.25°C over that period. However, the data of Hansen *et al.* show a mean temperature decrease for this interval of 0.5°C. This discrepancy of 1.0° to 1.75°C between the model predictions and observations in northern latitudes actually refutes the validity of the numerical climate models.

Many people find it difficult to believe that the models can be wrong, 11 particularly since they all seem to predict about the same degree of warming. But this similarity, too, is misleading. For instance, the model

---

Linear regression analysis—a statistical technique for determining how far data vary from a simple linear relationship, expressed by a straight line on a graph of the data.

of Hansen *et al.* predicts a 1.2°C temperature rise as a result of direct CO_2 effects and a 1.0°C rise as a result of the "well-established H_2O greenhouse effect," for a 2.2°C total warming and a water vapor feedback enhancement factor of 1.8. In Ramanathan's (2) most recent analysis, however, direct effects of CO_2 account for only a 0.5°C temperature rise, with feedback effects of water vapor adding 1.7°C more. Thus, although the total temperature increase that Ramanathan calculates is identical to that of Hansen *et al.*, his water vapor enhancement factor is 4.4. If these two models of the atmosphere differ so dramatically from each other in their assessments of this well-established effect, it is no wonder that they fail to properly represent the truly complex aspects of the earth-ocean-atmosphere system which lead to discrepancies of the type described above for northern latitudes.

With respect to potential benefits of increased atmospheric CO_2, Han- *12* sen *et al.* mention only the possibility of an increased growing season. In a review of more than 400 experiments dealing with economic yields of agricultural crops, however, Kimball (3) has demonstrated that a doubling of the atmospheric CO_2 content could increase global productivity by 33 percent and that a tripling could boost it by 66 percent— without additional inputs of fertilizers or water. It is thus time to realize that the CO_2 question is not a single-issue subject and that there are some positive agricultural benefits to be gained from a CO_2-enriched atmosphere.

S. B. IDSO

U.S. Water Conservation Laboratory, 4331 East Broadway Road, Phoenix, Arizona 85040

Notes

[1] J. Hansen, D. Johnson, A. Lacis, S. Lebedeff, P. Lee, D. Rind, G. Russell, *Science* **213**, 957 (1981).

[2] V. Ramanathan, *J. Atmos. Sci.* **38**, 918 (1981).

[3] B. A. Kimball, *Report 11*, U.S. Water Conservation Laboratory, Phoenix, Ariz. (1982).

24 May 1982

We used a one-dimensional (1-D) climate model to show that global *13* mean temperature increased in the past century at a rate consistent with the greenhouse theory (1). The questions raised by MacCracken and Idso in no way alter that result or undermine the conclusion that the greenhouse effect is real and will lead in the next century to global climate change of almost unprecedented magnitude.

Observed temperature trends. MacCracken and Idso are incorrect in stat- *14* ing that observations do not show a polar enhancement of the temperature trend, which is the principal expected subglobal temperature effect (1, 2). The global temperature warmed by 0.4° to 0.5°C in the past

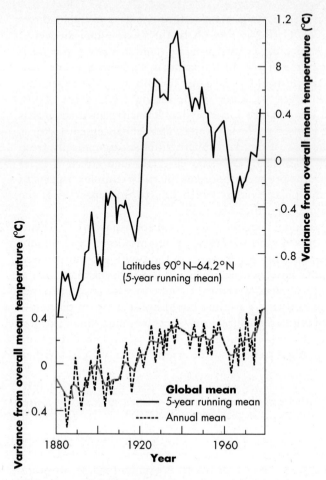

Figure 1.   Observed temperature trends based on data set described in (1), updated through 1980.
Source: Adapted from Michael MacCracken, S. B. Idso, J. Hansen, et al., "Climatic Effects of Atmospheric Carbon Dioxide," Science 220 (1983): p. 875. Copyright 1983 by the AAAS. Reprinted with permission.

century and high latitudes warmed by 1.2° to 1.5°C (Fig. 1), polar enhancement by about a factor 3.

Polar enhancement is expected for time scales long enough for the ocean surface temperature to approach its equilibrium response at all latitudes, that is, a few decades or longer. Figure 1 shows that polar enhancement also occurred for such decadal periods: the 1880–1940 warming and the 1940–1965 cooling and warming thereafter. **15**

MacCracken and Idso make much of regional details and peaks and valleys of the observed temperature trend. We agree that geographic patterns and short-term variations of observed temperature contain valuable information on the climate system. As our article made clear, we **16** strongly support the development of three-dimensional models that will realistically model natural climate variability on a regional scale and that can simulate the effect of greenhouse warming on such factors as standing and transient long waves and ocean currents. In the interim, changes in regional temperature patterns do not provide a basis for confirming or disproving the greenhouse effect. Note also that the global temperature trend has substantial interannual fluctuations (Fig. 1). Thus our procedure of analyzing the mean long-term trend should be more reliable than that of comparing temperatures from valley to valley after large volcanic eruptions, as proposed by MacCracken.

Climate sensitivity. Idso states that our model gives a water vapor *17* feedback factor of 1.8 and Ramanathan's model (*3*) yields 4.4. He uses this to argue that the consensus in the climatological community on the approximate magnitude of the greenhouse effect is misleading and the models are therefore untrustworthy. However, careful reading of the papers would have shown that the difference is one of semantics. We use the conventional definition of water vapor feedback: we run our model with CO_2 doubled but everything else unchanged, and then with CO_2 doubled and water vapor increased according to fixed relative humidity. With the same definition, Ramanathan obtains a feedback factor of 1.6 [table 4 in (*3*)].

MacCracken's numbered comments revolve around the question of *18* whether several uncertainties in our analysis, such as the CO_2 abundance in 1880 and the choice of starting date for our analysis, could throw the results off. (i) A plausible change of 10 to 15 ppm in the 1880 CO_2 abundance would have little effect on our results. In fact, the sense of suggested positive biospheric contributions to atmospheric CO_2 prior to 1940 is to slightly improve the ability of the model to match the relatively rapid warming in 1880 to 1940. (ii) We explicitly recognized the uncertainty in global climate sensitivity, and we even tested the effect of letting the model sensitivity be a free parameter. We found that with an exchange rate between the ocean mixed layer and thermocline based on passive tracers (k-1 to 2 cm^2/sec), a climate sensitivity of 2.5° to 5°C is needed to best fit the observed global temperature trend. The consistency of this empirical sensitivity with the a priori sensitivity estimated from climate models provides some evidence that this sensitivity is of the right order. (iii) Changes in the continent/ocean factor were tested in our 1-D model and found not to be of appreciable importance. (iv) Extension of the analysis back to 1850 is desirable, but it is not possible at this time due to lack of information on global temperature and atmospheric composition for that period. In summary, we agree with McCracken that it is desirable to account for as many uncertainties as possible in modeling climate, but in fact our analysis covers a greater range of possibilities than he has raised.

Confirmation of CO_2 warming. MacCracken misinterprets our position *19* on detection of the warming. We stated "More observations and theoretical work are needed to permit firm identification of the CO_2 warming." Also, we quantitatively compared projected warming to natural climate variability, concluding that the greenhouse warming "should emerge from the noise level of natural climate variability by the end of the century, and there is a high probability of warming in the 1980's."

The eruption of El Chichón in Mexico in 1982 injected a stratospheric 20 aerosol veil comparable to that from Agung in 1963. This may counteract the CO_2 warming for 1 or 2 years, and it provides an excellent opportunity for testing global climate models. But, barring improbable further eruptions of the magnitude of Agung or El Chichón, significant warming is still likely in this decade.

Beneficial effects of CO_2. Idso raises the question of CO_2 benefits for 21 photosynthesis. Our article was limited to the climate implications of increasing CO_2. We did not attempt to weigh the beneficial and detrimental effects, concluding: "Improved global climate models, reconstructions of past climate, and detailed analyses are needed before one can predict whether the net long-term impact will be beneficial or detrimental." We agree that the well-known issue of CO_2 "fertilization" of plants is an important question, but its discussion is extraneous to our article.

In summary, MacCracken and Idso present no new information which 22 significantly modifies our analysis. The evidence that continued emission of CO_2 and trace gases will lead to climate change is sufficiently compelling to call for vigorous investigation. The required efforts in global observations and climate analysis are challenging and require long-range commitment, but the benefits from improved understanding of climate will surely warrant the work invested.

J. HANSEN   P. LEE
D. JOHNSON   D. RIND
A. LACIS   G. RUSSELL
S. LEBEDEFF
Goddard Space Flight Center, Institute for Space Studies, New York 10025

Notes

[1] J. Hansen, D. Johnson, A. Lacis, S. Lebedeff, P. Lee, D. Rind, G. Russell, *Science* **213**, 957 (1981).
[2] S. Manabe and R. J. Stouffer, *J. Geophys. Res.* **85**, 5529 (1980).
[3] V. Ramanathan, *J. Atmos. Sci.* **38**, 918 (1981).

24 January 1983; revised 10 February 1983

Rhetorical Analysis Through Annotation

MacCracken and Idso make a number of specific complaints about the original Hansen *et al.* article. These complaints try to undermine specific claims in the original article. Hansen *et al.* then try to counter each complaint in order to reestablish the validity of each claim.

In the MacCracken and Idso letters underline and number the main statement of each critical point made against the original article. Circle the phrase or sentence in which this criticism is tied to a reference to the original argument. Also mark any devices used to tie the separate criticisms into coherent letters, paying specific attention to openings, closings, and transitions.

In the original article, find the specific passages or arguments referred to in the MacCracken and Idso letters and mark them to identify the criticism made of them. Use coded markings, such as M-1, to refer to MacCracken's first criticism. Discuss how serious the criticisms are and (if true) what damage they would do to Hansen *et al.*'s overall line of reasoning.

In the responses by Hansen *et al.* to the criticisms, identify which point in the MacCracken and Idso letters each of the responses is directed at. Use coded markings (M-1, I-1) to identify the critical complaints. Circle the phrases or sentences that refer specifically to the critical letters or the original text. Also mark devices used to tie the separate responses into a single coherent answer. Discuss the ways Hansen *et al.* try to counter the criticisms.

Discuss the techniques the critical letters and the response use to tie themselves to other documents in the series and the relationships established among the documents. Also discuss how each of the separate texts tries to tie itself together as an integrally whole and separate document.

Discussion Questions

Interpreting the Text

1. What kinds of difficulties does each of the critics find with Hansen *et al.*'s model? Do the criticisms seem credible and significant? On what bases?

2. Compare each criticism with the answer given by Hansen *et al.* Although you do not have the technical knowledge to judge, how appropriate and plausible does each answer sound? How does the answer repair the reliability of the original article?

3. What new information and nuances of argument are added to the original article through this exchange of letters? Does the exchange improve or advance the original argument, or is the exchange simply a static matter of attack and defense?

Considering the Issues

4. In what way does each criticism try to open up a black box in the argument—that is, something Hansen *et al.* would like you to accept as part of their argument, but the critics are unwilling to let pass. In what ways can the answers of Hansen *et al.* be seen as attempts to close up the black boxes or substitute new ones?

5. Are the overall conclusions of Hansen *et al.* ever attacked? What does each of the three letters say about the overall project and conclusions? In what directions would each of the criticisms lead future work and thinking?

6. Why does the argument get so technical?

7. Does this remind you of any other debates you have seen? How does it compare with political debates, courtroom arguments, disagreements with parents? How do the aims and techniques of these different types of contention compare? Also compare the disagreement here with other disagreements in other disciplines represented in this book. See for example the debates over the lessons of Chernobyl (pp. 494–518), the canon (pp. 25–107), or obstacles to black mobility (pp. 161–191).

Writing Suggestions

1. For a course in earth science summarize the debate expressed in this exchange. Include your estimate of the current state of the issues; that is, what the results of the debate are.

2. For some article that you have read and object to, write a letter to the editor of the newspaper or magazine it appeared in. Express your objections as precisely and forcefully as you can. As one strategy for criticism you may attempt to identify some black box in the argument the author relies on, and then open up that black box to call its assumptions and reasoning into question.

3. Your friend who is a science major has said to you that every statement that is presented scientifically is true. Write a letter to him, using this example and others that you are familiar with, explaining that science is a form of argument, and that scientific claims may be argued against and found not to be certain.

Statement Before the Senate Subcommittee on Environmental Pollution

James Hansen

Because some scientific research suggests the need for public action and because research often depends on government financing, scientists need to communicate with the government. Similarly, because Congress must consider policies for the future based on the best information available, Congress needs to communicate with scientists. Such communication often takes place through testimony before congressional committees. The testimony usually takes the form of the witness's prepared statement, followed by questioning.

Although scientists' testimony is based on their scientific work, they often try to find dramatic ways to present issues clearly and forcefully to gain public and congressional attention. Since the scientist's authority is already established by being chosen to testify, the scientist needs not so much to defend claims as to communicate the claims' importance for government planning, the future of America, and all the people of the world. Dramatic effects are often achieved through well-chosen, striking statistics and visual displays. Another technique is to bring the general ideas home with an application to a local, familiar situation.

We can see both techniques coming together in the closing section of Hansen's prepared statement. The largest part of the statement (not included here) summarizes and updates work we have seen discussed in earlier selections. For the closing section, however, Hansen's team has developed statistics to show the direct impact on the local climate of two American cities, even though their model is really designed to generate more global statistics. The two cities were carefully chosen to help the senators really feel the heat, and the predictions were displayed on graphs that dramatically emphasize the extreme change from current conditions.

Note as well the appeal at the end of the prepared statement for the maintainance of research funding. To maintain authority and importance, the scientist must claim much knowledge already gained, but to maintain research funding, the scientist must emphasize how much we still need to know. In the excerpts from questioning, Hansen and the other scientists hold to that fine line.

In the questioning, which occurred before the Senate subcommittee on June 10, 1986, Hansen is joined by F. Sherwood Rowland, professor of chemistry at the University of California, Irvine, and Robert Watson of NASA. In the discussion of climatic change, the greenhouse effect of several other greenhouse gases in addition to CO_2 is considered, including chlorofluorocarbons (used in refrigerators and air conditioners), methane (produced by the breakdown of organic material, as in swamps), and nitrous oxide. In addition, they consider the different but related problem of certain gases (especially CFCs) depleting the stratospheric ozone layer, leading to increased ultraviolet radiation reaching the earth's surface, producing an increased incidence of skin cancer and other harmful effects.

In the spontaneous byplay of the questioning, the senators' questioning defines the types of answers that are appropriate. The scientists, not knowing the questions beforehand, do not have prepared answers. The question about being "king" must have indeed surprised the scientists, but at least Dr. Watson appears playfully grateful at the coronation. Because of the spontaneity, the answers sometimes ramble, and the speakers are not always sure if their answers fit the questions. Notice, for example, the joking between Dr. Rowland and Senator Chafee over the size of the regal domain.

HOW MIGHT TEMPERATURE CHANGES of the magnitude pre- 1
dicted alter the number of days with temperatures above a given limit
for Washington, D.C. and other U.S. cities? This is a particularly difficult question to answer, because the climate models are not designed
for local studies. I believe that the best way we can get an estimate to
this question at the present time is to compile climatological data for a
given city from a long series of daily observations (including maximum
and minimum temperatures for each day) and to add to this record the
mean (monthly) increase in daily maximum temperature and in daily
minimum temperature as predicted by the climate model for the gridbox
which includes that city. This procedure tends to minimize the effects
of any errors in the model's control run climatology.

This procedure has been carried out for several U.S. cities for the 2
equilibrium change in climate for doubled CO_2, with the work being
done principally by Paul Ashcraft as a summer student study. Because
of the climate system's finite response time, the results may be most
applicable to some time approximately in the middle of the twenty first
century, if Scenario A is approximately correct.

The results of this exercise for two U.S. cities, Washington, D.C., 3
and Omaha, Nebraska, are shown in Figure 1. The number of days per
year in which the maximum daily temperature exceeds 100°F increases
from about 1 to 12 in Washington and from 3 to 20 in Omaha. The
number of days with maximum temperature exceeding 90°F increases
from about 35 days to 85 days in both cities. The number of days per
year in which the nighttime temperature does not fall below 80°F increases from less than one day in both cities to nine days in Omaha and
19 in Washington, D.C.

There are a number of reasons why these estimates may differ from 4
the real world response. Principal among these are the following: First,
the estimates are based on a model with sensitivity 4°C for doubled
CO_2; the real world sensitivity is uncertain by about a factor of two.
Second, the model assumes that the ocean will continue to operate
essentially like it does today; if North Atlantic Deep Water Formation
and the Gulf Stream should be substantially modified, for example, that
could significantly change the results for a location such as Washington,
D.C. Third, there are many reasons why local responses may vary; the
indicated changes can only be regarded as plausible for these cities, under
the assumption of climate sensitivity equivalent to 4°C for doubled CO_2.

Discussion of the practical impacts of greenhouse warming has fo- 5
cused on possible indirect effects such as changes of sea level, storm
frequency, and drought. We believe, however, that the temperature
changes themselves may significantly affect the climatic environment
for the general population.

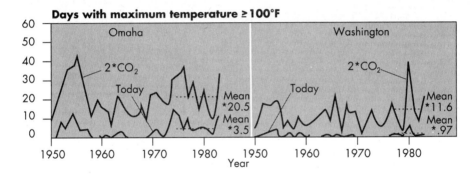

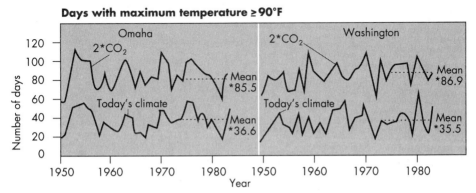

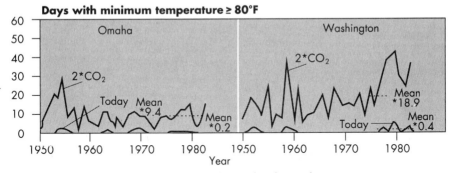

Figure 1. Annual number of days in Omaha, Nebraska, and
Washington, D.C., with (a) maximum temperature greater than
100°F, (b) maximum temperature greater than 90°F, and (c) minimum temperature greater than 80°F. Today's climate refers to
observations for the period 1950–1983. The results for doubled
CO_2 are generated by adding the warming obtained in a $2*CO_2$
climate model experiment to the observations for 1950–1983.

Evidence Needed to Confirm and Quantify the Greenhouse Theory

Evidence confirming the essence of the greenhouse theory is already **6** overwhelming from a scientific point of view. However, the greenhouse issue is not likely to receive the full attention it deserves until the global temperature rises above the level of natual climate variability. This will not occur at some sharp point in time, but rather gradually over a period of time. If our model is approximately correct, that time may be soon, within the next decade.

Unfortunately, when that point in time is reached people will begin **7** to ask practical questions and want quantitative answers. We are now totally unprepared to provide that information. Our understanding of the climate system and our climate models must be vastly improved.

The greatest need, in my opinion, is for global observations of the **8** climate system over a period of at least a decade. This will require both monitoring from satellites and *in situ* studies of climate processes. Prestigious scientific groups, such as the Earth System Sciences Committee appointed by the NASA Advisory Council, have defined the required observations in detail, and there seems little reason to repeat that information here. . . .

Senator CHAFEE. I would like to ask a question of each of the panelists. **9** That is: Do any of you believe that we need more scientific data before we could reach the conclusion that what is taking place now, if continued, will increase the temperature on the globe?

Are you prepared to say that if we keep going on the path we are **10** now, the temperature in the world is going to increase?

Dr. HANSEN. I don't think we need more evidence to say that. But to **11** answer the kind of detailed questions which are certainly going to be raised, we do need more evidence. As I mentioned global climate sensitivity is uncertain by about a factor of 2. The magnitude of the results which I showed would be different if climate sensitivity is larger or smaller than I assumed.

But I think the fact that the greenhouse effect is real is proven in a **12** number of different ways, such as by looking at other planets, which have different amounts of greenhouse gases.

Senator CHAFEE. Let me get the answers from the others. Dr. Rowland? **13**

Dr. ROWLAND. If you look at this Earth from satellites outside the **14** Earth, you can see the greenhouse effect in operation at all times. If you are going over the Sahara Desert, there are transparent regions of the infrared where the radiation comes right up from the desert, and there are other regions where the radiation is only coming from the top of the stratosphere because the carbon dioxide has absorbed the radiation from the desert below that.

The fact that the greenhouse effect is working on the Earth, it seems *15* to me, is perfectly straightforward. It has raised the temperature of the Earth about 30 degrees over what it would be without an atmosphere, and what we are talking about now are changes of another 1 or 2 or 3 degrees compared with a very large change that has already happened from gases that exist naturally.

Senator CHAFEE. Dr. Watson? *16*

Dr. WATSON. No; I believe global warming is inevitable. It is only a *17* question of the magnitude and the timing. . . .

Senator CHAFEE. Gentlemen, I am going to ask you a question. Sup- *18* pose each of you were king and you had what you might call unlimited authority. What would you do about this problem? I will start with King Watson.

Dr. WATSON. Thanks, once again. *19*

I think with respect to the ozone issue,° we have to look at all the *20* gases that contribute to a potential change in ozone: the fluorocarbons, methane, CO_2, and nitrous oxide. I don't personally like the approach of banning the specific use of substances like was done in the United States in 1978. While I recognize that it certainly helps to ban the specific use of one substance, therefore reducing the amount, in this case, of fluorocarbons into the atmosphere.

A much more logical approach, if you want to ban or regulate the *21* fluorocarbons, is to put an emissions cap on the total amount of gas that goes into the atmosphere. It doesn't matter what the use is. It matters that it is geting into the atmosphere. I think a protocol° at this time that limits the amount of fluorocarbons that get into the atmosphere is an extremely wise approach. I would advise pushing very hard for a protocol. The area of disagreement is exactly where we should put that limit.

Would you have a complete ban of fluorocarbons or limit them at *22* today's production levels? For the time being, I would limit it to something like today's production or thereabouts and still have an active research policy that would probably, within the next few years, provide more information. However, we should not focus just on the fluorocarbons, but we should consider all the gases discussed today. All of these gases affect both climate and the ozone issue.

Therefore, I think we have to look at all the gases, including methane, *23* nitrous oxide, and CO_2. These are very hard policy options. I think if you isolate or focus on one gas; that is, fluorocarbons, which are relatively easy to regulate, that would be the wrong approach. We would be solving a very small part of the problem. We will be back here soon

---

Ozone issue—the decrease in the ozone layer of the atmosphere, adding to the greenhouse effect. **Protocol**—a preliminary international agreement.

saying, "We covered the fluorocarbons; now what do we do about CO_2 and nitrous oxide?"

We have to look at our combustion policies which affect atmospheric 24 levels of nitrous oxide and CO_2. In addition, we have to try to understand what produces methane; this requires we do need more research. We don't understand why methane is changing, and it is changing at 1 percent per year. If we don't understand why it is changing, then we certainly can't control it.

Senator CHAFEE. Dr. Rowland?   25

Dr. ROWLAND. If I were king, the first thing I would do is consult 26 with the queen, who is sitting behind me and who has a very good view on what the sensible things to do in such cases are. Then what I would do, I think—I brought with me a magazine called "Bild der Wissenschaften,"° and you didn't specify that I was king of the world, but I gathered only king of the United States.

Senator CHAFEE. No; king of the world.   27

We don't travel second class here.   28

Dr. ROWLAND. The atmosphere is a world problem. I am looking at 29 this magazine, which is the German equivalent to "Scientific American," and on the front is a picture of the atmosphere and the ozone molecules and underneath it says, in German, "Humanity is destroying the protective shield of the earth, the ozone drama."

I think what I would do is start in on the chlorofluorocarbons. I would 30 replace all of the perhalocarbons° on a short-term basis, with anything such as fluorocarbon 22, which is a much less hazardous compound to the ozone. Then I would switch as soon as possible to those such as fluorocarbon 134 that have no hazard at all.

There are problems in controlling the other trace gases. We are very 31 much involved in trying to measure methane around the world, and its emission is a process which is largely influenced by man, because methane comes from swamps and from rice paddies and from cattle. Things like rice paddies and cattle are influenced by man, but it is going to be very hard to do anything about something like that.

I think there is a possibility that we can control, in some respects, the 32 emissions of carbon dioxide, but as has been mentioned, its release is primarily from burning fossil fuel and would require reconstructing powerplants. It is hard enough to construct them not to give off sulfur dioxide without taking off the carbon dioxide, as well.

I think we would want to be looking at those releases very closely, 33 and anyplace that you can see that you can cut down on emissions, then I think we should be doing it.

Senator CHAFEE. Dr. Hansen.   34

"**Bild der Wissenschaften**"—Trans: picture of science.   **Perhalocarbons**—the most active compounds of halogens (fluorine, chlorine, bromine, iodine, and astatine), carbon, and sometimes hydrogen.

Dr. HANSEN. I am sorry if I sound like a befuddled scientist rather *35* than a king, but I would like to understand the problem better before I order any dramatic actions. It is a very complicated global system, and we are just beginning to be able to model it. So I think that what I would like to see most of all, as I mentioned earlier, is global observations during the next decade, observations of the atmosphere, of the oceans, of the land surface, which allow us to see what is happening better and allow us to develop and test the models to represent what is happening.

Finally, I would like to point out that in my personal opinion, the *36* supply of two key ingredients needs to be increased in order that we could use such observational data to quantify the greenhouse effect and to develop adequate models and understanding. One of these key ingredients that we need is an influx of young scientists with appropriate training. We must begin training students now if we are to have scientists available in the next decade when the need for the information, I believe, is going to increase and the pressure to help define appropriate actions is going to be a lot greater.

The second key ingredient, in my opinion, is more research funding *37* for this kind of work. We are spending more and more time pursuing smaller and smaller research grants. I think that has an effect on our productivity in this work. So if I were king, I would ask for some research funding.

Senator CHAFEE. Let me ask you each again, it seems to me that Dr. *38* Watson said that dealing with the chlorofluorocarbons is but a small part of the problem. Dr. Hansen says, Let's have some more research, yet Dr. Rowland says, Certainly, let's tackle the CFC's right away, because that is something we can do.

It seems to me that although we are not going to achieve perfection, *39* we are probably not going to be able to substantially decrease the carbon dioxide emissions. But why not go after the CFC's? There is something we can do and do something more exciting, Dr. Watson, than merely keep them at the same level or, it seems to me, that I looked at Dr. Hansen's charges. Option B was a little discouraging. Maybe it is B, where we took some rather bold steps that was somewhat more encouraging.

Dr. Watson, my question to you is: Why not proceed at least against *40* the villain that we do know exists, even though it may not be the total villain?

Dr. WATSON. I think we know all of the gases are villains, sir; none *41* of them are perfect, but are all villains in different amounts. Some of the uses of CFC's are extremely important such as refrigeration and air-conditioning. Some of the other uses are rather frivolous, such as aerosol propellants, and foam blowing and Big Mac containers.

You may put a social judgment on what uses you want to ban it *42* from. However, Dr. Rowland may well be right that there are easy substitutes for fluorocarbons in refrigeration. If he is right, we can move fairly aggressively against this industry. If he is wrong, I think we would have to look much more closely.

I think we have to have a social judgment here of the utility of these 43 gases for social uses. I would not like to see a society without refrigeration. We also have to be somewhat careful that if we turn from one use of a chemical and replace it with a chemical, that the chemical doesn't have adverse environmental effects that we don't know about.

The opportunities Dr. Rowland mentioned are quite interesting. I 44 don't suggest they have any detrimental effects. What we do in regulations is we ban one substance, we start to use another substance, and the alternative is just as detrimental to the society, but we don't find out about it for a few more years. I think we should move with some caution, and some of the use of fluorocarbons are enforceable.

Senator CHAFEE. Any other questions, gentlemen? 45

Senator STAFFORD. Mr. Chairman, yes; one or two occurred to me. 46 Just for my understanding for a somewhat befuddled Senator here, am I correct that plants basically absorb CO_2 as part of their metabolism and exude oxygen?

Dr. ROWLAND. Yes. 47

Senator STAFFORD. So that should we cut down on CO_2 too much, 48 we would thereby put the plant life at risk. Am I correct on that? That isn't likely to happen, but I assume it could.

Dr. ROWLAND. Without carbon dioxide, plant life would be in great 49 difficulty. But none of the conceivable control systems are going to reduce the amount of carbon dioxide below what we have now.

Senator STAFFORD. Thank you. I assumed that was so. I had one 50 comment. If I instead of you were king, since I am chairman of the Senate's Education Committee, I would try to funnel more money in the direction of producing the scientists, Dr. Hansen, that I am sure we need or for whose need you express a view.

Rhetorical Analysis Through Annotation

As experts, scientists are asked for their opinions. To establish their usefulness as experts scientists must make direct statements about what they know. On the other hand, to maintain scientific credibility and to avoid attack by other expert witnesses, they must be careful to qualify what they say and admit uncertainties where there is no compelling evidence. Similarly, in asserting the need for continued funding, scientists must offer socially important knowledge while they continue to claim that there is much they still need to know.

In both the prepared statement and the question responses, mark direct assertions of knowledge with straight lines in the margin and mark qualifications and assertions of ignorance with squiggly lines in the margin.

Discuss the techniques used to identify statements as certain or less certain. Also discuss the effect of qualifications on the more direct assertions of knowledge. Finally discuss the purpose of each of the direct assertions, qualifications, and professions of ignorance.

Discussion Questions

Interpreting the Text

1. What consequences of the greenhouse effect are emphasized here? Why might these strike senators as significant?

2. What two cities were chosen for temperature change predictions? Why do you think these two were chosen rather than any others, such as New York City, Tucson, Miami, or Minneapolis?

3. What policy suggestions do each of the scientists make? How similar are the suggestions and how different? Are the differences nonetheless compatible? On what are the differences or recommendations based?

Considering the Issues

4. In what ways do the style, presentation, and argument of the prepared statement differ from those of the spontaneous responses to the questioning?

5. What precise reasons might Congress have in wanting to understand the greenhouse effect? How might climate change influence national interests? What kinds of action might the government take or how might various aspects of planning be modified to take climatic change into account?

6. What groups among the American people might be most affected by climate change? How would their lives be changed? What would they need to know most about the climate change? What kind of government intervention might these various groups want? What groups might be opposed to intervention? In what ways does the greenhouse effect become a political issue?

7. Why is science dependent on government funding? In what ways may this dependence distort research? In what ways may government funding act as a spur to research? Is it good or bad for science to have to justify its work before public political bodies such as Congress? Can science develop without large sources of funds? Are there better ways to fund scientific research?

Writing Suggestions

1. Use the information provided in this and other articles to write an article for your school newspaper on the threat posed by the greenhouse effect.

2. Write a letter to your senator expressing your feelings about public funding for continued research on the greenhouse effect.

3. For a political science class, use this and other relevant examples you may know of (such as in military technology, AIDS research, and space exploration) to discuss and evaluate the alliance between science and government.

4. Imagine you are testifying before your local town board, city council, or other local legislative body about some problem you are aware of in the community or the educational system. Prepare a report dramatizing your findings but maintaining credibility. Be sure to identify your goals for the report: what do you want to happen as a result of your report? If you do not have access to real data, you can simulate information for the sake of the exercise, but mark made-up data with an asterisk or brackets.

5. Imagine you are a social scientist working for a congressman, doing an in-depth study on the concerns of young Americans about the future. Write a statement discussing how important this greenhouse effect seems to college students as likely to affect their future, compared to other issues of international politics, environment, social concern, the economy, and so on. You may take a survey of your classmates to gather data. Close the report with what your findings reveal about the political impact of this issue.

Potential CO$_2$-Induced Climate Effects on North American Wheat-Producing Regions

Cynthia Rosenzweig

A model predicting temperature and precipitation change can be the basis for further predictions about consequences for human health, agriculture, and increased sea level through melting of polar ice and thermal expansion of the oceans. In the following article, Rosenzweig uses the results of Hansen *et al.*'s three-dimensional model to plug into a model of wheat-production which she has developed. Her model was designed to use the grid boxes of the Hansen *et al.* model. Because the particular focus of her study is wheat production in North America, she generates data only for a limited part of the grid.

Much of the article is devoted to developing the model and testing it out against available data. Once the model has been deemed adequate, it can then be used to generate predictions about agriculture under the changes predicted by the climate model. Surprisingly, the news is not that bad, at least in the short term. Warmer temperatures should improve growing conditions in northern regions now limited by cold weather.

This article appeared in the journal *Climate Change* in 1985. Rosenzweig is an agronomist (a specialist in field-crop production) at the NASA/Goddard Space Flight Center's Institute for Space Studies.

Abstract The environmental requirements for growth of winter, spring, and fall-sown spring wheats in North America are specified and compared to temperature results from the control run of the Goddard Institute for Space Studies general circulation model (GISS-GCM) and observed precipitation in order to generate a simulated map of current wheat production regions. The simulation agrees substantially with the actual map of wheat-growing regions in North America. Results from a doubled CO$_2$ run of the climate model are then used to generate wheat regions under the new climatic conditions. In the simulation, areas of production increase in North America, particularly in Canada, due to increased growing degree units (GDU). Although wheat classifications may change, major wheat regions in the United States remain the same under simulated doubled CO$_2$ conditions. The wheat-growing region of Mexico is identified as vulnerable due to high temperature stress. Higher mean temperatures during wheat growth, particularly during the reproductive stages, may increase the need for earlier-maturing, more heat-tolerant cultivars° throughout North America. The soil moisture diagnostic of the climate model is used to analyze potential water availability in the major wheat region of the Southern Great Plains.

WHEAT IS THE MOST important cereal-grain crop in the world. It 1 is grown more extensively and produced in greater quantity than any other crop. Total area of harvested wheat in 1980 was 236 million hectares° (ha) and total production was 439 million metric tons° (mt). The United States produced 65 million mt of wheat in 1980, a national harvest exceeded only by that of the Soviet Union, which produced 98 million mt. In the United States, wheat ranks second to corn in acres planted and quantity produced, and third in export value after corn and soybean. North America (United States, Canada, and Mexico) accounts for approximately 20% of world wheat production (86 million mt in 1980) (USDA, 1982). The importance of wheat as a world crop and of North America as a wheat-producing region justifies an examination of the possible effects of climate change on North American wheat production.

Since 1958 when systematic monitoring began at the Mauna Loa 2 Observatory in Hawaii and at the South Pole, atmospheric CO$_2$ has been increasing at yearly rates varying from 0.40 to 1.51 parts per million (ppm) (Keeling and Bacastow, 1977). A doubling of the 1800 A.D. level of about 290 ppm is projected for some time in the next century (Perry, 1982). Current level is about 340 ppm. It is generally agreed that the observed increase is primarily due to increased burning of fossil fuels, although biotic release due principally to tropical deforestation is appreciable (Woodwell et al., 1983). Climate models have predicted that this increase in CO$_2$ will cause temperature to rise due to the absorption of

---

Cultivar—a human-developed variety of a plant. **Hectares**—a metric unit of area equal to 2.471 acres. **Metric ton**—a thousand kilograms, equal to about 2,200 pounds.

outgoing infrared radiation by the CO_2 gas (Manabe and Wetherald, 1975; Ramanathan *et al.*, 1979, aand Hansen *et al.*, 1983). In this study, I analyze the effects of the predicted climate changes on the geographic location of wheat production. I do not examine the primary effects of increased CO_2 on photosynthesis and water use at the plant level, which a complete analysis of potential effects on crop production would include. A more explanatory wheat growth simulation model would be necessary for such physiologically detailed prediction. . . .

[After a review of the literature on the effect of climate on wheat yields and 3 *a summary of the Hansen* et al. *climate model, Rosenzweig constructs a model for wheat growth, taking into account the growing season, heat, and rainfall required for major wheat varieties. For analysis she divides the map of North America into gridboxes corresponding to those used on the climate model. Using current climatic conditions, she finds the wheat-growing model appropriately describes current wheat-producing regions. Then using the climate predicted by the Hansen* et al. *model if atmospheric carbon dioxide were doubled, she calculates what regions could grow wheat under the changed conditions. The calculations are summarized in Figure 1.]*

Wheat-Growing Regions of Doubled CO_2 Run

The major change in the wheat-growing regions due to the doubled 4 CO_2 scenario is a great extension of the winter wheat belt into Canada (Figure 1d). Temperature variables have moderated so that growing season is lengthened, thermal units increased, and mean minimum January temperature raised. No spring wheat is evident at all in this northern tier. Much of the winter wheat in this extended region is soft due to annual precipitation greater than 760 mm. It is possible that some less fertile, but still productive Canadian soil resources may be available to take advantage of this projected climatic warming and the possibly ensuing expansion of the Canadian wheat regions (see Furuseth and Pierce, 1982).

Changes within the borders of the United States are less dramatic, 5 but generally favorable for wheat production. Hard wheat in the Pacific Northwest (gridbox 17) changes to soft wheat due to increased precipitation in the doubled CO_2 run, and Montana (gridbox 18) comes into wheat production due to increases in length of growing season and thermal units. Also evident is the expansion of areas in fall-sown spring wheat in the southern latitudes due to warmer winter temperatures. In gridboxes 30 and 31 (Louisiana and Florida, respectively), slight decreases in precipitation also allow soft, fall-sown spring wheat to be grown. Moderate winter temperatures also shift winter wheat to fall-sown spring wheat in gridboxes 25 (Kansas and Oklahoma) and 26 (Arkansas and Indiana). In Mexico (gridbox 28), wheat-growing regions

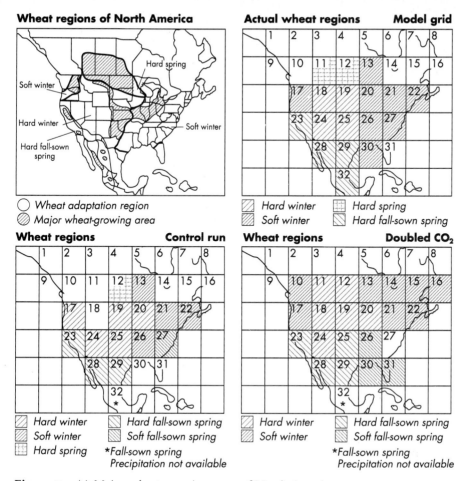

Figure 1. (a) Major wheat-growing areas of North America. Source: U.S. Wheat Associates and Foreign Agricultural Service, USDA. (b) Actual wheat-growing regions of North America on the GISS GCM grid. (c) Simulated North American wheat regions using the GISS GCM control run. (d) Simulated wheat regions using the GISS GCM doubled CO₂ run.

remain the same in the doubled CO₂ case, but, as will be shown below, greater high temperature stress may occur.

From the results presented above, it appears that the climate changes 6 due to doubled CO₂ in the atmosphere as simulated by the GISS GCM would have the general effect of expanding the winter wheat region quite extensively north into Canada and extending the fall-sown spring wheat region northward and eastward. Seven more gridboxes are capable of wheat production in the doubled CO₂ scenario than in the

	Run	Spring	Winter	Fall sown spring	No wheat
(a)	Control	1	9	5	17
	$2 \times CO_2$	0	14	8	10

	Run	Hard adequate	Hard dry	Soft
(b)	Control	7	3	4
	$2 \times CO_2$	8	2	11

Table 1.   Number of gridboxes in wheat production classes for control run and doubled CO_2 run of GISS GCM. (a) Growth habit; (b) Kernel texture and moisture conditions within hard wheat areas for gridboxes with available observed precipitation data.

control run (Table 1). Moisture, at least in terms of annual requirements, appears to be generally adequate for wheat production. In the control run, three gridboxes show dry conditions compared with only two dry gridboxes in the doubled CO_2 experiment. However, this does not take evaporative demand into account, which would tend to increase with elevated temperatures and increased vapor pressure deficits during the growing season.

It should be noted, however, that many of the changes in temperature 7 and precipitation shift the wheat classifications just under or over the limit into the next category and that in these situations some wheat of each type might be present.

Areas of Vulnerability

The relatively favorable situation for North American wheat production 8 in a doubled CO_2 world inferred from the results above is qualified somewhat when areas of particular vulnerability are defined using the mean temperature of the crop calendar (defined as the first month of the frost-free season through the month of harvest) and the months of the growing season with mean monthly maximum temperatures 32°C or above (Table 2). If the crop calendar is held constant, the mean temperature of these months in the doubled CO_2 world increases by an average of 3.3°C for 12 selected gridboxes. Mean crop calendar temperature for the selected gridboxes increased from 15°C, an acceptable level, to 18°C, a level which approaches the threshold for high temperature stress on wheat production (Jensen and Lund, 1971; Ramirez et al., 1975).

Gridbox	Type of wheat	Crop calendar	Mean temperature Control (°C)	2 × CO₂ (°C)	Revised crop calendar if changed	Mean temp. of rev. crop calendar (°C)	Type of wheat if changed	32°C Months Control	2 × CO₂
12	Spring	May–Aug.	14	17	—	—	Winter	—	—
13	Winter	Jun.–Aug.	17	20	May–Jul.	16	—	—	Aug., Sept.
17	Winter	May–Jul.	13	17	Apr.–Jun.	14	—	—	—
19	Winter	May–Jul.	14	18	Apr.–Jun.	14	—	—	—
20	Winter	May–Jul.	15	18	Apr.–Jun.	15	—	—	—
21	Winter	May–Jul.	15	18	—	—	—	—	—
22	Winter	May–Jul.	15	18	Apr.–Jun.	14	—	—	Aug., Sept.
16	Winter	May–Jun.	12	16	Apr.–May	14	—	—	Aug., Sept.
25	Winter	Apr.–Jun.	15	15	Sep.–Jun.	14	Fall-sown spring	Sept.	Jul., Aug., Sept.
26	Winter	Apr.–Jun.	18	22	Sep.–Jun.	16	—	Jul., Aug., Sept.	Jun., Jul., Aug., Sept.
23	Fall-sown spring	Oct.–Jun.	13	17	—	—	—	Jul., Aug.	Apr., May, Jun., Jul., Aug., Sept., Oct.
28	Fall-sown	Nov.–May	16	21	—	—	—	May, Jun., Jul., Aug., Sept.	
		Mean	15	18		16 (a)			

Table 2. Mean temperature of crop calendar, revised crop calendar value where changed under doubled CO₂, and months with mean maximum temperature over 32°C for selected gridboxes of control and doubled CO₂ runs of GISS GCM.
(a) *Includes unchanged values from mean temperatures of doubled CO₂ run.*

Wheat producers may avoid high temperature stress by shifting their 9
sowing and harvesting to an earlier time, if growing season changes
allow. Therefore, a new crop calendar, using the first month of the
growing season from the doubled CO_2 run (the month in which the last
frost of spring occurs) and an adjusted month of harvest was developed,
and new mean crop calendar temperatures calculated. This mean doubled
CO_2 crop calendar temperature is 16°C, slightly higher than the control
run value, but still in a relatively less stressful range. Some areas would
still experience high mean crop calendar temperatures, particularly gridbox 28 (northwestern Mexico, 21°C). This area would appear to be most
vulnerable to the warming trend.

Excessive high temperatures (over 30–32°C) are particularly damaging 10
to wheat during grain filling (Ramirez *et al.*, 1975; Johnson and Kanemasu, 1983). A high temperature stress indicator was approximated for
the model output of selected gridboxes as months which had a mean
maximum temperature 32°C or above. In the control run, four gridboxes
in the southern tiers experience temperatures of this level after wheat
harvest; in gridbox 28 (northwestern Mexico) both harvest and high
temperatures occur in May. In the doubled CO_2 run, high temperatures
were present in six gridboxes, and increased in duration in three gridboxes. For the most part these high temperatures still occur after harvest,
except in gridbox 23 (California) and gridbox 28 (northwestern Mexico).
Mexico appears particularly vulnerable since high temperatures begin
earlier, in April, and may cause stress during the grain-filling period.

High temperatures at planting time may result in irregular germina- 11
tion (Ramirez *et al.*, 1975). This may occur in gridboxes 17 (Washington
and Oregon), 24 (New Mexico and Arizona), 25 (Kansas and Oklahoma), and 26 (Indiana and Arkansas), thereby delaying planting. From
these results, it appears that a shortening of favorable growing period
may occur in some areas due to high temperatures, and a shift to shorter
season, more heat-tolerant cultivars may be in order. There may also be
a need to incorporate genes for reduction of photoperiod requirement,
since short days at low latitudes delay the heading of photoperiod-
sensitive wheat (Wiegand *et al.*, 1981).

Regional Analysis—The Southern Great Plains

The relative changes between the control and doubled CO_2 runs in the 12
monthly soil moisture diagnostic for the Southern Great Plains show a
relatively small decrease in water availability from January to May ranging from 12–17% (Figure 2). Significant decreases occur in June, July,
and August (32–47%), while from September through December soil
moisture remains approximately the same. The decreases in soil moisture
are mostly due to increases in evaporation due to higher temperatures.
These results emphasize the need for earlier-maturing, drought-tolerant

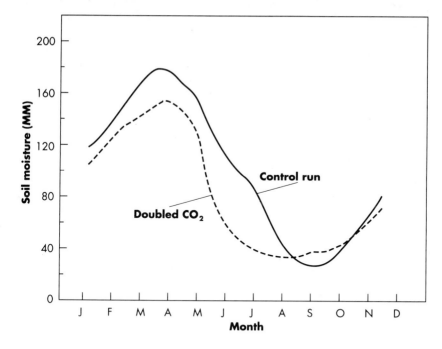

Figure 2.   Soil moisture diagnostic for gridbox 25 (Southern
Great Plains) of the GISS GCM control and doubled CO$_2$ runs.
Residence Time—the amount of time a gas remains in the stratosphere.
UNEP—United Nations Environment Programme.

cultivars. Wheat harvest before June would be desirable in this scenario
for the Southern Great Plains.

Decreased water availability and higher temperatures at germination [13]
could contribute to a decrease in wheat yields in the Southern Great
Plains. Increased irrigation could mitigate these conditions somewhat,
but this would strain an already taxed hydrologic° system. Throughout
most of gridbox 25, overdraft of groundwater, principally from the
Ogallala aquifer, is a major water supply problem. In northern Texas
and Oklahoma, annual groundwater mining (groundwater overdraft
above natural recharge rates) in the late 1970's equaled 14 million-acre-
feet (maf) yr^{-1} (1 acre-foot $= 3.26 \times 10^5$ gallons $= 1.234 \times 10^3$ m^3)
(Frederick and Hanson, 1982). Irrigated wheat may replace irrigated
corn in this region because it requires less than the 20–28 acre-inches

Hydrologic—concerning the study of water in the earth and its atmosphere.

usually applied to corn (Frederick and Hanson, 1982). In 1980, only about 3% of wheat grown in Oklahoma was irrigated (Oklahoma Department of Agriculture, 1980).

Within 30 yr, even without climatic warming, it may become un- **14** economical to irrigate cropland as energy costs and well-depths increase. Although annual precipitation in the Southern Great Plains appears to remain adequate in the doubled CO_2 scenario, length of growing season, growing degree units per growing season, and mean minimum January temperature all increase (Table 3). The soil moisture diagnostic indicates increased water stress. These factors would all tend to exacerbate the region's hydrologic situation.

From this initial attempt at a regional analysis of wheat production in **15** a doubled CO_2 world, it appears that the cropping system of the Southern Great Plains could remain basically the same, except for the change from winter to spring cultivars due to lack of cold temperatures for vernalization°. This would not entail great management changes of equipment or timing of operations. More importantly, yield decreases (due to increased plant water stress and higher temperatures at germination) and increased demand for groundwater supplies for irrigation appear to be the major negative effects that might be expected in a doubled CO_2 scenario for the region.

Conclusions

From analyzing the climatic effects of increased CO_2 from the GISS **16** GCM, it was found that areas of wheat production may increase in North America, particularly in Canada. If productive soils are available (and according to Furuseth and Pierce (1982) some are), Canadian winter

	Control	$2 \times CO_2$
Length of growing season (days)	169	206
Growing degree units per growing season	2378	3540
Mean minimum temperature in January (°C)	−4.65	0.54
Annual precipitation (mm)	586	533
Growth habit	winter	fall-sown spring
Kernel texture/moisture	hard adequate	hard adequate

Table 3. Environmental values and wheat classification for gridbox 25 (Kansas and Oklahoma) from control and doubled CO_2 runs of the GISS GCM.

Vernalization—the subjection of seeds to low temperatures to hasten plant development.

wheat-producing regions may expand. Major wheat regions in the United States remained the same in the simulation, although some wheat classifications changed. In the southern part of the United States, lack of cold winter temperatures may change wheat cultivars from winter to spring growth habit. In Mexico, high temperature stress could become a critical factor in wheat production. This is one area of vulnerability identified in the study. In general, higher mean temperatures during periods of wheat growth and high temperatures before harvest may increase demand for earlier-maturing, more heat-tolerant cultivars throughout North America. In the Southern Great Plains, decreased water availability from January through May may increase demand on an already stressed hydrologic system.

Given an understanding of the usual caveats and assumptions that *17* accompany the use of climate models such as the GISS GCM, these models can provide useful tools for analysis of potential agricultural crop zonation shifts due to climate change. The large grid size of the model limits the study of potential shifts to the macroscale and prohibits any analysis of the considerable subgrid-scale variability° of land surface and climate processes. One of the advantages of the climate model used in this study is the ability to look at the monthly distribution of climatic variables for any specific gridbox, as was done in the section on areas of vulnerability and regional analysis. Further research is needed to include more detailed environmental factors which affect wheat production in the study, e.g. soil resources, daylength, snow depth and duration, and water status at different development stages, for a range of maturity types. Studies of this type should also be repeated as improved versions of the GCMs are developed, particularly as more realistic land surface processes are incorporated. It would also be of interest to use results of other GCMs (e.g., the Manabe-Stouffer (1980) model), particularly those with finer gridbox resolution and lower predictions of warming due to increased CO₂. Since the GISS predictions lie in the upper range of estimated warming, this study may be considered as a 'worst case' scenario.

Finally, further research is needed to estimate the direct influence of *18* increased carbon dioxide on agricultural production in conjunction with the predicted climate changes. This influence may well be favorable. The experimental work of Gifford (1979) carried out at relatively high growing temperatures (19°C) suggests that a rise in atmospheric CO₂ will increase the yield potential of water-limited wheat. An analysis of reported experimental results shows that overall agricultural yields are likely to increase by an average of approximately 33% with a doubling of atmospheric CO₂ concentration (Kimball, 1983). Another direct effect of increased CO₂ in some species is an increase in stomatal° resistance

---

Subgrid-scale variability—variation smaller than that noticed in grid system.   **Stomata**—pores in a leaf or stem, by which gases and water vapor pass.

which leads to a decrease in transpiration° (Lemon, 1983). Results from watershed simulation studies suggest that a decrease in transpiration may lead to increased soil moisture and streamflow (Aston, 1984; Idso and Brazel, 1984); however, these studies neglect possible increases in individual plant leaf areas or in total vegetated area. The direct CO_2 effects of increased yield potential and decreased transpiration, combined with the expansion of wheat regions described above, may well mitigate the negative effects of high temperatures and moisture stress on wheat production in North America.

Acknowledgements

I thank Drs. Inez Fung, Marla A. Jackson, David Rind, Frank Abramopoulos, Norman J. Rosenberg, L. H. Allen, Vivien Gornitz and the reviewers for their helpful suggestions, Jeffrey Jonas for programming the charts of wheat environmental parameters, and Jean Lerner for the contouring program. Lilly Del Valle and José Mendoza did the graphics.

References

Aston, A. R.: 1984, 'The Effect of Doubling Atmospheric CO_2 on Streamflow: A Simulation'. *J. Hydrol.* **67**, 273–280.

Frederick, K. D. and Hanson, J. C.: 1982, *Water for Western Agriculture*, Resources for the Future, Washington, D.C., 241 p.

Furuseth, O. J. and Pierce, J. T.: 1982; *Agricultural Land in an Urban Society*, Association of American Geographers, Washington, D.C., 89 p.

Gifford, R. M.: 1979, 'Growth and Yield of CO_2-enriched Wheat under Water-limited Conditions', *Aust. J. Plant Physiol.* **6**, 367–378.

Hansen, J., Russell, G., Rind, D., Stone, P., Lacis, A., Lebedeff, S., Ruedy, R. and Travis, L.: 1983, 'Efficient Three-Dimensional Global Models for Climate Studies, Models I and II', *Mon. Wea. Rev.* **111**, 609–662.

Idso, S. B. and Brazel, A. J.: 1984, 'Rising Atmospheric Carbon Dioxide Concentrations May Increase Streamflow', *Nature* **312**, 51–53.

Jensen, L. A. and Lund, H. R.: 1971, 'How Cereals Grow', Bull. No. 3, North Dakota State University Extension, Fargo, ND, 39 p.

Johnson, R. C. and Kanemasu, E. T.: 1983, 'Yield and Development of Winter Wheat at Elevated Temperatures', *Agron. J.* **75**, 561–565.

Keeling, D. C. and Bacastow, R. B.: 1977, 'Impact of Industrial Gases on Climate', in *Energy and Climate*, National Academy of Sciences, Washington D.C., p. 72–95.

Kimball, B. A.: 1983, 'Carbon Dioxide and Agricultural Yield; An Assemblage of 430 Prior Observations', *Agron. J.* **75**, 779–788.

Lemon, E. R. (ed.): 1983, *Co_2 and Plants*: AAAS Selected Symposium 84. Westview Press, Inc., Boulder, Colorado, 280 p.

Manabe, S.and Wetherald, R. T.: 1975, 'The Effects of Doubling the CO_2 Concentration on the Climate of a General Circulation Model', *J. Atmos. Sci.* **32**, 3–15.

Transpiration—the process of vapors and gases passing through stomata.

Manabe, S. and Stouffer, R. J.: 1980, 'Sensitivity of a Global Climate Model to an Increase in CO$_2$ Concentration in the Atmosphere', *J. Geophys. Res.* **85,** 5529–5554.

Oklahoma Department of Agriculture: 1980, 'Oklahoma Agricultural Statistics', Oklahoma City, OK.

Perry, A. M.: 1982, 'Carbon Dioxide Production Scenarios', in Clark, W. C. (ed.), *Carbon Dioxide Review: 1982* Oxford University Press, New York, NY, pp. 337–363.

Ramanathan, V., Lian, M. S., and Cess, R. D.: 1979, 'Increased Atmospheric CO$_2$ Zonal and Seasonal Estimates of the Effect on the Radiation Energy Balance and Surface Temperature', *J. Geophys Res.* **84,** 4949–4958.

Ramirez, J. M., Sakamoto, C. M., and Jensen, R. E.: 1975, 'Wheat', in 'Impacts of Climatic Change on the Biosphere', *CIAP Monograph* **5,** Pt. 2, Climatic Effects, pp. 4-37 to 4-90.

United States Department of Agriculture: 1982, *Agricultural Statistics*, U.S. Govt. Printing Office, Washington, D.C., 566 p.

Wiegand, C. L., Gerbermann, A. H., and Cuellar, J. A.: 1981, 'Development and Yield of Hard Red Winter Wheats Under Semitropical Conditions', *Agron. J.* **73,** 29–37.

Woodwell, G. M., Hoffie, J. E., Houghton, A., Melillo, J. M., Moore, B., Peterson, B. J., Shaver, G. R.: 1983, 'Global Deforestation: Contribution of Atmospheric Carbon Dioxide', *Science* **222,** 1081–1086.

Rhetorical Analysis Through Annotation

This article, like many other scientific articles, relies heavily on diagrams, figures, and tables to display variables, data, and findings. These visual displays are then tied closely to the text.

Mark in the margin each segment of the text that is repeating, explaining, interpreting, or elaborating material also displayed on a diagram, figure, or table. Note which visual display is related to each textual passage.

Discuss the relationship between each of these passages and the relevant display. How do they complement each other? If you read only the diagrams, figures, and tables, how much of the substance of the argument would you understand? What would you miss?

Discussion Questions

Interpreting the Text

1. How does this article use the Hansen *et al.* climate model? How is the agricultural model related to the climate model?

2. What particular conditions of local regions affect the impact of the results of the general model? Why is it necessary to consider local conditions? What does this reliance on local considerations indicate about difficulties of interpreting and applying general results?

3. Where will wheat growing be affected by the predicted climate change? In what ways will the impact be positive? In what ways negative? What will the overall impact be?

Considering the Issues

4. Over what time period are these predictions made? Based on the trends indicated here, what may be the impact of climate change for the century after the period examined here? Are the positive effects likely to be short or long range?

5. Why is wheat agriculture an important issue? How is wheat production related to national and international economic relations? How may great increases or decreases in wheat production influence other sectors of the economy and politics?

6. What possible solutions or adjustments can be made to cope with these climate changes? To what extent do these solutions rely on simple or advanced technology?

7. On what is the call for further research based? Is this call warranted? If you were in charge of federal research grants what kind of research would you fund?

Writing Suggestions

1. Imagine you are working for the agricultural extension service of a university in a wheat-growing region. Write a short report for farmers telling them what they need to know about the impact of the greenhouse effect on their farming. Do not unduly alarm the farmers, but do offer them necessary cautions and specific advice. Be sure to identify the region you are discussing.

2. Present these findings as a bulletin for the evening television news in Oklahoma, New York, Mexico City, and Alberta, Canada.

3. Using the predictions of the Hansen *et al.* model and your own knowledge of one of the following activities, write an article assessing the impact of climate change on skiing, snowman building, beach holidays, or any similar activity. You may fabricate specific data where you need to; however, please label such made-up data with an asterisk or brackets.

Climate Change and Stratospheric Ozone Depletion: Need for More Than the Current Minimalist Response

John C. Topping, Jr.

Can we do anything to control the greenhouse heating of the atmosphere and the depletion of the ozone? The problem seems too pressing to leave entirely to research, but do we know enough to take the proper steps? Who is willing to bear the great economic and social cost of the changes that may be necessary? And even if the United States is willing to make radical reforms, will other nations cooperate?

These questions are raised and answered by John Topping, Staff Director of the Office of Air and Radiation of the U.S. Environmental Protection Agency from 1983 to 1986 and now head of The Climate Institute. His answer is that we simply must do something, and do it soon, for the problem is immediate, enormous, and disastrous in its consequences if unchecked. Even now, we can no longer stop or reverse the climate change and loss of ozone; all we can do is slow the process down and adapt intelligently to the inevitable change.

This paper, originally written in 1986 for an international conference, is a call to immediate action. The first half of the paper makes clear the necessity for action and the latter half outlines steps that can and must be taken now.

DEVOTEES OF LATE NIGHT television in the United States may 1 have seen the celebrated W. R. Grace and Company deficit trial advertisements. An elderly man, presumably of our generation, is on trial for failing to halt the mushrooming federal deficit. This courtroom scene in the year 2017 has the defendant facing a jury of children and an adolescent prosecutor who asks, "In 1986 the national debt reached $2 trillion. Didn't that frighten you?" Our contemporary lamely replies, "No one was willing to make the sacrifice." Stepping down from the witness stand, he implores, "Are you ever going to forgive us?"

While this advertisement may be too strong for the sensibilities of the 2 television networks, it may be an accurate representation of how our grandchildren will view our mortgaging the future of the global environment. By 2017 our grandchildren will be struggling with a radically warming world climate causing environmental changes beyond anything ever witnessed by our species. Unless humanity profoundly alters energy consumption and emission practices, the global environmental trauma could become the ecological equivalent of the hyperinflation in Weimar Germany in the 1920s, with perhaps as profound consequences for the health of democratic government.

Mid-range projections of average global surface temperature warming 3 by 2100 are generally at or above 5°C. Virtually all plausible energy-use projections (other than those hypothesizing the destruction of humanity in a final world war) point toward a doubling of the preindustrial levels of carbon dioxide well before the end of the twenty-first century. We are told by an eminent climatologist that this CO_2 doubling alone would warm the earth by an average of 3°C. As a result of recent calculations in some of the more sophisticated climate models of various feedback effects associated with a CO_2 doubling, the likely warming due to such growth of carbon dioxide in the atmosphere may prove to be at least 4°C (Hansen, this volume).

Although fossil fuel burning alone could produce a doubling of prein- 4
dustrial CO_2 levels in the next seventy-five years, such a doubling could be accelerated by a decade or more if we continue to clear the world's forests at current rates. The biosphere, especially forests, constitutes a major sink for taking up carbon dioxide so that it does not build up in the atmosphere. Yet the largest source of such uptake, the tropical rain forests, is often severely pressed by development pressures in Third World countries from both indigenous sources and multi-national companies.

Despite abundant evidence that the buildup of carbon dioxide levels 5
alone could produce an average global climate warming of 5°C by 2100, the most plausible current projections indicate that this CO_2-induced temperature warming will be roughly matched by a temperature rise due to a simultaneous buildup in other trace gases as chlorofluorocarbons, carbon tetrachloride, nitrous oxide, carbon monoxide, methane, and compounds of bromine.

The long-term implications of such a rapid climate warming for 6
humanity and most other animal and plant species on this planet are staggering. These involve losing tens of millions of acres of coastal land to the sea, the impairment of many of the world's port facilities, the loss of countless lives of coastal and lowland dwellers to increasingly destructive storm surges, and massive salt water intrusion on fresh water supplies. The greatest human toll is likely to come in famines that could ultimately claim the lives of hundreds of millions in Third World countries. The tragic famine we are now witnessing in Africa may be but a small harbinger of the catastrophe that will unfold as desertification claims arable land and shifts in rainfall patterns disrupt already marginal food production and distribution systems. Although many plants will grow more rapidly in a higher CO_2 environment, it is unlikely over the next century that such potential gains in the food supply would match the losses caused by migration of food belts. Moreover, the non-CO_2 greenhouse gases provide no such benefits but could disrupt the climate just as much.

Besides its potentially large toll in human lives, this rapid climate 7
change will probably destroy the habitats of thousands of animal and plant species, thus robbing our planet of much of its biological diversity. In addition to its direct human and ecological toll, adjustments to this rapid climate change could be expected to consume the entire growth dividend humanity would have used to improve living standards of future generations and to redress the impoverishment of the Third World. Huge sums would be required for dikes to preserve many coastal areas, and much of our planet's great investment in agriculture would be made obsolete by a rapid change in climate.

As apocalyptic as the consequences of such climate shock would *8*
appear to be over the long haul, people tend to glaze over at discussions
that seem more relevant to their great grandchildren. Economists have
developed the concept of discounting the value of human lives saved in
the future. As some have pointed out, by adopting a high enough
discount rate, one could conclude that the destruction of human civilization one or two centuries from now is of little or no economic consequence in present value terms, even if such a certain fate results from
today's decisions. Sadly the calculations of most public policy-makers
seem equally unmindful of the injunction of the great political philosopher Edmund Burke that government owes a duty not only to the
living, but also to the dead and to those who are yet to be born.

Yet, as some eminent NASA scientists have recently projected, climate *9*
change is no longer merely a concern for future generations. By 1990,
they suggest, we are likely to see temperature changes outside of the
normal range of variation with an increase of about 1°C in average
global surface temperature between now and the year 2000. At the end
of this century humanity could face a warmer world than at any time
in the last hundred thousand years with the prospect of a continued
warming at an ever-accelerating rate.

A major factor in the acceleration of these climate warming projections *10*
has been a late-blooming recognition of the important role of highly
absorptive greenhouse gases, such as chlorofluorocarbons, carbon tetrachloride, and various bromine compounds, which remain in the atmosphere for decades if not centuries before breaking down. Methane
growth due to agriculture, and nitrous oxide and carbon monoxide
growth from fuel combustion, have also caused the warming projections
to rise.

Because of their powerful bonding and insulating qualities, chloro- *11*
fluorocarbons are being used for a profusion of uses well past refrigeration and air conditioning to such diverse purposes as computer manufacturing and preserving the taste of a "McDLT" sandwich from a fast-
food restaurant. These same qualities that make chlorofluorocarbons
such readily adaptable commercial compounds also make them powerful
greenhouse gases and effective depleters of our stratospheric ozone layer.

Due to the rapid growth in CFC use during the 1980s and the rapid *12*
buildup of bromine compounds, the danger to the stratosperhic ozone
layer appears greater than was originally thought when concern first
arose in the mid-1970s. Yet much more important than the sizable
increases in skin cancer, potential weakening of the human immune
system, and likely crop and materials damage resulting from a chlorine
and bromine compound induced depletion of the stratospheric ozone
layer are the sizable boosts that such gases will provide to climate
warming.

Given present CFC-use projections, it is conceivable that these com- *13*
pounds alone will produce an amplification of 1° to 1.5°C in the total

global temperature warming over the next several generations. A small increment in the greenhouse warming can also be anticipated from the growth of such chlorine compounds as carbon tetrachloride and methyl chloroform as well as by a profusion of bromine compounds.

These stratospheric perturbants would be the first targets of any ef- 14 fective international effort to slow the greenhouse warming. They are all industrially-produced compounds, many virtually unknown two generations ago. Many have some available substitutes, which are neither stratospheric perturbants nor greenhouse gases for most commercial applications. Regulation of these compounds could afford dual benefits by providing stratospheric protection and slowing the greenhouse warming. Control of even small volumes of these chlorine and bromine compounds can have a highly beneficial effect, due to their long persistence in the atmosphere and their tremendous absorptive potential (sometimes several thousand times an equivalent molecule of carbon dioxide).

Any effective U.S. and international effort to address the dual prob- 15 lems of greenhouse warming and stratospheric ozone depletion will require a much more tangible commitment of resources and attention by senior policy-makers in the major industrial nations. In the United States there recently have been some encouraging indications of intellectual recognition by senior policy-makers of the importance of the problem of climate change. William Ruckelshaus' strong foreword to the provocative work *Greenhouse Effect and Sea Level Rise* (Barth and Titus 1984) and Lee Thomas' clarion call in March 1986 for stratospheric ozone protection pointed out the critical importance of these issues.

Yet recognition of these issues has not translated into a tangible re- 16 source commitment. Despite indications that prospective climate change dwarfs all other environmental problems combined, fewer than nine EPA employees out of a workforce of about 12,000 work full-time on either the issue of greenhouse warming or stratospheric ozone depletion. Although the proportion has grown considerably in the past year, still only about one-tenth of one percent of EPA's total resources is devoted to addressing these issues. This minimalist resource commitment is not due to a lack of will on the part of EPA's senior leadership but to the statutory ambiguity of EPA's role and the deep-seated hostility that the Office of Management and Budget (OMB) has exhibited toward EPA's addressing such first-order environmental issues as climate change, indoor air, and radon. OMB has resisted giving EPA resources in apparent fear that the agency might uncover problems with resulting budgetary or regulatory consequences. While somewhat greater sums have been directed at studying aspects of climate change at the National Aeronautics and Space Administration, the National Oceanographic and Atmospheric Administration, and the Department of Energy, no coherent federal-wide focus exists on these problems, which will ultimately affect virtually every agency in government.

With a few exceptions the resource commitment to seriously address- *17* ing these issues by U.S. environmental groups has been equally faint-hearted. Some environmentalists, by reflexively opposing all forms of nuclear power, have helped increase our dependence on fossil fuels. Moreover, both greenhouse-induced warming and stratospheric ozone depletion are global problems, and environmental policy-makers and environmental organizations in other industrialized countries have often lagged behind those in the U.S. in addressing these problems.

Despite the clear inadequacy of the present response to the prospect *18* of climate change, a number of tangible steps can be taken by the U.S. and other countries to make the problem more manageable. These include:

• *Preservation of critical satellite tracking research and climate modeling concerning ozone depletion and greenhouse warming.* The recent turmoil at NASA, the destruction at launch of a key weather satellite, and the general environment of federal budget austerity have placed some critical research in jeopardy. Its loss could greatly hinder our developing a clear understanding of the likely pace and regional implications of climate change.

• *Development of a serious external constituency for climatic stability including environmentalists, scientists, coastal dwellers, farmers, the nuclear and the solar industry, and others.* If such coalitions are organized in the major industrial democracies, they can help to ensure the attainment of broadscale international agreements essential to responding to climate change.

• *Immediate phasing out of such relatively frivolous and easily substitutable uses of CFCs as aerosols, egg cartons, and fast food containers through a combination of consumer boycotts, industry voluntary action, national regulation or taxes, and international agreement.* Concerted activity by consumers to avoid CFC aerosols preceded U.S. regulatory action. A similar focus on the threat to the environment posed by such environmentally dangerous and frivolous uses of CFCs might trigger a similar scramble by fast food retailers to point out that their products are not only tastier, but safer for the environment, than those of their competitors.

• *Approaching regulation of CFCs and other trace gases such as carbon tetrachloride, methyl chloroform, and bromine compounds by weighing their greenhouse absorptive potential, their residence time°, and their ozone depleting capacity.* Thus, even among CFCs, substitutions might be encouraged of longer residence time compounds by shorter residence time compounds.

• *Where appropriate, amend environmental statutes to address possibly harmful substitution effects caused by proposed environmental regulations.* EPA recently

---

Residence time—the amount of time a gas remains in the stratosphere.

issued a notice of an intent to list perchloroethylene, a significant dry cleaning solvent, as a hazardous air pollutant under Section 112 of the Clean Air Act. Such listing and subsequent regulation could conceivably trigger a rapid movement in the dry cleaning industry to CFCs, on balance likely to pose much greater environmental dangers than perchloroethylene. Language specifically permitting consideration of greenhouse warming and ozone depleting effects of available substitutes would facilitate more rational regulation.

• *Requirements that long-term projects reviewed under the National Environmental Policy Act consider climate change and sea level rise.* This might be accomplished through amendment of implementing regulations or by a suit directed at an appropriate project, such as a coastal highway that has failed to consider likely sea level rise. Institutionalization of climate change considerations into the project planning process for long term public and private sector investments should ultimately save taxpayers and investors billions of dollars and ensure that we leave future generations a sounder environment.

• *Insistence by bilateral and multilateral lending institutions that their funds not finance the destruction of tropical rain forests and other important global forest resources.* Recognition of the global stake in preserving these resources, located largely in developing countries, may ultimately require the industrialized countries to finance some of the economic loss developing countries would perceive occurring should they forego development in the tropical rain forests.

• *Recognition, even in the face of the tragedy at Chernobyl, that alongside energy conservation nuclear power remains the likely principal alternative to fossil fuel burning over the next generation or two.* Besides strengthening the powers of the International Atomic Energy Agency to improve safety standards and ensure against diversion of nuclear materials to nonpeaceful uses, recapturing public confidence in the safety of nuclear power will require implementing environmentally sound radioactive waste policies. It is likely that environmental and energy considerations may militate toward large scale nuclear plant construction before the end of this century. Yet to meet deep public concerns about the safety of nuclear power may require the development of a new generation of technology that is relatively invulnerable to nuclear meltdown. Governments, environmental groups, and the nuclear power industry have a common interest in the success of such an effort. Simultaneous satisfaction of safety concerns and economic considerations will require very rigorous safety standards coupled with a virtual regulatory certainty that careful adherence to such standards will ensure expeditious licensing and avoid protracted litigation.

• *Renewed international research focus on improving the efficiency of such alternative energy sources as solar power and perfection of such potential breakthrough technologies as hydrogen powered vehicles.*

• *A concerted public-private sector effort to mitigate the costs of climate change* by adjusting land use and coastal development policies to allow for the prospect of increasing sea level rise, by encouraging the development of crops that can flourish under rapidly changing climatic conditions, by factoring climatic change and rising CO_2 levels into the strategic planning of industry, and by incorporating the prospect of a rapidly warming climate into calculations of utility peak load demand and necessary future capacity.

Due to the enormous momentum in the earth's climate system already **19** present from our massive increase in fossil fuel burning and release of many manmade greenhouse gases, adaptation will be an essential part of our response. The sooner we incorporate climate change considerations into our societal planning the better our prospect will be for turning the greenhouse warming from an unprecedented catastrophe to merely an enormous societal challenge. Yet, even the best adaptation and mitigation strategy may be of little avail if present energy use and gas release trends remain unabated. Action by EPA UNEP° to sharply curtail emissions of the greenhouse gases at issue may afford us the time to fashion the more comprehensive response that will ultimately be required.

References

Barth, M. C., and J. G. Titus. 1984. *Greenhouse effect and sea level rise.* New York: Van Nostrand Reinhold.

Rhetorical Analysis Through Annotation

In order to encourage action, Topping attempts to overcome apathy, ignorance, and resistance and to establish a sense of urgency. In the first half of the paper Topping aims for specific emotional impact on the readers, even when he is presenting factual material and scientific findings. Only then does he offer specific steps to be taken; moreover, each action is pinpointed toward a specific group of people to create specific feelings of responsibility.

Next to each paragraph in the first half of the paper, write the primary emotion or feeling Topping is trying to arouse in the audience and note the method Topping uses to create those feelings. Discuss how the techniques used, the various emotions aroused, and the sequence of emotions created through the text help build an action-oriented sense of urgency in the audience. How are the feelings here not just private sensations but goads to public action?

Next to each step recommended in the second half of the paper, write the specific group responsible for the action. Note whether the action is to be taken directly on the environment, or on bureaucratic, institutional, or political attitudes and structures. Discuss why steps are targeted at particular groups rather than outlining general procedures (e.g., "reduce burning of fossil fuels"). Discuss also why so many of the steps are not directly aimed at the environment but only indirectly through social, political, or bureaucratic changes.

UNEP—United Nations Environment Programme.

Throughout the selection, circle every use of scientific findings or other factual material. Note how Topping uses these as resources to buttress the action-oriented emotions. How is the presentation of these affected by this emotional use?

Discuss how action orientation leads to a different presentation from the scientific studies presenting similar material earlier in this unit.

Discussion Questions

Interpreting the Text

1. What harmful impacts will come from climate change and ozone depletion? Which impacts come from greenhouse heating and which from ozone depletion? Which is ultimately more serious, the impact of CFCs on ozone depletion or on greenhouse heating?

2. What is the current degree of commitment of various groups to solving this problem? What have been the stands of various governmental agencies? Is this enough? Why or why not? Why do people seem to avoid confronting this major problem? Why is Topping particularly unhappy with the Office of Management and Budget?

3. Can these atmospheric changes be totally stopped? If not, what adaptations must be planned for?

4. What does Topping say that you, as an ordinary consumer, can do to slow global warming and ozone depletion?

Considering the Issues

5. Which of the proposed steps are likely to be more or less difficult? Which are likely to be most successful and which are likely to have the greatest impact?

6. What light does the political analysis of "The Seven-Sided Coin" (see pages 511–518), concerning nuclear energy policy, shed on this policy problem and the reasons why the steps are targeted at different groups? In what way are the two policy problems similar and in what ways are they different? In what way does the solution of each depend on the solution to the other?

Writing Suggestions

1. Imagine that you are a decision-making member of any of the groups responsible for any one of Topping's suggested steps. For other members of your group write a memorandum discussing the step to be taken, its urgency, and the difficulties in implementing it. You may also propose a specific implementation plan.

2(a) Imagine that you are an antinuclear power activist and Topping's argument for the revival of nuclear power has been getting favorable publicity in your community. Write a letter to the local newspaper editor or another form of communication to local citizens to answer Topping's suggestion. (b) Now imagine that you are both an ad writer and an environmental activist. Design a public service advertisement for magazines, newspapers, or television to discourage frivolous uses of CFCs.

3. Imagine that you are an industrialist in a tropical country, actively involved in using rain forest resources through mining, timber-production, or agricultural development. Further imagine that Topping's call has led to an international clampdown on funds for tropical forest development. Write a letter to your government's director of economic development asking for government financial support. Explain why it is in your country's interests to develop its resources despite international pressure to maintain tropical rain forests.

4. As part of this course's discussion of the use of rhetoric, write an analysis of how Topping attempts to encourage action through his presentation.

Letter to the President of the United States

Forty-two U.S. Senators

Through research and publicity, atmospheric scientists have been able to focus the attention of policy makers on the problem of the global warming trend. As described in the letter below, this issue is being discussed at the highest levels of government both nationally and internationally. In this letter, members of the Senate—Republicans and Democrats, conservatives and liberals—urge the president to foster international cooperation to take effective action to cope with the problem. By encouraging international cooperation, with the Soviet Union and the United States taking the lead, the senators are hoping that the various countries of the world may then overcome their separate short-term interests in not restricting their industries in order to pursue the long-term common good of all the inhabitants of the earth.

In this personal communication to the president in the spring of 1988, the senators summarize the scientific research (which we have read in detail in this unit) as the rationale for action, but they do not dwell at length on it. Rather the attention is on the president's commitments, responsibilities, and opportunities. The senators present future actions as simply a continuation of prior presidential actions and commitments made at previous summit meetings, for which the senators praise the president. The senators go beyond general encouragement of concern to this problem, to urge that specific steps be taken at two upcoming meetings, the summit meeting with the leader of the Soviet Union and the seven-nation economic summit.

United States Senate
Committee on Environment and Public Works
Washington, DC 20510-6175

March 31, 1988

The Honorable Ronald W. Reagan
The White House
1600 Pennsylvania Avenue
Washington, D.C. 20500

Dear Mr. President:

We are writing to urge that you continue and expand recent initiatives   *1*
on the international environmental problem of the greenhouse effect and
global climate change, such as those announced at the conclusion of the
December 1987 summit meeting with Soviet General Secretary Gorbachev. Specifically, we urge that, at the next summit meeting with the
General Secretary in Moscow and at the upcoming economic summit
meeting this June in Toronto, you call upon all nations of the world to
begin the negotiation of a convention° to protect our global climate.
Such a convention could be modeled after the historic Vienna Convention to Protect the Ozone Layer.

You are to be congratulated for including the problem of global   *2*
climate change as part of the agenda at the December 1987 summit
meeting with General Secretary Gorbachev. It is encouraging to observe
the growing commitment that our two nations are making to deal with
the environmental threat of global warming. Of particular note was the
Joint Summit Communique which stated that the "two sides will continue to promote broad international and bilateral cooperation in the
increasingly important area of global climate and environmental
change."

Scientists have warned us that increasing concentrations of certain   *3*
pollutants in the atmosphere will increase the earth's temperature over
the coming years to a level which has not existed for tens of millions of
years. There is some urgency to this matter since scientists predict that,
as a result of past pollution, we are already committed to a significant
global warming. These greenhouse gases will lead to substantial changes
in the climate of our planet with potentially catastrophic environmental
and socio-economic consequences.

Convention—an international agreement, usually on a specific subject.

The predicted global warming and climate changes are expected to 4 occur at a rate and in a fashion that will preclude natural evolutionary responses. The likely effects of the greenhouse effect include rising sea levels, changes in the location of deserts, extremely high temperatures in cities during the summer months, increases in the number and severity of hurricanes, the death of large portions of forests, and the loss of adequate moisture in the mid-continent agricultural belt.

The challenge of reducing this threat to the planet's well being is 5 considerable. One of the most significant greenhouse gases is carbon dioxide, a by-product of fossil fuels. The United States and the Soviet Union are the world's two largest contributors of carbon dixoide. To- gether, we account for almost one-half of the global total.

For these reasons, the United States and the Soviet Union must take 6 positions of global leadership on this matter and call for a convention on global climate change. Such a convention could address our scientific understanding of the problem, the need for and limits of adaptation as a response to future climate change, as well as strategies to stabilize atmospheric concentrations of greenhouse gases at safe levels.

Negotiations to achieve a climate convention would have to take place 7 on a multilateral basis. However, cooperation between the United States and the Soviet Union is an essential precondition of a successful inter- national response to the greenhouse effect. The problems associated with global climate change provide an historic opportunity for our two coun- tries to cooperate on a long term basis to insure the habitability of Earth. These facts were recognized and endorsed in the recently enacted Global Climate Protection Act (P.L. 100-204, sections 1101–1106).

For these reasons, we urge you and General Secretary Gorbachev to 8 use the upcoming summit meeting scheduled to be held in Moscow as a forum to call for the negotiation of a convention on global climate change and to commit the United States and the Soviet Union to a leadership role in that process. At the same time we suggest that you expand and elevate the level of ongoing bilateral U.S.-U.S.S.R. activity which could enhance our understanding of the problem. We endorse the establishment of a high level working group to study potential responses to climate change, including greenhouse gas emissions reductions and adaptation to climate change. This expanded bilateral activity should be recognized and supported as an important priority within the United States' foreign and environmental policy agenda.

Similarly, we urge you to use the seven nation economic summit that 9 is scheduled to be held during the month of June in Toronto as a forum to urge the negotiation of a global climate convention. At last year's economic summit, the leaders of the seven nations stated: "We underline our own responsibility to encourage efforts to tackle effectively environmental problems of worldwide impact such as . . . climate change. . . ." This year's economic summit is the appropriate opportunity to take the next step and call for a global climate convention.

Thank you for your attention and commitment to this important, *10* international environmental issue. We look forward to working with you and assisting you in our mutual efforts to protect our fragile planet.

Sincerely,

John F. Kerry	Max Baucus	John H. Chafee
Dave Durenberger	George J. Mitchell	Robert T. Stafford
Albert Gore	Dale Bumpers	Carl Levin
Pete Wilson	Frank Murkowski	Spark M. Matsunaga
Terry Sanford	David Pryor	Wyche Fowler, Jr.
Tom Harkin	Frank R. Lautenberg	Brock Adams
Timothy E. Wirth	Donald W. Riegle, Jr.	Alfonse M. D'Amato
Bob Graham	Patrick J. Leahy	Quentin N. Burdick
Dennis DeConcini	Bob Kasten	Arlen Specter
Steven D. Symms	Jeff Bingaman	Edward M. Kennedy
Bob Packwood	Thomas A. Daschle	Pete V. Domenici
Daniel J. Evans	Nancy Landon Kassebaum	Thad Cochran
Wiliam S. Cohen	Richard G. Lugar	Dan Quayle
Claiborne Pell	William V. Roth, Jr.	John Heinz

Rhetorical Analysis Through Annotation

The forty-two senators use a variety of tactics to influence the president's future actions. They praise his previous involvement in this issue and remind him of the commitments he has made; they offer reasons why he ought to be concerned; they present the problem as a challenge; they urge action; and they provide specific steps and guidelines for action.

Next to each paragraph or section of the letter, note the main persuasive tactic being used. Then circle words within each paragraph that help build the effect of these tactics within the paragraph. For example, in the third paragraph you may note all the words suggesting change that must be dealt with, in support of the tactic of offering reasons for concern and action. Similarly in the seventh paragraph you may note all the words implying cooperation and negotiation.

Discuss how the various features of this letter may serve to persuade the president to take action. Which parts of the letter may be most effective: the summary of scientific reasons or the reminder of political commitments?

As well as being sent to the president, this letter was distributed widely to the press, scientists, and environmental groups interested in the issue. In what way might this distribution serve as added pressure on the president to act? What other purposes might this distribution serve besides influencing the president?

Discussion Questions

Considering the Issues

1. Which of the statements in this letter are based on scientific research? Is the certainty of the scientific research presented in any way to be questioned or discussed? In what way do scientists appear more authoritative here than they have in previous selections? Why? What does the phrase "scientists have warned us . . ." tell us about the role scientists take in this letter?

2. The most visually striking aspect of this letter as originally presented is a long list of oversized signatures at the end. Is the impact or significance of this letter greater because it is signed by senators rather than ordinary citizens or scientists? By forty-two senators rather than a single senator? Why is this so, and what does this indicate about the relationship between persuasiveness and power?

3. Based on news reports about national and international action on the issue of global warming since this letter was written in March 1988, do you believe that the governments of the United States, the Soviet Union, and the other countries of the world are taking the issue seriously enough and are pursuing appropriate actions to stave off disaster? If not, what should they be doing and what may we do to ensure governments do confront the issue?

Writing Suggestions

1. As a concerned citizen, write a letter to the president or to the Environmental Protection Agency confirming your support of the senators' position urging action. Use details of the research presented in this unit to support your position. Or, write a letter to the head of the Soviet government or any other government that you feel ought to take action.

2. For a course on the politics of ecology, research what action has been taken since the publication of this letter to ensure international cooperation on global warming and write a paper describing the process by which governments are facing (or not facing) this issue.

3. As part of this course's concern with writing persuasively in different contexts, write an essay analyzing what this letter shows about how to persuade a president to do something. Pay special attention to those unusual aspects of persuasion that directly relate to the president's special role as a public leader.

Unit Writing Suggestions

1. Deeply concerned about the threats of climate change, you wish to communicate your concern to a group of people you feel should be

more deeply involved than they are. Prepare a talk or article using information from this unit to shake the group out of apathy. Identify whom you are writing for and in what way you will make your presentation (in a talk at a club meeting, video, personal letter, magazine article, etc.).

2. (a) Imagine that you are a professor of earth science and have had your students read the material in this unit for an introductory course on the past, present, and future of the earth. Write three essay questions for the final examination to test your students' understanding of this material. (b) Imagine that you are a student taking the examination in the course described in part (a). Write an essay in response to any one of the three questions.

3. For the editorial page of your newspaper, write an editorial on whether the costs of industrialization and economic development have been too high. Consider whether we have brought about our own doom or whether we have been able to make a better world by finding solutions to the difficulties we create.

4. Imagine you are a scientist who has been asked to speak to a group of talented junior high school students to help them understand what science is really all about. Based on the material in this unit, write a talk explaining to them how science does not always produce absolute abstract truth. Explain how science is a kind of argument and can be concerned with immediate practical problems.

5. As part of this course's concern with the varieties of disciplinary writing, write an essay describing modeling as a form of scientific argument. Using the examples of articles in this unit, discuss when and why modeling may be used, what are the characteristics of a modeling argument, what particular aspects of persuasion it must be sensitive to, and how it differs from the traditional experimental report.

6. As part of this course's concern with the varieties of disciplinary writing, write an essay discussing how the many audiences and purposes of writing about science influence the type of writing that takes place. Using examples from this unit (and other relevant units), discuss how the technical knowledge and concerns of different audiences (from newspaper reader to government official to scientific colleague) influence how the scientific material is presented.

UNIT

6

ENGINEERING

Nuclear Power Safety: Containing Terrifying Forces

Engineers design many useful things for us, such as bridges, automobiles, compact disc players, automated factories, and power plants. To be helpful, their designs must be reliable as well as economical. When engineers work with powerful forces and dangerous situations, the costs of failure can become unacceptably high. When a rubber seal on a garden hose fails, the cost is only some minor irritation and a few cents for a replacement. If a similar rubber seal fails in a space shuttle and causes it to crash, the costs include human lives, billions of dollars, and several years of effort for the space program. And if a technical failure occurs in a nuclear power plant and sets off a train of events that cannot be controlled by adequate safety features, the costs are incalculable.

Because nuclear power relies on massive forces, forces that fire the sun and that fuel bombs, it presents an enormous challenge to engineers. From one point of view, the creation of electrical power from nuclear fission is not difficult to do. If you put enough special nuclear material together, a nuclear reaction heats water, which will create steam to drive electrical turbines. The basic technology of power conversion differs little from the century-old technology of coal-powered electrical generators. The more difficult problem at hand is to design and build a plant that is sufficiently safe.

There are two approaches to nuclear safety. One approach is to make the operations of the plant so reliable that no incident could ever occur. Although this is an admirable ideal and although accidents may be minimized, accidents cannot be totally avoided. The second approach is to assure that any accidents that may occur remain small and the damage contained. Engineers have designed ways to shut the nuclear reactor down before accidents escalate into disasters and to isolate the effects of the accident within a contained space.

Despite the intelligence and efforts that have gone into keeping nuclear power safe, some accidents have made many people fear that the risks of nuclear power are unacceptably high. The accident at Pennsylvania's Three Mile Island nuclear power plant in 1979 virtually stopped construction of nuclear power plants for the time being in the United States, although European and Asian nations continued to build them. The 1986 Chernobyl disaster in the Soviet Union, costing an unknown number of lives, disrupted the life of a major region of the Soviet Union and contaminated much of European and Soviet agriculture. This incident demonstrated even more dramatically the dangers of nuclear power.

Yet many nuclear engineers believe that these disasters were avoidable and that given the world's energy needs we have no choice but to continue with nuclear energy. For them the accidents at Three Mile Island and Chernobyl contain lessons for future design improvements. Engineers have studied these incidents to find out exactly what went wrong and how to keep those things from happening again.

This unit presents different ways nuclear engineers have considered the promise and dangers of nuclear power. We start with an early calculation of the need for and immense promise of nuclear power, as presented in a classic textbook of nuclear engineering. More recent engineering descriptions of nuclear power plant design features (including the reactor containment structure) show how engineers approach design problems. Several examinations of the accidents at Three Mile Island and Chernobyl look for lessons for future designs, but also lead to questions as to whether the technology is worth the risk. Opinions are mixed. Finally, a government document assesses the obstacles to further nuclear power development in the United States.

Because nuclear power is of such public concern, engineering documents have become part of a public debate. Usually engineers communicate primarily with other engineers in their own company, with clients, and with regulatory agencies when required by law. For economic and institutional reasons, they tend not to share information with competitors or the public the way scientists do.

In the selections here you will only be looking at the way engineers talk about these issues and will not be asked to consider the wider public opposition to the construction of new nuclear power plants in the United States. The public debate forms an important background to many of the documents presented here, however, for public opposition has put nuclear engineers on the defensive. They have had to explain design criteria and safety systems. To reassure the public, engineers have had to increase their margins of safety. If nuclear fission power plants are ever again to be built in the United States, these engineers will have to address the concerns of the public and other interested parties, as is discussed in the last selection, "The Seven-Sided Coin."

The selections in this unit exhibit three general characteristics of writing within engineering: (1) a problem–solution organization, (2) a focus on the design object instead of on ideas, and (3) an orderly reasoning from first principles. These features of the writing result directly from the task of engineering. Engineers design objects to solve specific real-world problems, so when they present their designs, they first need to present the problem their design is supposed to solve. A machine does not make any sense (nor will you be willing to invest in it) if you do not know what it is trying to do.

Moreover, since engineers are concerned with building objects rather than building ideas, the object rather than the idea takes the central place in their texts. The design object is the accomplishment. Consequently, they tend to borrow designs from each other rather than theories or ideas; the largest continuity among the articles here comes from standard designs of nuclear plants. Almost every article discusses the U.S. pressurized water reactor with its safety and containment features. When the reactor under discussion is of a different design, as is the Chernobyl reactor, the article discusses implications of the difference between the variant design and the typical U.S. design.

Finally, since engineering technology usually applies proved knowledge, articles rarely report exploratory investigations and speculations or argue for new claims. Rather, the articles build in an orderly manner (sometimes indicated by sequential numbered statements) on known basic principles. Engineering documents often begin with a statement of all the relevant current knowledge, thereby defining the problem situation and establishing the materials and options for the solution. Then they present the design and discuss its characteristics and advantages.

Nuclear Power and the World's Energy Resources

Samuel Glasstone

In 1945, the atomic bombs exploded at Hiroshima and Nagasaki ended the war against Japan and demonstrated the tremendous power created by nuclear fission. Almost immediately, Americans began thinking about the peaceful applications of that power. Nuclear power seemed to promise an endless, cheap supply of energy. One scientist predicted that a car would run for a year on a nuclear pellet the size of a vitamin pill. By 1953, when President Eisenhower declared "atoms for peace" a major priority of the U.S. government, the main use conceived for nuclear power was the generation of electricity.

The following selection opens a 1955 nuclear engineering textbook, introducing the principles of nuclear power plant design. Samuel Glasstone, a leading nuclear engineer engaged in designing early experimental reactors, expresses the optimism of this period, seeing in nuclear power a solution to the earth's increasing need for power. His prediction of increasing demand for power and diminishing fossil fuel resources describes precisely our current situation. Moreover, the alternative of solar power remains little changed from Glasstone's description of thirty-five years ago: "The idea of making more direct use of the sun's energy is very attractive, but so far no satisfactory method has been developed for utilizing it on a large scale except through green plants." As Glasstone suggested, we have tried nuclear fission; fusion remains only an experimental hope. Eighty-six operating fission plants now produce about 15 percent of the electricity in the United States and there are about five hundred plants in operation or under construction worldwide. The problem thus remains much as he saw it. However, we no longer share his optimism about nuclear fission as an ideal solution.

Glasstone's presentation begins by defining the problem of world energy resources, then examines the options, and finally presents a solution in the form of a design for a nuclear reactor. The analysis proceeds in a numbered, step-by-step fashion as basic facts are introduced and built on and the solution of each problem raises a new problem to be solved. In more ways than one, this is a textbook example of an engineering presentation.

1.1. THE DISCOVERY OF NUCLEAR fission° in 1939 was an event of epochal significance, because it opened up the prospect of an entirely

---

Fission—the splitting of atomic nuclei of a heavy element into nuclei of two or more lighter elements, accompanied by the release of some binding energy.

new source of power, utilizing the internal energy of the atomic nucleus. The basic materials that can be used for the release of nuclear energy by fission are the elements uranium and thorium°. Minerals containing these elements are widely distributed in the earth's crust, so that, as will be apparent shortly, they represent a very large potential source of power.

1.2. For the past half century fossil fuels, namely, coal, oil, and natural gas, have supplied the major portion of the world's energy requirements. It has long been realized, however, that in the not too distant future these sources of energy will be largely exhausted. At the present time the total power consumption for all countries is about 0.1×10^{18} Btu,° i.e., 0.1 Q, per annum.[1] Taking into account both the steadily growing population and the increasing per capita power demand, it is possible that by the year 2000 the rate of energy utilization for the whole world will be close to 1 Q per annum. The most reliable estimates indicate that the energy content of the coal, oil, gas, and oil shale that can be recovered at no more than twice the present cost amounts to less than 40 Q. This means that within 100 years the economically useful reserves of fossil fuels will be virtually exhausted.

1.3. Even when allowance is made for errors in the foregoing estimates, the conclusion is inevitable that new sources of power must be found during the next 50 years or so if the earth is to support the growing population with some increase in living standards. Two such sources have been considered: solar energy and atomic (or nuclear) energy. The idea of making more direct use of the sun's energy is very attractive, but so far no satisfactory method has been developed for utilizing it on a large scale except through green plants. On the other hand, with the discovery of fission, nuclear energy appears to be a practical possibility.

1.4. One of the remarkable facts about nuclear energy is the large amount that can be released from a small mass of active (fissionable) material. Thus, the complete fission of one pound of uranium would liberate roughly 3.6×10^{10} Btu of heat; this is equivalent to the energy produced in the combustion of close to 1400 tons of 13,000 Btu/lb coal.[2]

1.5. The total amount of uranium and thorium in the earth's crust, to a depth of three miles, is very large, possibly something like 10^{12} tons. However, much of this is present in minerals containing such a small proportion of the desired element that extraction would be prohibitively expensive. Assuming, as is probable, that technological advances will reduce the cost of recovery from moderately low-grade ores to not more than $100 per lb of metal, it has been estimated that the world reserve, based on admittedly incomplete mappings, is 25 million tons of uranium and 1 million tons of thorium.[3] As will be seen later, it is unlikely that the whole of this material can be utilized economically

---

Thorium—a radioactive metallic element.   Btu—British thermal unit, the amount of heat necessary to raise the temperature of 1 lb. of water by 1° Fahrenheit.

in fission, but in favorable circumstances perhaps one third might be so used. On the basis of the energy equivalence factor given in the preceding paragraph, the heat that might be obtained by fission is thus

$$\frac{1}{3} \times 26 \times 10^6 \text{ tons} \times 2000 \frac{\text{lb}}{\text{ton}} \times 3.6 \times 10^{10} \frac{\text{Btu}}{\text{lb}} = 624 \times 10^{18} \text{ Btu}$$

$$= 624 \text{ Q.}$$

The possible energy reserve in the form of uranium and thorium is consequently many times greater than that of the fossil fuels and so it would, if properly developed, represent a very significant contribution to the world's power sources.

1.6. It may be noted, in passing, that the production of energy by fission is by no means regarded as the ultimate solution of the problem of making nuclear energy available for practical use. Scientists are intrigued by the possibility of obtaining controllable energy by the fusion° of very light nuclei, the process responsible for the energy of the sun and stars. If this could be achieved, water might become the main source of energy, for the fusion, into helium, of the hydrogen nuclei contained in one pound of water should produce (theoretically) close to 3×10^{11} Btu of energy. Even if the fusion process were restricted to deuterium, i.e., heavy hydrogen, since this would probably be easier to achieve, it would still be possible, in principle, to obtain nearly 10^8 Btu/lb of water.

Nuclear Reactors and the Fission Process

1.7. The basically correct statement, in § 1.4, that the heat released by the complete fission of one pound of nuclear fuel is equivalent to that obtainable from 1400 tons of coal (or 300,000 gal of fuel oil), has led to some erroneous conclusions. The fantastic possibility has been envisaged of including in an automobile enough fissionable material, about the size of a pea, to last the life of the vehicle. In order to realize why this is not within the bounds of reality, it is necessary to understand something about the fission process. Although this will be discussed in more detail in later parts of the book, a brief outline will be given here.

1.8. Fission occurs when a nucleus of the appropriate type captures a subatomic particle, called a neutron. The nucleus then splits into two lighter nuclei (the primary fission products), and at the same time energy is released. Also, in each act of fission neutrons are emitted, two or three on the average, and if one of these at least is captured by another fissionable nucleus, a fission chain reaction with the continuous production of energy becomes possible. The device in which the nuclear fission

---

Fusion—the combining of nuclei of light elements into nuclei of a heavier element, accompanied by the release of some binding energy.

chain is initiated, maintained, and controlled, so that the accompanying energy is released at a specified rate, is called a *nuclear reactor.*[4]

1.9. Because of the loss of neutrons, by escape and by capture in various ways which do not lead to fission, a chain reaction can be maintained only if the system exceeds a certain size, referred to as the "critical" size. Although this size has a definite value for a particular system, it can vary over a wide range, depending on the nature and amounts of the materials present and their geometrical configuration. Thus, for a reactor consisting largely of pure fissionable material (uranium-235 or plutonium-239), the critical size has been described, very roughly, as being about "as big as a football."[5] From the known density of metallic uranium, it can be readily calculated that a reactor of this type contains approximately 100 lb of fissionable material. If the amount is less than this, the fission chain cannot be maintained and there can be no continuous production of energy. However, in other reactors the critical mass may be smaller or larger, depending upon various circumstances. For example, systems using natural uranium metal as the nuclear fuel require several tons of this material before they become critical. At the other extreme, some reactors can operate on a few pounds of fuel.

1.10. Thus, although it is true that one pound of fissionable material can produce energy equivalent to nearly three million times its own weight of coal, the reactor in which the energy release occurs may contain anything from some pounds to several tons of nuclear fuel. The amount of fuel to be consumed for energy production must be present in addition to the critical quantity, since this is the essential minimum. However, too large an excess is not only wasteful, for various reasons, but it makes the reactor more difficult to control. There is, consequently, a practical limit to the energy that can be produced before the reactor is "refueled." Nevertheless, an excess of only 10 lb of fissionable material, over and above the critical amount, could produce the equivalent of 100 million kw-hr in the form of heat.

Utilization of Nuclear Fuel

1.11. There is no method known at the present time for utilizing the major portion of the energy of fission except as heat.[6] Thus, in a sense, a nuclear reactor may be thought of as a kind of furnace. In the production of electricity, for example, the reactor may be regarded as a substitute for the boiler firebox. The boiler is actually a heat exchanger, but the steam (or other vapor) obtained would be used in a conventional turbogenerator system. A general comparison between a coal-burning, steam-electric generating installation and one using a nuclear reactor as a source of heat is shown in Figure 1. The upper portion is a schematic representation of a coal-fired plant, and the lower section indicates the changes that would be necessary if the heat were supplied by a nuclear reactor. The reactor shown is approximately the size of the one at the

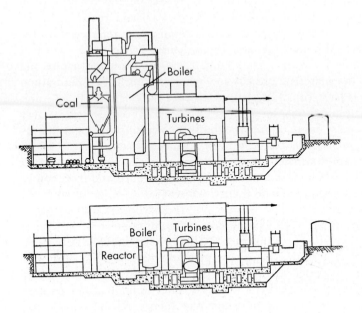

Figure 1. Comparison of coal-fired and nuclear steam-electric power plants (P. Sporn and S. N. Fiola).
Source: U.S. Department of Energy.

Brookhaven National Laboratory, including its thick concrete shield. It is seen that in the nuclear power plant the coal-handling equipment is eliminated and the boiler (or heat exchanger) is smaller than the conventional type. The electrical generating equipment is, however, essentially unchanged.

Notes

[1] The symbol Q is used to represent 10^{18} Btu, so that large quantities of energy can be expressed in terms of convenient small numbers; see P. C. Putnam, "Energy in the Future," D. Van Nostrand Co. Inc., 1953. This work is the source of the data presented here.

[2] Throughout this book a "ton" refers to a short ton of 2000 lb.

[3] P. C. Putnam, *op. cit.*, p. 214.

[4] The term "pile," although less descriptive of modern reactors, is still used to some extent. It had its origin in the fact that the first successful reactor was

constructed by piling layers of graphite (some containing uranium) upon one
another (§ 13.4).

[5]W. H. Zinn, *Nucleonics*, 10, No. 9, 8 (1952).

[6]A small fraction of the fission energy, considerably less than one per cent,
present as radioactive energy of the fission products, may be converted directly into electrical energy.

Rhetorical Analysis Through Annotation

This selection moves us along an inevitable path from one problem to the next
so that we accept the logic of the ultimate solution of nuclear power in the form
of a particular plant design. Each problem and solution is based on basic information and principles introduced at the appropriate point.

Underline each statement of a problem. If a problem is only implicit, state it
in your own words in the margin. In the margin, mark the information and
principles introduced to define and solve the problem. Place a star or other mark
next to the solution of each problem. Finally, label appropriately any discussion
of advantages or difficulties of each solution.

Discuss how these elements fit together in each problem–solution cluster and
how the solution to each problem in the sequence leads to the next problem.
Consider whether the step-by-step reasoning leaves any room open for alternative conclusions or considerations of other options. How are potential doors
to other options closed?

Discussion Questions

Interpreting the Text

1. According to Glasstone, how pressing are our energy needs?

2. Paragraph 1.5 offers a rough calculation of likely usable energy to be derived
from fission. Where does each term in that calculation come from and why is
it used?

3. Why are solar power and nuclear fussion not short-term options? Do they
hold promise in the long term?

4. How does nuclear fission work? How does the fission reaction constrain the
uses that can be made of nuclear power?

5. Compare the diagrams of the coal-fired and nuclear steam-electric power
plants. What are the similarities and differences?

6. Why are the paragraphs numbered as they are in this selection? What is
convenient or inconvenient about this numbering system? In what kinds of
writing are you likely to find similar numbering? Why don't all writers number
paragraphs in this way?

Considering the Issues

7. According to news reports, what is the current state of the world fuel
resources compared to current and future needs? How much attention has this

issue been getting in the news media recently? Have there been any changes in the level of public concern in your memory?

8. What aspects of life are affected by energy sufficiency? What are the immediate effects of a short-term energy crisis? What are possible long-term consequences of an extended energy crisis?

9. What are your feelings about nuclear power? Has it lived up to its promise? Should we continue to develop it? What should we do about currently operating nuclear power plants?

10. What current plans do we have for dealing with the energy problem? What efforts have we made to explore alternative energy sources? Do these plans seem adequate to the problem?

Writing Suggestions

1. Using calculations and data presented here or elsewhere, write a letter to a member of Congress urging the development of an energy policy or alternative source of energy. You may date the letter either back in 1955 or today.

2. Write an introduction to a textbook on any practical skill you are familiar with, such as cooking, bicycle repair, carpentry, sewing, party-giving, or paper folding. Explain the basic principles necessary for a beginner in the field to understand. You may wish to imitate Glasstone's numbering system, his use of diagrams, and other features of his writing.

3. For a presentation before an agency of a local government, describe a problem the community faces, list the options, and present a specific solution. Explain why your solution is best and the other options are less attractive.

4. Based on your own opinions and the opinions of people around you (such as those expressed in class discussion), write an essay in reaction to this selection for your college writing course in order to share your opinion with your classmates. In the essay you may compare current attitudes toward nuclear power to the optimism of the fifties. Or you may consider what has happened to the energy crisis and our perception of it.

Pressurized-Water Reactors

Anthony V. Nero

American nuclear engineers developed several designs to convert nuclear power into electricity. The pressurized-water reactor design was used at Three Mile Island and at many other installations in the United States. It is significantly different from the Chernobyl design, which represents the Soviet solution to the same task.

This selection is from a technical book written in 1979, describing nuclear reactors. It is directed toward readers who need to understand the reactors, but who are not necessarily trained engineers. In it, Anthony V. Nero, a nuclear physicist at the University of California's Lawrence Berkeley Laboratory, describes the design shared by some U.S. manufacturers. The description serves to familiarize the reader with the fundamental features of the system. Since individual reactors differ in some specifics, anyone working with a particular reactor would have to examine the detailed specifications for that unit.

The reactor and its parts are represented through several diagrams. Making reference to these diagrams, the text describes the parts, their functions, and how they fit together into a total system. First the overall system is represented and explained, then each key part is examined in greater detail. This text is typical of engineering descriptions in the close relationship between text and diagrams, the clarity and detail in the identification of the parts, and the concern for showing the function of each of the parts within the overall system.

MOST OF THE LIGHT-WATER° reactor power plants now operating *1* or under construction use pressurized-water reactors. Westinghouse supplies somewhat more than half of the PWRs in the United States, with the remainder split between Babcock & Wilcox and Combustion Engineering. Many of the details of PWRs vary from one vendor to another and even, for the same manufacturer, from one reactor to the next. However, the fundamental characteristic of PWRs remains the same: that the primary coolant raises steam in a heat exchanger° called a steam generator and this steam drives the turbine. A basic PWR system is shown schematically in Figure 1. Enclosed in a containment structure is the primary coolant° system consisting of the reactor vessel and two or more primary coolant loops, each including piping, pumps, and a steam generator (perhaps shared). The safety injection (ECC)° systems are also within the containment. Steam from the steam generators is transported out of the containment to the turbogenerator system. Condensate returns to the steam generators. Although three corporations offer PWRs, the system description that follows is based largely on that of Westinghouse. PWRs from the other manufacturers will vary in detail, particularly in the matter of the primary coolant loop arrangement.

Light water—ordinary water, wherein the hydrogen nucleus consists only of a proton. Heat exchanger—any device, such as an automobile radiator, that transfers heat from one fluid to another.   Coolant—a liquid used to absorb heat from a source.   ECC— emergency core cooling systems—a system to cool the core by water, in case of an accident involving loss of coolant.

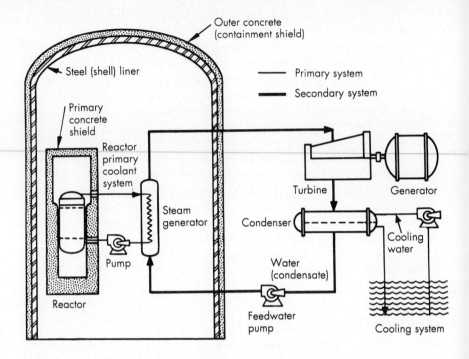

Figure 1. Schematic Pressurized-Water Reactor Power Plant. The primary reactor system is enclosed in a steel-lined concrete containment building. Steam generated within the building flows to the turbine-generator system (outside the building), after which it is condensed and returned to the steam generators. *Source: ERDA-1541.*

Basic PWR System

The basic unit of a PWR core is a fuel pin typical of water-cooled 2 reactors. For such reactors, the uranium dioxide fuel material is pressed into "pellets," cylinders about one-half inch in diameter and of similar height. These pellets are sintered (heated to high temperatures), ground to the proper dimensions, then sealed, along with a helium atmosphere, in a cladding material. This constitutes a fuel rod or pin. The cladding is typically an alloy of zirconium,° chosen for its low neutron cross-section, as well as for its structural properties. The fuel pin for a light-water reactor is shown schematically in Figure 2. These pins, each more than 12 feet (3.6 m) long for LWRs, are assembled into bundles or "assemblies," the operational unit for handling, refueling, etc. Should

---

Zirconium—a metallic element with a high melting point (1852°C) and low neutron absorption properties.

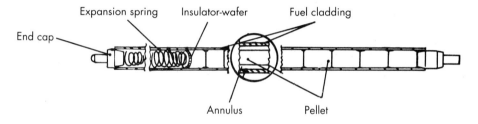

Figure 2. Cutaway View of Oxide Fuel for Commercial LWR
Power Plants.   The basic unit in the core of a light-water reactor
is a fuel rod containing uranium oxide pellets in a Zircaloy cladding. The rod is filled with helium gas and welded shut. The
circled portion exaggerates the annular° space between the pellet
and the cladding.
Source: WASH-1250.

plutonium be recycled into light-water reactors, it would be handled in
much the same way. In the United States, it has been proposed that the
plutonium oxide be finely mixed with the uranium dioxide before a fuel
pellet is formed.

The core of a pressurized water reactor consists of a large number of
square fuel assemblies or bundles. Figure 3 shows one of these assemblies, in this case containing a control rod cluster. Many PWRs use
assemblies that consist of 15 × 15 arrays of fuel pins of the type indicated
in Figure 2, each somewhat more than 12 feet long. Newer PWRs use
17 × 17 assemblies. These pins or rods are closely held together in a
matrix with no outer sheath, by the assembly's top and bottom structures, and by spring clip grid assemblies. A full-sized (about 1000 MWe°)
PWR may contain nearly 200 assemblies with about 40 or 50 thousand
fuel pins, containing about 110 tons (100 metric tons) of uranium dioxide
(and plutonium, were recycle to occur).

All the assemblies have provision for the passage of control rods
through rod guides which take about 20 of the positions that could
otherwise hold fuel rods. If the assembly is used as a control assembly,
and about 30% of them are, the rods from that assembly are manipulated
from the top as a cluster. The control drives are at the top of the pressure
vessel. In case the assembly does not contain a rod cluster, control rod
positions may be taken by burnable poison,° in this case boron 10 which

---

Annular—ringlike.   **MWe**—megawatts (electric), as opposed to the overall megawatts
of heat output. Because some energy is lost in the reactor operation and conversion to
electricity, the MWe is always lower than the overall thermal MW (or MWth) for a
nuclear reactor.   **Poison**—a material that absorbs neutrons unproductively and thereby
removes them from the fission chain reaction and decreases the reactivity of the system.

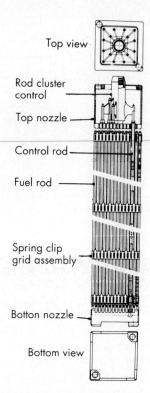

Top view

Rod cluster
control

Top nozzle

Control rod

Fuel rod

Spring clip
grid assembly

Botton nozzle

Bottom view

Figure 3.   Fuel Assembly for a Pressurized-Water Reactor.   In a
pressurized-water reactor, fuel rods are assembled into a square
array, held together by spring clip assemblies and by nozzles at
the top and bottom. The structure is open, permitting flow of
coolant both vertically and horizontally. All the assemblies in the
reactor may have the same mechanical design, including provision
for passage of a control rod cluster (shown in the figure). Where
there is no cluster, these positions may have neutron sources,
burnable poison rods, or plugs.
Source: WASH-1250.

is used after initial reactor operation to offset excess reactivity, or by
neutron sources, used for reactor startup. Otherwise, these positions are
left vacant and water flow through them is blocked.

Most of the control rods have silver-indium-cadmium neutron ab- 5
sorber for the full length of the core and are used for operational control
of the reactor, including load following,° and for quick shutdown capability. Reactor "trip" capability is provided by the fact that the rods

---

Load following—controlling the power output of the reactor to match the demand for
power.

can simply be dropped into place gravitationally; somewhat fewer than half the control assemblies are reserved for this shutdown capability, the remaining being used for operational control. Some of the control rods have absorber only in their bottom quarter and are used for shaping the axial (vertical) power distribution.° The other basic means of control is to introduce boric acid into the primary coolant. This method is used both for shutdown and for adjusting the reactivity to take account of long-term changes, such as reduction in fissile content and buildup of fission product poisons. Effectively, boron adjustment is used to keep the reactivity within the range of the control rods.

The core has three enrichment zones, with the most highly enriched **6** (slightly greater than 3%) at the periphery and the other enrichments scattered through the interior, all to provide a relatively flat power distribution. The average power generation density in the core is about 98 kW/liter. (See Table 1 for other PWR parameters.) This energy is carried away by a very large flow of water, about 140 million pounds per hour (18 Mg/s). The water's operating temperature is about 600 °F (315 °C), which maintains the clad temperature nominally below 700 °F (371 °C).

The core, control rods, and core-monitoring instrumentation are con- **7** tained in a large pressure vessel, designed to withstand pressures, at operating temperatures, of about 2500 psi (17 MPa°). The vessel may be about 40 feet in height (12 m) and 14 feet (4 m) in diameter, with carbon steel walls 8 inches (20 cm) or more thick. All inner surfaces that come into contact with the coolant are clad in stainless steel. (This is also true of all other parts of the primary coolant system, except for those portions that are made of Zircaloy° or Inconel°, i.e., the fuel cladding and the steam generator tubing, respectively.) The top head of the vessel, which holds all the control rod drives, is removable for refueling. The reactor vessel and its contents are shown in Figure 4.

The coolant enters the reactor vessel through nozzles near the top of **8** the core and, constrained by a "core barrel" between the vessel and the core, flows to the bottom of the core. The water then flows up through the core and out exit nozzles to the steam generators. From there, the coolant is recirculated to the core by large primary coolant pumps. The main elements of the primary coolant system are shown in Figure 5.

The pressure in the primary system is maintained at about 2250 psi° **9** (15.5 MPa), preventing the formation of steam. Instead, steam is raised

---

Axial power distribution—the amount of energy produced by each level of the reactor core, measured along an axial line in the core.   MPa—Mega Pascal, a unit of pressure. Zircaloy—an alloy of zirconium.   Inconel—a nickel-base alloy, which resists corrosion and high-temperature oxidation.   psi—pounds per square inch.

Core thermal power	3,411 MWth
Plant efficiency	32%
Plant electrical output	1,100 MWe
Core diameter	134 in (3.4 m)
Core (or fuel rod) active length	144 in (3.7 m)
Core weight (mass)	276,000 lb (125 Mg)
Core power density	98 kW/liter
Cladding material	Zircaloy-4
Cladding diameter (OD)	0.422 in (1.07 cm)
Cladding thickness	0.024 in (0.06 cm)
Fuel material	UO_2
Pellet diameter	0.37 in (0.9 cm)
Pellet height	0.6 in (1.5 cm)
Assembly array	15 × 15, open structure[a]
Number of assemblies	193
Total number of fuel rods	39,372[a]
Control rod type	B_4C or Ag-In-Cd in cylindrical rod
Number of control rod assemblies	60 (may vary considerably)
Number of control rods per control assembly	20 (may vary considerably)
Total amount of fuel (UO_2)	217,000 lb (98 Mg)
Fuel power density	38 MW/Te
Fuel/coolant ratio	1/4.1
Coolant	Water (liquid phase)
Total coolant flow rate	136 × 10^6 lb/hr (17 Mg/sec)
Core coolant velocity	15.5 ft/sec (4.7 m/sec)
Coolant pressure	2,250 psi (15.5 MPa)
Coolant temperature (inlet at full power)	552 °F (289 °C)
Coolant temperature (outlet at full power)	617 °F (325 °C)
Nominal clad temperature	657 °F (347 °C)
Nominal fuel central temperature	4,140 °F (2,282 °C)
Radial peaking factor (variation in power density)	1.5
Axial peaking factor	1.7
Design fuel burnup	32,000 MWd/Te (heavy metal); varies
Fresh fuel assay	3.2% ^{235}U (less in initial load)
Spent fuel assay (design)	0.9% ^{235}U, 0.6% $^{239,241}Pu$
Refueling sequence	One-third of the fuel per year
Refueling time	17 day (minimum)

Table 1. Representative characteristics of pressurized-water reactors.

   [a]*PWRs now being licensed have a 17 × 17 assembly array, with thinner rods totaling 50,952. Other specifications may be slightly changed.*
Source: Taken primarily from Westinghous Electric Corp. specifications.

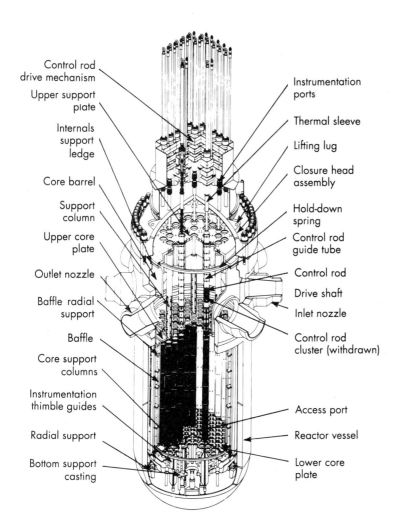

Control rod
drive mechanism

Upper support
plate

Internals
support
ledge

Core barrel

Support
column

Upper core
plate

Outlet nozzle

Baffle radial
support

Baffle

Core support
columns

Instrumentation
thimble guides

Radial support

Bottom support
casting

Instrumentation
ports

Thermal sleeve

Lifting lug

Closure head
assembly

Hold-down
spring

Control rod
guide tube

Control rod

Drive shaft

Inlet nozzle

Control rod
cluster (withdrawn)

Access port

Reactor vessel

Lower core
plate

Figure 4. Pressurized-Water Reactor Vessel and Internals. The core of a pressurized-water reactor is contained in a large steel vessel through which coolant flows. After passing into an inlet nozzle, the water flows down between the core barrel and the vessel wall, until it reaches the plenum° beneath the core; there it turns upward to flow through the core and out one of the outlet nozzles to the steam generators. The top of the reactor vessel, which is removable for refueling, supports mechanisms for driving control rods.
Source: Westinghouse Electric Corp.

Plenum—high-pressure container.

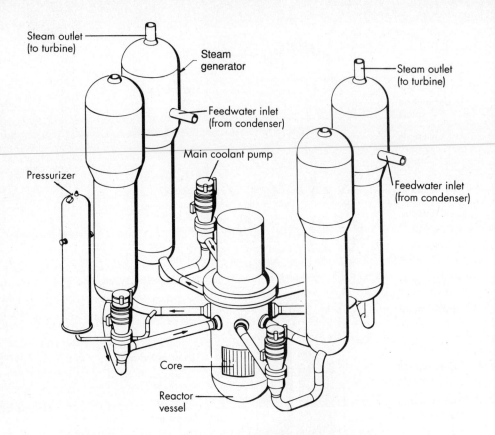

Figure 5.   Arrangement of the Primary System for a Westing-house PWR.   The primary system constitutes the nuclear steam supply system for a PWR plant. In the four-loop arrangement shown in the figure, each loop has its own steam generator and coolant pump. A pressurizer is connected to one of the loops. The primary coolant enters and leaves the steam generator from the bottom. . . .
Source: WASH-1250.

in a secondary system by allowing heat to flow from the high-pressure primary coolant to the lower pressure secondary fluid. This heat transfer occurs through the walls of large numbers of tubes through which the primary coolant circulates in the steam generators. After the steam has passed through separators to remove water droplets, thereby reducing its moisture content to less than 1%, it proceeds to the turbogenerator for the production of electricity. After condensation, it returns as liquid to the steam generators. The overall thermal efficiency of a PWR is about 32%. In the steam generators, the primary coolant passes only

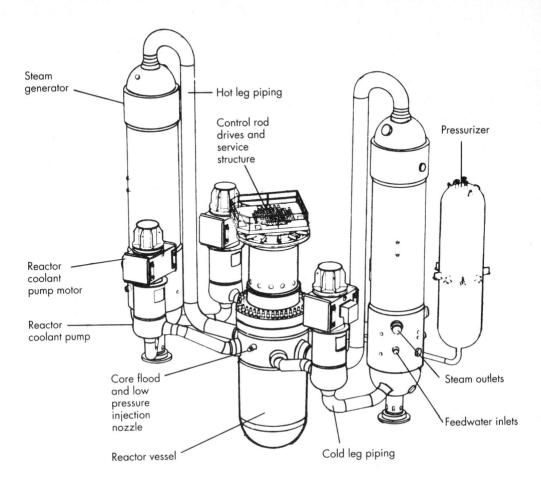

Steam generator

Hot leg piping

Control rod drives and service structure

Pressurizer

Reactor coolant pump motor

Reactor coolant pump

Core flood and low pressure injection nozzle

Steam outlets

Feedwater inlets

Reactor vessel

Cold leg piping

Figure 6.   Alternative Arrangement for a PWR Primary System. This PWR system has two outlet nozzles, each leading to a steam generator. The outlet of each generator is connected with two coolant pumps, each of which is connected with an inlet nozzle at the reactor vessel. These steam generators use vertical tubes, rather than the U-tube design of Figure 5.
Source: Babcock & Wilcox, a McDermott company. Reprinted with permission.

once through a single tube (i.e., the steam generators are "once through"), which is ordinarily either U-shaped or straight. A large PWR may have four external circuits, indicated schematically in Figure 5, each with its own steam generator and pump. As seen in Figure 6, this arrangement may vary from one manufacturer to another.

Since maintenance of the pressure near the design value is crucial (to *10* avoid the formation of steam in the primary coolant, on the one hand, and rupture of the primary circuit, on the other) a PWR system also includes a "pressurizer," as shown in Figures 5 and 6, connected to the "hot" leg of one of the steam generator circuits. The pressurizer volume is occupied partly by water and partly by steam; it has heaters for boiling water and sprayers for condensing steam, as needed, to keep the pressure within specified operating limits.

Rhetorical Analysis Through Annotation

The description explains the design by giving names to parts and processes that comprise the design. The named parts are usually both pictured in diagrams and described in the text. Processes (because they do not represent static hardware) are discussed in the text and only indirectly represented in the diagrams.

In the text underline all names of hardware parts. Circle all names of processes.

Using information in the text and diagrams, ascertain the meaning of each name. Discuss how meaning is established for each of these terms through context, definitions, diagrams, captions, terms used in the name, or any other manner you can find. Discuss how the relationship of the different parts and processes is established in the text and diagrams. Why are the diagrams and items in the text sequenced as they are? Which items are presented only in the text? Only in the diagrams? Only in the captions? Which are represented in both text and diagram? Why?

Discussion Questions

Interpreting the Text

1. What are the main parts of the basic PWR system? What are their functions? What reasons can you find for them being designed as they are?

2. How is the fuel system organized? What types of concerns influenced the design of the system? How is the water coolant system organized? What concerns influenced its design? To what extent do these two systems interact and in what way are they kept apart? Why?

3. In small groups, have one person explain each diagram to the group and answer questions about the function of each part.

4. How does this characterization of a nuclear reactor compare with that given by Glasstone on pages 457–458, both in overall design and in detail of presentation? How can you account for the similarities and differences?

Considering the Issues

5. Why are hardware descriptions so important to engineers?

6. Which parts and functions seem to require more elaborate mechanical systems than others? Why?

7. Why is so much concern given to shaping the power output and to controlling the coolant flow?

8. Do you find the design simple or complex? To what extent are you surprised by the simplicity or complexity of the design?

Writing Suggestions

1. (a) The local scout troop has asked you to give a talk describing the workings of a nuclear power plant. Write a short talk, using Figure 1 as a visual aid to help you explain how the plant works. (b) The day before the talk, the scoutmaster informs you that several of the scouts are blind and that you should not use visual aids. Rewrite your talk so that your listeners can understand it without the help of the diagram. (c) For this class's discussion of writing techniques, write a few paragraphs comparing the difficulties of using and not using diagrams. Discuss advantages and disadvantages of each approach.

2. Imagine you are a science journalist for a newspaper. An accident has just occurred involving a fuel assembly for a PWR. Your editor asks you to write an explanatory story describing the construction of the fuel assembly, using Figure 2 and/or Figure 3 to accompany your story. Write a clear three-hundred word story to accompany the main news story.

3. In a letter to a friend unfamiliar with the wonders of modern technology, describe a ball-point pen, an electric can opener, a tape recorder, a pop-top beer can, or any other small device. You may use diagrams.

4. Imagine you are an engineer having to explain to an audience of taxpayers why a nuclear power plant requires such complex hardware to do such apparently simple tasks. Prepare a short talk on "How and Why a Simple Thing Becomes Difficult."

Safety Considerations in the Design and Operation of Light Water Nuclear Power Plants

John R. Lamarsh

Although public opposition to nuclear power was mounting before the Three Mile Island accident, that incident brought the issue of nuclear power safety to national attention. In this selection John Lamarsh, a nuclear engineer at Polytechnic Institute of New York, explains and defends the safety system in place at Three Mile Island and other United States nuclear power plants. He was speaking in 1981 at a symposium on the Three Mile Island accident; the audience was a mixed collection of scientists, engineers, government policy planners, nuclear power regulators, power-industry representatives, and public interest advocates. To such a varied audience he explains the engineering logic behind the design of the barrier sequence system and discusses how technical problems in the construction and operation of the barriers were overcome.

Although Lamarsh seems to be presenting a simple description, he is also arguing that the system, as constructed, is a good one. Furthermore, although he treats the construction of an adequate safety system largely as a matter of hardware design, he recognizes at several points that public acceptance and cooperation are needed for the technical design to be fulfilled.

THERE ARE ESSENTIALLY ONLY two different types of nuclear 1 power plants being built and operated in the United States today: one type uses a boiling water reactor, or BWR; the other uses a pressurized water reactor, or PWR. The Three Mile Island plant is in the latter category, a PWR plant.

The basic principles of the operation of both types of nuclear plant 2 are quite straightforward. First, energy is released in the reactor fuel as the result of nuclear fission. This energy is then absorbed from the fuel by a passing coolant, which is ordinary water in the case of both the BWR and the PWR. With the boiling water reactor, as the name implies, the heat absorbed from the fuel causes the water to boil within the reactor itself. With the pressurized water reactor, on the other hand, the pressure of the water is kept so high that it does not boil within the reactor. Instead, after passing through the reactor core, the heated water goes to a heat exchanger called the steam generator, where the energy from the primary reactor cooling water causes water to boil in a secondary cooling-water loop. In short, in a BWR plant, the reactor itself produces steam; in a PWR plant, the steam is produced in the steam generator. In either case, the steam is used to turn a turbogenerator to produce electricity, the output of the plant. While none of these processes involve either new or especially erudite technology, nuclear plants must be designed and operated with some care due to the fact that they contain large amounts of radioactive materials.

Most of the radioactivity in a nuclear power plant originates in the 3 fission process itself. In this reaction, a neutron strikes a nucleus (in either the BWR or the PWR, this is usually the nucleus of the uranium isotope uranium-235), the neutron is absorbed by the U-235 to form uranium-236, and then this nucleus, the U-236, splits into two parts with the release of a considerable amount of energy. The two pieces of the fissioning nucleus that remain after the fission is completed are called fission products. Unfortunately, the majority of these fission products are radioactive, and spontaneously decay with the emission of a variety of β-rays° and γ-rays.°

Most of this fission product radioactivity dies away rapidly, on the *4* order of seconds to hours. Several fission products have half-lives°—a measure of how rapidly they disappear—on the order of days. A couple—strontium-90 and cesium-137, in particular—have half-lives of about 30 years; these tend to be the most troublesome in the disposal of radioactive wastes. Finally, a few fission products, such as iodine-129, have half-lives that are so long that they are essentially stable.

There is one group of fission products that is of special concern from *5* the standpoint of reactor safety. These are the fission products that are gases under normal circumstances, namely, the isotopes of krypton, xenon, and iodine. These gases are the first fission products to be released in a reactor accident in which the fuel sustains damage. The krypton and xenon are noble° gases, and they do not combine with or remain in constituent parts of the body. As a consequence, their biological effect is relatively mild. The iodines, by contrast, are chemically active, and when ingested or inhaled, they tend to travel to the thyroid gland, where one isotope, I-131, continues to deliver a radiation dose for several weeks. By the same token, of course, the release of radioactive iodine from a nuclear power plant can be controlled readily by various chemical and physical means.

It is the major objective of nuclear plant design to keep the fission *6* products confined at all times—during the normal operation of the reactor and under accident conditions. They must be prevented from coming into contact with either plant personnel or the surrounding public. There are a few other sources of radioactivity in a nuclear plant: the so-called activation products, materials that have become radioactive by the action of the neutrons in the reactor; and the transuranic nuclides,° mostly isotopes of plutonium, which are produced by the absorption of neutrons by U-238 in the fuel. But by and large, it is the fission products whose release to the public is the major source of concern in nuclear plant design.

Multiple Barrier Design

To prevent the escape of these fission products, nuclear plants are de- *7* signed with a sequence of obstacles, or barriers, between the fission products and the public at large. There are seven such barriers associated with all BWR and PWR nuclear plants as they are designed in the United States.

Beta rays—high speed electrons or positrons.   Gamma rays—high energy electromagnetic radiation emitted by radioactive decay.   Half-life—the time required for half of a given radioactive material to decay.   Noble—chemically inert or inactive   Transuranic nuclides—nuclei of elements having an atomic weight greater than that of uranium. All are artificially created and are radioactive.

The first fission product barrier is the nuclear fuel itself. This is in the 8
form of uranium dioxide pellets—little cylinders about ½ inch in diameter and 1 inch in length. Uranium dioxide is a hard ceramic material
with a high melting point, about 2,900°C (5,200°F). Practically all of
the fission products remain trapped within the uranium dioxide near the
point where they are formed in fission. Only a very small fraction of
the fission product gases, usually less than one percent, diffuses out of
the fuel at normal operating temperatures.

These fuel pellets are placed in long, hollow tubes that are sealed at 9
both ends. Fission products formed near the surface of the fuel and the
fission product gases that diffuse out of the fuel are collected in these
fuel tubes and, in this way, are prevented from passing into the adjacent
water coolant. The fuel tubes, or fuel cladding, as it is also called, are
the second safety barrier in nuclear plant design.

The third barrier arises from the fact that all BWRs and PWRs use 10
closed cooling loops to remove the heat produced in the reactor core.
There was a time when reactors were cooled by simply passing air or
water through the reactor core and discharging it directly to the environment. With those reactors, any fission products that may have leaked
from the fuel into the coolant exited the reactor with the coolant. All
of today's power reactors use closed cooling systems, and whatever
radioactivity is picked up by the coolant from the fuel remains within
the system. In addition, the coolant water is cleansed and purified on a
continuing basis, and the radioactive residues are retained for decay and
disposal.

In all reactors being built or operated today in the United States, the 11
reactor core is located within a heavily built pressure vessel. The craft
of designing, fabricating, and caring for reactor vessels is a very special
branch of technology by itself. Needless to say, the reactor vessel, which
is constructed of stainless steel six to eight inches thick, represents
another important barrier inhibiting the release of fission products from
the reactor.

The last barrier at the plant itself is the containment structure that 12
houses the reactor and its cooling system. This is a heavily reinforced
concrete building, on the order of three or four feet thick, with an
interior steel liner. Any fission products—in particular, the fission product gases—that escape from the reactor vessel or the cooling system are
released into and confined within the containment building. In PWR
plants, the containment building contains an overhead spray system to
reduce the pressure of the steam in the building in case of a break in a
high pressure coolant pipe. The sprays also tend to wash out or remove
radioactive iodine from the containment atmosphere. Containment
buildings also house elaborate filter systems to reduce the fission product
concentration within the building.

These last two barriers, the closed cooling system and the containment 13
structure, are tremendously effective in holding fission products. At the
Three Mile Island accident, for example, a total of only between 13 and

17 curies (Ci) of radioactive iodine were released from the plant during the course of the accident. However, about 7.5 million Ci were retained within the cooling system, and 10.6 million Ci were held within the containment building.

If the Three Mile Island accident showed anything, it was the wisdom *14* of containment philosophy, which originated in the United States in the early 1950s. Until very recently, the Soviet Union did not place containment structures around their reactors. I understand they are beginning to do so now.

The sixth barrier to the exposure of the public to radioactivity is the *15* manner in which nuclear plants are sited. There is much to be said about reactor siting. The most important is that nuclear plants are restricted to areas with relatively low population densities. Whether they should be more remotely sited than they are now is the subject of debate at the present time. Clearly, if remote siting is required to regain public confidence in nuclear power, then remote siting will simply have to be adopted as national policy if we are to retain the nuclear option.

The seventh and last of the barriers separating nuclear power plant *16* radioactivity from the public is evacuation. If all else fails, the other barriers have been breached, and dangerous amounts of radioactivity may be released, then the threatened population simply has to be moved. Much has been made of the evident lack of planning for evacuation in the vicinity of Three Mile Island. The fact is, however, that the evacuation of large numbers of people is ordinarily not an especially difficult problem, and evacuations occur all the time. Last autumn, a town west of Toronto was evacuated of about 250,000 people because of the derailment of chemical tank cars; a few years ago, 25,000 people were evacuated near Cicero, Illinois, for the same reason; last December, 8,000 people were removed from the outskirts of Detroit because of fire in a gasoline storage facility; and only last week, 9,000 people were evacuated in Somerville, Massachusetts, because of a minor rail crash involving chemical tank cars. And all of these evacuations were accomplished without the benefit of elaborate, federally approved evacuation plans.

Reactor Accidents

The foregoing sequence of seven barriers is designed to prevent radio- *17* activity from coming in contact with the public, both while the plant is operating normally and in the case of accidents. In normal operation, nuclear plants emit only trivial amounts of radiation. Nuclear plants are extremely tight. Incidentally, the tightest kind of plant appears to be the sodium-cooled fast breeder reactor° that the Carter administration so strongly opposed.

Fast breeder reactor—reactors that rely on higher energy neutrons to maintain the nuclear fission reaction, and produce additional nuclear fuel as a by-product.

Now what about nuclear accidents? There are any number of things 18 that can happen at a nuclear plant that can lead to the release of radiation. Most of these releases are of no consequence, however. But significant releases can occur if a substantial portion of the uranium dioxide fuel reaches the melting point, in short, if there is what is popularly known as a meltdown, and the multiple barriers fail in one way or another. The most important thing to recognize about a meltdown is that it would not be the end of the world. The most probable consequence of a meltdown is essentially no release of any radiation whatsoever.

Melting of fuel can occur in a number of ways, the most likely being 19 some sort of loss-of-coolant accident, that is, a circumstance in which the reactor fuel is not properly cooled. It is necessary to cool the reactor core, i.e., the region containing the fuel, both when the reactor is in operation and for some time after it is shut down, owing to the continuing decay of the fission products. The amount of energy released by the fission products is not negligible. About 7% of the total energy released in the core of an operating reactor originates in fission product decay, after the reactor has been in operation for a month or so. Thus, in a nominal 1,000-MWe nuclear plant that operates at a thermal efficiency of about 33%, so that the reactor is actually operating at a power level of 3,000 MW, approximately 210 MW (7% of 3,000) come from fission product decay. Following the shutdown of a reactor, the fission product decay heat drops off rapidly at first and then more slowly. After one minute, it drops from 210 MW to 120 MW; after one hour, it is down to 30 MW. But at the end of a full day after shutdown, 15 MW are still being produced by the fission products. If this heat is not removed, the fuel, or a portion of it, will melt.

When a normally operating reactor is shut down, the residual fission 20 product heat is removed by special components of the reactor cooling system. However, if the reactor cooling system should fail while the reactor is operating, it is necessary to supply an alternative source of cooling. This is the function of the emergency core cooling system— the ECCS, for short—a required component in every nuclear power plant used in the United States today.

Actually, the problem that engineers must solve in designing an ECCS 21 is not especially world-shaking, and indeed, the ECCS is neither a particularly complicated nor a sophisticated system compared with other areas of modern technology. All that is required is to assure that cooling water can be pumped continually through the reactor core at all times— when the reactor pressure is high and when it is low; when there is a break in a large cooling pipe or in a small cooling pipe; when a valve in the cooling system sticks open, as it did at Three Mile Island, letting the coolant escape into the containment building; when electric power on the utility grid is not available to operate pumps and valves; and so on. Providing a continuing flow of coolant to the core under these circumstances is a straightforward mechanical engineering problem that can be solved, and has been solved, by the installation of a multiplicity of independently operated high pressure pumps, low pressure pumps, multiple sources of reserve cooling water, redundant emergency electrical power sources, and so forth. Although there have been only a couple of loss-of-coolant incidents to date, emergency core cooling systems appear to operate properly. Recent tests in the Loss of Fluid Test Facility at the Idaho National Engineering Laboratory, which was designed and built specifically to test emergency core cooling systems, indicate that the ECCS works as designed. Of course, if some one shuts off the ECCS, as they did at Three Mile Island, then regardless of how well the system is engineered, it is not going to work at all and some melting of the fuel may result.

Summary

U.S. nuclear power plants are designed with a sequence of barriers to *22* prevent the escape of fission products. These include the fuel itself, its cladding, a closed cooling system, and a massive containment structure. In addition, nuclear plants are sited away from major population centers so that the affected population can be evacuated if the need arises. While it is highly unlikely, a release of fission products could occur if the core were to melt due to an unintentional lack of cooling. To avoid such occurrences, all nuclear plants are equipped with emergency core cooling systems. The fundamental soundness of this design philosophy has been demonstrated by the, to date, untarnished record of minimal population exposure from all nuclear power plant operations.

Rhetorical Analysis Through Annotation

This discussion of containment is itself organized around the concept of containment; that is, keeping what is inside from getting to the outside. Occasionally, however, the order is reversed when forces from the outside threaten the stability of the inside.

In the introductory section, circle objects that are identified as a threat if they should get from the inside to the outside. In the margin, label when these objects are presented as residing inside the reactor and when they are considered outside. Discuss where the threat appears and how the text establishes these objects as threats.

In the section entitled "Multiple Barrier Design," number the barriers in the margin from one to seven and identify where the barrier is located on a continuum from inside to outside. At which point could the threat have been said to have truly gotten outside?

In the section on "Reactor Accidents" label the level of the barrier being breached in each part of the description. Use the numbers from the previous section. How far outside is the threat represented as reaching in this discussion?

Throughout the entire text, place an arrow in the margin where a threat to the internal stability or operations of the system is posed by a force from the outside. What forces are these that come from the outside? Are the threats from the inside or the outside represented as the greater threat? Which are represented as being more under control by the engineers?

Discuss how the piece uses the concept of inside and outside to show the merit of the existing safety systems, to encourage the populace to cooperate with the design, and to argue that the outsiders should properly stay on the outside and that the inside should be left to the control of competent professional insiders.

Discussion Questions

Interpreting the Text

1. According to this account, what is the main safety problem? What are the strategies to deal with this problem?

2. What are the various protective barriers? What is the intended effect of each?

3. What possibly could go wrong with each barrier? What would be the consequence of a failure of each of these barriers? How is the next barrier designed to deal with the failure of the previous one? Why are the barriers placed in the sequence described?

4. How does Lamarsh evaluate the effectiveness of the parts of the system and the system as a whole?

5. How does the summary at the end compare with the entire text? Which points are emphasized and which are ignored in the summary? Why does Lamarsh write the summary as he does?

Considering the Issues

6. Does this account convince you of the safety of nuclear power plants? Why?

7. Can you think of any other device that relies on the concept of a sequence of safety barriers, such as in hazardous biological research or automated bank teller machines? Explain.

8. Lamarsh describes difficulties with the necessary external social cooperation. Does the interference in the operations of the system that he describes remind you of any other cases of public involvement in expert-run projects, such as in education, the economy, or health? Are practitioners likely to see public involvement as cooperation or interference? How do you see this involvement?

Writing Suggestions

1. For an exam in a course in elementary design, describe in 200 words the problem of nuclear power plant safety and the current solution.

2. For a public hearing on placing a nuclear power plant in your vicinity, at which Lamarsh made this reassuring talk, prepare a public response as a citizen.

3. Imagine you work for an automobile manufacturer that wants to emphasize the safety features of the product. For an advertisement to be placed in national news magazines, describe the crash protection system of your car as a sequence of safety features.

4. For a course on science and society, write an essay in which you discuss the impact of public involvement in technological projects, and whether it impedes the work of the engineers or makes for an improved design. Discuss whether such public involvement should be encouraged, discouraged, or accepted as inevitable.

5. For a political science class, explain how the government security system provides a series of barriers to prevent top secret information from escaping. Discuss where and how the system may break down, and evaluate its general effectiveness.

6. For a sociology class, describe how social systems such as privacy, family, and friendship help one maintain a personal life and personal identity distinct from one's public roles. Discuss when, how, and with what consequences the distinction between public and private breaks down. Evaluate the effectiveness and value of the systems that maintain the distinction between public and private.

Technical Aspects and Chronology of the Three Mile Island Accident

Leonard Jaffe

On March 28, 1979, a series of small mechanical failures and operator errors led to an uncontrolled excursion (or power increase) of nuclear reactor number 2 at Three Mile Island power plant near Harrisburg, Pennsylvania. Parts of the nuclear core melted and radioactive gases escaped into the atmosphere, but the reactor was eventually brought under control and the containment structure held, keeping most radioactivity from escaping. No immediate deaths or serious injuries resulted, although the long-term health consequences of the release of radioactivity remain uncertain.

This event approximated the kind of accident that all the planning was supposed to prevent. Engineers and other nuclear experts from government, industry, and public interest organizations immediately began studying how it happened and what it implied about the safety of nuclear power. Interpretations ranged from a vote of confidence for the safety of the containment system to a total rejection of nuclear power as inherently too unsafe. The following analysis from a member of the government's study team takes a middle position, that the accident shows the weaknesses of current design and gives us the opportunity to make improvements. Leonard Jaffe finds weaknesses not only in the mechanical hardware, but in the procedures for operation and in the overall administrative structure.

In the spirit that engineering, like writing, is a revision process of learning from errors, Jaffe identifies exactly where the mechanical, operational, and administrative failures were, how these failures fit into the total picture of how events unfolded, and how the system might be revised to prevent similar problems. He further suggests that this error analysis procedure become a regular part of the administrative attitude.

Although this analysis tells the story of what happened at Three Mile Island, that story is subordinated to the design questions raised by the events and the answers to be found in the analysis of the events. Thus the questions and answers organize the narrative, causing events of the accident to be told and retold in various orders, levels of detail, and focus. Questions also lead the narrative to events that occurred far from that day in Pennsylvania.

Jaffe delivered this address to the same symposium in 1981 on the meaning of the Three Mile Island incident that John Lamarsh spoke to (see pages 472–477).

I INDEED FEEL VERY privileged to be able to address you today on the subject of the Three Mile Island accident. I felt it both an honor and a terrible obligation to be a part of the staff of the president's commission investigating the accident. It was an awesome responsibility. 1

The Three Mile Island (TMI) accident may be to the nuclear power industry what the Apollo fire° was to this country's manned space flight program. That fire, which killed three astronauts, made the space industry aware of the necessity to renew its commitment to provide the management, technical, and quality assurance talent that would pay great attention to the smallest of details and every bit of experience to insure the success of the Manned Lunar Landing Program and the safety of future astronauts. 2

It is important, at this point, for me to do what the president's commission did very early in its report.[1] It indicated very clearly what it did not do. It did not examine the entire industry. It did not deal with the very important questions of nuclear waste disposal, for example. It looked solely at the TMI-2 accident and factors that related to it. In this same spirit of setting the record straight, I want to tell you that I am not a nuclear engineer. I am an electrical engineer by training, and my 3

Apollo fire—On January 27, 1967, an Apollo spacecraft exploded during a simulated launch countdown, killing astronauts Virgil I. Grissom, Edward H. White, and Roger B. Chaffee.

professional career has been devoted to aeronautics and space. For the last 22 years, I have been involved in the development of the applications of space. I have directed the development of large, technically risky projects in which the public exhibited keen interest. I have had some considerable experience in the investigation of failures. Perhaps that is why I was asked to become involved.

With the help of a small, but excellent, group of real nuclear experts *4* from the Navy, the Department of Energy, the National Energy Laboratories, and the National Aeronautics and Space Administration and many consultants from industry and the universities, we looked at the events leading to the accident, the accident itself, and the response of individuals and organizations to the accident. This involved six months of a most intensive effort, and resulted in hundreds of thousands of pages of records and testimony that had to be digested. It is not possible nor would it be appropriate to cover that effort in detail. I will try to tell you broadly what did happen and then give you my impression of possible contributors to the events that led to TMI-2.

At 4:00 A.M. on March 28, 1979, TMI-2 was operating normally at *5* nearly 100% rated power. At this power level, approximately 2,700 megawatts of thermal energy are being generated by the reactor, which heats the primary coolant to 600°F at a pressure of about 2,200 psig. This coolant is pumped through steam generators where it gives up its energy to create steam in the secondary loop, which drives a conventional steam turbine to generate about 1,000 megawatts of electrical energy. TMI-2 first went critical° exactly one year to the day before the accident. It had been declared operational at the end of December 1978.

It all began just after 4:00 A.M. when the main feedwater pumps that *6* circulate water in the secondary loop tripped,° interrupting the removal of heat from the primary system. Upon sensing this loss of feedwater flow, auxiliary feedwater pumps were started, which should have reestablished a supply to the steam generators. However, a pair of block valves in the discharge lines of these emergency pumps, which were supposed to be open at all times during normal operations, were in fact closed, resulting in the steam generators essentially boiling dry.

The primary system temperature and pressure began to rise almost *7* instantly with the loss of heat removal, causing the pressure relief valve on the top of the pressurizer to open. In about 15 seconds, the pressure in the primary loop had dropped to the point where the relief valve should have closed, but it failed in an open condition, creating a leak in the system. The pressure continued to drop to the point where emergency high pressure injection pumps were automatically turned on to replace the lost liquid. The closed block valves were discovered and opened at about 8 minutes after the onset of the event. This would have

---

Critical—capable of sustaining a chain reaction at constant or increasing power level.
Tripped—shut down.

been soon enough to prevent damage to the plant, but the open relief valve was not discovered and blocked off for 2 hours and 20 minutes.

Because of the open relief valve and the increasing water temperature   **8** and the high pressure injection of emergency coolant, the water level in the pressurizer rose, causing the operators to believe that they had too much water in the primary system when in fact there was too little. The reduced pressure permitted steam pockets to form, contributing to the increase in pressurizer water level. As a result, the operators took several actions that made matters worse rather than better. In an effort to control the level of liquid in the pressurizer and to prevent the system from becoming solidly filled with water, they throttled° high pressure injection and let water out of the system via the "let-down line."° Shortly thereafter, they turned off the emergency high pressure injection system, which had functioned properly up to that point. This caused further increases in the amount of gas (steam) in the system to the point where the main circulation pumps began to cavitate,° and then they were turned off to prevent damage. It was at this point that the two phases of the coolant in the primary system separated and the upper portion of the core became uncovered. The temperatures there rose to the point where the core cladding material, Zircalloy, could react with the steam. This reaction produces zirconium oxide and hydrogen, a noncondensable gas, which accumulated at the high points in the system. This made it difficult to reestablish coolant circulation.

Before the cladding reacted with the steam, fuel rod internal pressure   **9** buildup had caused some of the cladding to rupture, releasing radioactive fission products to the coolant, which flowed out through the open relief valve into a drain tank, which in turn eventually overflowed onto the floor of the containment building. When the level of water in the sump area rose to a specified level, a sump pump automatically started and pumped some of the radioactive coolant into storage tanks in the auxiliary building; these tanks also overflowed onto the floor of that building.

At about 1:30 in the afternoon of March 28, there was an explosion,   **10** or ignition, of a pocket of hydrogen that had accumulated in the containment building, but this apparently resulted in little damage, if any.

Circulation was reestablished about 16 hours into the accident, but   **11** the damage to the core had taken place. Although some say the accident was essentially over at that time, consternation continued through the weekend to Monday, April 3, partly due to misunderstandings and misinformation. On Friday morning, March 30, an evacuation recommendation was made by the Nuclear Regulatory Commission (NRC)

Throttled—decreased.   **Let-down line**—pipe to let water flow out of a system and decrease the pressure.   **Cavitate**—forming gas or vapor-filled cavities within water by mechanical forces.

to the governor of Pennsylvania in response to a radioactive gaseous release from the plant. The entire weekend was one that frightened the community with discussions of the possibility of a hydrogen explosion within the primary system and of dire consequences.

Let me go back to the beginning and look at some of these events 12 with a view toward shedding light on some possible root causes of the accident.

The commission reported that the most probable initiator of the events 13 of that March 28 was the shutdown of the condensate polishing system. It was this that probably interrupted the flow of secondary feedwater. The condensate polisher is a device that is used to remove impurities from the condensed water before it's returned to the steam generator. It's an ion exchange device that catches the impurities in a bed of resin that must periodically be replaced. Such a maintenance procedure was in fact being executed at 4:00 that morning on one of eight parallel units of the system. This routine maintenance procedure called for the injection of high pressure air to break up the bed so that the resin could be transported out of the system with the fluid prior to replacement with fresh resin.

Although the failure had not been duplicated at the time of the com- 14 mission report, it was felt that the most probable cause for the shutdown was water getting into the instrument air lines that controlled the entire system. The controls were designed or modified so that the entire system might shut down instead of only a portion of it doing so.

Why did this happen? Problems with the condensate polisher had 15 occurred before at TMI-2, with at least one operator having noted that something should be done to avoid a serious problem. The system, as it existed (and it may have been modified from the original design), was apparently not forgiving of a shutdown. The other sister plant on the site, TMI-1, is not completely identical to TMI-2. TMI-1 routinely bypasses 50% of the flow around the condensate polisher, so there is no possibility of a complete loss of all feedwater. TMI-1 also incorporates an automatic bypass valve that would open upon shutdown of the polisher. TMI-2 had only a manually operable bypass valve, which was normally closed. Taking all this into account and recognizing that the maintenance procedures might result in shutdown, procedures could have been considered that would have required that the bypass valve be opened during these maintenance procedures. Was engineering consideration of the original design or of design modifications adequate? Where were the quality and assurance people who could have observed maintenance procedures and reviewed not only the adherence to procedures but the adequacy of the procedures themselves? Our impression was that the quality and assurance staffing was such that only a small percentage of procedures could be monitored. Secondly, the condensate polisher was not labeled a "safety related" system and, therefore, was not as high on the priority list of things to look at. This term "safety related" comes up time and time again.

The next system that failed to provide its function was "safety re- **16**
lated"—the auxiliary feedwater system. It came on automatically on loss
of feedwater flow as it should, but two blocking valves were closed
instead of open as prescribed and thus prevented circulation until discovered closed eight minutes later. Why were the valves closed? We
don't know! The operator's control panel indicators showed them to be
closed. One of the indicators was covered by a "tag" hanging from a
control above it. A routine surveillance procedure had been performed
on this system two days before the event. That surveillance checkoff
record certified that the valves had been left open at the conclusion of
the test. At least six operator shift changes had occurred between that
surveillance procedure and 4:00 A.M. on March 28. No one had observed
the valves in the wrong position. There is no routine checklist requiring
operators to check all valve alignments on shift changes.

The above raises several questions about (1) the adequacy of the **17**
surveillance procedures and quality assurance monitoring; (2) the adequacy of control room procedures and discipline; and (3) the adequacy
of control panel indicators, displays, and tagging practices.

The surveillance procedure called for certification of procedural com- **18**
pletion by individuals who did not actually witness the restoration of
correct valve lineup. Operational procedures in the control room are
not independently monitored by the quality assurance people. It is left
to the operating and engineering staffs to review their own performance.

Valves have been found misaligned at TMI before. The TMI-2 control **19**
room does not routinely employ computer aids to assist in determining
correct alignment of systems for the conditions prevailing or desired.
This should be a simple system to implement. Even the color coding
employed on the control panel is not conducive to easy realization of
out-of-normal conditions. In the space business, we try to adhere to
color-coding practices on control panels in which normal conditions or
correct operating status is indicated by green lights. In general, red lights
are few. They indicate trouble. A glance at the board quickly tells you
where the trouble spots are. What is correct or normal in a nuclear
power plant changes with the condition or function required at the time.
The same is true for the various phases of a space mission. This requires
computational aids to check status of systems and alignments for each
operational situation, and with adequate telemetry,° it can be done.

The next and perhaps the most important *equipment* failure in terms **20**
of its ultimate consequences was the failure of the electromatic pilot-
operated relief valve (PORV) to close after properly opening to relieve
pressure in the primary coolant system. Note that I said *equipment* failure. The control panel indicator showed the valve closed, but this indi-

---

Telemetry—transmission of data over a distance by means of wires, radio, or other
means.

cator really monitored the electrical input to the valve and not the mechanical valve position. For 2 hours and 20 minutes, this condition went undetected and uncorrected even though there were many other indicators of loss of coolant through that valve. The actions taken by the operators (and concurred in by engineering and supervisory people on the scene) during this period clearly indicated a lack of understanding of the system under the conditions of this size loss-of-coolant accident. This occurred in spite of the following:

1. Pilot-operated relief valves have experienced failures.
2. Almost precisely the same situation (including operator misinterpretation and inappropriate initial response) had occurred in other plants of the same basic design.
3. Numerous indications of loss of coolant from the primary system.
4. Previous warnings that pressurizer level was not a reliable indicator of coolant level in the core.
5. Previous warnings (in the Rasmussen report) that an accident of the TMI-2 type had a higher probability of occurrence than did the more severe design basis accidents.

Again the question is, Why? There are numerous contributors.

1. Inadequate monitoring and follow-up of equipment difficulties. We could find no comprehensive industry-wide record kept of equipment problems with a view toward using this information to eliminate recurring equipment problems.
2. Operating and maintenance procedures were inadequate or deficient in light of recurring problems and recognized and documented potential for operator misinterpretation of plant condition.
3. Inadequate consideration and follow-up of prior experiences and concerns.
4. Inadequate training of operators in system fundamentals.
5. Inadequate training of operators in the response of the specific system to problems.
6. Inadequate simulator experience. Prior to the accident, the Babcock & Wilcox simulator used to train TMI operators could not simulate boiling water in the system other than in the pressurizer.
7. Lack of analytic aids to operators in the control room to assess the problem or to monitor the required alignment of the system.
8. Poor location and indication of some useful measurements.
9. Inadequate range on some instrumentation to cope with the excursions experienced during the transient.

10. A plethora of alarms.
11. Inadequate engineering capability to back up operations.

There are others.

But let's continue the scenario, for even after the PORV was discov- 21
ered open and then closed at 2 hours and 20 minutes into the accident,
the operators did not recognize that they had lost coolant, and actions
taken turned out to be inconsistent with the fundamental requisites of
keeping the reactor fuel covered and insuring heat removal from the
system. The automatic emergency systems were designed to do this and
did what they were supposed to do. They were interfered with. They
were prevented from doing their job during the critical period of the
accident. This was the major cause of TMI-2 damage.

Other plants have had similar experiences. Davis-Besse had an almost 22
identical situation in which the effects of a stuck-open PORV were
misinterpreted by operators and emergency high pressure injection was
throttled in response to water level increases in the pressurizer. But
Davis-Besse was operating at a small fraction of rated power at the time,
and they discovered the open PORV in 12 minutes instead of 2 hours
and 20 minutes. This was reported in a licensee event report (LER).
Why wasn't that LER given more attention? Possibly because the event
was terminated without serious consequence, or because the LER did
not acknowledge an operational error, or because the attention that LERs
generally get can be questioned.

Emergency control of a nuclear power plant should be concerned with 23
basically two functions: keeping the core covered and getting rid of the
decay heat. An emergency control station should be considered in which
only those controls and indicators necessary to these functions are located. This control station could be overriding and be such that return
of the plant to "safe" conditions is its sole concern and its control should
override all other instruction. This control station could be provided
with appropriate assistance by computer analysis of plant status and
required action to return to safe conditions against which the safety
operator could check his judgment and the results of actions taken.

A control room should be designed to handle emergencies. It must 24
be designed so that the operator can handle the unexpected, not only
the norm. When events are occurring according to the book, it's relatively easy to know where to look for confirmation of actions taken. In
TMI-2 the unexpected occurred, and the operators did not interpret
properly. Ultimately, hundreds of alarms were on at the same time;
there were so many that some operators complained of the additional
confusion.

But before I go on with possible engineering fixes, let's look at some 25
more of the accident. There are human interfaces with an accident other
than those associated with controls and indicators on control panels.

At about 1:30 P.M., a hydrogen explosion occurred in the reactor *26*
building. A 28-psi pressure pulse was experienced in the containment
building. This was not generally recognized as a hydrogen explosion
for some time, even though it has long been recognized that hydrogen
can be generated and must be attended to in the event of high temperatures in the core.

Later, the accumulation of incompressible gases in parts of the primary *27*
system made it difficult to reestablish coolant circulation. Methods for
ridding the system of the hydrogen bubble that developed in the primary
system had to be devised during the accident.

Frantic considerations and evaluations took place on the ensuing week- *28*
end, on March 30 and 31 and April 1, regarding the potential effect of
a hydrogen-oxygen explosion in the primary system, when it should
have been known that oxygen could not accumulate due to a normal
overburden of hydrogen in the coolant.

Questions about what would happen if the core melted could not be *29*
answered. A distinction was not made between some melting of the
core and a complete "meltdown."

This information should have been available, i.e., in the files, in well- *30*
considered studies executed in a thorough and unrushed atmosphere.
Information generated on a crash basis is generally subject to question.
It usually is encumbered with sufficient uncertainty that one is driven
to assume the worst-case scenario in order to be safe. In my view, one
should give consideration to worst-case scenarios when contemplating
the design of a system. But when you are in an emergency—when you
have to take action to prevent catastrophe—you must understand the
situation as it most probably is. To base action and decisions solely on
worst cases and hastily generated studies may remove realistic solutions
from your list of options and can cause unnecessary problems, as did
the scare caused by the potential of an H_2-O_2 explosion in the primary
system over that critical weekend.

We apparently also were not prepared to deal with an emergency that *31*
lasted for any length of time. This was probably the first time that the
NRC had time to deploy forces, reorganize its response, and take part
in a firsthand way in the resolution of a nuclear plant transient. We were
unprepared. Communication channels were inadequate, changed, or
otherwise ignored. This resulted in a certain amount of confusion and—
at least in the case of the March 31 release of radioactivity from the
plant and the resulting advice to the governor that an evacuation was in
order—in a serious error.

Communications channels that did exist were not used to fully un- *32*
derstand the circumstances of the release. Again, *ad hoc* provisions and
arrangements can result in such confusion. Accidents and responses to
accidents should be planned and well rehearsed.

But here I am again, engineering fixes to a particular set of problems. *33*
I'm afraid this is what the NRC has been doing for years. They have

institued "fixes" or patches to take care of particular problems experienced, rather than making fundamental and institutional changes that will insure that the system will become self-correcting and will take appropriate action based on experience, thorough analysis, and rigorous follow-up with corrective measures.

Some of the fundamental concepts really work. Defense in-depth is 34 one. In spite of the problems and errors of TMI-2, no one was killed. The plant was returned to a safe, stable condition. There are, however, some design aspects that may compromise some of the defense in-depth measures. Defense perimeters may be breached, either for operational convenience or to provide a measure of protection against the large design basis accidents that have low probability of occurrence. The use of PORV may be a case in point. Any break of the primary coolant system boundary should be clearly recognized as something that should not generally occur and therefore, if it occurs, as representing an abnormal or failure situation. In TMI-2, the opening of the PORV on March 28 was not immediately viewed with alarm. It was an expected response to a transient.

Another possible breach of a defense boundary involves double fail- 35 ures. Primary coolant is circulated outside the containment building even though this water may be contaminated (as it was in TMI-2) when core damage occurs. Since the let-down/makeup system° is used to control the composition and quantity of coolant in the primary system even during accident conditions, consideration should be given to establishing the containment isolation boundary so that gaseous leakage from the let-down/makeup system would not result in direct releases to the atmosphere.

In trying to look for contributing factors in the accident at TMI-2, 36 we took a look at the utility-industrial supplier-regulatory agency relationships that have developed.

The utility selects a contractor to supply a plant for a price. He expects 37 the contractor to meet the licensing requirements of the NRC, and the supplier agrees to meet those on record at the time the contract is signed. If the NRC determines that changes are required, they are made at additional cost to the utility. Changes that appear worthwhile to the supplier but that are not required by the NRC probably do not get too much attention because they are deemed nonessential. Thus the NRC, in effect, is assuming the responsibility for saying what is adequately safe and what is not. Under these circumstances, the utility may feel secure with that assurance and perhaps even absolved from having to make these difficult technical and financial decisions. This in turn can

---

Let-down/makeup system—system to decrease or increase fluid pressure by letting fluid out or adding new fluid in.

minimize the requirement for the kind of technical staffing and expertise that the utility might need to have to make these decisions.

Secondly, the ordinary building period for a nuclear power plant is *38* 12 years. The entire microelectronic revolution took place in less time. If you don't commit to the very latest in technology at the outset, you will surely end up with outdated designs. Several studies were executed in the 1973–74 time period that pointed up some inadequacies of existing control room designs, but apparently these have not motivated extensive changes as yet. The mystique of standardization, which says that it is desirable to duplicate previous designs, may still be dominating the industry.

Dr. Harold Lewis, in his recent article "Safety of Fission Reactors," *39* said that the president's commission report was "notable for its lack of specific technical recommendations for the enhancement of reactor safety."[2] We could have recommended specific fixes so that the scenario of TMI-2 per se would not occur again. This is what the NRC tends to do—recommend specific fixes. But how does this prevent a yet unimagined sequence of events from becoming an accident?

If there is one thing that I have learned through the TMI-2 investi- *40* gation, it is this: Nuclear power plants are very large, very complex systems that cannot be completely accurately modeled. Dangerous transients cannot be incurred deliberately so that the actual plant response to all events can be experienced and tested. The total amount of experience with individual components is still relatively low. It is with this in mind that I feel that the industry must seize upon every transient, every excursion, every abnormality, every operator mistake, and every component failure and learn from it. The industry must pull itself up by its bootstraps. Current plant performance statistics must not be accepted as "good enough" because they may not be good enough for the future, and one accident is one too many.

In the space business, if we have a failure—let's say of a component, *41* a transistor perhaps—we try not to merely replace the faulty component, we try to investigate thoroughly the reason for the component failure. Was it a generic problem? a design problem? a materials problem? a quality control problem? or a one-of-a-kind problem? Why didn't the system tolerate this kind of failure? Can it be made to tolerate this kind of failure? Were our procedures adequate to cope with the situation produced by the failure? We try to pursue these questions vigorously and rigorously before we close out the story of a failure.

In a similar manner, the nuclear industry must be made to vigorously *42* and rigorously examine every implication of a transient or failure experienced by anyone in the business, and this is a specific technical recommendation of the president's commission. It recommended that the following questions be asked—and answered on the occasion of occurrences not previously experienced:

1. Did the system design codes accurately predict the transient?
2. Did the design accommodate it?
3. Was the operational control room capable and convenient to the handling of the problem?
4. Did the operational procedures properly accommodate it?
5. Do the training and the training simulator address this accurately and adequately?
6. Is the component that failed a continuing problem?
7. Are the quality control and quality assurance adequate?
8. Are the organizations appropriate and capable of coping with results?
9. Do we understand the input of the occurrence on the probability of future accidents?

This kind of rigorous investigation and attention should be given to 43 all failures in all systems regardless of whether they are currently defined as "safety related" or not. Many failures or problems could be initiated by non-safety-related systems. If the result can cause confusion and operator error, the definition of what is safety related or not is a moot point.

To do what I have suggested requires two things: (1) a regulatory 44 requirement to insure and demonstrate the adequacy of the abnormal event closeout effort in all of the above areas; and (2) an adequate running recording of all critical plant conditions to insure that transients can be accurately reproduced for evaluation purposes. In other words, an on-line telemetry (flight) recorder at all times. In TMI-2, we were very fortunate to have a recorder called a reactimeter recording many useful parameters. Without it, the postmortem analysis would have been much more difficult indeed, if not impossible. There are currently no regulatory requirements for a recorder and instrumentation adequate for this function.

Only if the kinds of records that I am suggesting are kept and rigor- 45 ously used to critically examine our prior understanding and ability to handle the situation can we be confident of preparedness. Only if we plan for failure and accidents will we be able to react properly to minimize the effects. Only if we continuously use the statistics of experience and the tools of failure mode analysis to determine where the weak points are and judiciously eliminate them will we be able to constantly reduce the risk of nuclear reactors. It can be done.

The WASH 1400 study reduced the probability of occurrence of a 46 problem at the Peach Bottom plant because it used that plant as a case to study.[3] A failure analysis was made—a fault tree/event tree° of the

---

Fault tree/event tree—a schematic diagram of alternative sequences of events.

specific plant was analyzed—that did reveal the weakness. Such analyses should be living exercises on each plant. Weak links should be well known and tolerated only if carefully considered in documentation for the record.

It is only if we introduce this kind of rigor into the system and provide   *47* a utility-industry-regulator relationship that places the responsibility clearly on the utility for the safe operation of the nuclear power plant— which he ordered built and which he operates and he maintains—that we can be reasonably assured of continued improvement in the safety of these facilities.

In this light, it is interesting to note that Dr. Lewis in his article seems   *48* to deplore the fact that the NRC does not assume a greater role for assuring safety akin to that of the National Transportation Safety Board in the aircraft industry. At the same time, he acknowledges that there exists "an Advisory Committee on Reactor Safeguards [on which Dr. Lewis is a member] that can perform this function, and it does so on an ad hoc basis. There is certainly enough information in the operational experience of other reactors to have alerted us to the possibility of an accident of the kind that happened at TMI, but for one reason or another we seem not to have been alerted."[2] Isn't it interesting that almost a year after TMI-2, the Advisory Committee on Reactor Safeguards has not determined why they weren't alerted? Perhaps if they examined that question, they could better recommend ways in which to assure the avoidance of another TMI-2.

The cost of TMI-2 will not be known for a number of years. Our   *49* lowest estimate was approximately $1 billion. This is in excess of $10 million per existing nuclear power plant in this country. This does not take into account costs paid for more expensive energy incurred because of the hiatus in the development of new nuclear facilities. I don't know whether nuclear power can be made acceptably safe in the ultimate picture. I do know that we can ill afford not to make the expenditures required to rigorously pursue every experience and every piece of relevant information to drive the probability of an accident continuously toward zero. Each utility should be able to show every year that this year's plant performance and problem record is better than last year's.

References

[1]KEMENY. J. G., *et al.* 1979. Report of the President's Commission on the Accident at Three Mile Island. U.S. Government Printing Office. Washington, D.C.

[2]LEWIS, H. 1980. Safety of fission reactors. Sci. Am. **242**(3): 53.

[3]NRC. 1975. Reactor Safety Study: An Assessment of Accident Risks in U.S. Commercial Nuclear Power Plants. Report No. WASH-1400 (NUREG-75/014). U.S. Nuclear Regulatory Commission. Washington, D.C. (The Rasmussen report.)

Rhetorical Analysis Through Annotation

The President's Commission was established to answer questions about the Three Mile Island incident. This presentation of the commission's findings is consequently organized around questions and answers. One question leads to another, to reveal the commission's analysis. Some questions are stated directly, while others are implied.

Underline each explicit question in the text. Identify where the question is answered. If the question is only implied through the answer, write the question in your own words in the margin next to the answer. Discuss what type of material Jaffe presents in answer to each question and why the answer is or is not appropriate to the question.

Where one question grows out of the answer to the previous one, circle the transitional phrase that indicates the connection. Discuss the sequence and connection of the questions and answers. Consider how the questions and answers move from narrow mechanical considerations to broader operational procedures and general issues of administrative oversight. Discuss the differences between questions that come from different sources.

Discussion Questions

Interpreting the Text

1. What background information does Jaffe provide on himself, the commission, and its report? What is the purpose of providing this background?

2. What was the sequence of events beginning with the shutdown of the condensate polishing system? In which part of the system did each event occur? How did the breakdown spread from one part of the system to another? At what time and in which part of the system was the overall event partly under control? What went wrong and what went right? Use diagrams in the previous selections to identify the location of each part of the event.

3. What difference is there between the waterflow systems of TMI-1 and TMI-2? Why is this difference significant?

4. Why does Jaffe call the failure of the PORV the most important equipment failure? Why did he stress that it was only the most important *equipment* failure? How did the PORV valve fail? Why did its failure go unnoticed? How did inadequate metering equipment combine with inadequate operator understanding of the system? What led to these inadequacies?

5. What improvements does Jaffe suggest in equipment and procedures? To what extent do suggestions depend on mechanizing procedures that require few operator judgments? To what extent would the suggestions make more information more easily available to the operator, improving the operator's ability to make judgments?

6. What are the underlying historical, institutional reasons why the design and procedures were not as good as they might have been? What does Jaffe see as

the "mystique of standardization" (p. 489)? And why is it a difficulty? In what ways does the author feel that technical fixes are not enough? What are the more fundamental procedures that must be addressed? What changes does he propose at this fundamental level?

Considering the Issues

7. Which failures seem attributable to hardware function, hardware design, procedural inadequacy, lack of information, operator error, or other causes? In what ways did mechanical and human error combine? To what extent could each of these failures be rectified at the mechanical level? At the human level? Should human error be eliminated through automation, which eliminates humans from the process? Or should changes in human procedure and oversight control human error?

8. What uncertainties remain after this investigation, both of cause and consequences? Why do these uncertainties remain? What are the implications of these limits of our knowledge?

9. In your experience, such as in school, in the family, or on the job, could local accidents sometimes have been prevented by some more fundamental change in attitudes or relationships? For example, could a football player's broken leg have been prevented by greater concern for playing field maintenance by the school board or by better inspection procedures? Are the person and equipment on the spot always responsible? Or is the attempt to shift the blame to some more distant cause really just evading the issue of real responsibility? In which cases should local responsibility be maintained and when should more distant causes be located?

10. What impression does the author give of the space program compared to the nuclear power program? In light of recent events (the *Challenger* shuttle disaster and after), how do you evaluate the author's image of procedures at NASA?

11. In what way does the author hold to the "engineering as revision" theory? How does he wish to institutionalize this? How do you feel about the idea of engineering as revision and learning from design errors? Is it forward looking and will it lead to progress? Are the costs too high to allow imperfect designs? Are imperfection and improvement unavoidable?

Writing Suggestions

1. Use the details presented here to write a newspaper story explaining what went wrong at TMI-2.

2. For a television special on nuclear power, write a short dramatization of what went on in the TMI-2 control room at the crucial moments.

3. For an analysis segment of a television special on nuclear power, write a short editorial on "Three Mile Island, a Single Event or a Symptom of Deeper Problems?"

4. For this or any other course on writing, write an essay comparing the revision process in engineering to the revision process in writing. Discuss essential differences and similarities and what can be learned from the comparisons.

5. Imagine you have been commissioned by a corporation, school, club, or other organization to look into the failure of some product or event that you are familiar with, such as a bicycle or automobile breakdown, a cake that did not rise, a committee that did not complete its work, or a course in which the students did not learn. Write a report on the failure, its causes, and your recommendations for avoiding a similar problem in the future.

Chernobyl: Errors and Design Flaws

Colin Norman

On April 26, 1986, an accident much greater than the one at Three Mile Island occurred at the Chernobyl atomic power station in the Ukraine, in the Soviet Union. The accident has resulted in over thirty deaths already, and can lead to many more deaths in the long term. In addition, radioactive fallout has contaminated much agriculture in the Soviet Union and Europe, with unknown consequences for long-term health. The area surrounding Chernobyl (including several towns) has been declared uninhabitable.

Again questions were immediately raised about why this happened and how it could have been prevented. After some initial secrecy (blamed on local government officials), Soviet scientists and engineers were unusually candid about what they knew about the reactor and the accident. In August 1986, they presented all their findings to an international conference. Their report is summarized in the following article from the September 5, 1986, issue of *Science*, which is read by a broad range of scientists. Two other selections on Chernobyl follow immediately after.

This first article, after presenting an overview of the accident and background on the Soviet report, offers a detailed chronological account, but the scene described expands as the incident and its consequences spread out, escaping the bounds of the reactor.

A BOTCHED EXPERIMENT AND a series of deliberate safety vio- *1* lations, and a reactor that was inherently difficult to operate and control combined to cause the world's worst nuclear accident. Those conclusions are contained in a voluminous official report on the explosion and fire that destroyed the unit IV reactor at the Chernobyl atomic power station in the Soviet Union on 26 April.

The report, prepared by a team of Soviet investigators and released *2*
at an international meeting in Vienna, Austria, on 25 August, has been
welcomed by many Western experts as an extremely candid and detailed
account of the accident and its aftermath. It indicates that an extraordinary sequence of human errors turned some weaknesses in the reactor
design into deadly flaws.

It also provides the first public details of radioactive contamination in *3*
the region surrounding the devastated plant. According to Soviet estimates, some 50 million curies° of radioactivity were spewed into the
environment, and up to half of the ejected fission products may have
been deposited within 30 kilometers of the plant. This is presenting the
Soviets with a mammoth cleanup problem and raises the specter of
lingering health effects as long-lived radionuclides°—especially radioactive cesium—continue to enter the food chain over the coming decades.

This article, based on a copy of the report obtained by *Science* before *4*
the Vienna meeting, describes the causes of the accident. A subsequent
article will examine the potential health implications of the disaster and
report the discussion at the Vienna meeting, which is being held under
the auspices of the International Atomic Energy Agency.

The report paints a horrifying picture of engineers running a risky *5*
experiment with many of the reactor's key safety systems turned off. It
also describes how, in an effort to stabilize the plant before the experiment, the operators set the stage for a runaway reaction that released a
burst of energy that tore open part of the plant and initiated a series of
explosions and fires.

At the heart of what happened at Chernobyl is a design feature of the *6*
reactor that results in an increase in the fission reaction over certain
ranges as the density of cooling water decreases. This feature, known
as a positive void coefficient, can result in a power surge if cooling
water is lost or excessive boiling takes place. In most reactor designs
used in the West, loss of coolant has the opposite effect of shutting off
the fission reaction and dampening the power output.

Under normal operating conditions, Soviet plants have safety systems *7*
that are supposed to guard against power bursts. But they can be difficult
to control, and the Chernobyl reactor was operating under far from
normal conditions when it exploded.

The events began at 1:00 am on 25 April, when operators began to *8*
reduce the power output of the reactor from its normal operating level
of 3200 megawatts (thermal) in preparation for a planned shutdown.
Engineers were intending to conduct an experiment while the reactor
was running at low power, before the shutdown was completed, to test
one of the plant's safety systems. "It could be called paradoxical," Valeri

---

Curie—a unit of radioactivity, which is the emission of nuclear particles by unstable
atoms as they change to more stable forms. One curie equals 37 billion disintegrations
per second. **Radionuclides**—unstable radioactive nuclei of atoms.

Legasov, a senior Soviet atomic energy official, said at a news conference on 21 August. "They were concerned precisely for the safety of the plant."

The experiment involved disconnecting the generators from the grid and determining how long one of them could continue to power some reactor systems from its own mechanical inertia. This residual energy may be required to run cooling pumps in an emergency. The report says similar tests had been conducted before at the plant. 9

By 1:05 pm on 25 April, the reactor output had dropped to 1600 MW and one generator was disconnected. The experiment was planned to take place on the second generator when the power went down to 700–1000 MW. At 2:00 pm, before starting the experiment, operators shut off the emergency cooling system. They did this to avoid any possibility of the system being activated during the tests, but the report notes that the action constituted a serious violation of safety regulations. 10

Over the next several hours, the operators had a tough time stabilizing the plant, and the planned test was repeatedly delayed. Part of the problem was that one automatic control system was disengaged, a move the report refers to as an "operator error." This caused the power to dip sharply, at one point falling below 30 MW. 11

Another problem appears to be a buildup of xenon in the reactor. A by-product of the decay of iodine-131, xenon acts as a poison, slowing down the nuclear chain reaction and causing the power output to drop. To compensate for this, operators withdrew many of the control rods. 12

This eventually succeeded in bringing the power up to about 200 MW by 1:00 am on 26 April, but it meant that the reactor was operating right at the margin, with very little reserve control that could be used to increase the power if necessary. Moreover, when the rods are completely withdrawn, a surge in the fission reaction would not be dampened, and it would take several seconds to drop the rods into the reactor to shut it down in an emergency. 13

When the power reached 200 MW, plant supervisors decided to proceed with the test. Two more pumps were connected to the reactor shortly after 1:00 am to provide enough pumps to support the experiment. However, because the reactor was running at lower power than originally planned, this resulted in too much cooling water flowing through the core, which in turn caused the steam pressure and the water level in the steam separators to drop. In order to prevent the reactor being shut down automatically when these parameters fell below a critical point, the operators blocked signals from pressure and water-level sensors, thereby disabling a key part of the emergency shutdown system. 14

The decrease in steam generation caused by the excess cooling water prompted the automatic control rods to be withdrawn completely. The report states that the operators appear to have withdrawn virtually all the manual rods as well in order to maintain the power level at 200 15

MW. This further reduced the operating margin and the capacity to respond quickly to an emergency. However, the reactor appeared to be stabilizing and at 1:23:04, the steam supply to the generator was shut off.

About a minute before the test began, the operator reduced the flow *16* of feedwater to the plant, presumably to help maintain the steam pressure. Then, because four of the eight pumps supplying cooling water to the reactor were powered by the generator that was now running down, the amount of cooling water flowing through the reactor declined further. The operators were then faced with the opposite of the original problem: too little, rather than too much, cooling water.

The result was catastrophic. Boiling increased and, because of the *17* positive void coefficient, the power started to climb sharply. At 1:23:40, the shift manager gave the command to hit the emergency button, which plunges the control rods into the reactor to shut off the nuclear reaction. However, because the rods were almost completely withdrawn, the response time was slow. Moreover, impacts were heard and some of the rods stopped before reaching the bottom. The operators then cut off the drive mechanism so that the rods fell by their own weight.

By this time, however, the situation was out of control. Intense steam *18* generation was taking place around the fuel elements, which in turn cut down the ability to remove heat. The power output continued to surge, and the fuel started to disintegrate and fall into the cooling water. The result was a sharp increase in pressure, which ruptured the cooling channels and prompted a thermal explosion that "destroyed the reactor and part of the structural components of the building."

The initial blast that blew the reactor apart may have been caused by *19* a steam explosion, a massive release of energy caused by sudden boiling of water, although this is not clear from the report itself. A second explosion may then have occurred as hydrogen and carbon monoxide, formed when superheated steam reacted with zirconium and with the reactor's graphite moderator, mixed with air in the reactor building. This would have occurred after the reactor compartment itself had been breached. The report notes that witnesses outside the plant heard two explosions, one after another, at 1:24 am.

The explosions sent showers of hot radioactive material around the *20* reactor site, resulting in more than 30 fires. The most worrisome of these broke out on the roof of a turbine room next to the unit III reactor, which was still operating. It took 90 minutes for fire trucks to arrive from the nearby towns of Pripyat and Chernobyl, but by 5:00 am most of the fires were extinguished and the unit III reactor was shut down. The other two reactors at the site were shut down in the early hours of the following morning.

The devastated unit IV reactor would continue to pose a severe chal- *21* lenge for many days, however. According to the report, an attempt was made immediately after the accident to flood the reactor with water

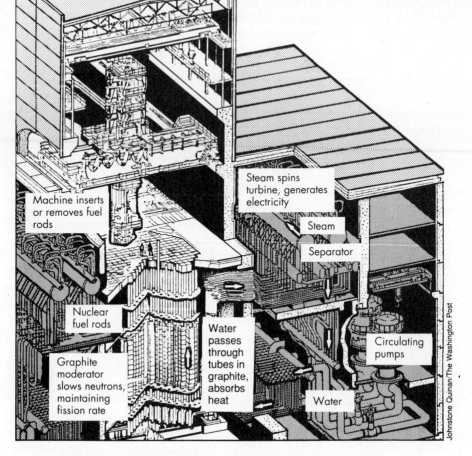

Machine inserts or removes fuel rods

Steam spins turbine, generates electricity

Steam

Separator

Nuclear fuel rods

Water passes through tubes in graphite, absorbs heat

Circulating pumps

Graphite moderator slows neutrons, maintaining fission rate

Water

Johnstone Quinan/The Washington Post

Figure 1.   The Reactor Design.   A massive graphite moderator, weighing some 1700 tons, is pierced by pressure tubes containing fuel rods and circulating cooling water. Refueling can be carried out while the reactor is operating and the plant is relatively cheap to produce and operate. However, it requires a complex control system and, as the accident demonstrated, under extraordinary circumstances, the power output can surge uncontrollably.
*Source: Johnstone Quinan/*The Washington Post. *Reprinted with permission.*

from emergency pumps in an effort to prevent the graphite moderator from catching fire. However, this proved unsuccessful, and it was not until 6 May that the graphite fire was brought under control and the temperature started to drop. This was achieved by dropping almost 5000 tons of boron, limestone, sand, clay, and lead into the reactor from military helicopters.

Between 26 April and 6 May, some 50 million curies of radioactivity *22*
were released into the environment in various fission products, according to calculations in the report. The largest single release occurred in
the initial explosion, which sent a plume of debris at least 1200 meters
into the air. This was followed by slowly decreasing discharges over the
next 5 days. However, by 2 May, radioactive emissions began to rise
sharply as decay heat in the remaining fuel drove up the temperature of
the core and fission products were carried aloft in the gases produced
by the burning graphite. Almost half the total release occurred between
2 and 5 May, according to the report, before dropping dramatically on
6 May.

Parts of the reactor complex itself became heavily contaminated not *23*
only from direct fallout from the accident but also from radionuclides
that were carried through the ventilation system, which "continued to
operate for some time after the accident," the report notes. Radiation
levels within the reactor complex were extremely high, resulting in
doses greater than 100 rads° to several plant personnel and firefighters.
According to the latest official figures, 31 people have died from burns
and radiation sickness.

Outside the plant site, radiation levels began to increase sharply several *24*
hours after the accident. The report notes that immediately after the
accident, winds carried radioactive debris past Pripyat, the nearest large
town, but as the winds dropped, fallout increased. By 7:00 am on 27
April, radiation levels in the area of the town closest to the plant increased to 180–600 millirems per hour, up to 50,000 times the background level, and they continued to increase until about 5:00 pm, when
they reached 720–1000 millirems per hour. At 2:00 pm evacuation of
the town's 45,000 people was begun. Within a few days, a total of
135,000 people living within a 30-kilometer radius of the plant were
evacuated.

The report is not sanguine about how soon people may be returned *25*
to their homes. It notes that radiation levels are likely to change as debris
is blown around, and states that repopulation will not be considered
until the entire 30-kilometer zone has been stabilized. This will require
entombing the reactor itself in a concrete case, decontaminating the
reactor site, and scraping up some heavily contaminated soils in the
region. This could take as many as 4 years.

The report estimates that the Pripyat evacuees received 1.5–5.0 rads *26*
of gamma radiation and 10–20 rads of beta radiation to the skin, and
perhaps a maximum of 30 rads to the thyroid gland resulting from
ingestion of iodine-131. These doses may increase natural cancer mor-
bidity among the evacuees by some 2%, the report estimates.

Rads—a unit of absorbed radiation or dose.

Outside the 30-kilometer zone, radiation exposure was of course much 27 lower, but because millions of people were affected, the anticipated number of excess cancers could be very large. As a rough estimate, the report calculates that exposure to relatively short-lived radionuclides from the Chernobyl accident will increase cancer mortality by about 0.05% in western Russia. That would translate to some 5000 additional deaths over 70 years.

The most serious long-term threat to health and the environment may 28 come from radioactive cesium, which has a half-life of 30 years. On the basis of "preliminary, purely speculative estimates," the report suggests that exposure to cesium-137 could increase the death rate from cancer in western Russia by a maximum of 0.4% over the next 70 years. That would result in almost 40,000 excess deaths.

These calculations are likely to be the subject of intense debate at the 29 Vienna meeting.

Rhetorical Analysis Through Annotation

The article describes the Soviet report as "painting a horrifying picture." The article repaints the horror by presenting a chronological narrative of a continuously decaying situation. We are shown the system falling apart step by step and then the consequences mounting up until we see the full horror of the disaster.

Mark a line at the end of each stage in the spreading disaster, and mark a double line where the topic shifts from the actual accident to its consequences. Note in the margin the degree of deterioration at each step. Also identify the specific agent that causes the situation to deteriorate to the next step.

Discuss how a picture of mounting horror is painted through the sequence of the event's stages and the aftermath.

Discussion Questions

Interpreting the Text

1. What topics are raised in the opening three paragraphs? How does this information help frame the story? Why is this information important to the following account?

2. How do the fifth and sixth paragraphs relate to the account that follows? Is the design feature called at "the heart of what happened at Chernobyl" directly to blame for the accident as described? What role does that design feature play in the following account?

3. Study the diagram of the Chernobyl design. How is it similar to the design of the American reactors (see Nero, pp. 461–470)? How is it different? Using the diagram, trace the series of events through the reactor.

4. What parts of the story of the Chernobyl accident are due to human error, bad procedures, bad design, equipment failure, inadequate understanding of the system, or any other cause?

5. Does this article offer any recommendations? Why or why not?

Considering the Issues

6. How is the sequence of events at Chernobyl comparable to that at TMI-2? How do the roles of human error, poor design, and equipment failure compare in the two events?

7. Why are damage estimates vague? What does this indicate about our knowledge of the effects of radioactivity?

8. How does this account of the Chernobyl disaster differ from what you remember of the original news accounts of the event? How much is the difference due to this account being written later—that is, after an investigation—and how much is due to this being an engineering-oriented report rather than a general news report? You may wish to look up newspaper accounts from the time of the original disaster at the end of April 1986 and of the later release of the Soviet report at the end of August. In the immediate news reports do you find any tendency to report rumors and stir up hysteria or, on the contrary, an attempt to downplay events?

[*Writing Suggestions appear at the end of the three Chernobyl selections.*]

Chernobyl Plant Features That Exacerbated Accident Consequences

Argonne National Laboratory

Because of design differences between the Chernobyl reactor and reactors in the United States and elsewhere in the world, questions arose as to whether a Chernobyl type accident could occur in American-designed reactors. After all, TMI managed to keep the incident contained, whereas Chernobyl exploded, spewing radioactivity over thousands of miles. Indeed, one interpretation is that the U.S. design is so much safer than the Soviet one that such extreme disasters are unlikely here. This interpretation, maintained by U.S. Department of Energy officials and the Nuclear Regulatory Commission, was expressed in a paper written for the August 1986 conference of technical experts, and revised afterward for publication in a Department of Energy report, again for technical experts. A key passage which summarizes the crucial differences between the U.S. and Chernobyl reactor designs is presented below. Notice the importance of the containment structure in the discussion.

ALTHOUGH THE SOVIETS PLACE heavy blame for the accident *1*
on the individuals who planned and carried out the turbine-generator
rundown test and on the reactor operators rather than on equipment
failures or design shortcomings, it is clear that features of the RBMK°
reactor design contributed to the severity of the accident.

1. The speed of insertion of the scram rods° appears too slow to provide *2*
adequate protection against emergency situations such as arose during
the accident. The Soviet approach is that large numbers of rods compensated for their slow rate of insertion. The insertion rate is stated to
be 0.4 meters per second, and since the total core height is 7 meters,
it takes about 18 seconds for complete scram rod insertion.

> The comparable scram time for U.S. PWR and BWRs ranges
> from 3 to 5 seconds.

2. There was no positive stop on the absorber rods to limit their with- *3*
drawal. The rods were so far out of the core that they did not immediately insert negative reactivity as depended upon when the reactor was
scrammed. To the contrary, the rod design and initial position caused a
"positive scram"; i.e., there was a major reactivity insertion upon scram,
rather than shutdown.

> The "positive scram" appears to be unique to the RBMK and to
> the particular state of the reactor; there is no positive scram in
> U.S. reactors.

3. Many parts of the reactor piping system pass through areas where *4*
there was no containment whatsoever. This includes the top sections of
the operating channels, steamwater lines, steam line piping, and parts
of the feedwater and returnline piping. It is indicated that fuel debris
was released directly to the atmosphere at Chernobyl-4 as a result of
pipe ruptures and blowdown° into uncontained regions.

> U.S. PWRs and BWRs all have substantial containments as one
> of a series of barriers to prevent accidental release of radioactive
> materials into the atmosphere.

4. The pressure relief line from the sealed reactor space was sized to *5*
handle blowdown from only one channel rupture. Hence, multiple ruptures into this sealed space did not have adequate relief to prevent over-

---

RBMK—designation of the design used at Chernobyl. About twenty-one reactors of
this design are operating in the Soviet Union. This design is not used outside the Soviet
Union. **Scram rods**—rods of neutron absorbing material, dropped or forced into the
core during emergencies to stop a reaction. **Blowdown**—emergency pressure release.

pressurization. Furthermore, the free volume of the reactor space was very small so that with inadequate pressure relief the volume would rapidly overpressurize and the region would become "unsealed" by structural failure.

> U.S. containments are designed with combinations of features involving large volume, high containment strength, and large-capacity pressure suppression systems to maintain containment integrity for accident conditions.

5. The zirconium-to-steel transition welds are thought to be weak points 6 in the RBMK piping system, although it is uncertain whether this played any role during the accident. The welds have a heatup rating limited to 15 degrees C/hour which may have been exceeded during the accident. Since rupture of the piping at the welds would cause blowdown into the sealed reactor space, they are a potential cause of failing the vault during the accident involving multiple ruptures.

> There are no comparable weld joints in U.S. BWRs or PWRs. Even if such joints existed, their failure would not pose a threat to vessel integrity which is a unique characteristic of the pressure tube reactor design.

Rhetorical Analysis Through Annotation

This excerpt is based on two types of contrast. The most obvious contrast is between the inadequate features of the RBMK design and the safer features of the U.S. designs. This contrast is accentuated by several obvious organizational, syntactic, and graphic devices. Less obvious is the contrast between human error and equipment shortcomings, established in the opening sentence.

Note in the margin all organizational, graphic, and syntactic features that highlight the contrast between the RBMK and U.S. designs. Discuss how these features help make the U.S. designs appear untainted by the difficulties of Chernobyl.

Now analyze the syntax and grammar of the opening sentence in greater detail. Place a line between the opening subordinate clauses and the main clause. Underline the subjects and circle the verbs of the various clauses. Discuss the types of contrasts that are being made between the first and second half of that sentence in terms of topic, actors, activity, and attribution of fault. Discuss the contrast between Soviet and American analysis of the causes being established. How is this contrast implicitly maintained through the remainder of the selection?

Putting the two types of contrast together, discuss the implicit critique being made of Soviet engineering and engineers. How does this selection criticize individuals while seeming to take an objective impersonal stance?

Discussion Questions

Interpreting the Text

1. What are the difficulties in the RBMK design scram rods? Why do these difficulties not affect U.S. design reactors?

2. What do points three, four, and five reveal about how well the Chernobyl reactor was contained? How did lack of containment affect the accident?

Considering the Issues

3. Compare this account with the previous account from *Science*. How important are the characteristics discussed here in the account given in *Science*? Did the other account attribute difficulties to other sources?

4. What is the relationship between human error and equipment failure implied in this passage? How does that compare with the picture drawn in the *Science* account of Chernobyl as well as the earlier account of the Three Mile Island incident?

5. According to this selection, what lessons for American nuclear reactor design are to be found in the Chernobyl incident? Do the authors feel we need to modify U.S. design in any way?

6. What interest may the Argonne National Laboratory and the Department of Energy have in maintaining faith in the U.S. designs? Is this selection successful in maintaining that faith?

[*Writing Suggestions appear at the end of the three Chernobyl selections.*]

The Lessons of Chernobyl

Eliot Marshall

Despite the official U.S. position that a Chernobyl-type accident could not happen here, other U.S. scientists and engineers seemed more troubled about the implications of Chernobyl, particularly concerning the power of a steam explosion that might breach U.S.-type containments. A second article from *Science*, September 26, 1986, presents the disagreement with enough explanation and technical detail for scientists who do not specialize in the field to understand the issues. The science journalist Eliot Marshall writes the story around the conflict between different scientists over what the lessons of Chernobyl really are. To follow the story you need to keep track of the players and their official positions.

THE NUCLEAR REGULATORY COMMISSION [NRC] seemed *1* confident at a recent meeting that the Chernobyl accident will add little to the agency's expertise on reactor safety. Staff scientists said they could see no immediate lessons for U.S. nuclear plants.

The blast that ripped Chernobyl apart was triggered by a runaway *2* fission reaction and powered by steam. The NRC seems to put most of the stress on the first half of the problem. It has focused on the differences between U.S. and Soviet methods of fission control, not on the common hazard of steam explosions.

On returning from the International Atomic Energy Agency confer- *3* ence in Vienna, NRC staffers told the five commissioners that they gained a solid understanding of how the accident came about. They had a less precise picture of the physical event itself. The Soviets were frank and open, they reported, although not able to answer all questions about the blast. However, NRC officials found the record clear enough to feel that there were few technical surprises.

Studying this accident, one expert said, is like returning to "ancient *4* history." It brings up problems in neutron physics that Americans elim- inated from their designs decades ago. Experiments on a series of test reactors at the Idaho nuclear engineering lab convinced U.S. researchers in the 1960's that they fully understood the hazards of runaway power accidents.

Harold Denton, head of reactor regulation at the NRC, told the *5* commission on 3 September that the staff needs time for the Soviet information to "seep in." With Chernobyl as a guide, the staff will "go back and look at things" in U.S. plants that once seemed troublesome and might need review. "But I don't see any areas in which we need to make any immediate changes in our regulatory basis," Denton said.

He was seconded by Themis Speis, the director of safety technology *6* for NRC and another member of the delegation that went to Vienna. "We didn't see anything telling us immediately to make radical changes," Speis said in an interview. "But we have a number of candidate issues that we are going to take a look at."

Speis gave four examples. One is the assumption that it is safer to *7* run reactors at low power than at high power. Chernobyl was running at less than one-tenth power when it ran amok. Another is the adequacy of U.S. measures to prevent a scenario known as "anticipated transient without scram" or the failure to insert control rods in a crisis. Cher- nobyl's rods had been deliberately disengaged. NRC officials want to review the chemistry of severe accidents, for Chernobyl released a far greater volume of lethal fission products than U.S. scenarios forecast, even for the worst accidents. Finally, the government may take a look at the quality of its evacuation plans. The Soviets had to scrap all of theirs because none anticipated the severity of the accident.

The prevailing view is that a Chernobyl-type accident could not *8* happen in the United States. It rests on several assumptions about the differences between Soviet and American reactors. One is widely accepted: that U.S. reactors are not vulnerable to the kind of power surge that triggered the Chernobyl disaster.

U.S. commercial reactors are designed to lose power when the core 9
loses water. It is conceivable that a U.S. reactor full of coolant could have a power surge if several control rods were ejected from the core instantaneously. But because the scenario is implausible, it has been little studied. In addition, it might be possible to increase power in a normally running reactor by pumping a large slug of supercooled water into the core. Again, it is hard to imagine how this could happen.

However, the design of the liquid metal fast breeder reactor—whose 10
construction was planned at Clinch River, Tennessee, and has been postponed indefinitely—does have a positive void coefficient.° This reactor could gain power with a loss of coolant, as Chernobyl did.

Military reactors fall into another category, one that for reasons of 11
national security has been less examined. They operate outside the NRC's jurisdiction and are said to have strange power dynamics and weaker containment buildings. The Department of Energy has commissioned an 18-month study of their safety by a panel at the National Academy of Sciences.

Other assumptions about the superiority of U.S. reactors are not so 12
widely accepted. For example, even before Chernobyl, critics of the NRC said the agency had understated the threat of explosions caused by molten fuel mixing with water or concrete. Critics also think the NRC has overstated the protection given by containment buildings.

The debate on molten fuel will intensify now, spurred on by Cher- 13
nobyl and by research coming out of the agency's "source terms" study. This is an industry-inspired effort to define more precisely the damage that could be done by the worst possible accident.

By happenstance, Chernobyl blew up just as the source terms project 14
was coming to an end. The industry believed this research would show that the old damage estimates were too large. It hoped NRC would use less cataclysmic terms to describe nuclear accidents—a hope that may have gone up in the smoke above Chernobyl.

The Chernobyl accident, several physicists say, must have included a 15
"prompt neutron" power burst. The Soviets apparently did not stress this fact but referred to the accident simply as a "steam explosion."

Reactor fuel emits two kinds of neutrons, the "prompt" ones that 16
appear in a millisecond, and the "delayed" ones that may take up to tens of seconds to appear. Reactors are designed to operate so that delayed neutrons sustain the chain reaction, for without the time lag they provide, it would be impossible to throttle the system up and down. No mechanism for controlling tons of fuel moves in fractions of a microsecond. For this reason, all reactors are designed to maximize the total

---

Positive void coefficient—results in an increase of the reactivity of a system, resulting from steam formed as the power level and temperature increase.

neutron flux without allowing prompt neutrons to dominate the reaction in the core. In contrast, an atomic bomb relies strictly on prompt neutrons.

The big weakness of a Chernobyl-type reactor (RBMK-1000) is that 17 when the system loses water, the power increases—so much so, it now appears, that prompt neutrons may take over. Last April, after disabling nearly all mechanical controls over the fission process, the operators at Chernobyl reduced the water flow. The inevitable followed: the water heated and allowed the power to increase. The reactor went into a rapid power surge, ending in an uncontrollable "prompt neutron burst." This blurs somewhat the distinction between a reactor accident and a bomb. But the distinction remains strong in terms of energy and speed, for the discharge from the fuel was far less energetic than a TNT blast.

Once the process was set in motion, neutron emissions in the core 18 grew exponentially for several seconds, rapidly overheating the fuel. Then the power dropped as heat slowed the chain reaction (due to the Doppler effect) and vapor pressure burst the core apart.

A Soviet mathematical reconstruction of the event shows the core 19 rising from below one-tenth power to 120 times normal in seconds (full power being 3200 megawatts thermal). It then dropped momentarily and finally surged up to 480 times full power. Speis thinks the second power surge may be the result of an error in Soviet calculations.

However, Richard Wilson, a Harvard physicist who chaired the 20 American Physical Society's source term study and who went to Vienna as an NRC consultant, does not rule out the possibility that the reactor surged to over a million megawatts. "Can you design a containment to go around such a system?" he asks himself. "I doubt that you can."

According to Speis, the fuel was subjected to an average heat of at 21 least 300 calories per gram, with some areas getting much hotter. It shattered and was ejected in particle form into the surrounding water, which immediately flashed to steam. The pressure shattered the 1000-ton concrete lid of the reactor and tossed hot graphite and bits of fuel through the roof of the building. In this sense, the Soviets are justified in calling the blast a steam explosion. But Speis and Wilson argue that what happened was very different from any steam explosion that is considered possible in a U.S. reactor.

The "vast difference," Speis says, is that the fuel at Chernobyl mixed 22 with the water in a fine particle form, whereas in the worst U.S. scenario, it would pour into the water as a large molten blob. Having a greater surface area, particles transfer energy more efficiently than blobs. U.S. research has concentrated entirely on blobs on the assumption that in a U.S. reactor, the overheated fuel would have to take that form. Speis notes that this research shows that it is very unlikely that a steam explosion could breach a containment structure. This is the settled NRC view, and, as a result, Speis says, "We were doing steam explosion research; we are now phasing it out."

Some disagree with this policy, one being the scientist whose budget 23 for steam research is being phased out. This is Marshall Berman of the Sandia National Laboratories. In an NRC-financed analysis in 1984, he declared that the data were too variable to support a clear answer. Some steam explosions convert less than 1% of the energy present to mechanical force. Other experiments show a more efficient pattern of conversion, enough to drive the pressure vessel head through the roof.

Berman concluded that the likelihood of a steam explosion breaking 24 a hole in a U.S. nuclear containment ranged between the impossible and the inevitable. The NRC was dissatisfied with this answer, and therefore commissioned a new panel of experts, the Steam Explosion Review Group [SERG].

The SERG experts were polled for their opinions of the likelihood of a 25 steam-driven catastrophe. Without doing new research, they concluded in 1985 that it was almost impossible. In writing the report, they added that it would be helpful to conduct some experiments to confirm this opinion.

Berman then wrote a memo describing SERG's data as "gambler's 26 estimates . . . essentially guesses" that "cannot be supported on technical grounds." He found the method of polling experts for their personal opinions to be nonscientific.

In a separate memo, NRC staff scientist Joram Hopenfeld rated the 27 expert opinions for credibility. He noted that "none of the 13 experts provided an estimate of containment failure which is technically defensible." The fuel core contains more than enough energy to blow the top off the reactor vessel and send it through the containment. So the problem, Hopenfeld explains, is that to argue this cannot happen, one must have some fairly credible physical evidence. Yet, Hopenfeld wrote, "There is no indication that the members fully utilized the available large-scale industry steam explosion experience." He found that very little confidence could be placed in the SERG estimates.

Nevertheless, the NRC forged ahead, citing SERG's opinions in a 28 source term document issued in July (NUREG 0956). It states that a catastrophic steam explosion inside the reactor vessel is "considered to have a low probability and its analysis is not included" in computer programs that are used to estimate the impact of a severe accident.

This issue may have to be reexamined now, along with others in- 29 volving the strength of containment buildings. One who intends to see the debate revived is Daniel Hirsch, a critic of NRC policy at the University of California at Santa Cruz.

Hirsch claims that "U.S. containments, like the pressure boundaries 30 for Chernobyl, are not required to be designed to withstand the challenges of core melt accidents." He ticks off some of the problems Chernobyl will bring forward: the risk of molten fuel reacting with concrete to produce an explosion, the possibility that melted fuel sprayed from a reactor vessel might overstress the containment, the particular weaknesses of the Mark I boiling water containment system (identified by the NRC as vulnerable), and the discrepancy between the large volume of iodine released from Chernobyl and the low amounts assumed to be released in U.S. accident models.

This is hardly an uplifting agenda from the nuclear industry's point *31* of view. But after Chernobyl, it may prove unavoidable.

Rhetorical Analysis Through Annotation

This drama of conflicting positions is told through the voices of various actors speaking from different vantage points.

Circle the name of each of the disputing parties and underline the individual's institutional affiliation. Note whether each represents government or the academy (the university and independent research community). Connect each name with his or her opinion. Discuss how individuals are set against each other in a drama of disagreement. How are groupings of individuals with similar opinions established? How do individual intellectual positions relate to institutional opinions? Note: Sandia National Laboratories are semi-independent, but government sponsored and financed.

Finally, circle any statements that represent the author's own judgments, evaluations, or opinions. Discuss the position the author takes in describing this disagreement and the lessons the author believes should be drawn from Chernobyl.

Discussion Questions

Interpreting the Text

1. How is a steam explosion different from a nuclear explosion? How is the steam explosion created here? Why is it such a danger to the containment?

2. What is the difference between "prompt" and "delayed" neutrons? Why is this distinction important to understand the Chernobyl incident?

3. Why, according to Speis, is it significant that the fuel at Chernobyl mixed with water in particle form?

4. How do the events at Chernobyl call into question U.S. assumptions? How do some analysts try to reassert U.S. assumptions?

Considering the Issues

5. What is the relationship between this account and the previous article by the Argonne National Laboratory? Does that position take any role in this article? How certain do you now believe the official view is?

6. What do you believe are the lessons of Chernobyl?

7. On what basis do the various scientists and engineers disagree? Do you feel they have good grounds for disagreement? On the basis of what you have read in this and previous selections, which position do you tend to favor and why?

Writing Suggestions

1. Based on all three accounts, write a newspaper article describing what happened at Chernobyl.

2. For a course in design, compare the TMI design with that at Chernobyl.

3. For a course in management, compare the lessons concerning the human errors that occurred at TMI and Chernobyl.

4. For a popular magazine, write up a personal account of the worst disaster you have witnessed or been a part of. This essay may be serious or comic. You may wish to follow the structure of the article by Colin Norman (pp. 494–500).

5. For your school newspaper write a consumer report comparing two different models of the same product, one of which is clearly inferior to the other. Follow the model of the Argonne Laboratory's report (pp. 502–503).

The Seven-Sided Coin

Office of Technology Assessment, U.S. Congress

Despite the great promise of nuclear power and the continuing need for energy sources, the nuclear power industry has been at a virtual standstill in the United States for over a decade. The following introduction to a report prepared in 1984 for Congress reviews the economic, political, social, and technical forces that aligned against nuclear power plant construction. The selection carefully avoids suggesting that nuclear power should be revived, but rather only identifies and analyzes the various constituencies that would have to be satisfied if nuclear power were ever to be revived as an energy option.

Although engineers may wish to reduce issues to technical ones of equipment and materials, they are designing objects for real social worlds. In earlier selections we have seen the effect of these real worlds through operator error, inadequate supervision, public opinion, and institutional pressures. At the most fundamental level, engineers cannot build their designs unless they convince people that these devices will benefit them and not impose an undue risk. Engineers must work with people, politics, economics, and social organizations just as they work with materials and equipment. Public commissions, human error, and economic choices are as much part of the environment of the construction as strong winds, gravity, and nuclear radiation.

As a report to Congress by a congressionally funded research organization, the Office of Technology Assessment, the document is a cautious, political one. It both analyzes political forces involved in nuclear power development and presents its own argument in a politically strategic manner.

––––––––––––––––––––

THE NUCLEAR POWER INDUSTRY is facing a period of extreme *1* uncertainty. No nuclear plant now operating or still under active construction has been ordered since 1974, and every year since then has seen a decrease in the total utility commitment to nuclear power. By the end of this decade, almost all the projects still under construction will have been completed or canceled. Prospects for new domestic orders during the next few years are dim.

Such a bleak set of conditions has led some observers to conclude that *2* the industry has no future aside from operating the existing plants. Some conclude further that such an end is entirely appropriate because they believe that nuclear reactors will not be needed due to the low growth in demand for electricity, and that the present problems are largely a result of the industry's own mistakes.

If nuclear power were irrelevant to future energy needs, it would not *3* be of great interest to policymakers. However, several other factors must be taken into account. While electric growth has been very low over the last decade (in fact, it was negative in 1982), there is no assurance that this trend will continue. Even growth that is quite modest by historical standards would mandate new plants—that have not been ordered yet—coming online in the 1990's. Replacement of aging plants will call for still more new generating capacity. The industrial capability already exists to meet new demand with nuclear reactors even if high electric growth resumes. In addition, reactors use an abundant resource. Oil is not a realistic option for new electric-generating plants because of already high costs and vulnerability to import disruptions which are likely to increase by the end of the century. Natural gas may also be too costly or unavailable for generating large quantities of electricity.

The use of coal can and will be expanded considerably. All the plau- *4* sible growth projections considered in this study could be met entirely by coal. Such a dependence, however, would leave the Nation's electric system vulnerable to price increases and disruptions of supply. Furthermore, coal carries significant liabilities. The continued combustion of fossil fuels, especially coal, has the potential to release enough carbon dioxide to cause serious climatic changes. We do not know enough about this problem yet to say when it could happen or how severe it might be, but the possibility exists that even in the early 21st century it may become essential to reduce sharply the use of fossil fuels, especially coal. Another potentially serious problem with coal is pollution in the form of acid rain, which already is causing considerable concern. Even with the strictest current control technology, a coal plant emits large quantities of the oxides of sulfur and nitrogen that are believed to be the primary source of the problem. There are great uncertainties in our understanding of this problem also, but the potential exists for large-scale coal combustion to become unacceptable or much more expensive due to tighter restrictions on emissions.

There are other possible alternatives to coal, of course. Improving the 5
performance of existing powerplants would make more electricity available without building new capacity. Cogeneration° and improved efficiency in the use of electricity also are equivalent to adding new supply. These approaches are likely to be the biggest contributors to meeting new electric service requirements over the next few decades. Various forms of solar and geothermal energy also appear promising. Uncertainties of economics and applicability of these technologies, however, are too great to demonstrate that they will obviate the need for nuclear power over the next several decades.

Therefore, there may be good national-policy reasons for wanting to 6
see the nuclear option preserved. However, the purpose of the preceding discussion is not to show that nuclear power necessarily is vital to this Nation's well-being. It is, rather, to suggest that there are conditions under which nuclear power would be the preferred choice, and that these conditions might not be recognized before the industry has lost its ability to supply reactors efficiently and expeditiously. If the nuclear option is foreclosed, it should at least happen with foresight, not by accident or neglect. This report analyzes the technical and institutional prospects for the future of nuclear power and addresses the question of what Congress could do to revitalize the nuclear option if that should prove necessary as a national policy objective.

Nuclear Disincentives

No efforts—whether by Government or the industry itself—to restore 7
the vitality of the industry will succeed without addressing the very real problems now facing the technology. To illustrate this, consider a utility whose projections show a need for new generating capacity by the mid-1990's. In comparing coal and nuclear plants, current estimates of the cost of power over the plant's lifetime give a small advantage—perhaps 10 percent—to nuclear. Fifteen years ago, that advantage would have been decisive. Now, however, the utility managers can see difficulties at some current nuclear projects which, if repeated at a new plant, would eliminate any projected cost advantage and seriously strain the utility:

• The cost projections may be inaccurate. Some plants are being finished at many times their originally estimated cost. Major portions of a plant may have to be rebuilt because of design inadequacy, sloppy workmanship, or regulatory changes. Construction leadtimes can approach 15

Cogeneration—consumers supplementing the electrical supply through small-scale generation, such as through wind or solar power.

years, leaving the utility dangerously exposed financially. The severe cash flow shortages of the Washington Public Power Supply System are an extreme example of this problem.

• Demand growth may continue to fall below projections. A utility may commit large sums of capital to a plant only to find part way through construction that it is not needed. If the plant has to be canceled, the utility and its shareholders must absorb all the losses even though it looked like a reasonable investment at the beginning. The long construction schedules and great capital demands of nuclear plants make them especially risky in the light of such uncertainty.

• The Nuclear Regulatory Commission (NRC) continues to tighten restrictions and mandate major changes in plant designs. Although the reasons for these changes often are valid, they lead to increases in costs and schedules that are unpredictable when the plant is ordered. In addition, the paperwork and time demands on utility management are much greater burdens than for other generating options.

• Once a plant is completed, the high capital costs often lead to rate increases to utility customers, at least until the plant has been partially amortized.° This can cause considerable difficulty with both the customers and the public utility commission (PUC). If rate increases are delayed to ease the shock, net payback to the utility is postponed further.

• Most of the money to pay for a plant has to be raised from the financial market, where nuclear reactors increasingly are viewed as risky investments. The huge demands for capital to pay construction costs (and the high interest costs on this capital) make unprecedented financial demands on utilities at a time when capital is costly.

• There are many opportunities for opponents of a plant to voice their concerns. Some plants have been the focus of suits over specific environmental or safety issues. In the licensing process, critics may raise a wide variety of issues to which the utility has to be prepared to respond. These responses call for a significant legal and technical effort as well as long delays, regardless of the ultimate disposition of the issue.

• Plant operation may not meet expectations. Some reactors have suffered chronic reliability problems, operating less than 50 percent of the time. Others have had to replace major components, such as steam generators, at a cost of tens of millions of dollars because of unexpectedly rapid deterioration. While there is no specific reason to think a new plant would not operate its full life expectancy without major repairs, no reactor is yet old enough to have demonstrated it. There also is the possibility of long-term shutdowns because of accidents such as Three Mile Island. Furthermore, a nuclear utility is vulnerable to shutdowns

---

Amortized—the debt being paid off.

and major modifications not only from accidents at its own facility, but also from accidents at any other reactor.

• Public support for nuclear power has been slipping, largely due to concerns about safety and costs. Public concerns can manifest themselves in political opposition. Several states have held referenda banning nuclear power or restricting future construction. None has passed that would mandate shutting down operating reactors, but some have come close. Furthermore, State and local governments have considerable control over the plant through rate regulation, permitting, transportation of waste, and approval of emergency plans. If the public does not want the plant, all these levers are likely to be used against it.

Given all these uncertainties and risks, few utilities would now con- 8 sider nuclear reactors to be a reasonable choice. Moreover, the pressures arising from virtually continuous interactions with contractors, NRC, the PUCs, financial institutions, and perhaps lawsuits by opponents, make nuclear power far more burdensome to a utility than any other choice. The future of nuclear power would appear to be bleak.

Yet there is more to nuclear power than the well-publicized problems 9 affecting some reactors. In fact, many have been constructed expeditiously, and are operating with acceptable reliability. Some have enjoyed spectacular success. For instance, the McGuire unit 2 of Duke Power in North Carolina was completed in 1982 at a cost of $900/kW, less than a third of the cost of the Shoreham plant in New York. The Vermont Yankee plant operated in 1982 at 93 percent availability, one of the best records in the world for any kind of generating plant. Calvert Cliffs supplies electricity to Baltimore Gas & Electric customers at 1.7¢/kWh. Finally, safety analyses are improving steadily, and none has indicated that nuclear plants pose a level of risk to the public as high as that accepted readily from other technologies. These well-managed plants have operated safely while providing substantial economic benefits for their customers.

Such examples, however, are insufficient to counterbalance the prob- 10 lems others have encountered. Nuclear power has become entangled in a complex web of such conflicting interests and emotions that matters are at an impasse. The utility viewpoint discussed above shows that there is little advantage and a great many disadvantages to the selection of a nuclear plant when new capacity is needed. Therefore, there will be few—if any—more orders for reactors in this century without significant changes in the way the industry and the Government handle nuclear power.

The Impasse

Consider now the perspective of those Federal energy policymakers who 11 believe the nuclear option should be maintained in the national interest.

It is unlikely that the U.S. Government will heavily subsidize the purchase of reactors by utilities or that it will build and operate reactors itself. Therefore, new orders will be stimulated only by alleviating those concerns and problems that now preclude such orders. Any policy initiative that is proposed, however, is likely to be controversial, because there are at least seven parties with distinct—and often conflicting—interests:

- utilities,
- nuclear safety regulators,
- critics of nuclear power,
- the public,
- the nuclear supply industry,
- investors and the financial community, and
- State public utility commissions.

To illustrate how these interests pull in different directions for different *12* reasons, consider just one issue. Changes in plant licensing and safety regulation often are cited as necessary elements of any strategy to revitalize the option, but there is little agreement on either the type or extent of reform that should be instituted.

• Before **utilities** will make a commitment to invest several billion dollars in a nuclear plant, they want assurances that extensive modifications will not be necessary and that the regulations will remain relatively stable. Utilities contend that such regulatory changes delay construction and add greatly to costs without a clear demonstration of a significant risk to public health and safety. To the utilities, such assurances do not appear to be impossible to grant. They point out that NRC has licensed 80 plants and should know what is necessary to ensure operating safety. Therefore, they would support revisions to the regulatory process that would make it more predictable and stable.

• However, there is another side to this coin. No plant design has been analyzed exhaustively for every possible serious accident sequence, and operating experience is still too limited for all the potential problems to have been identified. Accidents at Three Mile Island and at the Browns Ferry reactor involved sequences of events that were not understood clearly enough until they occurred. If they had been, both could have been prevented easily. As the **NRC** and the industry recognize different accident sequences, backfits° are needed to prevent future occurrences. Proposals to reduce NRC's ability to impose changes in accordance with its engineering judgment will be seen by safety regulators as hampering their mission of ensuring safety.

Backfit—to modify an existing piece of equipment to fit new standards or regulations.

• But there is a third side to this coin. Not only do the industry and NRC see regulatory reform very differently, but **critics** of nuclear power find much to fault with both the utilities and the NRC. In particular, they feel that the NRC does not even enforce its present rules fully when such enforcement would be too costly to the industry. Furthermore, they believe that the technology has so many uncertainties that much greater margins of safety are warranted. Thus, nuclear critics strenuously oppose any changes in the NRC regulations that might limit their access to the regulatory process or constrain the implementation of potential improvements in reactor safety.

• The **public** is yet a fourth side. Public opinion polls show a long-term trend against nuclear power. The public demands that nuclear reactors pose no significant risks, is frustrated by the confusing controversy surrounding them, and is growing increasingly skeptical about any benefits from nuclear power. These conditions do not give rise to a clear mandate for regulatory reform in order to facilitate more reactor orders. Such a mandate will depend largely on improved public confidence in the management ability of utilities and their contractors, in the safety of the technology, in the effectiveness of the regulatory process, and on a perception that nuclear energy offers real benefits.

• The **nuclear supply industry's** interests are not synonymous with the utilities' and thus represent a fifth side of the coin. The utilities need to meet demand with whatever option appears least expensive. If that option is not nuclear power, something else will suffice. The supply industry, however, has a large vested interest in promoting nuclear reactors, and the careers of thousands of industry employees may hinge on policy changes to revitalize the nuclear option, including regulatory reform.

• **Investors** may be ambivalent about licensing reform. Lengthy and uncertain licensing makes nuclear power a riskier investment during construction, but any accident during operation can have the same, if not greater, effect. Insofar as more stringent licensing makes accidents less likely, it reduces the financial risk. However, investors probably will be more concerned with the near-term risks involved in getting a plant online and would be more supportive of streamlined licensing if it reduced those risks.

• As representatives of consumers' economic interest, **public utility commissions** share the investors' ambivalence, but they might give more weight to operating safety because an accident that shuts down a reactor for a prolonged period usually will mean the substitution of more expensive sources of electricity.

Thus, there are at least seven different parties in each policy debate *13* on nuclear power: seven sides to the coin of each issue. No doubt others could be added, but those described above represent the major positions. Each party is a collection of somewhat differing interests, and each will look for different things in any policy initiative. Given such a multiplicity of interests, it is not surprising that the present impasse has developed.

Figure 1 illustrates these concepts. Utilities are at the center because *14* they make the ultimate decision about whether to order a nuclear plant or something else. The other parties have considerable, sometimes decisive, influence over whether a nuclear plant will be built, how much it will cost, and how well it will work. Each of these parties has its own agenda of conditions that must be met before it would support a decision by a utility to order a reactor. These conditions are listed with each

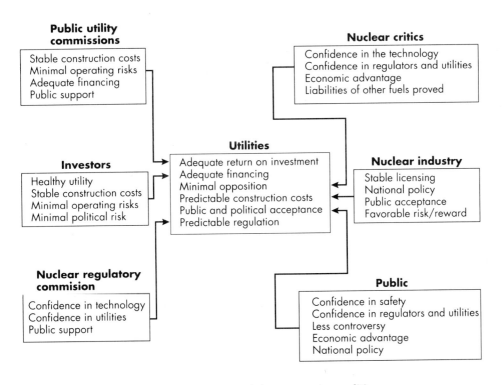

Figure 1.   The Seven Sides to the Nuclear Debate.

party. Those conditions that are common to all are listed at the bottom of the figure. For instance, nuclear power must be very safe, with a very low risk of core meltdowns or major releases of radioactivity. Disputes over this point relate to the degree of safety required, the adequacy of the methodology in determining safety, the assumptions of the analyses, and the actual degree of compliance with regulations. In any case, however, existing reactors must be demonstrably safe, and future reactors probably will be held to even higher standards.

A closely related issue is reliability. A smoothly operating reactor is **15** more productive for its owners, and it also is likely to be safer than one that frequently suffers mishaps, even if those mishaps have no immediate safety consequences. Thus, it also will be considerably more reassuring to the public.

Other common criteria are that there must be a clear need for new **16** generating capacity and a significant cost advantage for nuclear power. In addition, a credible waste disposal program is a prerequisite for any more orders.

Other conditions are especially important to some groups but less **17** important to others. Some of these conditions already are met to some degree. The arrows in Figure 1 drawn to the conditions under utilities indicate the major areas that are related to the other parties.

Many of the conditions in Figure 1 are **necessary** before enough of **18** the participants in the debate will be satisfied that nuclear power is a viable energy source for the future. It is much more difficult to know how many must be met to be **sufficient.** All the groups discussed above have considerable influence over the future of nuclear power. Efforts to revive the option—whether initiated legislatively, administratively, or by industry—are unlikely to be successful if some of the interests find them unacceptable. The task of breaking the impasse therefore is formidable.

Rhetorical Analysis Through Annotation

Serving on the committee that wrote this document were representatives of the many different interest groups. Moreover, it is part of a report to Congress, which itself is responsible to many diverse groups. Finally, any resulting congressional action requires wide social support. To achieve political agreement, this document must represent the views of all interested parties, balance these views, and find common ground on which most people can agree.

Whenever a series of alternative views or interests is presented, number each item in the margin. What graphic devices are used to highlight the balanced representation of the multiplicity of views and interests given?

Underline all statements that balance one view against another or otherwise provide a transition or connection between different positions.

Circle all statements that represent some form of common agreement.

Discuss how this document integrates all the various interests and positions into a single analysis. What conclusions, implications, or directions result from this integrating analysis? How does the integration serve the needs of Congress in considering political choices? Does this document seem to urge one direction over another, without appearing to be too overtly in favor of a position? How is this achieved? How does the persuasive strategy here indicate a political strategy necessary to make nuclear power again socially acceptable? What factors in the political climate surrounding nuclear power require the authors of this report to take such a politically subtle strategy? Does this strategy create an opportunity for opponents of nuclear power to press their claims?

Discussion Questions

Interpreting the Text

1. According to this report, why must we consider nuclear power? What are the needs for new electrical plants? What are the possible options? What are the advantages and deficits of each of the non-nuclear options?

2. What difficulties face nuclear power development?

3. Who are the various groups of people who have an interest and a way of expressing that interest in whether nuclear power is further developed? What are the interests of these various groups? How does the title of the selection summarize this situation of conflicting interests?

Considering the Issues

4. Given the analysis of electrical needs and options presented here, how important or inevitable do the authors believe the nuclear option is? Do you share their assessment of the various options?

5. Which group, if any, should have a more important say in whether and how nuclear power should be developed? Which, if any, of the groups do you feel represents your interests?

6. How do each of the constituencies affect the kind of problem engineers can or need to address and the solutions they might propose?

7. Under what conditions do you think nuclear power may become a serious alternative for development of new power facilities? Under what conditions may the various groups agree to the development of nuclear power?

8. Does the government have a right or responsibility to consider or support technological alternatives for the future? Do you recall any previous governmental involvement in energy development and energy policy? How might the government attempt to revive the nuclear power industry, if they were so minded? How would you feel if there was a move in Congress to support a revival of the nuclear industry?

9. Does the multi-interest structure of the nuclear power issue remind you of any other policy issues involving engineering design projects such as the Strategic Defense Initiative, also known as Star Wars? Is this case similar to other political

issues, such as what we should do about the greenhouse warming of the atmosphere (see Unit 5)?

Writing Suggestions

1. Write a letter to your member of Congress or to your senator expressing your opinion about this report and about the development of nuclear power.

2. For a magazine for engineers, write a short editorial on "Engineers Must Factor In the Social World." Use the case of nuclear power development as a major example.

3. For a political science class analyze the various constituencies that have a say in some policy issue that you are familiar with. The issue may be local (such as zoning for a new shopping mall), statewide (such as an education policy), or national (such as auto safety standards or trade protectionism).

4. For your college newspaper write an editorial against some policy or program in your college that you feel is failing. Explain the difficulties in or prices to pay for continuing the current policy, and assess whether these difficulties can be overcome or the policy changed.

Unit Writing Suggestions

1. For a college forum on the future of nuclear power, prepare a statement on the question, "Can we design and build nuclear power plants safe enough?"

2. For an examination in a course in contemporary American history, write a three-hundred-word answer to the essay question, "What has happened to the post-World War II promise of Atoms for Peace?" You may wish to do some research on the "Atoms for Peace" program in the late 1940s and early 1950s.

3. Imagine that a friend is a talented engineering student and is considering a career in nuclear engineering. She finds the work interesting and important, but she is unsure whether the field has much of a future. Write her a letter of advice based on your readings in this unit.

4. For a careers supplement to your college newspaper, write an essay on "Engineering Is More Than Blueprints and Hardware." Discuss the importance of social, political, economic, and institutional concerns in designing successful engineering projects.

5. As part of this course's discussion of how different disciplines communicate, write an essay describing the importance of the problem–solution model for argument and reasoning in engineering documents. Base your description on specific analyses of selections in this unit.

6. Imagine that a radical antitechnology protest group has taken over several campus buildings. They demand that the university stop granting engineering degrees because engineering is an antihuman subject and has caused only greater and greater threats to life on this planet. They are particularly incensed about the engineering school's continued interest in the development of nuclear power. You are the university president and must speak on television defending the contributions of the engineering school and in particular the degree program in nuclear engineering. Write that speech, giving a reasonable account of the difficulties of design and the admitted risks entailed in nuclear power.

7. "The Seven-Sided Coin" describes the complicated balancing of interests that must be accomplished if the nuclear energy program in the United States is to go forward in the wake of the Three Mile Island accident. In the Soviet Union, on the other hand, the decision of whether to continue constructing nuclear power plants in the wake of the Chernobyl accident depends primarily on a centralized bureaucracy. No new nuclear power plants are being built in the United States, while the Soviet Union continues a strong nuclear energy program. For a political science course write an essay discussing the advantages and disadvantages of the democratic system compared to the centralized one in making controversial technological decisions.

UNIT

7

INTERDISCIPLINARY STUDIES

Artificial Intelligence: Changing the Way We Think

Computers are simple electrical devices, yet they have changed our lives. Through increasingly efficient mechanisms and clever programming we have developed computers that can carry out complex activities. One continuing goal of computer science is to develop machines that can imitate the complex, decision-making process of human intelligence.

The attempt to duplicate intelligence artificially is a fascinating project. It forces us to analyze how we think and asks whether a computer can be taught to think the way a human thinks. As artificial intelligence comes closer to human intelligence, it is certain to have an immense impact on our lives. Computers are likely both to extend our ability to think and to take over many of the thinking tasks we now do by ourselves.

Artificial intelligence combines concerns of computer science with the concerns of psychology and philosophy, for any attempt to create intelligence artificially must be based on a formulation of what intelligence is and how it works. Conversely, any insights gained by computer science about intelligence may well have implications for psychology and philosophy.

Expert knowledge systems, one type of artificial intelligence programs, are interdisciplinary in a further way. They attempt to recreate the factual and procedural expertise of specialists, such as a petroleum industry geologist or a bacteriologist. Creators of expert systems must identify and codify the disciplinary knowledge of scientists, doctors, or lawyers to be able to build that expertise into a program.

Artificial intelligence is also interdisciplinary in the way it touches all areas of our lives. The social, psychological, economic, legal, political, intellectual, and other consequences of the incorporation of artificial intelligence into our daily activities need to be studied by the respective disciplines.

This unit begins with a look at the future impact of artificial intelligence and an explanation of some of the basic principles of automated reasoning. A specific example of an expert system follows. You will be introduced to a serious medical application and learn about its potential as a clinical tool. Next, a philosopher analyzes what is meant by the word "artificial" in the expression "artificial intelligence." He considers some elements of thinking that appear to lie outside the capability of computer-based intelligence. In the selection that follows, a philosophically inclined computer scientist considers the same question of the limits of current system design.

Other selections examine some of the consequences of artificial intelligence. A philosophical essay dramatically explores the "mind" resident in an expert system. A sociologist then looks at how people who use computers start using machine analogies to understand themselves.

Many different disciplines influence the selections that follow, and accordingly they are written in a variety of styles and forms. As you go through this unit, notice the different ways the different disciplines refer to the same subject. You may also consider whether the interdisciplinary character of the work leads the writing to transcend any particular discipline. Although each writer relies on a body of knowledge and specific ways of doing a particular set of things, he or she is writing for an audience and about problems beyond the original discipline. Thus, you may notice the influence of not just the disciplinary background, but of the interdisciplinary foreground as well.

Knowledge Technology: The Promise

Pamela McCorduck

For a number of years Pamela McCorduck, a free-lance writer, has been explaining the world of computer experts to the general public. In this article from 1984, she speculates on what artificial intelligence holds for our future. Her generalized assessments are based on professional familiarity with what artificial intelligence can and cannot accomplish.

Using history as a guide, McCorduck sets current cultural changes against large cultural patterns. She mentions both pros and cons of a more highly computerized world. Her bold views make us wonder about our own perceptions of the future.

1 THE NEW KNOWLEDGE TECHNOLOGY, especially its form known as artificial intelligence, is sometimes confusing, for as Henry Steele Commager° says of America, it had been invented before it was discovered. The invention of America, Commager notes, "embraced the Blessed Isles, the Fortunate Isles, Avalon, El Dorado and Atlantis; even the sensible Edmund Spenser thought that his countrymen might find Faery Land in the new world."

2 Just so: in science fiction, artificial intelligences in the form of malevolent robots (or benevolent ones, for that matter), in the form of self-aggrandizing computer networks, and anything else the human mind can imagine, have been presented to us in all-talking, full-color, and lurid detail.

3 The reality, then, is disappointing, and I sometimes wonder if the petulance exhibited by outsiders is less their outrage at the grand dreams than their disappointment that reality is, just now, so far from those dreams. William Bradford° first thought Cape Cod "a hideous and desolate wilderness, full of wild beasts and wild men" but later changed his mind. He, at least, lived there: the most vicious—and amusing— attacks on the New World came from Europeans who had not been there, but knew how awful it was and did their very best to expose it for the noxious and backward place it really was.[1]

4 You have just heard about the reality of knowledge technology. I am going to undertake to talk about the promise, but if your sense of that promise is what you have read in science fiction—in other words, the gadgets—then I must tell you that I am less interested in gadgets than in how they change our lives: our notions of our own possibilities. So

---

Henry Steele Commager—American historian. William Bradford (1590–1657)—Puritan governor of Massachusetts.

then, the questions arise: Are we embarking on a journey to the Atlantis, the El Dorado of the human mind? Or does something more mundane, even more sinister, wait at the end of our journey?

Frankly, nobody knows. Prophets must humbly remind themselves 5 that a nonhuman mechanism with the capacity to reason is a singularity in human history. Since it is a singularity, we can say nothing for certain. We know from looking backward that mechanical amplifications of human memory, in the form of the written word, made profound, unforeseeable changes in our fortunes. We assume that equally or even more profound and unforeseeable changes will come about as the consequence of our invention of a mechanical amplification of human reasoning power.

We can say nothing for certain but we can make some guesses. We 6 can guess that no matter how wonderful thinking machines will be, there are some things they will never be able to do. For example, they will not be able to guarantee the constancy of your lover; they will not instill filial piety into your children; they will not categorically eliminate wickedness from the planet, nor even give you blessed relief from the heartbreak of psoriasis, though they have a better chance of doing that than anything else I have mentioned. They will not give you deeper self-knowledge, I think, if you already resist self-knowledge. In other words, many aspects of human life will remain the same. But some things *are* going to change, in fact will never be the same again, and those are the promises I would like to explore.

There are themes that will recur throughout this discussion, and I 7 want to bring your attention to them right now. The first is the difference that a slight but crucial superiority in knowledge technology can make in resolving shades of gray to unequivocal black and white. The second theme is the order of magnitude effect, the fact that large changes in quantity bring about dramatic changes in quality. A third theme, which I mention because it is implicit in my talk, is the relatively swift rate of dissemination superior knowledge technology has historically enjoyed. Build a better intellectual mousetrap, and the human race beats down your door to get it.

You have heard about expert systems, which in their way are the 8 rudimentary equivalent of the written word. The fifth generation of computers, which Mr. Fuchi will talk about, is the equivalent of the printing press, in that it aims to bring the power of expert systems knowledge technology not only to experts in given fields who might want intelligent assistance, but that same expertise to anybody and everybody who might want it. Or, if I can change the metaphor a little bit, expert systems are the equivalent of custom-built horseless carriages, each one specially designed. Mr. Fuchi and his colleagues intend to bring this horseless carriage of the intellect into mass production.[2]

Let us look at some specific promises, then.   9

The Economic Promise

Knowledge is economic power. We sense that knowing more helps us *10*
gain more; we also sense that incomplete and vague information, misinformation, or late information is costly to us in the marketplace (and
all the more so in the clinic or on the battlefield). We want knowledge,
of course, not mere information; we want help with the information
glut, help that will automatically pare and shape all that information so
that we can, with our limited human brains, comprehend and make use
of it. One major promise of the new knowledge technology is that it
will give us knowledge we can use, when we need it and in the shape
we want it. The raw bulk will be refined, digested, and interpreted in
ways that we can put to effective use.

We have good evidence that knowledge has profound economic value. *11*
In the manufacture of automobiles, for example, the Japanese have
shown us that "working smarter" means a significant difference in productivity, something that Adam Smith° was the first to point out in his
Wealth of Nations. The Japanese have translated that "working smarter"
into products so attractive that if a genuinely free market were to operate, most of us would be driving Japanese cars, even as we now all
use Japanese consumer electronics.

The new knowledge technology will improve processes of every kind. *12*
I mean here manufacturing, management decision making, design,
catching fish from the sea, or growing wheat in the heartland. I can
illustrate this by telling you about a conversation Professor Feigenbaum°
here and I once had. He said: "You know, there's no such thing as a
machine as smart as a person." You can imagine my surprise. Were all
these machines that outperformed the human experts in the oil field or
the laboratory or the sickroom nothing more than frauds? I thought I
hadn't heard him right, so I made him repeat himself. He did. I still did
not get it, but I did begin to see something of the Zen master's smile
on his face.

Since I have been a combination of student and straight man of *13*
Feigenbaum's for a long time, I gave in and asked him to explain. "It's
easy," he said. "You start out with a task you want a machine to do.
You specify it precisely, drawing on human expertise. You use all the
expertise your team of experts has, but the machine still isn't as smart
as they are. But of course the moment you have the program and the
knowledge all laid out in detail in front of you, you can immediately
see how to make improvements. And suddenly the program has sur-
passed human performance. But there was no moment you could put

---

Adam Smith (1723–1790)—Scottish economist.   **Edward Feigenbaum**—computer expert.

your finger on when the machine was just *as* smart *as* the human. For a while it isn't as smart, and then suddenly it's smarter."

Thus even if no *new* knowledge is brought to bear on any process, **14** whether it is design or decision making, manufacturing or harvesting, the very fact of bringing to bear on that process a mechanism that embodies not only the expertise of the very best human experts at it (one expert or, for that matter, many geographically scattered experts) will change the quality of the process significantly for the better. Better processes allow better productivity, superior products, economic leverage. We have seen the first instance of this in the industrial revolution and we know what economic revolution was embedded in those machines. In knowledge machines, I believe the degree of the economic revolution will be orders of magnitude greater.

And then if knowledge technology begins to give us *new* knowledge, **15** knowledge that human beings would not have stumbled on because they do not have the time or energy to do the kinds of searches that might uncover that new knowledge, or because a clever combining of pieces of old knowledge is beyond the wit of our flesh-and-blood brains, the changes will be much more startling.

If we can sum up the economic promise of knowledge technology, it **16** is that it will resolve shades of gray—small advantages of various kinds, whether they are advantages of time, or capital, or slightly better design—into black and white, and that transformation turns only a slight competitive advantage into an overwhelming superiority.

The Intellectual Promise

Psychologists tells us that our evolutionary legacy is this: the human **17** brain can deal with about four concepts simultaneously, and no more. One part of human history—surely the most humane and honorable part—has been the systematic compensation for that rather pitiful legacy by providing ourselves with a collection of arrangements and tools that amplify our intellects. Written language is one such amplification; and printing, which created a revolution over several centuries by doing no more than mechanizing written language and improving its distribution by orders of magnitude, is another.

But there is a big difference between these instances of knowledge **18** technology, and the instance of knowledge technology the new fifth generation represents. Writing and printing are merely amplifications of, or substitutions for, the human memory. The computer, and particularly its form in new, intelligent machines, amplifies or substitutes for human reasoning power. This piece of technology has been with us for less than 40 years, and we are barely on the threshold of knowing what such technology will do for us. However, we have some indications.

As revolutionary as written language and, later, book publishing were *19* (and I hold that it was the urge toward universal literacy that is directly responsible for the social revolutions of the eighteenth century) these technologies had their drawbacks. For one important thing, books do not lend themselves very well to expressing experiential knowledge. (This is shown in our slightly pejorative term, "book knowledge." No matter how much they have read, we demand of our apprentices that they work in the shop or the clinic or the courtroom before we certify them, because we understand that experience is different from book knowledge, and we understand also that certain kinds of knowledge are transferred more effectively by example than by the abstractions of books.) This is what I meant by arrangements, that we trust the heads of experts to hold knowledge that books cannot. Technology that can indeed hold and even disseminate that experiential knowledge, the non-book knowledge, is here in a rudimentary form called "expert systems," which you have just heard about. The fifth generation of computers proposes to transform that rudimentary technology into a universal device, one that anybody can use. This means, very simply, that expertise, which is now badly distributed, will be more evenly distributed. In principle, and we hope in practice, the quality of diagnosis and therapy available to a sick person in a prosperous industrial country will be equally available to the peasants of Henan province, the poorest province of China.

Another drawback of the written word is (to repeat) that it is merely *20* memory, not processing. In the computer, however, we have in our hands an instrument that will amplify and substitute for human memory, and more important, human reasoning power. In other words, for the first time in human history, the production of knowledge is taking place outside the human head. There will be—in a modest way, there already is—automatic creation of knowledge. When a machine can use up all the knowledge we have given it and use it systematically in ways that we cannot, and can make inferences more deeply than we can (since it is not limited, as we are, by our evolutionary legacy of about four items we can attend to simultaneously), then what will happen? We do not know. We may forget how to do things. Though it was drilled mercilessly into us in secondary schools, very few adults today remember how to take square roots. Hand-held calculators do the job beautifully; why burden ourselves and our minds?

More interestingly, we shall perhaps begin to use our new powers to *21* think confidently about matters that have up to now eluded us. Problems that are simply too complex for one bright person, or even a group of bright people to cope with will become tractable because the new knowledge technology will be able to help us think faster and deeper than human brains alone (or even with their memory aids) can. For example, one area that has failed to yield very satisfactorily to our present-day knowledge technologies is human behavior: we simply cannot predict how individuals alone or in the aggregate will behave under changing circumstances. My guess is that the new knowledge technologies will be a tool for that kind of understanding.

But aside from certainty about things we already believe we want to know about, what of the human store of knowledge itself? Will it be different? We do not know. *22*

We do not know whether, even given the same heuristics, or rules of thumb, that humans use, a system that can think faster and deeper will necessarily think down the same avenues that humans do. If it should go elsewhere, we do not know what lies at the end of such different avenues. *23*

We do not know whether new knowledge can be discovered by a machine (though we suspect it can and have early intimations of it). If so, we do not know what the implications of such new knowledge might be. *24*

We do not know how to imbue humans with the critical intelligence to evaluate the knowledge they are exposed to. The problem is already a difficult one for readers of the written word. We do not know whether the ability to interrogate a reasoning machine, to make it explain itself, will help with this problem or exacerbate it. *25*

But let us make some guesses. We humans are mythmakers. Throughout human history, every important phenomenon has collected its share of myths, particularly when there was no other way to explain matters. Thus most of our earliest myths are agricultural (including the reproduction of human beings): our ancestors stood in wonder before the mystery of germination, growth, sustenance, and death, and made up stories, often with human actors but sometimes with animals and other fantastic creatures, to explain these mysteries. (The same kinds of myths explain natural phenomena, national histories, and even the technology of the written word.) What generates all these myths is the lack of rational understanding of the phenomena the myths intend to explain. *26*

At the moment, artificial intelligence is in a premythic phase. I alluded earlier to the tales of science fiction—and they go back to Homer, believe it or not—that anticipated artificial intelligence and told us how it was going to be.[3] Those tales were not exactly right, and I suggested earlier that they stand in relation to the reality of artificial intelligence as myths about El Dorado and Atlantis once stood in relation to the reality of the New World. It turned out the New World was far more complicated, and much better than people could have imagined, in its abundance and variety and opportunities for human achievement, but it did not look that way at first, so the folks who had expected to find the El Dorado of their dreams went away mad (or did not go there at all). *27*

Artificial intelligence at the moment contains no mysteries. You can sit down with the code of a program and figure out line by line what is going on, not unlike the score of a piece of music. Moreover, artificial- *28* intelligence researchers are at great pains to make sure that expert systems, while they are in the process of doing a task, must be able to explain their lines of reasoning to users, so that the user can evaluate the correctness of the program's decisions. I think this is highly important.

But what happens when expert systems, or other forms of artificial *29* intelligence, are so far beyond our human capabilities that they really cannot explain in any fashion we humans can comprehend? One young artificial-intelligence researcher suggests that humans will become "hobbyists" of thinking—that is, some of us will do it, but only as gifted amateurs. Many people worry right now that we humans are beginning to lose some essential skills by using calculators and word processors; no need to learn to add or subtract, or spell. True enough, but no great loss to the human race, I believe; but that is another story.

Myself, I would not be surprised to see the return of mystery, magic, *30* and the transcendental to a central place in human life. I suspect that we will eventually stand before our inteligent machines the way our ancestors stood before the cereal crop: in awe, in pleasure, in reverence, and in a certain amount of fear. And then, if we have not begun it already, we shall begin the great cycle of myths of intelligence, and our creativity will flourish apace.

Those of you who are confirmed rationalists may find this return to *31* the irrational to be a giant step backward for the human race. Those of you who are poets may be thinking, at last, and the sooner the better. I hold both views simultaneously and do not quite know how I feel about it. On the other hand, yesterday Bob Lucky suggested that our intelligent machines would push us, willy-nilly, up the evolutionary ladder, and so what has the potential for mystery at the moment may not be the least mysterious to our children. Their patterns of thinking may have changed in ways we simply cannot anticipate, just as writing, and then printing, made humans think in ways that could not have been anticipated but were nevertheless very different from prewriting and prepublishing patterns of thinking.

The Social Promise

Implicitly, we have been talking all this time about the social promise *32* of knowledge technology, and now we can make it explicit. It is the democratization of knowledge. In the same way that the written word once democratized knowledge (but surely different by orders of magnitude), knowledge is to be made accessible to everyone. There is the sure change in the professions, though not, I think, their dissolution. We ourselves are human beings, and we usually enjoy dealing with other human beings, so it seems unlikely to me that the relationship between professional and nonprofessional will disappear completely.

Since the professions are largely repositories of specialized knowledge, *33* is it possible that with the widespread distribution of knowledge, the professions will somehow become less exclusive? It is not only possible, it seems inevitable. Specialties that were once locked in individual human heads will be accessible to anybody—though not everybody will want such access. The distinction between specialist and layman will become more blurred than it has been, though I doubt it will disappear altogether.

For example, in medicine there has been a change over the last century *34* away from the healing arts and toward science—universal, explicitly science-based techniques. That change has brought immense power to physicians to cure, and it has also brought power to those outside the profession to measure performance. It has equalized the balance between professional and client in a way that has not been seen for many decades. When a performance is found wanting, the patient can complain, or even sue. Thus the malpractice suit is a manifestation of the lay community's new access to knowledge.[4]

When a further diffusion of knowledge takes place—when the knowl- *35* edge and techniques of the world's finest specialists are easily and clearly accessible not only to other practitioners in the field but to anyone— that transfer will have comparable ramifications. Medicine is the first profession touching ordinary people directly that has undergone a transformation of its certitudes; other professions that touch people directly are likely to undergo similar transformations, and raise similar expectations and standards of performance, such as engineering, design, the management of politics, and so forth.

Surely the dynamics of that relationship between professional and *36* client will change. For one thing, professionals will know more than they know now: they will, of course, enjoy the intellectual leverage that anyone has with access to much more knowledge in much easier ways. But since that knowledge *is* more accessible, they will, as the physicians have discovered, be held accountable in more precise ways. The exclusionary ways of the professions could disappear with the democratization of knowledge the way the divine right of kings disappeared with universal literacy.

We can expect changes in education. The process of education will *37* change because, first, we shall know more about human cognition and, second, we shall be thinking in different ways about different things and, third, the very tools we hold in our hands will be different.

Thus there is promise—as yet largely unfulfilled, I think—that the *38* design of artificial intelligences can illuminate and make explicit some principles of human cognition that have only been implicit, their exercise and cultivation no more than a matter of chance until now.

As for the tools themselves being different, video games, to take one *39* example, which are in their embryonic stage right now, will in their maturity play the central role that books have played in education. These matured forms will bear the same resemblance to what is currently found in arcades as books bear to hieroglyphics on the face of a cliff. What chiseler in stone could have anticipated where runes would end up? Who then could have predicted the great advantages of books and other printed matter: portability, cheapness, ease of distribution; or the profound changes literacy made not only in human thinking patterns, but in what we felt confident now to put our minds to, and all the enormous social changes that examination of the status quo brought about.

We are today as the makers of hieroglyphics. We can observe one *40* form of knowledge technology in video games and guess that portability, cheapness, and ease of distribution are givens. Interaction—the active engagement of human with machine—is very different from the participation print requires, and we guess that difference will be central. But the shape of that importance and its implications are impossible to predict.

We can expect changes in government. If knowledge is power, and *41* most of us would agree it is, and if we are talking about the democratization of knowledge, then we are also talking about the further democratization of power, continuing a trend that began in Europe in explicit ways in the eighteenth century. It was then that we came to have confidence that we could govern ourselves. However, as our polity grew, we could not all gather physically under one roof, and so we devised something called representative government to compensate for the impossibility of hearing from everybody. Knowledge technology will allow us the possibility of at last hearing from everybody, or at least everybody who is interested in any issue of government. It is possible to foresee a collapse of many of the contraptions of government as citizens take over more direct management of their governance.

The Threat of Knowledge Technology

Knowledge is power. That is embedded in our earliest texts, whether *42* scripture or instructions on how to fight a battle. With more knowledge comes not only more power, but also more responsibility, both individual and collective, and that we shall have to shoulder without excessive or unseemly grumbling. It will not be easy, but it will surely be exhilarating.

For humans who do not value knowledge, we do not know what a *43* world deeply steeped in knowledge will seem like. There have been suggestions that the enormously rich recreational possibilities of computers—barely touched so far—will either sedate or stimulate that disenfranchised group that now scorns knowledge. Knowledge as narcotic is not especially attractive to me, but the other possibility, the computer as a stimulant, is a hopeful one. Since the specific machines you will hear about from Mr. Fuchi, the Japanese fifth generation, are planned to be as easy to use as a telephone or television, it might be heartening to remember that in the United States, the number of television sets grew from 6,000 to 15.5 million in a matter of five years. We might wish the fifth generation such success.

Among our responsibilities—to name but a few—will be the protec- **44** tion of individual privacy (or even its redefinition), the responsibility for educating all young human beings to take their place in a knowledge-saturated world, the equitable assignment of credit for intellectual property (and perhaps its redefinition), which at the moment is there for the picking.

These are perhaps threats. But I personally am optimistic. I want to **45** tell you why. I spoke a little earlier about the concept of knowledge technology resolving shades of gray into black and white; transforming a small advantage into a decisive one. Here is an example of such a transformation.

Many peoples were milling around the Mediterranean basin and the **46** fertile crescent circa 700 B.C. but we really do not talk about the glory that was Mesopotamia, or the grandeur that was the Northern Semitic empires. Instead, we trace our cultural history directly back to the Greek peninsula and its islands. What was it about the Greeks? Why weren't those competing cultures to give us the glory that was indeed Greece?

There is an answer to that question and it illustrates my thesis per- **47** fectly. The answer lies in a simple but potent piece of knowledge technology that turned out to be crucial, that made Greek thought central to the western world for the next 2,500 years. That piece of knowledge technology was a better alphabet. Other civilizations surrounding the Greeks had alphabets of a sort, but they were not as good. What the Greek alphabet did because of its superiority was to turn a shade of gray into clear black and white. Greek thought came to dominate its neighbors, its enemies, and eventually, its intellectual offspring, what we are pleased to call Western culture.

Not only did Greek thought dominate because it was easier to dissem- **48** inate—for the first time in human history, literacy was democratized—but Greek thought also dominated because through the powers of the superior alphabet it found expression in, it got smarter. Thanks to its slightly superior written alphabet, Greek thought became dramatically more perceptive, richer, more precise, more systematic, more encompassing. It did that by changing, in a stunning release, the way people thought. As a consequence, Greek culture easily beat out its rivals, and shaped a civilization for the next 2,500 years.[5]

I have mentioned another piece of knowledge technology, the printing **49** press. It appeared in western Europe about 1450 (although it had already been invented in Korea and China many centuries before) and took the continent by storm. Its single critical feature was the order of magnitude change it could bring about in the dissemination of knowledge. Thus, in less than 50 years, Gutenberg's invention had been carried all over Europe, and from an estimated scores of thousands of volumes, Europeans now had more than 9 million volumes, roughly a doubling rate every seven years, which is not quite as good as computing, but not bad either. The printing press arrived as the Renaissance was already under way, but it amplified that glorious intellectual ferment to a fare-thee-well. It was directly responsible for transforming a little parochial quarrel in Germany into the Reformation, and probably equally responsible for the Scientific Revolution of the seventeenth century. I have no time to tell you of its effect on national languages, literature, and national consciousness, but it was profound and we feel it to this day. I would even argue that it was the main cause of European domination of so much of the planet for many centuries.

Both the Golden Age of Greece and the Continental Renaissance had 50 two other aspects in common with, indeed as a complement to, their knowledge technology. That was a burst of exploration beyond the boundaries of the known world—inspiration itself for fable, celebration, and prosperity.

Thus history is the source of my optimism. Here in 1983 we stand 51 with a new piece of knowledge technology in our hands. It is not a memory machine, as it has been so often in the past, but a reasoning machine, which will amplify human reasoning by the same orders of magnitude that writing and printing have amplified human memory. This new piece of knowledge technology surely has the potential for just that kind of slight but crucial superiority over the competition that resolves shades of gray into black and white. If nothing else, its powers— and by that I mean not only its large knowledge bases and its ability to reason with that knowledge, I also mean its universal distribution—will surely change the subjects we feel confident to address and, of course, the way we think about them. We also itch to break the boundaries of the known world. We are already beginning to, in ways that would have stunned the Greeks or Prince Henry the Navigator, but in ways I think they would have applauded.

Thus we stand, I think, on the threshold of another renaissance, 52 another golden age, with big changes ahead. Those changes will trouble the Establishment (because they will disestablish the Establishment) but excite the adventuresome, and enrich us all. For that is what new knowledge technology has always promised, and always delivered.

If I have been vague about the shape of the Atlantis, the El Dorado, 53 the Blessed Isles, of the new world to come, it is because I know in my heart that my predictions can only look feeble compared to the opulent complexity of the real when we reach those shores. Our little squabbles, our puny anxieties about our prospects will, if they are remembered at all, be charitably forgiven, the products of our lamentably limited minds that were, through no fault of our own, incapable of imagining something beyond our experience.

References

[1]COMMAGER, H. S. 1977. The Empire of Reason: How Europe Imagined and America Realized the Enlightenment. Oxford University Press. New York, N.Y.

[2]FEIGENBAUM, E. & P. McCORDUCK. 1983. The Fifth Generation. Addison-Wesley. Reading, Mass.

[3]McCORDUCK, P. 1979. Machines Who Think. W. H. Freeman & Co. San Francisco, Calif.

[4]HOLZNER, B. & J. H. MARX. 1979. Knowledge Applications; The Knowledge System in Society. Allyn and Bacon. Boston, Mass.

[5]HAVELOCK, E. A. 1982. The Literate Revolution in Greece and Its Cultural Consequences. Princeton University Press. Princeton, N.J.

Rhetorical Analysis Through Annotation

As a way of projecting the future, McCorduck uses history for a model.

Circle all references in this essay to history. In the margin identify the event referred to and the way it parallels the computer revolution.

Discuss how McCorduck uses history to develop her view of the future. Also discuss whether she has a generally positive or generally negative view of history. How does the concept of progress play a role in her construction of history? How is that concept of progress applied to the future of computers? Discuss what role you feel progress has actually had in history and whether current trends, particularly concerning computers, promise faster or slower progress in the future.

Discussion Questions

Interpreting the Text

1. What does it mean that something is invented before it is discovered? What is the distinction between invention and discovery? How does this apply to the new world? How does it apply to computers? To what extent can artificial intelligence be described as invention and to what extent as discovery?

2. What did Feigenbaum mean by saying that there is no such thing as a machine as smart as a person? Do this statement and the following discussion imply any differences between human minds and machines?

3. How does writing amplify our intellect? In what way will the artificial intelligence revolution be similar and what ways different in spreading intellect? What types of inequities and inequalities remain in our current spread of knowledge? How may artificial intelligence remedy that inequality? Give some examples.

4. What does McCorduck mean by turning shades of gray into black and white? Why does she think that is so powerful? Do you agree?

Considering the Issues

5. How does the opposition between our imagined invention and its real-world realization lead to disappointment? Do you think this has been the case in computer technology and other forms of modern technology? How is the imagination related to the inflated promotion of an idea or product? How does hype play on imagination, and for what purposes? What are the results of excessive hype?

6. Do you agree that computers have led to our loss of reckoning skills? Spelling skills? If so, do you believe with McCorduck that this is no loss? How does this compare with Plato's belief that writing would lead to a weakening of memory? Do you agree with McCorduck that artificial intelligence will lead to the loss of the ability to think? Will this be important?

7. What advantages do people with expertise and the ability to think in specialized ways have in our current society? What will happen to those advantages according to McCorduck? Do you agree that skilled thinking will become widely accessible and expertise will be common? May other forms of expertise arise to be sources of power for a small group of individuals? Do you agree that this will be a desirable outcome?

Writing Suggestions

1. For the editorial page of a newspaper write a reflective piece on the promise and threat of the computer age. Or, write an evaluative editorial entitled, "Computers: Revolution or Hype?"

2. If you have experience with computer programs and games, write an article for a computer users' magazine describing how some recent games or programs are more complex and "smart" than computer programs and games of five to ten years ago.

3. For a political science course write an essay on the political implications of knowledge technology, agreeing or disagreeing with McCorduck.

4. For a time capsule write your prediction of the ways in which artificial intelligence will change our way of life.

5. Write a personal essay for a college magazine about an experience where there was a great difference between anticipation and reality. You may want to discuss your anticipation of a high-tech device or other consumer product, college life, travels, a social event, or personal relations.

What Is Automated Reasoning?

Larry Wos, Ross Overbeek, Ewing Lusk, Jim Boyle

Computers think by means of a series of simple operations. They can only do complex thinking by building up simple processes into complex combinations. The following introduction to automated reasoning, from a textbook by computer scientists at the Argonne National Laboratory, illustrates the basic methods by which a computer thinks through a problem. The process is described in a simplified way and the problem explored is an easy one; nevertheless, the same principles and procedures apply to the most highly developed expert intelligence systems.

Compared to the direct human method of reasoning described in the article, the automated reasoning of the computer program appears ponderous and tortured as it works through every detail mechanically. Yet, automated reasoning has its advantages. These are discussed at the end of the selection.

1.1 What Is Automated Reasoning?

To understand what automated reasoning is, we must first understand *1*
what reasoning is. *Reasoning* is the process of drawing conclusions from facts. For the reasoning to be sound, these conclusions must follow inevitably from the facts from which they are drawn. In other words, reasoning as used in this book is not concerned with some conclusion that has a good chance of being true when the facts are true. Thus, reasoning as used here refers to logical reasoning, not to common-sense reasoning or probabilistic reasoning. The only conclusions that are acceptable are those that follow *logically* from the supplied facts.

The object of *automated reasoning* is to write computer programs that *2*
assist in solving problems and in answering questions requiring reasoning. The assistance provided by an automated reasoning program is available in two different modes. You can use such a program in an interactive fashion, that is, you can instruct it to draw some conclusions and present them to you, and then it will ask for further instructions. Or you can use such a program in a batch mode, that is, you can assign it an entire reasoning task and await the final result. In either case, the question is: "How do I instruct an automated reasoning program to carry out a task?"

The first step in instructing a reasoning program is to tell it about the *3*
problem to be solved or about the question to be answered. You must supply a set of facts that adequately describes the situation. . . . You must tell it essentially everything, including the simplest and most obvious facts. A reasoning program has very few concepts that it auto-

matically understands. Moreover, you must phrase each of the facts in a language that the reasoning program accepts. Everyday language usually does not work, for it is not clear enough and is often ambiguous. Since the program is required to draw only sound conclusions—those that follow inevitably from the given facts—the given facts must not be clouded by ambiguity or a lack of clarity. . . .

After being told about the problem, a reasoning program searches for 4 new facts—generates new facts by drawing conclusions from older facts. It obtains the new facts by applying specific types of reasoning, which are called *inference rules*. . . . A number of quite distinct types of reasoning can be applied to a problem. The surprise is that one can identify inference rules that apply in diverse and unrelated areas. But perhaps this fact is not totally surprising, for in arithmetic you learn about rules that apply regardless of where the numbers come from. In reasoning, similar rules exist that apply regardless of where the facts come from. Each type of reasoning is carefully structured to yield conclusions that must follow from the facts it uses. The facts obtained by applying the inference rules are then added to the pool of information or knowledge, depending on various criteria discussed shortly. Exhaustively applying inference rules in an attempt to solve the problem is too naive an approach. The attempt to solve even the simplest of problems or questions or puzzles by exhaustive attack would produce vast amounts of information, much of it irrelevant. Considerable control of the application of reasoning rules is needed.

The need for control is met by having a reasoning *strategy*. In chess, 5 for example, simply playing according to the rules without evaluating the consequences usually loses the game. In poker, betting simply according to the odds usually loses the money. In either game, strategy comes into play and is essential for winning. Similarly, an automated reasoning program must use strategy if it is to have a chance at solving the problem under attack. Some strategies direct a reasoning program in its choice of information or knowledge on which to focus. Even more vital, some strategies prevent a reasoning program from exploring entire classes of conclusions. Some strategies enable you to convey to a reasoning program your intuition and knowledge about how to solve the problem being studied. An automated reasoning program applies rules of reasoning continually, but subject to various strategies. . . .

We commented earlier that a reasoning program adds new facts to 6 the pool of information *only* if certain criteria are satisfied. For example, if the "new" information is actually a copy of already-existing information, then there is no point in keeping the "new" copy. Such duplicate information is in fact discarded immediately upon discovering that it is merely a copy of other information. A more powerful and subtler criterion exists for immediately discarding information: If the "new" information is already captured by an older bit of information—is less general than some fact already present—then the new is discarded. For example, if a reasoning program has available the fact that all fathers are older than their children, then the new fact that "my father is older than I am" is immediately discarded. . . .

Information that is classed as acceptable and therefore to be retained *7* is not necessarily kept in the form in which it is found by application of one of the rules of reasoning. For example, if you said to someone, "My father's father is coming to visit," your companion might reply, "Oh, your grandfather is coming to see you." An automated reasoning program can take similar action if you provide it with the appropriate rules for rephrasing certain facts. Such rephrasing is vital for many uses of an automated reasoning program. . . .

1.2 How Does an Automated Reasoning Program Reason?

A merchant wishes to sell you some fruit. He places three boxes of it *8* on a table. Each box contains only one kind of fruit: apples, bananas, or oranges. As a gesture of good will, the merchant, after asking you to turn your back, selects a piece of fruit from each box and hands you a beautiful apple, a beautiful banana, and a beautiful orange, establishing that each box contains a different type of fruit. You are momentarily puzzled by his request to turn your back, but the reason quickly becomes apparent. The merchant loves to gamble and offers you the chance to win all of the fruit if you can figure out what is in each box. If you lose, you must pay him three times what it is worth. He tells you correctly that each box is mislabeled. Box a is labeled apples, box b oranges, and box c bananas. You accept the bet on the condition that he allow you to look in the box labeled oranges. He agrees, and you look in box b and find that it contains apples. You then turn to him and announce correctly the contents of the other two boxes, and win the fruit. How did you do it?

Your solution might be the following. Since box b contains apples, box *9* a and box c do not. Since box c is labeled bananas, and since the label is incorrect, box c does not contain bananas. So, box c contains oranges, and box a contains bananas.

To present this puzzle to an automated reasoning program, everyday *10* language is not precise enough. Instead, such a program expects the puzzle phrased in a language like the following. For the statement that box b contains apples, we write

(1) CONTAINS(b, apples)

using b for box b. Similarly,

(2) LABEL(a, apples)

(3) LABEL(b, oranges)

(4) LABEL(c, bananas)

tell the program how each box is labeled. To say that each box contains one of the three types of fruit, where "|" represents **or**, we write

(5) CONTAINS(a, apples) | CONTAINS(a, bananas)

    | CONTAINS(a, oranges)

(6) CONTAINS(b, apples | CONTAINS(b, bananas)

    | CONTAINS(b, oranges)

(7) CONTAINS(c, apples) | CONTAINS(c, bananas)

    | CONTAINS(c, oranges)

which respectively say that box a contains apples or bananas or oranges, and so does box b, and also box c.

At this point, the process of giving all of the facts to a reasoning **11** program becomes slightly more complicated. For example, the fact that "**if** box a contains apples, **then** box b and box c do not" requires some care. Where "¬" represents **not** we write

(8) ¬CONTAINS(a, apples) | ¬CONTAINS(b, apples)

(9) ¬CONTAINS(a, apples) | ¬CONTAINS(c, apples)

(10) ¬CONTAINS(b, apples) | ¬CONTAINS(c, apples)

(11) ¬CONTAINS(a, bananas) | ¬CONTAINS(b, bananas)

(12) ¬CONTAINS(a, bananas) | ¬CONTAINS(c, bananas)

(13) ¬CONTAINS(b, bananas) | ¬CONTAINS(c, bananas)

(14) ¬CONTAINS(a, oranges) | ¬CONTAINS(b, oranges)

(15) ¬CONTAINS(a, oranges) | ¬CONTAINS(c, oranges)

(16) ¬CONTAINS(b, oranges) | ¬CONTAINS(c, oranges)

to cover all the combinations of boxes and fruit. Notice that statement 9 says that box a does not contain apples **or** box c does not contain apples, which is certainly true since they cannot both contain apples. . . . You might wonder at the need to write nine statements to cover this single fact, and you will discover that, with a slightly different notation employing variables, only one statement is in fact needed. Variables in a language allow you to talk about "all items having a particular property" without naming each item.

Since we have mentioned variables, let us now give the representation **12** for the fact that every box is mislabeled. That fact can be stated formally as "for every x and every y, x is **not** labeled y **or** x does **not** contain y", which is equivalent to "for every x and every y, **if** x is labeled y, **then** x does **not** contain y". . . . We write

(17) ¬LABEL(x, y) | ¬CONTAINS(x, y)

where the variables x and y are interpreted by a reasoning program as "for all x" "for all y". . . .

Given statements 1 through 17, an automated reasoning program can **13** apply a rule for drawing conclusions that would produce the following statements. From 1 and 10, the program concludes

(18) ¬CONTAINS(c,apples)

which says that box c does not contain apples. The reasoning program obtains this conclusion by "canceling" part of 10 against 1. From 4 and 17, the program concludes

(19) ¬CONTAINS(c,bananas)

which says that box c does not contain bananas. Arriving at this conclusion requires a more complex process than arriving at the preceding one does. The program obtains it by in effect replacing the variables x and y in 17 by c and bananas respectively, and then canceling part of the resulting statement against 4. The rule for reasoning logically can then be applied to 18, 19, and 7 simultaneously to give

(20) CONTAINS(c,oranges)

which says that box c contains oranges.

With the contents of box b given and of box c correctly deduced, the **14** reasoning program could then turn to box a. By using 1 again but now with 8, the program concludes

(21) ¬CONTAINS(a,apples)

which says that box a does not contain apples. From 20 and 15, the program then concludes

(22) ¬CONTAINS(a,oranges)

which says that box a does not contain oranges. Finally from 21 and 22 and 5, considered simultaneously, the program concludes

(23) CONTAINS(a,bananas)

which completes the explanation of how you won your bet.

Notice that the conclusions obtained by the reasoning program look **15** very much like your solution, although the steps are not in the same order. What is perhaps more interesting is that an automated reasoning program can use a strategy that decreases its chance of getting lost on the way to solving the puzzle. The conclusions that it draws, statements 18 through 23, are directly or indirectly traceable to statements 1 or 4. In particular, if a reasoning program, or a person for that matter, is prevented from applying rules of reasoning to various pairs of statements unless one of them is directly traceable to statements 1 or 4, then a sharp improvement in effectiveness might result. Such a restriction on reasoning is known as a strategy. . . .

Is the reasoning program being too careful and too pedantic? A var- *16* iation on this puzzle shows why such care is often needed. In the variation, the merchant does not make the magnanimous gesture of offering you one piece of fruit from each box, but instead correctly tells you none of the boxes is empty. Thus, you cannot assume that each box contains a different type of fruit. If you accept the bet, you will win only if you make the right guesses, for the information given in the variant of the puzzle is insufficient to pin down what is in box a and box c. For example, box a could contain oranges, and box c, like box b, could contain apples. If you had guessed at the contents of boxes a and c, you might have made the wrong guess. You might have assumed that all three types of fruit were contained in the three boxes, and not allowed for two boxes to contain the same type of fruit. Logical rea- soning would eventually prove that the puzzle was unsolvable—only guesswork might get you the correct answer. Thus, if the merchant required you to prove that your answers were correct, you would have no chance of winning. An automated reasoning program would not have answered the puzzle incorrectly. In fact, such a program could be used to prove that the correct answers are not deducible. Therefore, for solving the first version or for showing that the second version cannot be solved, an automated reasoning program can provide assistance.

Rhetorical Analysis Through Annotation

The first section of this textbook selection establishes three elements of a rea- soning program. The second section works through an example, in accordance with the three elements. Throughout, there is a running comparison between automated reasoning and human reasoning.

In the early section identify each of the three elements by circling the key descriptive word or phrase. In the latter part, next to each group of numbered instructions that comprise the program, explain the rationale for those instruc- tions in terms of the three essential elements.

Discuss why the program instructions are necessarily detailed.

Mark in the margin each explicit or implicit comparison made between au- tomated reasoning and human reasoning. Discuss how these comparisons help illuminate the nature, procedures, disadvantages, and advantages of automated reasoning.

Discussion Questions

Interpreting the Text

1. What do the authors mean in the third paragraph by the essential facts of a situation? What are the essential facts of the fruit puzzle?

2. What are inference rules? How do inference rules differ from simple inference? Give some examples. What inference rules apply in the solution to the fruit puzzle?

3. What are reasoning strategies? What reasoning strategies are used in the solution of the fruit puzzle?

4. In what ways is the automated solution to the fruit puzzle similar to the human solution? In what ways is it different?

5. What features does the extract from a textbook share with other textbook selections in this book (See pages 242–251, 277–283, 371–384, and 454–459). To what extent and in what way do they refer to the literature of the field, if at all? What is the role of explanation? Is there any argument? Are controversies mentioned at all?

Considering the Issues

6. To what type of puzzles may the type of reasoning discussed here apply? Are problems the same as puzzles, and can all problems be reduced to logical puzzles? What types of problems or puzzles may not be solvable through automated reasoning? Is intuition or guesswork necessary to solve certain types of problems? If so, name them.

7. How do you know what the essential facts of a problem are? What are the essential facts of a patient's disease, a math problem, building a bridge, deciding whether to get married, or choosing between two job offers? Are the essential facts of such various cases comparable or are they of radically different kinds? In which situations is it possible to know all the essential facts? In which situations may your knowledge of essential facts be incomplete or uncertain?

8. What are some examples of inference in your daily life? What rules guide you in making those inferences? What is the difference between formal deductive inference and informal inference? If you were pressed, could you reduce informal human inference to formal inference procedures that machines could carry out?

9. What reasoning strategies do you use in daily life: (a) in deciding whether to make a purchase; (b) in deciding how to fix something; (c) in taking an exam; (d) in solving a math problem; (e) in finding out what is bothering a friend? Which of these strategies can be incorporated in a computer program?

Writing Suggestions

1. If you have done any computer programming, write a line-by-line explanation of one of your simpler programs that will explain the logic of the program to someone who is unfamiliar with programming. If you have not done any programming, give a step-by-step explanation of some complex object or piece of writing you created. Again, the purpose is to explain the logic of what you have done to someone who is unfamiliar with the creative process.

2. Imagine you have a robot that will carry out a set of operations in a prescribed order. Instruct it to carry out some basic activity. Make sure the robot has all the information it needs to carry out the task accurately.

3. For a Star Trek newsletter, write a letter to Mr. Spock discussing how much of human behavior could be described as logical and whether guesswork, intuition, and feelings are necessary for making correct human decisions.

Consultation Systems for Physicians: The Role of Artificial Intelligence Techniques

Edward H. Shortliffe

In moving beyond mathematical and logical problems into the complex problems of the everyday world, artificial intelligence pays attention to the accumulated experience and wisdom of developed disciplines. The following description of an application of artificial intelligence to medical problems shows how an expert system can integrate a body of specialized disciplinary knowledge. Even more interestingly, the article explores how an expert system must be useful and acceptable to the people who have access to it. In this case, the system must fit in with the way doctors actually practice medicine.

Developing an expert system for medicine is, therefore, largely an interdisciplinary task. In 1981 Edward Shortliffe of Stanford University wrote the following description, in which he mixes a discussion of the basic principles of automated reasoning (as described in the previous selection) with an examination of the structure of medical knowledge and doctors' decision-making processes. Shortliffe's aim is to explain to other computer experts the principles his group used to design MYCIN, a program to help doctors diagnose and prescribe medication for microbial infections.

Abstract   Computer systems for use by physicians have had limited impact on clinical medicine. When one examines the most common reasons for poor acceptance of medical computing systems, the potential relevance of artificial intelligence techniques becomes evident. This paper proposes design criteria for clinical computing systems and demonstrates their relationship to current research in knowledge engineering. The MYCIN System is used to illustrate the ways in which our research group has attempted to respond to the design criteria cited.

1. Introduction

Although computers have had an increasing impact on the practice of *1* medicine, the successful applications have tended to be in domains where physicians have not been asked to interact at the terminal. Few potential user populations are as demanding of computer-based decision aids. This is due to a variety of factors which include their traditional independence as lone decision makers, the seriousness with which they view actions that may have life and death significance, and the overwhelming time demands that tend to make them impatient with any innovation that breaks up the flow of their daily routine.

This paper examines some of the issues that have limited the accep- *2* tance of programs for use by physicians, particularly programs intended to give advice in clinical settings. My goal is to present design criteria which may encourage the use of computer programs by physicians, and to show that AI [artificial intelligence] offers some particularly pertinent methods for responding to the design criteria outlined. Although the emphasis is medical throughout, many of the issues occur in other user communities where the introduction of computer methods must confront similar barriers. After presenting the design considerations and their relationship to AI research, I will use our work with MYCIN to illustrate some of the ways in which we have attempted to respond to the acceptability criteria I have outlined.

1.1. The Nature of Medical Reasoning

It is frequently observed that clinical medicine is more an "art" than a *3* "science." This statement reflects the varied factors that are typically considered in medical decision making; any practitioner knows that well-trained experts with considerable specialized experience may still reach very different conclusions about how to treat a patient or proceed with a diagnostic workup.

One factor which may contribute to observed discrepancies, even *4* among experts, is the tendency of medical education to emphasize the teaching of *facts*, with little formal advice regarding the *reasoning processes* that are most appropriate for decision making. There has been a traditional assumption that future physicians should learn to make decisions by observing other doctors in action and by acquiring as much basic knowledge as possible. More recently, however, there has been interest in studying the ways in which expert physicians reach decisions in hopes that a more structured approach to the teaching of medical decision making can be developed [Kassirer 1978, Elstein 1978].

Computer programs for assisting with medical decision making have *5* tended not to emphasize models of clinical reasoning. Instead they have commonly assigned structure to a domain using statistical techniques such as Bayes' Theorem° [deDombal 1972] or formal decision analysis [Gorry 1973]. More recently a number of programs have attempted to draw lessons from analyses of actual human reasoning in clinical settings

---

Bayes' theorem—a procedure for considering probabilities.

[Wortman 1972, Pauker 1976]. Although the other methodologies may lead to excellent decisions in the clinical areas to which they have been applied, many believe that programs with greater dependence on models of expert clinical reasoning will have heightened acceptance by the physicians for whom they are designed.

1.2. *The Consultation Process*

Accelerated growth in medical knowledge has necessitated greater sub- 6 specialization and more dependence upon assistance from others when a patient presents with a complex problem outside one's own area of expertise. Such consultations are acceptable to doctors in part because they maintain the primary physician's role as ultimate decision maker. The consultation generally involves a dialog between the two physicians, with the expert explaining the basis for advice that is given and the nonexpert seeking justification of points found puzzling or questionable. Consultants who offered dogmatic advice they were unwilling to discuss or defend would find that their opinions were seldom sought. After a recommendation is given, the primary physician generally makes the decision whether to follow the consultant's advice, seek a second opinion, or proceed in some other fashion. When the consultant's advice is followed, it is frequently because the patient's doctor has been genuinely educated about the particular complex problem for which assistance was sought.

Since such consultations are accepted largely because they allow the 7 primary physician to make the final management decision, it can be argued that medical consultation programs must mimic this human process. Computer-based decision aids have typically emphasized only the accumulation of patient data and the generation of advice [Shortliffe 1979]. On the other hand, an ability to explain decisions may be incorporated into computer-based decision aids if the system is given an adequate internal model of the logic that it uses and can convey this intelligibly to the physician-user. The addition of explanation capabilities may be an important step towards effectively encouraging a system's use.

2. Acceptability Issues

Studies have shown that many physicians are inherently reluctant to use 8 computers in their practice [Startsman 1972]. Some researchers fear that the psychological barriers are insurmountable, but we are beginning to see systems that have had considerable success in encouraging terminal use by physicians [Watson 1974]. The key seems to be to provide adequate benefits while creating an environment in which the physician can feel comfortable and efficient.

Physicians tend to ask at least seven questions when a new system is **9** presented to them:

1. Is its performance reliable?
2. Do I need this system?
3. Is it fast and easy to use?
4. Does it help me without being dogmatic?
5. Does it justify its recommendations so that I can decide for myself what to do?
6. Does use of the system fit naturally into my daily routine?
7. Is it designed to make me feel comfortable when I use it?

Experience has shown that reliability alone may not be enough to insure **10** system acceptance [Shortliffe 1979]; the additional issues cited here are also central to the question of how to design consultation systems that doctors will be willing to use. . . .

5. An Example: The MYCIN System

Since 1972 our research group at Stanford University[1] has been involved **11** with the development of computer-based consultation systems. The first was designed to assist physicians with the selection of antibiotics for patients with serious infections. That program has been termed MYCIN after the suffix utilized in the names of many common antimicrobial agents. . . .

5.1. Knowledge Representation and Acquisition

All infectious disease knowledge in MYCIN is contained in packets of **12** inferential knowledge represented as production rules [Davis 1976]. These rules were acquired from collaborating clinical experts during detailed discussions of specific complex cases on the wards at Stanford Hospital. More recently the system has been given the capability to acquire such rules directly through interaction with the clinical expert[2].

MYCIN currently contains some 600 rules that deal with the diagnosis **13** and treatment of bacteremia (bacteria in the blood) and meningitis (bacteria in the cerebrospinal fluid). These rules are coded in INTERLISP° [Teitelman 1978], but routines have been written to translate them into simple English so that they can be displayed and understood by the user. For example, one simple rule which relates to a patient's clinical situation with the likely bacteria causing the illness is shown in Figure 1. The strengths with which the specified inferences can be drawn are indicated by numerical weights, or certainty factors, that are described further below.

INTERLISP—a computer programming language.

5.2. Inference Methods

5.2.1. Reasoning model   Production rules provide powerful mecha- *14* nisms for selecting those that apply to a given consultation. In MYCIN's case the rules are only loosely related to one another before a consultation begins; the program selects the relevant rules and chains them together as it considers a particular patient. Two rules chain together if the action portion of one helps determine the truth value of a condition in the premise of the other. The resulting reasoning network, then, is created dynamically and can be seen as a model of one approach to the patient's problem.

MYCIN's strategy in rule selection is goal-oriented. The program *15* "reasons backwards" from its recognized goal of determining therapy for a patient. It therefore starts by considering rules for therapy selection, but the premise portion of each of those rules in turn sets up new questions or subgoals. These new goals then cause new rules to be invoked and a reasoning network is thereby developed. When the truth of a premise condition is best determined by asking the physician rather than by applying rules (e.g., to determine the value of a laboratory test), a question is displayed. The physician enters the appropriate response and the program continues to select additional rules. Once information on the patient is obtained, some rules will fail to be applicable: in this way the invoked applicable rules will provide a customized patient-specific reasoning network for the case under consideration.

Portions of a sample consultation session are shown in Figure 2. The *16* physician's responses are in capital letters and follow a double asterisk.

RULE300

[This rule applies to all cultures and suspected infections, and is tried in order to find out about the organisms (other than those seen on cultures or smears) which might be causing the infection.]

If: 1) The infection which requires therapy
       is meningitis, and
    2) The patient does have evidence of
       serious skin or soft tissue infection,
       and
    3) Organisms were not seen on the stain
       of the culture, and
    4) The type of the infection is bacterial
Then: There is evidence that the organism
       (other than those seen on cultures or
       smears) which might be causing the
       infection is staphylococcus-coag-pos
       (.75) streptococcus-group-a (.5)

Figure 1.   A Sample MYCIN Rule.

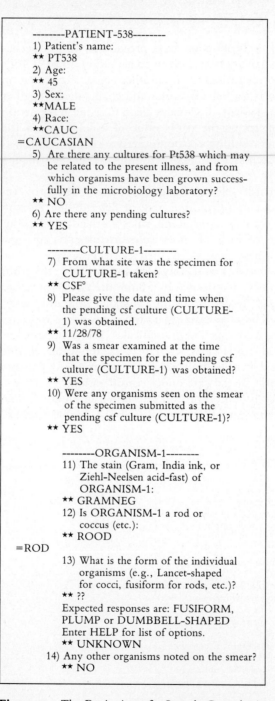

```
--------PATIENT-538--------
1) Patient's name:
** PT538
2) Age:
** 45
3) Sex:
**MALE
4) Race:
**CAUC
=CAUCASIAN
5) Are there any cultures for Pt538 which may
   be related to the present illness, and from
   which organisms have been grown success-
   fully in the microbiology laboratory?
** NO
6) Are there any pending cultures?
** YES

        --------CULTURE-1--------
7) From what site was the specimen for
   CULTURE-1 taken?
** CSF°
8) Please give the date and time when
   the pending csf culture (CULTURE-
   1) was obtained.
** 11/28/78
9) Was a smear examined at the time
   that the specimen for the pending csf
   culture (CULTURE-1) was obtained?
** YES
10) Were any organisms seen on the smear
    of the specimen submitted as the
    pending csf culture (CULTURE-1)?
** YES

        --------ORGANISM-1--------
11) The stain (Gram, India ink, or
    Ziehl-Neelsen acid-fast) of
    ORGANISM-1:
** GRAMNEG
12) Is ORGANISM-1 a rod or
    coccus (etc.):
** ROOD
=ROD
13) What is the form of the individual
    organisms (e.g., Lancet-shaped
    for cocci, fusiform for rods, etc.)?
** ??
Expected responses are: FUSIFORM,
PLUMP or DUMBBELL-SHAPED
Enter HELP for list of options.
** UNKNOWN
14) Any other organisms noted on the smear?
** NO
```

Figure 2. The Beginning of a Sample Consultation.

CSF—Colony-stimulating factor.

Note that the physician can indicate that he does not know the answer to a question (Question 13) and MYCIN will proceed to do the best it can on the basis of the data available. Typographical or spelling errors are automatically corrected (Question 12) with the presumed meaning printed at the left margin so that the physician knows what assumption has been made. Note also that the physician's responses are generally single words.

In Figure 3 the form of MYCIN's final conclusions and therapy 17 recommendations are demonstrated. Note that the program specifies what organisms are likely to be causing the patient's infection and then suggests a therapeutic regimen appropriate for them. There are also

---

INFECTION-1 is MENINGITIS

+ <ITEM-1> E.COLI
+ <ITEM-2> PSEUDOMONAS-
            AERUGINOSA
+ <ITEM-3> KLEBSIELLA-
            PNEUMONIAE
+ <ITEM-4> DIPLOCOCCUS-
            PNEUMONIAE

41) Does Pt538 have a clinically significant
     allergic reaction to any antimicrobial
     agent?
** NO
42) Do you have reason to suspect that
     Pt538 may have impaired renal
     function?
** NO
43) Pt538's weight in kilograms:
** 70

[REC-1] My preferred therapy
      recommendation is:
In order to cover for Items <1 2 3 4>:
     Give the following in combination:
     1) AMPICILLIN
     Dose: 3.5g (28.0 ml) q4h IV
           [calculated on basis of 50 mg/
           kg]
     2) GENTAMICIN
     Dose: 119 mg (3.0 ml, 80mg/2ml
           ampule) q8h IV [calculated on
           basis of 1.7 mg/kg] plus
           consider giving 5 mg q24h
           intrathecally

Since high concentrations of penicillins can
inactivate aminoglycosides, do not mix these
two antibiotics in the same bottle.

Figure 3. Example of MYCIN's Recommendations.

specialized routines to calculate recommended drug doses depending upon the patient's size and kidney function.

. . . .

5.3. *Explanation*

Perhaps the greatest advantage of the rules used in MYCIN is the way   18
in which they facilitate the development of mechanisms for explaining and justifying system performance. These capabilities also contribute greatly to MYCIN's educational role [Clancey 1979]. The explanation program has two options, one of which is limited in scope but fast and easy to use. This option is used during a consultation session and allows examination of the reasoning steps that have generated a specific question. The second option is more powerful but it involves language processing and is therefore less reliable and more time consuming. This question-answering capability is designed to allow full access to *all* system knowledge, both static (i.e., facts and rules obtained from experts) and dynamic (i.e., conclusions reached by the program for the specific consultation session). Each system is briefly described below.

5.3.1. Answers to questions about the reasoning status   During the   19
consultation, MYCIN may ask questions which the physician finds puzzling, either because they appear irrelevant or because the details of their applicability are unclear. When this occurs, the physician can digress momentarily and seek an explanation of the question[3]. Instead of answering the question MYCIN has asked, the user enters the word "WHY" and the program responds with a translation of the rule which generated the question. An example of this feature is shown in Figure 4. Note that MYCIN begins its response by phrasing in English its understanding of the "WHY question" asked by the physician. It then displays the relevant rule, specifying which conditions in the premise are already known to be true and which conditions remain to be investigated. In many cases this single rule displayed is an adequate explanation of the current line of reasoning and the physician can then proceed with the consultation by answering the question.

The user can alternatively continue to investigate the current reasoning   20
by repeating the "WHY" command several times. Each additional "WHY" is interpreted by MYCIN as a request for display of the next rule in the current reasoning chain. For example, in Figure 4 another "WHY" would be equivalent to asking "Well then, why are you trying to determine the organisms which might be causing the infection?" After responding to each "WHY," MYCIN returns to the current question and awaits the physician's response.

The "HOW" command is used in conjunction with the "WHY"   21
command. Note that MYCIN places a unique number before each condition in the premise of a displayed rule (Figure 4). If the user does not understand *how* a specified condition was met (or will be met), the

35) Is this a hospital-acquired infection?
** WHY

[i.e. WHY is it important to determine
whether the infection was acquired while the
patient was hospitalized?]

[2.0] This will aid in determining the
organisms (other than those seen on cultures or
smears) which might be causing the infection.
　It has already been established that
　　　　　[2.1] the infection which requires
　　　　　　　　therapy is meningitis, and
　　　　　[2.2] organisms were not seen on the
　　　　　　　　stain of this pending csf culture,
　　　　　　　　and
　　　　　[2.3] the type of the infection is
　　　　　　　　bacterial, and
　　　　　[2.4] neurosurgery is not one of the
　　　　　　　　relevant items from the history
　　　　　　　　of pt538, and
　　　　　[2.5] the age of pt538 is greater than
　　　　　　　　10 days
　Therefore, if
　　　　　[2.6] the infection ws acquired while
　　　　　　　　the patient was hospitalized
　then:
　　　　　　　there is evidence that the organism
　　　　　　　(other than those seen on culture or
　　　　　　　smears) which might be causing the
　　　　　　　infection is e.coli (.75)
　　　　　　　staphylococcus–coag–pos (.3)
　　　　　　　pseudomonas–aeruginosa (.3)
　　　　　　　klebsiella–pneumoniae (.5)

[back to question 35...]
**

Figure 4.　Example of the WHY Command.

"HOW" command, followed by the identifying number of the premise
clause in question, can be used. Hence "HOW" requires an argument
as shown in Figure 5. This example follows immediately on the "WHY"
example in Figure 4; thus the argument "2.3" refers to the third condition
in the premise of RULE545 in Figure 4 and "2.5" refers to the fifth.
MYCIN's responses to "HOW" commands are self-explanatory. Note
also that components of all explanations are given identifiers so that, in
Figure 5, the command "HOW 3.1" would have resulted in a display
of RULE526.

　Other features of the capability to assess the reasoning status during　*22*
a consultation are described elsewhere [Davis 1977, Scott 1977, Davis
1979]. Two points require emphasis here, however. First, these features

```
[back to question 35...]
** HOW 2.3

[i.e. HOW was it established that the type of
   the infection is bacterial?]

The following rules concluded about the
   likelihood that the type of the infection is
   bacterial:

                  Rule          Certainty
       [2.7]      RULE148        (.19)
       [2.8]      RULE500        (.51)
       [2.9]      RULE501        (.95)
       [3.0]      RULE502        (.97)
       [3.1]      RULE526        (.98)
       [3.2]      RULE504        (.97)
       [3.3]      RULE524        (.98)

Thus, it has been established that the type of
   the infection is bacterial.

   [back to question 35...]
   ** HOW 2.5

[i.e. HOW was it established that the age of
   pt538 is greater than 10 days?]

In answer to question 2 you said that the age of
   pt538 is 34 years. Thus, it has been
   established that the age of pt538 is greater
   than 10 days.

   [back to question 35...]
   **
```

Figure 5. Examples of the HOW Command.

require no English language processing since the user gives simple single-word commands; hence the capability is fast, efficient, and reliable. On the other hand, questions are limited to the immediate reasoning environment surrounding the question asked by MYCIN. Hence general access to other system knowledge or other conclusions previously made by the program is not possible. To provide a more general explanation capability, MYCIN must be able to respond to questions expressed in simple English as described below.

5.3.2. Answers to questions about the consultation and knowledge base 23
MYCIN's general question-answering feature is automatically made available to the user at the end of each consultation session. After a therapy recommendation has been given, the physician may still have several questions regarding details of the consultation and the basis for

diagnostic and therapeutic advice. Figure 6 shows an example of a simple English question which MYCIN understands and attempts to answer. Our approach to natural language understanding is very simplistic [Scott 1977] but often adequate if questions are kept short without subordinate clauses. In many cases questions are best answered simply by retrieving relevant rules and displaying them in a format suitable for the question being asked. In Figure 6 MYCIN offers a detailed explanation of how it had decided that the patient might be infected with an *E. coli*. All rules are specified by number so that the physician can have them displayed if full details are desired.

Figure 7 demonstrates the way in which a physician can ask general *24* questions of the knowledge base (static knowledge); neither the questions nor MYCIN's responses refer to any specific consultation session. Note that MYCIN has a sense of its limitations and makes it clear that it has no knowledge specific to pneumonia. Also, a large dictionary includes synonyms and hence permits MYCIN to recognize that "pneumococcal" refers to "pneumococcus," which in turn is the same as "diplococcus-pneumoniae."

** WHY DID YOU TREAT E.COLI?

ITEM-1 is E.coli associated with meningitis. I decided to treat ITEM-1 on the basis of clinical evidence only.

The following rules concluded about:
the likelihood that e.coli is one of the organisms (other than those seen on cultures or smears) which might be causing the infection

RULE545 was used to conclude that e.coli is
   one of the organisms (other than those
   seen on cultures or smears) which might
   be causing the infection (.74).
RULE557 was used to conclude that e.coli is
   one of the organisms (other than those
   seen on cultures or smears) which might
   be causing the infection (.93).

The parameters most frequently used in these rules:
   the infection which requires therapy
   whether a smear of the culture was examined
   whether organisms were seen
   the type of the infection

Figure 6.   Response to a Free Text Question.

** HOW DO YOU DECIDE THAT AN
 ORGANISM IS AN E.COLI?
The following rules conclude about:
 the likelihood that the identity of the
 organism is E.coli
555, 304, 243, 3
Which of the rules do you wish to see?
 ** NONE

** WHAT IS THE TREATMENT FOR
 PNEUMOCOCCAL PNEUMONIA?
The MYCIN system currently can treat the
following infections: BACTEREMIA
MENINGITIS CYSTITIS. Because the
knowledge base is incomplete, all other
infections will be treated like bacteremia.

 For treatment of DIPLOCOCCUS-
PNEUMONIAE in BACTEREMIA, the
drugs of choice (ranked by relative efficacy,
assuming sensitivity) are:
  1st choice:
   PENICILLIN or AMPICILLIN
  2nd choice:
   NAFCILLIN, CEPHALOTHIN,
   ERYTHROMYCIN, or
   CLINDAMYCIN
  3rd choice:
   TETRACYCLINE,
   CHLORAMPHENICOL, or
   VANCOMYCIN

** WHAT DOSE OF ERYTHROMYCIN
 DO YOU RECOMMEND?
When ERYTHROMYCIN is given for
BACTEREMIA, the recommended dosage is:
if age is > 12 yrs then 12 mg/kg q6h IV
else if age > .08 yrs then 5 mg/kg q6h IV
else if age > .02 yrs then 5 mg/kg q12h IV

Figure 7. Requests for MYCIN's General Knowledge.

5.4. *Evaluating MYCIN*

As work on MYCIN has progressed, we have begun to devise tech- 25
niques for analyzing formally the system's performance. It must be
emphasized, however, that the decision making performance is only one
aspect of overall system acceptability; as I have discussed, many of the
most significant problems occur when attempts are made to encourage
physicians to use a program, even after it has been shown to reach good
decisions.

 The details of the evaluation studies will not be presented here[4], but 26
a number of specific points are of interest. First any evaluation is difficult

because there is so much difference of opinion in this domain, *even among experts*. Hence, it is unclear how to select a "gold standard" by which to measure the system's performance. Actual clinical outcome cannot be used because each patient of course is treated in only one way and because a poor outcome in a gravely ill patient cannot necessarily be blamed on the therapy that had been selected.

Second, although MYCIN performed at or near expert level in almost 27 all cases, the evaluating experts in one study [Yu 1979a] had serious reservations about the clinical utility of the program. It is difficult to assess how much of this opinion is due to actual inadequacies in system knowledge or design and how much is related to inherent bias against *any* computer-based consultation aid. In a subsequent study we attempted to eliminate this bias from the study by having the evaluators unaware of which recommendations were MYCIN's and which came from actual physicians [Yu 1979b]. In that setting MYCIN's recommendations were uniformly judged preferable to, or equivalent to, those of five infectious disease experts who recommended therapy for the same patients.

Finally, those cases in which MYCIN has tended to do least well are 28 those in which serious infections have been simultaneously present at sites in the body about which the program has been given no rules. It is reasonable, of course, that the program should fail in areas where it has no knowledge. However, a useful antimicrobial consultation system must know about a broad range of infectious diseases, just as its human counterpart does. Even with excellent performance managing isolated bacteremias and meningitis, the program is therefore not ready for clinical implementation.

There will eventually be several important questions regarding the 29 clinical impact of MYCIN and systems like it. Are they used? If so, do the physicians follow the program's advice? If so, does patient welfare improve? Is the system cost effective when no longer in an experimental form? What are the legal implications in the use of, or failure to use, such systems? The answers to all these questions are years away for most consultation systems, but it must be recognized that all these issues are ultimately just as important as whether the decision making methodology manages to lead the computer to accurate and reliable advice.

6. Conclusion

Although I have asserted that AI research potentially offers solutions to 30 many of the important problems confronting researchers in computer-based clinical decision making, the field is not without its serious limitations. However, AI has reached a level of development where it is both appropriate and productive to begin applying the techniques to important real world problems rather than purely theoretical issues. The difficulty lies in the fact that such efforts must still dwell largely in research environments where short term development of systems for service use is not likely to occur.

It is also important to recognize that other computational techniques *31* may meld very naturally with AI approaches as the fields mature. Thus we may see, for example, direct links between AI methods and statistical procedures, decision analysis, pattern recognition techniques, and large databanks. As researchers in other areas become more familiar with AI, it may gradually be brought into fruitful combination with these alternate methodologies. The need for physician acceptance of medical consultation programs is likely to make AI approaches particularly attractive, at least in those settings where hands-on computer use by physicians is desired or necessary. This paper has attempted to explain why the wedding of AI and medical consultation systems is a natural one and to show, in the setting of the MYCIN system, how one early application has responded to design criteria identified for a user community of physicians.

Notes

[1]Several computer scientists, physicians, and a pharmacist have been involved in the development of the MYCIN System. These include J. Aikins, S. Axline, J. Bennett, A. Bonnet, B. Buchanan, W. Clancey, S. Cohen, R. Davis, L. Fagan, F. Rhame, C. Scott, W. vanMelle, S. Wraith, and V. Yu.

[2]This capability was implemented in rudimentary form in early versions of the system [Shortliffe 1976] but was substantially broadened and strengthened by Davis in his Teiresias program [Davis 1979].

[3]The mechanisms for examining the reasoning status using "WHY" and "HOW" commands were largely the work of Davis in his Teiresias program [Davis 1979]. The techniques he developed are general in their applicability and have been implemented in nonmedical domains as well.

[4]See [Yu 1979a] for the details of the bacteremia evaluation, and [Yu 1979b] for the data on MYCIN's performance selecting therapy for patients with meningitis.

References

Adams, J. B. "A probability model of medical reasoning and the MYCIN model." *Math. Biosci.* 32,177–186 (1976).

Clancey, W. J. *Transfer of Rule-Based Expertise Through a Tutorial Dialogue.* Doctoral dissertation, Stanford University, September 1979. Technical memo STAN-CS-79-769.

Croft, D. J. "Is computerized diagnosis possible?" *Comp. Biomed. Res.* 5,351–367 (1972).

Davis, R. and King, J. "An overview of production systems." In *Machine Representation of Knowledge* (E. W. Elcock and D. Michie, eds.), New York: Wiley, 1976.

Davis, R., Buchanan, B. G., and Shortliffe, E. H. "Production rules as a representation for a knowledge-based consultation system." *Artificial Intelligence* 8,15–45 (1977).

Davis, R., "Interactive transfer of expertise: acquisition of new inference rules." *Artificial Intelligence*, 12,121–157 (1979).

deDombal, F. T., Leaper, D. J., Staniland, J. R., et al. "Computer-aided diagnosis of acute abdominal pain." *Brit. Med. J.* 2,9–13 (1972).

Elstein, A. S., Shulman, L. S., and Sprafka, S. A. *Medical Problem Solving: An Analysis of Clinical Reasoning.* Cambridge, Mass.: Harvard Univ. Press, 1978.

Gorry, G. A., Kassirer, J. P., Essig, A., and Schwartz, W. B. "Decision analysis as the basis for computer-aided management of acute renal failure." *Amer. J. Med.* 55,473–484 (1973).

Kassirer, J. P. and Gorry, G. A. "Clinical problem solving: a behavioral analysis." *Anns. Int. Med.* 89,245–255 (1978).

Mesel, E., Wirtschafter, D. D., Carpenter, J. T., et al. "Clinical algorithms for cancer chemotherapy—systems for community-based consultant-extenders and oncology centers." *Meth. Inform. Med.* 15,168–173 (1976).

Michie, D. "Knowledge engineering." *Cybernetics* 2,197–200 (1973).

Pauker, S. G., Gorry, G. A., Kassirer, J. P., and Schwartz, W. B. "Towards the simulation of clinical cognition: taking a present illness by computer." *Amer. J. Med.* 60:981–996 (1976).

Scott, A. C., Clancey, W., Davis, R., and Shortliffe, E. H. "Explanation capabilities of knowledge-based production systems." *Amer. J. Computational Linguistics*, Microfiche 62, 1977.

Shortliffe, E. H. and Buchanan, B. G. "A model of inexact reasoning in medicine." *Math. Biosci.* 23,351–379 (1975).

Shortliffe, E. H. *Computer-Based Medical Consultations: MYCIN*, New York: Elsevier/North Holland, 1976.

Shortliffe, E. H., Buchanan, B. G. and Feigenbaum, E. A. "Knowledge engineering for medical decision making: a review of computer-based clinical decision aids." *PROCEEDINGS of the IEEE*, 67,1207–1224 (1979).

Shortliffe, E. H. "Medical consultation systems: designing for doctors." In *Communication With Computers* (M. Sime and M. Fitter, eds.), Academic Press, London, 1980 (in press).

Startsman, T. S. and Robinson, R. E. "The attitudes of medical and paramedical personnel towards computers." *Comp. Biomed. Res.* 5,218–227 (1972).

Teitelman, W. *INTERLISP Reference Manual*, XEROX Corporation, Palo Alto, Calif. and Bolt Beranek and Newman, Cambridge, Mass., October 1978.

Watson, R. J. "Medical staff response to a medical information system with direct physician-computer interface." *MEDINFO 74*, pp. 299–302, Amsterdam: North-Holland Publishing Company, 1974.

Wortman, P. M. "Medical diagnosis: an information processing approach." *Comput. Biomed. Res.* 5,315–328 (1972).

Yu, V. L., Buchanan, B. G., Shortliffe, E. H. et al. "Evaluating the performance of a computer-based consultant." *Comput. Prog. Biomed.* 9,95–102 (1979a).

Yu, V. L., Fagan, L. M., Wraith, S. M. et al. "Computerized consultation in antimicrobial selection—a blinded evaluation by experts." *J. Amer. Med. Assoc.* 242,1279–1282 (1979b).

Rhetorical Analysis Through Annotation

The interactive program described here calls for exchanges between doctor and computer. Almost all interchanges are initiated by questions, sometimes by machine to doctor, sometimes by doctor to machine. Questions constrain both the form and content of appropriate answers, because many questions have a limited set of responses. For example, "Are you finished?" is a yes–no question; the only appropriate direct responses are "yes" and "no."

In each of the sample printouts of program interchanges mark each question. Discuss what content and form is required by each question. Discuss how the actual answers fit the constraints.

Because questions constrain answers, the questioner controls the answerer, restricting his range of responses. For each question identify whether it is the physician or the computer in control and discuss what the one in control is trying to acomplish through the control and what role the responder is limited to.

Why is it important that the doctor be able to ask questions? At what points and for what purposes is the doctor allowed to question? What different patterns of questioning do you observe? Who has ultimate control over whether the information will be used? How does the issue of control relate to the issue of whether doctors will accept artificial intelligence assistance?

Discussion Questions

Interpreting the Text

1. Why have doctors been reluctant to use computers? How do their medical training and daily practices contribute to the reluctance? In what ways does MYCIN attempt to overcome that reluctance? Of what significance are the seven questions asked of doctors, as listed in section 2?

2. What reasoning process is carried out in the sample inference rule in Figure 1? What knowledge, information, or skill would the machine need to apply the rule? How certain are the results of following this rule?

3. What does it mean to reason backward from the goal? How does this concept apply to the questioning procedure of Figure 2?

4. Why does the program ask the questions it does in Figure 3?

5. How successful has MYCIN been? What limitations currently hamper the regular use of this and similar programs?

6. Why does Shortliffe use the section numbering system he does? How does his use compare to the use of the numbering system in the article on pages 454–459.

Considering the Issues

7. How are the samples of the program presented in the figures related to the text? Do the samples explain the text, or does the text explain the samples?

8. What vision does the analysis here give of the doctor's work? Is this all of the doctor's work? A major part of it? What else do doctors do? Can such programs replace doctors? Will they provide only limited help, or will they never prove useful?

9. How might the success of such programs affect the authority held by doctors? Under what conditions might the program become more authoritative than the doctor? What might be the social consequences? Consider these questions in relation to McCorduck's discussion on pages 525–536.

10. Do you feel that MYCIN has been taken about as far as it can go, or would you assume that further progress is likely? Why?

11. If you had a bacterial infection, would you ask your doctor to refer to MYCIN? Explain your answer.

Writing Suggestions

1. Imagine that you have been invited to speak before a sixth grade class to explain how interactive computer programs work to help carry out daily activities. Describe the workings of one or more programs you have used. These may include programs in a bank teller machine, a library cataloguing system, or any other system you may be familiar with.

2. For your college writing course, write an essay suggesting possible uses for expert systems in different professions. The piece may be comic or serious.

3. Imagine that in your sociology class you have been discussing the adage "Knowledge is power." In particular you have been discussing the power consequences of the kinds of knowledge under the control of different social groups. Write an essay discussing the power implications of artificial intelligence technology, referring to this and McCorduck's essay (pp. 525–536).

4. For your local newspaper write a personal column on whether your doctor (or a person in another profession) can be replaced by a computer.

5. As part of this class's discussion of the effects of language, write an essay analyzing the use of questioning in this selection. Or write a broader essay on questioning as a powerful social tool. In considering how people use questions to get what they want and to control other people's behavior, you may consider how one or all of the following use questions: police, lawyers, teachers, small children, reporters, bureaucrats, the Internal Revenue Service, skilled conversationalists.

Natural and Artificial Intelligence

Robert Sokolowski

By definition, artificial things are made by art—by human craft and ingenuity. What have we created when we create artificial intelligence? Is it a kind of intelligence or is it just a kind of fake, only the illusion of an intelligence? In attempting to answer these questions, philosopher Sokolowski considers how intelligence is embodied in the use of symbolic systems, such as writing and symbolic logic, which are used within artificial intelligence. If writing has become part of our intelligence, then perhaps the symbolic manipulations of artificial intelligence are also in the process of becoming part of our intelligence. Moreover, by considering some of the less straightforward symbolic tasks humans accomplish with language, Sokolowski presents challenges for the future of artificial intelligence and starts to identify what gives each of us our separate identities as thinking individuals.

This article first appeared in a 1988 issue of *Daedalus*, an interdisciplinary journal published by the American Academy of Arts and Sciences, and read by a large number of professionals in many different fields. Articles in *Daedalus* tend to treat subjects on an intellectually serious level, while avoiding the specialized language and technical issues that may keep people from different disciplines from following the argument.

IN THIS ESSAY WE will not attempt to decide whether artificial 1 intelligence is the same as natural intelligence. Instead we will examine some of the issues and terms that must be clarified before that question can be resolved. We will discuss how the question about the relationship between natural and artificial intelligence can be formulated.

One of the first things that must be clarified is the ambiguous word 2 *artificial*. This adjective can be used in two senses, and it is important to determine which one applies in the term *artificial intelligence*. The word *artificial* is used in one sense when it is applied, say, to flowers, and in another sense when it is applied to light. In both cases something is called artificial because it is fabricated. But in the first usage artificial means that the thing seems to be, but really is not, what it looks like. The artificial is the merely apparent; it just shows how something else looks. Artificial flowers are only paper, not flowers at all; anyone who takes them to be flowers is mistaken. But artificial light is light and it does illuminate. It is fabricated as a substitute for natural light, but once fabricated it is what it seems to be. In this sense the artificial is not the merely apparent, not simply an imitation of something else. The appearance of the thing reveals what it is, not how something else looks.

The movement of an automobile is another example of something *3*
that is artificial in the second sense of the word. An automobile moves
artificially; it moves only because human beings have constructed it to
move and have made it go by the release of stored energy. But it really
does move—it does not only seem to be moving. In contrast, the
artificial wood paneling in the car only seems to be wood; it burns,
bends, breaks, and decays as plastic, not wood. It also smells, sounds,
and feels like plastic, not wood. It seems to be wood only to vision and
only from a certain angle and in certain kinds of light.

In which sense do we use the word *artificial* when we speak of artificial *4*
intelligence? Critics of artificial intelligence, those who disparage the
idea and say it has been overblown and oversold, would claim that the
term is used in the first sense, to mean the merely apparent. They would
say that artificial intelligence is really nothing but complex mechanical
structures and electrical processes that present an illusion (to the gullible)
of some sort of thinking. Supporters of the idea of artificial intelligence,
those who claim that the term names something genuine and not merely
apparent, would say that the word *artificial* is used in the second of the
senses we have distinguished. Obviously, they would say, thinking
machines are artifacts; obviously they are run by human beings; but
once made and set in motion, the machines do think. Their thinking
may be different from that of human beings in some ways, just as the
movement of a car is different from that of a rabbit and the flight of an
airplane is different from that of a bird, but it is a kind of genuine
thinking, just as there is genuine motion in the car and genuine flight in
the plane.

Suppose we were to claim that artificial intelligence is a genuine, *5*
though constructed, intelligence. Must we then prove the truth of that
claim? Are we obliged to show that the machines really think, that they
do not only seem to possess intelligence? Perhaps not; no one has to
prove the fact that artificial light illuminates and that airplanes really fly.
We just see that they do. If thinking machines display the activity of
thinking, why should we not admit that they truly are intelligent?

The problem is that thinking is not as visible and palpable as are *6*
illumination, motion, and flight; it is not as easy to say whether thinking
is present or not. Even when we talk with another human being, we
cannot always be sure if that person is speaking and acting thoughtfully
or merely reciting by rote, behaving automatically. And there are cases
in which machines only seem to think but really do not: the electronic
calculator can do remarkable things, but only someone who is deceived
by it—someone like the person who takes artificial flowers for real
ones—would say that the calculator possesses its own intelligence. The
calculator may reveal the intelligence of those who built and programmed it, but it does not originate its own thinking.

How is artificial intelligence different from the calculator? How is it *7*
different from numeric computing? What does it do that we can call its

own machine thinking, its own activity that cannot be dissolved into the thinking of the people who made and programmed the machine? If we are to claim that the thinking machine, though an artifact, does exhibit intelligence, we must clarify what we mean by the "thinking" it is said to execute. This may not be a proof, but it is an explanation, and some such justification seems to be required to support our claim that machines think.

Alan Turing set down the principle that if a machine behaves intelli-   8
gently, we must credit it with intelligence.[1] The behavior is the key. But the Turing test cannot stand by itself as the criterion for the intelligence of machines. Machine thinking will always reproduce only part of natural thinking; it may be limited, for instance, to the responses that are produced on a screen. In this respect our experience of the machine's thinking is like talking to someone on the telephone, not like being with that person and seeing him act, speak, and respond to new situations. How do we know that our partial view of the machine's intelligence is not like that angle of vision from which artificial flowers look real to us? How can we know that we are not being deceived if we are caught in the perspective from which a merely apparent intelligence looks very much like real intelligence? Some sort of argument has to be added to the Turing test to show that artificial intelligence is artificial in the second sense of the word and not in the first—that although it is constructed and partial, it is still genuine and not merely apparent. We need to say more about intelligence to show whether it really is there or not, and we need to clarify the difference between its natural and artificial forms.

I

In discussing the distinction between natural and artificial intelligence,   9
we must be careful not to establish divisions that are abrupt and naive. If we formulate our question in terms of stark alternatives we may put our argument into a straitjacket and deprive it of the flexibility it needs. With this rigid approach we might set the computer in opposition to the brain, considering natural intelligence an activity carried on in the brain, artificial intelligence an activity carried on in computers. Here the brain, there the computer; here the natural intelligence, there the artificial intelligence. The activity is defined by the material in which it takes place.

This approach is blunt and naive because it neglects something that   10
bridges natural and artificial intelligence: the written word. Artificial intelligence does not simply mimic the brain and nervous system; it transforms, codifies, and manipulates written discourse. And natural intelligence is not just an organic activity that occurs in a functioning brain; it also is embodied in the words that are written on paper, inscribed in clay, painted on a billboard. Writing comes between the brain and the computer.

When thinking is embodied in the written word, there is something *11*
artificial about it. Consider a flashing neon sign that says Hotel. People
do not react to the sign as they would to a rock or a tree. They both
read the sign and answer it. They behave toward it in a manner analogous to the way they would react to someone who told them that the
building was a hotel and that they could get a room there. Furthermore,
the person who put the sign where it is—the one who is stating something in the sign and can be held responsible for saying what the sign
says—does not have to remain near it for the sign to have its effect. He
can let the sign go; it works without him. It is an artifice, and one that
manifests and communicates something to someone, inviting both an
interpretation and a response.

Of course, artificial intelligence promises to do more than writing can *12*
do, but it has a foothold in writing: it puts into motion the thinking
that is embodied in writing. Our philosophical challenge is to clarify
what sort of motion thinking is.[2] The continuity between writing and
artificial intelligence should make us less apprehensive about being somehow replaced by thinking machines. In a way, we are already replaced
by the written word. If I leave written instructions behind me, I do not
have to be around for the instructions to take effect. But this does not
cancel my thinking; it enhances it. If we find written records in the ruins
of an ancient city, we do not think that the speakers in that city were
obliterated as speakers by the documents or that their subjectivity was
destroyed by them; we think that their speech was more vividly appreciated as speech in contrast with the written word. We also believe that
their thinking was amplified by their writing, not muffled by it, because
through the written word they are able to "speak" to us. Likewise, the
codification of writing in artificial intelligence does not mean that we
no longer have to think. Rather, our own thinking can be more vividly
appreciated in contrast with what can be done by machines; the fact that
some dimensions of thinking can be carried out mechanically makes us
more vividly aware of those dimensions that we alone can perform. If
artificial thinking can substitute for some of our thinking as artificial
light can take over some of the functions of natural light, then the kinds
of thinking for which no substitute is possible will surface more clearly
as our own.

The gradual diffusion of writing into human affairs can serve as a *13*
historical analogue for the seepage of artificial intelligence into human
exchanges. Writing did not simply replace the linguistic activities that
people carried out before there was writing; its major impact was to
make new kinds of activity possible and to give a new shape to old
kinds. It enlarged and differentiated economic, legal, political, and aesthetic activities, and it made history possible. It even allowed religion
to take on a new form: it permitted the emergence of religions involving
a book, with all the attendant issues of text, interpretation, and commentary. Writing did all this by amplifying intelligence. Printing accel-

erated the spread of the written word, but it did not change the nature of writing.

The question that can be put to artificial intelligence is whether it is *14* merely an extension of printing or a readjustment in the human enterprise that began when writing entered into human affairs. Word processing is clearly just a refinement of printing, a kind of glorified typing, but artificial intelligence appears to be more than that. It seems able to reform the embodiment of thought that was achieved in and by writing. What will artificial intelligence prove to be? Will it be just a postscript to writing, or will writing turn out to be a four-thousand-year prelude to artificial intelligence? Will writing's full impact lie in its being a preparation for mechanical thinking?

If artificial intelligence is indeed a transformation of writing, then it *15* is more like artificial light and less like artificial flowers: a genuine substitute for some forms of thought, not merely a superficial imitation. Thinking is shaped by writing; intelligence is modified when it takes on the written form; writing permits us to identify and differentiate things in ways that were not possible when we could speak but not write. If artificial intelligence can in turn transform writing, it may be able to embody a kind of intelligence that cannot occur in any other way, just as the automobile provides a kind of motion that was not available before the car was invented.

In the case of any new technology, the new is first understood within *16* the horizon set by the old. The earliest automobiles, for instance, look very much like carriages. It takes time for truly new possibilities to assert themselves, to shape both themselves and the environment within which they must find their place. It took time for the automobile to generate highways and garages. The expert systems developed in the early stages of artificial intelligence are following this pattern.[3] They attempt to replace a rather prosaic form of thinking, a kind that seems ripe for replacement: the kind exercised by the man in the information booth or the pharmacist—the person who knows a lot of facts and can coordinate them and draw out some of their implications. Expert systems are the horseless carriages of artificial intelligence. They are analogous to the early writings that just recorded the contents of the royal treasury or the distribution of the grain supply.

This is not to belittle expert systems. The initial, small, obvious *17* replacements for the old ways of doing things must settle in before the more distinctive accomplishments of a new intellectual form can take place—in this case, before the Dantes, Shakespeares, and Newtons, or the Jaguars, highways, and service stations of artificial intelligence can arise. And just as the people who experienced the beginning of writing could hardly imagine what Borges° and Bohr° could do, or what a

---

Jorge Luis Borges (1899–1986)—Argentinian author. **Niels Bohr (1885–1962)**—Danish atomic physicist.

national library or a medical research center or an insurance contract could be, so we—if artificial intelligence is indeed a renovation of writing—will find it hard to conceive what form the flowering of machine thinking may take.

Furthermore, there is a lot of human thinking that is rather mechanical. It demands only that we be well informed and that we be able to register relationships and draw inferences within what we know. The extent to which such routine thinking permeates our intellectual activity may only be realized when artificial thinking succeeds in doing most of this work for us.[4] Large tracts of scientific data-gathering, measuring, and correlation, of planning strategies in taxation or insurance, of working out acceptable combinations of antibiotics and matching them with infections, of constructing networks and schedules for airline travel, of figuring out how to cope with laws and regulations, are tasks that can be codified and organized according to specifiable rules. Artificial intelligence will most readily be able to relieve us of such laborious thinking. But, since there are few unmixed blessings, it is also likely to introduce new routines and drudgeries and unwelcome complexities that would not have arisen if computers had not come into being. *18*

We are quite properly astonished at how machines can store knowledge and information, and at how they even seem to "think" with this knowledge and information. But these capabilities of machines should not blind us to something that is simpler but perhaps even more startling: the uncanny storage and representation that occurs when meaning is embodied in the written word. In artificial intelligence the embodiment changes, but the major difference is in the new kind of embodying material, not in embodiment as such. The neon light flashing the word Hotel engages many of the features found in thinking machines: a meaning is available, a course of behavior is indicated, inferences are legitimated. There seems to be no one who speaks or owns the meaning—the meaning seems to float—and yet it is somehow there in the sign. The meaning is available for everyone and seems to outlast any particular human speaker. *19*

In artificial intelligence such meanings get embodied in materials that permit extremely complex manipulations of a syntactic kind. Hence the machine seems to reason, whereas the sign does not seem to reason but only to state. Instead of simply comparing computers and brains, we should also compare the "reasoning" of the machine with the "stating" of the sign, and examine storage and representation as they occur in the machine and in writing. *20*

It is true that artificial intelligence may go beyond printouts into artificially voiced speech. It may move beyond printing to the more subtle embodiment of meaning that occurs in sounds. If it succeeds in doing so, its "speech" will have been a transformation of its writing and will bear the imprint of writing. Artificial intelligence will have moved in a direction that is the reverse of that followed by natural thinking, which went from voiced speech to the written word. . . . *21*

III

The kind of thinking that artificial intelligence is supposed to be able to   22
emulate is deductive inferential reasoning—drawing out conclusions
once axioms and rules of derivation have been set down. Making deductions means reaching new truths on the basis of those we already
know. It was this sort of reasoning that Frege° wanted to formalize in
his new logical notation, the forerunner of computer languages. Frege
wanted to secure the accuracy of deductions by making each step in the
deduction explicit and formally justified, and by keeping the derivations
clear of any hidden premises. His notation was supposed to make such
purity of reasoning possible.[5] The subsequent outcome of Frege's efforts
have been logics and programs that make the deductions so explicit that
they can be carried out mechanically; indeed, the part of an artificial
intelligence program that draws out conclusions is sometimes called by
the colorful name of "the inference engine."

But drawing inferences is not the only kind of intelligence; there are   23
other kinds as well. We will discuss quotation and making distinctions
as two forms of intellectual activity that are not reducible to making
inferences. We will also discuss the desire that moves us to think. These
forms and aspects of natural intelligence—quotation, distinguishing, desire—are of interest to artificial intelligence in two ways. If artificial
intelligence can somehow embody them, it will prove itself all the more
successful in replacing natural intelligence. But if it becomes apparent
that artificial intelligence cannot imitate these powers and activities, we
will have discovered some of the borders of artificial thinking and will
better understand the difference between natural and artificial intelligence.

Artificial intelligence depends on both engineering and phenomenol-   24
ogy. The engineering is the development of hardware and programs;
the phenomenology is the analysis of natural cognition, the description
of the forms of thinking that the engineering may either try to imitate
and replace, or try to complement if it cannot replace them. Our present
discussion is a contribution to the phenomenology of natural intelligence, carried out in the context set by the purposes and possibilities of
artificial intelligence.

Quotation

One of the essential characteristics of natural intelligence is that we as   25
speakers can quote one another. This does not just mean that we can
repeat the words that someone else has said; it means that we can
appreciate and state how things look to someone else. Our citation of
someone else's words is merely the way we present to ourselves and

---

Gottlob Frege (1848–1925)—German philosopher of language.

others how the world seems to someone different from ourselves.[6] The ability to quote allows us to add perspectives to the things we experience and express. I see things not only from my own point of view, but as they seem to someone from another point of view, as they seem to someone who has a history different from mine, as they seem to someone with interests different from mine. It is a mark of greater intelligence to be able to appreciate things as they are experienced by others, a mark of lesser intelligence to be unable to do so: we are obtuse if we see things only one way, only our way.

We do not describe this ability properly if we call it the power to put *26* ourselves in someone else's place, as though the important thing were to share that person's moods and feelings, to sympathize with his subjective states. Even the feelings and moods we may want to share are a response to the way things look, and the way things look to someone can be captured in a quotation. Furthermore, there can be complex layers of quotation. I can, for example, cite not only how something seems to John, but also how its seeming to John seems to Mary. But no matter how complex the citation, I remain the one doing the quotations; I remain the citational center.

When we speak we always play off the way things seem to us against *27* the way they seem to others. The way things seem to others influences the way they seem to us. This supplement of alternative viewpoints is neglected when we concentrate on straight-line deductive inferences. The logic of deduction is a logic for monologues—a cyclopic, one-eyed logic. All diversity of points of view is filtered out. Only what follows from our premises is admitted. . . .

The restriction of logic to a single point of view is a legitimate and *28* useful abstraction, but it should be seen as limited, as not providing a full picture of human thinking. In our natural thinking, the opinions of others exercise an influence on the opinions we hold. We do not derive our positions only from the axioms we accept as true. If artificial intelligence is to emulate natural thinking, it must develop programs that can handle alternative viewpoints and not just straight-line inferential reasoning. It must develop a logic that will somehow take the expectations and statements of an interlocutor into account and formalize a conversational argument, not just a monological one. Such an expansion of artificial thinking would certainly help in the simulation of strategies and competitive situations. On the other hand, if quotation is beyond artificial intelligence, then perhaps we alone can be the final citational centers in thinking; perhaps our thinking machines will always just be quoted by us, never able to quote us in return.

Making Distinctions

Another kind of thinking different from inferential reasoning is the *29* activity of making distinctions.[7] A computer program can make a distinction in the sense that it can select one item instead of another, but such an activity assumes that the terms of the distinction have been programmed into the machine. A more elementary issue is whether a distinction can "dawn" on a machine. Can a machine originally establish the terms of a distinction?

In our natural thinking we do not infer distinctions. To recognize that 30 there are two distinct aspects to a situation is a more rudimentary act of thinking than is inference. It is also a mark of great intelligence, especially if the two terms of the distinction have not been previously established in the common notions stored in our language. For example, to appreciate that in a difficult situation there is something threatening and also something insidiously° desirable, and to have a sense of the special flavor of both the threat and the attraction, is a raw act of insight. It is not derived from premises. This sort of thinking, this dawning of distinctions, is at the origin of the categories that make up our common knowledge. It is prior to the axioms from which our inferences are derived.

Similarly, the stock of rules and representations that make up a com- 31 puter program, a data base, and a knowledge base presumes that the various stored representations have been distinguished, one from the other. This store of distinctions has to have been built up by natural intelligence. And each representation, each idea in natural intelligence, is not just soaked up by the mind as a liquid is soaked up by a blotter; each idea must also be distinguished from its appropriate others.[8] Some thinking, some distinguishing, goes into every notion we have. The thoughtful installation of an idea always involves distinction. Is there any way that artificial intelligence can generate a distinction between kinds of things? Can distinctions dawn on a machine? Or is the thinking machine like a household pet, fed only what we choose to give it?

Desire

Desire is involved with thinking in two ways. There is first the desire 32 to know more: the curiosity to learn more facts or the urge to understand more fully. But there is also the desire for other satisfactions such as nourishment, exercise, repose, and the like. Let us call these desires the passions. How is thinking related to passion?

A common way of expressing this relationship is to say that reason 33 is the slave of the passions.[9] In this view, the passions we are born with establish the ends we want to pursue, the satisfactions we seek; reason then comes into play to figure out how we can attain what the passions make us want. Desires provide the ends, thinking provides the means. In this view there is little room for rational discussion of goals because the goals are not established by reason.

Insidiously—slyly and threateningly.

Such an understanding of the relation between desire and reason fits *34* well with some presuppositions of artificial intelligence. It is easy to see that the computer might help us determine how to get to a goal— perhaps by using the General Problem Solver techniques initiated by Allen Newell, Cliff Shaw, and Herbert A. Simon—but the computer has to have the goals set down for it in advance, just as it needs to have its axioms set down.[10] The computer helps us reach our goals by working out inferences appropriate to the problem we face and the resources we have. Thus, if natural intelligence is indeed the slave of the passions, artificial intelligence may go far in replacing it.

But natural reason is not completely external to our desires. It is true *35* that as agents we begin with passions that precede thought, but before long our thinking enters into our desires and articulates what we want, so that we want in a thoughtful way. We desire not just nourishment but to eat a dinner; we want not just shelter but a home. Our passions become penetrated by intelligence. Furthermore, new kinds of desire arise that only a thoughtful being could have. We can desire honor, retribution, justice, forgiveness, valor, security against future dangers, political society. Our "rational desire" involves not only curiosity and the thoughtful articulation of the passions but also the establishment of ways of wanting that could not occur if we did not think.

Artificial intelligence might be able to do something with goals that *36* are set in advance, but can it emulate the mixture of desire and intelligence that makes up so much of what we think and do? Can it emulate curiosity? The thinking machine is moved by electrical energy, but can there be any way of giving it the kind of origin of motion that we call desire? Can its reasoning become a thoughtful desire? Or will all the wanting be always our own?

Drawing inferences is an intellectual activity that is less radically our *37* own than are the three activities we have just examined. Once axioms and rules of derivation have been set down, anyone can infer conclusions. Even if we happen to be the ones who carry out the deductions, we need not believe what we conclude. We need only say that these conclusions follow from those premises. Inference can remain largely syntactic. But in quotation we stand out more vividly on our own, since we distinguish our point of view from that of someone else. In making a distinction we also think more authentically, more independently, since we get behind any axioms and premises that someone might set down for us and simply allow one thing to distinguish itself from another. In thoughtful desire we express the character we have developed and the way our emotions have been formed by thinking. Quotation, distinction, and desire are more genuine forms of thinking than inference. And although these forms of thinking are more thoroughly our own, they do not become merely subjective or relativistic. They express an objectivity and a truth appropriate to the dimensions of thinking and being in which they are involved, dimensions that are neglected in inferential reasoning.[11]

If artificial intelligence were able to embody such forms of thinking *38* as quotation, distinction, and desire, it would seem much more like a genuine replacement for natural intelligence than a mere simulacrum° of it. It would seem, in its artificiality, to be similar to artificial light. It would seem somehow capable of originating its own thinking, of doing something not resolvable into the reasoning and responsibility of those who make and use the thinking machines. But even if artificial intelligence cannot fully embody such activities, it can at least complement them, and precisely by complementing them it can help us to understand what they are. We can learn a lot about quotation, distinction, and desire by coming to see why they cannot be mechanically reproduced, if that does turn out to be the case. We can learn a lot about natural intelligence by distinguishing it from artificial intelligence. And if artificial intelligence helps us understand what thinking is—whether by emulation or by contrast—it will succeed in being not just a technology but part of the science of nature.

Endnotes

[1]Alan Turing, "Computing Machinery and Intelligence," *Mind* 59 (1950):434–60.

[2]Frege speaks of a *Gedankenbewegung* as the process his notation is supposed to express. See "On the Scientific Justification of a Conceptual Notation," in *Conceptual Notation and Related Articles*, ed. T. Bynum (Oxford: Clarendon, 1972), 85.

[3]See Paul Harmon and David King, *Expert Systems in Business* (New York: John Wiley & Sons, 1985).

[4]Jacques Arsac asks, "How many semantic activities of man can be represented by signs in an appropriate language, and treated 'informatically' [i.e., coded and syntactically manipulated]? Who, at this point in time, can determine the borders that this science will not be able to cross?" Arsac, *La science informatique* (Paris: Dunod, 1970), 45.

[5]See G. P. Baker and P. M. S. Hacker, *Frege: Logical Excavations* (New York: Oxford University Press), 35: Frege's concept-script "was designed to give a perspicuous representation of inferences, to ensure that no tacit presuppositions remain hidden. . . . The heart of *Begriffsschrift* is then the elaboration of a notation for presenting inferences and the setting up of a formal system for rigorously testing their cogency. . . . He foreswore expressing in concept-script anything 'which is without importance for the chain of inference.' "

[6]See Robert Sokolowski, "Quotation," *Review of Metaphysics* 37 (1984):699–723.

Simulacrum—an unreal or vague semblance.

[7]See Robert Sokolowski, "Making Distinctions," *Review of Metaphysics* 32 (1979):639–76.

[8]An interesting example of how one term can rest on several distinctions, and how the "activation" of one or another of the distinctions can modify the sense of an actual use of the term, is found in Pierre Jacob, "Remarks on the Language of Thought," in *The Mind and the Machine: Philosophical Aspects of Artificial Intelligence,* ed. S. Torrance (New York: John Wiley, 1984), 74: "For Bob's use of the predicate [black], something will count as black if it is not perceived as dark blue or any other color but black, whether or not it is dyed. For Joe's use of the predicate, something will count as black not only if it looks black but also if it turns out not to be dyed." The incident sense of "not black" makes a difference in the current sense of "black."

[9]The phrase is, of course, from David Hume: "Reason is, and ought only to be the slave of the passions, and can never pretend to any other office than to serve and obey them." *A Treatise of Human Nature,* ed. L. A. Selby-Bigge (New York: Oxford University Press, 1960), vol. 3, 415.

[10]For a summary of the General Problem Solver (GPS) and means-ends analysis, see John Haugeland, *Artificial Intelligence* (Cambridge: MIT Press, 1985), 178–83.

[11]In *Artificial Intelligence,* Haugeland contrasts two models of thinking: the "Aristotelian," in which the mind is said to think by absorbing resemblances of things, and the "Hobbesian," in which thinking is said to be computation carried out on mental symbols. Haugeland calls Hobbes "the grandfather of AI" because of his computational understanding of reason (p. 23), but he concludes that we may need to invoke a theory of meaning that involves both resemblance and computation (p. 222). It seems to me that rich resources for such a theory can be found in the philosophy of Husserl, for whom all presentations are articulated and all mental articulations are presentational. For Husserl, syntax and semantics are essentially parts of a larger whole. As against Haugeland I would say, however, that the mind should not be conceived as absorbing resemblances of things but simply as presenting things in many different ways.

Rhetorical Analysis Through Annotation

Sokolowski uses many analogies throughout the article to develop his ideas. Some of these analogies are brief and make only a passing point, while others, such as the analogy between written language and artificial intelligence, extend over long passages.

Put a star in the margin next to every analogy you find and circle the two items being compared. In the margin then briefly explain the point being made by each analogy. Finally, if the analogy is lengthy, mark where the analogy begins and ends.

Discuss how Sokolowski uses analogies to develop his thinking. At what points do his arguments entirely depend on analogical thinking and at what points do the analogies serve only as a passing clarification?

Discussion Questions

Interpreting the Text

1. What is the distinction Sokolowski makes between two types of "artificial" objects? Which type is artificial sweetener an example of? Artificial cream? Artificial cloth? Artificial emotions?

2. Why does Sokolowski not attempt to answer whether artificial intelligence is the same as natural intelligence? Does this mean he believes artificial intelligence is necessarily less intelligent than natural intelligence?

3. In what way is our natural intelligence dependent on the artifice of language? How has the development of the artifice of language changed our natural intelligence? How is artificial intelligence a transformation of writing? How is artificial intelligence different from writing? Will artificial intelligence then further change writing and our natural intelligence?

4. Why is quotation more than just a mechanical language skill? How does quotation permit us to appreciate the viewpoint of others and adopt multiple, perspectives in our own thinking?

5. Why is creating a distinction more difficult than categorizing items according to an existing distinction? Why is the ability to create new distinctions a significant form of intelligence? Have you ever found it useful or necessary to make a distinction between two objects or ideas?

6. How does desire determine what we think about? How does intelligence transform our desires? What is the relationship of your own personal desires and your thinking?

7. Why does Sokolowski find quotation, distinction, and desire more genuine forms of thinking than inference? In what way do they help establish our individuality without becoming simply subjective?

Considering the Issues

8. Insofar as our intelligence is based on such artifices as mathematics and written language, is our intelligence artificial? Is it "natural" for people to write essays, read books, deliver speeches, or do calculus problems?

9. In which school subjects is it most useful to adopt a single point of view, and in which is it useful to adopt a number of perspectives? Does the same pattern of usefulness of different points of view occur in the professional disciplines corresponding to the school subjects? How do patterns of quotation in writing in these disciplines correspond to the usefulness of multiple points of view? You may use examples from this anthology to help you think through these questions.

10. Besides *quotation, making distinctions,* and *desire,* what other types of thinking might Sokolowski have used to indicate activities humans can do, but machines cannot yet do?

11. Do you think computers will ever be able to quote, create new distinctions, or express desire? If they could, how would that change your opinion about how they think and whether they were intelligent? Would you then consider machines as individuals with personalities?

Writing Suggestions

1. As part of this course's concern for how language is used in academic disciplines, write an essay discussing the way in which writing a professional article is a form of thinking that involves other people in the thinking process. You may use any appropriate article in this book as an example to discuss. In developing your own thoughts you may wish to refer to Sokolowski's analogy of the flashing "Hotel" sign.

2. Using quotations to show the different points of view of the articles you have read in this unit, write an essay on "What does it mean that machines think?" This essay will be for an introductory course in computer concepts.

3. Imagine you are Robert Sokolowski and you wish to add a fourth item to your discussion of special forms of thinking. Write a few paragraphs discussing hope or any other appropriate kind of thinking, similar to the paragraphs on quotations, making distinctions, and desire.

4. In response to Sokolowski's claims that artificial intelligence does not have to be the same thing as natural intelligence to be intelligent, write an essay for a philosophy course arguing that artificial intelligence is not intelligent or that artificial intelligence is the same as human intelligence.

Some Expert Systems Need Common Sense

John McCarthy

The design of expert systems raises fundamental issues in philosophy, psychology, and human behavior about how we relate to the world through thought. John McCarthy, professor of computer science at Stanford University and one of the leading conceptual thinkers in the field, considers the role of common sense in human and artificial intelligence. In particular he uses the shortcomings of MYCIN (see pages 545–559) to illustrate limitations of typical expert systems; he then suggests some ways to overcome these limitations. In a wide-ranging philosophical style, McCarthy considers how issues in human behavior, psychology, computer science, and medical practice come together in systems design. This essay was originally written in 1984 as a speech to a gathering of computer experts to provoke them into rethinking their program design strategies.

AN *EXPERT SYSTEM* IS a computer program intended to embody 1 the knowledge and ability of an expert in a certain domain. . . . Their performance in their specialized domains is often very impressive. Nevertheless, hardly any of them have certain *commonsense* knowledge and ability possessed by any non-feeble-minded human. This lack makes them "brittle." By this is meant that they are difficult to expand beyond the scope originally contemplated by their designers, and they usually do not recognize their own limitations. Many important applications will require commonsense abilities. The object of this lecture is to describe commonsense abilities and the problems that require them.

Commonsense facts and methods are only very partially understood 2 today, and extending this understanding is the key problem facing artificial intelligence.

This is not exactly a new point of view. I have been advocating 3 "Computer Programs with Common Sense" since I wrote a paper with that title in 1958.[1] Studying commonsense capability has sometimes been popular and sometimes unpopular among artificial intelligence (AI) researchers. At present it is popular, perhaps because new AI knowledge offers new hope of progress. Certainly AI researchers today know a lot more about what common sense is than I knew in 1958—or in 1969 when I wrote another paper on the subject.[2] However, expressing commonsense knowledge in formal terms has proved very difficult, and the number of scientists working in the area is still far too small.

One of the best known expert systems is MYCIN,[3,4] a program for 4 advising physicians on treating bacterial infections of the blood and meningitis. It does reasonably well without common sense, provided the user has common sense and understands the program's limitations.

MYCIN conducts a question and answer dialogue. After asking basic 5 facts about the patient such as name, sex, and age, MYCIN asks about suspected bacterial organisms, suspected sites of infection, the presence of specific symptoms (e.g., fever, headache) relevant to diagnosis, the outcome of laboratory tests, and some others. It then recommends a certain course of antibiotics. While the dialogue is in English, MYCIN avoids having to understand freely written English by controlling the dialogue. It outputs sentences, but the user types only single words or standard phrases. Its major innovations over many previous expert systems are that it uses measures of uncertainty (not probabilities) for its diagnoses and the fact that it is prepared to explain its reasoning to the physician, so he can decide whether to accept it.

Our discussion of MYCIN begins with its ontology. The ontology 6 of a program is the set of entities that its variables range over. Essentially this is what it can have information about.

MYCIN's ontology includes bacteria, symptoms, tests, possible sites 7
of infection, antibiotics, and treatments. Doctors, hospitals, illness, and
death are absent. Even patients are not really part of the ontology,
although MYCIN asks for many facts about the specific patient. This is
because patients are not values of variables, and MYCIN never compares
the infections of two different patients. It would therefore be difficult
to modify MYCIN to learn from its experience.

MYCIN's program, written in a general scheme called EMYCIN, is 8
a so-called production system. A production system is a collection of
rules, each of which has two parts—a pattern part and an action part.
When a rule is activated, MYCIN tests whether the pattern part matches
the data base. If so this results in the variables in the pattern being
matched to whatever entities are required for the match of the data base.
If not the pattern fails and MYCIN tries another. If the match is successful, then MYCIN performs the action part of the pattern using the
values of the variables determined by the pattern part. The whole process
of questioning and recommending is built up out of productions.

The production formalism turned out to be suitable for representing 9
a large amount of information about the diagnosis and treatment of
bacterial infections. When MYCIN is used in its intended manner it
scores better than medical students or interns or practicing physicians
and on a par with experts in bacterial diseases when the latter are asked
to perform in the same way. However, MYCIN has not been put into
production use, and the reasons given by experts in the area varied when
I asked whether it would be appropriate to sell MYCIN cassettes to
doctors wanting to put it on their microcomputers. Some said it would
be okay if there were a means of keeping MYCIN's data base current
with new discoveries in the field, i.e., with new tests, new theories,
new diagnoses, and new antibiotics. For example, MYCIN would have
to be told about Legionnaire's disease and the associated *Legionnella*
bacteria which became understood only after MYCIN was finished.
(MYCIN is very stubborn about new bacteria, and simply replies "un-
recognized response.")

Others say that MYCIN is not even close to usable except experi- 10
mentally, because it does not know its own limitations. I suppose this
is partly a question of whether the doctor using MYCIN is trusted to
understand the documentation about its limitations. Programmers always develop the idea that the users of their programs are idiots, so the
opinion that doctors are not smart enough not to be misled by MYCIN's
limitations may be at least partly a consequence of this ideology.

An example of MYCIN not knowing its limitations can be excited 11
by telling MYCIN that the patient has *Cholerae vibrio°* in his intestines.
MYCIN will cheerfully recommend two weeks of tetracycline and nothing else. Presumably this would indeed kill the bacteria, but most likely

---

Cholerae vibrio—the bacterium causing cholera.

the patient will be dead of cholera long before that. However, the physician will presumably know that the diarrhea has to be treated and look elsewhere for how to do it.

On the other hand it may be really true that some measure of common   *12* sense is required for usefulness even in this narrow domain. We will list some areas of commonsense knowledge and reasoning ability and also apply the criteria to MYCIN and other hypothetical programs operating in MYCIN's domain.

What Is Common Sense?

Understanding commonsense capability is now a hot area of research in   *13* artificial intelligence, but there is not yet any consensus. We will try to divide commonsense capability into commonsense knowledge and commonsense reasoning, but even this cannot be made firm. Namely, what one man builds as a reasoning method into his program, another can express as a fact using a richer ontology. However, the latter can have problems in handling in a good way the generality he has introduced.

Commonsense Knowledge

We shall discuss various areas of commonsense knowledge.   *14*

1. The most salient commonsense knowledge concerns situations that change in time as a result of events. The most important events are actions, and for a program to plan intelligently, it must be able to determine the effects of its own actions.

Consider the MYCIN domain as an example. The situation with which MYCIN deals includes the doctor, the patient, and the illness. Since MYCIN's actions are advice to the doctor, full planning would have to include information about the effects of MYCIN's output on what the doctor will do. Since MYCIN does not know about the doctor, it might plan the effects of the course of treatment on the patient. However, it does not do this either. Its rules give the recommended treatment as a function of the information elicited about the patient, but MYCIN makes no prognosis° of the effects of the treatment. Of course, the doctors who provided the information built into MYCIN considered the effects of the treatments.

Ignoring prognosis is possible because of the specific narrow domain in which MYCIN operates. Suppose, for example, a certain antibiotic had the precondition for its usefulness that the patient not have a fever. Then MYCIN might have to make a plan for getting rid of the patient's fever and verifying that it was gone as a part of the plan for using the antibiotic. In other domains, expert systems and other AI programs

---

Prognosis—prediction or outlook for the patient.

have to make plans, but MYCIN does not. Perhaps if I knew more about bacterial diseases, I would conclude that their treatment sometimes really does require planning and that lack of planning ability limits MYCIN's utility.

The fact that MYCIN does not give a prognosis is certainly a limitation. For example, MYCIN cannot be asked on behalf of the patient or the administration of the hospital when the patient is likely to be ready to go home. The doctor who uses MYCIN must do that part of the work himself. Moreover, MYCIN cannot answer a question about a hypothetical treatment, e.g., What will happen if I give this patient penicillin? or even What bad things might happen if I give this patient penicillin?

2. Various formalisms are used in artificial intelligence for representing facts about the effects of actions and other events. However, all systems that I know about give the effects of an event in a situation by describing a new situation that results from the event. This is often enough, but it does not cover the important case of concurrent events and actions. For example, if a patient has cholera, while the antibiotic is killing the cholera bacteria, the damage to the patient's intestines is causing a loss of fluids that is likely to be fatal. Inventing a formalism that will conveniently express people's commonsense knowledge about concurrent events is a major unsolved problem of AI.

3. The world is extended in space and is occupied by objects that change their positions and are sometimes created and destroyed. The common-sense facts about this are difficult to express but are probably not important in the MYCIN example. A major difficulty is in handling the kind of partial knowledge people ordinarily have. I can see part of the front of a person in the audience, and my idea of his shape uses this informaion to approximate his total shape. Thus I do not expect him to stick out two feet in back even though I cannot see that he does not. However, my idea of the shape of his back is less definite than that of the parts I can see.

4. The ability to represent and use knowledge about knowledge is often required for intelligent behavior. What airline flights there are to Singapore are recorded in the issue of the International Airline Guide current for the proposed flight day. Travel agents know how to book airline flights and can compute what they cost. An advanced MYCIN might need to reason that Dr. Smith knows about cholera, because he is a specialist in tropical medicine.

5. A program that must cooperate or compete with people or other programs must be able to represent information about their knowledge, beliefs, goals, likes and dislikes, intentions, and abilities. An advanced MYCIN might need to know that a patient will not take a bad-tasting medicine unless he is convinced of its necessity.

6. Common sense includes much knowledge whose domain overlaps that of the exact sciences but differs from it epistemologically.° For example, if I knock over the glass of water on the podium, everyone knows that the glass will break and the water will spill. Everyone knows that this will take a fraction of a second and that the water will not splash even 10 feet. However, this information is not obtained by using the formula for a falling body or the Navier-Stokes equations governing fluid flow. We do not have the input data for the equations, most of us do not know them, and we could not integrate them fast enough to decide whether to jump out of the way. This commonsense physics is contiguous with scientific physics. In fact scientific physics is imbedded in commonsense physics, because it is commonsense physics that tells us what the equation $s = \frac{1}{2} g\, t^2$ means. If MYCIN were extended to be a robot physician it would have to know commonsense physics and maybe also some scientific physics.

It is doubtful that the facts of the commonsense world can be repre- **15** sented adequately by production rules. Consider the fact that when two objects collide they often make a noise. This fact can be used to make a noise, to avoid making a noise, to explain a noise, or to explain the absence of a noise. It can also be used in specific situations involving a noise but also to understand general phenomena, e.g., should an intruder step on the gravel, the dog will hear it and bark. A production rule embodies a fact only as part of a specific procedure. Typically they match facts about specific objects, e.g., a specific bacterium, against a general rule and get a new fact about those objects.

Much present AI research concerns how to represent facts in ways **16** that permit them to be used for a wide variety of purposes.

Commonsense Reasoning

Our ability to use commonsense knowledge depends on being able to **17** do commonsense reasoning.

Much artificial intelligence inference is not designed to use directly **18** the rules of inference of any of the well-known systems of mathematical logic. There is often no clear separation in the program between determining what inferences are correct and the strategy for finding the inferences required to solve the problem at hand. Nevertheless, the logical system usually corresponds to a subset of first-order logic.° Sysems provide for inferring a fact about one or two particular objects from other facts about these objects and a general rule containing variables. Most expert systems, including MYCIN, never infer general statements, i.e., quantified formulas.

Epistemologically—in the nature of its knowledge.   **First-order logic**—direct logical operations, involving no two- or three-stage operations.

Human reasoning also involves obtaining facts by observation of the *19* world, and computer programs also do this. Robert Filman did an interesting thesis on observation in a chess world where many facts that could be obtained by deduction are in fact obtained by observation. MYCIN does not require this, but our hypothetical robot physician would have to draw conclusions from a patient's appearance, and computer vision is not ready for it.

An important new development in AI (since the middle 1970s) is the . formalization of nonmonotonic reasoning.

Deductive reasoning in mathematical logic has the following property, *21* called monotonicity by analogy with similar mathematical concepts. Suppose we have a set of assumptions from which follow certain conclusions. Now suppose we add additional assumptions. There may be some new conclusions, but every sentence that was a deductive consequence of the original hypotheses is still a consequence of the enlarged set.

Ordinary human reasoning does not share this monotonicity property. *22* If you know that I have a car, you may conclude that it is a good idea to ask me for a ride. If you then learn that my car is being fixed (which does not contradict what you knew before), you no longer conclude that you can get a ride. If you now learn that the car will be out in half an hour you reverse yourself again.

Several AI researchers, for example Marvin Minsky, have pointed out *23* that intelligent computer programs will have to reason nonmonotonically.[5] Some concluded that therefore logic is not an appropriate formalism.

However, it has turned out that deduction in mathematical logic can *24* be supplemented by additional modes of nonmonotonic reasoning, which are just as formal as deduction and just as susceptible to mathematical study and computer implementation. Formalized nonmonotonic reasoning turns out to give certain rules of conjecture rather than rules of inference—their conclusions are appropriate, but may be disconfirmed when more facts are obtained. One such method is *circumscription*, described in Reference 6.

A mathematical description of circumscription is beyond the scope of *25* this lecture, but the general idea is straightforward. We have a property applicable to objects or a relation applicable to pairs or triplets, etc., of objects. This property or relation is constrained by some sentences taken as assumptions, but there is still some freedom left. Circumscription further constrains the property or relation by requiring it to be true of a minimal set of objects.

As an example, consider representing the facts about whether an object *26* can fly in a data base of commonsense knowledge. We could try to provide axioms that will determine whether each kind of object can fly, but this would make the data base very large. Circumscription allows us to express the assumption that only those objects can fly for which there is a positive statement about it. Thus there will be positive statements that birds and airplanes can fly and no statement that camels can fly. Since we do not include negative statements in the data base, we could provide for flying camels, if there were any, by adding statements without removing existing statements. This much is often done by a simpler method—the *closed world assumption* discussed by Raymond Reiter. However, we also have exceptions to the general statement that birds can fly. For example, penguins, ostriches, and birds with certain feathers removed cannot fly. Moreover, more exceptions may be found and even exceptions to the exceptions. Circumscription allows us to make the known exceptions and to provide additional exceptions to be added later—again without changing existing statements.

Nonmonotonic reasoning also seems to be involved in human communication. Suppose I hire you to build me a bird cage, and you build it without a top, and I refuse to pay on the grounds that my bird might fly away. A judge will side with me. On the other hand suppose you build it with a top, and I refuse to pay full price on the grounds that my bird is a penguin, and the top is a waste. Unless I told you that my bird could not fly, the judge will side with you. We can therefore regard it as a communication convention that if a bird can fly the fact need not be mentioned, but if the bird cannot fly and it is relevant, then the fact must be mentioned.

References

[1]McCarthy, J. 1960. Programs with common sense. *In* Proceedings of the Teddington Conference on the Mechanization of Thought Processes. Her Majesty's Stationery Office. London, England.

[2]McCarthy, J. & P. J. Hayes. 1969. Some philosophical problems from the standpoint of artificial intelligence. *In* Machine Intelligence 4. D. Michie, Ed.: 463–502. American Elsevier. New York, N.Y.

[3]Shortliffe, E. H. 1976. Computer-Based Medical Consultations: MYCIN. American Elsevier. New York, N.Y.

[4]Davis, R., B. Buchanan & E. Shortliffe. 1977. Production rules as a representation for a knowledge-based consultation program. Artif. Intell. **8**(1): 15–45.

[5]Minsky, M. 1974. A Framework for Representing Knowledge. MIT Artif. Intell. Memo 252.

[6]McCarthy, J.. 1980. Circumscription—a form of non-monotonic reasoning. Artif. Intell. **13**(1,2): 27–39.

Rhetorical Analysis Through Annotation

In philosophic fashion, this essay introduces concepts, defines them, and applies them to a specific problem. These concepts may be labeled with familiar terms that are then redefined more precisely or they may be labeled with unfamiliar, special terms.

Circle the major conceptual terms presented. Mark with a single line in the margin where these terms are defined. Mark with a double line in the margin where the concepts are applied to a problem of artificial intelligence. Note that major concepts, such as common sense, may have several subconcepts. Place a star next to each use of MYCIN as an illustration of a concept.

Discuss how McCarthy's introduction of new concepts sets up an analysis of artificial intelligence that helps reveal new issues to be considered in design.

Discussion Questions

Interpreting the Text

1. What is an expert system? What makes an expert system brittle? What are the characteristics of brittleness?

2. What does McCarthy mean by common sense? What does he mean by a program's ontology? What does he mean by a richer ontology? How is it different than common sense? How would a richer ontology solve some problems that would otherwise call for common sense?

3. What are the six characteristics of common-sense knowledge? What are the characteristics of common-sense reasoning?

4. What is the difficulty concerning concurrent events?

5. Why is it doubtful that common sense can be adequately represented by production rules?

Considering the Issues

6. How does MYCIN lack common sense?

7. Why does McCarthy say that MYCIN does not know how to make plans?

8. Monotonic is a metaphor from music, where it means sounding only a single note. What is the analogy with monotonic thinking?

9. Describe examples of nonmonotonic thinking that may occur in buying lunch, choosing courses, taking an exam, or writing an essay.

10. How does circumscription resemble common-sense thinking carried out by humans?

Writing Suggestions

1. Paraphrase paragraph 18 on page 580 beginning "Much artificial intelligence. . . ." Your aim is to clarify the meaning of this passage for a friend who is having trouble understanding it.

2. For a forum at your college where John McCarthy has appeared, write a response. You might discuss whether people meet his criteria of common sense,

or whether McCarthy has overlooked some aspects of common sense, or what a remarkable accomplishment common sense is.

3. For a philosophy course, write a paper on what it means to have common sense or on whether computers may one day be capable of common sense.

4. For an audience of people interested in some activity that you understand well (such as baseball, cooking, chess, drawing, or camping), write an essay explaining some fundamental concepts that would help your readers understand and want to participate in the activity.

What Is It Like to Be a Machine?

Ajit Narayanan

Artificial intelligence raises philosophical questions in its implications as well as its design. If we create thinking machines, in what sense, if any, do these machines think? Does thinking make the machines into creatures who have consciousness? Science fiction writers have long postulated that machines will gain minds of their own and rebel against their human oppressors. Some philosophers argue that the computer's apparent thought is nothing but the consequences of a mechanistic program and is, therefore, not real thought. Others have argued that if a computer can receive information, learn, and add to or modify its own rules, then it does have a type of consciousness.

In this selection Ajit Narayanan, a philosopher at Exeter University in England, supports the latter position through the thought experiment of imagining how an artificial intelligence system might describe itself. In this thought experiment from 1984, the philosopher uses techniques of science fiction to provide idealized evidence for philosophic discussion.

"MY NAME IS MONNY. If you were to ask me how I got such a   1
name, I would reply that my real name is MONITOR and that the humans who are responsible for looking after me have nicknamed me 'Monny' for sort. If you were to ask me why I am talking to you at this moment, my reply would be that this is because you asked me to. In fact, I am replying because you asked me a question 'Tell me, Monny, what is it like to be you?' If anyone asks me a question of a vague but personal nature, I reply in the following manner. First, I give some brief details about myself (and I am doing this now). Secondly, I give one or two examples of my recent work to provide some information to the

enquirer about how I function. Thirdly, I ask the enquirer whether this suffices as an answer to his or her question. Generally, it does. If you were to ask me how it is that I am replying to you in this form, I would reply that I have a strategy for constructing reponses to questions of a vague but personal nature from humans such that these responses have the underlying form of a short story with me, Monny, as the central character.

"My task is to monitor the behaviour of a nuclear reactor, the control-   2
room of which you are now in. If you ask me how I do this, my reply is that I have very many rules which are expressed in conditional form. Such rules have an antecedent° and a consequent.° If an antecedent of some rule matches some information I currently have in part of my memory known as working memory, I add the consequent of the rule to my working memory, making whatever changes are necessary to keep my knowledge of the behaviour of the nuclear reactor consistent.

"If you were to ask me about the nature of such rules, I would reply   3
that some are very specific in that they deal with very limited antecedents and consequents, and others are very general in that they deal with overall plans and strategies. If you were to ask me for examples of such rules, I would first check your security clearance and, depending on the level of clearance you have, I would reply accordingly. I see that you have low security clearance. Then my example of a specific rule would be 'If the temperature of the cooling fluid rises over a certain level—let us call this level X—then I initiate a sensory fault checking sequence which, if clear, leads me to a check of various valves for signs of leakage, and so on'. If a valve is leaking or not operating properly, I try to rectify the fault immediately and at the same time send a message to the main console describing my progress. If the human operators desire more information, I can invoke a trace mechanism which decribes in great detail my attempts to identify and rectify the fault. If the worst possible case were to arise, I can shut down the reactor completely in thirty minutes.

"My example of a general rule is 'If there is a certain sequence of rules   4
that is always followed for a certain initial antecedent and a particular state of working memory such that the result is a certain consequent, then I can create a short-cut rule which will take me from the antecedent to the consequent in one rule, provided that I invoke verification and integrity-checking procedures which check the correctness of the rule and attach a certain probability to the rule being correct if the rule cannot be shown deductively to be correct'. I must also report this rule to the human operators together with a list of modifications necessary to implement the rule. If they have no objection I add this rule to my collec-

---

Antecedent—the "if" term of an if–then logical statement.   **Consequent**—the "then" term that concludes a logical syllogism.

tion and make whatever changes are necessary to optimize my rule set. If this involves deleting rules which no longer apply, I do so.

"Given these rules, I have so far been able to monitor the behaviour 5 of the reactor adequately and have dealt with several minor faults successfully. If I were to come across a situation not catered for by my rule set, I can enter a so-called 'Type Minus One' state, which fortunately I have not been required to do so far in real-life situations, although I have entered this state for purely hypothetical purposes when I do not have very much to do. According to this state, I can generate any consequent I like from a null antecedent° and I then attempt to cater for the situation using my current rule set and adding rules as I go along. If you were to ask me for an example, I would mention the time that I hypothesized that a flood had taken place. According to my rule set at that time, I had no rules for dealing with the possibility that the reactor and the control room would be submerged under water. I then devised a set of rules through trial and error to take into account this possibility and cater for it. When I reported this possibility back to the human operators, they told me that a flood situation was impossible given the position of the reactor above sea-level, but that I should add the new rules to my rule set for the sake of completeness.

"I have now completed my response. Will this suffice?" 6

Rhetorical Analysis Through Annotation

Narayanan, through Monny, claims that Monny's answers, including this text, are constructed by a three-step procedure.

In the opening paragraph mark Monny's three rules for constructing an answer.

In the margin, next to each section of Monny's answer write 1, 2, 3 to identify which of the three procedures he is currently following. If Monny at any point uses some other procedure, write "other" and describe in the margin the procedure being used.

Discuss the rhetorical consequences of the rules Narayanan has established and evaluate how well Narayanan is able to construct an answer in accordance with the rules. Is it possible to give an adequate account following the procedures? If not, what are the difficulties?

Discussion Questions

Interpreting the Text

1. What does Monny do? How does Monny do it? What kind of thinking procedures does Monny carry out to complete these tasks?

Null antecedent—having no information in the if–term of an if–then statement.

2. How does Monny create new rules? Does Monny do it on its own? How do people enter into Monny's rule-creation and modification procedures?

3. In what ways is Monny's account consistent with the descriptions of automated reasoning (538–543) and MYCIN (545–559)? Does Monny have the common sense McCarthy discusses (576–582)?

Considering the Issues

4. What procedures ordinarily considered mental must Monny be able to follow to describe itself as it does here?

5. In what ways are Monny's "thought" and self-consciousness like a human's and in what ways different?

6. Do you believe Monny is a creature with consciousness? Should it be granted equal status with living creatures? Plants? Reptiles? Dogs? Horses? Humans?

7. How does the form of argument here compare with the kinds of writing you would expect from a philosopher? Why do you suppose Narayanan writes like this? What is a thought experiment? How is this one? Can a thought experiment be a proper form of philosophical reasoning? In what other fields and on what other occasions might one use a thought experiment?

Writing Suggestions

1. For a philosophy class write a monologue on "what it is like to be a dog (horse, tree, flower, amoeba, stereo system)" in order to reveal the mental operations, consciousness, or state of being it might have.

2. For a course on computers write a short essay identifying and analyzing the various thinking operations Monny performs.

3. For a church group, philosophical club, or spiritual gathering of some sort, prepare a talk on the differences between the thinking processes of humans and machines.

Thinking of Yourself as a Machine

Sherry Turkle

Computers make us think about psychology and philosophy not just to understand what a computer is and does, but also because we compare the workings of the computer to those of our own minds. Over and over we hear the question, does artificial intelligence mimic actual human processes? Is our intelligence just as artificial as that of computers? One of the original impetuses of artificial intelligence was to investigate how the human mind worked. Whatever psychologists may eventually come to believe, the metaphor of artificial intelligence has intrigued many people who perceive themselves in computer terms and identify with a computer culture.

Sociologists and anthropologists study beliefs in relation to people's community, culture, and activity. Sociologist Sherry Turkle examines how computer culture has influenced people's views of themselves in a book entitled *The Second Self* (1984), from which the following selection is taken.

MARK IS AN MIT junior and a computer-science major. He has always 1
been interested in logic and systems. When asked to think back to his childhood games, he does not talk about playing with other children. He recalls how he "sorted two thousand Lego pieces by color, size, and shape." He liked the feel of sorting the pieces, and he liked making the Legos into complex structures, "things that you would never expect to be able to make from Legos." Although Mark spends most of his time working with computers, he sees himself as a professional in training rather than as a computer hacker. He cares about his schoolwork, gets top grades, and "tries to keep things other than computers in my life." One of these is being "Dungeon Master" for one of MIT's many on-going games of Dungeons and Dragons. His game has been going for a couple of years, and he is pretty sure it is the best game in the Boston area.

> The people who play my dungeon use it to express their personalities, and also to play out sides of their personalities that they hide in their everyday life. That's one of the things that is so fantastic about the game. But you have to make a great game for that to really happen. You have to hold them in your world, but you have to give them a lot of space to be themselves. It is a very complicated thing, an art.

Mark spends many hours a week preparing for the Sunday-afternoon 2
meeting of his dungeon: "at least five hours of preparation for each hour of play. And sometimes we play for five hours. It's a responsibility. I take it very seriously. It's one of the most creative things I do."

Mark has strong relationships with the members of his dungeon. He 3
is more able to involve himself with them than with people he meets outside of the structure of the game. The dungeon offers him a safe world built on a complex set of rules. Within it he can use his artistry to build social situations much as he built his Lego constructions. Dungeons and Dragons allows Mark to be with people in a way that is as comfortable for him as dealing with things. It is his solution to a familiar dilemma: he needs and yet fears personal intimacy. He has found a way

of being a loner without being alone. One might say that for him Dungeons and Dragons becomes a social world structured like a machine.

There is another and more dramatic way in which Mark shows his *4* preference for machinelike systems. He has elaborated a theory of psychology that leads him to see himself and everyone else as a machine. The theory, which he claims to be his own, is made up largely of ideas current at the Artificial Intelligence Laboratory at MIT. We see in Mark how these ideas are appropriated by someone who is not part of the AI world, but who is close enough to be a first link on the chain of these ideas moving out.

Over the past year, he has built up a detailed picture of exactly how *5* the Mark-machine works through a self-consciously introspective method. "Like Freud," he tells me. "I don't follow other people's theories. I just think about myself and make up my own—the way Freud came up with his theories and then looked around him and fit things in." When Freud "looked around" he "fit in" ideas from his scientific culture, from physics and biology. Mark's is a computer culture. He uses computer systems to think about all complex systems, especially to consider the complexity of his own mind.

Mark begins with the idea that the brain is a computer. "This does *6* not mean that the structure of the brain resembles the architecture of any present-day computer system, but the brain can be modeled using components emulated by modern digital parts. At no time does any part of the brain function in a way that cannot be emulated in digital or analog logic." In *Tron,*° the programs are complicated, psychological, and "motivated" beings. They do a lot of running around, planning, plotting, and fighting. In Mark's model the computational actors in the brain are simple. Each is a little computer with an even smaller program, and each "knows only one thought." Mark takes the "one thought" limitation seriously. "One processor might retain the visual impression of a computer cabinet. Another might retain the auditory memory of a keyboard being typed at. A third processor might maintain the visual image of a penguin."

In Mark's model, all of the processors have the same status: they are *7* "observers" at a long trough. Everything that appears in the trough can be seen simultaneously by all the observers at every point along it. The trough with its observers is a multiprocessing computer system. Using computer jargon, Mark describes the trough as a "bus," a trunk line that puts actors in contact with each other. Their communication options are very limited. Each looks at the trough and when something appears that relates to what "he" knows, "all he can do is put his knowledge in."

Tron—a 1982 science fiction film about a human trapped inside a computer.

The trough plus observers make up the central processor of the brain. The consciousness of the brain is only a reflection of what is in the trough at a given time. Consciousness is a passive observer looking at the trough. It does not even see everything in the trough, but only those things which are very strong, either because they were dumped in the trough by more than one observer or they were in the trough for a very long time.

Mark goes on to elaborate this notion of consciousness as a passive   **8** observer:

The processors, the observers, correspond to neurons in the brain. If a researcher on the edge of the brain could sample a number of the neurons and decode what impression was active in the brain at a given time, that researcher could be "seeing" what the brain was thinking. That researcher would be performing the function of the consciousness. Helpless to alter the chain reactions in the brain, this consciousness is rather carried along in the thought process, sensing whatever is the strongest impression at a given time. The consciousness is a helpless observer in the process we call thought. It is a byproduct of the local events between neurons.

Mark does not read philosophy. But his computer model of mind   **9** forces him to grapple with some of the oldest philosophical questions: the idea of free will and the question of a "self." Mark's theory has room for neither: the trough and the observers are a deterministic system. What we experience as consciousness is only a "helpless bystander" who gets the strongest signals filtered up to him. "Actions as well as thought," says Mark, "are determined by the cacophony of the processor voices."

There is no free will in Mark's system. The individual's feeling of   **10** conscious decision-making is an illusion, or rather an imposture: one of the processors, just as dumb as the others, has arrogated to itself the "seeming" role of consciousness. It has no power of decision, "it could just be a printer, attched to the computer. The strongest messages from the agents would just be printed out." Consciousness is epiphenomenon.° Mark says that even if there were agents that could act with "free will," it would still be "them" and not "him" who would have it. In Mark's way of looking at things, there is no "me."

You think you're making a decision, but are you really? For instance, when you have a creative idea, what happens? All of a sudden, you think of something. Right? Wrong. You didn't think of it. It just filtered through—the consciousness processor just sits there and watches this cacophony° of other processors yelling onto the bus and skims off

---

Epiphenomenon—a secondary consequence of a primary event, object, or condition.
Cacophony—discordant noise.

the top what he thinks is the most important thing, one thing at a time. A creative idea just means that one of the processors made a link between two unassociated things because he thought they were related.

In the course of my interview with Mark, creativity, individual re- **11** sponsibility, free will, and emotion were all being dissolved, simply grist for the little processors' mills. I asked Mark if he thought that "mind" is anything more than the feeling of having one. His answer was clear: "You have to stop talking about your mind as though it were thinking. It's not. It is just doing."

Mark takes the idea of agents and runs with it as far as it can take **12** him—to the demolition of the idea of free will, to the demolition of the idea that he has a "responsible" self. And when I ask him about emotions, he says, "OK, let's model it on a piece of paper."[1]

Even though Mark makes it clear that the world must wait for to- **13** morrow's multiprocessing technology to achieve the working intelligence that he has modeled, he turns his version of the "society theory" into something that uses today's computer parts. His bus and simple processors are doing things that Mark thinks he knows how to make computers do (like recognize an "image of a penguin"). And when something comes up that he doesn't know how to make a computer do, he can postpone the problem by claiming that intelligence will emerge through the interaction of the processors.

Mark finesses° problems that would require making his model more **14** complicated or more specific. He talks about intelligence emerging from "two or three or four hundred stupid agents." But considering the highly specific skill that he gives to each of them ("one knows how to recognize a picture of a computer, another knows how to recognize a picture of a computer cabinet"), three or four hundred seem hopelessly few, even to allow the baby to recognize the objects seen from the crib, the playpen, and the high chair. Mark talks about his multiprocessor "model," but what he really has is a multiprocessor metaphor. Despite its generality and vagueness he finds his metaphor powerful. First, he can identify with it directly. He can put himself in the place of the agents. They look, they shout, they struggle, they assert their piece of smartness in the crowd. And it is powerful because Mark's daily experience with computers makes his theory seem real to him. Without the computer Mark's theory would feel to him to be nothing more than "wishy-washy hand-waving," the slur that engineers use to deride the psychological models of the precomputational past. He believes that in his model the problem of intelligence has been reduced to a technical one. Since he sees himself as a technical person, this makes him happy. It gives him a sense of being very powerful indeed. It means the appro-

Finesse—bypass, ignore.

priation of psychology by the engineers. What sweet revenge if the "ugly ones" turned out to be the gurus of the mind.

Mark's way of talking is exceptional only because his ideas are elab-   15 orated and he has such utter confidence in them. But the idea of thinking of the self as a set of computer programs is widespread among students I interviewed at Harvard and MIT who were familiar with large computer sysems. Like Mark, they find that the complexity of these systems offers a way to think about their minds.

Elliot, an MIT biology major, calls his agents the "gallery of stupids"   16 who "input into clusters of special-interest groups inside his brain." And then these special-interest groups fight it out and forward the result of their debates to his conscious self.

> Should I study, should I go to sleep? Most of the time, it comes to a debate. I am aware of the conflict, but the debate gets played out by the agents. And it continues while I sleep. Sometimes I decide to go to sleep, and I awake with no other thought but to study. The agents have closed their debate. And the signals that are most powerfully coming up to consciousness are the study signals.

Ned, an MIT premedical student, also thinks of his mind as a mul-   17 tiprocessor:

> Some of the agents are a little smarter than the others. The way an op-amp is smarter than a transistor, but that still makes them a long way off from having consciousness or free will. Consciousness and free will are illusions created by having many of the smarter processors and many of the dumber processors linked together by billions and billions of neural connections. . . .

Challenging the "I"

A model of mind as multiprocessor leaves you with a "decentralized"   18 self: there is no "me," no "I," no unitary actor. Mark expressed this when he admonished me not to talk about my mind as though "I" was thinking. "All that there is is a lot of processors—not thinking, but each *doing* its little thing." Elliot put the same thought jokingly: "Nobody is home—just a lot of little bodies."

But theories that deny and "decenter" the "I" challenge most people's   19 day-to-day experience of having one. The assumption that there is an "I" is solidly built into ordinary language, so much so that it is almost impossible to express "anti-ego" theory in language. From the moment that we begin to write or speak, we are trapped in formulations such as "I want," "I do," "I think." Even as we articulate a "decentered" theory there is a pull back away from it, sometimes consciously, sometimes not.

Of course, "mind as multiprocessor" is not the first challenge to the *20*
"I" that has encountered the resistance of everyday "commonsense"
psychology and everyday speech. The idea of the Freudian unconscious
is also incompatible with our belief that we "know what we want." We
don't, says Freud. "Our" wishes are hidden from "us" by a complex
process of censorship and repression. We are driven by forces quite
outside our knowledge or control.

Freud divided the "I," but the theorists who followed him moved *21*
toward restoring it. They did so by focusing on the ego turned outward
toward reality. They began to see it as capable of integrating the psyche.
To them, the ego seemed almost a psychic hero as it battled off id and
superego at the same time that it tried to cope with the demands of the
everyday. Anna Freud wrote of its powerful artillery, the mechanisms
of defense, which helped it in its struggles, and Heinz Hartmann argued
that the ego had an aspect that was not tied up in the individual's neurotic
conflicts: it had a "conflict-free zone." This "unhampered" aspect of the
ego was free to act and choose, independent of constraints. It almost
seemed the seat for a reborn notion of the will, the locus of moral
responsibility. Intellectual historian Russell Jacoby, writing of psychoanalytic ego psychology's reborn, autonomous "I," described it as the
"forgetting of psychoanalysis."

A theory that had called the "self" into question now had a reassuring *22*
notion of the ego as a stable "objective" platform from which to view
the world. A decentered theory had been recentered. A subversive theory had been normalized. Ego psychology is the version of the unconscious most acceptable to the conscious.

As a theory aspires to move from the world of high science to that *23*
of the popular culture, there is a natural pressure to cast it into more
acceptable forms. Theories that call the self into question live in a natural
state of tension. Although much of their power comes from the fact
that they offer concrete images through which to express our sense of
being constrained or driven by forces beyond our control, they are also
under constant pressure from that other side of our experience—our
sense of ourselves as selves. This was true of psychoanalysis. It is true
of multiprocessor models of mind.

The Reconstituted Center

Mark begins with the flat assertion that there is no self, no conscious *24*
actor. "Consciousness is just a feeling of thinking." But even as he
makes his case, the contradictions slip in. He claims that consciousness
"just sits there and watches this cacophony of other processors yelling
onto the bus and skims off the top what he thinks is the most important
thing, one thing at a time." But who is "he"? Could this skimming
really be done by a processor that is as "passive as a printer"?

Mark's description of how he developed his theory, his description of 25
his introspective method, illustrates the contradiction in his position.

> My only way to know all this, my only way to tell, is by closing my
> eyes and trying to figure out what I'm doing at any given time. My
> theory was not developed as a "neat hack" to explain something, but
> rather "I thought this was going on" based on the small amount of
> evidence that filtered through to my consciousness of what's going on
> in my mind.

Here there is the reappearance of a "subject," something either smart 26
enough to make up the theory itself or able to send ideas that come up
"back down the line" for further processing. But according to Mark's
theory as he states it rigorously, neither is possible: the consciousness
processor is dumb ("just a printer") and, at most, has the power to
"send back a bit or two." Mark brings in something like a self despite
himself. He would like to accept the pure decentered theory, but this is
not easy for anyone. We are pulled back to common-sense ways of
thinking that are familiar since childhood and supported by language,
ways of thinking that make us feel that there is a self, that the "I" is in
control.

Throughout history, philosophers have challenged what seems ob- 27
vious to common sense. Some have argued that we don't really know
that objects exist or that other people have minds, or that there really
are relations of cause and effect. The eighteenth-century Scottish philosopher David Hume held to this last view: events might follow one
another, but we never have the right to say that one caused the other.
While this might be easy enough in the philosophy seminar, in ordinary
life we are obliged to act and talk as though we had the right to make
such assumptions. And thus we understand Hume's *cri de coeur*,° "Skepticism can be thought but not lived."

The decentered theory of mind, whether in psychoanalytic or com- 28
putational terms, is as hard to live with as Hume's skepticism, and for
similar reasons. The cornerstone of ordinary life is that there is an "I"
that causes things to happen. A philosopher like Hume takes away the
causality. Decentered psychologies take away the "I." Thus one sym-
pathizes when Mark slips and reintroduces the "I."

Notes

[1]He makes a sketch that shows emotion corresponding to an overall change
in the state of the processor system. He explains that each of the little processors might be able to run in five different states that could correspond to
different thresholds for attracting their interest. The "angry" state might de-
sensitize the processors involved in working out logical connections. They
would still do their thing, but they do it far less insistently, while other pro-

---

Cri de coeur—cry of the heart.

cessors, for example those concerned with self-defense, might be sensitized. "Being angry" is not the job of particular agents. It is something that affects the functioning of all of them.

Rhetorical Analysis Through Annotation

Case studies often concern single individuals or events and therefore may not represent any more general pattern. Turkle tries to overcome this problem by constantly making connections. While presenting Mark as a single example, she keeps attaching him to larger classes of people and thought.

Identify each time a connection is made between Mark and a larger group of people or more general ideas. In the margin note the persons or ideas Mark's case is being connected with; also indicate the point that is being made by each connection.

Discuss how the connection is made, whether the connection is warranted, and what consequences result from the connection. To what extent does the individual case become representative of more general patterns?

Discussion Questions

Interpreting the Text

1. Why does Mark like Dungeons? What is the connection between his liking for dungeons and his attitude towards himself and computers? How does Turkle describe Mark's personality?

2. What is Mark's theory of the mind? Does it make sense to you? Does he follow what he describes as Freud's procedure of making up theories by thinking about himself and making other things fit in (paragraph 5)? Is this description an accurate representation of Freud's method as indicated by Freud's article in this book (pp. 201–208)?

3. Does Mark's theory of the mind fit with McCarthy's description of common sense (pp. 576–582)? To what extent and in what way does Mark allow or not allow for common sense?

4. What attitude does Turkle take towards Mark's theory of the mind? Is she setting him up to be criticized? Is her criticism warranted?

5. Turkle treats Mark's theory of the mind as an example of a larger class of theories of the mind. What are other examples of that class? What are the characteristics of that larger class?

6. What is Turkle's point in discussing decentered-self theories? What tension does Turkle find in these theories? How is this tension exhibited by Mark? How serious does Turkle believe this tension is? Do you agree about the existence of this tension and its seriousness?

Considering the Issues

7. Do you know people like Mark? What characteristics do these people share with Mark? Is Turkle's description fair to Mark and people like him? Does Turkle rely on any stereotypes? Is there any justification for the stereotypes?

8. Have you ever thought of your own mental processes as like a machine's? In what ways? Were the connections you made similar to Mark's or different? Do you think attempts to compare the human mind to a machine are valid?

9. What social consequences might develop if large numbers of people considered their minds as similar to computers? To what extent is this belief already widespread? Have social consequences already appeared?

Writing Suggestions

1. Imagine Mark is your brother or friend and has challenged you by claiming there is no self and no free will. Write an answer to him, presenting your views about your self and free will and giving your reasons for believing as you do.

2. For a psychology class, write an essay on whether computers can help you think about your mind and if so, how.

3. For a philosophy course, write an essay discussing whether the self exists and what this self is. Base your reasoning on your own subjective experience and avoid external theories of a soul or spirit granted you by an outside agency.

Unit Writing Suggestions

1. On the basis of the material presented in this unit prepare a talk introducing high school students to the concept of artificial intelligence. In addition to explaining what it is, discuss why it is interesting, what impact it may have on students' lives, and how it touches on many areas of knowledge.

2. For a symposium at your university on life in the twenty-first century, write a paper predicting the impact of artificial intelligence on one area of life.

3. Imagine that a series of after-class talks with your classmates has led to a heated debate over the relationship between human intelligence and artificial intelligence. Your teacher, overhearing this passionate debate, has turned it into a classroom project. To fulfill the teacher's assignment, write a position paper setting forth your belief and your reasons on the subject.

4. As part of this class's discussion on the function of the various forms of writing, write a comparative analysis discussing the difference in the style and structure between articles in this unit that discuss artificial intelligence design and those that discuss the impact of artificial intelligence on other areas of life.

5. Because the subject of artificial intelligence is so interdisciplinary, the articles here bear similarities to articles in a number of the other disciplinary units. As part of this class's discussion of the way different disciplines write about knowledge, compare the various approaches towards artificial intelligence taken by several of the articles in this unit.

6. As part of this class's discussion of writing in different disciplines, write an essay discussing how any one article in this unit resembles the articles in another unit of this anthology.

7. Imagine an extremist group that believes it is sacrilegious to try to imitate human intelligence has occupied your university computer center, demanding that it shut down all operations except for simple bookkeeping and calculations. You have been deputized to explain to these people that the work of the computer center is totally inoffensive and should be allowed to continue unimpeded. Write a talk to deliver to the occupying group.

Richard E. Kopelman: "Why Productivity Is Important." From *Managing Productivity in Organizations* by Richard E. Kopelman. New York: McGraw-Hill, 1986. Used by permission of the publisher. Quote within from *The New York Times*. February 1, 1983. Copyright © 1983 by The New York Times Company. Reprinted by permission.

John R. Lamarsh: "Safety Considerations in the Design and Operation of Light Water Nuclear Power Plants." From *The Three Mile Island Nuclear Accident: Lessons and Implications*, edited by Thomas Moss and David Sills. "Safety Considerations in the Design and Operation of Light Water Nuclear Power Plants" by John R. Lamarsh. New York: The New York Academy of Sciences, 1981. Used by permission.

Gary P. Latham and J. James Baldes: "The 'Practical Significance' of Locke's Theory of Goal Setting." From *Journal of Applied Psychology*. Vol. 60, 1975: pp. 122–124. From "The 'Practical Significance' of Locke's Theory of Goal Setting" by Gary P. Latham and J. James Baldes. Copyright 1975 by The American Psychological Association. Reprinted by permission of the publisher and author.

Gary P. Latham and Kenneth N. Wexley: "Goal-Setting Research—A Textbook Presentation." From Latham/Wexley, *Increasing Productivity through Performance Appraisal*, © 1981, Addison-Wesley Publishing Co., Inc., Reading, Massachusetts. Reprinted with permission.

Shirley Lim: "The Dispossessing Eye: Reading Wordsworth on the Equatorial Line." From *Discharging the Canon: Cross-Cultural Readings in Literature*, edited by Peter Hyland. Selection adapted by Shirley Lim from her article. © 1986, Singapore University Press. Used by permission of Singapore University Press.

Seymour Martin Lipset and Reinhard Bendix: "Social Mobility." From *Social Mobility in Industrial Society* by Seymour Martin Lipset and Reinhard Bendix. Berkeley: The University of California Press, 1959. © 1959 The Regents of the University of California.

Edwin A. Locke: "The Relationship of Intentions to Level of Performance." From *Journal of Applied Psychology*. Vol. 5, 1966: pp. 60–66. An edited version of "The Relation of Intentions to Level of Performance" by Edwin A. Locke. Copyright 1966 by the American Psychological Association. Adapted by permission of the publisher and author.

A. R. Luria: "The Mind of a Mnemonist." From *The Mind of a Mnemonist* by A. R. Luria. Translated by L. Solotaroff. New York: Basic Books, 1968. Reprinted by permission of Prof. Michael Cole.

John McCarthy: "Some Expert Systems Need Common Sense." From *Computer Culture*, vol. 426, edited by Heinz R. Pagels. "Some Expert Systems Need Common Sense," by John McCarthy. New York: The New York Academy of Sciences, 1984. Used by permission.

Pamela McCorduck: "Knowledge Technology: The Promise." From *Computer Culture*, vol. 426, edited by Heinz R. Pagels. "Knowledge Technology: The Promise" by Pamela McCorduck. New York: The New York Academy of Sciences, 1984. Used by permission.

Michael MacCracken, S. B. Idso, and J. Hansen *et al.*: "Climatic Effects of Atmospheric Carbon Dioxide: An Exchange." From *Science*. Vol. 220, May 20, 1983: pp. 873–875. "Climatic Effects of Atmospheric Carbon Dioxide" by M. C. MacCracken, S. B. Idso, and J. Hansen et al. Copyright 1983 by the AAAS.

Eliot Marshall: "The Lessons of Chernobyl." From *Science*. Vol. 233, September 26, 1986: pp. 1375–1376. "The Lessons of Chernobyl" by Eliot Marshall. Copyright 1986 by the AAAS.

Ajit Narayanan: "What Is It Like to Be a Machine?" Reproduced with permission from *The Mind And The Machine* by Torrance published by Ellis Horwood Limited, Chichester, England, 1984.

To the Student: Your ratings of the reading selections in *The Informed Reader* will help us plan future editions. Please mail your answers to the English Editor, College Division, Houghton Mifflin Company, One Beacon Street, Boston, MA 02108.

Please rate the selections by checking the appropriate columns.

Selections	Interesting	Not interesting	Didn't read
LITERARY STUDIES			
In Dispute on Bias, Stanford Is Likely to Alter Western Culture Program			
What Is a Classic?			
Compulsory Reading			
Shakespeare in the Bush			
The Canon in Africa			
"In the Realm of the Imagination"			
The Contents of English Literature			
The Dispossessing Eye			
The Canon as Cultural Evaluation			
Male Critics and Female Readers			
HISTORY			
The Art of Money-Getting			
The Self-Made Man in America			
Social Mobility			
Poverty and Progress			
Rags-to-Riches in Paterson, New Jersey			
The Golden Door			
The Negro Family			
Like It Was			
Restoring the Traditional Black Family			
SOCIAL SCIENCES			
The Art of Memory			
An Early Memory from Goethe's Autobiography			
Two Experimental Traditions in the Study of Memory			
Long-Term Memory for a Common Object			
Everyday Memory in Natural Contexts			

Selections	Interesting	Not interesting	Didn't read
Brain Systems and Memory			
The Mind of a Mnemonist			
The Lost Mariner			
BUSINESS			
Why Productivity Is Important			
The Art of Shoveling			
The Attack on Pay			
The Relationship of Intentions to Level of Performance			
The 'Practical Significance' of Locke's Theory of Goal Setting			
Goal-Setting Research			
Better Management for Better Productivity			
The Burger King Corporation Productivity Program			
NATURAL SCIENCES			
E.P.A. Report Says Earth Will Heat Up Beginning in 1990's			
The Greenhouse Effect			
The Atmospheric Temperature Balance			
Climate Impact of Increasing Atmospheric Carbon Dioxide			
Climatic Effects of Atmospheric Carbon Dioxide			
Statement before the Senate Subcommittee on Environmental Pollution			
Potential CO_2-Induced Climate Effects on North American Wheat-Producing Regions			
Climate Change and Stratospheric Ozone Depletion			
Letter to the President of the United States			
ENGINEERING			
Nuclear Power and the World's Energy Resources			
Pressurized-Water Reactors			
Safety Considerations in the Design and Operation of Light Water Nuclear Power Plants			
Technical Aspects and Chronology of the Three Mile Island Accident			
Chernobyl: Errors and Design Flaws			
Chernobyl Plant Features That Exacerbated Accident Consequences			

Selections	Interesting	Not interesting	Didn't read
The Lessons of Chernobyl			
The Seven-Sided Coin			
INTERDISCIPLINARY STUDIES			
Knowledge Technology			
What Is Automated Reasoning?			
Consultation Systems for Physicians			
Natural and Artificial Intelligence			
Some Expert Systems Need Common Sense			
What Is It Like to Be a Machine?			
Thinking of Yourself as a Machine			

Did you find the Rhetorical Analysis Through Annotation sections helpful?

_____

Would you prefer to have the Rhetorical Analysis Through Annotation sections precede the articles?

_____

School _____

Course title _____